The Shell Book of English Villages

The Shell Book of English
Villages

Edited by John Hadfield

Introductory Essays by

Ronald Blythe
Alec Clifton-Taylor, F.S.A., HON. F.R.I.B.A.
Olive Cook
Gillian Darley
Tom Girtin, F.R.HIST.S.
Professor W. G. Hoskins, F.B.A.
Paul Jennings, F.R.S.L.
'Miss Read'

Gazetteer entries by

Professor M. W. Barley
Anthony Brode
Christopher Hanson-Smith
Alan Jenkins
Dr Roger Kain
Charles Lines, F.R.S.A.
Sir Jasper More
Dr Richard Muir
Dr Patrick Nuttgens, A.R.I.B.A.
Biddy Nuttgens
David L. Roberts, F.S.A. (SCOT.)
David Verey, A.R.I.B.A.
Elliott Viney, F.S.A.
His Honour Judge Lyall Wilkes

Michael Joseph

First published in Great Britain by Michael Joseph Ltd
44 Bedford Square, London WC1, 1980
© The Rainbird Publishing Group 1980

The name Shell and the Shell emblem are registered
trademarks.

ISBN 0 7181 1900 2

This book was designed and produced by
George Rainbird Ltd
36 Park Street, London W1Y 4DE

Design: Trevor Vincent and John Hadfield
Picture Research: Mary Corcoran
Maps: Eugene Fleury

Filmset in Great Britain by
SX Composing Ltd, Rayleigh, Essex

Printed and bound in Great Britain by
W. S. Cowell Ltd, Ipswich, Suffolk

The picture on the cover is from a painting of
Chilham in Kent, by Rowland Hilder.

Endpapers: (front) Hambleden, Bucks.
             Photo: J. Allan Cash Ltd
          (back) Lustleigh, Devon
             Photo: Richard Gee,
             Spectrum Colour Library

Shell U.K. Ltd would point out that the
contributors' views are not necessarily those
of this company.

Contents

Colour Plates

Most of the colour plates have been chosen not necessarily to depict villages mentioned in the book but to give impressions of characteristic landscape scenes in the various regions by representative English artists. The photographic illustrations on the other hand all relate to places and buildings mentioned in the text.

Editor's Preface

Drawing by Thomas Rowlandson

Even more than Big Ben or Westminster Abbey the English village is the visual symbol of our way of life. Although many people have, perforce, to live in Coronation Street, or a tower block, or a suburban housing estate, their ideal is probably a home in the country. Their castles in the air, whether they have roses round the door or elegant Georgian façades, are a reflection of the traditional English scene: the annual flower show, the Boxing Day meet of hounds outside the pub, cricket on the green.

I almost wrote 'British' instead of English; but the environment and activities I have quoted are peculiarly English. In England the village, as a historical development and entity, is a far more dominant feature of the landscape than in Scotland or Wales. There the countryside tends to be dominated by natural features such as lochs and mountains, while the human habitations are more scattered, and less based upon ancient field patterns, manorial rights and parish history.

The purpose of this book is to survey the villages of England and to examine their differing characteristics in terms of history, layout, building materials and architecture. The contributors to the gazetteer have all been asked to choose a representative selection of villages within their special areas, for description and comment. Given a certain over-all specification the selections of our contributors have been made according to their own preferences. Beauty of buildings and environment are obviously two of the chief criteria, but many other factors have been considered, such as origins, historical associations, architectural detail, and that indefinable quality, 'atmosphere'. The Editor is prepared for many indignant readers to complain that *their* favourite villages have been omitted; but there are some 13,000 villages in England, and it required a total of 42 volumes of Sir Nikolaus Pevsner's invaluable *Buildings of England* series to record merely their architectural features. Our contributors, with less specialized terms of reference, have had to content themselves with commenting on roughly a tenth of the total.

All of them live in, or have long been familiar with, the areas about which they write. Some are architects; but the book is in no sense a supplement to Pevsner. The writers include professional geographers and historians, two former Members of Parliament, two former High Sheriffs, a provincial journalist, an official of the National Trust, even a Circuit Judge. All, of course, are profoundly interested in buildings, but some are more concerned with the origins and historical development of their villages, while others respond especially to personal associations, or are connoisseurs of what Peacock's Mr Milestone would have called 'the picturesque'. But these variations in response will, I hope, be matched by variations in response among readers. This is not one of those impersonal, made-to-a-formula digests of information. I have welcomed, and not ironed out, personal judgments and prejudices.

At the outset, inevitably, a distinction had to be made between villages and towns. I have to admit that this has usually been an arbitrary distinction. Many settlements have at some time in their history acquired the status of boroughs, but have latterly declined, through industrial or social change, into being regarded as large villages. In general, a rural environment was preferred, and several attractive village communities had to be omitted because they had been absorbed by urban sprawl. Nevertheless no consideration of the history of the village would be complete without reference to the villages that came into being during the Industrial Revolution and the 'model villages' created by employers and idealists in the nineteenth century to house people working in factories or mills.

When the original plan for the book was drawn up it was agreed that the qualifications for a selected village, apart from its beauty, layout, architecture and historical interest, should be a church, a 'big house', a village green, a river or pond, some farms and cottages, a school, a shop, and a pub or two. Admittedly, some of our contributors have occasionally ignored these desiderata, because of some special single feature in a chosen village which they considered to be of outstanding interest. Indeed, one contributor has written most interestingly about a village that now no longer exists!

But all too many of the basic elements of the English village have, alas, disappeared or are disappearing in our own times, under the stress of social and economic forces. The village shop is being put out of business by the multiple store, though, as Paul Jennings points out, it can provide an inestimable service not only for the retired and elderly who increasingly populate the village, but also as a village meeting place. Dedication on the part of a few courageous individual shopkeepers can arrest this process. But a change in *public* policy could save the disappearance of that equally valuable element in village life – the primary school. Hundreds of thousands of people, of different generations, will echo Miss Read's sadness at the passing of the village school where they, their parents and their children learned to read and write.

What are the other distress signals? The duckpond may have been filled in. There is less cricket on the village green: enthusiasts would rather watch Test matches on television. The green itself has probably been surrounded by concrete kerbs. The elm trees have died – though that is nobody's fault. And the church has been declared 'redundant' (surely one of the most sinister words of our time), a fact not entirely due to decline in religious conviction but also to competition by the motor car and television. These are inevitable manifestations of social change; and perhaps little more can be done about them than can be done about Dutch elm disease. But one aspect of change in the village *is* within our control – and that is to safeguard the 'faces' of our villages for generations to come.

One cannot drive people to church, or compel them to run unprofitable village shops, or to form a cricket club if they are too lazy to play. But it *is* possible, and usually no more expensive, to build and rebuild houses and cottages in materials appropriate to their environment, to replace or install windows of visually pleasant proportions, to get the slope of roofs right, to replace tiles with tiles – instead of asbestos or corrugated iron.

It is a great misfortune that the word 'planner' has become almost a term of abuse. The town-planning acts could have been the saving of our countryside – and still can be, if only those engaged in the planning departments can be better educated in the architectural use of their eyes.

For twenty-five years I lived near a town where one of the most delightful and conspicuous eighteenth-century buildings was disfigured by having had the glazing bars in the ground-floor windows torn out and replaced by large bleak sheets of plate glass. At intervals during the years I pointed this out to the local authorities – the building was, in fact, the Education Office – but nothing has been done to this day, either because the vast County Council budget couldn't afford the few hundred pounds required to put it right, or, what I fear is more likely, the authorities just couldn't see what was wrong.

According to the jeremiahs, the village is on the way out. But is it? Is a book like this merely a sentimental tribute – a swan song? Is Everyman's domestic ideal, as I described it in my first paragraph, to become unattainable?

There are several scathing references in the following pages to commuters and commuterland. One gets the point, and raises an eyebrow at the pseudo-Georgian front doors, the carriage lamps, the bottle-glass window panes, the poker-burnt name plates, the swimming pools, and the firms' cars lining the lanes. But in fact it may well be the commuter who is the saviour of the village.

He has taken over and restored the tumbledown cottage vacated by the farm-worker. The commuter may be absent all day, but in the evenings or at weekends he will attend meetings of the parish council, he will help to organize the flower show, he will join in a game of darts at the pub, he may roll the cricket pitch, he may even join the local preservation society. His wife may become President of the Women's Institute, and on Sundays – yes, I have seen this happen – he and she may fill the church pews where once the Lord and Lady of the Manor sat.

Cavendish, Suffolk

Kenneth Scowen

The Making of the Village

W. G. Hoskins

We always assume that outside the towns the 'typical' settlement is the village. Even this simple statement is not true everywhere, for there are considerable blanks on the 1:50,000 map (the old one-inch roughly) where villages do not figure but only single farmsteads or tiny hamlets. This is particularly true of the upland country of the North and the West, though even in lowland parts like Suffolk we find scatterings of hamlets or single farmsteads, a symptom for those who can decipher the map of clearance long ago (chiefly in the twelfth and thirteenth centuries) from original woodland. They are tiny settlements that for various reasons never made the grade to the status of village.

Taking the true villages, however, they used to be characterized as more or less compact settlements, with a parish church and a resident parson; a few shops that sold nearly everything between them, a school – sometimes one for boys and one for girls – two or three pubs, each with its own faithful clientèle, and less frequently a 'great house' on the edge of the village or standing isolated in a park. This was once the classic set-up, but it is rare to find it in its complete form today.

The parish church still stands, but the parson now serves two or three parishes (sometimes as many as four) and the vacated rectories or vicarages are sold off to well-to-do retired people and called The Old Vicarage or The Old Rectory. The historical name is kept but the house has changed its use. If you want to see the extent of the changes over the last hundred years or so, look in any county directory round about 1850–70. Some villages then possessed their own minor gentry, doctors, solicitors, as well as blacksmiths, wheelwrights, and a dozen other rural craftsmen; and a carrier took most of the population (those who did not possess private carriages or 'traps' as we called them in Devon) into the market town once a week, picking up parcels also and bringing back whatever villagers had ordered. A large market town would have housed a small army of carriers, going in and out from their chosen inns and pubs. Sixty years ago or more I embarked from the Bull Inn in Goldsmith Street in Exeter to be taken for my holidays ten miles along the byroads: making our slow progress through the lanes (I dare say the old horse was tired by then) with frequent stops for deliveries, and chats, and the final delivery of one small boy, half-unconscious with sleep, at the predestined cottage. A few villages had a railway station, and some hamlets had what were called 'halts'. But the railway network was far from complete, you might well have to walk two or three miles to the nearest station. Now that too is either a ruin with weed-strewn battered platforms, or a neat Gothic house transformed from the old station if it was fortunate. Many of the smaller branch-lines that served these Gothic stations were built in the 1880s and 1890s, in the same architectural style that had been fashionable half a century earlier.

The village, where it survives and has not been taken over by commuters (the most recent stage in its long evolution), looks as if it had stood there, apart from some Victorian red-brick villas, from time immemorial. Thousands indeed are mentioned by name in Domesday Book, the gigantic survey of England that William the Conqueror ordered to be made twenty years after the Norman Conquest. Order had been largely restored, for England was not conquered all at one go in 1066 – that was only the start of a lot of local resistance movements – but by 1086 it seemed necessary for the King to see exactly what sort of country he had acquired, who owned what, and what it consisted of – woodland, marsh, arable meadow, common pasture, and so on, and what it was worth. That is why so many village histories written by devoted parsons, schoolmasters, and scholarly retired men, begin with a bald statement from Domesday Book (1086). Yet many, if not most, of our villages had already existed for several centuries before the Norman Conquest. There are very few documents to give us a clue as to their age, unless an Anglo-Saxon land-charter exists – that is, the gift of some ancient estate, usually by the king to a monastic house. Or the present village may stand on top of extensive Roman remains which make it clear that it was several hundred years old even when the Normans moved in. Quite often the place-name of a particularly archaic type tells us that the village was established well back in Saxon times. And of course the existence of a Saxon church, of which there are scores still standing in this country, is irrefutable evidence that it served an established village, as at, say, Brixworth in Northamptonshire where the church dates very largely from the seventh century. Some parts of England are particularly well off for Anglo-Saxon churches; others have none, or, more strictly, none that is visible above ground.

This is not surprising as the Angles, Saxons, and Frisians began moving into this country from the beginning of the fifth century, sometimes taking over existing Romano-British sites. This is especially true of eastern and south-eastern England; but the antiquity of an English village is a subject about which it is hard to generalize.

Often the name of a place tells us something of its origin. We thought for a long time, thanks to the great Swedish scholar Ekwall, that place-names ending in -ing or -ingham belonged to the earliest phase of the Anglo-Saxon Conquest, from the fifth century onwards: in recent years doubts have been cast upon this useful clue and other early place-name types have been elevated to the primary stages of the Conquest. Moreover, at the risk of complicating what seems a simple subject, we have to bear in mind that villages could change their names, perhaps with the arrival of a new lord with a different name, so we are not dealing with the aboriginal name but a later one. In Leicestershire the large village of Wigston means literally 'viking's *tun* or village', suggesting a date sometime in the late ninth century or early tenth, a settlement first made at the Danish partition of Mercia in 877. But back in the late eighteenth century a large Anglo-Saxon cemetery was accidentally discovered which produced a quantity of grave-goods that dated from the early sixth century. So the village with the unmistakable Scandinavian name had existed for centuries before the Danes moved in, and must have had an Old English name that was changed when the new conquerors took over. Down in Somerset the present village of Biddisham near Axbridge was formerly called *Tarnuc*. Biddisham is a pure English name, but Tarnuc is Celtic. It is only by accident, or for the sake of legal clarity, that a charter of 1065 tells us that the old name had been superseded and that Tarnuc began life as a Celtic settlement.

Edwin Smith

Brixworth, Northamptonshire: the largest Saxon Church remaining in England;
dating mainly from the seventh century. The Saxon tower was heightened by the Normans.

A final complication in putting a date to the beginnings of a village, whatever its
present name, is that archaeologists are now uncovering in various places early
villages that disappeared beneath the ground and a new village was built some
distance away. This is apparently why, in East Anglia especially, many parish
churches stand all alone in the windswept fields, far from any village. Thus at
Longham in the depths of Norfolk the church stands alone. Excavations have
proved that the first village started in mid-Saxon times and lasted into the late
Saxon, and that it was based upon the village church. For some reason the original
farmsteads and cottages were abandoned, probably over a period of time. By medieval times the village was an entirely different shape, elongated along a street and
partly around a green, some distance from the church. By 1816 a map shows that
the medieval village too had disappeared, and Longham is now a small scattering
of cottages in the fields: the church is left all alone. So the village of Longham
has a very complicated history of mobility and the present plan is quite deceptive:
only archaeologists could have given us this below-ground evidence, plus a
sixteenth-century map which happened to survive to fill in some of the gaps in
the story.

There were recognizable villages long before early Saxon times, but they were
few and far between. Suffice it to say that most of our villages were centuries old
when Domesday Book was compiled and that many had changed their plans
perhaps more than once. Just why, we do not know. At West Stow, near Bury St
Edmunds – the site accidentally discovered when it was chosen for a municipal
rubbish dump, and now rescued for a Countryside Park – excavations have shown
inexplicable changes of site. The same is true of Maxey in Cambridgeshire
where the splendid twelfth-century church stands alone. But excavations have
shown what was probably continuous occupation around it since pre-Roman times.

The noble church of St Mary at Stoke-by-Nayland looms over a compact, largely Tudor village.
It was built from legacies left by local merchants between 1439 and 1462.

Domesday Book, except for the parts of the North of England where it remains a blank, tells us a good deal about our villages, more in some parts of England than others. Perhaps the most irritating omission (to scholars at least) is the inexplicable way in which it deals with village churches. Thus in Suffolk no fewer than 417 churches are recorded in Domesday Book, whereas in neighbouring Essex, which was equally populous, only sixteen are named; and in the large county of Devon scarcely a dozen. This apparently haphazard treatment simply cannot be explained; even in Devon, if one studies it closely enough, one can add to the short recorded list from place-name clues. So Honeychurch (which means 'Huna's church') is recorded as a village name in 1086, revealing that a church founded by one Huna, a local landowner, already stood there; and similar clues can be found abundantly elsewhere in England even though Domesday Book is silent on the subject.

Looking at a village church may well reveal considerable evidence of Norman work (especially the south doorway and the font) but unless it is Early Norman this is no proof that a church stood there as early as 1086. Probably it did, but these clues are not sufficient by themselves. Many village churches were rebuilt in stone during the twelfth century, replacing probably an older timber structure, and the greater part of these were rebuilt again in the fifteenth century and early sixteenth. Even so, the south doorway and the font of the twelfth-century church were carefully preserved *in situ* and are the only clues to the existence of an earlier Norman building. The reason for their survival is usually that the south doorway, which was the principal entrance to the church from time immemorial, was by far the most ornate and worthy of its position. It was therefore carefully preserved. As for the font, it was the visible symbol that the church possessed full parochial rights, i.e. the right to baptize and the right of burial, both of which meant *inter alia* fees for the parson not to be lightly let go. As few written documents specifically state these rights, the stone font was carefully preserved as the unchallengeable evidence of the ancient right to baptize.

The village church almost invariably occupies the site originally chosen for it. The village may have moved away, probably for economic reasons, but the church stayed on its original site. Sometimes it is now a ruin (Norfolk has more ruined churches than the rest of England put together) and often neglected beyond repair.

At the other extreme, some of the East Anglian churches are magnificent buildings, both in size and fittings. It is doubtful whether they were ever filled, even when the village population was higher than it is today. Such churches were built usually by two or three rich landowners or even one rich man; but sometimes they were built, as at Bodmin in Cornwall, with the pennies and even halfpennies of the poor. Even the wonderful coloured windows were often paid for by the villagers, like those at St Neots on the edge of Bodmin Moor, where by some miracle they survive intact.

Villages come in all shapes and sizes, depending on their history, and, above all perhaps, on their ownership. Some are simple 'street-villages', i.e. one long street and no more; others are grouped around a village green, sometimes of immense size, though some of these greens have been shrunk by encroachments; some villages have no distinct shape except that they are relatively compact, and yet others straggle about without any obvious plan. These probably originated from spasmodic 'squatting' on a piece of common land. It used to be said that if you could put up a cottage on the common and have smoke coming out of the chimney within 24 hours you had the freehold for ever. Another nice variation of this belief was that when the cottage was completed, the new owner could claim as much land as he could cover by throwing a stone around. That is why there are so many small patches around scattered cottages in those parts of England where common land is concentrated.

Villages owe a good deal of their present shape, and indeed their size, to the squires of the past, or more truly to the social structure of the countryside as a whole. Not every village had a resident squire – far from it – for example, in Elizabethan Suffolk only one village in five or six had one, though squires in neighbouring villages might own a good deal of land without residing. The determining factor was between what we call 'open' and 'closed' villages. If a big landowner owned most or all of the parish he had absolute control over any building, and might for his own reasons prevent any new building at all, or a bare minimum to keep up the labour supply. On the other hand, many villages, especially in the Midlands and parts of the North, possessed a regiment of small freeholders – a score or two perhaps – and these could build as they wished. No squire could stop them. The best example were the 'statesmen' of the Lake District, the sturdy freeholders of Wordsworth's time, the word being a shortened version of 'estates men', men who owned their own small estate. But many villages further south were ruled by a more or less feudal aristocracy and all change was subject to the lord's will. There was no appeal. These were the 'closed' villages. An 'open village' was, as its name implies, one in which there was an active land-market, with much buying and selling among the peasantry and much new building as the population increased, as it did remarkably at certain historical periods.

Farming was, of course, the major industry in the English countryside, together with all the ancillary occupations that went with it, such as smithies, saddlers and other leather-workers, and the basic textile trades. Mostly in the West and North, and old woodland country even in the Midlands, the fields were small and enclosed with thick hedges. Occasionally these enclosed fields were only a few acres in size, some as little as an acre or two, though they have been much enlarged since. In contrast to these tiny enclosed fields were the huge 'open fields' of the lowland country, sometimes called the three-field system, in which each field ran to hundreds of acres and was divided into a multitude of strips. Though called the three-field system for the sake of brevity, there were many more complex patterns as time went by, so that the three-field system developed in an obvious way into six fields, or a two-field system could develop into four. All this gave greater flexibility of farming, with a multitude of rules and regulations to get the best out of the land, and to prevent bad farmers from ruining other men's crops with their weeds and neglect.

In the old enclosed countryside, developed mostly from natural woodland, life was very different. Here the abundance of wood, even after centuries of clearance, gave winter fuel and as much wood as was needed for building. It is in these parts, such as the Midland forests of Arden and Rockingham or in the Weald of Kent, that we find whole villages built of timber with plaster infilling. The Weald and considerable parts of the West Midlands are still notable for their 'black-and-white' farmhouses and cottages, many of them dating from the sixteenth and seventeenth centuries. Something which William Cobbett noticed in the early nineteenth century was how much more comfortable these woodland villages were in winter, because of the plenty of wood for the gathering, whereas in chalk country, where the great bare downs supplied practically no fuel for the winter hearth, life was cold and miserable.

Changes in farming and in field systems had their effects on the villages themselves. In the open-field country of the Midlands (but in other regions also) enclosures came quite early, and the new enclosures, still hundreds of acres in extent, were used for large-scale cattle and sheep farming. In these villages there grew up local cloth and leather trades which gave much new employment in addition to the standard farming. For this reason alone many villages grew considerably in size. Many others declined because the large pastures required less labour than the former arable.

But the so-called parliamentary enclosures from the late-seventeenth century to about the mid-nineteenth had more devastating effects than the earlier pasture-enclosures of the fifteenth and sixteenth centuries. They involved millions of acres of arable land, and in the earlier half of the nineteenth century the ancient common lands also came under attack. The enclosures of the decades between about 1750 and 1850 led in some cases to the disintegration of old villages, either completely or in part. With open-field farming all the farmhouses and cottages had been gathered together in the village itself: the strip system of farming, with very mixed ownership of strips, and complicated regulations about such matters as the rights of pasture over the harvested lands, absolutely prevented new building outside the old village. But once the enclosure acts had reshaped the fields into the pattern we take for granted today, and produced compact farms instead of hundreds of scattered strips, there was a strong tendency for the bigger farmers at least to leave their ancestral villages and build new farmhouses and buildings in the midst of their new lands. Back in the village the old farmhouses were divided into two or three cottages, which housed the labourers. Not every village suffered in this way, but it was a fairly common change in the fabric of the village. The farmhouses newly built in the fields after the enclosures often betray themselves by names redolent of eighteenth-century events, mostly celebrating battles such as Waterloo, Quebec, Bunkers Hill and so on.

By the eighteenth century and sometimes earlier there were other social changes. In earlier times villagers had drunk bad ale in private houses, ale-houses mostly of ill repute, where the poor were alleged to waste most of their time. By Elizabethan times the more respectable village inn began to appear, with its own name that has often persisted to this day. So, too, many village schools were founded in this period – not always the grander grammar schools usually founded by villagers who had gone away to make a fortune and repaid their native village by a handsome grammar school, like the remarkable one at Appleby Parva in Leicestershire. All over England these village schools, large or small, went up usually in close proximity to the village church.

Nonconformity also grew rapidly in the later seventeenth century and many villages contain one or two chapels, some of them very handsome and worth seeking out. In several counties they have been the subject of special study and many are listed buildings.

There are two other kinds of villages that need mentioning – villages wholly replanned by the squire or the principal landowner, and the special industrial villages which were built in the days of the Industrial Revolution. Church and Chapel go together in the same industrial village, as by this date the Anglican Church had gone to sleep and was not prepared for the newcomers. Moreover, partly because of this neglect, the new industrial population was (if anything at all) staunchly nonconformist. The mining districts of Cornwall can still show hundreds of Nonconformist Chapels of various denominations, but they are also to be found in many other parts of England.

However, to return to the landlord-planned villages, these belong mainly to the eighteenth century when the Great House was enlarging its small old park into something grander in order to set off the house and to separate it physically from the village. This often involved the complete demolition of the original village and rebuilding it a mile or so away. One of the best examples of such a village is Milton Abbas in Dorset, beautifully sited and planned. In Northumberland the village of Blanchland was replanned by the Crewes in the latter half of the eighteenth century. The latest example of a completely replanned village I know is Horninghold in

south-east Leicestershire, rebuilt in the almost-golden ironstone of the district, as late as the early years of this century. The careful observer will be able to spot such villages all over England, not very frequently, but revealed by the similarity in style of the cottages all along the main street. Such villages were built with the immense wealth of the landed class in the nineteenth century, the age of enormous estates and of vast royalties from coal and other minerals, though not all great landowners felt impelled to spend their money in this way. This rich class received its death-blow – or nearly so – with World War I and the continuously high taxation since. Almost the only planned villages built since then have been those built by local authorities, with varying degrees of success.

The villages of the Industrial Revolution, from about 1760 onwards, are a very special class, not the less interesting because they are relatively modern and tend to be in ravaged industrial districts. Some, indeed, are extremely presentable, despite their origins and surroundings. They arose in the first place because the new industries used waterpower, often in unpopulated valleys. The factories and work-shops needed a labour supply and this had to be provided with houses in places that had hitherto been more or less uninhabited.

One of the most remarkable examples of this new growth is Cromford, in the Derwent valley of mid-Derbyshire. There may have been a few cottages here a long time back, but when the great Richard Arkwright (later Sir Richard) moved here to set up his own cotton factories he had to build a completely new village to house his workers. Many of the streets he built then (mostly in the 1770s) still stand solidly. We forget that many of the early factory-owners built well: they were the counterpart of the benevolent squires of earlier generations. Arkwright built in other villages also; and lower down the Derwent his great rivals in the cotton industry – the Strutts, now Lords Belper – created a new village at Milford. The Arkwrights and the Strutts supplied all the needs of the workers – churches, chapels, Sunday schools, as well as the mills where they worked.

In the Black Country, where the Industrial Revolution came a little earlier, industrial hamlets and villages can still be found – relics of the eighteenth century like Mushroom Green, and many others like it, which were probably built not by some industrialist but by squatters on the numerous bits of common land that are a feature of Black Country landscape, or were so originally. On these patches of land, of little or no agricultural value, the impoverished labouring class bunged up cottages almost overnight. The Lord of the Manor did not mind, as he collected yet another rent, and the local industrialists in the metal trades got the cheap labour they wanted.

In some ways the middle decades of the nineteenth century mark the apogee of Village England. Over much of rural England village populations reached their maximum in the 1850s. Thereafter came the decades of decline, with the Great Depression in farming and the collapse of mining in many places, above all the tin and copper mines of Cornwall. The classic account of the period is (to my mind) George Bourne's *Change in the Village*, first published in 1912, which deals mostly with the dying village of his younger days and the social changes that ensued. We tend to sentimentalize old village life but for many it was a lifetime of poverty and extreme hardship and not of roses round the door.

Opposite: Milton Abbas in Dorset, one of the best of the landlord-planned villages   *Edwin Smith*

The Fabric of the Village

Alec Clifton-Taylor

Perhaps the first thing to be said about our village buildings is that scarcely ever did they know an architect. Although, as we shall see, there are great variations from one part of the country to another, they are nearly all the outcome of gradually evolving traditions, dependent upon the needs and financial resources of the community and above all on the nature of the materials available.

Building materials are heavy, and until the advent of the railways – or, in certain limited areas, the canals – the most expensive item was not labour nor the materials themselves, but the cost of transporting them. So there was every incentive to make use of whatever was to hand on or very near the site. And here nature has, in England, been bountiful. Villagers had almost everything to satisfy their needs.

In the first place there was a great abundance of wood. Until the end of the Middle Ages some parts of England were wooded even to excess : in Sussex the oak used to be known as the 'Sussex weed'. Only in a few areas was there any shortage. So the very large majority of village buildings were originally timber-framed. The preferred wood was always oak, immensely strong and durable; even the laths between the studs (uprights) of a timber-framed building were, for preference, of riven oak, although frequently they were of beech. Where inferior kinds of wood were used the buildings have not usually survived. Other woods, especially elm, were useful for floors; others again, sticks of willow, ash or hazel, for the more primitive wattles which preceded the adoption of laths; and common rafters might be sawn from almost any wood that was available.

Many parts of the country were also very well supplied with clay. Long before the days of bricks and tiles this provided the 'daub' in wattle-and-daub construction, and in some areas the principal material for cottage building. Indeed, in London itself it is known that in 1212 some of the houses were built of mud. To obtain the best results some chopped straw was needed as a binder, and usually sand or gravel too, and even road scrapings; to be suitable for building the clay had to contain enough lime to enable it to set. The more lime the better, in fact: some of the best preserved mud walls are very chalky. Mud walls were thick and always erected on a solid base of stone, flint or, later, brick, to guard against rising damp. Since they were also rendered, they are not always easily recognizable; by far the largest number that now survive are in Devon and Dorset, where the usual term is cob. So long as such walls are kept dry they can last up to 300 years or even more.

The usual roofing material in the Middle Ages was thatch. The best, then as now, was made from reeds, which were very plentiful in the low-lying areas of eastern England, including the fens before they were drained, but seldom available elsewhere. So most people's thatching was done with straw, the longer the better, and long straw was available in almost every part of the country before the invention

Edwin Smith

Straw-thatching at Selworthy in Somerset

of the combine-harvester. Where no corn was grown, as in moorland regions, or sometimes on commons, resort had to be made to heather, which is hardly ever seen today but which in wet areas was regarded as more durable than straw.

Wood, mud and thatch: these were the principal domestic building materials of the English villages of the Middle Ages; and so far stone has hardly entered into the story, and brick not at all.

There was, however, even as far back as the twelfth century, one building in every village which was nearly always constructed of stone, and that was the church. In Saxon times the tiny churches were often built of wood, but the Normans came from a land with a stronger stone tradition, and for churches they did not regard wood as good enough. So began the exploitation of that most glorious of England's building materials, stone. Quarrying, with such tools as they had, must have posed many problems, although fortunately for them the sedimentary rocks have the characteristic of being much softer when first dug out, and of hardening on exposure to the air. But here again the most difficult problem was transport: stone of course is far heavier than wood. So, once again, they used what was available locally. Where there was serviceable stone, they quarried it; in regions such as Cornwall, where the principal materials are not sedimentary but igneous (granite and elvan) or metamorphic (slate), both very hard and intractable, they availed themselves wherever possible of 'presents'; hunks of stone, that is, lying about on the land or washed down by the streams. The choice of stone was marvellously wide; among the limestone and sandstones, of which the large majority of our churches are built, there was serviceable stone of many different colours and textures, drawn from a wide range of geological strata, some much better suited to ornamental carving than others, and some, it is true, not nearly so durable as the best.

The region least well endowed with stone suitable for building was East Anglia. Here, therefore, recourse had to be made to flint, a material which had been used extensively both here and along the South coast since Roman times, and even for camps dating from the Early Iron Age. Flint is so hard as to be in itself indestructible, but unless it is squared (a laborious undertaking not often practised before the nineteenth century) it can only be used for building with the help of a great deal of mortar. Fortunately the chalk which yielded the flints also provided plenty of lime, so that problem was easily solved. Thus even to this day the very large majority of East Anglian churches, and many later buildings too, are made of flint, which is also one of the commonest materials in villages all over the South-Eastern counties, wherever there is an abundance of chalk.

Where there was no local stone, not even flint, recourse had to be made to transport, usually by water, and here our long coastline and numerous rivers were a great boon. Some of the quarries were close to the sea; many others were close to rivers. Stone was also brought across the Channel, notably from near Caen.

Most of the flint churches were originally roofed with thatch, as some still are: elsewhere the favourite roofing materials were wooden shingles, 'slates' of fissile limestone or sandstone (which made, and still make, the most beautiful roofs of any) and, especially in the Perpendicular period when church roofs often became much flatter and hidden behind parapets, sheets of lead, much of it brought by barge from Derbyshire.

Except where wood was scarce, and in those parts of the country like the Cotswolds in which stone was specially abundant and not difficult to work, the church would probably have been the only stone building in the village at least until the fifteenth century, unless there happened also to be, presiding over the whole place

The Greyhound at Folkingham in Lincolnshire

Russell Read

as at Conisbrough or Corfe, a castle. Failing a castle, and therefore in almost all villages, the next most important building after the church was the manor house. Where the owner could afford it and circumstances allowed, this would also be built or rebuilt in stone. The dates, and therefore the architectural styles, vary greatly; of these there will be more to say presently, when we pass on to a consideration of the principal regions in turn.

Where no stone was readily available, the manor house is likely to have been the first building in the village to have turned to brick. In the medieval village brick was virtually unknown. Until Tudor times the use of brick, rare in England before the fifteenth century, was almost wholly confined to buildings of importance: schools, colleges and a few large houses. It was also used for a few churches, or parts of churches, in East Yorkshire and, especially in the early Tudor period, in the eastern half of Essex, which had no stone, not even flint. In Norfolk Sir Ralph Shelton employed it to great effect in the 1480s for his eponymous church, a Perpendicular work of outstanding quality. But, in general, brick made a late arrival in the villages. In the sixteenth century it was exceptional; in the seventeenth century still fairly uncommon. Only in the Georgian age did this material really make a considerable impact, and even from that period there is less brick than would at first appear. For a good many owners of timber-framed houses, wanting to look up-to-date but being unable or unwilling to afford a complete rebuilding, added a sometimes quite elegant façade, usually in brick, or, if the site allowed, built out two complete Georgian rooms and a hall, in front of the older timber-framed house. No architectural experience is more curious, nor in my view more disappointing, than to visit what appears to be a gracious classically-proportioned Georgian house and to find oneself in the low oak-beamed rooms of a building perhaps 150 years older.

After the church and the manor house, the most important house in the village in Georgian days would usually have been the rectory. Before the Reformation this was not the case: the country priests were usually poor men, and their houses were very modest. But in the eighteenth century the rector was often a man of some social standing: where the squire, or perhaps some local peer, was the patron of the living, this could be a comfortable niche for a younger brother or some other relation. And where an Oxford or Cambridge college held the patronage, the job often went to a superannuated Fellow. Hence the profusion of handsome Georgian rectories, usually built of brick, of which that at Ripple in Worcestershire, dating from 1726, will serve as an example. Happily many of these fine houses survive, though very rarely are they now inhabited by the rector.

Another large house in some villages, particularly in those on trunk roads frequented by coach traffic, was the inn. An excellent example is the Greyhound Inn at Folkingham in Lincolnshire. This is a stately Georgian coaching inn, on the direct road from the city of London to Lincoln, which dominates the broad village square. Although situated on limestone, the Greyhound Inn is but one of many Georgian buildings for which, because it then cost less, brick was preferred. In addition to quarries there were also, at Folkingham, good brickfields not far away.

Other large buildings which only a few villages were fortunate enough to possess before the nineteenth century were schools, hospitals and almshouses. These were always the result of private munificence, and, although a few are earlier, the large majority date from the seventeenth and eighteenth centuries. An outstanding example of the first is the Grammar School in the little village of

Appleby Parva in Leicestershire. Built in 1693–7 of now mellow pink brick, with
stone dressings, by the architect Sir William Wilson for Sir John Moore, a local
boy who grocered so successfully that in 1697 he became Lord Mayor of London,
this school, which is happily still in use, makes an astonishing impact when
suddenly encountered, beyond a broad mown lawn. In North Yorkshire the munificence of the Turner family endowed another small village, Kirkleatham, with
Turner's Hospital, a very handsome almshouse, founded in 1676 but mostly
rebuilt 66 years later on a most lavish scale. The material is again brick: reddish
brown here, also with dressings of stone. These are but two charitable foundations
which add lustre to a handful of villages in every county, all over England.

Some villages have a good mill-house, with a water-mill attached, which in
former days was of great importance for grinding the corn from the surrounding
fields. Doctors and lawyers and other professional men usually lived in the
market towns, but merchants sometimes set up house in the villages. William
Grevel built a fine stone house at Chipping Campden as early as 1400 out of the
profits of his trade in wool. By the eighteenth century most villages of any consequence had a number of good houses built or acquired by successful tradesmen.

But until the Industrial Revolution the chief source of employment in the
large majority of villages was farming; and with increasing prosperity the yeoman farmers were sometimes able to build themselves houses of very much better
quality than the cottages of their labourers. It is not unusual to find, close to the
Manor House, the Manor Farm, and next to the church the Church Farm. Other
farmhouses tend to be sited on the periphery of their villages, if not further afield.
It is an interesting fact that, although some manor houses were originally moated,
English villages, in contrast to many on the Continent, were scarcely ever provided with defences. The principal factors determining the siting of most of our
villages were the proximity of good farmland, an abundant water supply and
shelter from the wind. Hence the strong preference for valley sites, where the
rivers, even when they were only small and shallow streams, also provided a
means of transport and waterpower for the mills.

Very few English villages were consciously planned: none, in fact, except those
which were built, all of a piece, usually by Georgian landowners, of which Milton
Abbas in Dorset is deservedly the best known example. Nor is there any village
in which the classical style of architecture predominates. Classical buildings
there are of course (including some excellent Georgian churches), and often they
are among the most handsome of any; but because, until the Industrial Revolution, the same local materials continued to be used, the visual harmony was
maintained. In fact, variations of style seldom fail to enrich a village's architectural
impact, so long as the materials are right. That is a lesson which today we badly
need to re-learn.

Such, then, is the bird's-eye view of the English village. But as we travel about the
country, we cannot fail to notice many regional variations. These were due to the
accidents of history and geographical situation and to gradations in material
prosperity, and above all to geological differences, which directly controlled the
nature of the building materials. These will be treated in detail in the Gazetteer
section; here I can do no more than indicate some of the local specialities for which
the visitor should be particularly on the look-out, if he wants to savour his experience to the full.

Russell Read

The Grammar School in the little village of Appleby Parva in Leicestershire, 1693–7

The villages of the three south-eastern counties, Surrey, Sussex and Kent, are memorable above all for the radiant richness of their reds. The clays yield the finest bricks in England, and not only bricks but gorgeous tiles, which were used both for roofing and also for adorning walls. The builders so much enjoyed their plain tiles that sometimes, especially in Kent, they would carry down the roofs to within a few feet of the ground: the delightfully named cat-slides. The roofs are often high-pitched, with excellent, centrally placed chimney-stacks. The original purpose of the wall tiles was to give additional protection against bad weather to timber-framed houses, so they are often confined to the upper storey. They were usually hung with wooden pegs on to laths nailed to the oak studs, and their upper ends might also be bedded into lime mortar. Later, especially on south- and west-facing walls, bricks themselves might be provided with this additional covering, even on the humblest cottage, which never fails to add a note of richness. The finest collections of tile-hung houses are in Wealden places such as Tenterden, Smarden and Burwash, but many villages in the South-East can offer at least a few examples.

Other materials specially characteristic of the Weald villages are weatherboarding and the so-called Horsham slate roofs. Weatherboarding is much commoner on the other side of the Atlantic than in England; anyone familiar with New England will know with what resourcefulness those horizontal 'clapboards' of pine or cedarwood, painted in an enchanting range of colours, were used all over a terrain ill-provided with workable building stone. In England we have been shy of colour: most weatherboarding is white or, for farm buildings, tar-black. Usually these boards are chamfered at the lower edge and laid so that they overlap; when the light is right, the effect is one of thin, straight horizontal shadows rhythmically disposed across the white surface, and on freshly painted houses looks extremely good.

Horsham slates have nothing to do with slate, and are by no means confined to the Horsham area. This is a generic term applied to the products of those beds of Cretaceous sandstone which are widely scattered over the whole length of the Weald, between the North and South Downs. The special characteristic of all these rocks is that they are fissile, but they cannot be split, like true slate, into small thin slabs; on the contrary, the slabs are large, thick and enormously heavy. But they make a grand roof. It goes without saying that very strong rafters were needed to support such weights, yet hundreds have survived, in Sussex particularly, and, what is more, many of the houses which have such roofs are themselves timber-framed: an impressive tribute to the immense strength of the local oaks. The colour of this stone is dark brown, but as it is very (sometimes excessively) attractive to moss and lichen, the over-all effect is often somewhat green.

Across the Thames, in Essex, we are in the most stoneless county in the country. So here brick appeared early: to grand effect in the fifteenth century at Faulk-bourne Hall, so imposing that one almost forgets about the village, and under Henry VIII at a number of country churches, of which Layer Marney is notable. This church stands cheek-by-jowl with the immense brick gatehouse of a never-to-be-completed Tudor mansion.

Timber-framing at Lavenham in Suffolk

Edwin Smith

There is also a great deal of weather-boarding, generally applied in the Georgian period to older timber-framed structures, of which Essex has more than any other county. The chief difference from the South-East lies in the far greater use of external plaster.

Surrounding these four counties is a broad belt of flint stretching from the chalk downs of East Dorset to the north coast of Norfolk. This material is by no means rare in parts of the South-East, but in the downland country of Hampshire and Berkshire, along the whole length of the Chilterns, and above all in Suffolk and Norfolk its presence is ubiquitous. As a result these are pepper-and-salt villages, with an overall greyish tonality. It cannot be said that such places have the charm of many others. Until the mortar fails, flint buildings are virtually indestructible, and stand foursquare to every wind that blows – which is just as well, for in East Anglia, especially near the coast, the winter winds can blow very hard indeed. But flint is best used in conjunction with limestone, as can be seen in many excellent examples of alternating bands in Dorset, chequerwork in Wiltshire, and flushwork (knapped flint used decoratively in conjunction with dressed limestone to form patterns, tracery, monograms and so on) in Suffolk and Norfolk.

Associated with the flint belt is a good deal of brick, which varies considerably in colour and character. It is at its best at the southern end. In Hampshire, Berkshire and South Oxfordshire, in addition to excellent reds, there are places where the presence of plenty of lime in the clays yielded those elegant silver-grey bricks so much esteemed, as we would expect, in the Georgian age. Wickham in Hampshire has many examples, and so has Watlington in Oxfordshire. From Bedford through Cambridgeshire into western Suffolk the colour changes: here are those bricks that are euphemistically called 'white' but which in fact are a somewhat anaemic-looking pale brown. They account for very sober-sided villages, with no radiance at all, although the local habit of roofing with plain tiles of mixed colours, yellows, pinks and browns, all rather pale, can be attractive. Reds reappear in East Suffolk and Norfolk, where the brickwork, although not as good as in Kent, is often very pleasing, particularly in the outcrop of fanciful Tudor chimney-stacks and Netherlands-influenced gables.

But the most enjoyable villages in Suffolk are those in which neither brick nor flint prevails. This county, like its neighbour Essex, still preserves a great deal of timber-framing, some of it exposed and some plastered over but immediately recognizable wherever there is a jetty (projecting upper storey). Lavenham is deservedly famous for its timber-framing. The oak in East Anglia (where it is also the glory of many churches) and in the South-East is fortunately very seldom blackened, but left in its natural state, often an exquisite silver-brown. The plaster is more colourful than anywhere else in England, several shades of pink being specially favoured. The Suffolk villages are also (with a few in Essex) the best in which to enjoy the craft of pargeting: the application of ornamental patterns, either in relief or incised, to (usually external) plasterwork.

We cannot leave Norfolk without mentioning the roofs. This is the great area for reed thatch, obtained by dint of strenuous work in very cold conditions – for it must be cut in winter – from the fringes of the Broads. Since the advent of the combine-harvester, which has so crushed and bruised wheat straw as to render it useless for thatching, Norfolk reed has travelled widely across the country, but in its home county it is still seen at its best. It is the ideal roofing material for flint walls: the right colour and the right weight – which is to say, exceptionally light. Norfolk villages can still show more than 50 thatched churches, which is more than the whole of the rest of England. The best reed thatch is craftsmanship of a very high order: a joy to behold.

Where a Norfolk roof is not thatched, it is likely to be covered with good red pantiles. These are sometimes to be seen in Suffolk, but hardly at all in any of the other counties mentioned so far. But in Norfolk there are plenty, and they continue up the eastern side of England all the way to Northumberland. Apart from an area around Bridgwater, they are seldom found elsewhere in England. Their aesthetic appeal is considerable. They are larger than plain tiles, and the rhythmic surging of the courses yields a surface richness which never fails to give pleasure.

Moving now to the west and north-west of the flint, the brick, the plaster, the timber-framing and the thatch, we quickly find ourselves in an entirely different world. For we have reached the belt of Jurassic limestone which sweeps across the centre of the country in a great ogee curve from Portland Bill to the Cleveland Hills. Here, on the Oolite, are the majority of our most famous quarries; here are the classic villages, the show-pieces of our vernacular architecture. The prevailing colours are grey, pale brown and buff, with deep rust browns on the Somerset–Dorset border and in the neighbourhood of Banbury. Reds are hardly to be seen, and this is as it should be; only in parts of Lincolnshire, where the belt becomes very narrow and where limestone roofing slates were not always locally available, do we sometimes find stone houses with roofs of red pantiles. At the southern end of the belt there is still a good deal of thatch. But, in between, lovely roofs of graded limestone slates were the rule, and happily thousands survive. Around Stamford most of these slates came from Collyweston, where even today they are still obtainable. Farther south the average size is smaller: the most famous source of supply was Stonesfield, near Woodstock.

The Jurassic belt comprises two principal strands, the Oolite and the Lias. With the single exception of the Ham Hill stone of South Somerset, which used to be classified with the Oolites but which geologists now place in the Upper Lias, all the best Jurassic limestones are oolitic. And by 'best' I mean homogeneous enough in structure and of sufficiently fine grain to produce freestone: stone, that is to say, which can be cut 'freely', in any direction, either with a saw or with a mallet and chisel. The masonry thus produced is known as ashlar, and until the invention of power-driven saws it was the most expensive kind. Nevertheless, a good deal of it is to be found in the Cotswolds, even in the villages. The Cotswold villages, followed by those around Stamford, are the best built in England.

Even in the Cotswolds, however, the masonry of the cottages is usually rubble-stone, as is invariably the case on the Lias, apart from the Ham Hill area. For the humbler buildings this is, of course, perfectly appropriate, especially since the dressings, even of cottages, as can be seen to perfection at Rockingham, are often of freestone. The contrast, indeed, between the more refined stonework of the church or the manor house or other larger village buildings and the rubble-stone (which is usually coursed) of the others is entirely satisfying. On the limestone belt, even more than in the South-East, we think first not of the landscape but of the towns and villages, which are as 'jewels set in a silver sea'. Except that in some places the sea is inclined to be golden!

Owing to the persistence even into the eighteenth century of features derived from Tudor, and ultimately from Gothic, architecture, mullioned and transomed

J. Allan Cash

Cotswold stone at Lower Slaughter in Gloucestershire

windows and gables in particular, the villages of these regions preserve to an unusual degree a sense of architectural unity, greatly enhanced, of course, by the ubiquity of the limestone. Today stone is unhappily too expensive for many pockets, but the local authorities have rightly insisted on the employment of stone-coloured brick throughout this area.

If we care for architecture, we have now seen all England's finest villages, even though local patriots will be certain to demur. Beyond the limestone belt – still, that is to say, moving away from London – the large majority of churches are built of sandstone of one kind or another, New Red, usually rather soft, and Millstone Grit being the most frequent.

In the western Midlands, however, stone is much less characteristic of the villages, where the principal materials are timber and brick. If there was plenty of stone, there was also an abundance of oak trees, and in Worcestershire and the Welsh Border counties many of the smaller village buildings are still timber-framed. This is the region of 'black-and-white': the wood (but probably only in the nineteenth century, when industrial tar became available) was blackened and the interstices, the original wattle and daub or lath and plaster having often been replaced by brick-nogging, were limewashed. This shrill colour combination has its devotees, but is best seen in isolation, as at Little Moreton Hall; in a village street such buildings tend to 'jump', and a movement in recent years to de-black is surely greatly to be encouraged, for oak is much too fine a wood to be subjected to such harsh treatment.

In this part of England people were still erecting timber-framed buildings in the eighteenth century, for even then some of the forests had not been cleared.

But many of them are Elizabethan or Jacobean. Compared with the East and South-East, they are decidedly artless: Weobley cannot hold a candle to Lavenham. Some of this West of England black-and-white has a lively exuberance, but often one feels that the houses 'just growed'. The most ostentatious are usually to be found in the towns, for if a prosperous local tradesman was spending all that money on his house, he naturally wanted it to be seen. Village black-and-white is often rather crude: white squares or rectangles in somewhat clumsy frames, redeemed only by the roof when this is of sandstone slates.

It has also to be said that brick in the West of England, and in the North, is not nearly as pleasing as in the South and East. This is largely due to the less favourable composition of the available clays. It is also because a high proportion of the brickwork to be seen in these once sparsely populated areas is Victorian and machine-made.

Roofs in the western counties are now all too often of Welsh slate, a useful but unenjoyable material in which all the slates are of uniform size and can be somewhat purple, an unfortunate colour. More recently machine-made plain tiles have been the rule, and these are no better.

In the North, apart from East Yorkshire and the Vale of York, and leaving aside the industrial areas of the past 150 years, the usual building material was the local stone. This varied a good deal, but, except for the fine Magnesian limestone of central Yorkshire, was usually somewhat difficult to work. This, combined with other factors, which include the harsher climate, the less favourable economic circumstances before the Industrial Revolution and the no-nonsense-about-art attitude of most northern villages, has resulted in an architecture of

Walls of cob at Widecombe in Devon

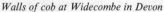

Edwin Smith

considerable austerity, which is usually subordinate to the grandeur of the landscape. The villages are not without dignity, but their spirit is reticent. Windows may be small, and house walls very roughly built; they often look better when whitewashed. Their most memorable feature is their roofs. The flagstones from the Coal Measures which are much in evidence in West Yorkshire and East Lancashire may be heavy, clumsy and dour, but, like the Horsham slates, they have a tremendous presence. In the North-West the grey-blues and grey-greens of the Cumbrian slates yield the loveliest roofs in England away from the limestone belt.

Red brick is the standard building material of many of the northern industrial villages, and a very harsh unattractive brick it is, particularly in Lancashire. In the Vale of York much of it is browner and older; on Humberside redder again and some of it still earlier: but seldom is any of this northern brickwork other than strictly utilitarian. The principal 'red pleasure' in this part of England is derived again from the roofs. Bright red pantiles are scattered over the whole of East and North-East Yorkshire, most of County Durham, and on or near the eastern seaboard all the way to Berwick-on-Tweed.

And so, finally, to the other end of England: the South-West. West Somerset and Devon may be thought to possess our most seductive countryside, as well as a splendid coastline; it is also another area in which the impact of the villages is subordinate to that of the landscape. The churches are, again, mostly built of sandstone, of many different colours; their towers, sometimes very tall, strive to dominate the villages, but as often as not the surrounding hills, as at Widecombe-in-the-Moor, rise far higher. The manor house and some of the other buildings will often be of sandstone rubble, but in many villages the predominant material is cob, with walls at least 2 feet thick. In either case a coat of whitewash or colourwash was popular: with cob invariable. Since no shuttering was used in building a cob cottage, the walls are liable to undulate; curved corners are frequent, and some cottages have projecting ovens of rounded form below the chimney-stacks. The usual roofing was, and in many villages still is, thatch. These are very rural villages, without architectural pretensions but perfectly in tune with their settings.

Cornwall is very different. Except that timber-framing and pre-nineteenth-century brick are even less common here than in Devon and West Somerset, one could hardly imagine a greater contrast. There is no cob and very little thatch. The local stone is among the toughest in the country: granite and slate. There are also a number of other rocks peculiar to the Duchy: elvan, polyphant, catacleuse, serpentine. (This last, a beautiful stone, and not at all tough, can be seen to excellent effect at St Keverne). For centuries the great quarry at Delabole near Camelford, a mile round and 400 feet deep, and still working, has supplied slate for most of the roofs in Cornwall and for many beyond. Otherwise, the rocks are mostly so hard that they were quarried very little before the eighteenth century; wherever they could, builders relied, as mentioned earlier, on 'presents'. Yet no English villages outside the Cotswolds are more completely stone-built than those of Cornwall. And because of the difficulty of cutting granite, the size of the blocks was sometimes gargantuan. Cornishmen have always enjoyed declaring that across the Tamar one enters another land, which is not England. Of their villages, most of them markedly unpicturesque, this is indeed the truth.

The Parish Church

Ronald Blythe

The most compelling building in almost every English village is a parish church. It is not architecture alone which concentrates our lingering attention upon this structure, but our recognition in its stony infusion of all that we are, or were, or hope to be. These thousands of old churches are broadly similar to each other and at the same time individually unique. They are easy to find but mysterious to discover. It is taken for granted that the average parish church is by far the most beautiful edifice in a place. It is also the most history-soaked artifact in the possession of a community, and whether a local person utilizes it for its sacred function or not, its presence in his landscape alters him. The sensitive traveller will often be overwhelmed by what might be called the quintessence of localism after an hour or two's exploration of it. The very silence of the huge arcaded room around which he casts his eye warns him not to draw hollow, echoing conclusions, for these are the walls within which everything was said. Centuries of birth words, marriage words, death words, gossip, the language of the hymn-poets and of the Latin liturgy and all the great Bible translation language have been spoken aloud here in the local accent. An imaginative glance at the List of Incumbents board will prove that most parish churches witnessed (heard) the very creation of colloquial English as six or eight hundred years of sermons battered away at erring minds. So it is a house of words as well as a house of wood and stone. No parish church can be understood if one omits the eloquence factor.

Most of these wonderful temples were built during the Middle Ages on sites which had often been held sacred long before Christianity itself arrived in the neighbourhood. When you open the churchyard gate you could be entering some Celtic field of the dead, or some wooded spot where Nature herself was worshipped. Or where one of St Augustine's travelling missionaries drew the crowds. Thus these familiar architectural pleasures stand with their feet in the primal faith, or in the beliefs it superseded.

The ordinary parish churchyards, those often steep little islands around which the modern traffic roars, or which are moor-locked or corn-locked in the countryside, have a fascination all of their own. They are botanical, elegiac and crammed with information about the latest 'old families', or the people who have constituted the heart of the local community since the late eighteenth century. In village graveyards the contrast between the north and south areas can still be seen and felt. In the south stand all the best tombs, in the north there is a bumpy desolation, for it was here that the parish interred its paupers, unbaptised babies, trouble-makers, bastards (and their mothers), thieves and the unfortunate generally. Being buried 'on the dog' was how they described it in East Anglia. The north side of a parish church will often reveal its greatest age, for over the years improvement money was usually only spent on the south, and many a nave presents

SAMUEL PALMER (1805–81): Coming from Evening Church. Tempera, 1830 (*Tate Gallery, London*).
One of the most notable examples of the 'visionary' paintings, charged with Christian symbolism,
by this follower of William Blake. It was painted at Shoreham, Kent, the background to
Palmer's most strikingly individual pastoral scenes.

JAMES CHARLES (1851–1906): Christening Sunday. Oils, 1887 (*City of Manchester Art Galleries*).
James Charles, one of the first artists to practise *plein-air* painting in England,
specialized in studies of country life. This picture, which was exhibited at the Royal Academy
in 1887, was painted at South Harting, Sussex.

a magnificent Decorated façade towards the sun, and its first simple Norman wall to the cold quarter. Many ancient graveyards, if they have not suffered ignorant attempts to turn them into suburban gardens, will be seen to contain rare plants as well as remarkable memorials. To shift the latter about for the sake of tidiness, as sometimes happens now, is tasteless and unfeeling. For those addicted to the delights of church exploration, a graveyard is the quiet overture to the surprises and satisfactions to come.

While a church will display the highest historic artistry of a community, it will also present what is in effect an ecological statement about its particular region, for it will have been constructed out of the best stone, wood and clays in the district. Sometimes having to make do with seemingly limited material, such as flint in Suffolk, forced the church-builders into dazzling ingenuity; hence the splendours of flushwork in which split flints set in panels of ashlared stone provide an exterior decoration which is like nothing so much as an architectural version of the magnificent garnets-and-gold ornaments found in the Sutton Hoo ship burial. The parish churches lift up the heart-stone of geological England in all its variety, from the oolite of the West Midlands to Cornish granite, from the 'red' and 'white' sandstone of Staffordshire, so soft that the air can eat its surface away, to stone from the great limestone belt which stretches from Dorset to Yorkshire, and from whose celebrated quarries many hundreds of our finest buildings have emerged. All down the east-coast counties can be found churches made of brick or roofed in orange or dull red tiles. These warmly-coloured shrines are especially harmonious to everything that surrounds them. In them we see the elevation of the very earth itself to inspirational heights.

Tucked away among these chiefly local materials lie the oddments and fragments, the bits of carving from a Saxon chancel, the tiles from a Roman villa, and, usually in the base of the tower, some great sarsen. Sarsen or saracen (stranger) stones are sandstone boulders which used to lie about in the fields rather strangely, like sheep, so that sometimes our ancestors called them grey wethers. They may have been mortared into the parish churches for other reasons than their usefulness, for there was something inexplicable and mysterious about them. Stonehenge is partly built of sarsens. Finally, in the full impact which these building materials make, on the awareness, comes wood. Outside, the wooden porches and doors, inside a medieval carpentry so superb that there is nothing like it, nothing that can be measured against it. Oak chiefly, though occasionally chestnut, woods that were maturing in forests long before the Conquest.

Most churches were built entirely of wood to begin with, and we have that intriguing survival at Greensted, Essex, to show us what they were like, where the eleventh-century nave has been made from huge tree trunks halved down the middle and set upright in a sill with their flat surfaces turned inwards. Although some of our parish churches originated as Christianized versions of classical temples, the majority began their long and ever-changing and yet immutable history as little shelters set up, probably by the priest himself, to protect altars from the weather. Soon the worshippers themselves sought shelter in a great adjoining building from which they could observe the mysteries through a lattice (cancelli) or chancel. The congregation called their part of the church the nave (navis meaning 'ship') both because it looked like an upturned vessel and because it represented for them a safe craft in which to voyage across the risky seas of life. Over the centuries a tradition emerged of priestly authority for the architecture and decorations of the chancel, and a local congregation's taste in most matters governing the nave. Both of them grew more and more splendid, partly because of the need for a pictorial theology and morality when few could read, which meant education by artists rather than scholars, partly as an attempt by men to reflect the divine creativity, and partly, no doubt, from solid, no-nonsense local ambition and pride. But whether the beautiful carvings or painted glass we see now resulted from the decision of some hard-nosed medieval trade guild or from the true piety of some uncalendared saint, time has unified them into a spiritual whole, and what we feel as we walk around any parish church, from the barest to the breathtakingly glorious, is that we are at the epicentre of all the shifts and formations which produced a regional society.

To the basic structure of chancel and nave must be added the most typical feature of all, a tall tower full of bells and often bearing a clock. It was the height of these towers which kept numerous parishes within sight and sound of each other through the ages. They had endless practical purposes as beacons, strong rooms for local funds and valuables, weather-testers, forts and as pointers to the infinite. There is no evidence to prove that the famous round towers of Norfolk, for example, were built purely for defence; but we do have a fascinating record from all over England of their varied uses as observation posts. From their Saxon beginnings parish church towers grew in their ability to make confident statements about the security of a man's home and his spiritual future. They elevated his vision, drawing his sight upwards, and also, when he climbed them, outwards beyond his own parochial ditches. And within England's thousands of church towers hang such a wealth of bells that it is no wonder that Handel described them as our national musical instrument, because for centuries we have made them 'speak', as the ringers would say, an ultimate wordless language to convey exultation or grief and, up until the last war, to spell out, as they did in Shakespeare's day, all kinds of local messages.

There is now a great revival in campanology, but the bells themselves, remote in their dizzy cages, remain the least seen wonders of a parish church. A high proportion of them are of the fifteenth century and part of the original fittings of a church erected during the finest period of parish architecture. Pre-reformation bells are usually inscribed with prayers, but later on we have them bearing legends such as that on an eighteenth-century bell in St Nicholas church, Ipswich, which says *Marlburio duce castra cano vestate* – 'I sound the ravaging of enemy strongholds under Marlborough's leadership'. The clash between what is eternal and what is national can be felt at all levels in these old buildings where every generation expresses its patriotism as well as its religious belief. Once incorporated within these hold-alls of what a local community found valuable or expedient, very little ever escaped, so that every parish church is a museum of political attitudes and social behaviour as well as a sacred place designed to accommodate the everlasting.

With over 11,000 churches to choose from, how is one to select their delights? For some of us association is the thing. To enter the tiny churches of Bemerton and Little Gidding, and to realize that *their* parish is that of a great Anglican literature stretching from George Herbert to T. S. Eliot, is one way of exploring these edifices. Writers draw the modern pilgrim to many a shrine up and down the land, from Hardy's Stinsford, a parish church without which, one could say, there would have been no Thomas Hardy, for although he escaped from its belief it yet remained in his blood, to Haworth, with its reek of doomed brilliance. Gray's Stoke Poges churchyard is the ultimate literary source of the thoughts which crowd in on us when we open any lych ('corpse' – Old English) gate, and our novels and poetry are more permeated with what philosophically and roman- tically exudes from this ancient building and its surrounds than from almost anything else. Never before was there such a traipsing through other people's parochial heart centres as there is now – and no wonder! For they are irresistible. It is because there is no limit to their artistry and to what they are able to say about the human condition that we brake suddenly and say, like Wemmick in *Great Expectations*, 'Halloa! Here's a church! . . . Let's go in!'

With such a vast number of parish churches to choose from, not one of which is without something worth looking at or thinking about, how invidious it may seem to pick out a recommended dozen or so. The following selection aims at nothing more than an attempt to contain such a huge and fascinating subject within a few parochial boundaries and make it manageable. Thus, if one wished to find a particularly fascinating example of what might be called immemorial parochial continuity where a tangible timelessness is still all above ground, so to speak, from the days of our Celtic ancestors to the present, and the average village church's slow awakening to the realities of the post-Vatican II world, then a little tour of the Winterbornes (Dorset) would provide it. There are ten of them and they lie on the steep chalky bank of the stream which gives them their name, and not very far from the quarries out of which St Paul's Cathedral was hewn. The most ancient of their churches is Winterborne Steepleton, which has fixed on an outside wall of the nave an amazing Saxon angel in full flight, with upturned toes and a great grave face turned backwards in a scanning motion. The church is dedicated to St Michael, the saint of the hilltops, so perhaps this is he, for the parish wanders upwards to the tall South Dorset Ridgeway with its stepped contours of 'Celtic' fields, known as lynchets, and a proliferation of barrows; and the vigorous sculpture is that of a being who soars up and down the human time-scale. Then there is Winterborne Abbas (because the church belonged to the Abbey of Cerne) where there is a whole range of minor delights from a 1440 bell to some fifteenth-century slip-tiles; Winterborne Came (because the church belonged to the Abbey of Caen, Normandy) where one of a number of grand tombs tells us that the Christian name of the first Countess of Dorset was Wil- liamsea; Winterborne Farringdon, which is a deserted medieval village where the church is just an oblong of green banks and a scrap of window tracery; Winterborne Monkton (because the church belonged to the monks of St Vaast in Aras) and where one needs an imaginative eye, for here the past is much frag- mented; Winterborne Herringston, where there is no church and no village, only a great Tudor house; and Winterborne St Martin, that lovely church which is crammed with parochial statements of every kind from eighteenth-century coffin stools to an unusual number of seventeenth-century headstones in the graveyard, with their deeply incised melancholy and strangely lively names. Yet the overwhelming structure within the parish boundaries here is Maiden Castle, that immense temple-cum-fort which Ptolemy called 'the city of Dunium' and whose juxtaposition to an old English village church is one of those things which stop the traveller in his tracks. As to its juxtaposition to that hill-dedicated angel St Michael at neighbouring Winterborne Steepleton, this is indeed food for theological thought on a parish level.

There are churches, of course, whose treasures are unique: buildings which contain something incomparable or which are themselves the highest example of their kind. Such a church is St Mary's, Fairford (Glos.), built by a wool merchant, John Tame, and which has retained all its original stained glass (*see coloured plate facing page 224*). Much of this came from the workshop of Barnard Flower, Henry VII's 'Master Glass Painter', who glazed the first windows in King's College Chapel, Cambridge. Reading from north to south, this set of windows is a picture rendering of the Catholic faith from beginning to end. William Morris, who lived nearby, often sat in this church to immerse himself in its glorious imagery. Or there are churches for looking at the rich iconography which preceded painted glass – painted walls, Copford (Essex) or Barfreston (Kent), for example, where we can still 'read' the illustrations which provided our Norman ancestors with their education. The artists who covered the interiors of churches with this picture-teaching, either in carvings or paint, were themselves the very reverse of parochial. They dealt in the great themes of Christendom itself, and even in cosmic abstractions, as at Copford, where the Signs of the Zodiac can be seen on the soffit of the chancel arch, and we can tell by looking at their work, hidden for so long under puritan whitewash, how swiftly ideas spread across Europe. At Wiston (Suffolk) there is a wall painting of St Francis preaching to the birds which is almost contemporary to that event in faraway Italy, and which is equivalent to one of today's news-pictures.

Hundreds of parish churches contain masterpieces of carpentry, and one of the first things which strikes the dedicated or compulsive church explorer is that, in spite of his skill with stone, wood is the Englishman's natural material for expressing utility in majestic terms. There are the Wealden churches with their extravagant wood, the celebrated timber roofs of East Anglia which are miracles of joinery, the bench-ends of the West Country, the superb black or silver-grey oak doors edged with carved kings, grapes and bishops, the early porches with their outer arches formed by 'splitting images' (from which the corruption 'spitting' image) or identical boards sawn from the same trunk, and the exquisite fretted rood and parclose screens which are so finely carved by countrymen that they look like attempts to create an undying foliage around chantries and tombs. Many parish churches have their chancels lined with fourteenth-century stalls with tip-up miserere seats, or misericords, whose fanciful and often Rabelaisian decorations seem to mock their purpose. Sometimes the carpenter's art makes a handsome and very decided social statement, such as in the Jacobean manorial pew at Bourn (Cambridgeshire). Often it was profound and intellectual, as at Trull (Somerset) where the four learned doctors of the Church, SS Gregory, Jerome, Ambrose and Augustine of Hippo, surround the medieval pulpit to lend their authority to all that was pronounced from it. One of the first pleasures to be found in church-crawling, as this activity has been recently and aptly described, is that it takes us into a realm where human nature and the Divine nature have been artistically and poetically inter-related. One minute a sublime wooden face catches our eye with its eternal implications, the next we are staring at some jolly figure of Lust or Gluttony, or simply, most likely, some all too earthy portrait of the carpenter's mistress or enemy.

Nor could one see many parish churches without becoming addicted to memorials. For the most part, they are erected to our betters. Only a fraction of the inhabitants of a parish ever got their names carved, although the majority of

people had them written down three times in the registers, when they were bap-
tised, when they were wed, and when they were buried. These parish registers
began to be kept in 1538 and it is only by studying them that we can begin to
understand the forces which produced the distinctive atmosphere of a certain
church. But it is the carved names, inside and out, which make the compulsive
reading and which arrest our gaze. Funerary sculpture offers a virtually illimitable
field for the addict and ranges from supreme works of art to today's dim, lawn-
mower-respecting little tiles in the cremation corner. Time and time again throughout our national literary history it has caught the eye of our greatest writers, from
Ben Jonson's 'Underneath this stone doth lie, as much beauty as could die' to
Kilvert's classic reaction to reading so many names he knew while wandering
around the churchyard at Langley Burrell after celebrating the Communion and
waiting for his clerk to put the chalice away. Listing them all, from Jane Hatherell
to Limpedy Buckland the gypsy girl, he adds the familiar conclusion: 'There they
lay, the squire and the peasant, the landlord and the labourer, young men and
maidens, old men and children, sister, brother . . .'. Thomas Gray, of course, had
put such thoughts in their most perfect language at Stoke Poges where he lies
in a simple tomb with his mother; this is as good a place as any for sombre enjoy-
ment.

As the average visitors book shows, there never was a time when so many non-
parishioners found their way into a local church, and certainly there never
was a time when they could interpret what they saw so knowingly. We have come
a long way since Thomas Rickman invented his names for Gothic styles – Early
English, Decorated, Perpendicular, etc. – in the nineteenth century, and we
are now educated in an appreciation of Victorian additions to these glorious
buildings. For the one thing which our increasing fascination for them tells us
is that, liturgically, architecturally or socially, they have never stood still. They
carry the marks of every progressive attitude as well as incorporating in their
fabric all the evidence of history's errors. If we whisper and shuffle a bit as we
tour through them it is not simply out of politeness but because they still awe us,
although exactly how and why it is hard to say.

The Village School

Miss Read

The traveller in Britain, pausing to cast an appraising or critical look at our villages, cannot fail to notice the local school, usually located in a central position. Sometimes it lies in the shadow of the parish church, and frequently it echoes its architectural style in modest form. Sometimes it is an integral part of the village street, blending with the cottages and small shops which flank it. Often all these buildings were built with the local stone, and designed by a sympathetic architect, and the result is harmonious.

But all too frequently the village schools were built in late Victorian times, after William Edward Forster's Education Act of 1870 was passed. This was the Act which set up locally elected school boards with power to build schools, appoint staff and supervise attendance. It made sure that no part of the country would be without a school, and that no child, however poor, would grow up uneducated.

It was a great step forward, but it was an unfortunate time for building, and not even the most ardent follower of Sir John Betjeman could admire some of the semi-ecclesiastical designs, often executed in a harsh red brick quite alien to their ancient surroundings, and embellished with bands of stonework which, however skilfully incorporated, present a certain fussiness to the eye.

Yet they have their charm. If the traveller stops to talk to the villagers he will soon discover that our village schools are regarded with deep affection and sincere admiration by a surprisingly large and varied number of people.

Naturally, those in the village are – or have been – directly involved with the school as scholars, parents, teachers, helpers or managers. They have worked at those desks, played hopscotch in that playground, and popped the blisters on the sun-baked school door. As grown-ups they have squeezed into too-small chairs at village meetings, sat through their children's Christmas plays, dutifully attended talks by the head teacher about New Mathematics, and gone home none the wiser. The village school remains part of their lives.

But there are others, often town dwellers, who feel the same affection for some particular village school. Many men and women, now in middle age, were evacuees in war-time Britain, and exchanged the city streets for life in the country. They spent a number of their most impressionable years as pupils in these foreign parts and a great many never broke the ties they made then with their adopted school. Others were sent to stay with grandparents or other relatives if illness cropped up in their town-based family, or any other crisis occurred. Usually the village schoolmaster would be willing to take in these temporary scholars, and another lasting link would be forged.

But it is the older villagers who give the clearest picture of how much the village school contributes to the community it serves. They remember when the school leaving age was 14, although many left before that time. This meant that from the age of five – sometimes four – until 14, the child stayed in the same school. A good thing? That is debatable, but it certainly made a strong bond between the pupils themselves and the grown-ups who lived around them.

It made for continuity, for tolerance of others' foibles, for time to watch the growth, not only of knowledge, but also of the formation of character.

A good village school teacher can be of enormous benefit to a small community. By the very nature of his position he is expected to set the same sort of standards of behaviour as the local vicar, the doctor or the squire. If his school is a church school, then he may well find himself actively involved in the choir or a church-warden's duties.

The older generation remembers well the vital part that the schoolmaster or mistress played in the parish. The schoolhouse, adjoining the school, was lived in then by the schoolmaster, and parents who wanted advice about their children knew where to find him. Today, more often than not, the house has been sold to strangers, or is used for the school dining room and kitchen, or a place for stores, and the head teacher comes to school by car from his home miles away.

Better transport is one of the reasons for the sad decline of the village school. In earlier times the children walked to school from their homes, walked home for their midday dinner, and back again for afternoon school. (I did it myself, thinking nothing of a mile and a half's trot four times a day in all weathers, and learning more about Kentish flowers and birds in that short time than ever I learnt since.)

Now parents can take their children farther afield if they prefer to. They too have no need to look for work in their immediate environs – nor could they find it in changed agricultural conditions.

Early in the century the little school of 16 pupils in which I once taught used to have a roll of over 100. Then the fathers were needed in great numbers as plough-men, carters, carpenters, foresters or gamekeepers, and the mothers as domestic workers on the big farms and estates. The families stayed put, and the school thrived. Now a 1000-acre farm can work with only a handful of men, and those who want to drive away to different employment do so.

Transport is not the only nail in the coffin of the village school. Families are smaller. Some of those earlier families had ten or twelve children. Now mothers need to go to work, usually farther afield, setting off as soon as their one or two children are of school age. They know that school dinner will be provided. Their houses are compact and easily cleaned. They have time to return to their careers and to earn something. But it means fewer children at the local school.

The obvious answer is closure of the school when numbers become really small. The traveller, looking for the village school, may well find the building, but no children playing round it, and no sound of youthful singing coming from it. It has probably been transformed into an attractive domestic dwelling. The playground has been overlaid with lawns, the shaky bell tower has been removed. Only the Gothic windows and the basic ecclesiastical architecture reveal the building's origin, although an elegant wooden name plate, swinging from a wrought-iron support may state unequivocally 'The Old School'.

There are very few schools which have closed without a stout battle. Affection, loyalty and a strong sense of the need for continuity unite a village when its old school is threatened. That indignation is justified. The first reason for parents' wrath is the removal of young children farther afield, away from their familiar background. There are plenty of other good reasons. Let's say the schooling has been efficient. The small classes have meant individual attention, which may not be the case when the child goes to a larger establishment. Then there is the loss of the head teacher and any other staff who may have played a great part in the life of the village. Why should they be uprooted?

And, above all, is the sense of loss. If the church represents the soul of the village, then the school is its heart. The school has served the people well, their parents and probably their grandparents. They like to see their own young blood there, learning these new-fangled metric tables where once they wrote £ s. d. in their best copperplate. They like to see them screaming around the playground, or hanging over the railings to shout at their mothers as they make their way to the shop. They like to hear the whistle which obtains partial – if not the desired complete – silence as playtime ends. It happened in their own day. It is as unchanging as the seasons, they feel, and rightly so. Memories forge strong bonds, and local authorities ignore this fact at their peril.

But one can see the local authorities' point of view. Financial advantages aside, there are real problems in these small schools. Staffing is difficult. The more remote the village, the shorter is the list of applicants for any post advertised. With railway branch lines closed, and buses few and far between, teachers need to have a car. In the old days there were usually one or two of the houses in the village whose owners would be willing to accommodate a teacher. Now the landladies of yore are out at work, and even if they wanted to take in a lodger there are few teachers who would want to spend their evenings, as well as their days, among their pupils. The nearest town is where they want to live, and who can blame them now that village activities, which once offered scope for talent and initiative, have declined as sadly as the small schools themselves? It is an uphill job, as any villager will tell you, to keep going the football and cricket clubs, the Women's Institute, the choir, and the upkeep of the village hall itself. Small wonder that teachers, particularly young ones, look to the town schools for their livelihood and their recreation.

Getting staff is not the only difficulty. *Keeping* staff is another. A two-teacher school needs a greater degree of compatibility between the staff members than is usual. It is easy enough if you are Mr Perrin, in a comprehensive school of 1000 children, to dodge Mr Traill, your *bête noir*, among the labyrinthine corridors. It is less simple when only a frail partition of glass and marmalade-coloured pitch pine separates you from your sole colleague, and you share every playtime and dinnertime in his company.

Of course, it can be even worse if there are three on the staff. Some very ugly triangles can be formed. But worse still, perhaps, is the plight of the teacher who is in sole charge, and it is right, I think, that the one-teacher school is on its way out. As I have mentioned, I taught myself in just such a tiny school for about two months until a new head could be appointed. I count that period as one of the happiest times of my teaching career, but it opened my eyes to the problems faced by one-teacher schools.

With an age-range from five years to eleven it is virtually impossible to find a story or music which all can enjoy at the same time. All work has to be individual, and there is no hardship in that when numbers are small. But there are things which the eight- and nine-year-olds miss. At that competitive stage they love, and need, team games, which are impossible with 16 children.

The sole teacher too is dangerously vulnerable when accidents or sudden illness arise. She must guard too against becoming neurotic or taking an unreasonable dislike to one of her number. It is a lonely life, particularly for a single woman who returns to her own solitary life after school hours.

Nevertheless, I was as sad as the rest when that little school closed. It seemed to me that the heart of that village had stopped beating, and the knowledge that this is happening all over the country only makes the whole business more piteous.

But one wonders if there is not some change of heart about rural communities. Anything affecting our children makes a swift impact on people, and the closing of village schools and all it implies may have given the impetus to a good deal of thought about living in the country.

For, more than ever, people are rebelling against the congestion of town life. If they have children they want a garden, somewhere for them to play, somewhere to hang out the washing, somewhere to rest in a deck chair, somewhere to put the pram. A garden is a rare commodity in a town centre, and whereas suburbia offers space, pleasant surroundings, shops, company and usually decent modern schools, there is the disadvantage for the wage earners of travelling to work. The cost of fares or the frustration of trying to park a car, and more and more frequent strikes make this business of commuting a hazardous affair.

With the coming of the motorways many young people have decided that it is probably more sensible to buy a house in a village within striking distance of a motorway junction and to rely entirely on a car to get to work. In the old days they might have been in a position to pay for private education for their children – some still are – but a great many simply cannot afford the fees which these schools are now obliged to ask, especially if there are three or four children to educate. They look to the state schools with increasing interest, and this is a good thing from all points of view.

Village schools today are staffed by teachers as well qualified as their town counterparts. The discrepancy in salaries which tended to concentrate capable teachers in the urban areas years ago has now gone. Parental and staff participation is mutually stimulating and helps to improve the standard of education.

Is it too much to hope that our existing village schools will remain open? They have so much to offer. A great many, up and down the country, have already celebrated their centenaries, and the ravages of age may show in crumbling plaster and leaking skylights. But the spirit within is as lively as ever, and the friendships made and the lessons learnt, in the family atmosphere of a village school, can warm a lifetime, as I am fortunate enough to know.

The Big House

Olive Cook

Edwin Smith

Madeley Court in Shropshire

> *One England blots out another. The England of the Squire Winters*
> *and the Wragby Halls was gone, dead . . . What would come after?*

We know more than D. H. Lawrence could of what came after, and that knowledge
has sharpened our interest in the paternalist, compact community of which the
Wragby Halls were the pivot. Despite the collapse of the society to which they
owed their association, the essential elements of the village scene remain, often
visually and always in our imagination, the parish church, the rectory and the
home of the squire, the 'big house', dominating a cluster of cottages. In image
after recollected image the ever-varying relationship of 'hamlet and Hall' delights
the mind's eye: Aynho grandly and sternly presiding over neat cottages from the
recessions of its courtyard; Warmington Manor, mullioned, gabled, of warm
brown stone, a more imposing version of its humble dependents, standing like a
hen with its chicks directly on the green without a garden; Cranborne rising
above its gatehouse to drench the village street with Arcadian poety; gabled
Kelmscott hovering with homely informality over the flat river landscape and

the 'old grey beehives' as Rossetti called the neighbouring cottages. So keenly do we recognize the symbolic as well as the aesthetic power of such images that when we come upon houses which were once vital forces in rural life lying half derelict or rent and ruinous like Madeley Court and Moreton Corbet Castle in Shropshire or torn down like Weeting Hall, Norfolk, to make way for an eruption of bungalows, we are overwhelmed by an almost personal sense of loss.

The most obvious reminders in the landscape of early feudal society are the ruined castles of Norman magnates. Their purpose was to subjugate a conquered people, and even in decay the stone bulk of one of these fortresses, where it is associated with a village, looms, as at Corfe (*see page 150*), and at Middleham (*see page 335*) with menacing, repressive power above the dwellings at its feet. Nonetheless the stark donjon-keep of the Norman castle, with rooms for storage and domestic chambers piled one above another, made its own contribution to the type of manor house which, under the Plantagenets, replaced castles as the hub of the social system.

The manorial economy, the origin of the village community, already existed in Saxon England. The manor comprised the whole estate of the lord, and both villeins and rent-paying tenants were bound to him. All attended the lord's court of justice, his moot (hence Ightham *Mote*) which was held fortnightly either in the manorial hall or under the venerable oak tree in the middle of the village; and it was significant for the peculiarly English relationship between landowner and villager that this was the lord's court and not the King's. The medieval ancestors of the country squires were knights who had acquired land in return for military service or on the principle of scutage, the payment of money instead of the performance of service. In times of peace the feudal system gave them the leisure essential to the development of the arts of civilized life. Thus they gradually became country gentlemen, improving their lands, embellishing their homes, patronizing craftsmen, musicians and men of letters and devoting themselves to local administration. In the reign of Edward III squires were appointed to the newly created office of Justice of the Peace, and for 400 years their power and authority continued to increase.

The manor house itself took two forms in Norman England. The more usual type consisted of a single huge aisled room, the character of which can be most vividly experienced in some well-preserved medieval barn such as the noble examples at Little Coggeshall in Essex, and Abbotsbury (*see page 144*). The aisles were used for storage, for the stalling of animals and for the accommodation of servants. The arrangement of the hall otherwise followed a set pattern. Near one end were doors opposite to one another, and the gable wall at the same end was pierced by three openings leading to the buttery, pantry and kitchen. The smoke from a central hearth, such as can still be seen in the hall at Penshurst, found its way through a louver in the roof. In order to control draughts, short movable screens like the flamboyant survival at Rufford Old Hall, Lancashire, were set at right angles to each exit. Eventually these screens became a continuous structure reaching from wall to wall, as at Penshurst Place and at Coker Court, Somerset. Two doors led through it into what was called the 'screens passage'. Opposite the screen at the other end of the hall a raised, paved space was reserved for the Lord of the Manor and his family. Despite the litter and disorder of the apartment the serving of dinner was a precisely conducted ceremony which foreshadowed the meticulous organization of the later squire's household.

The earliest brick-built house in England: Little Wenham Hall, Suffolk

The second form of manor house found in eleventh-century England was a small two-storeyed rectangular stone building of French origin. Very few such houses still stand, but of these Hemingford Manor has been continuously inhabited since it was built by Payne de Hemingford in about 1150. Although altered in the sixteenth century, and modestly enlarged by eighteenth-century additions, the plan of the simple little Norman house is perfectly clear. The low, vaulted ground floor comprised two chambers for storage and offices; the upper floor was occupied by the great hall, entered by an external stair. Manor house design evolved from combinations of the Norman tower-keep, the Norman two-storeyed house and the hall. L-shaped Little Wenham Hall, Suffolk, is an early instance of the union of tower and two-storeyed house, while tower and great hall are magnificently fused at Longthorpe, Cambridgeshire, and in many later houses – at Horeham Hall, in Essex, for instance, and at Daneways, Sapperton, Gloucestershire, where the High Building was only added to the hall house in the seventeenth century. The amalgamation of the hall and the two-storeyed house is far commoner than either of these arrangements. The two-storeyed house might be set across one end of the hall, as at Old Soar, Plaxtol, Kent, or it might, perhaps in answer to a nascent desire for symmetry, be matched by a further rectangular block at the other end, as at Little Chesterford Manor, Essex. The resulting H-shape dominated manor house design for many generations. Gifford's Hall, at Wickhambrook in Suffolk, Charney Bassett in Berkshire, Great Chalfield Manor in Wiltshire, and The Ley, at Weobley in Herefordshire are among countless houses exhibiting these components. All three basic units of the medieval manor house often occur in conjunction in the courtyard house, which derived from the early moat-protected timber enclosure. At Ightham (*see page 81*) the tower forms the gatehouse and this is its role in later houses such as Hoghton Tower, Oxburgh Hall, Layer Marney, and Sissinghurst *(see page 89)*. In all these buildings the tower-gatehouse becomes a spectacular mock fortification, parading the attributes of defence when it had ceased to be necessary.

These gatehouses reveal something of the tremendous aesthetic advances which distinguished domestic architecture in the late fifteenth and sixteenth centuries. With the addition of other rooms the great hall could dispense with aisles and had become a stately apartment lit by large windows and covered by an ingeniously contrived open timber roof, as at Ightham Mote, Penshurst Place, Gifford's Hall, Stoke-by-Nayland, and Great Dixter *(see page 85)*. But its most conspicuous features were all prompted and surpassed by ecclesiastical example. Now, at the close of the Middle Ages, with glimpses of horizons beyond the narrow confines of the medieval world and the stirrings of a new, secular habit of mind, the builders of houses became independent of church architecture. The great hall was long retained as the most important room in the house, and the esteem in which it was held is commemorated by the custom which lingers yet in some villages of referring to the squire's house as the 'hall'. But this retention of the hall was often the expression of a new, romantic, stimulating awareness of the historic past. It was the free association of feeling for the vernacular with a vision of classical forms which gave rise to the bizarre, dynamic and poetic houses of Elizabethan England. For, owing to the fact that through the break with Rome England had been cut off from direct contact with Italy, the high imagination of the builders was not hampered by first-hand knowledge of the classical disciplines.

With violent shifts in the upper levels of society and more land changing hands than at any time since the Conquest, brand new 'big houses' were transforming the aspect of many villages, while others witnessed extraordinary conversions. Lacock (*see page 235*), a former Augustinian abbey, was purchased by the Vice-Treasurer of the Bristol Mint, Sir William Sharrington, for £750. He himself planned the remarkable alterations, screening the monastic cloister and gatehouse with a startlingly novel balustraded classical front with a polygonal balustraded corner tower. The classical and the traditional were even more arrestingly and more harmoniously united in the great new houses of the period the designers of which were now for the first time called architects. At Barlborough (*see page 200*) John Smythson electrified the village with a metamorphosis of the traditional quadrangular house into a tall, compact, castellated mansion with a tiny inner courtyard and coronetted bays like turrets shooting up above the roof-line. At Hardwick his brilliant plan is a play upon the traditional H-design with the cross-bar of the letter projecting on either side of the uprights, but the elevation sensationally transfigures the plan for cross-bar and uprights terminate in immense square towers rising above the already lofty core of the house. The size, magnificence and extreme sophistication of these prodigious houses and their peers, such as Longleat, Burghley, Montacute, Wollaton and Burton Agnes, set them apart, but the spirit of drama and romance with which they imbue the village scene informs a profusion of lesser and incredibly diverse Elizabethan manors. Long Melford Hall shows none of the more surprising innovations of the period; yet it is an astonishing sight with its extravagant chimney shafts and gay pepper-pot domes flashing across the village green and contrasting so oddly with the classical, centrally placed porch in the open courtyard. At Ablington Manor, Bibury, ball-topped gables consort delightfully with an asymmetrically set porch consisting of Gothic buttresses flanking a Tudor arch framed by a Renaissance entablature and pilasters; and at Hammoon Manor, Dorset, a thatched, truly rustic house is suffused with sudden 'Midsummer Night's Dream' magic by a stone porch with a scrolled gable and a round Renaissance arch supported by swelling banded columns.

Very often Elizabethan invention and ebullience find an outlet in exaggerations of vernacular styles. With its jostling, multi-gabled bays and fabulous, soaring gatehouse completely covered with zigzags, lozenge-shapes, cusped circles and quatrefoils and ball-ended crosses, the well-known Little Moreton Hall, Cheshire, exalts the medieval timber-framed dwelling into a dazzling black-and-white conceit that never ceases to astound. And at Pitchford Hall, Salop, a symmetrical courtyard plan is galvanized by dynamic zebra stripes of hallucinatory regularity.

The interiors of such houses display many novel features – halls divided horizontally, halls placed centrally and at right angles to the façade as at Hardwick, and a bewildering number of bedrooms and parlours and often a long gallery, a many-windowed room on an upper floor used for the exhibition of pictures and tapestry, for music making and for gentle exercise. It might be a formal apartment as at Chastleton, with a rich plaster vault; it might be timbered and homely as at Little Moreton Hall.

The struggle between Crown and Parliament which disrupted the seventeenth century and which ended in Parliamentary supremacy, the Crown accepting its constitutional status, was of much consequence to the squires, for the government of the country was henceforth in the hands of the landowners wielding control through Parliament. Although building enterprises were considerably checked by the upheavals of this period the increased power of the squires was reflected in many new country mansions. The examples of Inigo Jones and of Sir Christopher Wren encouraged a more academic attitude to the principles of classical architecture, but the conflicting thought of the whole age was reflected in a hybrid style, and a century passed before Jones's unadulterated classicism was fully accepted. Groombridge Place, Kent, and Honington Hall, (*see page 187*) are typical houses built by seventeenth-century squires. Groombridge Place, russet-coloured above its broad green moat (for it stands on the site of an earlier house) preserves the H-shape of the medieval house, but the roofs of the cross-wings are hipped to create a continuous eaves-line marked by a modilioned wooden cornice. The entrance takes the form of an Ionic portico. At Honington the cross-wings still exist but merely as shallow projections, so that the house becomes almost a square block, thus foreshadowing the typical Georgian plan. The tall chimneys, however, recall past predilections for verticality, and are strangely moving seen in conjunction with the eloquent Italianate motif of imperial busts in niches.

The eighteenth century was the landlords' heyday, and if some of them were boozy and bucolic they seem on the whole to have resembled Squire Allworthy

Edwin Smith

The garden front of Long Melford Hall, Suffolk

rather than Squire Western. Inspired by an ideal of order, authority and concord, which is mirrored in the literature and painting of the period no less than in architecture, predisposed by a classical education and by the experience of the fashionable Grand Tour to adopt the Palladian style, the rules of which had now been firmly established by Lord Burlington, the foremost landowners and small squires alike set about creating houses for themselves which had the proportions and often the aspect of antique temples. The big house was now frequently built away from the village in a landscaped park which, adorned with pagan temples, statues, triumphal arches and obelisks as at Stourhead, Stowe, Rousham, Hagley,

Great Barrington and Hovingham, was part of the same transporting dream of a golden age. The houses themselves, whether of glowing red brick or shining stone or stucco, take the form of an absolutely symmetrical square or oblong block, isolated as at Clandon or, as at Houghton, rusticated and pilastered like an actual villa by Palladio, flanked by low service blocks. There is no end to the variations on these basic themes. The rectangular block may, as at Houghton and Hagley, be towered at the corners; it may be domed, as at Mereworth; sometimes there may be so little façade articulation that the impression is cliff-like and almost daunting, as at Overbury Court, Worcestershire, and Courteen-hall Hall, Northamptonshire; sometimes the temple-portico overshadows the entire house with the nobility of its stupendous proportions, as at Attingham; sometimes enthusiasm for antiquity flowers in an amazing image as in the giant south-front colonnade at West Wycombe – two-storeyed, Tuscan below, Corinthian above.

All these houses are attributed to well-known architects, and were the homes of wealthy landowners. Lesser squires employed local craftsmen. Guided by pattern books explaining the new architectural idiom, they tempered it to a peculiarly English form. Two examples must suffice. At Finchcocks, Goudhurst, Kent, tall chimneys continue the lines of the projecting central bays with impressive individuality and these bays themselves soar up uniquely above a large pediment which is purely ornamental. At Shepreth in Cambridgeshire the villager peers at Docraie's Manor between the ball-topped piers of a gate of wrought-iron scrolls and tulips and sees a ravishing and improbable Palladian window, the arch of which is filled with a wiry fretwork of interlaced ogees, the like of which the carpenter could never have seen in any book of instructions.

On the walls of a basement room in Lower Slaughter Manor, Gloucestershire, which was where the upper servants were generally housed in Georgian mansions, a servant named Richard White painted the following words in 1771: 'A good character is valuable to everyone but especially to servants for it is their bread and without it they cannot be admitted to a creditable family; and happy it is that the best of characters is in everyone's power to deserve.' The inscription reveals the mutual dependence of master and servant even in a small country house like Lower Slaughter Manor. The organization of larger households could not be maintained without a whole retinue of domestics. Entertaining was on a lavish scale, and guests, who stayed for weeks and sometimes months, spent their time looking at their host's collections of antiquities, marbles and paintings and at the splendidly illustrated volumes of history and travel books of engravings in the library, which now for the first time was considered an essential room in every big house. Outdoor pursuits included archery, field sports, especially fox hunting, and antiquarian and archaeological expeditions.

The reticent exterior of the Georgian squire's house was often a foil to the most luxuriant interior decoration. This at first, as in the Stone Hall and the dining room at Houghton, resplendent with Kent's glorious chimney pieces and golden furniture and Ruysbrack's exquisitely serene yet romantic reliefs of antique subjects, fully conformed to the Palladian ideal. But soon Rococo, Chinese and Gothic fantasies in wood, plaster, hangings and wallpapers (a fashionable innovation), as at Claydon, Arbury Hall (*see page 181*) and Ramsbury Manor, began to threaten that ideal. The Gothic tradition had never indeed been quite forgotten. Vanbrugh, for instance, never a Palladian although he used the classical idiom,

Edwin Smith

The Chinese room at Claydon House, Buckinghamshire

designed the little Manor at Somersby, Lincolnshire, with battlements and a strong
allusion to the screens passage as early as 1720. Gothic cottages and mock Gothic
ruins were introduced into landscape gardens among the classical temples as part of
the cult of the Picturesque; and in the last quarter of the eighteenth century
Gothic details began to adorn the façades of squires' houses. Ogee-headed
windows impart a sparkle to the front of Elton Hall, Herefordshire, and Hampden
House, Buckinghamshire; circular angle towers, an ogee-headed entrance and
crenellated parapets animate Fillingham Castle, Lincolnshire.

The order and symmetry of the Georgian mode were not immediately assailed
by these trimmings. But soon, in answer to the mounting craze for all that was
irregular and exotic, Nash was building totally asymmetrical, castellated, towered

and turreted houses at Luscombe and Caerhays; and the great Gothic piles of Ashridge and Belvoir Castle were rising theatrically in the fields of Hertfordshire and Leicestershire. They were the forerunners of a spate of monstrous palaces built by a new commercial plutocracy. The scholarly interest in medieval architecture stimulated by Pugin failed to establish Gothic as the accepted mode for these huge mansions. The wealth and importance of the Victorian squirearchy were proclaimed in a frenzied parade of revived styles – Greek, Gothic, French, Flemish, Venetian, Tudor, Elizabethan and Queen Anne. Harlaxton Manor is a huge, thunderous caricature of the Elizabethan mansion, a nightmarishly blown-up Burghley; multi-gabled Aldermaston Court, Buckinghamshire, all of patterned brick, brandishes a forest of Tudor chimneys and a square Gothic tower surmounted by a fantastic steeple with square-headed lights. At Somerleyton Hall, Suffolk, the vaguely Jacobean house is furnished with an Italianate tower and consorts uneasily with strange sculptured colonnades, neither Gothic nor classic. Millichope Park, Shropshire, parodies the classical style in a colossal Ionic portico with the entrance directly *beneath* it set between grotesquely short Doric columns; Waddesdon Manor takes the form of an immense French château in golden Bath stone; Ford Manor, Lingfield, combines a Gothic tower with a French pavilion and Dutch gables in a forbiddingly hard composition.

Inside these houses there were many rooms previously unknown – smoking rooms, gun rooms, billiard rooms and ballrooms; and the domestic offices included still-rooms, lamp rooms, knife rooms, china closets, drying rooms, ironing and folding rooms, as well as pantries and sculleries. They were symptomatic of the departmentalization which was disorganizing instead of organizing society.

The life led in this multiplicity of rooms was more elaborate than ever before, and with the continual weekend parties made possible by the railways it was pursued at a far hotter pace. But the quality had declined. Gladstone's daughter, visiting Waddesdon in 1885, wrote in her diary: 'There is not a book in the house save 20 improper French novels.' The unreal architectural pageant was but one expression of the make-believe that pervaded much of upper-class country life. The occupants of the big house were no more than superficially connected with the village: they had ceased to live from agricultural rents and were merely playing the part of the traditional squire on money drawn from industry and investments. Their actual power had been undermined when in the General Election of 1885 the newly enfranchised agricultural labourers voted Liberal. Three years later, when the Local Government Act of 1888 established county councils and elective urban and rural district councils, the patriarchal rule of the gentry came to an end. But for years after the close of Victoria's reign the trappings of manorial privilege disguised the revolutionary change in the social structure. The squire and his lady presided at annual village fêtes and conspicuously adorned the family pew in the parish church Sunday after Sunday, while their daughters visited sick tenants with jellies and broths and, like Miss Celia Thellusson of Rendlesham Hall in the years just before World War I, went round the village with what was called 'the babies' basket' full of linen and blankets for the poorest new born.

Now the pageant is undeniably and irrevocably over; but wherever the big house still stands it continues to impart a reassuring sense of ordered existence and to translate us to the lilac summer of a secure and aristocratic disposition.

The Village Shop

Paul Jennings

My late brother-in-law, a Tipperary man whose youth was spent in a village where the shop was even more all-embracing than the English version (you had only to move two feet along the counter where you got the stamps and it turned into a kind of bar) was once asked the following question by a man from one of those rather strict teetotal sects, in the Coventry factory where later he spent most of his working life:

'One thing I've never understood about Roman Catholics, Eddie, especially Irish Roman Catholics. They go to church on Sundays, and that's fine. But then they go straight out into the pub. Why is that?'

'It's because you can't get a drink in church,' was the faultlessly logical reply.

You can't get ham or washing-up liquid in church, either. Now while it is equally true that you can't get married, or enjoy communal contact with the things of the spirit, in a shop, until twenty odd years ago most people would have said that it had more chance of surviving as a popular, essential and unchanging feature of village life than the church.

Obviously we are not concerned here with the church, for so many centuries the focal centre of the village before village shops had been invented. As a matter of fact, though, the kind of village shop most of us have at the back of our minds is an ideal version: a marvellous, rather dark Aladdin's cave, with every inch of space utilized: Wellington boots, fireguards, coal scuttles, and perhaps even baby carriages and rugs hanging from the ceiling; a lot of sacks from which things were made up into paper bags twisted on the spot; a hand-turned bacon machine; patent medicines like Mother Siegel's Digestive Syrup and George's Pills for the Piles; sweets, gloves, hammers, screws and nails from dark oak shallow drawers with brass knobs, brooms, vinegar, tinned salmon, paraffin out at the back (and if there was anything they hadn't got they would have it from the town nine miles away by the carrier in the afternoon), newspapers, magazines of a blessedly pre-pornographic age – and, of course, the post office bit behind a kind of fireguard of its own – is in itself, for all its magic, a stage in the retreat from something even nearer the ideal of the village as a self-sufficient unit.

By 1965, when the 2600 village scrapbooks entered in the Women's Institute golden jubilee year competition provided a marvellously accurate picture of modern village life (since it was provided by the people themselves, not by thesis-writers or axe-grinding sociologists), it was clear from any of them (and I read around four million words of the best of them) that all villages had been losing specialist shops for generations, from Bellingham in Northumberland, now without its blacksmith, cobbler, watchmaker, sadler and tailor, via Kimcote, Leicestershire (baker's, butcher's, tailor's and 'several' other shops gone since 1846) to Laugharne, Carmarthenshire, the Llaregyb of Dylan Thomas's *Under Milk Wood*, where the butcher's had become a betting shop.

A great deal more has happened since 1965, when Drigg, in Cumberland (and never mind what dismal civil-service-region appellation has been since foisted on to that historic county) could report:

... practically everything is delivered to the door, including the car when serviced at the garage. Food is delivered from shops in Holmbrook, Seascale, Ravenglass, Egremont and Whitehaven. Travelling shops bring round bread, groceries, vegetables, fish and meat on different days of the week. ...

Even granted those special fringe-of-Lake-District conditions, that kind of thing sounds sadly out-of-date already as a picture of village shopping. Everywhere you ask about the mobile shop you are told that they have either ceased operating or will cease when the remaining vehicles finally become unroadworthy. And when you enquire into the economic future of 'the village shop' you run into a welter of statistics which, however much they vary in detail, point remorselessly to two things; decline, and the need for streamlining.

A survey of the South-West by the Conference of Rural Community Councils revealed a general fall between 1972 and 1977 in the percentage of villages with their own shop from the 70s and 80s (Somerset highest with 84 per cent) down into the 60s and 70s (Wiltshire lowest with 68 per cent). SPAR, one of the 'voluntary' groups that supply an increasing number of independent shops, and as such sharply differentiated from the 'multiples' like Tesco and Sainsbury which own their outlets, estimate that 5000 independent groceries went out of business in 1977.

Whatever statistics you choose (a *Guardian* article put the 1977 independent closures at 3000, 4 per cent of their total, and multiple branch closures at 1000, 11 per cent of *their* total) you come to the crux of the matter with the multiples, with their High Street monopolies and their huge, new, everything-under-one-roof depots on strategic town outskirts and, above all, their price war.

'A lot of people now, perhaps especially those in dormitory villages, tend to regard the village shop as simply a place to top up their deep-freeze supplies,' says Mr Leslie Seeney of the National Chamber of Trade. 'Even in the village where I myself live I've seen the number of shops go from three down to one. To run a village store today you need a real sense of social vocation, and you need to be practically a lawyer to cope with all the VAT and other ever-increasing regulations. And all this in a situation where all the time the tendency is to be forced to think in terms of profitability per square foot rather than "did old George want his bootlaces?"'

All this makes it very clear that there is no escape from the need for some kind of streamlining. The fact is that 20 years ago buying an old-established village shop, where there could still be a profit margin around 20 per cent, could be an attractive semi-retirement proposition (or, of course, something offering a future to the owner's children), and those who ran them could *afford* the wonderful higgledy-piggledy arrangement of stock, and the concern for old George's bootlaces. Now, with 5 to 8 per cent over the last ten years being steadily eroded, they can't.

What seems unavoidable is a change from the static to the moving. The concept of *moving on*, implicit in the very idea of the modern self-service shop, with price stickers put on everything by the appliance known in the trade as 'the gun', destroys the notion of the shop as a place where you might dash in quickly for half a dozen eggs or stay gossiping for an hour. Once you get into a self-service shop, however well you know the shopowner, the assistants *and* the customers, you are, like a patron of that other modern invention, the cafeteria, on a kind of human conveyor belt. Keep moving, or it will all build up behind you.

Of the 73,000 small grocers in this country, many of the 21,000 among them that belong to the efficiently-delivering, computerized-account 'voluntary buying groups' like SPAR, VG and others, are in rural areas. It is true that many people make their weekly, or even just monthly, trips to vast multiples and deep-freeze suppliers. But it is equally true that people are belatedly waking up to the hidden cost of this cheapness, even if they have their own cars, let alone if they are carless housewives for whom an erstwhile 1s. 6d. bus journey now costs 90p, and who can't carry all that much anyway. It is also true that for the elderly and immobile, whose shopping has always been not on a week-to-week, but on a *day-to-day* basis, their own village shop is more than ever a necessity.

I suppose Napoleon thought it was a tremendously smart insult to call us a nation of shopkeepers. I've never been able to see it myself. True, the Hindus, who went into all this a great deal more subtly many centuries ago, put the Kshatriya or military caste above the Vaishya, the trading and agricultural caste. But that was in the days when war was a pleasant aristocratic hobby, an extended version of hunting, for people who liked that kind of thing. Napoleon invented conscription in 1798; and the whole notion of total war, of *everybody* in one country wanting to kill everybody in another, was born. Some of my best friends are soldiers; indeed I was one myself for a time, by pure luck of an unadventurous kind; but as a national persona, commend me to the shopkeeper, not the soldier with his dreams of wading to glory through puddles of blood, who has eventually to be stopped by shopkeepers compelled to take up arms in, they hope, the nick of time.

To take on the (I say again) essential role of village shopkeeper nowadays as a career, as a life, when you are young, you need to belong to the Vaishya caste, and like it. You need to have some sort of grip on week-to-week cost accounting. You may be totally independent and do your own buying, although this will become increasingly difficult. If you belong to a 'voluntary group' such as VG or SPAR (purely contractual, it's *your* shop) their huge lorries will call on you regularly, with invoices from a computerized accounting system, on which you can work out a 'notional' profit statement each week. A total sum of £75 on a £900 turnover in a village of 3000 is not untypical; and handling £900 worth of stuff is a lot of work.

In a manual put out by VG they say if your net profit before taking out your salary is £3000 and you use goods from the shop to the value of £500, then: £3000 + £500 = £3500. Subtract from this what you could earn as a competent manager – say £3000 – and you have £500. £500 on an investment of £11,000 is only 4.5 per cent. You would be far better off with your money in a building society, and have no risks and less responsibility.

In other words you'll have to aim a bit higher. You have to be capable of deciding what your stock limit is. Would it be profitable to increase the range by adding, say, wines and spirits (what is the local competition?) What about staff?

Only the broadest generalizations are possible; but I think the common denominator of several successful village shopkeepers whom I have interviewed is a combination of this efficiency with a genuine love of village life and its people; and you can't really have this 'central' quality if your shop isn't a post office as well.

'I was a sales rep till we started here,' said one, 'and we decided to go in for this partly because I was too long away from the children and partly because we love this village. I do the shop, and my wife does the post office.'

'I had one week to learn,' said his wife. 'Three bureaucrats came and stood by me – one of them had a rubber with a special hole in it so that he knew it was *his* – and at the end of the week one of them did say "you seem to have picked this up quite well". It was a great moment. The Post Office pay a salary, which is supposed to cover heating, lighting, the premises – we found after we came that the only way was to have that separate room for the post office. We start at six, and sort out the letters into walks – or drives – for four postmen. And you really have to know people's names. Often in the early days I would have to say "Good morning, Mrs ——" and read her name upside down on her pension book if I could get a look. No one can teach you how long to listen to some old lady, sending a greetings telegram on the birth of a grandchild, and going on at some length about its unsuitable Christian name, before you realize the queue is getting impatient. Sometimes of course there isn't a queue; then it could be half an hour. When the snow was on . . .'

'. . . bit of luck, there,' put in her husband, 'somehow I knew it was coming, I don't usually do this but I asked the bank manager if I could go over the top. Well, you saw the crowds we had in; and we always had basics like bread and milk for them while we were cut off. I heard others weren't so lucky.' So prescient, more like.

'. . . an old man came in and said "Ah, the post office is one place that never runs out of money." They think it's a kind of bottomless well. But in fact we have to make up a strict balance every Friday.'

'It may sound silly, but we always look first at the deaths column in the local paper – ever since one of our girls asked a lady how her husband was, and he had died two days previously. We're very lucky with our staff. They're all local, they love the work. Even so, as an example, I have to tell you that since we started here five years ago staff wages have gone up 295 per cent – and that's with a *smaller* staff than we originally had.'

One gloomy estimate is that in 1984 (!) there will be only 50,000 independent groceries, the majority of the closures being rural ones. On the other hand, Mr Len Jackson, Vice-President of the Wholesale Grocers' Federation, thinks that the drift from giant corporations to 'convenience' and specialist shops ('I believe that bacon service counters have not gone, they are just resting') in America will, as usual, take place later in Britain. 'We may even become "a registered trade" in the manner of some continental countries, where it is necessary for food retailers to be registered and have a certificate of competence to trade.'

But certificates imply examinations, tests, some kind of abstract standards, uniformity. The whole point about the village shop is that while some kind of attempt has to be made to assess future prospects, these remain abstract too. The actual shop you go to in a village may still be the good old jumble. It may be a streamlined self-service. It may be a marvellously neat and well-ordered affair, fluorescent tubes on the low old ceiling beams, with a kind of stock island in the middle, that you can walk round – 'kind of half-way,' says the owner, 'self-service *is* convenient for the customer, but we prefer it this way. Everybody in this village has their *own* basket, and yes, people do like to stop and talk here. I've heard different accounts of the voluntary chains, some say they're marvellous, some say the opposite. I deal with three wholesalers, and try to keep stock to a minimum' (odd, since this shop seems to contain *more* varieties than the self-service in the next village), 'and we manage, we manage.'

Your true village shopkeeper, however much modern trends force rational order on to empirical higgledy-piggledy, will always 'manage'. That's about the only valid generalization possible. He will always manage, he will somehow always know about old George's bootlaces and Mrs Smith's rheumatism, as well as stock control. Long live the Vaishya caste!

The lithographs reproduced on pages 37, 38 and 51 are drawn by J. Scarlett Davis from designs by Peter F. Robinson in his Village Architecture, *1830.*

The Village Pub

Tom Girtin

The grander title 'Village Inn' evokes a clichéd image compounded of Falstaffian Merrie England and Dickensian jollity. Belated travellers spurring to get there, coach horns blowing, a genial rubicund host and complacent black-eyed serving wenches with flagons of foaming ale. There can, in fact, have been relatively few villages that ever boasted an Inn. Only those on the main lines of communication, at the cross roads, or along the turnpike road, would have needed or been able to support such an institution. The Inn was for the town; for the village it was the tavern or the ale-house or, in later terms, the 'local', the pub.

So, in spite of all those pubs whose signs – which blazon the course of England's history or folk-lore or which chart its topography – declare them to be inns, there are but few that fulfil the legal requirements, few that provide both food and lodging and may not turn away the customer for whom there is room.

Between the World Wars the tavern had its own romantic cliché formulated for it, largely through the gusty enthusiasm of such writers as G. K. Chesterton, Hilaire Belloc and J. B. Morton. To the averagely romantic townsman the words 'village pub' conjured up a low-built, probably thatched, rose- or wisteria-hung cottage with rustic benches for the Oldest Inhabitants outside, under a large tree, and, inside, log-fires, inglenooks, oak settles and scrubbed whitewood tables at which the hikers, the cyclists and, later, the motorists could refresh themselves with bread and cheese and pickled onions. And, of course, flagons of foaming ale.

No townsman seems to have admitted the simplest and most crucial of facts that, basically, the village pub was the working villager's club. Here was his recreational centre, where he could play darts and dominoes, cribbage and nap, shove-ha'penny and skittles and bar-billiards and various esoteric and largely regional games involving immense skill in throwing or swinging rings or balls.

Here, too, was the clearing-house for local gossip and information. The prices at the local livestock market were of no less importance than those of the Stock Market to a West End clubman. And what clubman actually welcomes strangers to his preserves? Tolerant he may be, and perhaps even polite, but glad he is not. The result was that, wherever possible, in the smallest and more remote ale-houses the better class of strangers were ushered into the landlord's or landlady's private sitting-room ('There now! You'll be more comfortable in here!'), where, sipping genteelly and not at their ease, they could enviously hear from the bar the low murmur of conversation, the click of dominoes, the sudden bursts of laughter.

In other, larger, pubs there was a Saloon Bar that was frequently only another larger version of the sitting-room. An upright piano by Collard & Collard, vases made from brass shell-cases and filled with Honesty and Chinese lanterns, a copper coal purdonium, a folded fan of red crepe-paper in the fire-place. It was comfortable, but, like a 'Residents' Lounge', it was not companionable.

In the more frequented pubs the physical distinction between the bars was less marked: the so-called Saloon Bar had the somewhat better furniture that the higher cost of drinking there demanded. But it was not greatly patronized if compared with the Public Bar, where the villagers were well aware of their economic importance. 'You may get your jam from Them', they would tell the landlord, 'but this is where your bread and butter is.'

The social distinctions were usually fairly strictly observed and, when necessary, enforced. If some shabby fellow, in working clothes, entered the Saloon Bar either by mistake or by over-weening presumption, he was likely to be greeted from behind the bar with the unequivocal and stentorian command: 'Other side!'

It is hard to realize that this shaming cry was still to be heard as late as the 1950s; but, dreadfully undemocratic as it was, segregation into two (or even more) bars had its advantages: a drinker, if appropriately dressed, could always avoid those he did not wish to meet. There was usually a corner in which, if he so wished, he could find privacy.

It was thus possible, from behind the bar, to see and hear the tenant farmer fulminating against the local poacher and publicly wishing that he might lay his hands upon him, quite unaware that no more than two feet away from him, on the other side of the class-dividing wall, the grinning villain had just finished entertaining the company with a joyous account of his latest exploit.

But even though this sort of pub survived World War II (and may still be found by the connoisseur) changes of the most fundamental order were taking place.

To begin with, the clientele began to be upgraded. In the ten years during which food rationing was a serious factor a snack at the pub was the surest way of supplementing the minuscule domestic allowance. The upper-middle classes of the older generation who perhaps had never before visited a pub except, possibly, on horseback for a stirrup-cup in the yard on the occasions when the Hunt met there, became fairly regular patrons. And even the women among them, once they had made the initial rather *declassé* plunge, acquired the habit. The Saloon Bar became increasingly and far more profitably in demand. To this development some brewers reacted quite quickly: in order to keep the new-found trade they appear to have felt it necessary to upgrade the type of licensee. Demobilized officers and (sometimes) gentlemen provided a handy solution. They could 'speak the language' of the new customers and understood their ways: at the same time, having usually also served for some time in the ranks, they were able to get along with those in the Public Bar.

The experiment was, on the whole, a success – at any rate it carried the evolution of the pub through what might have been a difficult period. But it led to some uneasy relationships. The brewers (and, still less, their District Managers) were not used to being treated by the tenants as equals. And the conservative traditional Licensees, resistant to change, reacted with a mixture of scorn and rage to which they often gave vent in the columns of *The Morning Advertiser*.

A change in drinking habits was also going on. More spirits were being drunk and the upgraded clientele were apt to demand something better than British sherry. The new landlords were, on the whole, responsible for introducing the pleasures of foreign wines to a wider circle of drinkers. The vast increase in Continental travel reinforced the habit and added a demand for other drinks once considered impossibly exotic, a demand strengthened by the ever-increasing number of female pub-goers. An order for a Martini no longer meant a more predominantly gin-based concoction; Dubonnet became in many areas more readily obtainable than in parts of France; Pernod made a surprising appearance ('Why not try a Pernod and Bitter-Lemon!') and there evolved a number of drinks based on sparkling perry. But it was not entirely the fault of women that the addition of lime-juice to lager became a commonplace.

Concurrently with these trends a far more serious change was in progress. A very large proportion of village pubs had always belonged to small family-owned breweries, no further than a dray-horse journey away, whose sole interest lay in maintaining outlets for their beer. Their tenants enjoyed cheap accommodation and, at worst, a tiny income which they sometimes supplemented by daytime working on the land, leaving the pub in charge of their wife or the Old Chap – the parent of one or other of the couple.

Now the small breweries were swallowed up by the great combines, whose interests extended far beyond the brewing and selling of beer into chains of hotels, restaurants, casinos, shipping lines and newspapers. Great areas of the country-side were carved up into monopolies. Every pub was expected to shew the share-holders a reasonable percentage of profit on the financial empire's balance sheet. Considerations other than social became increasingly influential. Although the brewers' propaganda leaflets proclaimed that 'Every Community Should Have Its Local', in fact in many small villages the now insufficiently profitable pub was closed – and the villagers were left without their social centre.

Elsewhere in many places where the pub was flourishing under a good and popular tenant the brewers thought it logical to take more of the profits to them-selves. They ejected the tenant and replaced him by a salaried manager – a step which to the more critical local senses indefinably but definitely altered for the worse the atmosphere of the pub. The licensee was no longer master in his own house. It is agreeable to note that this trend appears to have been halted, and per-haps even reversed: in an occupation where a hundred hours a week may quite usually be worked a man should be, at any rate, his own master.

The personality of the publican – and his wife – is of the essence. The dreadful cliché 'mine host' precisely defines his role: the directing spirit of a continual (and, often, personally boring) party at which he must be, above all, a good and sym-pathetic listener and, if possible, where circumstances demand, a good entertainer. He should never show boredom or favouritism or air troubles of his own. He must respect and modestly enjoy the beer he serves. He must control the over-ebullient guest and, sometimes, encourage the diffident. He must suffer fools gladly. He must, especially, like and be interested in People.

There is a touch of theatricality about his trade: at opening time the doors are unlocked, the lights go on, the curtain rises, metaphorically speaking, on yet another unscripted act which may turn out to include many dramatic forms, through farce and domestic comedy to, occasionally, melodrama.

The theatrical effect is often heightened by the rather bogus nature of the setting. The brewers had always echoed architecturally the public taste for the imagined 'olden days'. The Tudor period had always fatally attracted them. The interiors, and sometimes the façades too, of decent Georgian pubs would age almost overnight. Tendentious 'histories' were hung in their bars:

> *Bluff King Hal was often to be found here, quaffing a stoup of ale with Catherine Howard. Queen Elizabeth I and Charles II both patronized . . .*

Inside, cheap wrought-ironwork and reproduction horse-brasses proliferated. Outside, on the car park ('No Coaches Served') might stand a stage-coach; wagon wheels were disparbled about.

Now another profitable notion affected the social structure of the pub. As public self-regrading, from working to middle class, occurred, and with the ever-increasing use of the car, Saloon Bars became fuller and Public Bars emptier, it was an obvious step to convert the whole premises into one single bar – a classless society in which the higher prices could be charged throughout. Where this happened it was the end of that pub as a social centre for village life. No longer was there any privacy, no longer was there any escape from unwanted acquaintances. Where once the herdsman's dog lay dutifully beneath its master's chair and occasionally sighed and looked towards the doorway, the hearty beasts of local weekend gentry bound uncontrollably around. ('Don't take any notice of him! He's quite harmless! He's only after a bit of your sandwich!').

Where once space-demanding pub games were played, only darts universally survives: the flashing fruit machine of itself contributes more to the profits than all the drinkers in the Public Bar ever did. (It is, indeed, claimed that one large chain of pubs makes no less than 25 per cent of its annual profits from the machines.) Canned music plays continuously and over-loudly – often, apparently, more for the benefit of the staff than of the customer.

The one tradition that the brewers have scrupulously maintained is that of the glass of foaming ale. By raising beer from the cellar with the aid of carbon dioxide it froths more uncontrollably than ever it can have done in the old days. But here the customer has at last struck back. Supporters of the Campaign for Real Ale, at first disdained by the brewers and derided by much of the trade press, have achieved considerable success in bringing back beers that have more the quality of wine than the stuff for which the brewers created a 'public demand'.

Now that so many villages have become, in essence, an extension of whatever may be the local town, their pubs have become suburban pubs, and the old social life, with its segregation, with its games of dominoes and cribbage, has been driven underground. You are likely to find it going on behind some unpromising Victorian façade, outside which stand no company cars and inside which the landlord still goes down two steps into his back room behind the bar to draw your pint and fetch you a couple of dozen free-range eggs.

For the traditional, imagined, pub is still to be found for the searching. Ideally the traveller should look for either a Free House or a pub which still belongs to a small local brewery, a pub where there are still two bars, a pub which has not been architecturally over-developed in a village which is not a suburban extension of a town.

Even where the pub has been 'improved', where it has all the faults which are so apparent to the old pub-goer, the place is nevertheless still likely to be worth a visit. The atmosphere is unique in the world: often copied or exported abroad the pub has always proved obstinately and inimitably British. Pub food – even though there are not many actual ploughmen buying the 'Ploughman's Lunch' (which is the old bread and cheese and pickled onions upgraded) – is often the best value for money that you will find anywhere. In the Age of Envy the stranger is still likely to find a friendly welcome. And even where those who live in the village, those who are regular customers, know that their pub has been slightly spoiled for them, to the traveller it will still provide pleasant entertainment.

The Ideal Village

Gillian Darley

Gillian Darley

Chippenham, near Newmarket: the earliest Ideal Village

The traditional village is rather like a geological fragment: it consists of strata, the layers which have built up over the centuries. Reading these layers, clues emerge which point to the history of the settlement but which, nevertheless, only sketch in the outline. The ideal village, far from being made up of historical accretions, is a distinct creation. It is, whatever the nature of the guiding principles behind it, the expression of a single idea and purpose. Frequently, that idea has been the brainchild of one individual.

It might appear from such a description that such villages are relatively rare. Yet a careful count produces an astonishingly high figure, though many of these 'purpose-built' settlements have been swallowed up within later phases of development within the last century or two. For the purposes of this essay, I have kept to those planned, model or ideal villages (the three words are almost interchangeable) which most clearly have kept their own identity and which were planned as real villages, rather than as hamlets or satellites to existing villages.

As there are many such villages, so too there are many motives behind their creation. The aspirations were practical (often expedient), architectural, philanthropic or idealistic. Sometimes the motives were mixed together so that elements of all these four concerns can be detected. The majority of ideal villages were instigated by one person: a landlord, employer or philanthropist, who continued to exercise control over the activities within the village long after it had been completed. Just a few villages were the creation of the villagers themselves; perhaps a scheme had been suggested by a religious or political leader, but the conception and realization of the community remained in the hands of the people living there. Socially, these are the most intriguing of all the categories of ideal village; they tend, loosely speaking, to be 'utopian' experiments and, in history, have usually been short-lived.

There is a clear starting point for the chronology of the ideal village. In 1700 the future Lord Orford, First Lord of the Admiralty, began the reconstruction of the village of Chippenham, near Newmarket. His was not the first *scheme* for such a village: there are drawings for a small hamlet incorporated in the landscape designs for the Castle Howard park, dated *c.* 1699, but this was the first to be constructed. Orford's motives were, in common with those of most of the eighteenth-century landowners who became village builders, connected with the improving of his house and surrounding park and the necessity to retain his tenantry nearby, for employment on the estate. He demolished a number of cottages dotted around the area earmarked for the park, reorganized the provision of common lands, and set down a line of neat, traditional double cottages parallel with the thoroughfare and leading up to the lodge gates. The cottages, of one and a half storeys, have outbuildings attached which link the entire row into a single chain, with large garden plots for each half cottage in front. Beyond stands an elegant school, in architectural form rather resembling an orangery of that period, adding the last touch to the picture.

Enclosure meant that the gardens had replaced the open field strips; grazing rights were still allowed to the villagers, but they had been curtailed. This story, the emparking process and the resultant need for new accommodation to replace that which had been lost, was repeated frequently in the eighteenth century. East Anglia led the field, for agricultural prosperity allowed generous spending earlier there than elsewhere. The cottages, though generally more spacious than those provided at Chippenham, were hardly sufficient for families with perhaps six to eight children.

The plan of eighteenth-century ideal villages was formal. It was common for the line of cottages to take up the axis of an avenue leading up to the entrance gates. The small village at New Houghton, Norfolk, built to accompany Houghton Hall, is a typical example, dating from 1729. Like many others the village church has been left behind, stranded within the confines of the park.

Against the background of the threat of the Poor House, the spectre of rural destitution, the new villagers, provided with a sound new cottage and garden, even, perhaps, with almshouses for their old age, were a stable community. Re-established symbolically at the gates of the estate, the village was likely to contain faithful employees.

The concept of the village as an *architectural* ideal becomes a factor in the second half of the eighteenth century. When Sir James Lowther and the 1st Earl of Harewood commissioned, respectively, the Adam brothers and John Carr of York – among the most eminent architects of their age – to design their estate villages, a turning point had been reached. Architects were venturing into uncharted seas here. Traditionally the master builder dealt with cottages, lodges and farm buildings. The architect designed the mansion, possibly the stables, and the church. Certainly both the Adams and Carr produced remarkably urban schemes for the rural sites they were given, but in detail they restrained themselves and built sturdy cottages well suited to remotest Cumbria and West Yorkshire. Both villages date from the 1760s.

Although Lowther was built as a giant truncated Greek cross plan, Harewood followed the lines of a T-junction on the Leeds–York turnpike. Plan generally reflected the site and at Milton Abbas, best known of all the ideal villages, a formal outline of double cottages lines the shallow sweep of a long valley over the hill from Milton Abbey itself. Milton Abbas, probably owing its inspired site to Capability Brown, was a village built to replace a sizeable market town. For this reason it is one of the largest of all model villages (see page 18).

Oliver Goldsmith's poem *The Deserted Village* chronicles one such village destruction, and it is thought that he was referring to the rebuilding of Nuneham Courtenay near Oxford; another among the many new villages of the mid-eighteenth century.

Ideal villages in both the eighteenth and the nineteenth centuries were usually estate villages. But the eighteenth century saw the first attempts to improve the industrial housing situation, which was to lead on to more sophisticated philanthropic endeavours in the following century; it also saw the first communal experiments, in the exemplary villages built by the Moravians. Fulneck, near Pudsey, was the first of a number, and like Ockbrook, near Derby, still stands in a relatively rural setting. Built on a tricky hillside site, which put up the costs of the venture considerably, it was designed in a restrained classical style with its chapel and school as the dominant buildings. Fulneck, like the last and most

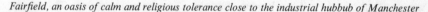

Fairfield, an oasis of calm and religious tolerance close to the industrial hubbub of Manchester

Gillian Darley

Gillian Darley

Chapel and school in classical style in the Moravian village of Fulneck, Yorkshire

developed of the Moravian villages, Fairfield (which is now enclosed by Droylesden), managed to sustain a relatively self-sufficient economy and an excellent school, and was a community which, though religious in origin (the Moravians being a Nonconformist sect originating from Northern Europe) was not authoritarian or repressive.

Where the industrial model village was concerned it appeared important that the settlement should be, as far as possible, a self-contained unit. Saltaire, the most elaborate such village, which dates from the 1850s, was carefully organized. There were schools, both for children and for adult education, almshouses, chapels, shops, a communal laundry and a wide range of housing all surrounding the woollen mill that provided Titus Salt's great wealth. Although by the end of the nineteenth century such wholesale provision of facilities by an employer for his employees had come to represent oppressive paternalism, in the mid-century the extraordinarily high standard of planning, landscaping, architecture and social provision was entirely novel.

The very circumstances that led to the foundation of new industrial communities also brought about the first attempts to find a complete alternative. The miseries that the Industrial Revolution had visited upon the majority of the workforce tempted many to try and find an escape. The Moravians undoubtedly attracted people from the northern industrial towns, even in the eighteenth century, but it was in the early nineteenth century that the prevailing living conditions led to an upsurge of reform. Robert Owen, himself an industrialist, was the first and best known to propose new kinds of villages, but the output of volumes of theory, from Owen and many others, far outweighed any practical actions. New villages in a rural setting were regarded as the ideal – that same ideal that links nineteenth-century theory with twentieth-century practice in the Garden City movement.

Like the Moravians, the Chartists were another group which set up villages administered by and for themselves, despite the zealous leadership of Feargus O'Connor. This time the principles were political. The Chartist land colonies, one of which remains at Minster Lovell, consisted of identical cottages set in three to four acres, with a school. Neither chapel nor public house was allowed. Despite the collapse of the scheme, the settlements continued to depend on the land as smallholding communities.

Existing housing conditions were, on the whole, little better in the countryside than in the expanding cities. The newly built mid-nineteenth-century estate village represented a great improvement in standards of accommodation, at a time when basic minimum requirements were being laid down. Sindlesham Green, for example, was a completely new village, built by the Walter family at the gates of their new mansion, Bearwood. It included an inn (the Walter Arms), church, almshouses, a school and a variety of cottages.

The necessity for decent living space had to be combined, however, with the prevailing winds of fashion. These dictated for much of the nineteenth century that cottages should be designed in the Picturesque style. At Somerleyton, near Lowestoft, Sir Morton Peto's architect dressed up the plain, stock-brick cottages with three bedrooms and the best of modern sanitation, by adding half-timbering, carved barge-boards, elaborate chimneys, and dotting them around a village green.

Here the visual ideal of the village was a guiding principle. The writers who had elaborated the theories of the Picturesque envisaged a sylvan, pastoral countryside well removed from the harsh realities of rural existence. Starting with Nash's Blaise Hamlet, this idiom was the most popular one for ideal villages, in firm reaction to the formal lines of cottages favoured in the eighteenth century. Old Warden, Ilam and Somerleyton are all exercises in the same manner, following a firmly held architectural idea. The Picturesque was also larded onto existing villages, as at Harlaxton where distinctive decorative detail unified the older cottages with those newly built. Here, in particular, the maxims of the pattern-book writers were closely followed, to the extent that the occupation of each inhabitant of a cottage should be denoted in architectural terms.

On a grander scale, owing to its function, but still definitely Picturesque, is Edensor, on the Chatsworth estate. One of a number of villages serving the

FRANCIS DANBY, A.R.A. (1793–1861): Cottages at Blaise Hamlet (detail). Watercolour, *c.* 1822
(*City of Bristol Museum and Art Gallery*). Francis Danby, best known for poetic and imaginery
landscapes, lived in Bristol from 1813 to 1823. Blaise Hamlet, the prototype of the
Picturesque village, was built on the outskirts of Bristol in 1810.

JOHN BUONAROTTI PAPWORTH (1775–1847): Gothic Cottage, 1818 (*Library of the Royal Institute of British Architects*). This is a hand-coloured lithograph from Papworth's *Rural Residences, consisting of a series of Designs for Cottages, Decorated Cottages, Small Villas and other Ornamental Buildings,* one of the many books of architect's plans and drawings published in the Regency period as expressions of the Picturesque movement and the Gothic revival.

Gillian Darley

Twentieth-century Picturesque: cottages round the village green at Ardeley, near Walkern, in Hertfordshire

enormous estate, it consists mostly of sizeable villas, built for the professional members of the Chatsworth staff. Here Paxton, who seems to have master-minded the design, put together an historic catalogue of building styles, a most unlikely combination of periods and derivations, their only unifying feature being the local stone. With its castellated entrance lodge, it has much in common with the villa estates of the northern towns in which the prosperous citizens played at living in a village.

Similarly the industrial villages of the later nineteenth century also took up rural imagery. The cottages of Port Sunlight are half-timbered, tile-hung and very much more rustic than the rest of Birkenhead. Its country cousin, Thornton Hough, built nearby for the same man, Lord Leverhulme, and designed by the same architects, looks very similar – but, as an estate village, seems more appropriate.

This self-conscious pursuit of vernacular architecture was the last manifesta-tion of the Picturesque in the nineteenth century. When Joseph Rowntree com-missioned Parker and Unwin (the partnership responsible for Letchworth Garden City) to design a village outside York he successfully combined the best features of the rural and the urban to create probably the most pleasant industrial com-munity of all. New Earswick was sited well away from the chocolate factory (unlike Port Sunlight, which was beset by soapy smoke) and the residents of the village were not exclusively Rowntree employees. The cottages were simply detailed, with open, light rooms, and were sited informally within a well landscaped area. A large hall was provided for communal activities and gave a visual focus, stand-ing to one side of a green. A similar unfussy design was chosen for Ardeley, a small village in Hertfordshire, with thatched cottages grouped around the village green and well, with a village hall and, beyond the pond, the lychgate leading to the church which serves as a reminder of an earlier village. Dating from 1918, this is one of the relatively few twentieth-century estate villages. Landowners

Gillian Darley
Whiteley Village, founded in 1911, as a memorial to the owner of the Bayswater store in London

built cottages, but it took a brave, or very rich, man to build an entirely new village. The last of all was Rushbrook, outside Bury St Edmunds, completed in 1965. Here Lord Rothschild rebuilt the existing cottages for his tenants and provided a village hall alongside.

Like the landowner, the twentieth-century industrialist rarely had to provide housing for his employees. The responsibility had passed to the State, and to the private speculative builder; and the housing philanthropist had become, by and large, a figure of the past. Nevertheless, sustaining the long-established tradition of the benevolent nonconformist employer, F. H. Crittall built in the late 1920s a village to house the employees working at his metal window factory in Essex. Oddly situated in agricultural countryside, a mixture of neo-Georgian and flat-roofed International Modern style cottages were built at Silver End. There were also a shopping centre, a hotel, a thatched church and well landscaped public gardens. It is, in many respects, the most unlikely of all industrial villages.

Another unlikely village is Whiteley Village in Surrey. This was built as a result of a huge legacy left by William Whiteley, the Bayswater store owner, and was a series of almshouses, with shops, church and chapel, and communal rooms – the equivalent to a village hall. The plan was an octagon and each section of the eight sides was designed by a different architect, though all used the same materials, red-brick and tiles. The form of a village was a favourite choice for builders of institutions in the nineteenth century; Dr Barnardo's first home in Ilford, for example, was designed as a series of cottages. As at Whiteley Village, which had housed the first of its 350 pensioners in 1917, the humane scale and appealing image of the village were found to be ideal antedotes to the usual atmosphere of large-scale institutions.

One other unusual type of created village is that designed as a holiday resort. There are few of them and certainly the most idiosyncratic is to be found on the Suffolk coast at Thorpeness. Here a motley collection of buildings of virtually every style and design conceivable was built for the use of holidaymakers, who would rent accommodation from the developers, the owners of the estate. It offered a wide range of facilities and functioned as something akin to a Country Club, attracting back the same families year after year. Built before World War I, it was in its heyday in the 1920s and 30s. The *pièce de resistance* is a water tower disguised as a cottage high above the trees. In reality the iron legs enclose a cottage, and the 'cottage' is the metal tank.

As has been said, in the twentieth century the responsibility for the provision of improved housing – whether in industrial areas or in the countryside – had passed to public and local authorities. In addition the developer was contributing a far larger proportion of necessary housing, much of it in the suburbs along the lines of communication of road or rail. The contribution of the philan-thropic individual had become an anachronism. Nevertheless, the basic idea of the village has remained highly attractive. Apart from connotations of rural peace – villages are still painted in the Picturesque image of the eighteenth century where advertising is concerned – the village continues to represent an appropriate scale of community. Most of the new ideal villages are now the 'neighbourhood units' of the recent generation of New Towns. Milton Keynes, for example, consists of numerous villages, even some of the original scattered settlements that existed long before the city was conceived.

However, there have been a few attempts to found new villages. New Ash Green in Kent faced the obstacles of modern planning regulations, with limita-tions on providing local industry in particular, and passed through numerous difficulties as the financial climate changed during the years of its development. Such new villages as have been created are based on their accessibility to existing towns and places of employment; none exist independently and none come any-where within the definition of self sufficiency – the aim of the early utopian founda-tions. Undoubtedly some of the ideal villages created since 1700 are clever counter-feits. They emulate features of the traditional village, yet cannot lay claim to its complex character, its subtle social composition or its intricate fabric. Neverthe-less over a period of 250 years many of our greatest thinkers and designers have been engaged in creating villages. Whether their approach was that of the social reformer, the fashionable architect, the efficient landowner, or the dreaming idealist, the building of a small, relatively self-contained community was an essential ingredient in their plans. To judge the success or failure of their efforts is, inevitably, a subjective process. Some are physically more attractive than others; some seem to be more confident and active communities than others. The 1970s have suggested new types of villages, reverting to the ideas of self-sufficiency. All this shows that the village continues, as ever, an intriguing ideal and it seems likely to continue to produce as many forms as men have ideas.

The Garden of England

KENT SURREY EAST SUSSEX

Alan Jenkins

The area we are covering in this section of the book is Kent, Surrey and East Sussex. West Sussex is often nearer, in the character of its villages, to its neighbour Hampshire. And yet we are on dangerous ground if we claim that this or that village 'could not be in any other county' than the one in which it is. We may know we are in or near the Cotswolds by the lichened stone and walled fields, or in Warwickshire by a certain kind of red brickwork. It would be easy to generalize and, whipping off a blindfold, say: 'Here are oasthouses: we must be in Kent.' But hops are grown in other counties too although Kent grows over half of those in the UK: you will find oasthouses in Puttenham and near Farnham, both in Surrey. We are not much safer if we think of old Surrey cottages as being tiled or weatherboarded, for, as the Weald mixes Surrey, Sussex and Kent together, we find much the same kind.

The character of villages in this region, as in any other, owes much to geology, history, farming and industry. Millions of years ago it was a huge mountain range. Erosion of the top of it exposed what we now call the Weald: two tentacles or escarpments of chalk, the North and South Downs, holding between them rings or outcrops of Upper Greensand, Gault Clay, Lower Greensand, Weald Clay and, in the middle and at the bottom, the Hastings Sands. Over most of it, two thousand years ago, lay a dense forest, called by the Romans *Silva Anderida*, after their port of Pevensey (we shall see, when we look at the Romney Marsh villages, how sea and the hand of man have altered the coastline and reclaimed the soil). The Saxons, arriving in the fifth century, knew this forest as Andresweald, the Forest of Anderida. Even in the fourteenth century the forest almost roadless and unmapped as it was, was impenetrable enough for Edward III to require twenty-two guides to get him from London to Rye.

Edward III left an important legacy to South-East England: he encouraged Flemish craftsmen to settle here, bringing with them a more sophisticated technology of weaving, new styles of building, and glassmaking, especially for stained-glass windows. You see their houses in Wealden Kent, and the church they rebuilt at Cranbrook, one of several towns or villages which have an ancient Cloth Hall.

This weaving industry, and the wool it needed, depended on sheep raising. The North Downs,

with their rather coarse grass, can nourish sheep, but it is the short grass of the South Downs that has made famous the Southdown breed – not that they are found in such numbers as formerly: the Romney Marsh breed is now far more important than Southdown in the UK and in Australia and New Zealand. But sheep can graze on many kinds of terrain and this fact was responsible for the loss of more forest land in the Middle Ages, as clearings were made. Later, trees were damaged by deer, which love to strip off the bark, and by squirrels and rabbits, which attack the young saplings.

Reafforestation was an unknown science until comparatively recent times (the Forestry Commission was born in 1919). We have all heard the story of Nelson's friend Admiral Collingwood,

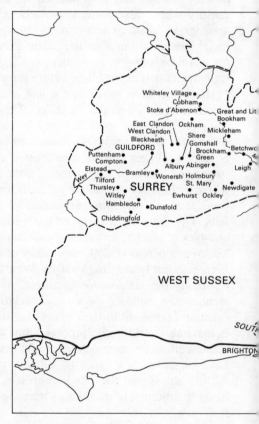

who, on country walks, used to carry a pocketful of acorns to plant haphazardly, hoping they would grow into huge oaks for building warships. The first scientific attempt to solve the problem was a paper read by John Evelyn (a Surrey man) to the Royal Society in 1662, from which modern British interest in arboriculture probably dates.

The depredation of the Forest of Anderida, however, had begun many centuries before this. From Roman times and earlier iron had been mined and smelted: for this, fuel was needed, and there was timber in plenty: oaks for charcoal, later on for the ships of England. Ironworks existed on either side of what is now the Surrey–Sussex border, and eastwards into Kent. The industry reached the height of its importance in the sixteenth and seventeenth centuries, and died out in the nineteenth as the Industrial Revolution converted a quasi-cottage industry into 'dark satanic mills' elsewhere.

Place names, especially their last syllables, tell us something of the social history of the South-East. Any village ending in -ly or -leigh (both, in this region, usually pronounced lye) means that it began as a settlement in a forest clearing – Ardingly and Hoathly in Sussex, Leigh in Surrey and Kent. A feature of Kentish place names is the ending -den (Horsmonden, Tenterden, Smarden), meaning dene or dean, a wooded vale, a forest retreat; -hurst (as in Goudhurst, Lamberhurst)

means a copse on a hillock. Thursley in Surrey and Woodnesborough in East Kent suggest that Thor and Woden were worshipped here before St Augustine came.

From the Weald flow the rivers that drain it – Surrey's Wey and Mole, their waters entering the Thames; Kent's Medway, Stour, Cray and Darent, entering the Thames Estuary and North Sea respectively; Sussex's Ouse and Rother (the eastern one), entering the English Channel – though for some miles the Rother's left bank can be claimed by Kent, since it is here on the county boundary.

The Weald's most fertile soil is in the Hastings Beds with Lower Greensand running close, which stretch from the Surrey–Sussex border to Romney Marsh. Loquacious Mrs Elton, in Jane Austen's *Emma*, will admit no county but Surrey to the title 'Garden of England'. Surrey manages pretty well with its sticky Wealden clay, Bagshot Sands and flinty chalk outcrops, but it has to award the palm to Kent, whose 36,000 acres of apple orchards and 8000 acres of hopfields it cannot hope to rival; but it is justly proud of its grain fields and pastures south of the Hog's Back.

Surrey is a little ashamed of some of its flat lands to the north of the North Downs: they are too near the sprawl of London for comfort, and large areas of them, as also of Kent, have been absorbed by the Greater London Council. Much of Surrey

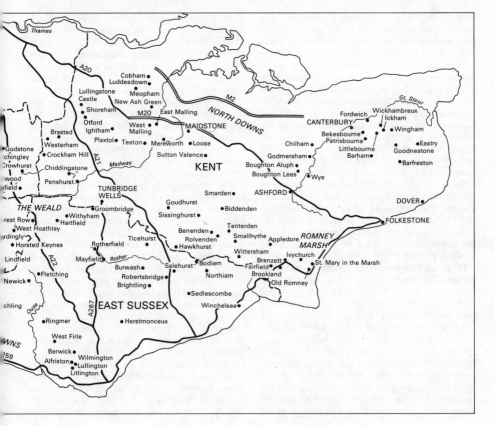

Kenneth Scowen

Four styles of architecture at Alfriston, Sussex

attracts the stigma 'commuter country'. The same can be said of Kent north-west of Sevenoaks, and Sussex around Haywards Heath. There is little profit in this kind of thinking. The townsman, whose love of the country may be 'sentimental' to the born countryman, has done much to preserve the best things in our villages. Architectural critics bewail the 'savage restorations' by Victorian architects of Saxon and medieval Surrey churches. Those churches are loved by the villagers who use them. The same critics allow a little cool praise to the prosperous nineteenth-century businessmen who, with the coming of railways, built mansions within thirty miles of London. To old villages modern housing estates are sometimes added: they can be discreetly designed and sited so as not to clash, Winchelsea and Chilham being good examples. A village is a community, and an expanding population has to live somewhere. We cannot for ever be bound by Ye Olde Worlde.

Let us rather rejoice in the variety of South-East villages, the luxury of their vistas, small or panoramic, with no hill as high as 1000 feet (Leith Hill the highest point, is 35 feet short of it), and rivers that meander rather than rush. Contrast the trimness of, say, Ewhurst in Surrey with the eeriness of certain Romney Marsh hamlets, which used to be islets before the Marsh was drained. Wealden villages in West Kent, especially east of Tunbridge Wells, were partly shaped by the Jutes' law of *gavelkind*, which, unchanged by the Normans, said that when a landowner died his estates were to be divided equally among all his

sons. Hence, instead of huge baronial estates, you find mansions built by generations of yeoman farmers and cottages built by smallholders. These are often of black-and-white timbering, often beside a millstream, with an oasthouse or two (which today may be dwellings). Weather-vane motifs on the oast cowl mainly depict the county symbol of the rampant horse in Kent and other variations include traction engines and animals. Not that the South-East, the most vulnerable part of Britain to foreign invasion, has ever lacked castles and defence works. Thus it is rich in ruins and the archaeological remains of two thousand years and more.

The sea has oddly interfered with the South-East. It has attacked the north coast of Kent so that the original Roman fort at Reculver, on which a seventh-century Saxon church was built, may have been as much as three miles inland. It has also silted up the south-east coast so that Winchelsea, once a flourishing Cinque Port, is now more than a mile inland, and the tongue of shingle called Dungeness was lengthened by the tides. No good has come of this other than two atomic power stations, a lighthouse and a bird sanctuary (in Denge Marsh behind).

We tend to expect of a village, in the South-East, that it should have a church, a pub, a manor house, a triangular green round which they should be pleasantly grouped, a pond or stream, a general store, and – cottages. These conditions cannot always be fulfilled, but we may be content if four are. In the South-East it is likely that only the church will be of stone, and that according to the nearest quarry. (But churches around Canterbury are sometimes of Caen stone, brought from Normandy.) Local builders, in the ages before speedy transport, used what was close at hand – flint, sandstone, Kentish ragstone, timber and local baked brick. There *are* stone cottages in Surrey, Kent and Sussex, but they are not what we expect. We expect, as one authority has said, the 'deep rosy glow of Kentish tiles' and the 'silvery toughness of old oak'.

Tilehanging is characteristic of the three counties as is weatherboarding. In the eighteenth century filling in timber with brick became common, and all through the South-East you find harmonious blends of tile, brick and board as ways of keeping out the cold. Thatch gets scarcer as the craft of thatching vanishes. Tiles have their fascination, and repay study. At Burwash, Sussex, you can see tile, brick and board in the same houses all down the street; at Witley, Surrey, fishtail tiles on a half-timbered cottage. Fishtail (or -scale) tiles are of many patterns: in Surrey, Hascombe, Ewhurst, Witley and Haslemere can all show local variations. Half-plastering is fairly common in Kent and Surrey. American visitors to South-East villages may well imagine themselves to be in Pennsylvania or in New England, whose older rural spots can show plenty of weatherboarding.

Should a village have grown organically, or can it be planned as a whole in modern times? We have found three of the latter for our Gazetteer. Visit them, and see what you think.

Kipling, who lived near Burwash, praised the Weald for its 'wooded, dim, blue goodness.' Perhaps he was seeing it on a misty day. Belloc, galumphing about the South Downs, and stopping at all the pubs, called them 'the great hills of the South Country': they made him long for the company of 'the men who were boys when I was a boys'. Of the two poets, Kipling came nearer to understanding the true South-East and its villages, whose names to him *were* poetry. He wished he had been born here. He would not be right to say today 'The Downs are sheep, the Weald is corn'; he perhaps overpraised those 'whale-backed Downs'; but he knew the hamlets that lay between the humps, and quotes their names all along the South-East country – Firle, Ditchling, Brenzett:

I'm just in love with all these three,
The Weald and the Marsh and the Down countree.

GAZETTEER

ABINGER, *Surrey*: two villages (Abinger Hammer and Abinger Common) in one parish, straggling roughly N and S from the 'Hammer' on the A25 Dorking–Guildford road, at the southern foot of the North Downs, to Abinger Bottom. The 'Hammer' takes its name not from the hammer clock ('Jack the Smith') but from an old forge where cannon balls (and perhaps the iron gates of Old Temple Bar) were made in the 16th c. This is one of the 'Tillingbourne villages', like Albury, Gomshall and Shere, following for 10m the little river which rises near Leith Hill and flows W to join the Wey at Shalford. The Tillingbourne used to power eight watermills for cornmilling, gunpowder making, iron furnaces, weaving and tanning. Beside it (near the A25) is Crossways Farm (17th-c) with Dutch-style windows surmounted by arches: the setting of George Meredith's *Diana of the Crossways*. The district is famous for watercress, which however grows better in well water than in rivers.

Abinger Common (2m SSE), is a triangular green with the Abinger Hatch Inn on the E side and St James's Church on the W. The church, parts of which date back to the 12th c, has been much reconstructed – badly in 1857 and well (by Frederick Etchells) in 1950, to repair great damage done by a flying bomb in 1944. In 1964 the tower was struck by lightning, and further reconstruction has made it one of the best village churches in the district. The War Memorial in the churchyard is by Lutyens. The E window of the chancel has some good modern stained glass ('The Living Cross' by Lawrence Lee, 1967). In the porch is a 15th-c alabaster Crucifixion, believed to have come from Leicestershire.

Next to the church is Abinger Manor House, built originally by Sir John Evelyn in the late 17th c but much restored after a 19th-c fire: only old floors and the Jacobean porch give any idea of the first building. In the garden is a Norman motte or private fortress, and in a nearby field a Mesolithic (4000–5000 BC) pit-dwelling excavated in 1950 by Sir Edward Beddington-Behrens assisted by Dr L. S. B. Leakey.

Keep your eyes open for an ancient whipping-post and stocks. Between the Manor House and the churchyard is the manorial pound, where the Evelyn family kept their cattle; and Abinger Manor Cottage, where Max Beerbohm lived during World War II. Abinger has always attracted writers, among them E. M. Forster, who named a collection of essays *Abinger Harvest*. The Leith Hill Festival, now a three-day affair with massed choirs at Dorking, began at Abinger village hall in 1904, when Dr Ralph Vaughan Williams conducted the first evening concert.

Friday Street is ¾m E, a few cottages by a pond deepset in a pine-wooded valley, a place of extraordinary peace, with a good inn, the Stephen Langton named after the famous archbishop. 1½m W is **Holmbury St Mary**, dating from the 1870s, after the railway came to Dorking; a pleasant valley village with G. E. Street's church of St Mary (1879) and a winding road to Holmbury Hill (magnificent views over several counties).

ALFRISTON, *E. Sussex* (4m NE of Seaford), in the Cuckmere Valley, is probably the most popular tourist village in Sussex, with a difficult parking problem. Out of season, disregarding coyly-named curio and teashops, its treasures can be seen. The Star Inn dates from the 15th c and so does the George; the Ship is a particularly fine timber-framed house. The Star, once a hostel for mendicant friars, has several wood carvings, among them a lion believed to have been a figure-head from a Dutch ship wrecked in the Channel *c.* 1670. The stem of a medieval Market Cross stands in the widening main street. Near the river is the Clergy House (14th c), timber-framed and thatched, thought to be the only building of its kind in England: it was restored after 1896 when it became the first building to be bought by the National Trust. The church of St Andrew, an unusual 14th-c mixture of Perp and Dec, is built on a Saxon barrow within an almost circular churchyard. Inside, it is generously proportioned, with triple sedilia and piscina.

In the neighbourhood are a long barrow, a round barrow and a Saxon cemetery (on a hill to the NW) which has yielded spearheads, drinking horns and other relics: these can be seen in the Barbican House Museum, Lewes.

Lullington and **Litlington** ($\frac{1}{2}$m and 1m SE), are pleasant villages, also over-patronized. The former has one of the smallest churches in England – really the chancel of an older church. Litlington church dates back to *c.* 1150: the village is chiefly a place to have tea. Not far away is Charleston Manor, described as 'a perfect house in a perfect setting': a mixture of Norman, Tudor and Georgian, it originally belonged to William the Conqueror's cup-bearer. Charleston is now a shrine for devotees of the Bloomsbury Group.

Wilmington (1m N), has a largely Norman church and a Benedictine Priory, but what everyone goes to see is the Long Man on the N side of Windover Hill – possibly the largest representation of a human being in the world (226ft high), cut in turf onto the white chalk. An archaeological puzzle: the first record of it was in 1779, yet it has been ascribed to both Saxons and Vikings.

At **Berwick** (1$\frac{1}{4}$m NNW) – pronounced 'Burwick' – the unique feature of the church is the wall paintings by Bloomsbury artists, done during World War II for Bishop Bell of Chichester by Duncan Grant and Vanessa and Quentin Bell, who lived nearby at Charleston. Grant's 'Christ in Glory' is the most impressive.

APPLEDORE, *Kent,* 8m NNE of Rye. On the edge of Romney Marsh, but not of it: you see the difference once you have crossed the Royal Military Canal (dug as a defence against Napoleon) which curves round the Marsh from the Rother, near Rye, to Hythe. A port before the Rother changed course in the 13th c, it sheltered 250 Danish ships threatening King Alfred in 892. Most of it lies along the wide turf-bordered main street with houses of various ages and styles from 16th c onwards, harmoniously mixed. The Swan Hotel (N of church), of 18th-c brick, and Swan House (timbered) opposite are among many attractive buildings. Horne's Place (1m N) is a

good (probably 17th-c) farmhouse on a medieval timber frame. It includes a stone private chapel (1366), 22ft long and 1ft higher than its length, beautifully designed and carved within. The house is said to have been attacked by Wat Tyler's rebels in 1381.

The church of St Peter and St Paul (EE) was rather clumsily rebuilt after being burnt by the French in 1380: nave and N aisle were combined. The tower doorway (1510) has the arms of Arch-bishop Warham above it. Much timber within: chancel arch, roof beams, screens. The stained glass is mostly modern by local artists, especially Godfrey Humphrey whose window at the W end of the nave shows Fairfield church (on the Marsh) as background to Christ the Shepherd with His flock amid rabbit, kingfisher, gulls and Marsh wildfowl.

BENENDEN, *Kent.* On a high ridge 4m SE of Cranbrook, its big tree-lined village green, where cricket is played at summer weekends, is famous. Tile-hung cottages and white weatherboarded post office mingle with 19th-c houses and sand-stone church. Benenden School for girls was built amid pines in Elizabethan style on what was the Earl of Cranbrook's Hemsted Park (1859–62) in 300 acres. Lord Cranbrook turned Benenden from a scattering of yeomen's Wealden houses into a true village, using mainly the Victorian architect, George Devey. The original church, struck by lightning in 1672, was well restored by David Brandon in 1862. It has traces of 14th-c masonry, and once boasted a strange three-stage timber belfry.

BIDDENDEN, *Kent.* An almost too-perfect village 5$\frac{1}{2}$m ENE of Cranbrook in which practically everything is an Ancient Monument – black-and-white houses, tithe barn, pond, the lot. Part of it is grouped round a small green planted with shrubs and with a quaint village sign incorporating the famous Biddenden Maids. The short High Street has a long line of half-timbered houses; not many Wealden ones. Biddenden was an important centre of the Flemish weaving industry – hence the beautiful Old Cloth Hall (16th–17th-c), seven-gabled, tile-hung and timbered. Hendon Hall and Biddenden Place are both 18th-c red brick, the latter with hipped roof and elements of a 17th-c house.

All Saints Church (14th-c with later additions) is an architectural puzzle, though it seems clear that a Dec church was enlarged into Perp style with wider aisles and bigger windows. The tower is probably 15th c and was a beacon tower, the font 13th c. Local families of four centuries are commemorated in about 70 brasses of varying quality. In the churchyard a stone commemorates Thomas Collings, who in 1815 at the age of 96 went reaping with his son of 74 and daughter of 66.

The legendary Biddenden Maids, 12th-c Siamese twins, Eliza and Mary Chulkhurst, originated the Easter charity by which bread and cheese is distributed to pensioners at the Old Workhouse.

BLETCHINGLEY, *Surrey*. (Sometimes spelt Blechingley.) An almost 'perfect village' alongside a wide main street on the A25 road 3½m W of Redhill, it stands to benefit from the by-passing M25 motorway. This will no doubt encourage the Morris dancers who can sometimes be seen here on summer evenings. The mainly 16th-c Whyte Harte Inn has been an inn all its life, which is something of a record. Like much of the village, it recreates the feeling of Tudor England amid more modern typically Wealden tile-hung houses. Once a market town, the original street line can be seen by walking along Middle Row.

The fine Perp church of St Mary (largely 15th-c with Norman W Tower) has been much rebuilt, some of it as recently as 1910. It can be approached by Church Walk which has some attractive old cottages, including the 1552 Nicholas Woolmer Cottage and 17th-c Legg's Cottages. The church tower dates from the late 11th c. but the crenellated top is modern. It had a spire until 1606 when it was destroyed by lightning. The heavy S door and porch are 15th c: the room above was used as an arms and ammunition store in Elizabeth I's reign.

Within, you cannot fail to note the monumental tomb of Sir Thomas Cawarden, Henry VIII's Master of the Revels and owner of Bletchingley Place, bequeathed to him by Anne of Cleves. Cawarden outdid the Vicar of Bray in his religious tergiversations. A reformer under Edward VI, he became a Catholic under Bloody Mary and a Protestant under Elizabeth. The 1707 monument in the S chancel chapel to Sir Robert Clayton, Lord Mayor of London in 1697, is an impressive larger-than-life composition including his wife: the only known sculpture of Richard Crutcher, greatly admired by Sacheverell Sitwell. Dryden satirized Sir Robert as 'As good a saint as usurer ever made'. Among many Victorian additions is a reredos (1870) by G. E. Street which curiously places Bishop Wilberforce (of Oxford and Winchester) among the apostles in his own lifetime.

The original manor of Bletchingley was granted by William the Conqueror to Richard de Tonbridge, whose son is thought to have built the 12th-c Castle, fragments of which can be seen in a private garden, Castle Hill, S of the main road.

For the rest, it is a village rich in cottages: in High Street The Cobbles, King Charles's House, the post office, the 16th-c Clerk's House; and many others in side lanes.

Pendell is ¾m NW, with an 18th-c manor house, the 17th-c Pendell Court and Pendell House.

Brewer Street is 1m N, a handful of cottages and a 15th-c half-timbered farmhouse in a quiet setting, with the 18th-c Place Farm and a Tudor gatehouse which is all that remains of Anne of Cleves' mansion. 1½m to the E, Tilburstow Hill (574ft) commands excellent views.

BOOKHAM, Great and Little, Surrey. Much developed since World War II, the Bookhams, despite the term 'commuter country', have much to offer. They are within easy reach of National Trust lands at Bookham Common, Polesden Lacey and Ranmore. The High Street still has plenty of villagey characteristics, and the district is rich in period pubs, notably the Anchor and the Windsor Castle.

The church of St Nicholas, on the corner of High Street and Lower Road, has an oddly proportioned yet attractive 12th-c flint W tower surmounted by weatherboarding and splayed spire. The chancel dates back to 1341, when the original church was built by John de Rutherwyke, Abbot of Chertsey (the grave N of the altar may be his). There was much restoration (on the whole tasteful) by Carpenter and Butterfield in the 19th c. The E window has six vivid scenes from the Life of Christ in stained glass, believed to be 15th-c Flemish, rescued from France during the Revolution. Among many memorials is a fine one to Robert Shiers, lawyer and lord of the manor from 1614. The estate was eventually acquired (1700) by Dr Hugh Shortrudge, Rector of nearby Fetcham, whose will left money to the vicars of four local churches on condition that they preached an annual sermon on the martyrdom of Charles I. The 'Shortrudge sermon' is still preached at St Nicholas on the last Sunday of January.

Little Bookham has a tiny (undedicated) church with timber belfry just off Lower Road. It is a single room (12th-c) restored in the 19th c with a tub font of uncertain date. The yew tree in the churchyard is supposed to be as old as the church. Within are many memorials of the Pollen-Boileau family, who lived in the fine 18th-c Manor (now a girls' school) next door.

Bookham has literary associations. Fanny Burney (1752–1840) and her husband General D'Arblay lived at the Hermitage (corner of East Street) where she wrote *Camilla*, whose profits enabled her to build a house near Box Hill. Jane Austen spent holidays at the old vicarage (demolished) of her godfather the Rev. Samuel Cooke (see tablet in the chancel of St Nicholas) who married her cousin Cassandra. Bookham is sometimes thought to be the 'Hartfield' of *Emma*.

2m S of Bookham is Polesden Lacey (open to the public), a Regency house by Thomas Cubitt on the site of a 17th-c house owned by the playwright Sheridan, but much extended by Mrs Ronald Greville (d. 1942) in sumptuous Edwardian-Louis XIV style. It is also a regional headquarters of the National Trust. In its lovely park is an open-air theatre with a summer Shakespeare season. George VI and his bride spent their honeymoon at Polesden. In summer the rose garden is superb.

BRAMLEY, *Surrey*. A sprawling village of mixed character on a tributary of the Wey 1m NE of Godalming, as valuable for its surroundings as for its contents. Like Holmbury St Mary it owes most of its existence to the railway's arrival in 1865. Yet it has some good Georgian and Regency houses, and, in the High Street, the fine 16th-c Bramley East Manor. Two Lutyens houses may be seen: Millmead (1907) built for

Kenneth Scowen

Cricket on the green at Brockham in Surrey

Gertrude Jekyll of garden fame, and Little Tangley (1899), an extension of a house built 22 years before, with remains of one of Miss Jekyll's gardens. Holy Trinity Church has bits of a Norman arch and a 13th-c chancel, but little else of interest except perhaps a monument to one Henry Ludlow (1730), a large well-carved urn and flambeau in a Palladian surround, a style called by Pevsner 'anti-baroque'.

A more interesting church is St John the Baptist at **Wonersh** (1m NE), mostly 18th c with traces of 12th–14th c in tower, chancel and arches. The church was well restored in 1901, though the redbrick porch spoils the effect. Wonersh, once a centre of the weaving industry, is well supplied with old cottages some of which still contain weavers' beams. The Grantley Arms, a good half-timbered 16th-c inn, is the true centre of the village. The Grantley family owned Great Tangley Manor, one of Surrey's finest Elizabethan houses (1584) but altered and extended by Philip Webb (1886).

Blackheath is 1m further NE, a neat and pleasant Victorian village with a small unremarkable church (1895), a Franciscan monastery (Gothic Revival, 1895) and 'The Hallams', a rather severe tiled and timbered house by Norman Shaw (1895). A village of the nineties!

BRENCHLEY, *Kent* (7m E of Tunbridge Wells), noted for fine Tudor cottages, gathers round a tree on a patch of grass, amid acres of orchards. Even the butcher's shop is timber-framed. The Old Workhouse, Marle Place (both 17th-c) and Brenchley Manor (16th-c) are among many interesting houses. Near the Manor (once known as the Old Parsonage) is an old oak 36ft round which was mentioned in the Domesday Book. An avenue of enormous yews 350 years old leads to a sandstone church, dating from the 13th c but restored in 1849. The rood screen (1536) is beautifully carved.

BRIGHTLING, *E. Sussex* (4½m W of Robertsbridge), is a village of charm on a hill with beech trees around. Its EE church of St Thomas à Becket (13th–14th c) had William of Wykeham for its rector in 1362. It was probably he who re-dedicated it from St Nicholas to St Thomas. It is full of monuments and brasses, and in the churchyard is the 60-ft pyramid mausoleum of a great English eccentric, Squire 'Mad Jack' Fuller (d. 1834), built by himself in 1810. He is said to have been buried in a sitting position holding a bottle of wine and wearing his top-hat.

The whole district is permeated by Mad Jack, who had the good taste to collect Turner's paintings, dabbled in astronomy and was a fiery MP for Lewes. His various follies are scattered about: his domed observatory in Brightling Park, the Needle on the highest hill (657ft) which commands a superb view across the Rother valley, and the Sugar Loaf, built near Woods Corner as a replica of Dallington Church spire (1¾m SW) to win a bet that he could see the spire from his house. Of the house, only the 1699 part remains – a two-storeyed block of nine bays.

BROCKHAM GREEN, *Surrey* (2m E of Dorking, just S of the main A25 road), is famous for its classic triangular village green where cricket has been played for over a century, with W. G. Grace among many famous visiting players. To the N is a beautiful view of Box Hill (563ft), and there was a touch of genius in siting the cruciform Christ Church (1846) by an architect (B. Ferrey) with a great sense of grouping. In 13th-c style, simple and solid, it has some good German stained glass. E of the green is Brockham Court (late 18th c). Court Farm was once used by the Dukes of Norfolk as an overnight stop on the way from London to Arundel Castle. Feltons Farm (to SW) dating from the 17th c, has a quadrangle of typical Surrey barns. Brockham (the name may refer either to badgers or a brook, though 'brook' is too small a description for the River Mole) has a village pump and a variety of cottages whose ages must be guessed, though two (in Wheelers Lane) are probably 16th-c. The green is locally celebrated, each 5 November, for its huge bonfire and sometimes too-boisterous firework display; atoned for at Christmas by its open-air carol service and brilliant Christmas tree.

Brockham is one of a trio of Mole-side villages, the other two being **Betchworth** and **Buckland**. Betchworth Castle (only fragments remain) was originally built by the river (on what is now a golf course) in the 14th–15th c. Unlike Buckland, Betchworth, a 'street village', has largely escaped the A25 road. Parts of St Michael's church date from Edward the Confessor, including (by tradition) a massive dug-out solid oak chest. The church must have fallen into great disrepair to have been so radically restored (by E. C. Hakewell) in 1851. The interest lies in guessing what it must have been like originally. The egg-cup-shaped font is by Eric Kennington (1951).

Outside the church is a little square of (mainly 17th-c) cottages, barns and the old Vicarage (1715). As you go down to the river, notice Old House, a long, thin Queen Anne house, and the Dolphin Inn (c. 1700).

BURWASH, *E. Sussex.* A lovely High Street on a ridge between the rivers Rother and Dudwell, with excellent views of the Weald; peaceful, although it is on the busy A265; lined with period cottages and houses, some timber-framed, with pollarded trees on the N side. Probably the best house is Rampyndene, built by a timber merchant in 1699. Many houses are tile-hung or brick-infilled, so that the general effect is a cheerful red-white-and-black. For descriptions of the countryside, see Kipling's *Puck of Pook's Hill.* St Bartholomew's Church tower might be as old as c. 1100. The wide chancel and S arcade are EE. Among monuments is the oldest known iron tomb-slab (14th-c) to John Colins, of an iron-founding family who lived at Socknersh (1½m SE). A bronze plaque near the door commemorates Kipling's only son John, killed at Loos in 1915.

Batemans (¾m SW), an ironmaster's house dated 1634, was Rudyard Kipling's home 1902–

36: a fine Jacobean house set in 33 acres of gardens designed by Kipling himself. It is now a National Trust museum, much of it (including his study) exactly as he left it at his death, littered with mementoes of his stories. He came here to escape the sightseers who had plagued him at Rottingdean. He is still remembered in the village, especially by men who as boys were allowed to fish in the Dudwell which ran through his garden. In a letter to a friend Kipling gave his first impressions of the place: 'Behold us lawful owners of a grey stone lichened house . . . beamed, panelled, with old oak staircase, all untouched and unfaked . . . a good and peaceable place.'

CHIDDINGFOLD, *Surrey.* The mental picture most people retain of this sizeable village in richly-wooded country, 3½m from the Sussex border, is the vaguely triangular green, with its tastefully converted Georgian cottages and the well-known (15th c, probably older) Crown Inn – a half-timbered house, claiming to be the oldest pub in the country, where Edward VI is supposed to have stayed over 400 years ago. There is also a pond with ducks and water-lilies. This, you feel, is South England as she was meant to be. Like many West Surrey villages Chiddingfold was a centre of both iron and glass industries in medieval times. Glassmaking continued as late as 1615, using local sand and wood, but declined as the Age of Coal approached. Not much Chiddingfold glass survives in local buildings (perhaps this is the Puritans' fault) but the church of St Mary has a little in the slender lancet window of its W wall – all the pieces were found on the sites of old glass-working forges.

St Mary's is another major restoration by Woodyer (1869). The original building dates from the 12th c (the first vicar was Geoffrey de Lechlade in 1180), but inside it is clear that we are standing in a 13th-c EE structure which has been heightened and lengthened subsequently. The W tower however may be 17th c. Its peal of eight bells includes one believed to be 500 years old. Note the priest's door in the S wall, thought to be as old as the church itself.

Chiddingfold used to have a fine 18th-c mansion, Shillinglee Park, destroyed not by enemy action but by Canadian troops billeted there. They set it on fire while celebrating the end of World War II: only the façade remains.

The ending *-fold* in several local village names (e.g. Dunsfold, Alfold) means 'forest clearing'. State afforestation is now replacing trees, and about 80,000 young oaks have been planted in 2000 acres nearby. The ash is also important for the old-established industry of making walking sticks.

At **Dunsfold** (5m E) we are almost in Sussex. It is a long (½m) string-bean of a village with brick and tile houses along a rough grass common, with bigger country houses nearby mostly dating from the 17th c when richer Londoners sought a refuge from the Plague (1665). The glory of this village is the church of St Mary and All Saints (*c.* 1270 and almost unaltered) with a 15th-c belfry. Strangely, it lies ½m E of the main village, possibly because of a 'holy well' whose waters were thought to cure blindness. A peaceful village, occasionally disturbed by jet-fighters from a local airfield.

Hambledon (5m NE, via Wormley) – don't confuse with Hambledon, Hants, of cricketing fame – is scattered, but the church (mainly 1846 but 14th c in parts), Court Farm (tile-hung) and the old Granary make an attractive group, and there are some good 16th- and 17th-c cottages, such as School Cottage, Malthouse Cottage and Malthouse Farm. Excellent views from surrounding hills of North and South Downs and Hydon's Ball (593ft), a memorial to Octavia Hill (1838–1912), housing reformer, open-space crusader and co-founder of the National Trust.

CHIDDINGSTONE, *Kent,* 6m W of Tonbridge. An unspoilt, justly famous single-street National Trust village, all 16th and 17th c except the 19th-c 'Castle', a rebuilding in mock-Gothic of the 17th-c home of the Streatfeild family, descended from Richard Streatfeild, ironmaster (d. 1601). The Castle has an exhibition of Royal Stuart pictures and furniture, and oriental relics. Legend says that the sandstone rock beside the footpath in the park is the Chiding Stone, where scolding wives were arraigned; more probably the village takes its name from a medieval patriarch named Chid. St Mary's Church, sheltered by trees, 13th c with Perp tower, was rebuilt after a fire in 1625. It contains many carvings, some grotesque (one is a head with two noses, two mouths and three eyes). Among the furnishings are a decorated font of 1628, and a pulpit of about the same date.

Hever Castle (2½m W), once the home of Anne Boleyn, is a fortified manor house lovingly restored by William Waldorf Astor in the early 1900s, set in magnificent gardens with long avenues of chestnuts and limes, a yew maze and topiary, and an Italian garden profusely dotted with (genuine) Roman and Renaissance sculpture. The castle and part of the grounds are often open to the public.

CHILHAM, *Kent,* 5½m SW of Canterbury. The centre of this extremely pretty village (best visited out of the tourist season) is a small square of Tudor and Jacobean houses, many of them timber-framed, with a variety of gables all accidentally harmonizing. All is compact: church at one end, castle gates at the other, houses festooned with camellias, jasmine, roses and creepers, the White Horse Inn and Tudor-style lodges to the Castle. At each corner of the square a lane leads to yet more period cottages. In The Street (NE corner) is a line of overhanging houses, especially Robin's Croft, once a vicarage, over whose door are the words: 'The sparrow hath found a house and the swallow a nest for herself'.

St Mary's Church, with tall Perp tower, is of flint and stone, mostly 15th-c but much restored by David Brandon (1863). Within, monuments and tombs (many 17th c) make good use of Bethersden marble. There is some nice carving near the roof, and 15th-c stained glass in N aisle windows. The yew tree by the gate may be as old as the church itself. All that remains of the Norman castle is the tall octagonal keep (rare). Beside it is a fine Jacobean house, built (in a hexagon with one side missing) for Sir Dudley Digges in 1616 and now the seat of Viscount Massereene and Ferrard. The grounds, laid out by Capability Brown, are open to the public.

The road from Chartham (3m NE) along the Chartham Downs to Street End gives one of the most beautiful views in Kent.

Julieberries Graves (½m SE), near an old mill by the railway, is a Neolithic long barrow dug into for a Roman grave, which may or may not be that of one Julius Laberius. The area is purported to be the site of the last battle between the Romans and the British.

Godmersham (2m S), may be reached on foot through the 500 acres of Chilham Park which joins Godmersham Park. It has no pub, a church and a few scattered buildings. The Palladian house (1732), beautifully situated overlooking the Stour valley, was owned by Jane Austen's brother Edward, adopted by the Knight family whose name he took. Jane and her sister Cassandra often stayed here. The flint church has a Norman chancel and tower. Among its monuments is a wall memorial to Edward Knight (d. 1852) and his wife Elizabeth.

CLANDON, EAST and WEST, *Surrey.* These villages, on the A246 Leatherhead–Guildford road, are the point at which commuterdom becomes genuine country. E. Clandon is a group of old cottages gathered round a small, mainly Norman church (St Thomas's) with a shingle belfry (1900). The old Manor, behind it, is a large farmhouse (*c.* 1700) and not far away is the Old Forge.

A National Trust signpost on the A246 points to Hatchlands, a noble red-brick mansion set in parkland, built in 1756–7 by Admiral Boscawen with the prize money of his victories over the French. Like Clandon Park it is open to the public, but in term-time is an international finishing school for girls. A rather severe front is relieved by an oriel window. Much of the interior decoration is early work by Robert Adam, fresh from his Italian travels: the best examples are the large Drawing Room and Library. The single-storey Music Room in the N side was added by Sir Reginald Blomfield in 1903. The last owner of the house was the architect H. S. Goodhart-Rendel who gave it to the nation in 1945.

West Clandon, an almost single-street village running N for a mile from the main road, has an excellent inn, The Onslow Arms. The church of St Peter and St Paul has a 19th-c N tower with wooden spire, remnants of a 13th-c nave and a splendid (probably 17th-c) pew for the Onslow family. Cottages are often half-timbered with flint infilling (as at Shere, q.v.). Clandon Park reaches from W. Clandon to Merrow. The original 1642 house was rebuilt by the Onslow family, to designs by the Venetian Leoni in the 1730s. Palladian in style, with ornate use of red-brick (unlike Hatchlands), its S front has been called 'Hampton Court Wren'. The entrance hall (two storeys high), with overmantels by Rysbrack, baroque plaster ceiling and painted panels, has been called 'one of the grandest early Palladian rooms in England'. The surrounding park, laid out (c. 1770) by Capability Brown, contains a tree-sheltered flint-and-brick Grotto with statues of the Three Graces, an unremarkable Ionic Temple (1833) and, of all things, a Maori house brought back from Waitoa by a Lord Onslow who was Governor of New Zealand.

COBHAM, *Kent* (5m W of Rochester), is famous for its Dickens associations, such as the half-timbered Leather Bottle Inn to which Mr Tupman retired after being jilted by Rachel Wardle, and Cobham Park, the novelist's favourite place to walk to from Gad's Hill. The park was designed by Humphry Repton and has many beautiful trees. Cobham Hall (now a multiracial girls' school) is one of the largest and most interesting houses in Kent. Set amid cedars, beeches and oaks of its Repton-designed park, its russet brick, long windows and spired turrets elegantly embrace its 17th-c middle block. The house may be visited during school holidays. Decorated by (among others) Inigo Jones and the Adams, its outstanding features are the Long Gallery, an astonishing Gilt Hall (1672) and two

fine staircases. In the park is a small Roman villa.

The chancel of St Mary Magdalene church (13th–14th-c) has a unique collection of some of the best brasses in England, all of the Cobham family in late medieval times, the figures and costumes exquisitely done. Nearby are almshouses, part of the ecclesiastical College founded by Sir John de Cobham (1362) and Stone House, the original schoolhouse of the College. The late 17th-c redbrick house Owletts (¼m NW), open to the public at stated times, was the home of Sir Herbert Baker, friend and collaborator of Lutyens: his work may be seen in several Kent villages.

At **Sole Street** (2m SW), Yeoman's House, half-timbered in Weald style, dates from the 15th c. **Luddesdown** (2½m S) is notable for its manor house, Luddesdown Court (early 13th c). **Meopham** (4½m SW), is a long straggling village (in danger of overgrowth) with a fine 13th–14th-c church, a smock windmill and a cricket green where the county side sometimes plays. From Meopham (pronounced 'Meppam') came the Tradescants, founders, with Elias Ashmole, of the first scientific museum in England.

DITCHLING, *E. Sussex,* 7½m NNE of Brighton. An overgrown village at a cross-roads, with a romantic past and a long tradition of arts and crafts. Its setting, with Ditchling Beacon (2½m S), looming behind, is impressive. The Beacon, at 813ft the third highest point of the South Downs, once boasted a gibbet. On it was lit one of the fires that warned of the coming of the Armada. It is best reached by the narrow road from Wick Farm, Westmeston.

Chiddingstone, a National Trust property

Kenneth Scowen

The oldest part of the village is west of the cross-roads. The mainly 13th-c parish church of St Margaret (the nave and aisle are older), later restored with the transept rebuilt in the 1860s, shows a good deal of EE work. Opposite the church is Anne of Cleves' House, an architectural jumble with plenty of the 16th c left, which has mellowed into something beautiful, even if it attracts the stigma of 'picturesque'. Like other Sussex houses of the same name, it may once have belonged to Anne as part of her gift from Henry VIII, but there is little evidence that she ever lived here. Among other nearby houses, notice Cotterells (black-tiled) and Pardons (date uncertain) with a gazebo in the garden.

Ditchling enjoyed fame in the 1920s as a Sussex Bohemia. It had an art printing press and a colony of artists among whom were Eric Gill, sculptor, designer and writer, and Frank Brangwyn the painter. Arts and crafts – weaving, pottery, leatherwork – still flourish here. In modern times Ditchling's most celebrated resident has been Dame Vera Lynn.

EASTRY, *Kent.* The best of this large village on the A256 3m SW of Sandwich is gathered near the spacious early 13th-c church of St Mary the Virgin, with its 66ft Norman tower and noble W doorway. Those who have been up it say that 17 other churches can be seen from the top. Within, it is clear that tower and nave are the same age: tower arches and nave arcades match. Furnishings and monuments include a heart-stirring hanging monument to Capt. John Harvey, one of Nelson's officers, who died of wounds (1794) off Brest on the 'glorious First of June' just before he was to have been promoted admiral. Above him are sculptured the three French ships he captured. On a column in the nave is a curious carved circle, believed to be a primitive calendar.

Eastry Court, next door, has an 18th-c front superimposed on remains of a medieval house. In its grounds, leaning over into the churchyard, is a huge evergreen oak of incalculable age. History and legend are intermingled in Eastry, reputed to be the site of a 'Palace of the Kings of Kent' (no trace remains) and the place where Thomas à Becket hid from his enemies.

We are in windmill country, and a little white one is visible on the way to **Goodnestone** (2m W – the *d* is not pronounced), whose 250-acre park contains, amid trees, Goodnestone House (18th-c with pillared porch), often visited by Jane Austen while staying with her brother Edward who had married the daughter of the house. The restored 13th-c church is adjacent. The village street has an attractive 17th-c brick house with curved Dutch gables, a style often found in E. Kent.

Barfreston (6m SW), a pleasant hamlet, must be visited for its superb unspoilt 12th-c church of flint and Caen stone, perhaps the finest of its kind in England. Less than 50ft long, it is rich in carvings, probably by craftsmen from Canterbury Cathedral. Monkeys, goats, a bishop, foliage, winged beasts of fantasy, men and animals fight-ing are all in this riot of design. The interior is dominated by the 19th-c EE-style wheel window above three Norman lancets. The bell is situated in a yew tree.

EWHURST, *Surrey.* The name, of course, means yew wood. Because it straggles between three clusters, guidebooks tend to overlook its many charms. You see it best from, Pitch Hill (843ft, 1m N) – a little square, then the church in a group of cottages, and Ewhurst Green ½m S of this. The Weald sandstone church, on a hillock, was rebuilt in 1837 after a disastrous attempt to underpin the central tower, which crashed, destroying the chancel and N transept. The tower was rebuilt in Norman style with broached spire by Robert Ebbels. The nave and S doorway (generally agreed to be the best in Surrey) are *real* Norman. The font, decorated with St Andrew's crosses and chevrons, is possibly 14th c; the pulpit Jacobean; the elegant altar rails (from Baynards Park, Cranleigh) 17th-c. Some of the cottages are nondescript, but there is a fine half-timbered one at the N end of the village (near the Bull's Head) called Deblins Green (*c.* 1700), and the 15th-c Tudor House. Hiding in the woods as you go up to Pitch Hill are some 19th-c residences, among them Alfred Powell's Long Copse (1897, thatched *and* tiled), owing much to William Morris and the Arts and Crafts movement; Philip Webb's Coneyhurst (1886, tile-hung in the Surrey manner); and George and Peto's Woolpit (1888), built for the Doulton chinaware family who provided the terracotta. The village also boasts a 19th-c mill which seems to have been used by smugglers as a 'bulk-breaking' point.

FLETCHING, *E. Sussex,* 3¼m NW of Uck-field. It appears in the Domesday Book as *Flesc-inge,* but there have been attempts to derive the name from *flèche,* an arrow, since the district was known in medieval times for the manufacture of arrow heads. These no doubt came in handy in 1264, when Simon de Montfort encamped here the night before the Battle of Lewes. The church of St Mary and St Andrew is largely 13th-c with a few later additions. Its tower is early Norman (possibly even late Saxon) with shingled spire. Some excellent monuments are here: a late 14th-c brass to a knight and lady of the Dalyngrugge family; a 15th-c one to a glover named Peter Denot. The handsome tomb of Richard Leche, High Sheriff of Sussex and Surrey (d. 1596), has his life-size effigy in alabaster, with his wife beside him, although as a widow she had been married again to the Earl of Nottingham. A mausoleum was added by the first Earl of Sheffield, who lived at Sheffield Park. Sheffield's great friend Edward Gibbon, historian of ancient Rome, is also buried here (1794). Near the church is Church Farm House (early 18th c) and, in the opposite direction, the gatehouse to Sheffield Park, famous for its splendid gardens (by Repton) which are especially beautiful in the rhododendron season. The house itself, built in 1779 by James Wyatt, is

Gothic Revival. Sheffield Park Station is on the Bluebell Line, a length of railway preserved by private enterprise and enthusiasm.

Newick (2m SW), has some good period houses, a well-restored church with a Perp sandstone tower, and a village pump of wrought-iron. The Bull Inn, on the green (the bull is Papal, not bovine) is so called because Newick lies on one of the Pilgrims' Ways to Canterbury. Piltdown (1m SE), famous for its missing-link 'Man', was the scene of an archaeological hoax (1912 – discovered 1953) and preserved in the name of the local pub.

FORDWICH, *Kent.* 3m NE of Canterbury on the River Stour, this largely Tudor village of about 300 people was a medieval port for unloading food for Canterbury's two great monasteries and Caen stone for repairing the Cathedral. It takes its name from the ford at the crooked part of the River Stour nearby. It had its own mayor until 1883 and still has an annually-elected 'deputy'. The timber-framed Town Hall (*c.* 1540), filled in with herringbone brickwork, thought to be the smallest town hall in England, has a court room and jury room on the first floor, a prison below and stocks outside. Dangling over the water is the ancient Town Crane which was still unloading barges a century ago. It was traditionally used to dip the ducking stool for scolding wives. The stool, with other museum pieces, can be seen in the town hall.

The unrestored 13th-c church of St Mary has a tall shingled steeple and box pews (a special one for the mayor with iron stands for his mace). There is a 17th-c wall painting, some good 14th- and 15th-c stained glass, a Norman stone tomb in which (with no known evidence) St Augustine once lay, and a wooden penitent's stool. Church, town hall, timbered houses, and old hostelry the George and Dragon, and river sum up the village in one picture.

FOREST ROW, *E. Sussex* (2½m SE of East Grinstead), is overgrown and suffers from being on the main A22 London–Eastbourne road; but, like Chelwood Gate (3½m S), it is a good starting point for exploring Ashdown Forest. It lies on a hillside overlooking an upper reach of the River Medway. ½m NW are the ruins of Brambletye House, 'Jacobethan' in style, built in 1631 for Sir Henry Compton and afterwards owned by Sir James Richards who, suspected of treason, fled the country in 1683. Towers and bays of the original shape can still be seen. Ashdown House (1m NE), built in the 1790s by Benjamin Latrobe (architect of Baltimore Cathedral and several buildings in Philadelphia) is as elegant as any 18th-c house in Sussex. Kidbrook Park (¾m SW), early 18th-c with Victorian additions, is the Freshfield family seat, in gardens laid out by Repton.

Hartfield (4½m E), is a likeable village on the road to Tunbridge Wells. The name is typical of Ashdown Forest, once famous for deer-hunting. Its 13th-c church (parts may be older) has a Perp

W tower with broach spire. Notice a churchyard cottage called the Lychgate, timber-framed and dating from *c.* 1520. Bolebrooke (1¼m outside the village) is a 16th-c brick manor house, once owned by the Dalyngrugges (*see* Fletching) who also built Bodiam Castle (*see* Northiam). Cotchford Farm (½m S), beside a stream which joins the Medway, was the home of A. A. Milne. The wooden bridge where Christopher Robin played Pooh-sticks has been saved for the nation by the County Council and Mr Milne's publishers.

Withyham (5¾m E), too scattered to be a true village, needs to be explored. The 17th-c church stands on a steep hill. It shows traces of a 14th-c church which was burnt by lightning. The interior is famous for its monuments, most of which are in the Sackville Chapel: here are sculptures by Nollekens, Flaxman and Chantrey, and a beautifully scripted slate tablet to Victoria Sackville-West, poet and gardener (d. 1962).

GODSTONE, *Surrey.* There is a *South* Godstone 3½m SW of Godstone proper: ignore it. The miracle is that this most attractive village, in a gap of the chalk North Downs at the dog-leg junction of two main roads (A22 to Eastbourne and A25 to Sevenoaks) has not been ruined by traffic. The M25 motorway is helping it to breathe. Its tree-girt square green has a cricket pitch and a small pond (Godstone has seven ponds altogether). The church of St Nicholas is ½m to the E in a district known as Church Town. Sir G. G. Scott the architect lived at Rooksnest House (now a school) and restored the church in 1873, leaving only fragments of the old Norman structure. In it is a monument (1641) to a cousin of John Evelyn, one of two immortal diarists whose families came from these parts (the Pepyses came from Tandridge, 2m ESE, famous for its golf course). The Evelyns seem to have made their money from gunpowder manufacture, once a Surrey industry.

Near the green, the White Hart Inn (probably 16th-c, though the name is said to refer to Richard II's badge) is one of several period hostelries here. Mentioned by Cobbett in *Rural Rides*, it was a famous coaching inn and (legend says) a stopping place for the Tsar of Russia and his party in 1815 on the way to see a prize fight at Blindley Heath.

5½m SW is **Outwood** (also accessible from Bletchingley, q.v.) which has Britain's oldest working windmill (1665) with a rural museum and small zoo for visitors' entertainment. There was a second 'smock' mill (1860) which collapsed in 1961. Together they were known as Cat and Fiddle. The village stands on a 400-ft hill from which, according to tradition, the glow of the Fire of London (1666) could be seen 25m away.

GOUDHURST, *Kent,* 10m E of Tunbridge Wells. A splendid village on a high hill sloping to the W (which is the best approach) surmounted by a square-towered church. Magnificent views of orchards, hop gardens, oasts and church spires, from Rochester to Hastings on a good day. 1m before climbing to the village you cross the site of the single-track old branch railway from Tonbridge to Hawkhurst: it never had more than two coaches. Railway enthusiasts have reopened part of the line and the public can take trips from Tenterden. Goudhurst Station is now a house called Haltwhistle, and the Railway Hotel became the Goudhurst Hotel. There are the usual tilehung and weatherboarded houses, often with timbering underneath. The Star and Eagle Hotel, once connected to the church by a tunnel, was a hideout of the notorious Hawkhurst Gang of smugglers, led by Richard Kingsmill, hanged at Horsmonden in 1796. There is still a house called Spyways. The Almshouses are worth noting with their figurines.

St Mary's Church (13th- and 14th-c, restored mid-19th-c), sandstone, has a 17th-c beacon tower with Gothic castellation and belfry windows: generally open to visitors wishing to admire the Wealden panorama. Within, many monuments (in brass, wood and stone) and tombs of the Culpeper and Bedgebury families, from the 15th c onwards – big landowners and later ironfounders. Local legend says that certain marks on the walls were made by archers sharpening their arrows before going with Sir John Bedgebury to the battle of Agincourt.

Finchcocks (1¾m S), is that rarity in Kent, a Baroque house in Vanbrugh style, red-brick, built for Edward Bathurst in 1725. Glassenbury Park (2m SE), thickly wooded, contains a moated house dating from the 15th c. It is approached by a lime avenue, at one end of which is the grave of Napoleon's charger, captured at Waterloo.

Scotney Castle (2m W) is well worth visiting in its romantic lake setting and with a beautiful garden.

Bedgebury National Pinetum (2½m S), 75 acres, is a branch of Kew Gardens, started here because, before the age of smokeless zones, conifers would not grow properly at Kew. Bedgebury has the largest collection of conifers in Europe. The park, open to visitors, has most kinds of tree and shrub, including Californian redwood and some cypresses, and there is a glorious display of rhododendrons in season. The big sandstone moated house (now a girls' school), originally 17th-c, was turned into a sort of Louis XIV château with a pavilion roof (two rows of dormer windows) and an odd spired tower. Nearby is Pattenden Manor, one of Henry VIII's hunting lodges.

GROOMBRIDGE, *Kent and E. Sussex,* 4m W of Tunbridge Wells. The county boundary runs along Kent Water, a tributary of the Medway. Trim and tidy, the original village centres on a triangular green with 18th-c cottages on two sides. It owes much to John Packer who established a private chapel (1625) which became the church of St John the Evangelist. This was a thankoffering for the safe return from Spain of the Prince of Wales, afterwards Charles I, having failed to woo the Infanta. Gothic in style, it retains some of its original furnishings, such as the font and pulpit. Chancel and nave are one. There

is some 17th-c stained glass with heraldic designs in one window; and monuments to John Packer and his son Philip, who rebuilt Groombridge Place in the second half of the 17th c. The Place, H-shaped and standing in a square moat, is of mellow red-brick, lovely to look at – architect unknown, but it may have been Wren. The house in its medieval form originally belonged to the Waller family: from it Sir Richard Waller set out for Agincourt, where he captured the Duke of Orleans. The gardens, laid out by John Evelyn the diarist, are open to the public in summer.

HAWKHURST, *Kent,* 4m S of Cranbrook. Village or town? In three parts, Gill's Green, Highgate and The Moor. Highgate is the newest part (yet with 18th-c weatherboarded houses in the middle of its colonnaded shopping centre), divided from The Moor (the true village) by a stream in a valley. The Moor is a large green with cottages on two sides. The church of St Lawrence, with its rather short Perp W tower, is long and built mainly of ragstone. The tall chancel window (late 14th c) is particularly fine, spacious like the chancel itself. Nearby are Church Court, half-timbered and brick, and Wetheringhope (18th-c red-brick) with its Venetian window. Beside the Royal Oak Inn is a weatherboarded house associated with the Hawkhurst smuggling gang who have left a trail of legend between Romney Marsh and London.

HERSTMONCEUX, *E. Sussex,* 5m NE of Hailsham. The last syllable is pronounced *soo.* A pleasant village which knows that people only come to look at the Castle. All Saints Church dates from *c.* 1180 with 14th- and 15th-c additions. It has a Norman font and some fine monuments. A brass in the chancel to Sir William Ffiennes (d. 1402) invites you to earn 120 days of pardon by saying a Paternoster and an Ave for him. A sculpture of Thomas Lord Dacre (d. 1533) and his son is the most impressive feature. Near the church is a 14th-c tithe barn. Woodworking is a traditional craft hereabouts, and Herstmonceux has a speciality: trug-making (a trug is a wooden basket used by gardeners) which dates only from the Great Exhibition (1851).

The castle, the only red-brick castle in Sussex, usually photographed with its reflection in the moat is 15th-c, well restored in the 1930s, and shows the medieval castle becoming a symmetrically beautiful fortified manor. Its design may have been influenced by Bodiam Castle (*see* Northiam) which is 55 years older. One of the great buildings of England, now housing the Royal Greenwich Observatory, it is unfortunately not open to the public except for a museum in a small part of it. The Newton Telescope Building and the gardens can be visited at stated times.

HORSTED KEYNES, *W. Sussex,* 3¾m NE of Haywards Heath. The name Keynes comes from De Cahanges, the Norman family who were Lords of the Manor after the Conquest. The village, a peaceful blend of old and new, is on two levels, the green (with Tudor houses and two pubs) above, the church below. The church, of local stone with shingled spire, is all Norman except for lancet windows added to the S transept in the 13th c and the N arcade, restored in 1888. Who was the small 13th-c knight whose effigy (27 inches long) in the chancel is among the monuments? Is this a heart-shrine, meaning that he was killed in the Crusades and his heart sent home? Several Wyatts are buried here, descendants of Sir Thomas, poet and courtier, beheaded by Mary Tudor. Horsted Keynes station, 1m from the village, is a terminus of the Bluebell Line (*see* Fletching), one of whose locomotives is named 'Birch Grove' after the home (at Chelwood Gate, 2m N) of Mr Harold Macmillan, Prime Minister 1957–63.

Ardingly (4m NW), is a straggling village with the 14th-c Perp-and-Dec church of St Peter outside it. The church has some fine brasses, protected by carpets, of the Wakehurst and Culpeper families. The Culpepers built Wakehurst Place (1m N) in 1590: it was much altered in the 17th and 18th c. The estate (462 acres) is now part of Kew Gardens specializing in rare marsh plants (National Trust: open to the public). Ardingly College (1½m S), one of the Woodard public schools (1864), has a noble chapel.

1m N is the South of England Agricultural Society's permanent showground.

IGHTHAM, *Kent,* 4½m E of Sevenoaks. A not-to-be-missed village whose unique feature, the Mote, lies 2m SW, nearer Plaxtol than Ightham. By-passed by the A25, it is rather a show village, with some good restored Tudor houses and the 16th-c George and Dragon Inn. Town House, at one corner of the village centre, with overhanging gables, was built about 1555. The church (14th–15th c), on a knoll apart from the centre, has some well-carved monuments, including one of Sir Thomas Cawne (1374), the two Sir William Selbys (d. 1611 and 1638) and Dorothy Selby (d. 1641), famous for her needlework, whose memorial bears some heroic couplets beginning:

She was a Dorcas
Whose curious needle turned th' abused stage
Of this lewd world into a Golden Age.

She is also said to have deciphered a code message which led to the discovery of Gunpowder Plot.

Oldbury Camp (1m W), amid trees, has Stone Age caves, and Iron Age Celtic earthworks, used by the Belgae (1st c) to resist Roman invaders.

Ightham Mote, home of the Selbys for three centuries, is an exceptionally fine moated manor house amid trees, meadows, a lake and gardens with peacocks. Mote means *moot*, a medieval council, not moat. The doorway leads straight into the faultless 14th-c Hall. The Solar (living room) and private chapel are both 16th-c, with a priest's room nearby. Lovingly preserved by its

Kenneth Scowen

The gatehouse of Ightham Mote

present American owner, the Mote is open to the public at stated times.

Plaxtol (2¼m S), a tiny village with some old houses pleasantly grouped, has an undedicated church of Cromwellian simplicity with a hammerbeam roof – the only completely 17th-c church in Kent. Once a chapel, rebuilt by Archbishop Laud, it became a parish church in 1649. Despite its severity it has a well-carved reredos showing scenes of the Passion, and carving on the old pulpit. There is an interesting museum of wrought ironwork at the foundry on the E side of the village.

Fairlawne House (built in the 17th-c) was once the home of the Puritan Vane family, notably of Sir Harry, who became Governor of Massachusetts in 1636.

LEIGH, *Surrey*. There are 14 villages called Leigh in Britain. The word, pronounced *lye*, means a forest clearing. This Leigh is 4m SW of Reigate. Some critics find it too trim, tidy and demure. It is difficult to believe that, like Charlwood and neighbouring villages, it was once a centre for the Weald iron industry. The whole district as far as Gatwick was known in the 14th c as 'Thunderfield-in-the-Forest'. To the E is a hamlet called Irons Bottom.

The village green is as nearly perfect as you will find – triangular with church at apex amid timbered and tiled cottages with roses round the doors. On one side is the weatherboarded Plough Inn (parts date from 14th c) which has real ale from the wood. On another is Priest's House, a long jumbled terrace of restored 15th-c houses of different heights, with much half-timbering:

probably used in medieval times to accommodate visiting clerics. Leigh Place, N of the church, was once a 15th-c house with a moat in which coins and cannon balls have been found. 'Gothic' windows and turrets were added recklessly in the early 19th c. St Bartholomew's Church, largely 15th-c, restored by Woodyer and Lees in 19th-c, is like a small box with 'picturesque' additions. Its Horsham slab roof is supported by Wealden oak. Inside are memorial brasses to the Arderne family: John Arderne of Leigh Place was High Sheriff of Surrey in 1432.

Another 'iron village' is **Newdigate** (5m SW), by no means compact, but it has some good features, such as the attractive (restored) 13th-c church of St Peter, once called 'Hunter's Church' because it is said to have been built by the Earl de Warenne, the great Norman landowner, for his lords and knights when deer hunting. The shingled tower, with spire, is all of wood, supported by huge cross-braced timbers which are supposed to be 500 years old. The best cottages are near the church – Dean House Farm (brick and timber, 16th c), White Cottage and Hasted Cottage, next to the Six Bells Inn.

LINDFIELD, *W. Sussex,* 1½m NE of Haywards Heath, and almost part of it. Pevsner calls its ½-m long High Street 'without any doubt the finest village street in Sussex.' A good example of how a truly beautiful village 'just grows', with Georgian and Tudor alternating behind grass verges and lime trees. Never mind the sneers at 'postcard prettiness'.

The 13th-c church of St John the Baptist is at one end and a pond and large village green at the other. To see it properly you must visit it out of season – motor-coach parties and tea-queues obscure one's vision otherwise. The church, mainly 14th-c, is a mixture of Perp and Dec. Close by is Church Cottage (timber-framed, 15th-c) and Old Place (timber and brick, 1590). Lindfield House and Lindfield Place are both 18th-c. Going S down the street, everything enchants: Bower House, Malling Priory, Nash House, Manor House. One or two houses have become bow-fronted shops.

The two famous names associated with the village are very different. Philip Henslowe (d. 1616), theatrical and bear-baiting impresario, Edward Alleyn's partner and founder of the Admiral's Men (a rival company to Shakespeare's), was born here and graduated to Bankside via dyeing and starch-making. Lindfield owes more to the Quaker William Allen, who settled here in 1824 and on the West Common built cottages with smallholdings for the poor, founded a school, fought slavery with Wilberforce, joined Robert Owen in the cooperative movement, and counted among his friends both the Duke of Sussex and the Tsar of Russia.

LINGFIELD, *Surrey.* With 7000 population, this can claim to be Surrey's largest village; almost a town. 2m off the A22 and ½m from its railway station, it is famous (to the outside world) for its racecourse. It is certainly the most attractive centre in E. Surrey, where country roads converge in a way that suggests it was once an important market town. Its mineral spring and local ale were both praised by John Aubrey (1626–97). The district is permeated with relics of the Cobham family, who from medieval times lived at Starborough Castle (1½m E) of which only stumps of towers and traces of a moat remain – the present house is Victorian.

St Peter and St Paul ('the Westminster Abbey of Surrey') is the county's best unspoilt Perp church, rebuilt and enlarged from a 14th-c church (of which a tower remains) by Sir Reginald Cobham in 1431, who also founded a Carthusian college here. There is an unusual double nave. The tall N aisle and chancel contain several Cobham tombs. The first Lord Cobham's effigy is soldierly; his head rests on a Saracen's head to show his descent from a Crusader. He fought at Crécy and died of the plague in 1361. In the chancel lie Sir Reginald Cobham and his wife; in the N chapel Sir Thomas Cobham (1471); in front of the altar the third Lord Cobham and his wife: he fought at Agincourt. There are some splendid brasses, the best in Surrey, and not only of Cobhams.

The Carthusian college disappeared in the 16th c. On its site is a 17th-c tile-hung farmhouse, and (N of the church) the Guest House, now the County Library. If Lingfield has a centre, it is Plaistow Street, around a duckpond. Here, tree-shaded, are the two principal curiosities of the village: St Peter's Cross (said to be 15th-c) and the Cage, added to it in 1773 as a tiny village jail, last used in 1882 to lock up a poacher. Nearby are some good tile-hung and weatherboarded cottages; but the best ones are grouped in a square leading to the church (S side). Star Inn Cottages are c. 1700, the timber-framed Old Town Stores 16th-c; and Pollard Cottage, used as a butcher's shop until recently, retains a rare 15th-c shop front.

Crowhurst (3½m N), almost on the Kent border, is a fairly unspoilt hamlet with a row of single-storey cottages, a hilltop church dating back to the 12th c, and a yew tree 99-ft round, said to be at least 1000 years old. It was hollowed out c. 1820 and used as a sort of café with tables and chairs. Crowhurst Place (½m SW) once a beautiful moated 15th-c mansion built for the Gaynesford family, was much altered by George Crawley in 1918. There are the usual legends that Henry VIII stayed here on his way to visit Anne Boleyn at Hever Castle. There is beautiful heathland to the SW.

LOOSE, *Kent,* 2m S of Maidstone. An enchanting small village scattered about a valley, watered by two streams which are joined by others. They run through people's gardens and beside the church, and one once drove a mill. The Loose stream supported 13 mills in 3m at one time. Down the valley are the gabled Chequers Inn and the 18th-c red-brick Vale. The long, two-storeyed timbered Old Wool House, where wool was once cleaned before being fed to Wealden looms, is up near the top. So is All Saints Church, with its Norman tower, shingled spire and 15th-c windows. The nave was rebuilt in 1878 after a fire. Beside the church is an enormous yew, 36ft round, also said to be nearly 1000 years old. Buried in the churchyard is the Rev. Richard Boys, who before becoming vicar of this parish was chaplain to Napoleon on St Helena and may have been the last person to see him alive.

Leeds Castle (5½m E) seen from the A20 is the perfect romantic fortress-home surrounded by its lake and moat with black swans, and 500 acres of parkland. It belonged in the 12th c to Robert de Crevecoeur and became Royal property in 1272. Plantagenet and Tudor kings stayed, and Royal factions fought, here, notably Queen Isabelle ('the she-wolf of France') and her retinue in the rebellion against Edward II. It was for some time the home of Catherine of Aragon and the prison of Elizabeth I before she ascended the throne. About half the Castle dates only from 1822 and was renovated in the 1930s. It is open to the public except when being used as a medical conference centre or for special meetings. Leeds village has some old houses of various ages and a Norman towered church with Saxon windows. An early 13th-c ragstone watermill, one of the oldest in Britain, is attached to the barbican.

Sutton Valence (4m SE), built mostly on a ridge with tiered streets, commands superb views across the Weald. This is its most attractive feature; but there are some interesting houses – Lambe's Almshouses (1580), the Swan Inn, some 18th-c cottages on the green, and Valence House, half-timbered with overhanging gables (1598). Sutton Valence Boys School (founded 1578) is now in 20th-c buildings. There are remains of a Norman castle and a windmill.

MAYFIELD, *E. Sussex*, 8½m S of Tunbridge Wells. On a high ridge offering (especially by the windmill at Argos Hill to the NW) wide views of Weald and South Downs, spoilt only by the TV mast at Cross-in-Hand. The village sign shows children playing in a field, suggesting a derivation from Maids' Field (doubtful). There is a legend that St Dunstan, patron saint of ironworkers, had a forge here and, being tempted by the Devil, beat him off with a pair of tongs (said to be still kept at the Old Palace). When he became Archbishop of Canterbury in 959 he built a rough wooden church here. The present church is dedicated to him. The stubby W tower is EE, the rest Perp, with Jacobean pulpit and late-17th-c font. There are monuments to the Baker family (17th–18th c) who went in for such un-Sussex names as Philadelphia and Marthanna. From 1780 to 1912, all the vicars belonged to the Kirby family, one of them serving for 52 years. Fire swept through the village in 1389, thus the oldest houses in the main street date from the 15th c; these include Walnut Tree House and Middle House Hotel. London House is mixed 17th- and 18th-c.

The Archbishops of Canterbury had a palace here, the remains of which, with additions and extra Victorian buildings, are now a school, the Convent of the Holy Child Jesus. The impressive 14th-c Hall (68ft × 38ft) was converted into a chapel in the 1860s. In it are a sculptured Madonna (15th c, probably Dutch) and a 14th-c Italian painting of the Crucifixion. The Well House and Gate House are both 15th c. After the Reformation the Palace became the home of Sir Thomas Gresham.

Rotherfield (3m NW), is a spacious village with some nice houses (such as the 17th-c Old Manor) and much less traffic than Mayfield. Also on a hill, it has a church dedicated (unusually) to St Denys or Dionysius. There was a church here in Saxon times, given by Bertwald, Duke of the S. Saxons, in gratitude for a miraculous cure at the monastery of St Denys in France. The present building is an attractive mixture of early 13th-c (the arcades of the nave, e.g.) and Perp (the tower and E window). The E window has some excellent stained glass by William Morris and Burne-Jones (*c.* 1875), there are remains of frescoes from 13th–15th c, and in the Nevill chapel a good 15th-c ceiling with grotesque heads and badges of the landowning Nevill family.

MICKLEHAM, *Surrey*. The A24 London–Worthing road, beautifully landscaped as it sweeps through this glorious bit of the Mole Valley, by-passes Mickleham, a 'picture postcard' village and none the worse for it. Mickleham Downs, part of what is locally known as 'Little Switzerland', are said to support 70 kinds of butterflies and 300 of moths. Behind the village rises Box Hill (563ft), ruined by motorcycles and icecream parlours but magnificent out of season, and good for skiing when enough snow falls.

Juniper Hall (¾m S), now a field-study centre, is a mainly 18th-c house (decorated by Adam) built by David Jenkinson who sheltered French Revolution refugees such as Mme de Staël and General d'Arblay, who married novelist Fanny Burney in Mickleham church (1794). Another novelist, George Meredith, was married there in 1864. He lived for 20 years at Flint Cottage on Zigzag Hill. Down at the Burford Bridge Hotel (1800) Keats completed *Endymion*, R. L. Stevenson often stayed, and Nelson slept there before leaving England for the campaign that ended in Trafalgar.

St Michael's Church (Norman, with plenty surviving the 1891 restoration: Leigh Hunt said it was 'plump as an abbot') has some good Flemish stained glass in the E window. Note the rare 'grave boards' (wooden tombstones) in the churchyard. Opposite is The Running Horses Inn (17th c) and nearby the Dutch-gabled Old House (1636).

On the W side of the A24 are Norbury Park (½m) and West Humble. The former, a late 18th-c mansion, is sited so as to overlook the whole valley. From it you can sometimes see London. It was the home of the late Dr Marie Stopes. West

Humble is a high-class commuter hamlet, part of it (Camilla Lacey) on the site of Fanny Burney's house, built from her literary earnings. There is a curious old barn-church, and Box Hill Station, compared by some to a Gothic church, by others to 'the lodge of a French château'; somehow absolutely right for a country railway station.

NEW ASH GREEN, *Kent* (2m E of Kingsdown off the A20), is an experiment – a wholly 20th-c village planned from scratch on 430 acres of the North Downs. Designed by Span, a development company with environmental ideals ('planning is better than sprawl') which unfortunately went bankrupt, it was to have been a self-sufficient town for up to 6000 people with a pedestrian shopping precinct, church, school, recreation fields, even some light industry (which never came). A certain number of houses were set aside for G.L.C. overspill. About half the area is left as open space. Much use is made of slopes and split levels. Trees and plants counteract the austerity of planning. Punch Croft is a section where short terraces, black-tiled and brown weatherboarded, look out on to greens. The Primary School is particularly well designed. Knights Croft, with longer terraces, uses straw-coloured weatherboarding. This is not the sort of village coachloads of trippers go to see, but it should be studied as one way of making rural life tolerable in the future. (*See* 'West Kent and The Weald' in *The Buildings of England* series by John Newman, who lives in New Ash Green himself.)

NORTHIAM, *E. Sussex,* 6½m SE of Hawkhurst. A large village with a long main street, much white weatherboarding and a rich variety of houses of different periods – the 20th-c ones are mainly at the N end. On the green is an oak tree, reputed to be 1000 years old, under which Elizabeth I sat on 11 August 1573 to change her green, high-heeled shoes which she left to the village (where they are still kept) as a souvenir of her visit. St Mary's Church (mostly of ironstone) has a mixed Norman and EE tower; much of the nave and chancel is 14th c. The Frewen Mausoleum, added in 1846, contains graves of the Frewen family who were lords of the manor and rectors of the parish. One of the rectors in the 17th c was a Puritan who named two of his sons Thankful and Accepted. Accepted became President of Magdalen College, Oxford, and also a staunch Royalist, for which Charles I rewarded him with the Archbishopric of York.

On the outskirts of the village are several notable houses, among them Great Dixter (¾m N), a skilful conversion and enlargement by Lutyens of a 15th-c manor house. Lutyens added a complete timber-framed barn brought from Benenden (q.v.) and re-erected. The whole stands in lovely gardens rich in clematis, open to the public, with a nursery garden adjacent.

Bodiam (3m WNW) is a small village with a great late 14th-c castle which, like Herstmonceux (q.v.), stands in a lily-filled moat and is one of the great fortified houses of England. It was restored in 1919 and given to the nation by Lord Curzon of Kedleston. Built in 1385 to resist possible French invasion, it saw no action until the Civil War when it failed to resist General Waller's Parliamentarian Army. It is not habitable, being largely roofless, but the design is clear. More comfortable than most castles of its time, it seems to have had a primitive central heating system. There is a museum nearby: both Castle and museum are open to the public.

OCKHAM, *Surrey.* One of a group of villages in the flat agricultural part of Surrey S of the A3 London–Portsmouth road: all have benefited from the A3(M) section, but some are threatened by the M25 extension. Ockham lacks a true centre, and many cottages are 19th c. For comic awfulness, see the pseudo-Gothic Hautboy Hotel (1864), but the restaurant is excellent. N of the A3 is Ockham Mill (1862), five-storey brick. William of Occam (c. 1280–1349), schoolman and theologian who once accused the Pope of heresy, was probably born in the district.

Ockham Park, originally a Jacobean mansion remodelled by Hawksmoor (1724) and Voysey (1894) was badly burned in 1948. All that remains is the kitchen wing, the Italian-style tower, stables and orangery. In its parkland is All Saints Church, amid tall trees. Its sturdy square W tower is probably 15th-c, but the general framework, chancel arch and N arcade are 13th-c. The big surprise is the E window – seven lancets with beautifully carved capitals. The 1735 brick chapel was added as a mausoleum for the King family who lived at Ockham Park.

OCKLEY, *Surrey.* On Stane Street (Roman road, AD 70, London to Chichester, now A29), once known as Brandy or Silk Street because it was a smuggling route, Ockley has one of the biggest (600ft wide at one point) 'classic' village greens where cricket is played in summer and hounds meet in winter. A good variety of period cottages and a stone-pillared well like the one at Abinger (q.v.). Looking W and N you always have well-wooded Leith Hill (965ft with a 64-ft tower on top) as background. Oral tradition for 11 centuries says that Ockley was the site of a great battle (851) in which King Ethelwulf's W Saxons defeated the Danes. In Norman times the district was part of the Royal Deer Forest.

The church of St Margaret, oddly, is not on the green but ½m NE: as there was once a 12th-c castle nearby, this may have been the original village centre. The church's foundation date is uncertain, but the list of rectors begins in 1308 and the glass in the window E of the 15th-c porch may be 14th c. The whole church was rebuilt in 1873. Ockley Court (18th-c brick with bow windows) is opposite.

The pleasure of Ockley is in its setting, its atmosphere and its pubs. The Cricketers and the Red Lion are both 17th c. The Parrot (uncertain date) at Forest Green (2½m N) is worth a visit too.

The hall at Great Dixter

Among cottages of various ages on Stane Street and around the green, tiled, brick or weather-boarded, note Carpoles and Tanyards Cottages (W side) and Lime Tree Cottages (pleasantly odd) on N side.

On the way up to Leith Hill, nobly set amid trees and rhododendrons, is Leith Hill Place (17th–18th-c), owned successively by the Wedgwood and Vaughan Williams families. Open to the public at stated times in summer, it contains a collection of Wedgwood pottery and portraits of the family by Romney, Reynolds and Stubbs. Leith Hill itself, especially from the folly tower, gives splendid views as far as the Channel. John Evelyn, 300 years ago, claimed he could 'discern twelve or thirteen counties on a serene day'. The tower was built (1766) by Squire Richard Hull, also of Leith Hill Place; he is buried underneath it. It was afterwards said to have been used by Stane Street smugglers to store contraband goods.

OTFORD, *Kent*, 2½m N of Sevenoaks, with Shoreham and Eynsford, makes a village trio in the Darent valley, which is rich in Roman remains. The fact that it sits astride the A225 should not deter visitors. True, the duck-pond is now in the middle of a roundabout, but High Street contains some attractive old houses such as Broughton Manor, with its medieval hall and 16th-c gable, and the Bull Inn, whose panelling may have come from the Archbishop's Palace. The Palace, rebuilt from a manor house by Archbishop Warham (1518) who already owned Knole, is only a fragment of the original, and part of it has been converted into cottages. The church, by the green, has a 17th-c timbered porch leading into

a squat Norman tower, and the nave is 11th-c. Some good monuments within, notably of the Polhill family, one of whom, Elizabeth, was Cromwell's granddaughter, her father being General Ireton. The Church Hall (1909) was designed by Lutyens, whose brother was vicar here.

Shoreham (2m NW), lies off the main road, and though quite large is peaceful. The main street contains a number of old houses of various dates. The church, at the top end of the street that runs down to the river, is mostly Perp, Early and Late; the flint and red-brick tower 18th-c. Wesley often preached here, and it is recorded that the poet William Blake slept through one of his sermons. Blake used to come here to stay with Samuel Palmer, painter and etcher, at Water House (early-19th-c) where Palmer lived for five years.

Lullingstone Castle (4¼m N), is really an 18th-c house whose grounds contain a herb garden and a 14th-c church. Nearby is the best excavated Roman villa in Kent, showing remains of a Christian chapel (possibly 4th-c).

PATRIXBOURNE, *Kent* (3m SE of Canterbury), is a village of great charm, some of it accidental, some not, owing much to the antiquarian Lord Conyngham in the 1860s. His house Bifrons has been pulled down; only the Lodge, with its gables and curious chimneys, remains. Some cottages are 19th-c mock-Tudor, others are genuine Flemish-gabled. A stream runs through some of the gardens. A modern neo-Georgian close harmonizes unobjectionably with its surroundings. On his estate Lord Conyngham found and excavated more than 100 graves of Jutish settlers whose artifacts reveal much of NE Kent's early history.

The flint and Caen stone church of St Mary (late Norman, with 17th-c S door), set in a garden, is not to be missed. Inevitably compared with Barfreston, the N doorway is deeply carved; so is the stonework round the nave where the Norman tower cuts into it. Among many features are a rare wheel window at the E end, a mass clock, a 16th-c Dutch screen, and a glowing profusion of stained glass (16th- and 17th-c). They show pilgrims to Jerusalem, the story of Pyramus and Thisbe, and New Testament scenes, many of them by Peter Bock and Martin Moser, leading Swiss glass painters of the 16th c.

Bekesbourne (1m E), has charm, but is too near the main railway to Dover for comfort. The medieval Archbishops of Canterbury used to have a Palace here (a fragment remains). The Norman church of St Peter has, like Patrixbourne, an impressive N doorway. The church stands behind an orchard on a hillock, at the foot of which is the gatehouse where Cranmer fled on the death of Edward VI, awaiting arrest and martyrdom.

Howletts Zoo Park, with John Aspinall's collection of tigers and gorillas, is 1m NE.

Barham (4m SSE), just off the A2 Dover road at the beginning of the beautiful Elham Valley, is a group of mainly 18th-c red-brick houses on a wooded hillside with a green-spired church at the

Kenneth Scowen

The Leicester Square at Penshurst

top and an 18th-c manor house, Barham Court, nearby. The church, cruciform with late 13th-c chancel and transepts, is pleasant, but the stained-glass E window (1925) has its critics. The village is approached along Barham Downs, scene of Caesar's bloody battle against the ancient Britons, fought by the 7th Legion.

Broome Park (5m SE), built 1635–38 for Sir Basil Dixwell and the last home of Lord Kitchener, is a superb rosy-brick H-shaped Caroline house with tall bunches of chimneys and moulded brick gables; occasionally spoilt inside and out by Kitchener's additions, but very satisfying, set in 600 acres of rich parkland. The drawing-room is possibly the finest late 18th-c room in Kent, Adam-style (by James Wyatt) with a lovely marble fireplace. The great hall, nearly 100ft long, was decorated by Kitchener, who made the oak door himself and designed the two huge chimney-pieces after models he had seen at Hatfield House. Broome Park is now a country hotel.

PENSHURST, *Kent,* 5m NW of Tunbridge Wells. Penshurst Place, the finest 14th-c manor house in England, is so famous that people forget there is also an attractive village here. A village almost entirely 19th c, new or restored 'Pictur-esque', deliberately imitating earlier styles with timber and tiles, very expensive at the time and inhabited by commuters – yet the whole thing works and has mellowed and merged into its setting. William Wells gathered around him a group of artists and architects, of whom George

Devey was the best. Devey's ragstone and half-timbered cottages for Lord De L'Isle (owner of Penshurst Place and descendant of Sir Philip Sidney, Elizabethan poet and soldier) can be seen at the entrance to the churchyard. Devey also made additions to Home Farm and Swaylands, both outside the village proper. The rectory is early-18th-c. The church, much rebuilt by Sir G. G. Scott (1864), is basically 13th–14th-c. The Sidney Chapel contains monuments to the family.

Penshurst Place, with its ancient furnishings and Italian garden, is an experience not to be missed: it is open to the public in summer.

PUTTENHAM, *Surrey,* is the best of the Hog's Back villages which lie N and S of the high chalk ridge from Guildford to Farnham with panoramic views on both sides. N of the Hog's Back the villages are undistinguished – it is easy to be misled by the name Christmas Pie, which is mainly bungalows; and the most interesting fact about Normandy is that William Cobbett lived there. S of the Hog's Back you are often in deep farming country among sandstone hills and woods.

Puttenham is a 'long street' village along the Pilgrims' Way, on a slope where chalk meets sandstone and houses show tile, timber, stone and brick. The church of St John the Baptist has a Norman (c. 1160) N arcade and a Norman window in the S wall. There is a brass of Edward Cranford (rector 1400–31). The tower is early 15th-c. Otherwise it is a Woodyer restoration (1861) so thorough as to be called 'naughty' by Nairn and

Pevsner. Even the local guidebook quotes Betjeman's parody of 'The Church's One Foundation'. In the N aisle is a memorial to Esther Bellasis, who married Capt. George Bellasis of the East India Company: he killed a man in a duel and was transported to Botany Bay; poor Esther died of a broken heart in 1805.

Puttenham Priory (1762) is one of the best Palladian houses in Surrey; and to the W of the church is Greys Home Farm (18th c), brick and stone with weatherboarded barns, and beyond them a group of L-shaped barns ending in a quartet of oasts (there are more near Farnham) so that for a moment you imagine you are in Kent. In the village notice also Winter's Farm, Rosemary Cottage and Old Cottage (all 15th-c), Farm Cottage and Street Farm (16th-c). There are two good examples of Voysey's work, Greyfriars ($\frac{1}{2}$m NE; 1896), beautifully situated in harmonious gardens on a slope with S view, and ($\frac{1}{2}$m SE, on the way to Compton) Prior's Field (1900), extended by Voysey's pupil Muntzer when it was turned into a girls' school, which it is still.

Compton (2$\frac{1}{2}$m SE), has much charm and three special attractions. The oldest parts of St Nicholas's Church are 11th c, the tower may be Saxon, and the unique feature is the two-storey Romanesque sanctuary (12th c). But most people come here to visit the Watts Gallery, containing 200 works of the painter and sculptor G. F. Watts (1817–1904), and the Watts Chapel where he is buried. Designed by his wife, also a painter, the interior is a riot of Art Nouveau.

Elstead (4$\frac{1}{2}$m SW), on the river Wey, has a 14th-c church, a five-arched medieval bridge and an 18th-c watermill. Waverley Abbey (12th c), the ruins of England's first Cistercian monastery and inspiration of Scott's novel, can be reached by a walk along the river.

Tilford (2m further SW), has *two* medieval bridges and a large green. In All Saints Church (1867) a Bach Festival is held every spring.

RINGMER, *E. Sussex,* 2$\frac{1}{2}$m NE of Lewes. A good centre for exploring Southdown country, Ringmer is becoming rather too urbanized. The best of it is round the green. The village sign commemorates two 17th-c women who are part of American history – Ann Sadler, who married one of the founders of Harvard University, and Gulielma Springett, wife of William Penn; also Gilbert White, who used to visit his aunt Mrs Snooke, the Vicar's wife: she bequeathed him her tortoise Timothy.

The church has a flint tower and other 19th-c features but is basically 13th–14th c, the EE pillars standing on Norman bases. Inside, monuments to the Springett family, and one to William Childs, batman-butler to John Christie (the inscription says 'servant and friend').

The whole village owes much to the generosity of Christie. Glyndebourne Opera House (1m S, just over the hill), opened in 1934, was wholly his creation, added to a Victorian-Tudor house. Here a season of international opera is given

every year. Visitors in evening dress picnic in the superb gardens during the interval, cooling their white wine in the lake. There is a restaurant built so as not to disturb oak trees which act as pillars and grow through the roof.

West Firle (4m S) barely exists as a village, though it has an interesting church with a Norman doorway, 13th-c chancel and W tower, a 15th-c holy water stoup outside the porch, and the Late Perp Gage Chapel with brasses and monuments to the Gage family. The Gages owned Firle Place, an originally Tudor but mainly Georgian mansion, with its fine great hall, staircase hall and library, which has a rococo ceiling. The house contains mementoes of General Sir Thomas Gage, British Commander in the War of American Independence. From the village a footpath leads up to Firle Beacon (splendid views) where Neolithic, Bronze Age and Roman relics have been found.

Bentley Wildfowl Collection (3$\frac{1}{4}$m NE), is a 23-acre park where over 100 different species of birds may be seen in natural surroundings.

ROBERTSBRIDGE, *E. Sussex,* on the A21 Hasting road, is almost disqualified as a village because it has no parish church (though two Nonconformist chapels): it is in the parish of Salehurst. The village street is handsome, in spite of traffic, with many timbered and boarded houses (one of the best is the National Westminster Bank) and the 18th-c George Hotel. Abbey Farm, just outside the village, was built from the ruins of a Cistercian Abbey founded in 1176 by Robert de St Martin, the bridge-builder who gave his name to the village. Buried somewhere in it is Sir Edward Dalyngrugge, who built Bodiam Castle. 1m W along the road to Brightling (q.v.) is the Gray-Nicolls cricket-bat factory, founded 1876: with one of its bats W. G. Grace scored 2000 runs.

We cross the river Rother to **Salehurst** (1m NE), amid hopfields and oasts. The church of St Mary, on a hill, is visible through trees from Robertsbridge. Its 14th-c tower was heightened in Perp style in the next century; the body of the building is mingled EE and Dec with a very long nave. The font is 12th-c with salamanders (symbol of baptism) round it: local legend says it was a thankoffering from Richard I, part of whose ransom in 1194 was paid by the Abbot of Robertsbridge. There is some good stained glass, notably a window by Kempe in the S aisle. The Wigsall Chapel, endowed by the Culpepers of Wigsall Place (2m NE), is mostly taken up by the organ. Lord Milner (1854–1925), colonial administrator, is buried (in a Lutyens tomb) in the churchyard.

Sedlescombe (4$\frac{1}{2}$m SE), famous for the international Pestalozzi Children's Village (founded 1959), is a relatively unknown but extremely pretty village in its own right, with a long wide green flanked by 16th- and 17th-c houses. The restored Queen's Head Inn is basically 15th c. The village pump on the green is dated 1900. Of the original 14th–15th-c church, little but the W tower remains, most of the rest being Victorian.

Ivychurch, a Romney Marsh village

ROLVENDEN, *Kent,* 3m WSW of Tenterden. Its main street, leading to St Mary's Church, has wide grass verges instead of a village green, and beyond them rows of typical Wealden tile-hung and weatherboarded houses. Church tower, a splendid renovated black windmill with white sails and Rawlinson Farm (a big timbered house) make an attractive group as one approaches from the S. The church, built on a hillock, is light and spacious, with traces of its 13th-c origins and a 14th-c nave. Much was added in the 19th c, notably carved woodwork such as the family pew of the Gybbon-Monypennys (1825) in its own gallery (from which, oddly, the pulpit cannot be seen). Family monuments include one to H. J. Tennant (d. 1936), brother of Margot Asquith. For him Sir Edwin Lutyens built the big neo-Georgian Great Maytham Hall just outside the village. At Rolvenden Layne (1½m SE), a large green is edged with cottages, some 14th c, and a house from whose window John Wesley preached. Hole Park (1m W) has a lovely garden and is open to the public at certain times.

From Rolvenden to Tenterden runs a bit of the old single-line Kent and East Sussex Railway, built in 1900 for local farmers and immediately overtaken by the petrol age; it is now run by rail enthusiasts. **Tenterden,** a highly attractive market town whose main street is full of 16th–18th-c houses and shops, with the finest 15th-c church tower in Kent, is said to have been the birthplace (*c.* 1422) of William Caxton the printer. **Smallhythe** (2m further S), almost on Romney Marsh, was a medieval port and Smallhythe Place (1480) the Port House. Really two beautiful 16th-c cottages run together, with overhanging upper storey, it is now a theatrical museum in memory of Ellen Terry who lived here until her death in 1928. The 16th-c church and other ancient houses make this hamlet well worth visiting.

ROMNEY MARSH VILLAGES, *Kent.* The Marsh (including Romney Marsh proper as far S as Rhee Wall, Walland, Denge and Guildford Marshes) is an acquired taste. When mist settles suddenly and frogs croak, you are in limbo. Yet it has glorious dawns and sunsets. It is an ornithologist's delight. Sinister, often – an impression aided by tales of smuggling, in which most of its villages, or hamlets, were once involved. Some hamlets were once islets. Each has something of interest – usually its church, for this (in Betjeman's words) is 'church-crawling' country. Dikes and ditches make the lanes bend infuriatingly. Here the famous Romney sheep are bred, and tulips are grown. Distrust footpaths – they often lead into mud.

Wittersham (Isle of Oxney, on the border of the Marsh): an inn, a post office, an oast, a windmill, a Lutyens neo-Georgian house built for Alfred Lyttelton, 'athlete, lawyer, statesman', according to his memorial in the restored 13th–14th-c church with its handsome Dec tower.

Fairfield (Walland) has a very odd church, built of timber (13th c), later bricked in and completely rebuilt in 1913, keeping the 18th-c pulpit and 17th-c font.

Brookland (Walland) has a still odder church, largely unspoilt 13th–14th c, with a three-tiered belfry (made of timber salvaged from wrecks) standing beside it instead of on top because the subsoil was too soft to bear its weight. A Norman lead font with Zodiac signs is one of several surprises within.

Brenzett, a bunch of cottages at a crossroads, has a Norman church with timber tower and tiny spire. This church is dedicated to a Kentish patron saint, St Eanswith. Inside, a 17th-c alabaster monument to John Fagge of Rye and his son, lords of the manor. Sheep safely graze in the churchyard.

Old Romney, once a port, now a scattered village on Rhee Wall, the first retaining wall of Romney Marsh, has an unrestored 13th–15th-c church with a fine Purbeck marble 14th-c font. The box pews were painted pink for a film, *Dr Syn*, based on Russell Thorndike's smuggling parson. New Romney (3m E) is the terminus of the famous light railway that runs to Hythe.

Ivychurch has the spacious 14th-c church of St George, near the Bell Inn, and a cluster of cottages. With its big 'Kentish' W tower, its unspoilt nave and seven arches and its two-storeyed porch (which used to be the village school), it is the Marsh's most impressive church. The church at Newchurch (4m NE) has similar features but has been over-restored.

St Mary in the Marsh (2m SW of Dymchurch), has a few cottages, some tall trees, an inn and one of the best unrestored small 13th-c churches in Kent, EE with full Norman tower. Within, the font has holes for staples, to discourage witches; and St Mary's greatest treasure is a 1578 chalice. In the churchyard by a rosemary bush E. Nesbit (1858–1924) is buried, authoress of *The Railway Children* and other books for children.

SHERE, *Surrey.* This, one of the 'Tillingbourne villages' between North Downs and Weald, is often claimed as Surrey's most beautiful. The fact that it is over-exposed and too full of sightseers in summer is no reason to spurn it. It lacks a 'usual' pattern, but there are enchanting views and corners, one of Surrey's most interesting churches, half-timbered houses, a stream, an old cornmill (now a pumping station) and a profusion of watercress beds. Whistler's friend Seymour Haden did a well-known etching called 'Shere Mill Pond' which is probably Netley Mill. The Shere by-pass (A25) protects the village from traffic.

St James's Church (13th–14th-c, well restored in 20th c) to the E of Church Square, is approached from Lower Street between varied cottages (not all old). The lych-gate (1901) is by Lutyens. The general plan, the tower, the zigzag-patterned S door (look for pilgrims' crosses scratched on it) and the grand W doorway are all clearly Norman. The St Nicholas chapel was added about 1275. The work of Louis Osman (1956–66) did something very unusual for a Surrey church: he uncluttered it, combining the best points of the old building with a clean white modern effect, using stainless steel for the altar rail. The 13th-c font is of Purbeck marble. The big early 13th-c chest was probably used to collect money for the Crusades. There is some medieval stained glass in the aisle E window. In the N wall is an anchoress's cell (1329) built for Christine Carpenter who wished to be incarcerated for ever, taking part in Mass through a tiny hole.

Conveniently near the church is the White Horse Inn (16th-c with restored front). Interesting houses in Lower Street include a 1705 brick house, Ash Cottage (*c.* 1600) with overhanging first floor, and the Old Prison House (17th-c) – *very* 'picturesque'. In Upper Street, note Knapps Cottage

and the gate lodge (by Lutyens) of the 19th-c Manor House. In High Street, the post office and Bodryn are both timbered early 17th-c. There is even a Lutyens half-timbered shop (1892).

Gomshall (1½m ENE, on the A25), is more Victorian than at first appears. It is an ancient centre of the tanning industry: among the pottery and antique shops is a genuine tannery where leather goods are sold. More watercress beds, and a 16th-c packhorse bridge over the Tillingbourne. The early 18th-c Manor House lies S of the railway whose trains are so infrequent as to be more an event than a disturbance.

If it is true that **Albury** (2m W) means 'old village', there is little sign of it. 'Quaint' is probably the word. On a twisty road off the A25, it is largely the work of the Gothic-Revival architect, Pugin (1812–52). Originally called Weston Street, it became a sort of tentacle of Albury Park, built on the site of a Tudor house by John and George Evelyn (*c.* 1700) for the Duke of Norfolk, but since much altered by others, especially Pugin. Madly, it has 63 chimneys for 60 rooms, each of a different design. The house has been converted into 36 flats for retired people. What makes the place worth visiting are the gardens, laid out by the Evelyns on a hillside N of the house. The neighbourhood has three churches: St Peter and St Paul (Saxon foundation) in the park itself (attractive but disused since 1842); another St Peter and St Paul (1842) in Weston Street; and the 1840 Gothic-style Irvingite (Catholic Apostolic) church, N of the park, described by an architectural pundit as 'good fun'.

SISSINGHURST, *Kent,* 3m NE of Cranbrook. So famous is the Castle and its gardens that the village itself tends to be ignored. Formerly

The gatehouse of Sissinghurst Castle

Edwin Smith

known as Milkhouse Street, it is a pleasing street of Wealden houses (usual white weatherboard) some of them built by wealthy weavers before the 16th c. Sissinghurst Court (16th-c) and Sissinghurst Place, both with gardens open to the public, are worth a visit. There is an old forge, a small Victorian church and the site of Trinity Chapel which, in the 15th c, enabled villagers to go to Confession if the weather was too bad to tramp to Cranbrook.

The tall brick gatehouse tower of the Castle, in a wooded valley, is all that remains of a fortified Elizabethan manor house, probably on the site of a moated medieval house on which a courtyard had been superimposed. It was built by Sir Richard Baker (d. 1594) who received Queen Elizabeth I here in 1573. Two other fragments of Baker's house remain, the South House and the Priest's House (1560). During the Seven Years War (1756–63) the Castle was used to house 3000 French prisoners of war, who did much damage. The officer in charge of them at one time was Edward Gibbon of the Hampshire Militia, future historian of the Roman Empire. It was bought in a derelict condition (1930) by Sir Harold Nicolson and his wife Vita Sackville-West, who restored it and together made a lake and planned its famous gardens, including the White Garden (all flowers white, all leaves silver) and many fragrant herbs.

In South House Harold Nicolson had his study and there wrote his biography of George V. Vita had her writing-room in the tower, which also houses the printing press owned by Leonard and Virginia Woolf in the early days of the Hogarth Press. Priest's House was the last home of Richard Church (d. 1972), poet, novelist and writer on Kent.

When they decided to buy the Castle, which they could not really afford, the Nicolsons reasoned that they *ought* to buy it because one of the Bakers who built it had married a Sackville, Vita's family. The real reason, understood by everyone who visits the place, is contained in Vita's diary for 4 April 1930: 'Fell flat in love with it.'

SMARDEN, *Kent,* 4m NE of Biddenden. Is this the loveliest short street in Kent? The old Wealden wool-village has half-timbered and weatherboarded houses on both sides of the street, and the neighbourhood is rich in well-preserved houses, cottages and farms, among which the sluggish, tree-lined Beult stream meanders. The unaltered stone church of St Michael (14th-c), 36ft high with its big Perp W three-stage tower, is known as 'the Barn of Kent' because that is what it looks like. Its enormously wide nave is one reason; the other is its timber roof carrying 36ft without a beam (very rare in medieval times). An ancient charter, granting Smarden a market and a fair, signed by Elizabeth I, may be seen. Near the SE corner are hints of a very old wafer-oven for Communion. A strange poor-box bears an enamelled picture, apparently of Christ's Baptism, probably 13th-c French work

from Limoges. Nearby, notice Hartnup House (17th–18th c), the 16th-c Cloth Hall, and a group of cottages one of which forms a kind of lych-gate for the church.

Romden Castle (1m E), a curious 18th-c red-brick building with a tower, was probably once a fortified 15th-c manor house.

STOKE D'ABERNON, *Surrey*. This is a divided village: the N part merges into Cobham and is lost in suburban sprawl. The S part is what matters; beside the River Mole, meandering through fertile fields, a manor house and (not to be missed) St Mary's, one of the oldest churches in England whose fascination no charges of 'bad restoration' can spoil. How old? Parts certainly go back to the 7th c, a few years after St Augustine arrived; and the use of Roman bricks and cornices in the S wall shows that there must have been a Roman settlement here. The N aisle is 12th-c, the fine two-bay rib-vaulted chancel 13th-c. The N chapel (*c.* 1490) was given by Sir John Norbury in gratitude for victory at Bosworth Field: it has (unusual comfort) a fireplace. Much of the church was lost by restoration in 1866. But the world-famous feature inside is the oldest memorial brasses in the country. The two biggest are of Sir John D'Abernon (1277), 6ft 6in long, in armour with lance, standing on a monkey-like lion, and his son John (1327), 5ft, doing likewise. The 1620 seven-sided pulpit is decorated with seven hellish-looking monsters with animal paws, a male head and one female breast. The E window has some roundels of 15th-c Flemish stained glass. Much 17th-c ecclesiastical bric-à-brac among the furniture, and a 13th-c Crusaders' chest. Over the altar, an impressive 15th-c painting of the Annunciation (Flemish).

The nearby Manor House, dating mostly from 1757, is a mixture of Palladian and baroque with 20th-c additions. Of minor interest, but beautifully situated, it is threatened by the M25 motorway which, on a high embankment, will spoil the view.

Cobham (2½m NW), is another divided village: Street Cobham, on a sharp bend of the A3 Portsmouth Road, is a traffic bottleneck which even the A3(M) has not much relieved. Church Cobham (towards Leatherhead and Downside) has a few good features – the restored Norman church of St Andrew, the 19th-c mill (damaged) and neighbouring houses, The Cedars (15th-c with 18th-c front: National Trust) and Ham Manor (early 18th-c). Matthew Arnold lived in a cottage at Pain's Hill (1m W), an 18th-c house with gardens and a lake where he used to skate.

TESTON, *Kent*. Beautifully set in the 'cherry blossom area' of the Medway Valley 5¼m SW of Maidstone (despite the A26 main road), Teston has one of several medieval vaulted bridges across the river (others are at East Farleigh and Yalding). It is of ragstone; the extensions are 19th c but blend perfectly with the middle arches. The village has no pub or school but is notable for its cricket

Kenneth Scowen

A corner of Smarden

and hockey ball factory. The Saxon foundation church, also of ragstone, was rebuilt in 1710: it has a brick-topped tower with recessed spire; within is an impressive reredos of the same date. In the churchyard is an epitaph to James Ramsay, vicar of Teston (d. 1789), and his Negro servant Nestor whom he had rescued from slavery and who died aged 36. Ramsay had been a naval chaplain under Admiral Middleton, who lived at Barham Court nearby. The two men spent their last years campaigning for abolitionism, and inspired Hannah More's poem *Slavery* (1788). Barham Court, mainly 18th-c, was rebuilt in 1791, and again after a fire in 1932. It has stables and an orangery (1792). Overlooking the river are the remains of a Roman villa. In this area you can see mounting blocks hewn out of stone and watering troughs on the side of the road.

Mereworth (3m W), pronounced Merryworth, is for admirers of the Palladian style. The Castle (designed by Colin Campbell) is a copy of Palladio's Villa Rotonda at Vicenza, built to the order of the 7th Earl of Westmorland, who destroyed a medieval church to make room for it and built (1744–6) a largely Palladian one ¾m away. The Castle, with its 60-ft dome under which is the Hall, is sumptuously decorated inside. The ceiling of the Long Gallery is by the Venetian Francesco Sleter. Unfortunately the Castle is not open to the public although its gardens are occasionally. The church is an extraordinary mixture of London churches – the excessively high steeple from St Martin's-in-the-Fields, the porch from St Mary-

le-Strand. Many monuments and some stained glass were brought here from the old church. In the churchyard is the grave of Admiral Lucas, winner of the first VC in the Crimean War.

THURSLEY, *Surrey.* A well-looked-after, beautiful but little known village about 1m W of the A3 between Milford and Hindhead. An acacia on the green was planted in memory of William Cobbett (*Rural Rides*). Difficult to believe that there was an iron industry here 600 years ago, or that the name means 'field of Thor' the war god. On the N slope above Hindhead, it has a small green looking N to a view of the Hog's Back. There is a large nature reserve on Thursley Common. Most of the village clusters round two cul-de-sacs, The Lane and The Street which leads to St Michael's Church (Saxon foundation, ruthlessly restored in 19th c). Two Saxon windows, a Saxon oven in the chancel and a (possibly) Saxon font help one to imagine the original church. The wooden belfry and spire are 15th-c, so stoutly supported by posts (tree trunks 2ft 6in thick) with tie-beams and arched braces, as if the village lived in terror of its falling down. The churchyard contains a famous grave, that of an unknown sailor murdered at Hindhead in 1786: his three assassins were hanged on Gibbet Hill, the highest point on Hindhead Common.

Thursley was the birthplace of the architect Sir Edwin Lutyens (1869–1944) who, aged only 19, converted The Corner, a row of cottages, into one house. As a boy he lived at The Cottage (Lutyens

House) in The Street. There is a great variety of pretty cottages and houses, stone, tile-hung or timbered, including Old Hall, Old Parsonage and Wheeler's Farm (16th c), Badgers and The Lodge (18th c).

The spectacular Devil's Punchbowl (2¾m S), is a huge sandstone valley sloping to the N, like a bit of N Wales in Surrey.

Witley (3½m E), lacks a central pattern but has many attractions, including 500 acres of Witley Common and a beauty spot known as Sweet Water. In many ways it is more like a Sussex Weald village. In Victorian times it was a sort of 'summer Chelsea' for writers and artists. At her country home, The Heights (now Roslyn Court), George Eliot played tennis, met her neighbour Tennyson, was visited by Henry James and wrote her last novel, *Daniel Deronda*. The best-known house is Step Cottage, tiled and timber-framed in a group in Church Lane; and there are many other brick-and-timber cottages. All Saints Church, not over-restored, has a Saxon nave, extended in Norman times; the tower is mostly 17th c.

TICEHURST, *E. Sussex*, 8m SE of Tunbridge Wells. As you would expect on the Kent-Sussex border, lots of tile-hanging and weatherboarding, some genuinely old houses (18th-c and earlier), others modern to blend with them. Ticehurst, which dates back to at least 1180, looks like its name, *ticen-hyrst*, a wooded hillock where goats feed. Today the village, cut through by the main A266 road, is hardly safe for goats. The mainly 14th-c church of St Mary gathers the best of the village round it. It has Perp E and W windows, arch to the nave and W porch; other windows are Dec. The Courthope Chapel is named after a local family, whose home was at Whiligh, 2m NW on the way to Wadhurst. Whiligh, dating from 1586, has in its grounds an oak tree which (doubling the usual claim) is said to be 2000 years old. Oaks for the timber of Westminster Hall were cut here in the 14th c.

WESTERHAM, *Kent*. Traffic jams at the junction of the narrow winding A25 and the A233 on the village green make this a place to be avoided at summer weekends, though M25 now gives some relief. On the green are statues of General Wolfe, born here in 1727, victor of Quebec in 1759, and Sir Winston Churchill, the two most famous local residents. Wolfe spent his boyhood at Quebec House (then called Spiers), a gabled brick early 17th-c house which is now a museum of his life, open to the public. The Pheasantry (on the green), Grosvenor House and Squerryes Lodge are good 18th-c houses: the Lodge has bits of a 13th-c stone house at one corner. At the George and Dragon Inn Wolfe stayed (1758) on his last visit to Westerham. Squerryes Court (late 17th-c) was (and is) the home of the Warde family, friends of the Wolfes: in their Garden Wolfe was commissioned (1741). The house (open to the public in summer) has more mementoes of Wolfe and some Dutch paintings. In its park is the source

of the River Darent and a Celtic fortification (*c*. 3rd-c BC).

St Mary's Church, much restored in the 19th c, has traces of 13th-c work and some 16th- and 17th-c monuments. The tower spiral staircase is medieval. The Royal arms of Edward VI, painted on wood, are extremely rare. At the 14th-c font both Wolfe and some of Churchill's grandchildren were baptized.

At **Chartwell** (2m S), lived Sir Winston Churchill for nearly half a century. An older house was converted for him (1923) by Philip Tilden, using stepped gables with a Tudorish effect. The hillside position is glorious; the gardens, with stream, lake and nearby farm, delightful. Inside, the house is much as Churchill left it, with relics of the great man, including original typescripts of some of the speeches.

Crockham Hill (2½m S), commands one of the greatest views in Kent, which accounts for the several 1880-ish houses round about. The National Trust has kindly supplied a seat at the summit. Below is the church built (1842) by the squire of Squerryes, Charles Warde. By the altar is the grave of Octavia Hill (d. 1912), a founder of the National Trust.

Brasted (1¾m E), much disturbed by A25 traffic, is unjustly neglected. Its long street contains some good period houses and antique shops. Brasted Place (1784) was built by Robert Adam. The church is mostly Victorian, with features and furnishings going back to the 13th c. At the half-timbered White Horse Inn (looks old, but is only 1885) Battle of Britain pilots relaxed after the daily slaughter and wrote their names there.

WEST HOATHLY, *W. Sussex* (5m SSW of E. Grinstead), a hilltop village nearly 600ft up on the W fringe of Ashdown Forest. Its centre is St Margaret's Church, the Cat Inn and the Old Parsonage. Facing the church is the 17th-c stone Manor House, and just beyond it, the Priest's House, 15th-c timber-framed with wattle and daub (now a museum). The Norman church, founded in 1090, is mainly 13th-c, on the whole well restored. The Cat Inn has the usual smuggling stories. The lower lane leading S to Highbrook, by a house called Leams End, commands the widest panorama of the South Downs in Sussex, from The Long Man at Wilmington to Chanctonbury Ring (about 27m).

Gravetye Manor (1m N), is a splendid late-Elizabethan house (now a country hotel) built by Richard Infield, yet another Weald ironmaster (hence the wrought-iron memorial slabs in the church). In the early 20th c it belonged to William Robinson the landscape gardener, who designed the extensive grounds and woodlands.

WEST MALLING, *Kent* (5m WNW of Maidstone, just off the A20), is almost a small town. High Street and Swan Street contain many excellent 18th- and early 19th-c houses, brick and white stucco. The Swan Hotel, an old coaching inn, looks mostly Tudor. Cade House and Went

House (early 17th-c with wrought-iron gates) claim attention: opposite the latter, under a Gothic arch, is the cascade (1810) of a spring which rises near St Leonard's Tower ($\frac{1}{2}$m SW), built *c*. 1100 by Bishop Gundulf of Rochester to protect his manor. Gundulf also founded a Benedictine Abbey, destroyed by fire (which consumed much of the village). The ruins were used in the 18th c to build a house which since 1893 has been occupied by Anglican Benedictine nuns.

At the opposite end of the village, St Mary's Church has a squat Norman tower surmounted by a long, sharp Victorian spire. Much of the church is Norman, including chancel, N doorway, sedilia and vestry. The nave, whose original Norman length was probably 72ft, was rebuilt in 1901. The churchyard has gravestones believed to be 600 years old: some have grotesque faces carved on them. Manor House, next to the church, with a park and a lake, began as an 18th-c two-storey house and was altered in mid-19th c. West Malling airfield played an important part in the Battle of Britain. Today it is used for light aircraft and gliding.

East Malling (2m E), cannot be called beautiful – some parts are too built up – but it has some interesting features, such as Clare House and Paris House (both 18th-c and both a little way out of the village). St James's is an almost complete Late Perp church with a lofty W tower. Inside, some 14th-c stained glass, brasses and tombs, including that of Sir Thomas Twisden (d. 1683), one of the judges who tried the judges of Charles I for regicide. He married the sister of Matthew Thomlinson who, although a Roundhead, became both jailer and friend to the condemned king. On the scaffold, Charles gave him his gold toothpick. East Malling Research Station, incorporating the Wye College First Experimental Station was founded in 1921.

WHITELEY VILLAGE, *Surrey* (2m NW of Cobham), is a wholly 20th-c village built (1914–21) to the order of William Whiteley of Whiteley's Stores in Queensway, London. He died in 1907 leaving £1 million to found a village for 'thrifty old people'. It was the age of Garden Cities and Suburbs. For once we do not have to look for Perp, Saxon windows and villainous Victorian restorations. After a competition between six architects, Whiteley was laid out over 225 acres in 1911 by Frank Atkinson. Various other architects were engaged to design different areas and buildings. (*See page 66.*)

Atkinson did the very opposite to Sir Raymond Unwin's deliberately villagey asymmetry at Hampstead Garden Suburb: he made a classical pattern of circle and octagon with radiating avenues. A monument to Whiteley himself (by Frampton) is bang in the centre. Some houses are single-storey, some two-storey. Those in North Avenue are by Sir Reginald Blomfield, those in South Avenue by Sir Mervyn Macartney, and so on – architects were chosen by Whiteley himself for their grand manner and sensitivity to land-

scaping. St Mark's Church (13th-c style) is almost the only attempt to get back to the Middle Ages. Chestnut Walk contains shops, post office and a communal kitchen. Chapels for various denominations, a club with a licensed bar and a village hall. Lots of trees, avenues and lawns, but no garages. The whole is harmonious and peaceful.

WICKHAMBREUX, *Kent.* 'Perfect' small village 4$\frac{1}{2}$m E of Canterbury, best visited out of the coach-party season. Mill Corner, with its white weatherboarded mill (still in use), little bridges across the stream to cottage gardens, a triangular green shaded by chestnuts and limes, some good Georgian houses, timbered ones too, a pub and a 14th-c church – the picture is seen as a whole.

St Andrew's Church, approached through an avenue of limes, is nearly all of a piece, though the chancel was restored in 1878 and small 19th-c alterations were done with taste. 14th-c stained glass (S aisle) shows Salome waiting for the head of John the Baptist; but it is the E window you will remember: an Art Nouveau Annunciation (1896) by Arild Rosencrantz, the first American glassworker to decorate an English church. The window, donated by Count Gallatin of New York, shows the Virgin surrounded by angels and lilies. Round the green, notice Wickham Court (early 19th-c), the Old Rectory (18th-c), the mainly medieval flint-and-stone post office, and Old Willow Farm (early 19th-c).

Ickham ($\frac{3}{4}$m SSE), a long wide village street and green, lined with brick and weatherboarded houses (mostly 19th-c), is worth a pause: a tiny Norman church, a 17th-c farmhouse, and the Old Rectory, mixed 13th- and 18th-c.

Littlebourne (1$\frac{1}{4}$m SW), on the Nailbourne which becomes the Lesser Stour, is two groups of houses around the large short-spired 13th-c church of St Vincent, with a long 14th-c thatched barn, a few oasts and a (converted) white weatherboarded watermill. Unfortunately Lee Priory ($\frac{3}{4}$m S), a Gothic house belonging to Horace Walpole's friend Thomas Barrett, has been replaced. Walpole called it 'a child of Strawberry, prettier than the parent.' A model of one of its rooms is in the Victoria and Albert Museum as an example of neo-Gothic architecture. A 14th-c barn belonging to St Augustine's in Canterbury is one of the oldest aisled barns in Kent.

Wingham (2m ESE), on a violent double-bend of the busy A257, is more town than village, but has its attractions: a large restored 13th-c church, two basically 13th-c inns, half-timbered houses, an excavated Roman villa and a main street lined with copper beeches and chestnuts.

WINCHELSEA, *E. Sussex,* 2$\frac{1}{2}$m S of Rye. Village or town? Over the centuries there have been two Winchelseas – one a Cinque Port, washed away by the sea in the late 13th c, the other the orderly, peaceful, almost excessively pretty hill village we see today, when it is more than 1m inland. Edward I, our first town planner, laid out

Kenneth Scowen

The Strand Gate into Winchelsea

gridded streets with hospitals and defensive walls, of which only three gates remain – Strand Gate, New Gate and Pipewell. The idea was to create a special port for the Gascony wine trade. Several medieval wine-vaults can still be seen.

St Thomas's Church, intended to be almost the size of a cathedral, was never finished. The 14th-c chancel remains, with much subsequent and impressive decoration. There is both medieval and modern (Expressionist) stained glass. Tombs include those of two of the Alard family, Admirals of the Cinque Ports. The Court House or Hall in High Street dates from 14th c and is now a museum which illustrates Winchelsea's history with models and relics, including municipal maces of the 15th and 16th c. There is the ruin of a 14th-c Franciscan church in the garden of a house called Greyfriars in Friars Road. Many houses are 19th-c imitating earlier styles. The 18th-c New Inn in German Street and the Salutation Inn in Castle Street are worth visiting to see the cellars.

WYE, *Kent.* 7m NE of Ashford in the Great Stour valley, but well away from the A28 road. Almost a market town, with a racecourse, but irresistible. Its well-known agricultural college is part of London University: four early 20th-c quadrangles have been grafted on to the 15th-c theological College of St Gregory and St Martin, founded by John Kempe, Archbishop of Canter-

bury, who was born in Wye. It is entered from the churchyard. The church, 13th-c on an earlier foundation, also owes much to Archbishop Kempe. The steeple has been unlucky: it was burnt by lightning in 1572, and crashed into the chancel in 1686. The present tower is over the old N transept. The village part of Wye is mostly Georgian, with a few fine 16th- and 17th-c houses such as the Old Vicarage and Old Manor. Bridge Street crosses the river by a five-arched bridge on which are carved the names of six workmen who repaired it in 1683. Wye was the birthplace of Mrs Aphra Behn, a barber's daughter who became Britain's first woman novelist.

Boughton Aluph (3¾m NW), one of Kent's four Boughtons, is set in the 2000-acre arable and grassland areas of Eastwell Park, once home of the Earls of Winchelsea. Eastwell's ruined church contains a tomb said to be that of a natural son of Richard III and thus the last Plantagenet. The large, isolated church of All Saints, the parish church of **Challock** (14th-c with later additions) is on a 'Pilgrims' Way': it has a finely proportioned interior and 14th-c stained glass in the E window (Coronation of the Virgin). Some concerts of the Stour Music Festival are held here; others at Olantigh House, Wye.

Boughton Lees (1m S), a green with old cottages on two sides, has a timber-framed manor house with 17th-c brick front and fanciful later additions.

The Chilterns

SOUTH BUCKINGHAMSHIRE   HERTFORDSHIRE   EAST OXFORDSHIRE

Elliott Viney

The Chilterns form the central section of the great chalk belt which runs north-east from the Dorset coast to the Wash. The northern edge of this belt crosses Salisbury Plain, becomes the Berkshire Downs, reaches the Thames at Goring, then, as a prominent escarpment, crosses four counties until, near Royston, it merges into flatter country but continues up to the Norfolk coast. The Chilterns section is usually taken to run from Goring to the neighbourhood of Hitchin and to include all the country between the escarpment and the Thames and the outskirts of London to the south. For this book the boundaries of the region include most of Hertfordshire, Buckinghamshire south of the River Thame, and the south-east corner of Oxfordshire, bounded by the Thame to the North and the Thames to west and south. The historical core was the three Hundreds of Chiltern (Stoke, Burnham and Desborough in South Buckinghamshire), notoriously so wild and turbulent that they needed a special Steward to control them right up to the eighteenth century.

It was always a backward area. Celtic inhabitants built Iron Age hill forts along the escarpment (e.g. at Ivinghoe and Whiteleaf). The Belgic tribes who moved into Hertfordshire bringing a stronger plough and more sophisticated farming, put up a stout resistance to the Roman invader; the latter built their roads out of London and settled in some of the valleys but did not penetrate into the hills which also held little appeal for later Anglo-Saxon and Danish invaders at least until after the more fertile lowlands to the north had been cleared and settled. Late Celtic survival is shown by such names as Walden – 'valley of the foreigners', an Anglo-Saxon name for a surviving Celtic settlement.

This isolation in the hills, rather cut off from the developing life of London and the Thames Valley and the prosperous Midland plain, gave the dwellers in the Chilterns an independence of character and a strong streak of opposition to established views. So here the Lollards were centred in the fourteenth to fifteenth centuries, the Reformation was welcomed in the sixteenth and the Quaker movement began in the seventeenth century. John Hampden, the finest man Buckinghamshire has produced, led the early resistance to Charles I which developed into the Civil War but it is worth noting that he was

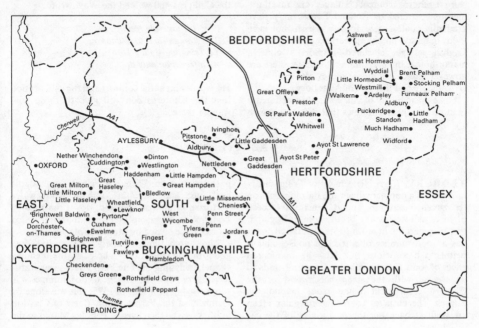

supported by almost every fellow squire, and of the 60 regicides who tried and condemned Charles I at least a quarter had Buckinghamshire connections. In the last two centuries the Chiltern valleys have been strong centres of Nonconformity. Even today it does not require much imagination to see in the short, dark-haired types who throng the streets of Chesham the distant descendants of those first Celtic settlers.

The physical character of the west end of the Chilterns is different from Hertfordshire; in the former the escarpment, rising to close on 900 feet in places, is clearly defined and crowned with beechwoods except for areas of clear downland such as Wallington Hill, Coombe Hill or Ivinghoe Beacon. South of the edge the land slopes gradually down to the Thames, becoming more urban as it reaches towards London, but still surprisingly remote in places like Stonor or Turville. Immense beechwoods still crown the valley sides although experts shake their heads and foretell their disappearance in a generation through disease and inadequate replanting. By contrast, in Hertfordshire the escarpment is less pronounced, descending more gently into the plain; here the beechwoods are less continuous, the countryside, although still hilly, more gently rolling.

Of the eight main roads which radiate from London through the region, five are Roman in origin. The canals, the railways and the motorways follow the same valleys that the Romans used. By contrast the lateral communications are still generally tortuous and difficult; there are innumerable lanes, steep, high-banked and winding, particularly in Hertfordshire, where the general configuration of the country has resulted in long, one-street villages, stretched along a valley bottom. In the Buckinghamshire and Oxfordshire Chilterns compact villages are rare; numerous scattered or isolated houses may have gradually coalesced to form a parish, but even today they have not the appearance of a traditional English village, clustered round its church, manor house, inn and mill. Of the latter there are however good examples within the region in Oxfordshire and the Vale of Aylesbury.

Since the majority of villages in this section are built on the chalk it follows that flint and clunch

(chalky limestone) were the only materials available, apart from wood, in the Middle Ages. So the Chiltern churches are built of flints, but because flint cannot 'turn a corner' stone had to be imported for the angles, the door frames, windows and arcades. This in many cases came from the quarries at Totternhoe, and was a clunch which generally had weathered badly so that many towers and walls were covered with pebbledash or cement in the nineteenth century. An attractive feature of some flint churches is the chequerboard effect of alternate flint and stone panels. This is not one of the outstanding church areas, in comparison with Somerset or Northamptonshire, but if the architecture is fairly uniform, the interiors have wonderful variety. The monuments are outstanding throughout the region, the 'Aylesbury' fonts are famous, while in Hertfordshire almost every church has a spike – the dwarf spire of lead or wood on the square tower. In the villages brick and half-timber houses abound while towards the Essex border many houses display ornamental pargeted designs on plaster.

The Icknield Way, which follows the chalk for its whole length, is the oldest road in England, dating from the Bronze Age, perhaps even older. It follows the spring-line on the escarpment on what was the lowest dry ground above the thick forests of the undrained lowlands; many settlements began where the springs bubble out from the chalk and seven have been included in this section. Maps show a Lower Icknield Way, running south-west from Ivinghoe, parallel and north; this dates from medieval times when the Vale had been cleared and drained. To walk the original way, where it is still a bridleway – say from Whiteleaf to Bledlow Cross – can be an evocative experience. Rupert Brooke, who loved the Chilterns and walked the Way, wrote:

> . . . . *I'll take the road . . .*
> *The Roman road to Wendover*
> *To Tring and Lilley Hoo*
> *As a free man may do.*

His words hint at the comfort and the exhilaration that the Chilterns can still give to those who wander there.

GAZETTEER

ALDBURY, *Herts.,* lies 3m W of Tring and N of A41. It is a popular village and the old stocks on the green beside the pond must have been pictured as often as any beauty spot in England. But in general it lives up to its reputation for it has a good number of attractive houses and is neither self-conscious nor has the manicured effect of some famous villages. Its setting adds to its charm, with the steep beechwood of the Chiltern escarpment rising from behind the houses. The cottages round the irregular green are well set back but the positioning of the car

park is a mistake. There is a friendly, unmodernized inn; and there are several Bridgewater Victorian estate cottages and, down the road to Ivinghoe (q.v.), a big Georgian mansion called Stocks, once owned by Mrs Humphry Ward.

The church, though heavily restored, has some good monuments. The whole of the Pendley chapel, including the fine Perp screen, was transferred here when the College of Bonhommes was suppressed at Ashridge in 1575; this was done by members of the Verney family (later of Claydon in Bucks.) who then lived at Pendley Manor in the

The classical church at Ayot St Lawrence

parish. There are good brasses of Sir Ralph and Lady Verney on their table tomb in the NW chapel. Just outside the S door stands a sundial on a 17th-c wooden post.

ASHWELL, *Herts.* (2m N of A505, the Baldock-Royston road), is the most northerly village in the county. Although N of the Icknield Way it is at spring level on the lower slopes where the bare downs above Baldock sweep down to the Midland plain. The spring is in fact the source of the River Cam, so it is no surprise to read in a local guide that 'a rare species of worm has lived in these waters since the Ice Age'. Ashwell is a sumptuous place with a great array of splendid old buildings, some fine contemporary ones, many trees and those four essentials of an English village – church, manor, mill and pub.

The great size of the church indicates 14th-c prosperity, but here the Black Death struck hard, vividly signified by some of the *graffiti* on a wall inside the tower; one says (in Latin) '1350. Miserable, wild, distracted, the dregs of the people alone survive'. Others – and they are a unique series – record more personal feeling such as the outburst of 'a frustrated medieval architect' who carved the words, 'The corners are not pointed correctly; I spit at them'. The tower itself is 176ft high and is propped by massive buttresses.

The best start for a perambulation of the village is at the mill, N of the church, which has been brilliantly adapted, with contemporary additions, as a dwelling; the mill wheel still turns. The former Maltings opposite have also been skilfully adapted. Moving up Mill Street, on the right is the small Merchant Taylors' school, built by the London livery company in 1681, and now used as a Further Education centre. The big manor house, seen down a drive, is called Ashwell Bury; it was much altered by Lutyens and is now used as

offices. In Swan Street the town hall is a small, gabled 16th-c building which houses a small but crowded museum of local bygones. The High Street has an array of notable houses, starting with the Rose and Crown at the W end, then Bear House (another former inn) and St John's Guild House, founded in 1476, half-timber and pargeting with a similar cottage adjoining. Further E on the opposite side, Forresters Cottages, another 15th-c row, has been well restored by the Hertfordshire Buildings Trust. Jessamine House which has an 18th-c façade concealing an earlier core faces the Three Tuns which is not only welcoming and picturesque but displays another antique in the form of a pensioned-off, double-decker London bus. E of this inn are the springs, and from here Springhead Lane runs back to the Mill, passing on the left Ducklake House, yet another 16th-c building.

Ashwell appears to have been a prosperous village, except when interrupted by plague or fire; various minerals have been extracted in the past, and barley grown for the Maltings. Yet it did not suffer from Victorian expansion and it survives as very well-kept village, proud of its architectural heritage but also with contemporary additions of considerable distinction.

AYOT ST LAWRENCE, *Herts.* (3m W of Welwyn), has a remarkable feeling of isolation set as it is on a wooded hilltop and approached only by a number of very narrow lanes. The unusual name may derive from the Anglo-Saxon *Aega's gaet*, or pass, which would refer to the valley between Ayot St Peter and St Lawrence. The village is not large, but most houses in it have some architectural interest. In the centre are the ruins of the medieval church which the owner of Ayot House, Sir Lionel Lyde, began to demolish *c.* 1770 because it spoilt his view; the indignant protests of the Bishop of Lincoln saved what is left today but Sir Lionel went on to build New St Lawrence mainly to form a spectacular 'eye-catcher' from the W windows of his house. His architect, Nicholas Revett, designed a classical temple with a portico at the E end (which meant that the altar is at the W end) and two low transepts to N and S. Sir Lionel and his lady were apparently an incompatible couple; they were buried in separate transepts, Sir Lionel's views being that 'as the Church has united them in life, it should make amends by separating them in death'. The whole ensemble certainly is still highly effective seen from the E; that side is of stucco but from the W the decaying brick gives a very different picture.

Near the old church the Brocket Arms is a house where the Sunday School is held in the tap-room; it is an excellent half-timbered and white-washed building. There are other excellent houses such as the Old Rectory and Bride Hall to the S; yet the most important house in the village is without question the ugliest; this is Shaw's Corner, the home of George Bernard Shaw for the last 44 years of his life, which he left to the National Trust on his death in 1950. Built in the late 19th c as the New Rectory it is featureless as a building, but of great interest for its contents. Preserved by the Trust exactly as Shaw left it, there is already a strong period attraction about its furnishings; and the innumerable relics, in-cluding the famous hats, vividly evoke the great man. Yet the furniture, the decorations and the pictures (with the exception of the magnificent Augustus John portrait) are of supreme ordina-riness; acute critic as G.B.S. was, he must surely have been lacking in any aesthetic sense.

Ayot St Peter, 2m SW is even smaller, but has two large 17th-c houses and a Victorian church with interesting Arts and Crafts furnishings.

BLEDLOW, *Bucks.*, on B4009, 2m W of Princes Risborough. The parishes along the Chiltern escarpment grew from Anglo-Saxon estates, and when these were formed the land in-cluded part of the fertile plain and some of the upland woods, the church usually being sited on the spring-line and therefore near the line of the Icknield Way. Thus the parishes were long and narrow. Bledlow parish, stretching almost from Ilmer to West Wycombe (q.v.), is 7m long but barely 2m across at its widest. As the village has not expanded significantly it still reflects this early pattern. Out in the plain to the N there is a scatter of tiny settlements – Forty Green, Holly Green, Pitch Green and Skittle Green – while high up in the hills Bledlow Ridge has another isolated group. The Icknield Way runs ½m above the village at the foot of the steep beechwoods of the escarpment; here it is a bridle way rather than a metalled road. The house at the county boundary called Wainhill was once the Leather Bottle, a simple alehouse where drovers put up for the night and where one of the present gardens is in fact an original sheepfold. Hidden in the

woods above Wainhill and just off the main path along the crest Bledlow Cross is carved in the chalk beside a tumulus; barely visible from the plain there is no evidence, beyond a dubious reference in 1350, that it is any older than the 17th c.

The main village stretches along one short road. At the E end the Manor House, 18th-c brick, and opposite a recent (1977) courtyard development Lyde End which won a Civic Award. Then the Lyde itself; this was described by John Nash in 1936: 'Lyde Brook flows from the chalk in the sides of a deep ravine near Bledlow Church. This is the only place in Bucks. where a river rises straight out of the hillside, and the gorge, at the bottom of which is a watercress bed, is cool and damp, even in the height of summer.' The local rhyme runs

They that live and do abide
Shall see the church fall in the Lyde

but fortunately the church survives for it is full of interest even if somewhat neglected inside. The S door is one of the oldest in Bucks. (*c.* 1280); above it a scrap of medieval wall painting shows Adam and Eve, the former leaning on his spade. There is a good example of the late 12th-c 'Aylesbury' type of font, stiff-leaf capitals on the aisle arcades and an 18th-c reredos in the S aisle, which also has a striking 14th-c window.

There are several good cottages with brick-nogging; these include Old Mill in the valley, on the Lyde brook, which was once a paper mill. The Lions of Bledlow Inn, handsomely placed at the W end of the village, makes a good base for ex-ploring the fine walking country around.

BRIGHTWELL BALDWIN, *Oxfordshire,* is 1m W of the Stadhampton–Watlington road (B480). It is a small but attractive village on the open farmlands a few miles N of the Chilterns. The big house has been demolished but the stables have been converted into a dwelling and are set in a pleasant park. Almost every house has some point of interest, particularly the Georgian Rectory and the Lord Nelson Inn which has an unusual verandah between the gabled wings. The church, which sits impressively on a low hill, has much to commend it. Although the S aisle has been 'scraped' and the arcades and font are the plainest of plain Dec while the chancel has a scrubbed and aseptic look, yet there is a fine array of old glass, mostly of saints but some heraldic. However, it is the Stone Chapel, now used as the vestry, which must be seen, not only for the glass, but also for the monuments of the Stone family who were Lords of the Manor in the 16th and 17th c. They will probably appeal to today's visitors more than they did to the guidebook writer in 1904 who bluntly dismissed them as 'ugly'. The largest and most spectacular fills the whole NE wall with such baroque exuberance that it spreads on to the ceiling; it was built in 1670 to commemorate several members of the family whose tombs had been destroyed in City churches in the Great Fire four years earlier. Some of the lettering is indifferent but that on a slate panel beneath the three great flaming urns is accomplished.

Cuxham, 1m E, is by no means a spectacular village but has the charm which a small stream always gives when it runs beside the road with pleasant houses on both sides.

CHECKENDON, *Oxfordshire* (N of the Reading–Wallingford road, A4074), is a scattered village reached by a tangle of narrow lanes and so heavily wooded that in summer it could easily be missed altogether. There are many other similar settlements in this S tip of the county where it runs down to the Thames valley, but Checkendon is probably the most typical. The small nucleus round the church has several half-timbered houses of merit. The church had associations with the Anglo-Saxon St Birinus (*see* Dorchester) which may account for the outstanding, sophisticated quality of the Norman work of this admirable stone and flint church. Although small in scale its view facing E is impressive, with the raised altar backed by an apse on which paintings of Christ in Majesty and Apostles were added in the 13th c. The nave is light and airy and has a Perp roof with gilded bosses. There are many wall tablets (several to former rectors, all from University College, Oxford, still the patrons of the living), the most outstanding being the Rothbath monument carved in 1960 by Eric Kennington who himself is commemorated in a large window in the S aisle, exquisitely engraved by Laurence Whistler. A tablet also records the bell ringers achieving 5056 changes in 1970.

CHENIES, *Bucks.,* little changed for a century, is a surprising 19th-c survival, still bearing everywhere signs of the family who dominated it for 400 years – the Russells, Earls and Dukes of Bedford. The name was originally Isenhamsted Chenies and it was the Cheney family who owned the manor from the 12th c to the 15th c when it descended in the female line to Anne Sapcote who married Sir John Russell, later the 1st Earl; this was in 1523 and very soon the Russells began to extend the modest brick manor house. Although much of their work has been lost in subsequent centuries the great S wing remains, with a magnificent range of Tudor chimneys, a long gallery in the roof and an unusual series of buttress-like projections which contain closets and privies. The gardens, restored in recent years, have an old well and a number of tunnels of uncertain age beneath the lawns. The house is open in the summer.

The manor remained with the Russell family until sold after the death of the 12th Duke in 1953, but ceased to be their main residence during the Civil War when they moved to Woburn; however, they continued to be buried in the large chapel which the 2nd Earl added on the N side of the parish church in 1556, with the result that the Bedford Chapel contains what is probably the finest sequence of monumental statuary in any parish church in the country, ranging from a whole series of Elizabethan and Jacobean monuments, to the immense classical tribute to the 1st Duke, and many others showing the varying tastes of the 19th and 20th c. Permission to enter the Chapel is rarely given; the ordinary visitor must be content with a frustrating glimpse through a glass screen. At the W end of the church are some good brasses.

In the 19th c the Dukes of Bedford were the greatest of the 'improving' landlords and the many villages they controlled on their various estates were virtually rebuilt between 1840 and World War I. Chenies is a good example, the houses being in a Tudor Revival style, well-spaced round the sloping green, giving an effect which is both picturesque and nostalgic. Apart from these houses there are three other buildings worth seeing, the Bedford Arms inn, the Baptist Chapel of 1760, little altered inside and with a pretty Regency Manse beside it, and the recent addition to the village school, a small hall with panels of flint and brick, an object-lesson in architectural 'good manners'.

CUDDINGTON, *Bucks.* (N of the A418 Aylesbury–Thame road), separated from Nether Winchendon (q.v.) by the breadth of the modest River Thame, is still a picturesque village, a jumble of small roads with names like Great Store, Spurt Street and Holly Tree Lane, sloping down towards the river, and lined with mainly old houses set at odd angles and heights. Many are 17th-c, some of stone, some half-timber and brick while a few are built of wichert (*see* Haddenham). None are showpieces, but the combination of pleasant materials, smallness of scale and irregularity of layout add up to a most satisfying effect. Exploration should be on foot starting from the little green on the Aylesbury road which has a pump in working order and, occasionally, a tethered goat in front of a colour-washed thatch cottage and the top-heavy lodge at the entrance to the drive to Nether Winchendon House. Down Church Street there are friendly inns, the Bernard Village Hall (built in 1927 with materials from the demolished almshouse at Dinton (q.v.) and, at the bottom a small stone Jacobean manor called Tyringham Hall.

The church is of architectural interest for it was enlarged no less than four times in the 13th c, leaving only the tower to be added two centuries later. Inside there is a Norman font and handsome altar rails. The road drops past the church down to Frog Lane and Lower Green which is surrounded by old houses. In several places new houses have been in-filled but even these seem usually to be half-hidden behind the old wichert walls. Beyond the green, the rich pastoral valley of the Thame stretches NE. Other lanes lead up the hill back to the upper green. In Spurt Street a rather splendid house dated 1884 has an elaborate display of Victorian ironwork.

DINTON, *Bucks.,* just S of A418, Aylesbury–Thame road, 4m W of Aylesbury. The turn off the

main road is at a cross-roads marked by an 18th-c
folly, Dinton Castle, which Sir John Vanhattem
built to display his collection of fossils – ammonites
are still imbedded in the walls. A chestnut avenue
leads down to the core of the village which lies on
a slight rise with magnificent views across the
Vale of Aylesbury to the Chilterns. The Hall was
mainly rebuilt in the 17th c and has had additions
since; the gabled N front can be seen from the
churchyard. The great feature of the church is the
fine carving of the Norman S doorway; within
good woodwork and a series of wall tablets and
brasses to Greenways, Lees, Maynes and Van-
hattems, all former owners of the Hall. The most
notorious of these was Simon Mayne, one of
several squires from Puritan Bucks, who signed
the death warrant of Charles I; he entertained
Cromwell, whose sword is still preserved at the
Hall. Simon Mayne met his death in the Tower.
His servant John Bigg was so distressed that he
spent the rest of his life foraging in the surrounding countryside as a hermit, providing the name of
the inn The Dinton Hermit at nearby Ford.

Just E of the church lies the Old Vicarage which
Sir Gilbert Scott built of wichert (see Haddenham)
c. 1850 and the remains of a Tudor hall house
which has been wantonly wrecked by turning the
two gabled ends into separate houses and de-
molishing the linking hall; a Tudor fireplace can
still be made out on the exterior wall.

½m W of the church is **Westlington** (a corruption of West Dinton), with many old cottages and
two inns.

DORCHESTER-ON-THAMES, *Oxford-
shire,* perhaps only just qualifies as a village but,
despite pressures of various kinds, it retains the
feel of a true village. Dorchester urgently needs a
by-pass, for the A423 carries heavy traffic and a
walk along the main street, so full of interest, is
both hazardous and noisy.

It is a very ancient site. The rich soils of the
Thames valley have attracted settlers from the
earliest times and Neolithic, Bronze and Iron Age
remains are all around; the confluence of the
River Thame with the Thames ½m downstream
gave an easily defended site which the Romans
were quick to exploit. But the most significant
event in the village's history occurred in 635 when
St Birinus, the Bishop of Dorchester, baptized
Cynegils, pagan king of the West Saxons, which
marked the coming of Christianity to the whole
of West and South England and also to the first
member of the family from whom the present
royal line descends.

A monastery founded in the 12th c was suppressed at the Reformation but fortunately the
village was able to acquire the church for the
parish. It is a glorious building. The earliest parts,
the nave and N transept, date from the first
monastic period, to be followed by the S aisle and
chancel in the 13th c and then, after another 100
years, the sanctuary which contains two of the
finest church windows in England. Other treasures
in the church are the shrine of St Birinus, recon-

structed with fragments of the original work in
1964, an ancient lead font, a vivid monument to a
13th-c knight in the act of drawing his sword, and
the glorious medieval glass of the E end windows.

A good idea of Dorchester's variety of houses
can be gained from a circular walk based on the
local Society's guide which can be obtained at the
small museum near the entrance to the Abbey.
Not surprisingly there are several fine old coaching inns on the main street and far too many
individual buildings of interest to be listed. One of
the main impressions is of the open space, either
greens or allotments, which help to give character
to the village. There are the Iron Age ramparts
called Dyke Hills, just outside the village, and a
hill fort of the same age on the Sinodun hills
(known as Wittenham Clumps) which are a
perpetual reminder of the 3000 years of history
that can be seen at Dorchester.

EWELME, *Oxfordshire.* The name derives from
Lawelme – a spring source – and the spring can be
seen today running down to extensive cress beds.
Ewelme is built on a steep slope to which brick and
flint houses cling at all angles but is notably chiefly
for one of the finest sets of unchanged 15th-c
buildings in England made up of a church,
almshouses and school, all built 1435–45. Geoffrey Chaucer, poet and royal official, had connections with nearby Wallingford; his son Thomas
became Chief Butler of England and married the
heiress of Ewelme and it was their daughter and
heiress Alice who made a great match with
William de la Pole, Earl and later Duke of Suffolk.
The Poles, starting as merchants in Hull, were the
first medieval family to attain the peerage and
great estates from comparatively humble origins.
In 1437 Henry VI licensed them to build an Almshouse – 'God's House in Ewelme' – for 13 poor
men and two clerks. Although the statutes have
been modified over the years (the inmates no
longer have to attend five church services every
day) the original building and its organization
have changed very little in five and a half centuries.
The almsmen, who now include women as well as
men, do have plumbing, electricity and a water
supply but Duchess Alice would have no difficulty in recognizing her foundation. By a curious
quirk of James I, the 'Master' of the Almshouse is
the Regius Professor of Medicine at Oxford.

The courtyard round which the lodgings are
grouped is built of brick – a very early use for
brick in Oxfordshire – and highly picturesque.
The adjoining church, also built by the Suffolks,
is a splendid Perp building, little altered either in
its structure or contents; for this we can thank
Col. Martin, the local Parliamentary commander
in the Civil War, who protected it from desecra-
tion. As a result it is a rich storehouse of church
furnishings of the 15th c and later. The font has a
breathtaking carved wood cover (only rivalled by
Ufford in Suffolk) over 10ft high; all the woodwork – screens, doors and roof – is of high quality.
There are 17 brasses and much heraldic glass but
the crowning glory is, appropriately, the great

tomb of Duchess Alice herself (1475); she lies, carved in alabaster, fierce and indomitable, in Garter robes, under a painted canopy supported by angels.

The third building of the foundation is the Grammar School adjoining the Almshouses, with a discreet modern addition and a master's house. Nothing remains of the manor house of the Chaucers, but a walk in the village will reveal a number of pleasant houses.

Swyncombe, 3m E of Ewelme, up across the open downland, near the wooded crest of the Chilterns is a group of 'big' house, church and rectory which, although almost hidden in beech woods, enjoys fine views to the N. The little Norman church is worth visiting; like Checkendon (q.v.) it has an apse at the E end.

FURNEAUX PELHAM, *Herts.,* lies 4m NW of Bishops Stortford; it is one of three Pelham villages each of which was owned by the Furneaux (pronounced Furnix) family in the 13th c. Like Much Hadham (q.v.) it had for long close connections with the Bishops of London and remained 'extra-parochial' until 1836. It is a picturesque village with a particularly pleasing group of cottages, between the church and the manor house, which are thatched, pargeted and colour-washed in pink. The manor house, hidden by high hedges and walls, is brick-built and gabled. The church is rather grand – fine Perp work in flint with a big tower and a two-storey embattled S porch; inside there is much to admire, particularly the stained glass by William Morris and Burne-Jones in the S chapel. The nave roof has been repainted to some effect. The interesting collection of old prints and the flower arrangements show how well this church is cared for.

The countryside around the Pelhams gives the impression of great remoteness; it combines the low hills and valleys of Hertfordshire with the large, hedgeless fields of East Anglia; the narrow lanes wander inconsequently between high banks.

1m NE of Furneaux Pelham the very small village of **Stocking Pelham** (Stocking originally meant 'built of logs') is rather dominated by a forest of electricity pylons misleadingly called a *sub*-station, but 2m further N, on B1038, **Brent Pelham** is worth a visit. Brent means burnt, after a 12th-c fire which destroyed the village. Here are the kennels of the Puckeridge hunt. The Barclay family who live at the handsome 17th-c Hall have hunted this pack since 1896.

GADDESDEN, LITTLE and GREAT, *Herts.* Little Gaddesden is best approached from Northchurch, the NW suburb of Berkhamsted; here B4506 leaves A41, crosses the railway, climbs to Northchurch Common and, after passing through part of Ashridge woods, reaches Little Gaddesden at Ringshall. The present village dates only from the 16th c, when the College of Bonhommes, on the site of Ashridge House, was suppressed and became royal property. The future Queen Elizabeth lived here during that critical

time when her sister Mary was queen; in 1553 she was arrested, sent to the Tower and was fortunate to escape with her life. During her reign Ashridge was let to various tenants but James I sold it to his future Lord Chancellor, Thomas Egerton Lord Ellesmere; his son was made Earl of Bridgewater and their descendants lived there until 1921. The monastic buildings were turned into a major house and Ashridge became the centre of a great estate; many houses in this and nearby villages display a coronet and 'B' showing that they were built for estate workers.

The form of the village is unusual. A single street has houses only on one side with a wide expanse of grass between them and the road beyond which is the park. The houses vary in age and provide a good exercise in dating. They include a Manor House which is genuinely Tudor, another, with a forest of yellow brick chimneys, which wants to be but is not, the Bridgewater Arms, and John of Gaddesden's House which is a timber-framed, whitewashed 15th-c building with topiary in front. A lane leads W to the church; its isolated position and the tell-tale mounds and banks beside it indicate a deserted village. As might be expected it has an array of Bridgewater monuments. The 1st Earl was Lord President of Wales, the 2nd and 3rd Earls and the 1st Duke were all Lord Lieutenants of Buckinghamshire in which county Ashridge lay until it was transferred to Hertfordshire in 1895. It was the 3rd Duke who achieved real fame as the 'father' of canals in England. This eccentric bachelor, of great wealth, had the acumen to foresee the commercial advantages of a canal system and the means to finance it and this was achieved through the genius of his engineer James Brindley. A column on the edge of the park, overlooking Aldbury (q.v.), commemorates the 'Canal Duke'. After his death his successor, the 7th Earl, decided to rebuild his house and this was carried out by James Wyatt in 1808–18 on the grandest possible scale with a façade 1000ft in length, an entrance hall nearly 100ft high and a private chapel larger than many parish churches; it is certainly one of the most spectacular monuments of the early Gothick revival. The gardens (open in summer) were one of Humphry Repton's favourite creations; in them is the first purpose-built skating rink in England, now converted into a rose garden.

When the estate was sold in 1921 the National Trust acquired the whole park, some 3500 acres of beechwood and downland, including Ivinghoe Beacon, the most glorious stretch of open country in the Chilterns. The house is now a Management College but visitors can drive through the park by using a toll road.

Nettleden, 2m S is no more than a hamlet of a dozen houses, reached by a road through beautiful, unspoilt scenery. Both the houses and the setting are pleasing. The church, at first glance, might be mistaken for Jacobean brickwork but in fact it dates from 1811 except for the flint tower now covered and painted with an ochre tint; the interior is wholly Victorian.

Great Gaddesden, 3m SE of Ashridge, is not a show village but its setting in the broad water-meadows of the Gade valley is pleasant enough. The church stands well on the hillside, backed by a line of trees, and showing to the E two gabled ends one of which, the chancel, has buttresses of re-used Roman tiles and the other, the Halsey Chapel, is of 18th-c brick. The churchyard is large and has been partially cleared of graves; a group of table tombs have now been placed in a close-packed row just beneath the E windows. The little flint and stone boilerhouse added at the SW corner in 1961 is, however, a model of how these things should be done. Inside there is good Perp work but the Halsey monuments are a really fine series of great interest. This family have been at Gaddesden Place, a standard Palladian block on the hill opposite, or at an earlier house, for over 450 years. Below the Place is the charming hamlet of Water End, a row of varied 17th-c half-timbered cottages, which suffer from heavy traffic on the Hemel Hempsted road. 1m S, a house at Piccotts End has some notable medieval wall paintings which are open to the public.

GREAT OFFLEY, *Herts.,* just S of the A505 Hitchin–Luton road. The old village is a single street; there is a much larger area of modern housing in a large estate to the W. The main road used to run through the N end of the village but has now, to the comfort of many (but not perhaps to the benefit of the five inns) been replaced by a massive by-pass further N, cutting off Westbury Farm, a distinctive Elizabethan building with barns and a dovecote, from the rest of the village.

Moving S down the village street, past the inns, Offley Place is on the left, a plain house of 1810 but of interest because it was the childhood home of Hester Salusbury, later to be remembered as Dr Johnson's friend Mrs Thrale. The church is a curiosity from the outside, with utterly disparate sections, a W brick tower of 1810, a 13th-c nave of stone and a massive high chancel of Portland stone, windowless to N and S looking like a high-class warehouse; its date is 1777. By contrast the interior has much to admire beginning with the elaborate 14th-c font. The monuments are numerous; that of Sir John Spencer (1699) is dramatic and moving, while in the chancel the unusual stucco moulding is set off by a whole series of 18th-c busts, mainly of members of the Salusbury family. Offley church is indeed a good example of the quite unexpected surprises which continually delight the visitor to English parish churches. The two framed medieval tiles in the S aisle which 'prove that King Offa was buried here' need not be taken too seriously.

HADDENHAM, *Bucks.* (2m NE of Thame), is now a very large village, surrounded by modern housing estates and some light industry on three sides, but the intricate core between Townside on the W and Churchway on the E is of great interest and highly attractive. The older houses are all built of wichert, the local marl which medieval craftsmen found, if mixed with straw and water, to be a reasonably stable building material. It is, however, pervious to water, so the walls had to have a base of stone and a capping of thatch or tiles. These walls – there must be a mile of them – still dominate the old village and help to give it its unique character. A good example is the footpath called Dragontail from Churchway to Skittles Green. The Bone House in High Street has, on its façade, examples of the wichert craftsmen's tools, made of knuckle bones and set in the roughcast.

Haddenham should be appreciated on foot. A visitor might start from Fort End, a wide cross-roads at the N end, with two contrasting houses, Old Hadden, 16th-c, and Maitland House, 18th-c, and move S down High Street for which, in keeping with the village's reputation for local eccentricity, if not daftness, ends in a cul-de-sac. Dove House, 16th-c, is on the right, and then Bone House and a cruck cottage, sadly spoilt by a garage, built just in front of it. Leave High Street by Crabtree Road and follow Gibson Lane past the small, elegant Skittles Green to emerge on the green at Church End. There is more worthwhile walking along Flint Street and Station Road even if the station no longer exists; nor are there flying machines operating from the airport beyond Townside.

The green is large, surrounded by modest houses of all ages (only the 1898 school strikes a jarring note), and has a well-stocked duckpond. Two ancient farmhouses flank the church, that to the E, Church Farm, is unusual for Bucks. in having a recessed centre section known as the Wealden type. Along Ashton Road is Tudor Grenville's Manor, for centuries the home of the Rose family. Walter Rose, woodcarver and local historian, wrote two minor classics, *The Village Carpenter* (1937) and *Good Neighbours* (1942), both pictures of village life in the late 19th c. His wood-carving business is still carried on next door.

The church is worthy of the village; seen across the green against a background of fields the fine EE tower stands up splendidly. A circuit will show windows of several centuries. Inside the restorers were restrained; the chief impression will be of light; the coloured glass is mainly modern and of good quality but there is much clear glass. One of the old bench ends (in the centre aisle at the W end) has a charming 15th-c carving of a con-temporary plough.

HAMBLEDEN, *Bucks.,* a rewarding Chiltern village, lies 1m N of the Thames and the Henley–Marlow road. Perfectly placed in the valley, the beech-clad hills seem to be breaking like waves down the slope on either side. It is a brick-and-flint village, the houses so uniform in style that they might almost have been built in one decade whereas in fact they range from the 17th to the 20th c. Much is comparatively recent 'estate' building, dating from 1871 when W. H. Smith, politician and founder of the bookshops of that name, bought the estate; he made his home at a large early-Victorian house on the river called

Kenneth Scowen

Hambleden

Greenlands; this is now the Administrative Staff College and his descendants live at the handsome flint Manor House of 1604 just E of the church.

The core of the village surrounds a small triangular green, with the churchyard on the N side, in which there is a large classical monument to members of the Kenrick family including Dr Scawen Kenrick who, when rector in 1724, built the imposing seven-bay brick house on a rise S of the village; this is no longer the Rectory and is now called Kenricks. The view N from the churchyard is attractive – cows in lush meadows with a small stream running between the cottages.

The church was drastically treated by 19th-c restorers, who cemented the tower turret and stripped the high nave walls of their old memorial tablets, which gives the nave a blank, unfurnished appearance. The tomb of Sir Cope d'Oyley, carved by John Hargrave in 1633, is vivid indeed, with his sons in armour kneeling behind him. This is in the N transept; in the S an intriguing new altar has recently been created using some fine oak carving originally made as a bedhead for Cardinal Wolsey.

Down near the Thames, Yewdon Manor is rambling and many-gabled and marks the site of a Roman villa excavated in 1912 (finds now in the County Museum, Aylesbury). Across the main road the large, weatherboarded mill stands near the weir; although the mill machinery has been removed it is a reminder of the vital part such mills played in the village economy for centuries.

Fawley, between Hambleden and Henley, is a very scattered parish stretching from Fawley Court on the Thames to the church up in the hills; the latter contains some notable woodwork for the pulpit, and stalls were originally carved by Grinling Gibbons for the chapel at Cannons, Middlesex, and were transferred when that great

house was demolished in 1748. Fawley Court, now a school, is a classic example of how an imposing Carolean house loses its character when plate glass windows are substituted for the original sashes. There are fragments of a formal garden and, on an island in the river, an elegant classical temple; Temple Island marks the start of the course for Henley Regatta.

HAMPDEN, GREAT and LITTLE, *Bucks.,* lie high on the Chilterns and are best approached either from Great Missenden or Princes Risborough. The name of Hampden is, and always will be, honoured in Bucks. Not only were the family of that name settled there before the Norman Conquest, but they remained by far the most influential family in the county for 700 years with several different branches holding manors all over the Vale of Aylesbury, With John Hampden (1594–1643), the 'Patriot', they became nationally known. His wisdom, firmness and moderation were universally acknowledged and many felt at the time that, but for his death in a skirmish early in the Civil War, an earlier and less drastic settlement of that conflict might have been achieved. For two centuries after his death he was the patron saint of the Whig party. His great-grandson, while Treasurer of the Navy, unwisely speculated (with Government funds) in the 'South Sea Bubble'; for this he lost most of his estates but such was the veneration for his ancestor that he was allowed to retain Hampden House and its surroundings, still owned by his descendants today.

Parts of Hampden House date back to the 14th c, but it was largely rebuilt early in the 17th c in brick, which was cemented over and given battlements a century later when the E front was rebuilt and some grand rooms created inside. This front looks down a long avenue, terminated by two small lodges known as the Pepperpots. The house is now a girls school. Nearby the parish church has Hampden monuments and hatchments. The small village, like so many in the Chilterns is no more than a scatter of detached cottages in clearings in the thick beechwoods.

Below the house the beautiful Hampden valley runs from Great Missenden to Chequers; on the lane running up to Prestwood, just above the great avenue, a cross has been erected on the actual piece of land on which John Hampden refused to pay the Ship Money tax. At any season this is a splendid view of Chiltern scenery.

Across the valley **Little Hampden** can be reached by a narrow lane which ends high in the woods at a church, three farms, an inn and a few houses. The church, entered under an ancient, two-storey porch is very small, but has some good wall paintings, a 12th-c sculpture of a bishop and the reinstated, pre-Reformation altar, a rare survival. In the churchyard are several gravestones with lettering by Eric Gill, who lived and worked at Pigotts, on a hill top nearby.

The Hampden estate marches on the E with that of Chequers, the fine Elizabethan brick house which derives its name from a 12th-c owner Helyas de Scaccacario, a clerk in the Exchequer. It was built by the Hawtrey family in 1580 and was purchased and restored by Lord Lee of Fareham, who gave it to the nation in 1919 as a country residence for the Prime Minister. Security precautions prevent a close view but it can be seen from the road and a public footpath crosses the park.

HASELEY, GREAT and LITTLE, Oxfordshire.

Great Haseley (1m S of A329, Stadhampton–Thame road and W of M40, exit 7), is a village of some character in breezy, open country on the Oxfordshire plain N of the Chilterns. It is largely stone-built, and has a single street; this should be walked from W to E. The houses vary in age and style; some are set high above the street with aubretia-covered walls below; many are thatched, and there is some half-timber among the stone. At the E end are church, manor house and Old Rectory; famous residents who have occupied the latter include John Leland, the pioneer British antiquary in Tudor times, and Dr Wren, Dean of Windsor and father of Sir Christopher. The manor, an imposing, early classical building with extensive outbuildings, including an ancient tithe barn, has a somewhat forlorn appearance. The church is a fine one; some Norman fragments remain but mostly it is Dec and Perp. In particular the Dec chancel is of good quality with windows which are reminiscent of Dorchester Abbey although it was the Abbots of Abingdon who owned the building and were probably responsible for the rebuilding. There are several monuments.

Little Haseley, ½m S, is a picturesque hamlet of stone, thatched cottages, scattered to no particular plan, and not prettified for the benefit of commuters. Haseley Court has a long history of rebuilding and additions. A 14th-15th-c wing was extended in the 16th c and Gothicized in the 18th; then, in 1710, a new, classical wing was added at right angles to the older building and this too was later extended. Part of the interior, which is mainly 18th-c, was damaged by fire in recent years. Among the outbuildings is a 15th-c tithe barn. There is some ancient topiary in the grounds which were rescued from complete dereliction after the last war by Mrs Lancaster, who restored them and made one of the finest gardens in Oxfordshire.

HORMEAD, GREAT and LITTLE, Herts.

(on B1038, 2m E of Buntingford). Great Hormead is a modest virgin of a village, unviolated by any ugly development, where almost every house hides shyly up a steep bank or behind thick hedges and trees. Its one street is worth exploring on foot because there are a number of delightful cottages to be discovered as well as one larger house, the Old Rectory. Up the hill to the S the one new development is appropriately chaste; this lane passes the church and soon reaches **Little Hormead,** only a straggle of houses, but

notable for its church. This is tiny, almost all Norman and very sparsely furnished, yet strangely moving; its ancient 12th-c N door, with original ironwork, is justly famous.

Wyddial, 2m NW, is only an apology for a village but again is distinguished by an unusual church. Here the N aisle and chapel were added in 1532, the first time bricks were used in church building in the county; there are some very fine carved wood screens, Flemish glass and some excellent monuments. The Hall, just to the N, is a handsome whitewashed house enlarged from an earlier building in the 18th-c.

IVINGHOE, Bucks.,

is on B489 between Tring and Dunstable, 1m W of Ivinghoe Beacon, the prominent triple-headed hill which dominates this part of the Chilterns and well illustrates the Anglo-Saxon word 'ho', meaning a spur of land. On its main top traces of an Iron Age fort, excavated in 1963, can be seen, particularly the banks of the main entrance which lies along the ridge running E towards the chalk-cut Whipsnade lion. All this windy downland is National Trust property, part of the great Ashridge estate (see Gaddesden), and is very popular at weekends, when the sky is thick with model planes, but it is splendid walking country. The Icknield Way curves round the base of the Beacon and turns into Ivinghoe village past the church, the modest Tudor manor house on the right and the Old Vicarage, a 16th-c house with a Gothick front on the corner. There is a spruced-up inn facing a green and a handsome Georgian house, now a Youth Hostel.

The church is a fine one, set in a very large churchyard. From any angle it 'composes' well, due partly to the central tower with a small spire. Built in the 13th c, it was altered and enlarged at least twice; the result was a tall, airy, light building, grand, but on a small scale. The unusual circular clerestory windows were blocked except in the N transept. The two outstanding features of the interior are the exquisite 'stiff-leaf' carving on the capitals of the nave arches, probably by the same craftsman or workshop who did similar work at the neighbouring churches of Pitstone and Eaton Bray, and the fascinating series of 'poppyheads', the carved terminals of the medieval benchends; these eerie, long-haired faces, only half human, were the 'green men' of the woods and forests, and show how pagan legends were still real to the medieval carvers. There is a sumptuous Jacobean pulpit with tester and reading desk but the preacher's hourglass was sadly stolen in recent years. Above, a fine Perp roof is carved with angels.

Ivinghoe merges on the W with **Pitstone,** an undistinguished sprawl dominated by the works of the Tunnel Cement Co. whose immense workings in the chalk are beginning to encroach on the Chiltern escarpment. The church, recently rescued and restored by the Redundant Churches Fund, is well worth a visit (open on Sunday afternoons); it has the oldest brass in Bucks. and

J. Allan Cash

Little Missenden

a chest which is 700 years old. At Pitstone Green Farm the local Historical Society have a small museum of early agricultural tools; it was also active in restoring the windmill, owned by the National Trust and believed to be the oldest post mill (1627) in England, normally open on summer weekends.

LEWKNOR, *Oxfordshire* (just W of exit 6 on the M40 and on B4009 Chinnor–Watlington road), has retained its charm despite the roar from the motorway. Although well below the escarpment, Lewknor is on the spring-line which appears in the middle of the village. S of the church there is a spacious area, often alive with the games of children released from the pretty school house of 1836. To the E stand a tall white rectory and a number of cottages, some with Gothick windows. W of the church more open space, the inn and a lane winding N, leading to Moor Court, an 18th-c manor house surrounded by a medieval moat. The church, a large one, stands up proudly with a fine battlemented tower. Although parts are Norman – the Chancel arch for instance – the bulk of the building is good 14th-c work with typical windows and elaborate sedilia. The font is Norman. Two large tombs, both of the 1620s, are now most awkwardly placed, having been moved from either side of the altar and losing their canopies in the process. There are more monuments in the Jodrell chapel and one to Bishop Howe of Hong Kong, beautifully lettered on slate.

Pyrton, a hamlet 3m SW, has a mellow Jacobean manor house set in a park; it was from here in 1619 that Elizabeth Symeon came to be married to John Hampden in the nearby church, now very dark and much restored. The vicarage, the inn and the farm are all 17th-c or earlier. **Wheatfield,** an even smaller settlement than Pyrton, 3m NW of Lewknor, is remote and evocative of an earlier century. Not far from the remains of a great house, now a farm, the little church sits solitary in the middle of a field. The interior of this simple, medieval building is a rare example of what an 18th-c church looked like, for all the contemporary fittings are intact. The surrounding landscape is beautiful; Charles I is said to have breakfasted nearby after a Civil War skirmish.

LITTLE MISSENDEN, *Bucks.* (just off the A413, Amersham–Aylesbury road), was lucky to be by-passed as early as 1930, so the usual main-road clutter of filling stations and cafés is missing and it remains a single street with only a few unobtrusive modern houses. The Misbourne stream occasionally flows through the village; this eccentric little river, which rises just W of Great Missenden, has often been known not only to vanish for a season but also (so it is said) to reverse its course on occasions. At the junction with the main road at the Amersham end there is a group of three half-timbered, brick houses, the Mill on the right and opposite a 16th-c hall house. Moving W a new village hall rather lets the side down, but Missenden House is a handsome Georgian house with two bay windows, past which a row of cottages and an inn lead to the Manor House, curiously reticent in what it shows to the road, but somehow giving the impression of containing treasures within.

The church, just beyond the Manor, is one of the best in the Chilterns, and packed with interest. The exterior, with a 15th-c porch and an 18th-c dormer window, hardly prepares the visitor for the interior, where the transformation of a simple Anglo-Saxon building into an aisled Norman one can be easily understood (with the help of an informative guidebook). There is a most graceful double-lancet E window, there are re-used Roman titles in the chancel arch, blocked Saxon windows, a Norman font and a fine series of wall paintings in good condition. St Christopher, with the Christ Child on his shoulder, stands in the river with fishes round his feet, facing, as was usual, the main entrance. There are scenes from the life of St Catherine and, on the W face of a N aisle pillar, a moving Crucifixion. Running S from the Manor, Penfold Lane passes the early Victorian, pink-washed Old Vicarage, Ridgewell House, which has Regency bows fronting an earlier house, and Town Farm before turning up the hill to Holmer Green on one of the prettiest lanes in the Chilterns.

Missenden Abbey, now the Adult Education Centre of Bucks. County Council, is 1m W along the valley. At the Reformation the abbey buildings were turned into a Tudor house, but this house was converted into a square Gothick mansion in 1808 which stands in a landscaped park, now bisected by the Great Missenden by-pass. It retains much contemporary decoration within.

MILTON, GREAT and LITTLE, *Oxfordshire*. Great Milton lies just N of the A329 Thame–Stadhampton road, 2m W of exit 7 on the M40. Its reputation as the finest village in south Oxfordshire is a justified one for it has an exceptional number of good houses both great and small, which have a pleasant unity through all being built of local stone. The High Street is wide, with ample grass verges to which the cottages are set at odd angles; the infilling of recent buildings is generally unobtrusive. The visitor who walks from the N end to the church will cover nearly 1m in which he will always have something of interest in sight, finishing with a climax at the church which is flanked by two exceptionally fine houses.

The village has grown, from its original nucleus round the church, N along a low ridge, and it is this outcrop of the Upper Portland beds from which the random rubble stone giving so much texture and character to the village was quarried. Milton Lodge, at the N end, the King's Head and the Old School House lead to a large triangular green which has a very satisfying row of 17th-c colour-washed cottages on the S side and two more inns. The road to the right then leads past the thatched cottages of Priory Bank to the Priory itself, one of two former Prebendal farms; the other, The Monkery across the road, dates

back in parts to the 15th c. The road then curves left uphill to the Great House, handsome mid-18th-c, with an addition of 1788 by James Paine; its impressive garden wall faces the Tudor manor house which has a large modern extension, sympathetic to the old in design although the yellow stone dressings are clearly not local stone.

The church is large, set in a secluded and well-maintained churchyard from which the elaborate buttress and stair-turrets can be admired. Inside there is much to please although Sir Gilbert Scott's restoration was as thorough as ever. There are a sequence of good wall monuments, all of which have been cleaned and repainted, but the magnificent tomb of Sir Michael and Lady Dormer (1616) has lost much of its grandeur by its removal to the base of the tower where he and his companions show only the soles of their feet to the visitor! Preserved in a glass case are the instruments – ophicleide, key-bugle, concertina and 'cello – used by the band before the introduction of the organ in 1861.

Little Milton, 2m SW on the main road, also has some good stone houses, but the heavy traffic through its narrow, winding street gives it the dusty, shuttered appearance of a French main-road village.

MUCH HADHAM, *Herts.,* is on B1004 between Bishops Stortford and Ware. It is the aristocrat of the county's villages, and has the air of knowing it. Although, like the majority of Herts. villages, it is strung along a narrow river valley the look of much of its buildings and of the surrounding countryside show that East Anglia begins only a few miles away. The village appears bigger than it really is for although the street is very long, there is little development outside it, and the little River Ash, flowing a few hundred yards away to the E, might be a remote country stream. A walk should start at Hadham Cross at the S end, distinguished by Yew Tree House, very picturesque, creeper-clad with thatch and tiles, dormers and an ancient wall; it is all much earlier than the displayed date of 1697. The Old Crown is opposite, and then follows a stretch of uninteresting houses, including some Victorian almshouses, until, after the playing fields, the White House is reached; this is an exquisite Regency Gothic building. There are other cottages, some with pargeting, beyond, and then, after a lane and on the opposite side, the first of Much Hadham's wealth of large 18th-c houses; this, the Hall, is an ambitious seven-bay brick house of 1730 with good iron gates and extensive stables. Interest now shifts back to the other side. Medieval Campden Cottage, which houses the Hertfordshire Society, is followed by the Bull Inn and the Red House, also of 18th-c brick, but more modest than the Hall. The street now reaches its climax with a whole succession of smaller houses, in rows, which, although varied in style, age and decoration, make a most satisfying picture. Pride of ownership is apparent in the fresh colourwash. A lane just past the Victorian manor house

Kenneth Scowen

Nether Winchendon

leads down to the church, set in a large churchyard which serves to emphasize the fine lines of the building – an impressive one. The base of the tower is massive, and the inevitable Hertfordshire spike on the top, a very small one, looks rather incongruous, like a grandfather wearing a hat from a Christmas cracker. Nothing else detracts from this grand church, very large for a village, but worthy of this particular one. For centuries the manor was owned by the Bishops of London, which may partly explain the size of the church and the lavishness of the interior, where the Perp fittings include font, screen, pulpit and stained glass. The piscina, the N door (which has ancient iron fittings) and the Easter Sepulchre are earlier. The village's most distinguished resident, the sculptor Henry Moore, has carved two head-stops for the W door. The long wall to the N divides the churchyard from the former Palace of the Bishops which is a large rambling brick house of many periods, now a private residence; here Edmund Tudor, father of Henry VII, was born. Opposite the churchyard gate, the former rectory was once the home of Dr Nowell, Dean of St Paul's, who is supposed to have invented bottled beer, but certainly wrote the first Catechism for the Church of England in 1570. There are two further large houses: The Lordship, N of the Palace, once the home of William Morris, and North Leys, 18th-c, with a fine doorway and ironwork.

Little Hadham, 3m N, is a cross-roads village with pleasant houses but with too much traffic for comfort. Hadham Hall, 1m E and N of the

Bishops Stortford–Royston road, is a fine Tudor house; like nearby Audley End, only one wing of a quadrangular house survives – mellow brick with mullioned windows, an entrance tower and a separate gatehouse. The Hall is now a school.

Widford, 2m S of Much Hadham, has an interesting church set above a deep valley; an ancient brick wall bounds the churchyard. The attractive, pink-washed Gothick house E of the church is only one of many pleasant buildings.

In this area there are numerous **Greens.** These may be hamlets or just a group of a few houses; there are at least ten within a 2-m radius of Much Hadham, of which **Bury Green** is probably the most attractive.

NETHER WINCHENDON, *Bucks.* (N of the A418 Aylesbury–Thame road), is closely linked with Cuddington (q.v.) historically (and by a footbridge) but by road they are 2m apart. Whatever the approach the traveller will find a small but wonderfully preserved village. The setting, half hidden in the valley of the River Thame, is pastoral and deceptively remote; a steep hillside protects it from the N. Unity of ownership (up to recent years) and unity of building styles give it a distinct character. Although almost all the houses are of brick and half-timber, they were, up to the last war, also plastered and coloured with an ochre wash which was very pleasing; since the war much restoration has been undertaken, usually exposing the brick-work, but one house (on the right approaching from Cuddington) retains its orange coat. The houses are mainly 16th- and 17th-c; the massive, gabled Manor Farmhouse just W of the church is of this period. Vine Cottage, opposite the churchyard gate, is probably pre-Reformation in origin.

The church should certainly be visited; it is not unique, but it is the best example in the county of how the majority of small village churches looked before the mid-Victorian restorers got to work; here although they did rebuild the chancel in a quite inoffensive way the remainder was left. Standing on the chancel steps and looking W today one sees an almost untouched 18th-c interior. There are box pews, a towering Jacobean pulpit, chandeliers, W gallery, Hanoverian Royal Arms and bequest boards; even the organ, although a later insertion, is 18th-c. Beneath the tower a vast clock pendulum swings above the boards recording famous peals by the bell-ringers.

Nether Winchendon House (open in summer months) was originally a grange or outlying farm of Notley Abbey; since the Reformation it has come by descent through the Goodwin, Tyringham and Bernard families. Originally a quadrangular stone house of which the W range survives little altered, the E and N sides were demolished, except for a corner tower. The S range is Tudor with great chimneys, but this had a Gothick facelift in 1780 resulting in a façade which is quite exceptionally picturesque.

PENN, *Bucks.*, lies on a ridge, 500ft up, running E and W in grand Chiltern country. It is a village which, despite the pressures from nearby Beaconsfield and High Wycombe, has managed to retain its identity. The view N from the Crown Inn of the uninterrupted sweep of beech woods, or S from the churchyard of the Hogs Back and Hindhead 50m away, are remarkably rural for a place only 30m from Central London. The church contains, along with a good collection of brasses, hatchments, consecration crosses and modern stained glass, one great treasure, a medieval 'doom', the painting of the Last Judgement which was usually placed above the rood cross on the chancel arch. All such paintings were removed and usually destroyed at the Reformation, but this one was found as 16 loose boards (and about to be burnt as 'scrap') in the roof in 1938 after which it was restored and rehung in the church. Only six such dooms survive in the country.

The houses along the ridge, W of the church, are mostly white, and have a Regency look about them, which in fact is deceptive for some are very much older, such as Stone House where the Grove family lived for five centuries until recently. When the road curves N and emerges on a large green it becomes the boundary with **Tylers Green.** Although geographically one, the two villages are separate parishes, with separate outlooks, and propinquity has bred intense rivalry. In the Middle Ages Penn was famous for its flooring tiles, still to be found in churches throughout

south England; so the origin of the name Tylers Green is self-evident. On the Penn side of the road, overlooking the pond are several attractive flint houses; Old Bank House which was built *c.* 1690 has two Dutch gables. A modern house called French Meadow recalls an episode in the French Revolutionary wars when Edmund Burke, the statesman, who lived at Beaconsfield, built a school for the children of French emigrés.

Jordans, 5m E of Penn, will always be associated with William Penn, the founder of the Society of Friends and the first 'Proprietor of Pennsylvania'. Although he liked to think so, he was not, in fact, one of the Penn family who were Lords of the Manor for five centuries; but he had many links with the neighbourhood, married a Chalfont girl, and is buried in the garden of the meeting house at Jordans, a movingly simple, unadorned building, the first (1688) Quaker centre, now lovingly preserved and a place of pilgrimage from all over the world. The village was largely built by Quaker families, on Garden City lines, in the 1920s.

Penn Street, almost lost in the woods 2m N of Penn, has an admirable Victorian church with an unexpected central tower and spire, built by Benjamin Ferrey in 1849, set against a magnificent backcloth of beech woods.

PIRTON, *Herts.* (3m NW of Hitchin), is a large village and one that clearly is proud of itself. Lying on the lower slopes of the chalk but above the Bedfordshire plain, its antiquity is immediately apparent from the mound of the 'motte and bailey' castle, very unkempt and overgrown despite being in the care of the Department of the Environment and making a sad contrast to the beautifully maintained lawns and gardens of the remainder of the village. The castle area is over 4 acres, still open space; the Norman builders almost certainly built on the site of much earlier fortifications. The church, near the mound, looks splendid, and the contrasting materials – flint, clunch and stone – give ever-varying textures and colours. The two-storey S porch in particular is impressive while in spring the large churchyard is gay with daffodils and drifts of speedwell. By contrast the interior is disappointingly stark.

There are old houses in plenty; the pretty cottage by the churchyard gate is typical – half-timbered and whitewashed. There are larger houses like Hammond's Farm (at the NW corner) which is handsome brick and timber except some parts which have been cemented. Great Green has several pleasant houses but one of the interests of the village is the amount, variety and quality of recent building. Much care has been taken with the layout of these new roads and 'closes'; ample space, much grass, seemly design and suitable materials all contribute to make these new developments worthy of holding their own with older villages. It is noticeable how much more satisfactory is the use of the local, light-coloured brick in contrast to the fiery red of the most recent houses. All this would not count for much if it was not obvious that those who live here take a special pride in their village, which has most of the ingredients the visitor hopes to find, including a well-stocked duckpond. High Down, on a hill 1 m S, is a quadrangular Elizabethan house, once the home of the Docwra family.

PRESTON, *Herts.*, is in the low wooded hills S of Hitchin. It was once an estate of the Knights Templars which accounts for the name – Temple Dinsley – of the large house E of the village, where an 18th-c front of seven bays has been enlarged, first by Lutyens in 1911, and then again in 1935 when it became a school. The whole village has a Lutyens feel about it and he did indeed build some houses, but the main impression is of a village version of one of the nearby Garden Cities, with large gardens, mature trees and a general air of conscious rectitude. Figtree Cottage, Vine Cottage, the Red Lion and the Well make an attractive group round the green. There is a simple church of 1900. John Bunyan once preached to a secret congregation in Wain Wood to the N, which somehow seems appropriate.

ROTHERFIELD GREYS, *Oxfordshire,* on a minor road 3 m W of Henley, is a small village which is important for Greys Court, one of the most interesting houses in the Chilterns. The Grey family, famous and widely-spread in the Middle Ages, owned the estate at the time of Domesday Book and for the next four centuries. In 1397 Sir John de Grey, one of the original Knights of the Garter, was licensed to 'crenellate' his manor house. In 1485 the estate reverted to the Crown and, in 1518, Henry VIII awarded it to Robert Knollys whose descendants lived there until 1708 when a daughter took it to the Stapletons; in 1935 it was bought by Sir Felix Brunner who gave it to the National Trust. The present house is a pleasant medley of periods – medieval kitchen, Tudor flint gables, 18th-c NW wing. Rotherfield means 'open fields where the cattle graze' and it is pleasant to see them grazing still in the small park beyond the ha-ha. Opposite the house is an intriguing mixture of buildings ranging from the walls and towers of Sir John de Grey's castle to a Tudor dower house and the Cromwellian stables, behind and within which are a brilliant and imaginative series of enclosed gardens, including what must be one of the largest and most ancient wistarias extant. On the far side of the house, in the stable-yard, there is an ancient well which, as late as 1914, was still worked by a donkey.

Across the fields to the SE, in a lovely setting, is a fine brick house, built and altered over three centuries, called Pindars; it was formerly the rectory. The church must be seen for the magnificent brass of Lord Robert de Grey (1387) and the elaborate tombs of Sir Francis and Lady Knollys (1596) and Lord William Knollys (1632), a marvellous display piece of Jacobean pride, described by John Piper as 'one of the richest works of art for miles around'.

Greys Green, S of the Court, has a College, a long, low block dated 1836 and recently restored by the Henley Housing Trust. SW on B481 **Rotherfield Peppard** has some good houses scattered round an immense green.

ST PAUL'S WALDEN, *Herts.,* is on B651, 3 m W of Stevenage, and should be coupled with Whitwell; St Paul has the big house, the church and a few estate cottages on a hill, Whitwell the population in the valley below. The Bury is a large brick mansion built by James Paine in 1767 for the daughter of Edward Gilbert who married George Bowes, a wealthy Durham landowner; their daughter and heiress brought the estate to her husband the 9th Earl of Strathmore from whom the Bowes-Lyon family, who still live there, descend. Queen Elizabeth the Queen Mother was born in the house. On the N side of the house is a formal layout with three radiating avenues terminated by 'eye-catchers' one of which is the church, a noble, battlemented flint building which has some surprises inside. Edward Gilbert, then owner of the Bury, transformed the chancel in 1727, in the taste of the time, with a tall, flamboyant screen leading to an elegant display of stucco and carving in low relief. Apart from an unusually fine Perp font the most intriguing feature is the number of ledger stones on the floor ranging from the 17th c to 1961, the latter a beautifully lettered one to Sir David Bowes-Lyon. Inside the tower there is a rare 14th-c stained glass Virgin and Child.

Whitwell is 1 m S of St Paul's Church. It has a typical Hertfordshire long village street with the infant River Mimram running behind the houses on the N side. A large new housing estate has been built to the S but as it is up the hill and parallel to the old village it makes no impact on the latter. There are good houses to be seen; at the S end the handsome 18th-c mill house has been converted into a Yough Hostel. Moving N several modest, timber-framed cottages are interspersed between three old inns, one of which, the Eagle and Dove, is prominently dated 1747 although it is very much older; the equally bold 1951 on the *graffiti*-covered bus shelter is probably accurate.

STANDON, *Herts.,* lies just E of A10, 4 m S of Buntingford. It is a substantial village at the junction of two Roman roads, the Stane Street from Colchester and Ermine Street, the old Great North Road. All the interest is on either side of the High Street, which runs S from the Bishops Stortford road; this is wide, with broad grass verges on the E side, and although there is no outstanding building in it, the effect, with modest houses from the 16th c onwards, is extremely pleasing. There is one Georgian brick house beside the church, which is a noble building with a detached tower, unique in Hertfordshire. Because it is built on a rise there are steep steps up from nave to chancel which itself slopes upwards; the effect from the W door is most impressive. The monument to Sir Ralph Sadleir, a local Elizabethan magnifico, is on the S wall of the chancel

Kenneth Scowen

The Norman tower at Fingest

and has his actual helm, sword and standard beside him on the wall.

Puckeridge, now linked to Standon on the N by half a mile of indifferent housing, had, until recently, a shell-shocked appearance, from the heavy traffic pouring through its narrow main street. Now happily by-passed it is coming to life again, with much painting and restoration of its many fine old houses, which are mainly coaching inns from the heyday of the Old North Road.

TURVILLE, *Bucks.,* is 4m N of the A4155 Marlow–Henley road, but it is best approached by leaving M40 at exit 5 and turning S through Ibstone; just before the road drops steeply, by the windmill, there is a panorama of some of the finest scenery of the 'deep Chilterns' – wide, low valleys and beech-clad ridges running down to the Thames valley. The monks of St Albans acquired the lands of Turville in 796 and held them until the Reformation. It is a village of small houses which has grown little over the past two centuries. The Old Rectory, a charming Gothicized house, stands just N of the well-maintained churchyard; the wooden fence recently erected on the S side has carved finials which copy those on the 18th-c grave boards. The church shows all the signs of being properly cared for and has been much improved by a recent restoration, commemorated on the N side by a small stained-glass window designed by John Piper. Apart from the 18th-c N aisle and a modern vestry the building retains its

Norman dimensions although it was modestly rebuilt in the 14th c. The walls are a mixture of flint, clunch and stone, part is cemented, while the parapet of the massive, squat tower is of 17th c brick. William Perry of Turville Park, whose monument by Thomas Cooper, a Henley sculptor, can be seen, added the Lord of the Manor's pew in 1733 with contemporary heraldic glass in the windows.

On the road to Watlington, 2m W, is Turville Heath, an attractive scatter of houses deep in the beech woods. Turville Park is a plain house of *c.* 1800 recently restored (and much improved) by the demolition of Victorian additions, which faces, across a green, Turville Grange, a fine mid-Georgian brick house.

Less than 1m E of Turville is the small village of **Fingest** which has, at Manor Farm, some of the finest flint barns in the Chilterns, a well-known inn and a church with a famous and much-photographed tower; this is tall, capped with a double saddleback roof and is so large inside that it may have been the nave of the Norman church with the present nave being the chancel.

WALKERN, *Herts.,* on B1037, E of Stevenage, is a long, single-street village, typical of so many in the N half of the county. Historically its only claim to be remembered is because in 1711, for the last time in England, a local woman was sentenced to death as a witch (commuted to life imprisonment). Moat Farm, the White Lion and

No. 80 are three of the more outstanding houses in the long High Street. At the N end there is a tall and dignified 18th-c house with a pink Regency front; this is the Old Rectory. The infant River Beane runs parallel with the street; a lane fords this stream and leads to the church which, although much altered both in the 15th and 19th c was once Norman as shown by the S aisle and porch. Yet even the Norman church was an enlargement of an even earlier building. This is proved by the late Anglo-Saxon sculptured head high on the S side of the arcade, just inside the door; Sir Nikolaus Pevsner consideres this moving carving was originally placed above the entrance of the first church. There are good brasses and monuments.

Ardeley, 1m NE (as the crow flies), is secluded and reached only by narrow lanes but is a surprise to come on unexpectedly. Most 'model' villages date from the late 18th or 19th c (e.g. Chenies) but the development here was in the unlikely year of 1917 when the Lord of the Manor commissioned F. C. Eden. The latter, an austere and imaginative architect, designed a ring of houses round a green N of the church. All are whitewashed thatched cottages but include a village hall in the same style and a well in the centre of the green. The whole concept, which might so easily have been quaint or nostalgic, is skilful and highly effective (*see illustration on page 65*).

The church, which also serves four neighbouring hamlets, contains monuments to the Chauncey family, long associated with the village. Sir Henry Chauncey, a 17th-c antiquary, wrote the classic *Historical Antiquites of Hertfordshire.*

WESTMILL, *Herts.,* on a minor road 2m due S of Buntingford, has a reputation as the most-photographed village in the county. It has a slightly self-conscious charm, with rows of colourwashed cottages set back from the road behind carefully shaven lawns and lime trees. The small triangular green has a good brick house on thé W side, picturesque cottages to the N, and the statutory pump in the middle. Past the church Westmill Bury is a very fine 18th-c house, set well back from the road with numerous outbuildings including a notable barn.

WEST WYCOMBE, *Bucks.,* is on A40, 2½m NW of the centre of High Wycombe. It is a famous village (one of only three entirely owned by the National Trust) which everywhere shows the works and influence of the Dashwood family who acquired the estate in 1698 and still live at the big house. Dominating the village on a steep hill is the church of St Lawrence, described at its opening in 1763 as 'the most beautiful country church in England' but by a guidebook writer in 1903 merely as 'full of eccentricities'. Sir Francis Dashwood, a typical, cultured country gentleman (he founded the Society of Dilettanti in the 1740s) entirely rebuilt it except for the base of the tower. It is a very fine example of a grand 18th-c church – great Corinthian columns, painted ceilings, good ironwork and everywhere fine wood carvings such as the lectern chairs. The font, which possibly is 'eccentric', has a snake creeping up the stem to attack a group of doves grouped round the bowl. There are the expected Dashwood monuments.

Visitors queue to climb the tower to the spectacular golden ball where Dashwood's convivial and much-maligned group of friends who called themselves the Knights of St Francis of Wycombe used occasionally to dine. From the tower there is a view of the Dashwood Mausoleum below; this hexagonal, flint building, open to the sky, is

The village green at Westmill

British Tourist Authority

one of the most ambitious of all follies, designed by Sir Francis to house the hearts of his friends – the urns to contain them can be seen high up on the inside wall. The view also shows the $2\frac{1}{2}$m of straight road Dashwood built when enlarging his park to divert the old Oxford turnpike which ran to near his house. It was the extraction of the chalk from quarries in the hill to make this road that produced the caves, now an additional tourist attraction. The park and house (National Trust) are a very fine example of late 18th-c landscape layout in which Humphry Repton played a major part; there are several follies such as the Temple of the Winds, a classical Temple of Music on an island in the lake, a farmhouse built to look like a distant church, and everywhere fine trees. So well did Sir Francis and Repton do their work that it is difficult to realize standing by the Cascade, that the new housing estates of High Wycombe are only a short distance away.

When the National Trust acquired the village in 1934 from the Royal Society of Arts, who had purchased it five years earlier, they were determined to keep it as a genuine village, lived in by those who work locally and in this they have been successful. Despite the relief brought about by the opening of the M40 motorway, heavy traffic still pours along the single street; however, West Wycombe should be explored on foot. On the S or park side there is a good coaching inn, the George and Dragon (1723), one of three which survive from the nine existing in the great days of the coaches. Nearer High Wycombe a pretty close of old cottages can be discovered; opposite these the Old Vicarage is a small classical villa in flint. The church loft, brick and half-timber, is 15th-c; from the arch beside it a steep lane, lined with attractive cottages, leads up towards the hill.

Sir Francis Dashwood's house at West Wycombe: a detail from an eighteenth-century engraving showing part of Humphry Repton's landscape layout

British Tourist Authority

East Anglia

NORFOLK SUFFOLK CAMBRIDGESHIRE ESSEX

Richard Muir

Although lying close to the overbearing influences of London, and lacking, with the possible exception of Norwich, a metropolitan focus of its own, East Anglia is still a very distinctive region. Jutting into the North Sea, with its broad waist bounded by the Thames and the Wash, and in the distant past made somewhat isolated from the rest of England by natural barriers of forest and fen, it has long possessed an individual identity. Within living memory the folk of Norfolk and Suffolk have looked upon immigrants from 'the shires' or the rest of England as being akin to foreigners. Essex has traditionally shared many of its outlooks with the other East Anglian counties, although much of its southern reaches have been engulfed by London's commuterland.

The region includes one shire – Cambridgeshire – and the ancient boundary between East Anglia and Mercia ran through the county along the River Rhee. The latest round of administrative boundary reforms has brought Huntingdonshire and the former Soke of Peterborough into the Cambridgeshire fold. Parts of Huntingdonshire resemble the Cambridgeshire Fens although others have an East Midlands character.

Although more isolated than its south-eastern location might suggest, and the home of people of an independent spirit, it would be wrong to regard East Anglia as being parochial. The neolithic flint mines of Grimes Graves were England's first factory, which exported its wares widely; during the medieval period East Anglia was far and away England's most dynamic industrial region; while the bustling little ships which sailed between East Anglian ports and the Low Countries kept the region in the mainstream of European life. Many innovations resulted from these fruitful contacts: the art of brickmaking, lost after the Roman departure, returned to England probably as a result of bricks being brought back as ballast in the medieval wool ships. Expert clothworkers, drainage engineers, Dutch and crow-stepped gables, and an improved farm-wagon design – all played a part in the developing rural landscape as a result of overseas contacts.

From the time when the immigrant neolithic farmers found the light soils of the chalk scarps and Brecklands responsive to their wooden ploughs, the region has supported quite a dense rural population. Iron Age remains abound, and the Romans established numerous camps, villas and communities; they built forts at Brancaster,

Burgh, and Bradwell to resist Saxon pirates and in due course the region felt the first force of the Saxon invasion before falling to the Danes. The villages of East Anglia yield remains of many phases of settlements. They are as diverse as the East Anglian landscape itself, which presents a host of contrasts, from the lushness of Dedham Vale or Grantchester meadows to the barren Brecklands, from the Brecklands to the man-made Broads and man-drained Fens, from the wind-blasted Norfolk shore to the bountiful granaries of Suffolk and Cambridgeshire.

Anyone who has studied villages closely will know that they do not fit easily into artificial categories – each village is an individual with its own unique personality. Still, a loose typology emerges. In the Fenlands the older villages tend to be found perched on what were formerly island ridges or mounds of sand and gravel; Thorney and Eye are examples. In Norfolk (where the isolated churches which so frequently occur present something of a mystery) there are several villages which straggle loosely around vast greens. Some villages, like Finchingfield in Essex, huddle tightly around a green, while others, like Foxton in Cambridgeshire, which follows a stream, have a linear form.

Then there is the generous endowment of villages which contain the fossilized remains of the textile industry, the golden fleece of East Anglia's prosperity in medieval times, when the symbols of industry were not the belching chimney and blackened terrace, but the richly endowed church palace, the timber-framed warehouse home of the wealthy clothier, and the waterside fulling mill. Lacking coal, East Anglia was unable to compete with the northern mills in an age of steam power, but the old cloth industry has left a rich legacy of glorious churches, like those at Lavenham and Long Melford, of large and attractive villages which were once towns in the forefront of the nation's leading industry.

East Anglia also contains the buried bones of villages which fell in an unequal struggle against landscape or landlord, like Great and Little Childerley and Brookhampton in Cambridgeshire. The Black Death was a convenient scapegoat for lost villages, but in East Anglia particularly it was the landlord with an eye for the profits of sheep rearing or the status of a great park who was usually to blame. By the eighteenth century it was less easy for the landlord to ride roughshod over peasant rights, and emparking

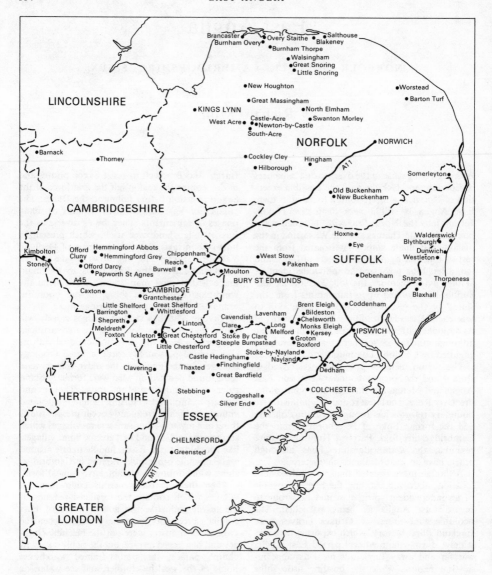

was usually accompanied by the construction of a new village for the displaced community, as at Holkham in Norfolk. Some landlords combined charity with their architectural whims and went out of their way to create model villages. There are several good examples in East Anglia, including Easton, Somerleyton and Houghton. The coasts of Norfolk and Suffolk are studded with villages which were once lively fishing and trading ports; the silting of a very mobile shoreline, land reclamation and the centralization of fishing in great mechanized ports has put paid to the old way of life, and now a safer life-style based on tourism and retirement is followed. Finally, in East Anglia there are two recent reconstructions of ancient villages: at West Stow there is a meticulous recreation of an early-Saxon village, and at Cockley Cley a more fanciful Iceni village.

The old historians have left us saddled with some myths about the English village. Firstly there was the notion that the Saxon invasion was a traumatic affair which swept away all former settlements and created our village landscape out of nothing; yet the reader of this section of the book will be struck by the frequency of villages with Saxon names which stand upon or close to Romano-British settlements. Secondly, the patterns of village growth have been over-simplified, while recent research is revealing that the village is a complex and dynamic feature of the landscape, thrusting this way and that, shuffling buildings around, and often, as at Duxford and Great Shelford, the remains of a Saxon village lie beneath the dwellings of the modern village.

The individuality and in many ways the richness of East Anglian village architecture derive partly from the region's general lack of good building materials. Much of the region is underlain by chalk, and this yields only flints, too small and intractable to be cut into blocks, and clunch, a soft building material which was quarried at some villages, such as Barrington, but has little to offer the builder. In the northern margin of Norfolk the Lower Greensand makes an appearance, and the soft biscuity sandstone known as Carstone is used locally. In the south and east of Essex Kentish rag and puddingstone conglomerate are used, while further north there is access to the beautiful oolitic limestone, the finest building material used in English village architecture. In general, though, East Anglian builders were obliged to make the best of what they had got. For instance, in the London clay on the Suffolk coast they found a muddy-looking stone called *septaria*, which was used in Orford castle and several coastal churches.

The medieval builders usually reserved stone for the building of churches and castles, and flint was all that was generally available. A few sponsors could afford to import expensive freestone from outside, and Barnack stone from the northwest was a favourite choice. Usually stone could only be used to face the corners of walls and edges of doorways and windows; and flint, either used as rubble or knapped, was used to build knobbly walls which are sombre in the shade but sparkle and flash in the sunlight.

East Anglia's timber-framed buildings are numerous and often excellent in the quality of their workmanship, and they were constructed from a rapidly dwindling supply of local oak forest. In comparison with the timber-framed buildings of north-western England, where an abundant supply of oak lasted much longer in a less heavily settled part of the country, many East Anglian timber buildings will reveal an economical usage of heavier timbers and the employment of more numerous, but lighter, struts. The village builders of the Fenlands were in the worst position of all, for there the native forest had long suffered a death by drowning, and blackened prehistoric bog oaks have emerged from the shrinking peat to warm many a Fenland hearth. The visitor will have to search hard in East Anglia to find a cruck-framed timber building of the type so common in the north and west of England, for in East Anglia the traditional style is that of box-framing with, as elsewhere, various types of wattle-and-daub being used to fill the spaces between the timbers.

As a result of contacts with the Low Countries where there was an older tradition of brick- and tile-making, and perhaps in response to the poor supply of local materials, bricks made an early appearance in the buildings of East Anglia, initially reserved for the homes of the wealthy and then appearing as bricknogging infilling the spaces in timber-framed homes. Essex probably saw the post-Roman rebirth of English brick-making, perhaps firstly in the twelfth century at Little Coggeshall and Copford, long before brick became a fashionable material for Tudor mansions. In due course a number of local brick industries developed, with the colour and character of the bricks depending upon the nature and firing of the local clays: red bricks from the north of Cambridgeshire, bricks of a washed-out white around Cambridge, and yellow bricks at Dengie. In some chalky areas unfired bricks of clay lump – a mixture of chalk and clay – were made. Although short of wall-building materials, East Anglia was rich in the raw materials for roofing, with straw from the abundant harvests of wheat and barley and reed from the Fens; reed is still grown for thatching at Wicken Fen. The typical East Anglian thatched roof is steep, with open gables, in contrast to the lower all-encircling pie-crust thatch of the West Country.

East Anglia is also rich in village landscape relics. There is a surprisingly large number of moated manor houses, of which Oxburgh Hall is the most splendid example. With its grainlands, marshland and lack of alternative sources of power, it is not surprising that East Anglia has a majority of England's windmills. They were mainly used for grinding grain, but some were harnessed to drainage machinery. A century ago there were around 1500 mills at work here, and today there are more than 60 which are in a fair state of preservation. A good post mill can be seen at Great Chishill in Cambridgeshire; and in the same county a smock mill is being restored at Fulbourn. There is a magnificent tower mill at Pakenham in Suffolk. Many East Anglian villages retain greens, and gigantic examples can be found at Barrington, Long Melford and Old Buckenham. Stocks and a whipping post can be seen at Meldreth; Caxton has a gibbet, and Papworth St Agnes a communal bakehouse, while many villages retain their old pumps. A number of Saxon churches remain: there is the unique log-walled church at Greensted, and excellent examples of all periods of medieval church building are to be seen, particularly in the Perp palaces of the old cloth towns. In Norfolk there are many round-towered churches where the need to provide freestone corners for flint buildings is avoided.

A land of character and diversity, East Anglia expresses itself especially through its village landscape. Many villages, like Cockley Cley, tell a tale whose beginning is lost in the mists of time; several, like Great Chesterford, have echoed to the steps of Roman legions. Some, like Long Melford, Thaxted and Clare, tell of immense former wealth; while others, like Burwell, where 82 villagers perished in a barn-theatre fire, remember disaster. Finally, East Anglia has been the source of some of our finest recent popular village history: Rowland Parker's *Common Stream* flows through Foxton; Blaxhall in Suffolk provides the substance for many of George Ewart Evans's oral histories, while not far away is Ronald Blythe's 'Akenfield', present under a different name, and, a little farther south, the farming county of Adrian Bell's *Corduroy* series.

GAZETTEER

BARNACK, *Cambridgeshire.* Whilst Colly-weston in Northants. is noted for its roofing tiles it can be argued that no village in England is more famous than Barnack as a source of good building stone. Barnack lies across the new county boundary in the N tip of Cambridgeshire, 2m E of A1. The honey-coloured local building stone is richly displayed throughout the pleasant village, though sadly, as is so often the case, overhead wires intrude upon the scene. The large and noble church stands in the heart of the village. The lower part of the tower is clearly Saxon, and may have served as a village refuge in troubled times. The extensive medieval stone quarries lie to the A1 side of the village where the deeply pocked and pitted landscape is becoming overgrown with bushes. Countless wagonloads of this stone were exported, many going to the chalklands in the S where good building stone was lacking.

BLAKENEY, *Norfolk*, is a beautiful place, a former port and fishing village which now faces a safer and more comfortable future as a village for retired folk and a resort for small-boat sailors. Braced by salty breezes blowing over the estuary marshes from the sea, the harbour is sheltered by the long spit of shingle and sand which is owned by the National Trust and supports colonies of sea birds and salt marsh flora and provides interesting field work for students of dune formation and coastal deposition.

Blakeney was a busy seaport in medieval times and the High Street has a guild hall with a brick-vaulted undercroft which may date from the 14th c. The church of St Nicholas is in the Perp style but it contains the nucleus of an older church in the 13th-c rib-vaulting of the chancel constructed by the Carmelite friars who had a friary just to the N. There is a tall W tower and a slender E turret which is said to have provided a beacon for shipping. The nave, with a hammerbeam angel roof, and the carved font belong to the 15th c, but the stalls with carved misericords in the chancel may belong to the end of the 13th c. Although the fisher cottages in the village changed hands for less than £50 before World War II, the old way of life has been completely displaced and the incoming population is a wealthy one.

1m or so along the coast to the E is the village of **Salthouse** whose name can be taken quite literally, for here in the 11th c was a warehouse at which salt collected along the N Norfolk coast was assembled. Above the village the heathland is underlain with coarse infertile glacial debris, and the village had to look to the narrow coastal strip for its arable land, while the sea rose to the edge of the present road at high tide. Unable to make much of the heathland, the villagers turned to the coastal marshes which were reclaimed by a piece-meal process of banking, ditching and grazing before falling to the plough. Marsh reclamation may have helped the village farmers, but eventually it put the local maritime interests out of business and in the 17th c the channel from the port to the sea was well and truly blocked.

However, the old port still has a salty air, and villagers have scratched graffiti of sailing ships in the choir stalls of the 15th-c church of St Nicholas. The church is built upon a slight elevation and provided a refuge and furniture store when the storms of 1953 backed up a tidal surge which caused severe damage in the village.

BLAXHALL, *Suffolk* (4½m S of Saxmundham), has been immortalized in the writings of George Ewart Evans, whose works are essential reading for all lovers of country lore. It is not an outstandingly beautiful village, but the largely unspoilt home of village families who once grazed their flocks on the former common lands beside the River Alde. The cottages which form small huddles between the fields are mainly of an unadorned brick-and-tile construction and there are some single-storey 'bedroom cottages' built by squatters on the common. The pastoral way of life was liberally spiced by the fruits of smuggling until relatively recently, and duty-free drinks were for sale in some of the more isolated Blaxhall cottages.

The church has a 14th-c nave, and a 12th-c carved stone stands at the base of the flushwork tower. There is a hammerbeam roof and a tall Tudor pulpit. The Ship Inn dates from the early 18th c and it is generally thought now that its name comes not from the boat, but from the Suffolk dialect word for 'sheep'. In the cellar are the old iron hooks once used for hanging poached game, and the Ship has been one of the surviving outposts of traditional English song and dance.

2m away, at **Snape**, the Crown Inn has a secret chamber that was once used by smugglers, while in the land to the E of the isolated Snape church, on the road to Aldeburgh, an Anglian ship burial was excavated in 1862 to reveal a mid-7th-c boat 48ft in length – but no treasure. The Maltings at Snape are 19th-c buildings and they received bargeloads of American barley, which was offloaded from the grainships standing offshore, until the revival of English barley growing and the centralization of the malting industry put an end to the Snape maltings in 1965. The buildings were then taken over and converted into an opera house and concert hall by the Aldeburgh Festival Committee. They were seriously damaged by fire in 1969, but were speedily rebuilt under the inspiration of the founders of the Aldeburgh Festival, Benjamin Britten and Peter Pears. The acoustics of Snape Maltings are considered to be among the finest in European concert halls; and the situation of the concert hall, on the edge of the salt marshes, is very beautiful.

BOXFORD, *Suffolk,* midway between Sudbury and Hadleigh on A1071. Nestling in a hollow, close to the stream from which it takes its name, Boxford is a most attractive village. In the days when it had a cloth industry it was a much grander and more dynamic place than it is today. At the start of the 17th c the village was the home of four weavers' guilds and supported 37 weavers, 11 clothmakers and a number of shearmen, dyers and fullers. In 1684 one employer alone had more than 200 workers on his payroll. This former importance is evident by the grandeur of the church, and the name of the Fleece Inn, which may date from the 15th c and contains a room lined with panels from the church.

The church of St Mary is partly the product of endowments received between 1441 and 1469; an impressive but airy building, it can lay claim to national distinction since the timber-built N porch is a remarkably old example of its kind, and it may be a century older than the showy mid-15th-c S porch. The tower belongs to the 14th c and the spirelet may date from the early 19th c. Inside the church there is a painting of Christ flanked by angels on the chancel arch while the mural of a crowned figure in the S chapel is thought by some to represent Richard II, and by others King Edmund. On the S wall there is a tablet to Elizabeth Hyan whose death in 1746 at the age of 113 was 'hastened' by a fall.

The village contains a number of timber-framed buildings, some of them concealed behind elegant later façades, and a variety of medieval, Elizabethan and Georgian styles are displayed. The Old School House was a Tudor Grammar School; Old Chequers in Church Street displays a carved bressumer; and Hendrick House in Swan Street has an 18th-c plastered front and pedimented gable. On Broad Street the yellow-brick former engine house dates from 1828.

The nearby village of **Groton** is a loose collection of neighbouring hamlets which have the Groton church of St Bartholomew as their focus. John Winthrop, who held the manor at Groton after 1618 and was born at nearby Edwardstone, founded the city of Boston, having led the first large-scale Puritan colonization of New England. The town of Groton, in Massachusetts, commemorates this link.

BURWELL, *Cambridgeshire* (5m NE of Newmarket), offers a great deal to those in search of relics of the old village landscape. The Fen edge site had long attracted settlement, and a variety of stone axes and bronze tools have been discovered nearby; at least three Romano-British house sites have been unearthed and there was an Anglo-Saxon cemetery. From a point 1m W of Burwell the famous Devil's Dyke ran SE towards Ditton Green for nearly 8m. This was the most impressive of the Cambridgeshire dykes, which include Fleam Dyke and Bran Ditch. There have

been several unsuccessful attempts to provide exact dates for these massive features of the Dark Age landscape; and the battered bones unearthed at Bran Ditch show their association with defence. They could be the product of a Romano-British attempt to resist Saxon penetration, but they might also reflect hostility between the early Saxon kingdoms. They span the open terrain between natural barriers, but whether they were built as an obstacle to cattle raiding, as features which could be defended, or as boundary markers, remains open to question. A speculative account of their nature is given by Rowland Parker in *The Common Stream.*

The church of St Mary is described by Pevsner as 'the most perfect example in the county of the Perp ideal of the glasshouse'. The church is very largely the product of generous endowments made in the 15th c, although fragments of Norman work can be found in the base of the tower. The interior is lined with the soft local chalky stone known as 'clunch' and contains fine carving and monuments, while the exterior is of sterner flint rubble. The tower rises from a square base to an octagonal upper section which is clearly inspired by the famous tower of Ely cathedral.

Burwell was once the scene of a terrible tragedy. On 8 September 1727 a host of villagers gathered in a barn to enjoy the novelty of a travelling puppet show. There were more spectators than the barn could accommodate, so the doors were nailed shut. Perhaps a discontented spectator took a terrible revenge, for a dying Fordham man admitted starting the fire which caused the death of 82 members of the audience. Their monument stands in the churchyard.

To the W of the church are the remains of Burwell castle moat; the walls which have disappeared were begun in 1143, but never completed.

The village runs in elongated form for 1m and contains a host of interesting buildings. To the S, at Malting Corner, there is a splendid long stone barn which terminates in a malthouse and which probably originated as a barn for the Priory of St John, which was established at Burwell around 1100 on the site of the present vicarage. The main street is lined with buildings which mainly belong to the 17th and 18th c. On Newnham Lane can be seen the old fire-engine house which previously served as a double lock-up. Overlooking the village there is a superb tower mill which was in business until quite recently; nearby there is the stump of a second mill, while a third, the Adventurers Fen mill, has been re-sited at Wicken Fen.

Features of great historical interest converge at the village of **Reach,** 1m W of Burwell. Here is the N end of Devil's Dyke and the remains of a Roman cut which led to the navigable River Cam near Upware; known as Reach Lode it resembled the better known Car Dyke at Waterbeach, and may have been used for irrigation and drainage as well as for transport. In medieval times Reach served as the main port for Cambridge, and both Reach and Burwell had complexes of basins and canals. The wealthy merchants who lived in these

Geoffrey N. Wright

Castle Acre: the priory church

villages had private docks at the backs of their houses which connected with the main lodes, and then via Fenland waterways to the North Sea.

CASTLE ACRE, *Norfolk*, 4m N of Swaffham. Standing in the outer bailey of what some believe to be the grandest castle earthworks in England, the village of Castle Acre has one of the most imposing situations in East Anglia. The castle, which lies beside the ancient trackway, Peddar's Way, was built shortly after the Conquest by the Conqueror's son-in-law, William de Warenne, and occupied by the family until the line died out in the 14th c. The castle was built on a scale befitting its noble master, and although only fragments of the shell-keep remain it is a full 160ft in diameter and within it there are the foundations of an oblong keep. The only castle building to survive intact is the 13th-c gateway with a pointed arch and flanking towers. The grooves for the portcullis can be seen. The castle is most impressive for the scale of its earthworks, the crescentic motte and the very deep ditch. Castle Acre is essential visiting for admirers of ruins, and those of the priory are splendidly evocative. The priory was founded about 1090. William de Warenne had been impressed by a visit to the great abbey at Cluny in Burgundy. When he returned he founded a Cluniac priory near his main castle in Lewes Castle Acre priory was a daughter establishment of the one at Lewes.

In the late 13th c the buildings were fortified. The priory benefited from its proximity to the great pilgrimage centre at Little Walsingham, and managed to divert a number of pilgrims with the counter-attraction of the arm of St Philip. Still standing is a little altar in the infirmary chapel where pilgrims who were dying in their attempts to reach Walsingham received the Last Sacrament.

Perhaps the most impressive feature of the ruins is the W front of the priory church, one of the finest examples of late-Norman architecture, with elaborate ornamentation in blind arcading. The gatehouse, pierced by entrances for pedestrians and vehicles, belongs to the early 16th c and is of stone with brick dressings and diagonal buttresses and mullioned windows; it bears the arms of Fitzalan, de Warenne, Maltravers and Royal arms. The cloisters are in ruins but the outlines of the Norman frater, chapter house and church can be traced. The village church of St James stands between the outer bailey of the castle and the priory precincts; it is mainly in the Perp style though it contains the remains of a much altered earlier church which may have been built about 1300, to which date the priest's doorway belongs. There is a 13th-c font, with a very tall 15th-c cover, an early 15th-c screen with painted figures, and on the pulpit are representations of the four Latin Fathers of the Church.

The village site was certainly well populated before the Norman castle and priory were built, for a large Saxon cemetery with burial urns has been excavated, and there is also a report that stone coffins which may have belonged to the castle founder and his wife were discovered during bridging of the Nar.

There is much of historical interest in this area; the church of All Saints at **Newton-by-Castle Acre,** to the E, has a Saxon crossing tower, windows and archway, while at **South Acre,** across a deep ford from Castle Acre, the church of St George contains the wooden effigy of a crusader, a brass of Sir John Harsyke who died in 1384 and the replica of a fine helm which is on loan to the Tower of London. At **West Acre,** which is 3m W of Castle Acre, there are the remains of a priory which was founded by the Augustinians only a few years after the Cluniac order was established at Castle Acre. It extends on both sides of the Nar, and work in the Norman and EE styles can be seen among the remains of the church and chapter house. The gatehouse is a 14th-c flint building.

CASTLE HEDINGHAM, *Essex* (4m NE of Halstead), is sometimes spoken of as being a town, but with only around 1000 occupants this is a tribute to its former glories rather than its present function. Glories there were indeed, for the dominating castle was, until its partial demolition in 1592, the principal residence of the mighty De Vere family, the Earls of Oxford. The castle stands on a hillock NE of the church, and the keep, which is the best-preserved example of its kind in England, was built around 1140. The keep is faced with imported Barnack stone and rises to over 100ft. The earthworks of the inner and outer baileys can be seen; and, when complete, the castle had a Great Hall standing SW of the keep, a chapel to the S, a turreted brick gatehouse and a forebuilding attached to the W wall of the keep, which may have been a prison, while in place of the two shortened-angle turrets there were four, complete with battlements. The keep is open to the public, and on the second floor can be seen the lofty Hall, almost 30ft in height, with an encircling gallery at half the height of the room.

The church of St Nicholas is an almost complete 12th-c Norman parish church, to which have been added a Tudor tower of brick and a late medieval double-hammerbeam roof to the nave. The five chancel choir stalls have misericords with carvings representing a fox with a distaff, two leopard's heads and a monk being carried away by a wolf. There is a monument in black marble to John, the 15th Earl of Oxford, who died in 1539; the Earl and his Lady are represented on the lid of the tomb, which is flanked by the kneeling figures of four sons and four daughters. This is the only monument to the De Veres, the remainder of whom were buried at Earls Colne Priory.

The town has a number of attractive timber-framed buildings, among them the 15th-c Falcon Inn, and some fine Georgian brick buildings, of which the vicarage is a good early example.

CAXTON, *Cambridgeshire* (5m E of St Neots), is notable for a rather grisly reminder: the gibbet which is situated near the spot where the A14 crosses the A45. Local tradition does not answer all the questions concerning the gibbet: some say one was erected in 1753 to dispose of Gatwood, a highwayman from Royston who had been at work on the Great North Road; others that a murderer was hung from the gibbet in an iron cage, and when a baker gave him bread the baker was hung along with him. It is thought that the last time the gibbet was used was at the start of the 19th c, when the victim was a local man.

But Caxton has more convivial claims on our attention. It contains two fine old inns. The Crown House was formerly the Crown Inn and has served as an inn since the early 16th c; the old timber building gained a carriageway in the early 17th c, and later a Georgian façade in five bays. The George Inn has also responded to changing fashions: to the rear can be seen the original Elizabethan brickwork while the front of the building is a Georgian addition. The church of St Andrew is a 13th- and 14th-c building, heavily restored in the Victorian era.

In the early 13th c the original village of Caxton was moved from around the church to exploit the Old North Road market trade.

CHELSWORTH, *Suffolk* (7m NW of Hadleigh), is one of a series of picturesque villages on the upper reaches of the River Brett. It consists largely of a charming row of houses lining the N side of the village street and facing the parkland of Chelsworth Hall. There are well-kept gardens and chestnut trees and one passes through the garden of a 17th-c house to reach the 14th-c church of All Saints, which was originally approached towards the 15th-c S porch, recently converted into a vestry. Above the chancel is a medieval Doom painting showing Christ enthroned on a rainbow.

1m SW is the attractive village of **Monks Eleigh,** where a small green runs between rows of cottages towards the church. Standing on the green is the parish pump built in 1854.

Little more than 1m further W is **Brent Eleigh**

Monks Eleigh

which consists of a group of thatched houses and a row of almshouses dating from 1731. The church also contains a medieval wall painting which in this case depicts the Crucifixion. **Bildeston,** to the NE, not on the River Brett, is full of picturesque old houses, and has almost the air of a small town. It was a place of importance in the days of the medieval cloth industry, producing a famous variety of blue cloth. The fine 15th-c church with its original carved door is reached after a steep ascent out of the village.

CLARE, *Suffolk*, although little more than a large village today, has a splendid past which is preserved in a number of buildings and monuments. W of Gosford Street, which is on the N side of the massive church, are the remains of Iron Age fortifications which guarded the Stour valley and reflect the fierce Celtic tribal rivalries of the years before the Roman invasion under Claudius in AD 43. The strategical significance of the later Saxon settlement at Clare was recognized by the Norman invaders, and shortly after the Conquest a huge motte was thrown up and capped by a fort commanding the ancient Icknield Way, which followed the chalk scarps between the Fenland to the N and the forest to the S. Clare was granted to one of King William's foremost warriors, Richard de Bienfaite, and it became the centre of the manorial empire known as the Honour of Clare. The family wielded great power in the realm and Gilbert de Clare married the daughter of King Edward I, although the male line of the family terminated when their son fell at Bannockburn in 1314, and the castle passed to a daughter, Elizabeth.

Edward III, the cousin of Elizabeth, was a frequent guest at the castle. During the construction of the Victorian railway yard workmen unearthed a priceless pearl-encrusted gold reliquary cross which is believed to have belonged to Edward. The castle motte remains impressive, and fragments of the 13th-c shell-keep can be seen, although the old railway station obliterated the inner bailey, and now attempts to atone for this vandalism by serving as an information centre for an imaginative little country park.

The imposing flint-built church of St Peter and St Paul lacks the grace of the church at nearby Long Melford (q.v.), but is a magnificent monument to the medieval prosperity of the town, which was based on the riches of the Suffolk wool and cloth trade. The tower dates from the 13th c; the N and S porches were added in the 14th c; and there was extensive enlargement and rebuilding in the 15th c. The chancel was remodelled in 1617 although the faithful retention of the medieval Perp style ensured that harmony was preserved. Sadly, the medieval stained glass perished in 1643 when Clare suffered a visitation from the official vandal, William Dowsing, who later boasted that he had 'brake down 1000 pictures superstitious.' The S porch sundial of 1790 admonishes the clock watcher to 'Go about your business'.

C. Righton Campin

Pargeting at Clare

Robert Godewyk, who was prior of the nearby priory in the early 14th c, is commemorated on a stone set into the church floor. The 16th-c brass eagle lectern is something of a novelty, serving as a money box, with money entering at the beak and exiting at the tail. Among its less imposing relics the church includes a bellringer's beer jug or 'gotch' and iron candlesticks on the gallery pew.

The Augustinian priory was built beside the Stour in 1248 by Gilbert de Clare, to provide the order with its first English house 124 years after the Benedictines had removed from Clare to establish themselves at nearby **Stoke-by-Clare.** The infirmary still stands, along with the remains of the walls of the church and the tomb of Joan of Acre, the daughter of Edward I who died in 1305. The priory was dissolved in 1538 and remains of the friary are incorporated in the 17th-c house built among the ruins, including the 14th-c doorway in the W wall. The Augustinians returned to their old home in 1953 to establish an institution for the training of novices.

Clare contains some fine old buildings and several examples of the pargeter's art. A superb exhibition of the decorative plasterwork which was popular in the E counties of England during the 17th and 18th c can be seen on the gable of the former priest's house which stands beside the churchyard and displays a vigorous floral design. The house, which now serves as a local museum, bears the date 1473, but the pargeting is at least two centuries later. Other notable buildings include the Globe Inn with its Georgian façade, the Swan Inn with its heraldic sign, and the Callis Street post office with its carved brackets.

Nethergate House is a fine 16th-c building which was remodelled in 1644; and a number of good Georgian houses stand on Nethergate

Street. Clifton House displays a 16th-c chimney with star tops. Red House is Georgian and beside it is a pargeted gable wall covered in a floral relief; this pargeting may well be quite recent, for this is one old craft which survived well into the present century. On Market Hill is a shop above a vaulted cellar dating back to the 14th c.

Cavendish, 1m or so to the E, is one of the most picturesque villages in East Anglia, with a number of pretty timber-framed and colour-washed cottages grouped around a large green. The tower of the medieval church of St Mary brings the vista to perfection as it rears upwards behind the thatched cottages. (*See illustration on page 10.*)

CLAVERING, *Essex,* 8m N of Bishops Stortford. Two roads skirt this pretty village, leaving in peace the main street, which runs between them and is lined with picturesque old houses. There are two abandoned tower mills NW of the village, which has the remains of a castle as well as a charming church in the Perp style. The castle, near the 17th-c house called The Bury, is N of the church. It was probably Norman, and although no castle buildings are to be seen the remains of the rectangular moat can be traced.

The church of St Mary and St Clement dates from the late 14th c and retains its original roof while the font of Purbeck marble dates from *c.* 1200 and must have come from an older building. Much of the original stained glass has survived in the N windows and a very old dug-out chest is kept in the nave. The pulpit is Elizabethan and the church has brasses of the 15th, 16th and 17th c.

There are two interesting old houses on the street which runs from the church: beside the churchgate is a 15th-c house with overhangs which may have originated as almshouses or as a guild hall, while the brick-fronted 17th-c house further along contains the remains of a late 17th-c shop and storeroom.

COCKLEY CLEY, *Norfolk,* 3m SW of Swaffham. A visit to this village will be valued by anyone interested in the early history of the English village, for here there is an imaginative reconstruction of an Iron Age Iceni village of about AD 60. Experts may find some of the features of the village, such as the snakepit, somewhat speculative, and with good timber more abundant at the period concerned one might expect some of the buildings to have been more substantial. Nevertheless the reconstruction captures the ethos of this turbulent age of stockaded villages as well as some of its detail. There was probably an original British village at Cockley Cley, perhaps destroyed as part of the reprisals which followed the Boudicca revolt. The reconstruction includes a stockade and a drawbridge which is topped by a tower, the round house of the chief, a long house for the warrior élite, huts for the poorer folk, a smoke house, a chariot house and a corn store. The interiors of the huts are complete with bedding, and there is an oven and a look-out platform perched in a tree. The Iceni village is part of a growing rural museum.

Across the road in a thicket behind the Forge Museum stands the former church of St Mary which was converted into a priest's house around 1540. With its round apse and doorway, the building looks like a small Norman parish church, but the guidebook argues that in fact the design of one of the windows suggests a date of AD 628 – which would make it a remarkably old church indeed. The operational church in Cockley Cley stands within the hamlet and has a round tower in the Norfolk manner; it is a medieval building which was heavily restored in 1866.

The cottage which houses the museum of local antiquities was built as a forge in the 15th c, and is constructed around a large brick chimney. A part of one wall has been opened to expose the original blackthorn laths tied with flax which supported the plasterwork of the original cottage building. At Cockley Cley one senses the convergence of different prehistoric and historical eras. Not very far away are the vast neolithic flint mines of Grimes Graves; in the museum there is the skeleton of a local Bronze Age man, in the former church a Roman coffin unearthed in the nearby estate. Running through the village is the prehistoric Icknield Way.

3m SE, the village of **Hilborough** has a very fine church which is associated with the family of Lord Nelson. His full title was Baron Nelson of the Nile and of Hilborough, and the family lived in the village in the 18th c. The great sailor's grandfather, father and brother all in turn served as rector. The great Duke of Wellington lived for a while at Hilborough Hall, a white brick house built in 1779. The church of All Saints is a beautiful building in a fine and secluded setting. It is largely in the Perp style, although the chancel is *c.* 1300. The front of the W tower is sumptuously decorated and the W doorway has canopied niches and a row of shields within quatrefoils.

CODDENHAM, *Suffolk* (7m N of Ipswich), is both a charming village and one which can boast ancient origins. The Roman settlement was known as Combretovium, and a fort stood at the intersection of four routeways and guarded the ford across the River Gipping. There was also a Roman posting station, and excavations in the fields around Baylham Mill have unearthed coins and medallions of the 1st c. Nero and Claudius are represented.

The oldest feature of the church of St Mary is a Norman chancel window, a part of the remains of the original Norman chancel. The tower, nave and S aisle are in the medieval Dec style and the clerestory and N porch are in the later Perp manner. The interior is rich, and the most striking feature is the double-hammerbeam roof decorated with flights of angels. There is a painting of Christ shown to the Multitude, in the style of Caravaggio, and a fine Jacobean pulpit, panelling and holy table. A 15th-c alabaster panel of the Crucifixion can be seen by the S aisle altar.

Kenneth Scowen

An essay in the Picturesque: Easton, Suffolk

The pretty village street is lined by some old buildings, notably the post office housed in a building which once served as an inn and dates back to *c.* 1500. It is timber-framed, with an over-hang and geometrical pargeting. Another former inn is Gryffon House, reputedly once the home of an archer called Wodehouse who was knighted by Henry V after the battle of Agincourt. The former vicarage stands in a park W of the church; it was built in 1770 and has an Adam-style interior.

COGGESHALL, *Essex.* The large village of Great Coggeshall is probably of considerable age and follows the Roman Stane Street which ran from Braintree to Colchester. It was one of a number of Essex centres which were important producers in the medieval cloth industry, and as a result Great Coggeshall contains one of England's finest timber-framed buildings, Paycocke's, which was built by the village's leading clothier, Thomas Paycocke, *c.* 1500. The house has experienced a number of alterations during its long history; the brick infilling between the closely spaced studwork is not original, and a plaster façade was added during the Georgian period and then removed as part of a restoration in 1905. The house, which has five bays, was clearly built to impress, and the large oriel windows of four and five lights would have made it much brighter inside than most contemporary buildings. The upper storey overhangs and there is a bressumer which includes Thomas Paycocke's initials amongst its wealth of carving.

Although Paycocke's is probably more famous than Great Coggeshall itself, the village contains a large number of attractive buildings, particularly inns: the Woolpack with its timber-framing near the church, the Lamb and Flag near Paycocke's, another timber-framed jettied building, and the White Hart.

The church of St Peter ad Vincula was all built to one plan in the 15th c, and its large size and its memorials to clothier families reflect the prosperous medieval cloth trade. The church suffered severe bomb damage in 1940 and the tomb of Robert Paycocke was badly damaged. The church also contains the tomb of Thomas Paycocke, whose death in 1580 signalled the extinction of the family whose grand house then became a cottage. In the S chapel there is a monument to Mary Honywood who died in 1620 and left, according to the inscription, no less than 367 descendants.

The adjacent village of **Little Coggeshall,** beside the upper reaches of the Blackwater, contains the fragmentary remains of an abbey which was founded by King Stephen and given over to the Cistercian order in 1148. The remains of a 13th-c dormitory can be seen, as well as those of a chapel, although the church has disappeared and the cloister has only recently been exposed by excavation. The Abbey is of particular architectural interest because of the widespread use of brick in the 12th- and early 13th-c remains – one of the very earliest post-Roman uses of brick to be found in England. Following the Dissolution, a house which has the date 1581 on the porch was set up among the Abbey buildings.

DEBENHAM, *Suffolk.* Located at the source of the River Deben, this is a picturesque large village of venerable houses and pollarded trees. The church of St Mary has a very old core and the lower parts of the tower seem to date from the Norman Conquest or a little before, and long and short work is displayed in its corners. The upper part of the tower, which lost its top in the 17th c, is Dec, as is the two-storey porch or galilee attached to the W face of the tower. Inside there is a fine roof of alternating hammerbeams and crested tie-beams on arched braces, a Jacobean pulpit and a sculpture of a bishop's head which dates from c. 1300, a tomb chest and brasses of members of the Framlingham family.

Although a fire in 1744 is believed to have destroyed no less than 38 houses, many attractive old buildings remain. The former guild hall at the top of the hill dates from c. 1500; it is a timber-framed building with a bricknogging infilling on the upper floor, a four-centred door-arch and charming porch. The detached building of Hitchams School dates from 1666 and has an overhanging upper storey and decorated beam. The Red Lion Hotel is c. 1600 and has its original decorated plaster ceiling.

Crow's Hall, 1¼m SE, is a splendid example of a moated mansion and dates from the early 17th c. Of brick construction, it contrasts with the older timber-framed moated manors of East Anglia. It abounds in oak panelling and the approaches to the mansion are lined with a fine range of old farm buildings known as 'the Barracks', perhaps reflecting the role of the mansion as a Cavalier base during the Civil War.

DEDHAM, *Essex*, in the Stour valley, lies in the heart of the Constable country, and its church tower appears in a number of the artists' paintings. It is another of the former East Anglian wool towns. It received a colony of Flemish cloth-workers, refugees from turmoil on the Continent, during the 14th c, and had a bay and saw mill which was used as a cloth factory. An adjacent watermill was used in the fulling of cloth, which was soaked in water and then beaten to felt, making it difficult to unravel. The village did not decay after the decline of the East Anglian cloth industry, and it now has relatively few medieval timber-framed frontages, deriving its character from the large number of Georgian brick houses which gracefully line its streets, some painted white and some displaying the natural brick. The village retained its market, and early in the 18th c two schools were established which enjoyed notable reputations, attracting a number of middle-class residents to settle in Dedham. It is to this period that many of the fine brick buildings belong, although several medieval buildings lie behind Georgian brick façades.

The church of St Mary was built on the wealth of prosperous 15th- and 16th-c clothier families. The magnificent flint-and-stone tower was financed by the Webbe, Hawke and Dunton families, and was the last part of the church to be built, with money provided for the battlements in 1518. The tower is breached by a passageway which was made to allow religious processions to circle the church without leaving holy ground.

The old grammar school at the side of the churchyard square was built in 1732 and was attended by John Constable, who had been unhappy at school in Lavenham. At Dedham his artistic day dreams met with greater toleration. The English School was housed in Sherman's Hall, built originally as the home of a clothier, an ancestor of Sherman, the American Civil War General. The classical brick façade was added to a much older building around 1735. Beyond, on Mill Lane, the Marlborough Head is a timber-framed building c. 1500; it began as the home and place of business of a prosperous clothier and was then occupied by a dyer before its conversion into an inn in 1704. Southfields, S of the church along The Thrift, is of a similar date, and the timber-framed building with its delightful disregard for the vertical and horizontal was again the home and warehouse of a wealthy clothier, John Webbe. It was built around a courtyard and the carriageway beneath the timber-framed gable would admit a loaded wagon.

Castle House, less than 1m SE, was the home of the famous horse painter, Sir Alfred Munnings, who died there in 1959; it is open to the public on Wednesdays and Sundays and many of the artist's works are on display. Constable's famous Flatford Mill lies 1m or so E of Dedham *(see illustration facing page 129.)*

DUNWICH, *Suffolk*, 4m S of Southwold. The handful of fairly recent cottages stands close to the submarine site of what was once a vigorous town. The origins of the town are uncertain but St Felix of Burgundy established the See of East Anglia at Dunwich about AD 632 and crowned Sigebert King of East Anglia there. His palace was built about the same time. Dunwich was a cathedral city until 870. When Domesday Book was compiled Dunwich had 508 men in its population, including 236 burgesses, three churches, a Benedictine monastery and Franciscan and Dominican friaries. It received a charter from King John in 1199, and at the height of its prosperity in the 13th c the port owned 80 ships, had nine churches and a church of the Knights Templar.

Even at the time of Domesday the low sandy cliff on which the town stood was under attack by the sea, and some of its farmland had been carried away. In 1239 the Franciscan friary had to be moved away from the coast, although Daniel Defoe recorded that Dunwich was still exporting cheese, butter and corn in the early 18th c. Last to go was the medieval church of All Saints, which began to topple into the sea in 1904, the tower falling in 1919. The last buttress of the tower was removed to the safety of St James's churchyard.

The church of St James in the modern hamlet was built in the early 19th c and in its graveyard are the ruins of the Norman leper hospital; the only other remains of old Dunwich are those of the Franciscan friary, between the hamlet and the sea.

EASTON, *Suffolk* (2m NW of Wickham Market), offers more for admirers of Victorian architecture than it does for travellers in quest of the Middle Ages. Most of the village was built during the 19th c by the local landlords of the time, the Earls of Rochford and Dukes of Hamilton, in a deliberately 'picturesque' manner. The villages *ornées* and cottages *ornées* which resulted from

Georgian and early Victorian romanticism were much ridiculed both at the time and in later years, but the cottage *ornée* may come to be valued as an expression of its era, and Easton has some fine examples.

The 'crinkle-crankle' wall which surrounds the park converges upon the church and provided the family of the Earl with its own private entrance through the N porch, although the big house has long been demolished. The church of All Saints is of much greater age than the village, and the plain 14th- and 15th-c exterior contains sedilia and piscina of around 1300 and some fine woodwork. Strangely located on each side of the altar are late 17th-c family pews, complete with canopies; and there are also box-pews dated 1816, 17th-c stained glass and a brass to John Brook who died in 1426 and Mary Wingfield who died in 1675.

The Easton Farm Park is well worth a visit. It incorporates a model farmstead and dairy built by the noble family in 1870. As well as being a museum of early farm machines and hand tools the farm still works, and visitors can watch the afternoon milking of the large dairy herd. A variety of now rare breeds of farm animals are on show, including the remarkable longhorn cattle.

EYE, *Suffolk.* The name Eye means 'island', recalling the days when the settlement was surrounded by marsh. In the Middle Ages this was a place of some importance, and after the Conquest a motte-and-bailey castle was built to the W of the present church, where a tributary joins the River Dove. A priory was built at Eye shortly after the castle, although both fell out of use in the reign of Henry VIII. The keep which stands on the castle site is a 19th-c folly. The church of St Peter and St Paul dates mainly from the 15th c and is noted for its very impressive 101ft tower and the flushwork tracery on the W front. Eye had a market early in the Middle Ages and became a borough in 1408; it was a parliamentary borough in the reign of Elizabeth I and provided two members of Parliament until 1832. It retains a garish Victorian town hall, but with fewer than 2000 inhabitants it ranks as little more than a large village today, though a walk around the rectangle of main streets reveals a number of 17th- and 18th-c houses testifying to its former importance. Linden House, in Lambseth Street, built of blue and red bricks, standing behind a row of trees, is a particularly fine example of a Georgian façade. Chandos Lodge, the home of Sir Frederick Ashton, has an undulating 'crinkle-crankle' garden wall, as have other gardens in Eye.

FINCHINGFIELD, *Essex,* 8m NW of Braintree. This former spinning village is one of the most photographed villages in England. There are villages with finer churches, taller windmills and larger greens; the attraction of Finchingfield derives from the way the different elements in the village landscape combine themselves into a vista which embodies most of the components of the 'typical' village scene. Approaching from the W, the visitor will see the green with its pond and bridge, and the houses which line the road climbing the hill towards the church, with their white fronts and gables reflected in the shallow stream-fed pond. Although the scene might have been designed to be seen through the view-finder of a camera, its charm lies in the lack of planned regimentation in the buildings, which clump together in uneven rows. Some are tall and some short, some have gables and some dormer windows; they are tightly packed around the green and seem to be edging forward, the better to view the scene.

The church of St John the Baptist is Norman; the tower was raised during the 15th c and was topped by a spire which fell during a storm in 1702, after which the cupola was added to round off the tower. The church includes a 15th-c font and chancel screen, and the chapel contains memorials to the Kempe family of nearby Spain's Hall. Interesting among these is one to William Kempe who died in 1628, and who did 'hold his peace for seaven yeares', not speaking for this length of time to honour his vow made after falsely accusing his young wife. Between 1806 and 1808 Patrick Brontë, father of the novelist sisters, was curate at Finchingfield. Scratched on a window sill in the S aisle is the framework of concentric squares used in playing the medieval game of Nine Men's Morris.

The tall, white-gabled, timber-framed and jettied building by the church is the former guild hall, which dates from *c.* 1500. A passage beneath it runs to the churchyard. The building standing closest to the pond was formerly the workhouse. The post windmill on the road which leads to the left from the bridge was purchased by the village and restored in 1949; further along the road can be seen an unusual octagonal thatched cottage, perhaps of Dutch design and built in the 17th or 18th c.

FOXTON, *Cambridgeshire,* 5m NE of Royston. The obscurity of Foxton ended with the publication of Rowland Parker's celebrated village study, *The Common Stream.* Visitors to Foxton should not expect to find a picture-postcard village: Foxton is a village which is pretty in parts, and its story, so skilfully woven by Parker, is similar to that of hundreds of other eastern villages. The famous stream which once played such an important role in the life of the community is now a mere trickle which is partly banked over.

The stream was once lined by the huts of a British village whose population was attracted to this water source in an otherwise dry chalk landscape. Parker has discussed the arrival of a Roman settler whose villa perished in the Boudicca revolt, and was pillaged for building materials by the villagers, who then suffered the full weight of a Roman reprisal. Burials of both Iron Age and Saxon date have been unearthed at Foxton, and the Saxon village of Foxton along with several nearby villages was granted to the Benedictine nunnery which was founded at Chatteris about AD 975.

A church of soft chalk may have been built *c.* 1140, and experienced several rebuildings before the greater part of the present church of St Laurence was set up in the early 14th c, apparently by a local man, Thomas de Foxton, whose name appears on one of the surviving original windows. The tower and clerestory were paid for by local subscription, and the work was completed about 1540. Parker's research shows that between 1550 and 1620 individual enterprise rebuilt the village; more than 50 new or rebuilt houses appeared, most of them of good timber and built to last, and no less than 20 of these homes have withstood the ravages of weather, time and fire, and stand today. The eye is sure to be caught by the home created out of a malthouse, which was converted in 1870, retaining a charming conical roof.

Rivalry between Foxton and nearby **Barrington** rumbled over many centuries. The old boundary between Mercia and East Anglia ran between the two villages. While Foxton consists of cottages tightly strung out along the old street and stream, Barrington is a large and nebulous place with an enormous green which must have appeared quite prairie-like before cottages began to encroach upon it in the 17th c. The village name suggests early-Saxon settlement by the followers of someone called Bara, and important Saxon cremation cemeteries have been found in the village, which dominated a crossing on the River Rhee and developed a chalk clunch mining industry. Although partly broken up by post-medieval settlement, the green remains impressive, and the village with its many timber-framed thatched cottages and a large 13th- and 14th-c church is a most attractive one. Graffiti, some of medieval date, can be found in the nave of the church, which has a medieval painting of the 'Three Quick and the Three Dead'. A good example of a cottage *ornée* can be seen on the S side of the green, consisting of a pair of cottages and dating from 1847.

GRANTCHESTER, *Cambridgeshire,* 2m SW of Cambridge. Though it is famed in Rupert Brooke's poem, and has the popular Orchard tea garden and punting through the meadows, there are nevertheless villages in Cambridgeshire which at least equal the appeal of Grantchester and are less overrun with visitors. The 'chester' in the place-name (from the Latin *castra* – a camp) suggests a Roman settlement, and beside the school there are the remains of a rectangular ditch-and-bank earthwork and of a Romano-British house. Excavations have shown that before the 12th c the original Saxon village of Grantchester was moved sideways across the village fields. This example shows that far from being fixed and staid, the early medieval village was lively and mobile. Fragments of 11th-c building in the walls of the 14th- and 15th-c church testify to the presence of an earlier church, and the church of St Andrew

and St Mary – the clock apart – is most noted for its fine chancel with its swirling tracery in the Dec style which may be the work of masons from Ely cathedral.

SW of the church is Manor Farm, the home of a 15th-c Chancellor of the Exchequer, but now there is only the much altered hall standing, and the cross-wing has been demolished. The old vicarage dates from the late 17th c, an attractive building of deep rich brick with a hipped roof. But perhaps the most attractive part of the village is formed by the old watermill and millpond at the S end below the church. A final and less obvious attraction is the Victorian letter box at Riverside.

GREAT BARDFIELD, *Essex* (7m NE of Great Dunmow), has an unusual form, and the two foci of the old village are well separated. The original green has been built upon and stood at the convergence of the three village streets. The other nucleus of the village consisted of the church and, beside it, the timber-framed and plastered hall, which dates from *c.* 1600 and has a 17th-c timber barn and a dovecote of brick with a pyramidal roof. The church of St Mary the Virgin appears to belong to different periods during the 14th c, with the tower, chancel, S aisle and S porch probably being the oldest parts of the building. The windows of the aisle are an outstanding feature of the building and their tracery is in a very individual style. Large fragments of the original stained glass can be seen in the windows of the N aisle.

A brick-built tower mill can be seen on the Shalford road and the village contains 16th-c timber-framed buildings, of which Place House is the best example. There are some fine Georgian brick houses and a weird Victorian town hall.

The inspiration for the remarkable stone screen which fills the chancel arch in Great Bardfield church came from the church of St Mary the Virgin in the nearby village of **Stebbing.** As well as being slightly the older, the Stebbing example is also judged to be the finer, and the centre of the three arches once contained an image of the Crucifixion flanked by Mary and Joseph.

GREAT and LITTLE CHESTERFORD, *Essex,* 3m N of Saffron Walden. Away from the roar of traffic on the A11 which skirts the village to the W, Great Chesterford is an attractive village with some pleasant corners. The 'ford' part of the name shows that, like many of the Cambridgeshire villages to the N, Great Chesterford stands at a ford on the River Cam. The 'chester' part of the name suggests a Roman camp and indeed, a Roman fort and town stood here. The Roman settlement was preceded by a settlement of the Celtic Belgae tribe and the Roman fort appears to have been established in the 1st c. The town may have belonged to the 4th-c. Apparently the walls of the Roman town were still visible in the 18th c, but subsequent excavations for road-building materials de-

stroyed them and they are now only visible from
the air. The walled town, which was protected by
a ditch, was oval in shape and covered more than
30 acres. The church of All Saints includes fragments of 13th-c building in the chancel and
arcades but the greater part of the church is of
15th-c date, including the tower which was rebuilt in 1792.

Little Chesterford close by is probably a
daughter settlement. To the W of the 13th-c
church of St Mary the Virgin is a very rare example
of an early 13th-c stone manor house whose thick
walls form the E wing. The centre section is also
old, belonging to the 14th c, while the solar wing
to the W is probably of 15th-c date. It is surrounded by a charming garden.

GREAT and LITTLE SHELFORD, *Cambridgeshire*, 3m S of Cambridge. Although much
colonized and developed by Victorian academics
from nearby Cambridge and by later generations
of commuters, the original pattern of the village –
or rather villages – can still be traced, and a number of good old buildings remain. It is now being
realized that the development of a great many
English villages was much more complex and
dynamic than was hitherto thought, and that
many villages contain the remains of more than
one old settlement. Great Shelford is of this type;
the core of the bustling modern village lies between two Saxon settlements, one, on the site of
an older Romano-British village, stood just N of
the level crossing on Granhams Road, the other
to the S, where Great Shelford straggles towards
Little Shelford. There were two triangular greens:
High Green which surrounded the road of that
name, and Ashen Green which was enclosed in
1834 and whose outline is traced by Tunwells
Lane, Woolards Lane and High Street.

Interesting old buildings are dotted among
the more recent infilling. No. 42 Granhams Road

has been converted from a timber-and-plaster
pigeon house of *c.* 1700. Jumbled together in this
locality are the remains of Romano-British and
Saxon villages. The De Freville Farm which
faces the road junction is a 16th-c timber-framed
house with hall and cross-wings of a high standard
of workmanship. Of a similar date is Oak Cottage
on High Street, a well-preserved building with a
richly carved bressumer which formerly looked
out over the green. Careful inspection will reveal
an old insurance marker above the doorway.
Moving towards Little Shelford, the Grange
with its overhanging E gable wing is an old house
altered and enlarged in the 16th, 17th and 19th c.
Next we come to the three timber-framed terraced cottages which were converted from a
single original building built *c.* 1660. The church
of St Mary includes fragments of an older Norman church which was rebuilt in the 14th c of a
mixture of local flint, rubble and clunch, with
freestone dressings. The original tower toppled
in 1798 and the replacement, which becomes octagonal in the Cambridgeshire manner, used the
original materials but not the design. On the
front of the church there is a sundial and a charming niche statue of the Virgin. Inside there is an
excellent nave roof of alternating tie-beams and
hammerbeams, a 15th-c Doom painting on the
chancel arch, and a Jacobean pulpit.

A part of the old 15th-c hall remains in Rectory
Farm House and near here there is thought to
have been an ancient hermitage. By now the
visitor is almost in **Little Shelford,** which began
at a crossing point on the Cam, extending E in a
linear form, then swinging S to follow the margins
of the manor grounds. The church of All Saints
includes fragments of Saxon ornamentation; a
Norman doorway and window survive in the nave,
while the chancel was rebuilt in the 13th c, the
tower in the 14th c and the S chapel in the 15th c.
The church was associated with the De Freville

A claimant to be Suffolk's most beautiful village: Kersey

J. Allan Cash

family, whose monuments include a 14th-c tomb and effigy. There are several old timber-framed buildings, of which Kings Farm is perhaps the most interesting, an old timber-plaster-and-brick two-bay cottage which was fashionably Gothick-ized in the 18th c. An old pigeon house similar to the one at Great Shelford stands in its grounds.

GREENSTED, *Essex* (7m SE of Harlow), is nationally renowned for possessing our only example of a Saxon log-built church. Pevsner thought that the church dated from 1013, when the body of St Edmund was carried through the village; but subsequent scientific tests have suggested a date *c.* 850 and revealed the remains of two earlier timber-walled chancels. Although the rotted bases of the logs were removed and the timbers raised to their original height on a brick plinth during a restoration of 1848, it is a remarkable tribute to the durability of English oak that the exposed logs have survived for over 1000 years. The original church was a simple building of split logs which were joined by tongues and grooves, pegged with dowels; the roof would have been thatched, and there may have been no windows as small auger holes can be seen in the logs to ventilate the building.

Various additions and alterations to the building were made in later ages; the Normans added a chancel of flint which was rebuilt in brick in the early 16th c and Tudor builders provided the six dormer windows. The wooden weatherboarded spire in the traditional Essex manner is of uncertain age. Greensted Hall nearby is an Elizabethan building which was completely remodelled in 1875.

HEMINGFORD GREY, *Cambridgeshire,* 4m E of Huntingdon. Standing beside the River Ouse, this is one of the most delightful of the villages in the former county of Huntingdonshire, and enjoys the reputation of having the oldest inhabited house in England. The early date of the house – about 1160 – was established by work carried out by the occupant, the authoress Mrs L. M. Boston. Northants. stone makes an appearance in the N of the county, and here it was used by the Norman owner to construct a house of two storeys, a ground-floor store room, with a hall and bedroom above. The stairway was on the outer wall, and the original windows and fireplace survive to give valuable insights into the domestic architecture of 800 years ago. The old house was knocked about by alterations made during the 16th and 18th c, but recently experienced a sympathetic restoration. Fragments of Norman work also survive in the N arcade of the village church, which may once have had a central tower. The W tower was decapitated during a storm in 1741, after which the remaining stump was topped off with eight decorative stone balls.

The manor house was the home of two sisters of celebrated beauty, who put their looks to good use. One married the Earl of Coventry in 1752, but eventually her face became her misfortune and she died from lead poisoning, which was traced to her cosmetics. The other sister married the Duke of Hamilton, and, after he died, the Marquis of Lorne. She gave birth in all to four more dukes.

A little further along the Ouse is **Hemingford Abbots,** once the property of Ramsey Abbey. The church contains a Roman coffin and has a painted E bay to the nave roof. This is a pleasant village with many thatched cottages which began as a huddle of cottages around the church and then grew in the direction of Godmanchester.

HOXNE, *Suffolk,* 4m NE of Eye. The name of this village is pronounced 'hoxen' and may refer to the village site, comparing it to the shape of muscles in the heel of a horse. According to legend, the young king Edmund who fled from a Danish invasion in AD 870 was captured here and slain when he refused to renounce Christianity. His severed head is said to have been found with a friendly wolf standing guard; the head was taken to Beodericsworth monastery (later Bury Abbey) where the supposed skull of Edmund became its chief relic.

From the middle of the 10th c until 1078, when the bishop moved on to Thetford, Hoxne, like North Elmham, had a cathedral. During the 13th c a colony of monks from Norwich established themselves beside the chapel which was built to St Edmund at Hoxne, and they may have been responsible for promulgating the legend of Edmund's death. Little remains today to testify to the former religious importance of Hoxne although the church of St Peter and St Paul is a fine building of 13th- to 15th-c construction. The chancel was rebuilt in 1879 using new stained glass for the windows. There are paintings of St Christopher and of the Seven Deadly Sins on the N wall, where dragons devour the sinners, while a carving on one of the bench-ends portrays the severed head of Edmund. Hoxne Abbey is a timber-and-brick house which stands on the site of the former monastery. The Swan Inn has served the public since the Middle Ages.

ICKLETON, *Cambridgeshire* (4m NW of Saffron Walden), originated at a ford crossing on the River Cam. It stands at the place where one of the branches of the prehistoric Icknield Way, which followed the chalk scarps from East Anglia to the South Midlands, crossed the river.

The nucleus of the village is the area around the church, which stands on a low river bluff and is flanked by two medieval halls and faces a small green. The church is an old one, dating from the early 11th c; three centuries later the central tower was heightened, the aisle widened, and the N transept rebuilt. Other additions were made in the 13th, 15th, and 16th c; it was extensively restored in the Victorian period. The church was sadly gutted by fire in 1979.

E of the church stands Norman Hall, which has a 15th-c hall range and solar wing, while, S of the church, Mowbrays is a 15th-c timber-framed building with a 17th-c brick façade. From the ford and church the main axis of the village runs to the SW, along Abbey Street, which traces the line of Icknield Way, and ends at the site of a medieval priory which was deserted during the 16th-c suppression of monasteries. Fragments of the priory seem to have been incorporated into the nearby Abbey Farm. Although the cottages along Abbey Street seem, with their brick walls, to belong to the 19th c, many are of medieval date, and behind the encasing brickwork the original walls of timber and daub lie concealed. One cottage is a rare example of a 15th-c aisled hall. Caldrees Manor at the church end of Abbey Street is a 16th-c building which was considerably enlarged in the 17th and 18th c, and the original building is masked by a remodelled façade. Ickleton is one of the many English villages which is much older than it appears at first glance, and a number of medieval buildings stand behind the cosmetic alterations of later ages.

KERSEY, *Suffolk* (2m NW of Hadleigh), formerly a cloth town, gave its name to a type of woollen cloth which was popular in the Middle Ages. But the origins of the village remain uncertain, although it is known to have attracted a small colony of Flemish clothworkers during the 14th c, and the stream which flows across the village street was used by the textile workers for soaking the newly made cloth. The village consists of one main street, and from the N end of the street, where the remains of a 12th-c Augustinian priory lie in the grounds of Priory Farm, the visitor can look across a vista of timber-framed cottages, with their red-tiled and pantiled roofs, to the ford and the rising land with its dominating church beyond.

The siting of the church is impressive, as is the church itself, with its Perp flint tower, grand S porch and the panelled roof which was revealed when a plaster ceiling was removed in 1927. High on the S wall is a painting of St George and the Dragon. The church seems to have faced several misfortunes; the building of the Dec-style nave and the carving of the incomplete arcade of the broad aisle may have been interrupted by an outbreak of the plague, while 17th-c Reformers vandalized the frieze above the aisle, the angels in the roof of the aisle, and several niches.

Kersey is deservedly one of the beauty spots of Suffolk, and is apt to be crowded with sightseers during fine weekends in the summer, but it should not be missed, and the surrounding countryside is singularly unspoilt.

KIMBOLTON, *Cambridgeshire*. Geoffrey Fitz Piers' establishment of a market at Kimbolton in 1200 technically qualifies the settlement as a town, but, large village or small town, it is a place of considerable charm, standing very much on its own in a rather empty countryside. To ensure the collection of market tolls, the village street was re-routed through the market place, which is represented by the long and spacious High Street. The market prospered and was complemented by a fair. As Kimbolton grew in the 13th c there seem to have been plans to expand the town across the River Kym, but for some reason perhaps declining prospects, it was not until recently that building took place on the new town site.

The present castle (now a school), which carries the scars of Civil War bullets on the oak door of the S porch, is largely the product of building in the 17th and 18th c although beneath much of the façade the nucleus of an older castle remains. The castle was formerly approached from the W through a now disused archway which faced the great hall across an inner courtyard. The old castle is best known as the enforced refuge of the luckless wife of Henry VIII, Catherine of Aragon. After it was decided that the castle should present its E face to the world Robert Adam was commissioned to design the gatehouse, *c.* 1765.

There are indications of an older castle at Kimbolton and on an overlooking hillside there is a moated castle mound which may have been the site of the castle of Geoffrey, the market maker. In 1522 stone and wood for castle building were granted to Sir Richard Winfield, and work began on the present castle. It is possible that an intermediate castle stood near the present vicarage, where the remains of a rectangular moat can be seen.

There are numerous monuments to the one-time owners of the castle, the Montagu family, within the parish church, which is a 13th-c building with a 14th-c broach tower, and their mortuary vault lies beneath the N chapel. A medieval screen depicts saints and Kings of England. **Stonely,** 1m SE, is a pretty village and was the location of Stonely Priory, an Augustinian foundation of 1180 which stood on high ground outside the village, on the way to Easton, although little remains of the priory today.

LAVENHAM, *Suffolk*. Although Lavenham has a population less than half of that of Long Melford, with which it is often compared, the houses here are more tightly clustered than those at Long Melford, and consequently Lavenham has a more town-like atmosphere. A Saxon village with two manors existed here in the area of the present High Street. The town rose to prominence as a centre for the export of wool, and it attracted a colony of Flemish clothworkers during the 14th c. It flourished during the cloth-making boom of the 15th c, when the blue cloth of Lavenham was famous. During the Tudor period more Dutch refugee clothworkers arrived at Lavenham, moving up the Stour valley from Colchester. During the 17th c the Lavenham cloth industry declined in the face of competition from northern and western weaving industries which were better endowed with the waterpower needed in the laborious process of fulling the cloth. Wars on the Continent closed many markets for East Anglian cloth, while the Civil War in England caused great disruption. During the 18th and 19th c the introduction of steam-powered textile machinery virtually killed textile making in coal-less East Anglia. Some clothworkers changed to spinning yarn for use in Norfolk weaving industries, while a small horsehair and silk-weaving industry developed in the 19th c.

The failure of Lavenham to develop adequate replacements for its moribund cloth industries at

PHILIP WILSON STEER (1860–1942): Walberswick Pier (detail from the painting known as 'Girls Running'). Oils, 1894 (*Tate Gallery, London*). Much of Wilson Steer's finest work was done in the 1890s, in a neo-Impressionistic style, at Walberswick and Southwold, vividly evoking the clear skies and brilliant atmosphere of the Suffolk seascape.

JOHN CONSTABLE, R.A. (1776–1837): Willy Lott's House at Flatford, 1824 (*Victoria and Albert Museum, London*). This oil sketch, done on paper measuring only $9\frac{1}{2} \times 7\frac{1}{8}$ inches, was one of a number done by Constable of a favourite Suffolk scene, 'the little farmhouse on the edge of the river, close to Flatford Mill'. The cottage is still to be seen.

least allowed the survival of the essentially medieval wool town, which was fossilized for the admiration of later generations. The medieval timber-framed buildings seldom gave way to Georgian brick houses and façades, as happened at Thaxted (q.v.) and Dedham (q.v.).

The church of St Peter and St Paul stands on the site of a 14th-c church, the chancel of which was incorporated into the new building, financed by a partnership between the Earls of Oxford and the wealthy clothier families of Spring and Branch. It was built between 1444 and 1525, when the cloth industry was at its height, and provides an imposing monument to Lavenham's former wealth. The tower of flint and Barnack stone is a landmark for miles around, rearing upwards for 141ft, and there is a legend that it would have been higher had not the master mason fallen off the top. This may or not be the case, but the tower lacks battlements and has an unfinished appearance. After work on the tower ended there was a lull in building, to allow the enormous structure to settle. Visitors to the church who have a head for heights can climb the tower for a small charge and obtain a magnificent view of the village beneath. Thomas Spring, who along with his father had helped to finance the tower, was apparently so proud of his newly awarded coat of arms that he had his arms engraved on the tower 36 times. The church contains numerous memorials to the family of the Earls of Oxford, the De Veres, who owned the manor from the Conquest until the 16th c. These include the emblems of the boar, a pun on the family name as *verres* is Latin for boar, and the star, awarded to the arms of De Vere after crusader Albericke de Vere recaptured the standard of St George from the Saracens. Unfortunately, like Clare (q.v.) and Walberswick, Lavenham did not escape the attention of the Puritan William Dowsing, who smashed all the glass. The coloured glass now is Victorian.

Apart from its motor traffic, the village is unspoilt, and credit is due to the Post Office for the removal of posts and wires in 1967. The Swan Hotel at the bottom of the hill is a fine example of timber-framing from the reigns of two Elizabeths, for some of the work was accomplished during a 1965 extension, when the old building technique was retained. One of Lavenham's three guild halls is now an extension at the back of the Swan (where notable music recitals are often given). The Corpus Christi guild hall in the market place was built in the early 16th c, when Lavenham received its charter from John de Vere, and it has since served the town as guild hall, prison, workhouse, almshouse, and wool store. Now, in the ownership of the National Trust, it acts as a community centre. The cross in the market place has stood there since 1502. The 15th-c Woolstaplers in Prentice Street was the home of Lavenham's last surviving wool merchant, and the De Vere House on Water Street is of a similar date. It stands on the site of the Saxon village and has recently been restored, following its destruction by vandals. Lavenham contains many other buildings that are worthy of mention, including several Tudor shops, with their original windows, and the old grammar school. Were it not for the traffic, the visitor could well imagine that he or she had been transported back to the late Middle Ages (*see illustration on page 26*).

(*see illustration on page 26*)

LINTON, *Cambridgeshire*, 6m N of Saffron Walden. This large and linear village has some small claims to modern fame as the home of the remarkable psychic Matthew Manning, and the establishment of a vineyard which produces one of the good new English wines. The village also harbours a small zoo. Unlike many of the larger East Anglian villages, Linton does not show signs of great former prosperity, and the houses lining the street which plunges down towards the River Granta and then up again are mainly of humble proportions. However, the neighbourhood was well-peopled in prehistoric times and an Iron Age settlement which stood less than $\frac{1}{2}$m to the SE of the station has yielded bone-weaving tools, pottery and traces of grain-storage pits and a rectangular siderable settlement in that era.

The church of St Mary incorporates the three styles of medieval church building. The EE style is apparent in the S arcade and tower, the Dec in the N arcade and chancel arch, and the Perp in the chancel chapels and the porches. Inside there is a brass of the armoured figure of Henry Paris who died in 1427 and a monument to Sir John Millicent who died in 1577. The village contains a number of picturesque houses and vistas. Chaundlers, on High Street, a timber-framed house which displays a pargeted front, is probably the best building. The Bell Inn beside it is a homely timber-framed building of the 16th c. To the N of the church the Trinity Guild Hall with its overhanging upper floor is another pleasant building of similar age. The village college, built in 1938 to the design of S. E. Unwin, is said to have had an important influence on modern school architecture. At Little Linton nearby can be seen Cambridgeshire's only example of a clapper stile; well-maintained, it has three rails which pivot downwards to assist the passage between the fields.

Journeying towards Cambridge on A604, the traveller will pass the famous Wandlebury hill fort, which crowns the Gog Magog hills. This enormous fort is less obvious than many others of its kind as the area has been emparked and forested. The area is open to the public, however, and among the towering deciduous trees can be seen the broad encircling ditch, 1000ft in diameter, with a second less prominent bank and ditch set inside the outer defences – a later addition when the defences may have been reactivated to meet the threat of Belgic tribes advancing from the S. It is held on quite good authority that until the area was emparked in the 18th c an ancient figure of a giant was engraved upon the Gog Magog chalk slopes. A crude representation of the figure of a giant is scratched on stone in Sawston Church, and the locality abounds in myths and legends.

LONG MELFORD, *Suffolk*, is justifiably one of the most popular villages in England, but unlike many of its competitors it is sufficiently spacious to be able to cope with its tourist traffic. The 'Melford' part of the name means 'ford by the mill', and 'Long' will require no explanation to anyone who has walked the length of the main street. The site was occupied first by a Romano-British village.

Long Melford was one of a number of East Anglian towns which rose with the fortunes of the medieval cloth industry. Until the 14th c East Anglia exported raw wool, and the growth of the cloth industry was stimulated by the settlement of Flemish weavers, refugees who settled in Long Melford in the 14th c. The village grew rich during the cloth boom of the 15th c. The industry survived in Long Melford during the 17th c, when it declined in many other East Anglian villages, but decayed in the following century. The great days of Long Melford as a centre of a leading English industry were over; but, unlike Lavenham, the village was a river port and saw some Georgian and Victorian prosperity, and consequently its medieval appearance was not fossilized. Although it still retains some small industries and attracts large numbers of tourists, Long Melford, with its enormous green and parish church, has the atmosphere of a village rather than a town.

There are several noteworthy buildings, but pride of place must go to the church of the Holy Trinity which, despite its largely 20th-c tower, has a claim to be the finest village church in England. The church is built of 'flushwork', of knapped flints sandwiched in a stone framework, and with its 97 windows the church fairly sparkles in the sunlight. Unlike many churches, it is not the accumulation of many stages of building. It was erected between 1460 and 1496 in the Perp style, with the wealthy Clopton family whose memorials are found throughout the church as the leading benefactors. The original tower was struck by lightning in 1709 and replaced by a discordant brick tower in 1725. In 1903 this tower was encased in stone and although some writers have criticized the new tower as being inspired more by Oxford than by Suffolk most onlookers will find it in harmony with the body of the church. Much of the original glass has been lost and the mistakes of an earlier attempt at reconstruction have recently been corrected. With the church built in the glasshouse style of the late Perp, the interior is light and airy and equally as impressive as the exterior.

The church is approached past the Trinity Hospital which was erected as almshouses in 1573 and reconstructed in 1847. The building looks out over the vast sloping green, formerly the place of a horse-trading fair and a resting place for gypsies. Facing the church across long acres of green is Long Melford Hall (see illustration on page 47). Built c. 1560, the hall incorporates the vaults of the hunting lodge used by the Abbots of Bury St Edmunds before the dissolution of the monastery. It passed to William Cordell, a crafty lawyer who became speaker of the House of Commons. He entertained Queen Elizabeth at his new hall in 1578 in a unique display of wealth, when he had a

Frederick Bantick
The 'wodewose' in the Bull at Long Melford

retinue of 2000 men on hand to greet her. The house has been occupied by members of the Hyde Parker family since 1786 and is now a National Trust property. The remains of the moat can be seen to the S of the house, along with some ornamental topiary. Similar octagonal towers to those at Melford Hall can be seen at Kentwell Hall, which was the home of the Clopton family; this hall is also moated and a distinctive feature is a mile-long avenue of limes planted in 1678. It is about ½m N of the church, and obviously a number of features are common to the two halls in Long Melford. Which influenced which is uncertain, but Kentwell Hall may well be a little older. At least there is no doubt as to the origin of Long Melford Hall, for the pit in the green from which the clay for the bricks was dug can still be seen.

Although it echoes the style of Long Melford Hall, the school opposite dates from 1860 and took over a function which had been performed for centuries in the Lady Chapel of the church. The Bull on the main street has been an inn for 400 years; the building dates from around 1450 and contains a number of carved beams including one which shows the traditional East Anglian figure of a wodewose or wild man of the woods.

MELDRETH, *Cambridgeshire*. The most remarkable features of this pleasant little village can easily be missed by the traveller; they are the stocks and whipping post which, well preserved, lurk in the shadows of the spreading chestnut tree at the road junction. Beside the stocks there can also be seen the stone base of an ancient praying cross. Close by stands the church of the Holy Trinity which has a Norman chancel built of clunch rubble; the tower, made of the same material, is in the Trans style, and the nave and aisles are in the Dec and Perp styles. Stained glass depicting the figure of St John and dating from early in the 14th c can be seen in the head of a window in the chancel.

The village of **Shepreth,** 1m or so NE, has yielded on a mound which rises from a marsh numerous fragments of flint implements which suggest New Stone Age occupation. From the late-Saxon period these and other lands around were owned by the nunnery at Chatteris; and Manor Farm, which has a partly 15th-c interior, was one of the possessions. The church of All Saints, like the church at Meldreth, has Norman work in the chancel; but this building is a mixture, and virtually every century from the 12th is represented.

MOULTON, *Suffolk*. This otherwise unremarkable village in the racehorse training countryside around Newmarket is given distinction by its possession of two 15th-c flint bridges, one of them a splendid four-arched packhorse bridge spanning the shrunken River Kennet. The church of St Peter has a rather spartan appearance but was judged by Pevsner to be over-restored. There are Norman nook-shafts on the S side of the nave, and the tower dates from the late 13th c. N of the tower there are the remains of an anchorite's cell.

5m N, across the border in Cambridgeshire, is the village of **Chippenham** which was laid out for Lord Orford in the early 18th c, and stands outside the park gates. So rustic is the appearance of the colour-washed cottages that only the regularly alternating cottage styles and roof heights betray the planned origins of the village, which still retains its pump at the road junction (*see illustration on page 60*). The school dates from 1712.

NAYLAND, *Suffolk*, charmingly located in a willow-flanked loop of the River Stour on the Suffolk–Essex border, is one of the numerous villages in the region which owed its former prosperity to the cloth trade. The village seems to focus on Alston Court, an adventurous building situated at the S end of a lane which connects it with the church. The core of the building appears to date from around 1480 and comprises the E wing where bricknogging infills the exposed timbers. The plastered front is dominated by an enormous hooded doorway of early 18th-c date, and there is a vast 16th-c nine-light window.

The church of St James received numerous generous endowments from wealthy clothiers, and is largely Perp although the 14th-c tower is topped by brickwork which dates from 1834. The ornate stone porch to the tower was built in 1525 as the gift of the prosperous clothier William Abell, and the more modest N porch was the result of an endowment of about a century earlier. In addition to its rich brasses, plate and linenfold panelling of earlier ages, the church is able to boast an altar painting of Christ blessing bread and wine by no less an artist than John Constable, completed in 1809.

In Church Street can be seen a Georgian obelisk milestone standing close to Alston Court and the village has a liberal sprinkling of fine timber-framed buildings including the White House, the Queen's Head, with its coaching yard, and the Butcher's Arms. These and other old buildings combine with the old bridge and Stour-side setting to produce a most appealing vista.

NEW HOUGHTON, *Norfolk*, 8m W of Fakenham. Many English villages have had to give way to the makers of grand parks. Some of the victims of emparking were lucky, and a new custom-built village was set up to take the place of the old. This was the case at Houghton, where the white cottages lining the road leading to the hall and park all date from 1729. When the old village went down, the medieval church of St Martin was left stranded in the park; it had obtained a new tower about the time of the destruction of old Houghton and went on to experience a rebuilding in Victorian times which largely transformed it. The new village of four-bay two-storey cottages, with pyramidal roofs, was completed with the addition of one-storeyed almshouses and two model farmhouses.

Houghton Hall was built between 1722 and 1735 to designs by Campbell and Ripley, with an interior and furnishings by Kent. The owner was no less than King George's prime minister, Sir Robert Walpole. The park is the home of a herd of white deer.

Great Massingham, 2m S, presents a complete contrast, and has a much more timeless atmosphere as it encircles a green whose ponds may be the fish ponds of an Augustinian Priory established in the early 13th c. Remains of the priory are contained in Abbey House, which only dates from the 19th c but includes a medieval doorway, lancet window and buttress. The outstanding feature of the church of St Mary is the beautiful 13th-c S porch with a roof of arched braces to collar beams. Inside the church there are a 14th-c font and a 15th-c screen, and fragments of original medieval stained glass can be seen in the tracery of the chancel.

NORTH ELMHAM, *Norfolk* (5m N of East Dereham), is remarkable because it contains the remnants of a Saxon cathedral. From the late 7th c to the mid-8th c the Bishop of Norfolk resided at North Elmham and there may have been a wooden cathedral or church here at this time. The see lapsed, until it was revived around AD 955; about 1078 it was transferred to Thetford, which was then one of the largest towns in England, finally becoming rooted in Norwich in 1096. The cathedral ruins are jumbled among those of a moated medieval manor house, but the outlines of the stone cathedral, which dates from about 50 years before the Conquest, can be clearly traced. The builders used blocks of conglomerate, an unusual choice of building stone. There was a rugged W tower with a stair turret, a semi-circular apse, the probable location of the bishop's throne, a transept with square towers in the angles of the nave and transept, and neither aisles nor chancel. In 1388 Bishop Despencer, presumably having been disturbed by the Peasants' Revolt a few years before, obtained a licence to build a fortified house among the cathedral ruins; a deep moat was dug, the walls were lined and partitioned with flint and rubble, and a hall was raised above the nave. The castle building was never completed. There was probably an earlier castle of the motte-and-bailey type in the neighbourhood on Tower Hills.

The church of St Mary is a 14th-c building with a tower of the 15th c and a 16th-c chancel. Norman work can be found inside, and probably represents the remains of an older church. Some of the original stained glass is preserved in the window tracery; the pulpit was built by Francis Floyd, the parish clerk, in 1626. On the dado of the rood screen there are paintings of 19 saints.

Swanton Morley, 3m S, was the ancestral home of the Lincoln family, of which Abraham Lincoln was a direct descendant. The Angel Inn was built as a family home by Richard Lincoln in 1616. He disinherited his eldest son who moved to Hingham and sent his son Samuel as an apprentice to a local weaver. When the weaver decided to emigrate to America in 1637, Samuel and two of his brothers went with him, to join Robert Peck, who served as vicar both at the Norfolk **Hingham** and at the new village of Hingham, Massachusetts, founded by people from the Norfolk village.

OLD BUCKENHAM, *Norfolk* (3m S of Attleborough), with its thatched church, vast green, windmill and castle remains, should satisfy the most exacting of village connoisseurs, while it is said that the cricketer Jack Hobbs rated the pitch at Old Buckenham Hall, with its imported Australian turf, as his favourite.

The castle earthworks are the oldest feature in the village. The rectangular embankments were probably constructed by the Romans, and within these earthworks a Norman castle was built. Only the castle mound and some fragmentary ruins near Abbey Farm remain, for in 1146 William d'Albini donated it to the Augustinians for use as a quarry for building materials for a priory. This too perished, and only rubble marks its traces. The green is of gigantic proportion, and the straggling clusters of cottages surrounding it form little nucleations with enchanting names like Cake Street, Hog's Snout, Puddledock and Loss Wroo.

The church of All Saints has Norman work in the N doorway and carstone of the W wall, while the polygonal tower, nave and chancel are in the Dec style. Whitened, thatched and with roses in the churchyard, the church is a delight to the eye.

When William d'Albini gave his old castle to the Augustinians he built a new one at **New Buckenham,** 2m SE. Although demolished in the 1640s, this castle is of considerable historical interest as the first English example of a round keep. There is a possibility that this castle, too, was built within Roman earthworks. A square gatehouse was added around 1200, joining the keep with the E bailey, while at some time during the 13th c a larger gatehouse was built to the W, the ramparts were made higher, and an additional bailey was made. The two-storeyed keep rose to around 40ft and had walls that were 10ft thick. Although it has lost its chancel, the 12th-c chapel survives as an outbuilding of a house.

The interest of New Buckenham does not end here, for in complete contrast to the random organization of Old Buckenham it is a rare example of a planned medieval settlement with a grid-iron street pattern, although experts disagree as to whether the planned layout is early- or late-medieval. The polygonal 17th-c Market House stands in the remains of the old market place; the upper floor is supported on wooden Tuscan columns, and the middle column served as a whipping post. Angels, harts, a gatehouse and heraldic shields are carved on the boards.

OVERY STAITHE, *Norfolk* (4m W of Wells-next-the-Sea), was probably built as a port after silting and a receding sea resulted in the loss of navigation at the upstream village of Burnham Overy. In the early 19th c Overy Staithe was a bustling little port, handling schooners, barges and brigs. But the coming of the railways wiped out its coastal traffic and the village was left with only an agricultural role, although today it attracts a number of small-boat sailors. The granaries and maltings are in the care of the National Trust. The truncated church, with its reduced Norman tower, reflects the changing fortunes of the village.

Burnham Overy, 1m upstream, displays both a windmill (1814) and a watermill (1737), with a three-storey brick-built miller's house. The church of St Clement at Burnham Overy has a Norman central tower, lowered and capped with a pretty cupola in the 17th c. The broken shaft and the remains of the base of an old churchyard cross can be seen to the W of the church.

Burnham Thorpe, 1m or so SE, is famous as the birthplace of Horatio, Lord Nelson. A local legend tells that Nelson's mother began to give birth while taking a drive in a pony cart, and, as she was unable to reach the vicarage, Nelson was born in the huge flint barn beside the pub. The barn may have begun its life as a warehouse in days when The Burn was navigable by barges at high tide. The old vicarage has been demolished, but Nelson memorabilia are displayed in the church, which is some distance from the village and may be flanked by the buried remains of cottages from a deserted village.

Seven villages, all containing 'Burnham' in their name cluster closely together, reflecting the medieval prosperity of this part of Norfolk. **Brancaster,** 4m W of Overy Staithe, was the site of a Roman fort built to defend the coast against Saxon invasion. The fort stood on Rack Hill; there is little to see today except the outlines of the large enclosure and the remains of the earth rampart.

PAKENHAM, *Suffolk* (6m NE of Bury St Edmunds), is best known now for its splendid towering windmill, but there is a very long history

New Buckenham, Norfolk, seen from the Market House

of settlement here. Late neolithic pottery, a Late
Bronze Age barrow and the remains of Roman
pottery kilns have all been discovered here, as
well as the remains of a Saxon settlement.

The mill is of the tower type and is *c*. 1820; it has
a tarred brick tower five storeys high, four sails
and a fantail, although the gallery running around
the cap is a recent addition. An enthusiastic owner
has been assisted in his preservation efforts by a
grant from the Historic Buildings Council, and
the milling machinery is in working order; the
village also has a watermill.

The church of St Mary has a Norman nucleus of
Barnack stone consisting of a nave, central space
and transept; the upper part of the tower is octagonal and 14th-c; the N transept was added in
the mid-19th c. Inside there is a very fine medieval
font with four figures carved around the stem, and
a dragon, unicorn, pelican and lamb are seen
against the bowl.

Newe House has an attractive Jacobean brick
façade of 1622; it is a symmetrical building with
three Dutch gables and mullioned and transomed
windows. It is locally famous for its previous
owner, 'American Reeve', a local smallholder who
ran away to the USA to become a buffalo hunter
and then a rancher and sheep herder, making his
fortune and returning to Pakenham to buy the big
house. Although snubbed by the gentry he was
popular in the village and is said to have shot at
bottles with his sixgun to entertain the village lads.

Roman remains abound in the local fields; a
villa lies in the grounds of Redcastle Farm; a
small fort is thought to lie near Mickle Mere; and
a section of Roman brickwork has been uncovered
on the track 600ft S of the church.

PAPWORTH ST AGNES, *Cambridgeshire,*
5m S of Huntingdon. The somewhat isolated
village of Papworth St Agnes is in a decline, as the
deserted cottages and spreading giant hogweed
show. The visitor may be taken by surprise by the
small factory-like building which stands upon a
grassy triangle in the road junction. It is a relic of
the old communal life, a 19th-c bakehouse built
for use by all the villagers and a reminder of the not
too distant days before gas and electric ovens – or
sometimes any oven at all – became standard
cottage fittings. It carries a Victorian letter box.

The strange church of St John is losing its roof
and the unusual chequered building in stone and
flint includes fragments of 14th- and 16th-c work,
but is essentially Victorian. Weeds are growing in
the moat of the manor, which is of a stone-and-
brick construction uncommon in the area. It was
built by Sir William Malory who died in 1586 and
was a descendant of Sir Thomas Malory whose
Morte d'Arthur did much to perpetuate the
Arthurian legend. The interior includes rich
plasterwork, particularly the Malory arms on the
hall ceiling, and the original dovecote still stands.

To the NW, but formerly across the boundary
in Huntingdonshire, are the Offords. **Offord Cluny,**
as its name suggests, once belonged to the Cluniac
order, but the name of **Offord Darcy** is misleading,
an aggrandization of the real name Offord Daneys.
Both the merging villages have churches and
manors; the spired church of Offord Darcy
includes much Norman work and that of Offord
Cluny, where six carved figures support the roof
of the nave, is of the 13th c. The Cluny manor is a
large 18th-c brick building, and that in Darcy was
built in 1613 as a two-storeyed timber-framed

building. Not grand enough for its 18th-c occupants, it was provided with a façade of three
storeys, the upper windows being quite useless.
The Three Horseshoes in Darcy dates from 1626
and was formerly a farmhouse. On the lane to
Buckden there stands a medieval stone bridge with
a watermill close by. At **Toseland,** 3m SW of Papworth, is a remarkable isolated Tudor farmhouse
with three brick bays, mullioned windows and
clusters of octagonal chimneys.

SILVER END, *Essex* (4m SE of Braintree), is
included as a reminder that not all English villages
have their origins shrouded in the mists of time.
The village expresses a vision by F. H. Crittall,
whose firm produced metal house fittings at
Braintree. Faced with the need to expand, Crittall,
rather than attaching an industrial suburb to an
existing town, chose to create a new village where
his firm's products could be prominently displayed. The result was Silver End, a village of
uncompromisingly box-like homes in the International Modern style, interspersed with rows of
houses built in brick to a neo-Georgian design. To
add to the incongruity, the editor of. *The Studio*
magazine provided a design for a thatched church.
While we may question the degree to which the
village harmonizes with the Essex landscape,
every provision was made for the convenience of
its community, with a shopping arcade, bank,
school, public garden and playing fields all featur-
ing in the design. Built during the late 1920s,
Silver End is a recent expression of a spirit of
radical Nonconformist paternalism in village
building which extends back through the 19th c.

SOMERLEYTON, *Suffolk,* 5m NW of Lowestoft. While the main events in the lives of many
villages may be lost in the mists of time Somerleyton presents no such problems. The village is
largely the product of a fortune made from railway
construction. The man responsible was Samuel
Morton Peto (who also provided most of Lowestoft harbour, and the Reform Club and Nelson's
Column in London). His architect was John
Thomas, best known as a sculptor, a favourite of
Prince Albert, and the carver of many of the
statues in the House of Commons. Peto bought the
manor of Somerleyton in 1844, and set about the
reconstruction of the old village and Hall. The
village is described by Pevsner as 'weird', and is
thought to have been inspired by Nash's Blaise
Hamlet near Bristol. It has a square green which is
railed and an iron pump of 1857. The school is
a mock-Tudor building, and the cottages, some
thatched, are of brick and sham timber-framing,
and occur in a bizarre range of designs.

The church of St Mary retains its 15th-c tower
of flint but was otherwise remodelled by Thomas,
and echoes local stone-and-flint church designs. It
has a 15th-c font with a 17th-c cover; it has four
lions on the stem and four angels around the bowl;
the 15th-c screen reveals 16 painted figures. A
former owner of the Hall, Sir Thomas Gernegan,
is commemorated in the 16th-c tomb chest.

The original Elizabethan and Queen Anne hall
was thoroughly rebuilt by Thomas, although the
shaped gables of the original house can be detected, and Queen Anne panelling is preserved in
the staircase hall. Thomas contributed an Itali-
ate tower, and in general the style adopted inside
and out is sham-Jacobean. When the house was
complete in 1857 it was highly praised in the
Illustrated London News, particular mention being
made of the scene of enchantment created when
the gas jets were lit. Later writers have been less
generous in their praise. In 1866 Peto's firm went
bankrupt and the house was bought by Sir Francis
Crossley. In partnership with Thomas, Peto left
behind a house and village which, while being far
removed from what some modern connoisseurs
would hope to find in the Suffolk countryside,
present an unusual contrast with the older houses
and villages of the county.

STEEPLE BUMPSTEAD, *Essex,* 2½m S of
Haverhill. This quaintly named village nestles in
the Essex-Suffolk borderlands. The church of St
Mary has an 11th-c core which is preserved in the
lower stages of the W tower. The remainder of the
church belongs to the 14th and 15th c, apart from
the Tudor brick upper section of the tower, the
clerestory and S porch, which are of the 16th c. On
the chancel door is a copy of an 8th-c Irish bronze
gilt boss, the original of which was sold by the
church and is now in the British Museum; it may
have found its way to Steeple Bumpstead as part of
a hoard of Viking plunder.

Moyns Park, 1m E of the church, is a gabled
Tudor brick building dating from *c.* 1580, and to
the rear is a timber-framed wing of around 1520.

The most interesting building in the village is the
Moot Hall which stands isolated at the road junction near the church. It appears to be a replica of
the Thaxted Guild Hall and the ground-floor
timber arcades were originally open. During the
17th c it served as a village school, and it is now
used by the parish council; it was restored by the
villagers as part of the 1977 Jubilee celebrations.

Beside the churchyard can be seen a cramped
19th-c brick-walled and slate-roofed lock-up.

STOKE-BY-NAYLAND, *Suffolk,* owes its
impressive air to the cloth trade, and the fame of its
magnificent church (*see illustration on page 14*)
partly to the paintings by John Constable in the
Victoria and Albert Museum. The church is in the
Perp style, with many fine brasses to the Howard
family, who were ancestors of two of the wives of
Henry VIII, Catherine Howard and Anne Boleyn.
The timber-framed maltings by the church is in
the care of the National Trust, as is the guild hall.
There are two grand old inns, the Black Horse and
The Crown, while Gifford's Hall, 2m NE of the
village, is a Tudor courtyard house with the
remains of a chapel of St Nicholas in its grounds.
On the way to Gifford's Hall one passes through
Scotland Street, which is lined with well-preserved
timber-framed and plastered houses. Leaving
Stoke-by-Nayland by the road to the SE one passes

Tendring Park, whose great house, Tendring Hall, built by Sir John Soane, has now been demolished, and comes to Thorington Hall, a 16th-c house with 18th-c additions. It now belongs to the National Trust but is privately occupied.

THAXTED, *Essex*. Even in a part of England so rich in small towns and villages Thaxted is outstandingly interesting. The Saxon name *Thec stede* denotes a place where thatching is found, and probably refers to reeds. The Saxon village at Thaxted was clustered around a small stream in the lower part of the village in the area of Copthall Lane, and recent excavations have discovered the traces of a Roman road nearby. The Saxon manor stood overlooking the peasant huts on the slopes of the hill where the church now stands.

During the Middle Ages Thaxted became important for its cutlery industry, and a community of cutlers was established beside the manor entrance, at the W end of the present Town Street. The manor rolls were destroyed during the peasant uprising of 1381 and the manor seems to have disappeared about this time; perhaps this represented a victory for the burgesses in an attempt to free themselves from feudal control. Thaxted does not appear to have had any special advantages as a base for the cutlery industry; nevertheless the Poll Tax Return of 1381 lists 79 cutlers, 11 smiths, four shethers and two goldsmiths; so obviously during the Middle Ages it was a place of great importance. As no iron is to be found in the area it is possible that knives and swords were brought to Thaxted for finishing. The cutlery industry declined towards the end of the Middle Ages, and the award of borough status to Thaxted in 1556, when the town was said to be in 'great Ruine and decay', may have been an attempt to restore prosperity, although the charter was extinguished in 1686, by which time Thaxted had established itself in its present role as a small market centre.

The village is still dominated by its hilltop medieval church of St John the Baptist, St Mary and St Lawrence. There were two churches in early medieval Thaxted. One, dedicated to St Catherine, stood on the hill where Rails Farm now stands; the other, nearby, provided a nucleus around which the present church was built between 1340 and 1510. The church is one of a number in England which have been described as being 'the finest parish church in England'. At least it is the finest in Essex. Its size and decoration reflect the wealth of the medieval cutlers and the patronage of the powerful de Clare family who owned the manor. The S aisle and nave appear to be the oldest parts of the building, followed by the S porch, the N transept and N aisle and then the tower and spire, which date from about 1475. The former church probably provided support and allowed services to proceed uninterrupted during the construction of the larger church. Part of the spire was struck by lightning and collapsed in 1814, and was rebuilt in 1822. There is a wealth of carving in both stone and wood. Gargoyles, a frieze of small animals, and heraldic emblems decorate the exterior.

Richard Muir

The Guild Hall at Thaxted

The magnificent guild hall which, with the church rearing on the hill behind, dominated Town Street, was built by the cutlers *c.* 1390. Inside the posts in the open ground floor was a stone-floored market area, and a second market was found on the floor above. The top floor was occupied by the guild warden. After the decline of the cutlery industry the building served as a town hall, and its subsequent history was chequered. It was restored in Georgian style in 1714, and accommodated a grammar school until 1878. It experienced a fearsome restoration in 1910, when the Georgian plaster was removed to expose the timber frame, and arches were introduced between the first-floor windows. During the restoration in 1975 the first floor was adapted as a council room.

Thaxted contains a wealth of memorable buildings, of which only a few can be mentioned. Walking S from the church, a group of almshouses can be seen. The thatched building on the left was built as a Priests' House, then served as four almshouses until it became derelict and was converted into a single dwelling in the 1930s. The almshouses to the right date from 1714, and the renovation of 1975 which provided homes for three elderly couples won a Heritage Year Certificate of Merit. The windmill which can be seen from the almshouses was built in 1804 on the site of an earlier mill and gave 100 years of service. By the 1960s it was in an advanced state of disrepair but a steady programme of restoration by a Windmill Trust has resulted in an excellent reconstruction, which will be completed with the addition of sails. The machinery of the upper floors is intact and the mill is open to the public. A rural museum occupies the lower floor.

Thaxted contains a number of houses which are much older than they appear to be and a number of timber frames are concealed by plasterwork façades of the Georgian period. One of the towering 15th-c jettied houses on Stoney Lane, which leads from the guild hall to the churchyard, is known as Dick Turpin's House. There is no known connection with the famous highwayman, but he was born only a few miles away, at Hempstead. Clarence House was built in 1715 and has a superb Queen Anne doorway; built as a private house it is now a Further Education centre.

Described by Sir John Betjeman as having few equals in England in terms of beauty, compactness and juxtaposition of medieval and Georgian architecture, Thaxted is also a tribute to what thoughtful conservation can achieve.

THORNEY, *Cambridgeshire,* 6m E of Peterborough. Before the drainage of the Fens in the 18th and 19th c Fenland villages were few and far between and had rather isolated existences perched on ridges or mounds which stood above the surrounding marshlands. These villages, whose names often include the element '-ey', denoting islands, were the homes of resourceful and independently minded farmers, shepherds and fishers who are still known as 'Fen Tigers'. Thorney is a typical example of a Fen island village. Various recent changes in administrative boundaries have caused it to shuttle between the Isle of Ely, Huntingdonshire and Peterborough, and now it is in Cambridgeshire. It is thought that the abbot of Medeshamstede (Peterborough) established a community of anchorites here sometime around AD 660, and a Saxon monastery here was destroyed by the Danish invaders a century later. A monastery was re-established here by St Ethelwold before the Conquest and given over to the Benedictine order, the Normans replacing the wooden buildings with ones of stone in the first years of the 12th c. After the Dissolution the buildings fell into ruin except for the church, which was colonized by the villagers, who had no church of their own. Two turrets stand among the accumulation of work of the 15th, 17th and 19th c.

Most of the present village is the product of a 19th-c Duke of Bedford, whose family did so much to transform the Fenland landscape. It is a thoroughly planned estate village, providing good accommodation for the estate workers, functional and attractive, but with a very strange building in Tank Yard, which is five storeys in height. There was a water tank which supplied the community on the top floor, while below was a chamber which received the village sewage *en route* for disposal – a strange and seemingly unhygienic combination.

THORPENESS, *Suffolk,* 2m N of Aldeburgh. Although there is a long history of occupation in this area, as the round barrows in the nearby heathland testify, Thorpeness is a relatively modern village with an unusual background. It is a planned holiday resort, the creation of the writer G. S. Ogilvie. While the mock-Tudor architecture is generally restrained, the intention was to re-create the atmosphere of Merrie England. There are very few comparable purpose-built resorts to be found anywhere in England.

Work began with the construction of The Meare, an artificial lake covering 65 acres. Then the nucleus of the resort was built, comprising The Dunes, The Haven, The Whinlands, The Benthills and the Country Club. After World War I building took place on the N side of The Meare. In 1928 the attractive group of almshouses was built; the Dolphin Inn is perhaps the most appealing building, but there is no doubt that the strangest is the House In The Clouds. This is an elaborate attempt to mask the water tower. A real dwelling is built into the structure. The early 19th-c post mill was moved to Thorpeness from nearby Aldringham and was converted from its original role as a corn mill into that of a waterpump. The church of St Mary was provided in 1936.

WALBERSWICK, *Suffolk* (1½m S of Southwold), whose name dates from the Dark Ages and means 'Walhbert's farm', nestles on a gently sloping cliff beside the artificial 17th-c channel of the River Blyth. When in the 14th c storms choked the harbour of Dunwich, which lies 5m S, Walberswick took over much of the Dunwich trade and developed an important fishing industry. In due course the industry declined, in the face of coastal changes, the reduced consumption of fish which followed the general adoption of the Protestant faith, and later, the centralization of the industry in a few large ports. Doubtless smuggling too played a part in the former prosperity of Walberswick, which is reflected in the massive and partly derelict church. The village is now the home of a small colony of artists and is a largely unspoilt small tourist resort. A Bailey bridge across the Blyth once carried the light railway which ran from Southwold to Halesworth 8m away.

The church of St Andrew, which stands on higher ground overlooking the coastal village, has a tower which dates from 1426, and the body of the church was built about 70 years later. The original contract for the building of the church by local masons, Adam Powle and Richard Russel, still survives, along with instructions that the W door and windows should be modelled on those at Halesworth church, and the tower should be like the one at Tunstall. The prosperity which supported the building of this mighty church did not last. The church suffered at the hands of Cromwell's iconoclast, William Dowsing, in 1643, when the windows and tombs were smashed. Shortly after, the village was in decline and the remaining Walberswick families petitioned to have part of the building closed down, leaving only the S aisle and tower in use.

The journey by car to Southwold across the River Blyth involves a lengthy detour via **Blythburgh,** another village which can look back to former glories as a port and fishing town. Like Southwold and Walberswick, Blythburgh experienced a series of very destructive fires during the 17th c. Early in the Middle Ages an Augustinian priory stood at Blythburgh, but little remains of it today. Like Walberswick, Blythburgh had inherited an overlarge church. The

Edwin Smith

The church of the Holy Trinity, Blythburgh: one of the most impressive in Suffolk

spire fell in a storm in 1577 when a sermon was being preached, and a number of the congregation were killed or injured. The church only dates from the 15th c but its size and the height of its tower make it one of the most impressive in Suffolk. There is a Jacobean pulpit and the bench-ends are carved with seated or kneeling figures representing not merely human beings engaged in various activities but also vices such as gluttony and pride. Now an old people's hospital, Bulcamp workhouse stands on the site of a Dark Age battle at which King Anna and his son fell. During the 17th c a Dutch community was invited to Blythburgh to

straighten the river and reclaim marshland. The White Hart, with its Dutch gables, echoes the contacts between East Anglia and the Low Countries.

WALSINGHAM, *Norfolk*, 5m N of Fakenham. Little Walsingham is larger than its neighbour, Great Walsingham, and of much greater historical importance for it was the target of one of medieval England's most important pilgrimages. According to the legend, in the early 12th c the widow de Faverches saw a vision of the house of the annunciation in Nazareth and was directed by Mary to memorize the house and build a replica in Norfolk.

Kenneth Scowen

Worstead, Norfolk

The site for the building was revealed by dry patches in a dewy field; the wrong patch was chosen and the house would not rest on its foundations until it was moved to a second dry patch. Then a small stone church was built around the wooden replica. Soon the legend sprang up that the spirit of Mary had deserted the Holy Land, which was overrun by infidels, and had taken up residence in Norfolk. In any event, **Little Walsingham** began to attract pilgrims from Britain and also from the Continent. In the 12th c the Augustinians set up a priory, and the Franciscans followed with a friary in 1347, both of which prospered until the Reformation when they were demolished. The largest survival of the priory is the gatehouse, which consists of two slender towers supporting an arch, while one chamber of the priory has been built into a house and its vaulted ceiling is still preserved. The friary stood outside the village on the road to Houghton; two cloisters and parts of the living quarters remain, but there is little left of the church. In 1921 Anglo-Catholic sponsorship produced a new statue of the Virgin, based on an old likeness of the original Little Walsingham statue, and in 1938, when a new shrine and brick church were completed, the statue was placed inside. The walls are set with stonework from many ruined churches and the shrine has become a focus for Anglo-Catholic pilgrimage.

The great priory gatehouse stands at the E side of the High Street and the village has a number of attractive old houses, a 16th-c octagonal pump house set atop with a beacon brazier in Common Place, and a market. There is an old grammar school and the College of Priests. The church of St Mary was sadly gutted by fire in 1961 and restoration work has been carried out on the interior. The N chapel contains Epstein's statue of the Risen Christ. The exterior displays good 14th- and 15th-c work.

Pilgrims approaching Little Walsingham from the S showed their devotion and humility by completing the last mile of their journey barefoot, leaving their footwear at the slipper chapel at Houghton St Giles, a small 14th-c building which was restored and reopened as a Roman Catholic chapel in 1934, providing a nucleus for religious activities which are held in the surrounding area.

A little more than 1m W are **Great** and **Little Snoring.** The most interesting feature in the former village is the opulent early 16th-c rectory, with octagonal turrets and fancy Victorian chimneys. The medieval church of St Mary contains a large 17th-c commandment board with the Four Last Things – heaven, hell, death and judgment – as a warning. The Norman church at Little Snoring has a beautiful carved Norman font and a detached round tower which may be Saxon. Of the 170 or so round towers in England, Norfolk has 119. The reason for this lies partly in the intractable nature of flint as a building material. Where square corners are required they must be of freestone or brick built into the flint walls. A round tower has no corners and can consequently be built entirely of flint. Edingthorpe is a good example.

WESTLETON, *Suffolk* (5m NE of Saxmundham), has an unusual thatched church in which the parishioners annually mount a flower festival, using only wild flowers. The village is also famous horticulturally for Fisk's nursery garden, which specializes in clematis. There are a number of fine buildings, mainly in brick, including the gabled Elizabethan Moor House, the Crown Inn, and the elegant early-19th-c Grange. There is a large green bordered by an avenue of lime trees beyond which is a large duckpond. The charming gardens of the White Horse Inn reach down to the pond, and visitors are often joined by hungry groups of ducklings. A summer fair is held on the green.

WEST STOW, *Suffolk*, 4m NW of Bury St Edmunds. About 1m from the present village can be seen not only the site of the first fully excavated English Anglo-Saxon village, but also an authentic and growing reconstruction of Saxon village buildings, such as existed near the site during the pagan Saxon period before AD 650. The setting is remote and beautiful, and the quality of the reconstruction, which is not officially open at the time of writing, superb. The original village was slowly abandoned early in the 7th c, and although the site was lightly ploughed in the early medieval period, the traces of the Saxon village were preserved when a sandstorm swept over the area around 1300.

The remains of 80 buildings were found, though not all will have been in use at the same time. The oldest huts dated from *c.* AD 400, overlapping the Roman occupation, and suggesting that the Saxon villagers, rather than being fearsome conquerors, came as the invited guests of the Romans or Romano-British people, and, that for a while, the Saxons coexisted with the villagers of a nearby British settlement. Two types of huts were found : sunken single-room wooden tent-like huts, which were apparently grouped around larger wooden halls. Roofs were of thatch, and the walls were of carefully joined split logs. There is little evidence of wattle-and-daub having been used. The site has provided much needed insights into the life-style and villages of our Saxon ancestors, and has yielded a number of objects including pottery, weaving implements, tools of iron, bronze and bone, and a beautiful brooch of bronze.

West Stow Hall has a remarkable three-storey brick gatehouse dating from the 1520s, and bearing the coat of arms of Mary Tudor. The turrets have double trefoil tops and brick pinnacles. The side of the gatehouse is timber-framed with brick-nogging. In a room above the gatehouse is an Elizabethan wall painting of the Four Ages of Man.

WHITTLESFORD, *Cambridgeshire* (6m S of Cambridge), like several of the villages nearby, including Duxford, Great Chesterford, Great Shelford and Stapleford, takes its name from an ancient ford on a branch of the River Cam. The original village was aligned in a SW–NE direction, along a road which ran down to the ford. The modern road from Cambridge to Duxford cuts this old road at right angles and has provided the village with a new axis along which more recent growth has taken place. The pleasant park-like area to the S and E of the cross-roads is not the original green, which now lies beneath the car park of the Tickle Arms, but the remains of a former manor-house garden. The medieval manor was moated and stood close to the river crossing, facing the church.

The church, which has a 12th-c nucleus, may stand on an ancient pagan site, and a fragment of pagan Saxon carving has been incorporated into the lower part of the tower, where it is clearly visible. The S aisle of the church belongs to the 13th c, while the tower was heightened and embattled in the 14th c. A charming feature of the carefully restored church is the unusual timber-framed porch of a pleasantly rustic appearance. In the churchyard can be seen the graves of many young British and Commonwealth airmen who served at the famous Battle of Britain airfield at Duxford, 2m S, which is now the home of an impressive collection of historic aircraft. Duxford was the base of the legless ace, Douglas Bader, whose Duxford wing frequently reinforced the hard-pressed squadrons which guarded London.

A number of old and appealing buildings can be found, most of them standing along the axis of the original village, which is now represented by West End, High Street and Church Lane. The guild hall stands at the cross-roads, and the timber-framed building was probably used by a guild connected with the church. It is *c.* 1500; the upper storey overhangs in the medieval manner, and the main posts are carved. This superb example of timber framing has been well restored, although the dove box on the W wall is a recent addition and post-dates the demolition of buildings which Victorian photographs show standing next to the guild hall. Markings Farm on West End has a 15th-c wing, and the position of the medieval smoke-hole can be seen at the top of the E gable; the W wing belongs to the 17th c.

WORSTEAD, *Norfolk* (3m SE of North Walsham), gave its name to the renowned worsted cloth. Little more than a large village today, with a square flanked by Georgian and Queen Anne houses, in medieval times Worstead was a bustling industrial town. The former prosperity which the cloth industry produced is reflected in the church of St Mary, which was created between 1379 and 1450. The chancel screen has a dado with the paintings of 16 saints, and in front there is a brass to John Alblastyr, who donated the screen before his death in 1520. The interior also boasts a fine hammerbeam roof, box pews and a traceried font.

4m SE of Worstead is the church of St Michael, **Barton Turf,** which stands quite isolated from any village. St Michael's is famous for its screens. Only the dado of the screen across the S aisle remains, with the painted figures of St Olaf, St Edmund, Edward the Confessor and Henry VI. Twelve figures decorating the base of the chancel screen are well-preserved, with coving and tracery above. The body of the church is of 14th- and 15th-c construction and there are figure pinnacles to the tower.

It is now known that the Norfolk Broads are artificial, the result of medieval peat-digging for fuel in a region which was lacking in timber, and the name Barton Turf probably refers to a place where turf was dug. There are a considerable number of isolated churches in Norfolk like the one at Barton Turf, and they remain something of a mystery in the English landscape. In a few cases, like that of Egmere, the church can be related to a declined surrounding village, but in many more cases the church has always stood in an isolated position, perhaps serving as a religious focus for dispersed and hamlet communities.

The South Country

BERKSHIRE HAMPSHIRE SOUTH WILTSHIRE DORSET
WEST SUSSEX ISLE OF WIGHT

Anthony Brode

The great hills of the South Country are less than half the story. The impressive chalk range which Hilaire Belloc recalled with such affection curves north and west out of his beloved Sussex through Hampshire to merge with the uplands on the Berkshire border and level out into the great spread of Salisbury Plain. But between chalk and Channel lie the remains of the Forest of Bere; the Hampshire basin and its trout streams; the New Forest; and Dorset's variegation of downland, woodland, farmland, stone strata and shale beds – with their deposits of oil and natural gas.

No one has tried to relate South Country man to his background as thoroughly as William Cobbett. In his *Rural Rides* he gave free rein to his favourite hobbyhorses – agricultural economy and parliamentary reform – but in his pages may be found shrewd observation as well as political propaganda. North of Winchester, for instance, he travelled 'over roads and lanes of flint and chalk. ... The country where soil is stiff loam upon chalk is never bad for corn. Not rich but never poor. There is at no time anything deserving to be called dirt on the road. The buildings last a long time, from the absence of fogs and also the absence of humidity in the ground. The absence of dirt makes the people habitually cleanly; and all along through this country the people appear in general to be very neat.'

So, just as a certain soil was good for certain crops (between Selborne and Thursley Cobbett noted 'a fine buttery stoneless loam upon a bottom of sand or sandstone – finer barley or turnip land it is impossible to see'), so a certain soil might be good for man.

Traces still remain of the South Country's earliest communities – such causeway camps as Windmill Hill in Wiltshire and the Trundle in West Sussex. The first inhabitants doubtless straggled up from the south before the waters of the Channel swept over the ancient land-link with the continent of Europe, and later the creeks and beaches of the new shoreline tempted intermittent waves of tribes and individuals from across the water. Often these invasions, major and minor, were the indirect result of migrations originating thousands of miles away to the south-east, but it was with the expansion of the Roman Empire that the process gathered impetus. Gaulish tribes including the Durotriges, the Atrebates and the Belgae crossed into England only to be followed in succeeding centuries by the Romans themselves.

The tribes had an effect on the landscape, since their ploughs opened up the more accessible terrain, and Roman Britain saw southern farmland worked from central homesteads. Few were on such a grand scale as the combination of palace and administrative headquarters at Fishbourne in West Sussex, but even a modest 'villa' might be the nucleus of a number of other buildings.

Empire builders take their architectural styles with them, to Fishbourne no less than to New Delhi. There was, however, a long time-gap between the use of Roman-style tiling at such outposts as Fishbourne and the widespread use for ordinary housing of any roofing material more sophisticated than thatch. Its use was perhaps the first of human crafts, as man tried to keep off the rain with heather, turf, reeds, leaves and branches, or varieties of straw: but of course a thatched roof is no longer an indication of the age of a property or the poverty of the inhabitants. In parts of the south a new thatched roof has become as much a status symbol as an ex-directory telephone number – and usually it merges with its neighbours better than the older buildings modernized in the last hundred years with roofs of slate or tile. Of corrugated sheeting, whether in metal or plastic, the less said the better – except by way of protest.

Apart from the individual decorations and signatures a master-thatcher may give a roof, there are several regional variations in style: one is the Sussex hip, in which the top few feet of thatch nearest the ridge are swept round the end wall of a cottage – usually to protect a window. At the beginning of the nineteenth century the Isle of Wight specialized in the cottage *ornée* with overhanging thatch – suddenly romantic rather than vulgar in upper-class eyes – supported by 'rustic' pillars. Michael Billett points out in *Thatch and Thatched Buildings* (1979) that Wiltshire and parts of Berkshire and Hampshire are the counties richest in thatched walls, though, just as the wall itself might be crumbling cob, the wall-thatch might not be allocated the best of materials, so usually it is only on the best-kept farms and estates that examples survive.

Reeds for thatching are cultivated along various stretches of the Hampshire and Dorset coastline, though not in such profusion as the Norfolk beds which give East Anglia a higher proportion of thatched roofs than the South Country. Abbotsbury and other local reeds are naturally to be found more commonly at the western end of the

Opposite: one of the standing stones in the village of Avebury

Janet and Colin Bord

area: elsewhere the material might be Norfolk reed, combed wheat reed (this is in fact wheat straw produced by a modification to the threshing-machine, which would otherwise mangle the stalks), as well as the cheaper, but comparatively short-lived, ordinary straw.

After the withdrawal of the Roman legions the rivers which debouch into the English Channel – Adur, Arun, Meon, Itchen, Test, Avon, Stour and Frome – offered subsequent incomers the easiest invasion routes. Between the fifth and seventh centuries Angles, Jutes and Saxons created (or more often, perhaps, enlarged) valley settlements which came to consist of hovels clustering round manors, churches and mills. In recent years it has

been suggested that these hovels were not as squalid as the word has now come to suggest; though the first versions may have been little more than a hole in the ground covered by branches, the timberwork grew more sophistic-ated, and later framed walls were filled in with cob. This mixture of clay and straw was being advocated as late as 1850 as suitable for the building of cottages; numerous examples of this building material may still be seen in cottages in, for instance, the New Forest, along with more stable varieties of walling material such as wattle-and-daub or lath-and-plaster.

Inevitably much use was made in the south of chalk – usually the harder, deeper layers known as

clunch. The flints found in the chalk were at first reserved for the manor (and sometimes for its barns) and for the church, a fact which has ensured that these are the only pre-fourteenth century buildings to be seen today.

Stone from the Nadder Valley in Wiltshire, from Portland in Dorset and from the Isle of Wight later began to be exported by local quarries to wherever in the south of England more durable building material was needed in the form of blocks or slabs or facings. Here and there various free-stones, requiring less in the way of quarrymen's special skills, were dug, shaped and used in the vicinity.

Clay deposits resulted in the establishment of numerous brick and tile works, notably in southern Hampshire. Though it takes an expert to identify unmarked bricks some firms marked their products very clearly. Few were as distinctive as those of the Bursledon Brick Company which turned out, well into the twentieth century, possibly to the mystification of archaeologists of the distant future, batch after batch incised with the initials BBC.

Variations major and minor in bricks, tiles and even chimney-pots are, however, only a few among the many factors that have helped to ensure that no matter how hard one looks – and it's fun looking – no such thing as a *typical* South Country village is to be found anywhere.

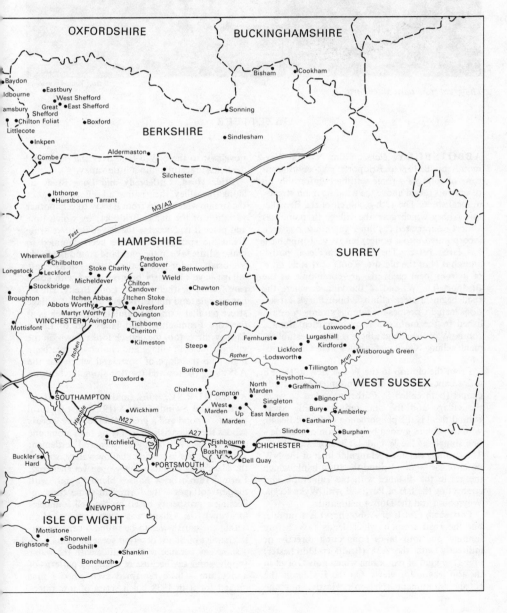

The great tithe barn at Abbotsbury

GAZETTEER

ABBOTSBURY, *Dorset* (10m NW of Weymouth on B3157 to Bridport), has continuous rows of cottages – some settling comfortably on pavements raised above the winding main street – in local stone. The 12th-c church of the Benedictine Abbey which gave the village its name has almost disappeared (its inner gatehouse has been incorporated into a house) but its vast tithe barn has fared better. The present medieval parish church is N of the old site. Roofs of thatch, most of it from local reedbeds, are commoner at the Bridport (i.e. W) end of the village, where the road begins a steep climb. Abbotsbury's attractions include, besides the famous swannery established by the monks, a tropical garden along a combe W of the village; there is also an establishment selling 'Garden Gnomes and Orniments' (*sic*).

From the clifftop to the W the view to the SE is dramatic – a round hill surmounted by a sturdy chapel (both called St Catherine's) lies between the village and the sea, and stretching away behind them is the phenomenon of Chesil Beach, with its pebbles graded by the action of the tide – fine shingle at the W end, large stones at the E. The swannery is in a rectangular inlet at the NW point of the lagoon behind the 10-m bank, which merges in the distance with the vulnerable spit connecting the Isle of Portland with Wyke Regis, Weymouth and the Dorset mainland.

Portesham (2m E of Abbotsbury) is a jumble, but the road from it which leads NW before fanning out into lanes connecting directly or indirectly with the A35 (Bridport–Dorchester) offers the kind of panorama which puts Dorset in the top league for views. On the E ridge is the Hardy Monument (Nelson's Hardy, not the

novelist); to the NW a lane over the downland descends gracefully into a little valley.

Bride Head, Littlebredy and **Long Bredy** lie along this valley, their names all reflecting that of the stream which flows from E to W to yet another variation of the name, Bridport; by which time and place it has become the River Brit. At Bride Head the spring-waters have been dammed to make a little lake in the parkland round the Early Victorian–Tudor house; the cottages of its estate village have obviously been grouped with equal care for the aesthetic effect. Long Bredy, 2m W, has a single (and not really very long) N–S village street parallel with a streamlet; the church is at the top. From either end lanes run to **Litton Cheney**: here, too, the church looks down on the village, but both village and church are relatively higher up the slope of downland which has the A35 along the top and the Brit along the bottom.

ALDBOURNE, *Wilts.* (midway between Hungerford and Swindon on A419), has two focal points – a pond and a green. On the latter a cross echoes the big parish church lying high along one side. Though it is really a downland settlement Aldbourne lies in a wide shallow valley, so that the place feels simultaneously open yet sheltered. Formal 18th-c brick houses blend happily with modest cottages – the former in some cases reflecting a prosperity based on the bell foundries for which the village was once famous. High within the parish was to be found a century ago the hamlet of Snap: deserted some 80 years back – some say because of difficulties with the water supply, some say because of changing patterns of agriculture – little remained even when I first looked for it in 1938 but a series of low ridges where perhaps a dozen cottages had stood.

Baydon (1m NE of Aldbourne) is on a Roman road – Ermine Street – and only just off the M4; the highest village in Wiltshire, it is said by some to be the Mons Badonicus at which King Arthur won a victory over the Saxon invaders.

ALDERMASTON, *Berks.* (12m SE of Reading on A340), is an essay, or rather a series of essays, in brick: mostly red, mostly mellow, mostly 17th- or 18th-c – though some new houses keep up the standard very well. These are up a hill SE of the village street, which is topped by the lodges of Aldermaston Court and finished off at the bottom by a handsome 18th-c pub on the road towards the Old Mill (more attractive brick).

Beyond the mill the road continues to its junction with the A4 midway between Reading and Newbury at Aldermaston Wharf – a name recalling busier days on the Kennet and Avon canal. Industry of a kind has come comparatively recently to Aldermaston itself, in the sprawl of the Atomic Energy Research Establishment: Pevsner found the original mid-20th-c administrative buildings in the grounds of Aldermaston Court 'impressive and architecturally well-designed'. This is more than can be said of the tatty tangle spreading along the Kingsclere road on the high ground S of the village: perhaps it is embarrassment rather than fear of espionage which is responsible for the notices forbidding photography. But the short main street of the village is neat and compact, combining the beautiful and functional. The same may be said of Alan Caiger-Smith's pottery, thrown and fired and displayed on premises occupying one of the red-brick buildings.

Silchester, 4m SE of Aldermaston, is now Hampshire farmland jutting into Berks.: the Romans, who made it a garrison town at the centre of a network of communications, called it Calleva of the Atrebates after the tribe in whose territory it was. Most of the Victorian excavations, which revealed traces of Forum, Basilica, public baths, guest house and shops, were filled in. The site belonged until 1974 to the Duke of Wellington; later a property company's plan to sell it off in small lots to American investors and others was dropped when Hampshire County Council agreed to buy all 141 acres.

ALRESFORD, *Hants.* Some say 'Awlsfd' and some say 'Arlsfd': once it seems to have been Aldersford, the ford by the alders, and the river now called Arle or Alre is possibly an awkward back-formation. Medieval church records refer to it merely as the River Itchen, into which, according to today's maps, it flows further downstream: and in these parts church records carry some weight since it was a Bishop of Winchester, de Lucy, who in the 12th c dammed up various little streams at Old Alresford to provide a head of water to make the Itchen navigable – though naturally it was always the lower half of the navigation, from Winchester to Southampton, which carried most of the traffic. The episcopal reservoir

has now dwindled to a pond rich in wildfowl, though the village is still connected to New Alresford on the main Alton–Winchester route by a road running N and S along the top of the original embankment. The old (early Georgian) rectory is another though less commendable example of clerical enterprise, having been enlarged and improved by a – technically – noble rector, Francis North, Earl of Guildford. He was also Master of St Cross, the religious foundation at Winchester: and in 1853 there was a judicial inquiry into his use, or rather misuse, of the foundation's endowments to endow himself with a larger house and a higher life-style. The reputation of Old Alresford's incumbents was however restored by his successor George Sumner (later Bishop of Guildford) and Mrs Sumner (founder of the Mothers' Union). The 18th-c church has a tablet commemorating this – and also a notable monument in multi-coloured marble, dated 1757, to the first wife of Admiral Lord Rodney. The family's connection with the village is also commemorated in Old Alresford House, nearby, built about the same time by Sir George Rodney Brydges.

'New' Alresford dates back to before the dam-building bishop, though it was he who enlarged the settlement. The road from Old Alresford widens dramatically, once over the bridge, into New Alresford's Broad Street. This makes a T-junction with the East Street and West Street sections of the Alton–Winchester road: broad indeed, but tree-lined and elegant in its mixture of shops selling books, bread, teas and other necessities, and of private houses. One was the birthplace in 1787 of the novelist Mary Russell Mitford. The half-urbanized village has lost its air of antiquity less through a natural regeneration of buildings than from a series of fires in the 12th, 15th, 17th (four of them in that particular century) and 18th centuries. The fire of 1644 was due to the 'scorched earth' policy of the Royalist troops defeated at the Battle of Cheriton. The Roundheads seem to have got the fire or fires under control as decisively as they had the battle, which actually took place in high open country S of New Alresford.

Cheriton, E of the battlefield, is now a quiet village where a green and streams create a much softer and friendlier atmosphere than that of the 'hard, iron village' described by Cobbett. Perhaps he was there on a cold day: on a warm one it is possible to survey much of Cheriton from the benches outside the HH – claimed to be the shortest name for a pub anywhere in the kingdom. The claim has, however, been challenged on the grounds that it is merely an abbreviation (for Hampshire Hunt). 1m S, over the Winchester–Petersfield road, the Ordnance Survey map marks the source of the River Itchen.

Kilmeston, $\frac{1}{2}$m further on, is enchanting but for its overhead power cables. The 18th-c manor house looks enormous but the cottages around remain unimpressed. Building materials include brick with tile roof, flint with slate, and timber frame with thatch; there is even a stretch of weatherboarding complete with busy dovecote *en suite*. There is room in front of many of the cottages not only for trim front gardens but for neat stretches of grass bordering the lanes which wind through the village and out into the surrounding woods and fields.

Tichborne lies 2m NE of Cheriton: turn W at Cheriton Mill and follow the course of the youthful Itchen. The hamlet with its pre-Conquest church lies W of the road, and Tichborne Park to the E. The Tichborne Dole, revived in recent years in the form of bags of flour for deserving local ladies, is said to have originated during the reign of Henry I in a callous promise by Sir Roger Tichborne to his bedridden wife that she could have, to provide funds for the needy, as much land as she could crawl round: the 20 acres she somehow managed to encompass became known as The Crawls. The family remained staunchly Roman Catholic and the parish church retains a Catholic side-chapel with memorials to various members. Their fortunes dwindled in the 19th c, with expensive lawsuits over a claim by Arthur Orton, a butcher from London, to be the heir to the estate; both seem to have met in Australia. Orton, though he produced impressive evidence suggesting that he was the young baronet (another Sir Roger), was jailed for 14 years as an impostor.

N of Tichborne the road divides: both branches cross the A31 (Alresford–Winchester) to follow the Itchen as it turns due W. The larger road, on the N bank, goes through **Itchen Stoke, Itchen Abbas** (where Charles Kingsley stayed at a pub, the predecessor of the present Plough; fished; and possibly got the idea for *The Water Babies*: his description of the stream fits the Itchen perfectly), **Martyr Worthy** and **Abbots Worthy** – ribbon development here and there, but a posh class of ribbon. The lane S of the river goes through **Ovington,** where the pub garden tends to fill with importunate ducklings, and intermittently follows the Pilgrims Way through **Avington** – 18th-c church, house, and stable block; a little terrace of cottages; and a cast-iron bridge.

AMBERLEY, *W. Sussex* (6m NE of Arundel on B2139), is a careful and successful exercise in conservation. Hereabouts the process began early, gathering momentum (if that's not a paradox in respect of a process which consists largely of putting a brake on development) in the twenties. That decade has somehow imposed itself on buildings dating from many centuries previously – just as women's make-up in Hollywood historicals was usually contemporary with the shooting of the film rather than the period of the action. The church is basically Norman and the castle – a manor house fortified in the 14th c to guard the gap where the Arun breaks through the South Downs – was also an ecclesiastical property, belonging to the Bishops of Chichester. Today a manor house – not the original – remains, hard up against the shell of the castle.

The village itself is almost a reference library of building materials – copybook examples of flintwork, brickwork, and timberwork topped here by tiles, there by thatch; though for many visitors it is the stretches of flint walling, rather than individual houses or cottages, which linger in the mind as characteristic of this trimly attractive place. The marshy tract of land N of the village is named, magically, Amberley Wild Brooks: rare plants, wildfowl and (except in the driest of summers) such squelchy terrain that unkind people from neighbouring villages pretend to believe Amberley folk are born with webbed feet.

Bury, on the opposite bank of the river, has a duckpond instead of a marsh – and stone cottages clustering about a cross-roads rather than a display of building techniques lining, as can be seen at Amberley, a rectangle of lanes.

AVEBURY, *Wilts.* (1m N of A4, midway between Marlborough and Calne), is according to Sir John Betjeman the place where the story of English architecture begins. The 17th-c diarist and antiquarian John Aubrey wrote that Avebury was a cathedral in comparison with the 'parish church' of Stonehenge: certainly the earthworks and arrays of standing stones at Avebury are more extensive, though they have never attracted the same amount of public interest. Perhaps this is because the circle at Avebury lacks the evidence, so impressive at Stonehenge, of man's first big advance in building technique – the laying of a horizontal slab on top of two verticals. This comparative sophistication apart, the biggest difference between the two sites today is that the 28-acre circle at Avebury has the greater part of a village actually inside it, and a busy road running right through the middle. While Stonehenge, bleak on Salisbury Plain, has lost much of its majesty with its popularity as a tourist attraction, Avebury, with a small but permanent population, remains impressive, unaffected and timeless.

The village itself is scarcely memorable, but it can hardly be expected to compete with its setting: in any case there are some very pleasant cottages, and on the fringe a beautiful juxtaposition of (largely Norman) church and (mostly 16th-c) manor. Seen from the circle they merge into their background of trees, which elsewhere grow too sparsely to break up the open aspect of this prehistoric landscape.

SE runs an avenue of standing stones to another circle-site 1m away at **West Overton**: Silbury Hill, the largest man-made mound in Europe, rises 1m S of Avebury above the A4, which here follows a rare curve in the Roman road to Bath to avoid this archaeological enigma. From its flat grassy top the view N includes Windmill Hill, a neolithic encampment which to judge by the quantities of animal bones discovered on the ditched site may have been a combination of cattle market, trading post and centre of ritual. Beyond, the Great Ridgeway offers walkers a magnificent track which goes N and then turns to the E, by way of Barbary Castle and Uffington, and on to the Thames Valley at Goring.

BONCHURCH, *Isle of Wight* (immediately E of Ventnor), takes its name from St Boniface Church, a 13th-c building on a Saxon site: it is symptomatic of the Victorian development of the island that there is a second church of St Boniface dating from the 1840s. It was built further inland, a sensible precaution on a spectacularly crumbling coastline. Whereas Ventnor has surmounted the problem of expanding up and down along the cliff-face, taking full advantage of a chine running down to the shore, Bonchurch has been able only to capitalize on its position by recognizing The Landslip as an attraction. Its terraced gardens are easy on the eye but hard on the calf-muscles.

Shanklin Old Village, 2m N (its 'Old Church' is mid-Victorian) is a manicured group of thatched buildings which contrast with the 19th- and 20th-c development now making a single urban sprawl of Shanklin, Lake and Sandown: but only a few miles inland all is green fields and peace.

BOSHAM, *W. Sussex,* is a yachtsman's delight. The village, built on a piece of land jutting out into an inlet of Chichester Harbour, boasts that Quay Meadow (a National Trust property) is where King Canute staged his confrontation with the tide, or more probably with his courtiers. Southampton backs its own claim to the royal 'demo' with the street name Canute Road, but Bosham offers as evidence a child's coffin, discovered in 1865 and re-examined in 1954, below the floor of the Saxon church where legend had long insisted that the Danish king's daughter had been buried. A memorial plaque in Copenhagen porcelain bears the black raven which was his emblem; but the Christian tradition in Bosham goes further back, possibly to a Roman building on the site of the present church, where a noble chancel arch and plain unbuttressed tower exemplify Saxon ecclesiastical architecture at its grandest. The building is even represented in the Bayeux Tapestry, for it was from Bosham that Harold set out in 1064 on his ill-starred voyage to Normandy. When William paid his notably more successful return visit a couple of years later Harold's Sussex estates were naturally among the first he seized.

N of the church, masonry from a 7th-c monastery is incorporated into a house and a cottage. 'Old' Bosham – much of it 1000 years younger than the monastery – lies along the foreshore: car parking is not forbidden, but vehicles tend to be submerged at high tide. There is no through route and despite extensive building all over the wooded peninsula or Hoe (most of it very well-mannered and some a little self-conscious) the brick and tile nucleus of the village remains largely unaffected.

Dell Quay is on the Chichester Channel, E of the Bosham peninsula; its cottages are grouped round a boatyard which replaced a silted-up port at **Appledram** (½m up-channel), of which little remains but a church and two manor houses.

Fishbourne has practically become a W suburb of Chichester. It was in digging the foundations of a house in 1806 that a Roman tesselated pavement was first discovered and when the area was about to be sold for housing in 1961, it was purchased by the Sussex Archaeological Trust. This enabled digging to continue until the ground plan of a whole series of elaborate buildings was unearthed round a courtyard 250ft wide, with further development stretching S across the present A27 to an artificial inlet from the sea. It has been identified as the Palace of Cogidubnus, a puppet or client king (more of a governor-general in today's terminology) of British origin who had acquired Roman citizenship – and backing; and it must have been a combination of private residence, administrative headquarters, and official guest house. The area of the N wing has now been covered by a functional but perfectly agreeable structure of wood, aluminium and glass which protects an impressive series of mosaics – some very fine indeed – in their original positions. It provides walkways from which the mosaics, wall-footings and underfloor heating system may be seen, and houses a superbly laid out museum showing various stages in the development, overrunning, neglect and rediscovery of the site. The project is, in fact, a model of its kind.

BOXFORD, *Berks.* (5m NW of Newbury), lies in the Lambourn Valley; which, with its stream, minor road and abandoned railway, is an odd mixture of the picturesque and the impromptu. Apart from the natural tendency of the settlements to follow these three – usually parallel – lines of communication, there are places where the problem of merging 20th-c practice in agriculture and architecture with the background has not been solved. Perhaps it has not been attempted: rusting farm machinery and vehicles, buildings displaying their guts (or at least their girders) and grey rectangles of building-blocks qualify at least one straggle for nomination as Berkshire's worst-kept village.

But persevere. Boxford's bungalows perch on a bank as though to avoid getting their feet – or at least their footings – wet; but it's a sensible precaution since this is very much a valley village with the flat landscape spiked by tall poplars. A lane leading away from the main cluster of buildings becomes a not-quite-separate hamlet called **Westbrook**; the lane is flanked on either side by thatched cottages – the chapel is thatched, too – and passes the much grander Westbrook House before it dwindles to a farm track. At its end the farm buildings make a mellow group against the rising ground along the top of which M4 now runs.

Great Shefford is W and upstream from Boxford; development round a cross-roads has left church, manor and farm almost isolated at the top end of the village. St Mary's is the only Berkshire church with an original, and very probably Norman, round tower. The old rectory is Georgian: the manor dates back to the 16th c.

East Shefford and **West Shefford** are more compact, tidier versions of Great Shefford: but **East Garston,** 1m or so upstream, is the only Garston there is, since it was a 'tun' or settlement named after Esgar, whose holding is recorded in Domesday Book. Most of its occupants live along the banks of the stream in thatched timber-framed cottages with brick or flint infilling.

Eastbury on the Lambourn side of Garston is a villagescape in miniature, with a little square reached by a small bridge. This is the beginning of Betjeman country, and appropriately the church and schoolhouse are, unflamboyantly, mid-19th-c.

This is also, of course, horse country. Studs and stables are big business in the Lambourn valley, with Berkshire downland providing ideal country for training gallops. Visitors should remember that strings of bloodstock take priority, by local custom if not by law, over motor traffic along the narrow lanes around Lambourn, where a once-busy market town grew up at the crossing of two roads.

BROADCHALKE, *Wilts.* (9m WSW of Salisbury), is the largest of a series of villages which shelter along the valley of the River Ebble. The quietest of the valleys whose streams come together in and around Salisbury, it runs into the Avon 3m S of the city. The 17th-c diarist John Aubrey lived in a modest family estate at Broadchalke before going to live in London: his home was at the Old Rectory. He was a warden at the parish church, which he said possessed one of the 'tunablest' ring of bells in Wiltshire.

Aubrey wrote affectionately of the village and its river ('There are not better trouts in the Kingdom of England than here') and the surrounding countryside with its gentle slopes and avenues of trees. There are groups of cottages N of the river, but the main village clusters round a quadrilateral of lanes sloping up to the S. Two continue uphill and one crosses the Oxdrove – the Roman road which forms the county boundary with Hampshire; and finally A354 (Salisbury–Blandford), *en route* for Martin and Rockbourne (q.v.).

Bowerchalke is reached by a continuation of another lane from Broadchalke which climbs a gentler slope up the line of a tributary stream: farm buildings, houses and cottages are grouped to take advantage of the shelter of the combe. Back again in the Ebble valley, **Fifield Bavant** (upstream from Broadchalke) is a hamlet with a Norman church – one of the smallest in the South Country – to match: on a rise at a road junction, this church can hardly be said to dominate the group of buildings below it even with the help of a bell-turret by way of a tower.

Ebbesbourne Wake (1m W), is in another S-climbing combe, and is in effect by-passed by the valley road which continues through Berwick St John to join the A30 (Salisbury–Shaftesbury) below Whiteshoot Hill. Here the ancient Herepath (military road) on the ridge between the Ebble and Nadder valleys became a turnpike busy with coaches on the long haul from London to the SW. Earthworks along the deserted track include Chiselbury Camp, but there is a whole series of barrows and ditches: walkers and skylarks have the ridge to themselves except where the grass

track is crossed by roads connecting the villages in the valleys on either side until, E of Wilton Park, it becomes a stretch of Salisbury Racecourse.

Bishopstone, 3m downstream from Broadchalke, has a medieval church large by the standards of the Ebble Valley, the lower reaches of which probably supported a larger population before the agricultural depression of the 19th c: some of the bigger houses – and there are attractive examples – today seem almost marooned in the gently sloping fields.

Coombe Bissett is a busy village where the A354 (Salisbury–Blandford) crosses the valley. Over the road and downstream, **Odstock** and **Nunton** have some remarkably pleasant brick buildings (notably a manor and farm at Odstock, and Nunton House itself) and thatched cottages; but infilling is erratic in quality though planned in appearance. Odstock Hospital sprawls over the downs from Salisbury to the N, and S there are woods and avenues of yew: the tree gives its name to a notable pub in Odstock.

BUCKLER'S HARD, *Hants.*, is the port that never was. In Nelson's time it flourished as a shipyard, producing his famous *Agamemnon* and other wooden men-o'-war; today its single wide street with a backcloth of sailing craft on Beaulieu River has the air of a slipway. On either side a row of redbrick 18th-c houses is fronted by lawns where once ships' timbers were stacked, and one row ends in The Master Builder. Now a hotel, it was from 1746 to 1805 the home of Henry Adams, and during his time and that of his sons 50 warships were launched from the yard.

Earlier, however, the Duke of Montagu, owner of the Beaulieu Estate and self-styled Lord Proprietor and Captain-General of the Islands of St Lucia and St Vincent – he actually *was* Master-General of Ordnance, Master of the Great Wardrobe, and Governor-General of the Isle of Wight – had planned to increase his fortunes still further by landing sugar and other goods from his plantations in the West Indies at a private port which was to rival Lymington and Southampton. The river is still privately owned (by Lord Montagu of Beaulieu) and a former inn at Buckler's Hard has been turned into a maritime museum as an adjunct to the Motor Museum at Beaulieu. Exhibits include guns and various items of ships' armament and equipment; prints and plans; and some impressive models – including one of *Agamemnon.*

BURLEY, *Hants.* 'A few houses, a pub and a church do not make a village,' wrote the vicar of this New Forest parish in 1972, offering as alternative ingredients the friendliness of the inhabitants and a community spirit. The former must be severely strained by the pressure of the coach operators who bring holidaymakers in their thousands from Bournemouth and Southampton, and the latter by an understandable split between those who can make money out of the visitors and those who cannot. The best times to see Burley are the early spring and the late autumn, when the trees are at their best and the coaches less obtrusive. Despite the number of shops which once served the local community and now sell antiques and 'giftes' to visitors, enough remains to provide an attractive centre from which to explore at least the SW quarter of the Forest.

It is worth reminding newcomers that the old sense of 'forest' was hunting preserve rather than woodland, and that acres of treeless heath form one of the attractions of the area – though possibly a less obvious one than the mixed plantations still surviving alongside the regiments of Forestry Commission conifers. Only the main roads through the Forest are fenced off – elsewhere, residents with common rights can let their ponies and cattle (and, in autumn, pigs) wander at will. These animals have right of way over motor traffic: hitting them may prove not only distressing but expensive. Owing to the poor soil, settlements are sparse, often straggling along lanes or streams: but the fact that many have no particular focus has saved them from the development which has turned (for instance) Brockenhurst and Lyndhurst into urban patches.

BURPHAM, *W. Sussex*, has one road into it which is also the road out: a downland track known as the Lepers' Way is the only alternative to the village's 3m S link with the A27 just E of Arundel. Thatched cottages – some brick, much flint – are set with their solid Norman church on rising ground above the water-meadows, with prospects up and down the valley of the River Arun. Here the river takes a wide lazy curve to which between 1816 and 1871 there was an alternative waterway in the form of the Wey and Arun Canal. This linked Godalming with Arundel, and hence London with Littlehampton, and the Thames with the English Channel – ultimately by way of Portsmouth Harbour.

BURTON BRADSTOCK, *Dorset*, has walls of yellow-lichened stone – an infallible sign of unpolluted air – and front doors neat in white and blue. In the oldest part of the village, where the road past the school and the church crosses a bridge and peters out among the fields, thatched cottages line a series of back streets and cross-lanes which take a little green in their intimate stride. To the E a road along the clifftop, where the hedges are combed and the trees sculpted by the prevailing onshore wind (clean air indeed!), provides a spectacular drive to Abbotsbury (q.v.). *En route*, or practically so, are **Puncknowle** (pronounced 'Punnel') – now dominated by awkwardly-stepped terraces as well as farm silos – and **Swyre**, where caravans have been allowed to trickle down the combe between village and sea.

CERNE ABBAS, *Dorset* (9m N of Dorchester on the Sherborne road, A352), is a happy film-set mixture of flint, brick and colour-washed plaster. The time-scale of the village is exemplified by the fact that the New Inn in Long Street is at least

250 years old. A row of unusual timber-fronted houses with stone party-walls overhangs one side of Abbey street, which leads briefly from Long Street up to the medieval church and abbey ruins. These last, like the banks of the sunken lanes leading E and W out of Cerne, are hung with ferns and ivy and look crumblingly romantic in a damp way. Only three structures now remain: a long barn, a two-storey guest house and what was the entrance to the abbot's hall. It is now an arch leading nowhere, and should you inadvertently happen to approach it from the rear you won't see until you emerge the notice about the danger of falling masonry. Tumbledown is, alas, the adjective for these reminders of medieval Cerne.

Prehistoric Cerne, as represented by the ithy-phallic giant cut into the chalk $\frac{1}{2}$m N of the village, is in much better nick; which may or may not say something for the relative grip over the centuries of Christianity and paganism on the local populace. Maypole dancing, another aspect of fertility cults, was traditionally held on a nearby earthwork called the Trendle – the name being perhaps a variation on the Trundle, which originally (as in the W. Sussex hill fort of that name above Goodwood) meant a circle.

Sydling St Nicholas (2m SW of Cerne Abbas over a ridge of downland), lies in the valley of Sydling Water, which runs parallel to the River Cerne but more erratically both in course and flow: whereas the latter's valley takes a main (Sherborne –Dorchester) N–S traffic artery the former peters out, along with its road, in a series of dry combes N of **Up Sydling**. Even travelling E–W from Cerne to Maiden Newton you may – if you risk a shallow ford N of the village – miss Sydling St Nicholas altogether. But don't. Its barn is as big as Cerne's but its high street must be one of the shortest – and quietest – in the country. Two of its houses bear their dates (one 1733 and the other, the former vicarage, 1640) but time, like the road system, has to a great extent by-passed this serene and delightful corner of Dorset.

CHALTON, *Hants*. (1m E of the A3 – turn off midway between Petersfield and Horndean), has a notable building either side of its informal-looking sloping stretch of green – a (partly) 13th-c church and a 16th-c (or earlier) pub. The Sussex border is not far away, but the Red Lion, with its overhanging upper storey like a Wealden farmhouse, suggests a style from even further E. Hard by the church its former rectory has 19th-c impositions on a medieval building – but this is also true of the village itself, where Victorian cottages sit happily among much older buildings.

Buriton lies 1m or so N along a lane which roughly parallels the A3 as both rise and fall over the W end of the South Downs. You can walk from a field behind the church to Ditchling Beacon, above Brighton, by way of Chanctonbury Ring; or if you prefer to stand and stare there are ducks, a pond, some well-converted stabling, and the manor house where the historian Edward Gibbon spent his childhood. 'An old mansion in

Edwin Smith

Corfe Castle, with the Greyhound Hotel in the foreground

a state of decay', he wrote, 'had been converted into the fashion and convenience of a modern house; and if strangers had nothing to see, the inhabitants had little to desire. The spot was not happily chosen, at the end of the village and the bottom of a hill; but the aspect of the adjacent grounds was various and cheerful: the downs commanded a noble prospect, and the long hanging woods in sight of the house could not perhaps have been improved by art or expense.'

Which of the two was the more important ingredient in the establishment of two adjacent attractions – Forestry Commission walks in what since the Silver Jubilee (1977) has been known as the Queen Elizabeth Forest, or the Stone Age Village established by Hampshire County Council on the summit of Butser Hill – is also a subject for Gibbonian speculation.

COMBE, *Berks.*, is almost cut off from the rest of the county, being a wooded cleft (combe-cwm-valley) in the highest shoulder of the downland. But for a quirk of the county boundary it would be in Hampshire: tucked into the S slope of the ridge, it is approached by a minor road from Hurstbourne Tarrant (q.v.) which at one point cuts right into the chalk to provide drivers of any long vehicles rash enough to make the ascent with room for an exercise in three-point turning. Farms and their cottages sheltering at this and other points include the nucleus of this tiny village – its 12th-c church and 18th-c manor.

Combe gibbet on the summit of the hill was erected in 1676 to hang George Broomham of Inkpen and Dorothy Newman of Combe. She was a widow with three children; they murdered the two youngest in their sleep and threw the bodies into a pond. The third was given poisoned porridge for breakfast but tried it on the dog;

the dog it was that died. From the ridge – the highest point in Berks. – the eye is led to the immediate prospect of Walbury Camp, an Iron Age encampment with defensive ditches 15ft across, and on to one of the widest panoramic views in all the South Country. N lies the Vale of the White Horse, transferred with a third of Berks. to Oxfordshire during the boundary revisions of 1974; while in the opposite direction a great sweep of alternately open and wooded landscape stretches away as far as the South Downs.

Inkpen lies on the Berks. slope, not so much a village as an irregular grid of lanes in which Higher Inkpen merges into Inkpen itself. The attractions of the latter include the former rectory, reflecting ecclesiastical prosperity and elegance of style in 1700 or thereabouts, and the parish church, reflecting architectural techniques and individual taste from the 13th c to the 19th – Pevsner cites the 'charming Arts-and-Crafts Gothic south window'. A 20th-c feature is the oak font cover for which a New Forest sculptor, the late Ron Lane, carved in walnut a series of water-creatures including a vole, a dipper, a newt, a kingfisher, and a teal.

COMPTON, *W. Sussex*, is 3m S of South Harting at a sudden bend on the B2146 from Petersfield to Funtington. It lies in one of a series of narrow wooded valleys running S from the ridge of the downs rising steeply from the Rother Valley: near Compton, cross-lanes run in from E and W and the junctions provide *raisons d'être* for a settlement of brick and flint cottages complete with church, pub and shop. Up Park (National Trust), 2m N, was built at the end of the 17th c. H. G. Wells spent part of his childhood here at the end of the 19th c when his mother was housekeeper in this William and Mary house stranded 600ft up on the downs. 'The place', he wrote in his autobiography, 'had a great effect on me.'

The Mardens – East, West, North and Up – all lie within a few miles of Compton and are connected by lanes which zigzag up and down between fields and copses. At Up Marden there is nothing but a farm and a church, the former partly hiding the latter, and little seems to have changed since St Michael's was built – for whom? – in the 13th c. This is one of the quietest corners of Sussex.

COOKHAM, *Berks.*, is a Thames-side village which hasn't quite grown up – into a town, that is: perhaps the Tarry Stone (a sarsen which would have been more at home on the Wiltshire Uplands) is partly responsible. A plaque notes that the Stone ('at which sports were held before 1507') was moved to its present position in 1909 by order of the parish council. It gives its name to one of the group of handsome brick houses across the main road from the wide cul-de-sac leading to the church, which looks suitably village-y with its exterior of flint and stone. Churchgate House and Churchgate Cottage lie on one side of the cul-de-sac confronted by Churchgate, which somehow looks American-Gothic. The cast-iron bridge over the Thames is unmistakeably Victorian but light and (for Victorian traffic) functional.

In the High Street, still free of blatant multiple stores, the Stanley Spencer Gallery recalls that Cookham was the artist's birthplace, home and inspiration. Buildings with names such as The Malting and Forge House recall earlier days when the timber-framed cottage called Moor End, now leaning backwards, must have been upright: this, like Moor Cottage nearby, recalls in turn the time when the grassy stretch which starts where the High Street stops was wilder than now: though it's still called Cookham Moor.

Cookham Rise and Cookham Dean lie this way *en route* to **Bisham**: as at Cookham, Bisham church lies by the river and when the water-level is high it looks as though it is moored in the meadows. It seems only fitting therefore that swans should be the supporters on the coat of arms of the Hoby family whose monuments (notably that dedicated in 1605 to Margaret, wife of Sir Edward Hoby) are a feature of the much restored building. Another is to Sir Philip Hoby, who at the Dissolution acquired the abbey upstream, beyond the village with its terraced brick cottages. The recurring name Temple – Mills, for instance, and Park – is a reminder that the abbey was originally a preceptory, or subordinate community, of the Knights Templar. Precepts ('authoritative commands', says the *Shorter Oxford English Dictionary*) are a great feature of Bisham: 'No Boating', 'No Camping', 'No Access to River'. Back at the E end of the village there is a path between the church and the school ending in a stretch of grass which leads down to the river, with handy rings set into a modest concrete embankment. But half-hidden by the ivy on a wall to one side is the inevitable notice 'No Mooring'. Fitting into this prohibitive atmosphere is a forbidding 20th-c brick fortress reminiscent of one of those emergency food stores built during World War II and given the title of Buffer Depots. Improbably, it is a Sports Centre.

CORFE CASTLE, *Dorset,* is 5m SE of Wareham on the A351. A community which cared more for visitors' opinions would not have allowed one of its finer buildings, dating from 1575, to be flanked by modern buildings so architecturally inappropriate. Perhaps a decline in general prosperity over the past two or three centuries may be blamed; but the Isle of Purbeck has always tended to go its own way. This seems true of Corfe Castle in particular. The state of the castle ruins high above the village is due less to the attacks of weather, time or even siege engines, than to deliberate retribution by outside authority. Norman in origin, the castle was a Royalist stronghold during the Civil War and held out until 1645, when one of its officers left on the pretext of bringing reinforcements from Somerset but returned with Roundhead troops from Lulworth and Weymouth. In the following year Parliament voted to have it blown up but the attempt was only partly successful – the massive stoneworks dominate both the ridge on which they stand and the buildings clustered below.

Corfe noisily remembers its prosperous past every Shrove Tuesday, when the Ancient Order of Marblers and Stonecutters meets – paradoxically enough – between the red-brick walls of the town hall. This modest room dates from the 1770s: the work of earlier marblers and stonecutters survives in fine buildings all over the country, and in the stone cottages and larger buildings – including the church – which still make up most of the centre of the village. These are perhaps more direct links with the past than the Order's erratic progress across the heathland to Ower Quay on the S edge of Poole Harbour, once the quarrymen's port for stone shipped to all parts of the kingdom. Nowadays the only dues paid are a pound of pepper and a football; which suggests a tradition slowly disintegrating in the same way that Corfe's West Street peters out, after some attractive variations in width and level, on to the Common, now that East Street has become the link with the road to Swanage. But among the barrows and ridges all around the village are traces of the sunken lanes along which marble and freestone were hauled by horse-drawn cart and sledge to be dressed, before shipment, by the craftsmen of Corfe.

The small market place is now dominated by the Greyhound Hotel, which has swallowed up a pair of cottages: but the process of digestion has proved successful, while the Bankes Hotel nearby remains unassimilated 20th-c. The 18th-c Town House, as it is now called (the ground floor is occupied by a bank), had a first-floor mayor's parlour entered from the higher level of the adjacent churchyard; the nearby Council Chamber had a similar arrangement, though the original lock-up has been made into a museum.

British Tourist Authority

Godshill, in the Isle of Wight

The Army holds 7000 acres of heathland at the W end of Purbeck, though as the poet Paul Hyland points out in his invaluable and evocative book *Purbeck – the Ingrained Island*, the name 'Battle Plain' in fact dates back to the scene of a minor skirmish during the Civil War. Elsewhere, wide tracts of heathland offer more to holidaymakers – especially walkers – than to those who have tried to farm the acid soil. Various forms of transport – quarrymen's sledges, clayworkers' tramways, the Wareham–Swanage branch of the London and South Western Railway – have left their scars, and many provide tracks for those seeking alternatives to the lures of the holiday areas. Wider scars are left by quarrying, and old clayworks vary in appearance from slimy rubbish-dumps to the romantic landscaping of The Blue Pool. The effect of the recent expansion in oil drilling, confined at one time to a modest operation at Kimmeridge, cannot yet be judged.

Kingston, SW of Corfe Castle, is an example less of organic village growth than of the vigorous craftsmanship of a group of 19th-c stonemasons. A trim-looking estate village, it belonged to the Scott family of Encombe, Earls of Eldon. The gigantic church, commissioned by the 3rd Earl and completed in 1880, was until 1921 their private chapel. Purbeck stone and Purbeck skill have combined to produce a cold memorial to Victorian pride and piety – not to mention a tower visible for miles.

Langton Matravers has a 15th-c church tower even lower than the 19th-c roof of its nave: the story goes that earlier roof-timbers were damaged by the weight of contraband stored there (by this time smuggling had replaced piracy for which the

Isle of Purbeck had once been notorious). As far as respectable trade is concerned, a village museum underlines the lessons of history – or at least a sense of the past – taught by the stone buildings themselves. The King's Arms retains a Purbeck marble fireplace perhaps in compensation for having changed its name – an upsurge of Royalist feeling, maybe – from the Masons' Arms, and a degree of continuity is maintained even in council-house design.

DURWESTON, *Dorset*, is in the Stour valley 2m NW of Blandford Forum. The approach from Blandford is over a stone bridge making a T-junction with the A350 Shaftesbury road; the bridge was provided in 1795 by the Portman family who owned **Bryanston,** downstream, and their estate housing at the Bryanston end of Durweston makes a formal beginning to the village, which spreads tidily between the high ground and the water-meadows. Bryanston village is, in contrast, a mess, apart from the 18th-c model farm with its wide shallow arches in red brick. The present grandiose school building was built by Norman Shaw at the turn of the century for the 2nd Viscount Portman: in the architectural circumstances Wyatt's 18th-c gateway, facing the town of Blandford, is deceitfully inviting.

Stourpaine faces Durweston across the meadows where the Shaftesbury road strikes N up the narrowing valley of the Iwerne – constricted almost immediately by Hod Hill rising square between the confluence of the two rivers. This Iron Age encampment, taken over and garrisoned by the Roman legions, still has the air of a natural fortress towering above the surrounding countryside. It is separated by a narrow combe on the N from what the poet Jeremy Hooker calls 'Hambledon's curved man-hewed back'. Higher, irregular in shape, less thoroughly investigated than Hod Hill, Hambledon presents a challenge to the archaeologist which has so far been taken up with little determination.

Iwerne Courtney, alias Shroton, lies between Hambledon and the A350 – the main road having deserted the stream for a stretch: stone cottages and long barns, some thatched.

GODSHILL, Isle of Wight, is probably the Isle of Wight's most photographed village – and not surprisingly, since the tower of the parish church rising from a cluster of cottages provides a picture-postcard combination of stone and thatch. The 14th-c church – the third on a prominent site which itself gives fine views over the S of the island – contains a unique medieval mural showing Christ crucified on a triple-branched flowering lily, the 'Lily Cross'. Climbing the mound on which the church stands is well worth the effort: gravestones share the churchyard not only with bracken, brambles, nettles and grass but with a well-populated rookery. Small patches are carefully tended, but following the narrow winding paths through the thickets and undergrowth is an eerie experience made stranger by sudden glimpses of the roofs of the village far below. Superior persons find Godshill self-conscious and commercialized, but the older buildings are undeniably pretty, from gabled hotel to private cottage (one near the church has a roof like a Norman helmet, with eye-slits for first-floor windows and a noseguard between the two which stretches down to protect the front door). And if a teashop wishes to proclaim itself one of Godshill's original six 16th-c cottages, why shouldn't it?

GRAFFHAM, *W. Sussex,* 4m S of Halfway Bridge on A272, which here runs W to E, N of the Rother: there is no parallel route S of the river, only a network of lanes loosely connecting the villages and hamlets which lie below the scarp of the South Downs. The gently undulating terrain is reminiscent of Surrey heathland – sandy knolls with bracken, silver birches, rhododendrons and pines. Lanes from Halfway Bridge and other points either side of the Midhurst–Petworth road converge on Graffham: efforts have rightly been made to obliterate the word 'only' from a signpost saying 'Graffham Church Only', for it is just at this point that the real village begins. A single street winds uphill between the houses (much flint – but practically every other building material as well) to the much-restored church and – across the road – a churchyard with suitably ecclesiastical trees. Beyond the church, the 30 m.p.h. speed limit through the village ends. So, in fact, does the road – only a track leads up to the hanger on the ridge of the downs and down the other side through woodland and farmland to the Lavant valley.

Heyshott is W of Graffham – 2m by crow, 4m by car – along the Rother valley: similar attractions plus a straggly green. Just E of Heyshott is the source of a stream which joins the Rother at Selham. In the angle between stream and river Ambersham Common runs NE to give all-round views of this very agreeable mixture of landscapes.

GREAT WISHFORD, *Wilts.* (6m NW of Salisbury), is the most southerly of a delightful series of villages in the valley of the Wylye, which gave its name to Wilton and hence to Wiltshire. 'Great' is a relative term since Little Wishford is a small group of buildings N of the river on the A36, which carries fast, heavy and constant traffic between Salisbury and Warminster – between Southampton and Bristol, in fact. Luckily, from Wilton to Heytesbury there is a pleasant alternative route which plays snakes-and-ladders with the old Great Western railway line and leaves its villages in peace.

Wishford villagers maintain an old reputation as fighters for their rights. The Earls of Pembroke in creating Wilton Park closed the E–W road S of the River Nadder. The villagers of Wishford reacted, and their victory over the family's efforts to close Grovely Wood on the ridge above the village is still commemorated. To celebrate their ancient right to cut and gather wood there, the people of Wishford rise at first light on Oakapple Day (29 May) and cut green branches from Grovely to decorate their church and cottages (and, it is said, to provide sticks for their runner beans). They go on to the cathedral at Salisbury, where at one time there were further celebrations in the form of dancing before the High Altar and a fair in the Close. But this Christianization of a pagan Rite of Spring was too much for the Victorians, and today's proceedings tend to be rather more seemly, in the style of a garden fête.

The church has a 17th-c monument to Sir Richard Grobham, said to have killed the last boar – or one of the last – in these parts; he also has a more functional memorial in the Grobham Almshouses, where stone walls and mullioned windows represent one building style among many in the village. Next door, for instance, there is an 18th-c school building in chequered brickwork. Nearby a high wall – cob and brick – is surmounted by thatch protected not only by netting but by a notice, 'Please keep off the thatch'. It can't be strictly for the birds: perhaps an unfortunate experience one Oakapple Day prompted it.

Little Langford, Steeple Langford and **Hanging Langford** lie upstream: cottages in stone, flint and brick either singly or – more frequently – in combination. There is some lovely chequerwork in squares of flint, and among the simple but effective decorative patterns are alternate bands of flint and brick.

Wylye village, beyond the Langfords, is where the A303 London–Exeter road crosses the valley. In recent years traffic has been diverted by way of a loop around and partly above the village: it was a kiss of life for a community choking to death – not a very gentle kiss, perhaps, but it came just in time.

Stockton, upstream again, maintains the Wylye Valley standards (no wonder Cobbett called it 'very fine') not only in its groups of cottages but also in a three-sided courtyard of almshouses, named after the Topp – an Elizabethan merchant – who built Stockton House. This has many of the ingredients which make the humbler dwellings such a delight – mullioned windows, banding of flintwork and stonework – but on the grand scale. Farmhouses of the same period or a little later help to separate the villages by two or three centuries from the trunk road ½m away.

HURSTBOURNE TARRANT, *Hants.*, was the termination of one of William Cobbett's *Rural Rides*. 'Uphusband', he called it, and made many references to it in his writings. Most were highly appreciative: 'The houses of the village', he recorded, 'are in great part scattered about, and are among very fine and lofty trees; and from many points round about, from the hilly fields, now covered in young wheat, or with scarcely less beautiful sainfoin, the village is a sight worth going many miles to see.'

A long steep slope precipitates travellers N from Andover on the A343 into the valley of the Bourne. The village grew up where the road crosses both the stream and the minor road (B3048) which follows its curving course down under a high brick railway viaduct at St Mary Bourne to its junction with the Test at Hurstbourne Priors (Cobbett's 'Downhusband') and hence by the side of the Test itself to Wherwell (q.v.). Hurstbourne Tarrant has survived the main road traffic. On the Newbury side of the cross-roads an old chapel and a group of thatched cottages have been converted into a craft gallery. ½m further on, a lane swings N to follow a wide dry valley – a favourite spot for picnics – which runs up to the county boundary (see Combe). Many of Hurstbourne Tarrant's visual attractions lie, however, along the minor road which follows the stream – dry in summer, like so many chalkland rivulets. **Ibthorpe** lies upstream. Georgian houses which Jane Austen knew lie among flint cottages (many of them abruptly end-on to the road) and add a touch of elegance to what is already one of the prettiest villages in one of Hampshire's quietest valleys. The road runs N through Upton and Vernham Dean to the high ground where Hants. meets Berks. and Wilts. E of Vernham Dean is Chute Causeway, the classic case of a Roman (Venta Belgarum–Cunetio, i.e. Winchester–Mildenhall, near Marlborough) road taking a vast detour, along a far older track, to by-pass natural obstacles – in this instance, Hippenscombe and Haydown Hill. Magnificent country!

IMBER, *Wilts.*, is in the middle of a battle-training area stretching over the NW quarter of Salisbury Plain. It may not be visited except by permission of the Ministry of Defence, which is normally granted once or twice a year. The ghost village is included in these pages to recall a promise made to the inhabitants, when the Army turned them out in 1943, that they would be allowed to return. One inhabitant, the village blacksmith, is reported to have died of a broken heart on finding, within a few weeks of the compulsory evacuation, that his smithy had been demolished and his much-prized bellows had 'disappeared'. The shell of the parish church remains: the houses and cottages of timber and brick have been replaced by concrete façades used to train men in street fighting.

LURGASHALL, *W. Sussex* (5m NW of Petworth), has a classic village green – triangular, it slopes down to the E side where most of the houses are grouped. To the NW, Blackdown, the final thrust of a high shoulder which stretches back to the meeting-point of Sussex, Hampshire and Surrey, makes an impressive backdrop to the village, with the middle distance filled by tall trees. The green is in itself a meeting-point – of architectural styles. These vary according to building materials but the stone cottages complement, rather than make a contrast to, the tile-hanging which recalls villages to the N and E. Some of the buildings appear at first sight squat, owing to the height of their brick chimney-stacks, but the overall effect is attractive indeed. **Lickfold** to the S and **Fernhurst** to the W (another green here, edged by cottages in stone or tile) typify the cosy villages and hamlets in this

fine area of woodland and streams bounded by the A283 (Guildford–Petworth) on the E and on the W by the A286 (Haslemere–Midhurst).

Lodsworth, further S towards Halfway Bridge, combines formal house with casual cottage along the main trunk of the village street and its short branches: much tiling, even a touch of weatherboarding.

Tillington, in the extreme SE of the rectangle, is abruptly ruled off by the high wall enclosing the park of Petworth House (National Trust): the harsh line matters less in this trim estate village than in Petworth itself, where the wall juts into a corner of the little town and adversely affects a layout which includes some elegant buildings.

MELBURY OSMOND, *Dorset*, hides successfully 7m S of Yeovil just off the A37 to Dorchester. Thatched cottages appear grouped together as though awaiting the next photographer. The road pattern is almost that of a swastika, with all lane-lines but one stopping abruptly, or almost so, or else petering out into tracks. One of these reaches a mill to the N, another crosses a ford to the S – the stream in both cases being one of the many which flow through this farmland of Dorset's NW frontier and join on the border of Somerset.

Melbury Sampford is where the stream rises – 1m S, in fact in the parkland of Melbury House, where a Tudor tower rising above 17th-c remodelling is echoed after a fashion by Victorian-Tudor extensions.

MICHELDEVER, *Hants.* (pronounced 'Mitchel-devver') is to most people a small railway station, in London and South Western Classical architecture – Tite, 1840 – on the main line from Waterloo to Southampton. Esmeralda and other abandoned relics of the Pullman Car Company no longer rust sadly away in the deep cutting from which chalk was taken for embankments further down the line and for reclaiming land during the building of Southampton Docks; but the sidings still have the air of an elephants' graveyard for Southern rolling stock. Until Andover, 10m away, had its own line, Micheldever Station, which came to give its name to the settlement which sprang up around it, was known as Andover Road. All this is preliminary to the real village of Micheldever, 2m S: both railway and main road (A33 Basingstoke–Winchester) missed it, thereby ensuring its compact survival around a staggered cross-roads.

The church is startling: it has a red-brick octagon plonked (1808) in the middle of a medieval building already equipped with a tower of flint and stone. In an unmarked grave in the churchyard – it used to be said that snow never settled on it – is buried a 19-year-old ploughboy from the village, Henry Cook, hanged during the agricultural riots of 1831 for allegedly striking a landowner, William Baring, with intent to murder. Inside the church, by way of contrast, three monuments commemorate the Barings, whose family vault lies beneath the floor of the chancel.

Stoke Charity is downstream and 2m W of Micheldever. The Dever, also known as the Bullington, has like so many other chalk streams in Hampshire been channelled and controlled for the commercial growing of watercress. At Stoke – it belonged in the 13th c to Henry de la Charité – the church appears to be emerging from the watercress beds: in fact it is on a slight rise in the meadows. Cottages almost dabble in the water; there is a lane on either side of the stream W to **Wonston,** where a medieval grouping of buildings beyond the church merges into the main-road settlement of Sutton Scotney.

MILTON ABBAS, *Dorset* (8m SE of Blandford Forum: turn N off A354 at Winterborne Whitchurch or Milborne St Andrew), is often cited as an early example of town – or rather village – planning: sometimes it is forgotten that the process involved wholesale demolition. The winding, sloping single street of thatched cottages, set in a continuous stretch of lawn (*see illustration on page 18*), was planned in the 1770s, and no doubt in those days a semi-detached two-up two-down with shared front door was a desirable enough residence, though the village could scarcely have provided accommodation for many of those who had lived and worked in the small market town which the Earl of Dorchester razed because it spoiled his view. But along with some of the inhabitants came to the new site a row of single-storey almshouses built 100 years previously and transferred bodily from the town to the village: a gesture, perhaps, towards what would today be called 'public relations' though – since there was accommodation only for six deserving persons – it was a modest gesture indeed. The almshouses were erected, or rather re-erected, in 1779: and seven years later a church was built opposite.

At the top of the village is some incongruous 19th-c brick: the 20th c has shown something between tact and cowardice in placing its council houses as far out of sight of 18th-c Milton Abbas as 18th-c Milton Abbas was out of sight of His Lordship's new house. The school which now occupies it has made no attempt to tuck away its own ancillary buildings, which hang about at the side and rear of the main Abbey House as though waiting for something to happen.

What happened to the original abbey, a 10th-c foundation, was that after the Dissolution its church became a parish church and then its main hall – dating from 1498 – was incorporated into the Earl's grandiose (his own architect called it 'ugly') residence. The mass is mitigated by Capability Brown's landscaping, with its artificial lake backed by decorous woodland, but the effect was partly lost when the school playing-fields were laid out in the grounds.

MORETON, *Dorset* (5m NE of Wool, 1m E of B3390, Affpuddle–Weymouth), is where Lawrence of Arabia is buried. Past the church – a mixture of Georgian elegance and Gothic complication, famous for its memorial windows engraved by Laurence Whistler – a track fords the River Frome and rises through plantations to a point on the Bovington Road at Clouds Hill, where Lawrence's cottage is now National Trust property. Notices about tank-training areas are reminders of the proximity of Bovington Camp, where he essayed one of his attempts at anonymity in the guise of Trooper Ross. Near Moreton Church a tall thatched post office stands at the entrance to a cul-de-sac of thatched cottages; opposite the church the graveyard extension where Lawrence lies has a lychgate with incongruously classical columns; but the common factor in many of Moreton's buildings is the diamond pattern on heavily leaded windows.

Woodsford, 3m NW of Moreton on a lane which crosses the B3390 and follows the course of the Frome in the direction of Dorchester, is a hamlet remarkable for a partially-thatched castle: a fortified manor house dating from the 14th c, it now towers (literally) over its farmyard below.

OKEFORD FITZPAINE, *Dorset* (4m SE of Sturminster Newton: 1m from A357 at Shillingstone or New Cross Gate), sits at a complicated cross-roads. The E–W road dips S on the outskirts of the village before curving back almost immediately to meet the lanes to N and E. From the curve a short spur leads to the church, which from below appears to be backing up the hill. The irregular pattern gives added interest to the mixed collection of cottages and houses, some built a little above road level: many are thatched, several have alternate bands of flintwork and brickwork. One has a section of timber frame with brick infilling (and thatch) at right angles to a stone section with mullioned windows.

Hammoon (3m N of Okeford Fitzpaine across the A357), lies on a wiggle of the River Stour: the closely grouped church, manor and farm are separated from the water by little more than the width of the short and narrow lane which serves them. Beyond the hamlet to the N the problems caused by the Stour's meanderings are emphasized by the provision of a lifebelt near the bridge, a notice 'Road Liable to Flooding', and the name on somebody's gate, 'The Lighthouse'.

Back through Hammoon and Okeford Fitzpaine the road to the S climbs the slope of Woolland Hill, where a ridge offers a series of views spectacular even by Dorset standards. At Bulbarrow a pedestal provided by the Automobile Association marks the direction of sundry towns and villages in Blackmoor Vale. From here the road SE to Cheselbourne and Puddletown (*see* Tolpuddle) passes through **Ansty,** where a remarkable pub, with a façade like a Victorian railway station and an interior decor which defies classification, provides delicious food and a remarkable beer under the name of Old Ansty Ale. This tends to encapsulate the drinker from the world for a while, so that a brief indifference prevails even to such sad sights as the intermittent replacement of thatch by corrugated sheeting.

Kenneth Scowen
The centre of Gilbert White's village of Selborne

RAMSBURY, *Wilts.*, was in Saxon times the centre of a flourishing diocese, complete with cathedral and bishop: three of the latter went on to become Archbishops of Canterbury. But it's a case of long time no See: and in fact Ramsbury has been a mere parish for nine centuries and more. Nevertheless the church has Anglo-Saxon remains and even part of a Viking-style cross which probably dates from the 9th c. Many houses in the main street, which ends in a triangle in front of a notably hospitable pub, have gardens stretching down to the Kennet; and downstream Ramsbury Manor in 17th-c brick and stone takes fine advantage of its riverside setting.

Littlecote, still further down, has a notable Tudor-Elizabethan mansion, and **Chilton Foliat,** 1m E on the Berks. boundary, allows villagers as well as those at the big house to enjoy the amenities of living by the river.

ROCKBOURNE, *Hants.*, is 4m NW of Fordingbridge, where its bourne joins the River Avon. 'The village street in Rockbourne', says Pevsner, 'is one of the prettiest in Hampshire.' Quite so, though actually it has been in Hampshire only since a revision of county boundaries in 1895, and most of the houses and cottages which alternate so attractively – with a good pub half way – along the course of the winding little stream were in Wiltshire when they were built. Pre-dating the notion of counties altogether are the (originally Norman) church and adjacent manor, whose cluster of farm buildings include a 14th-c barn. But the oldest homestead in the village is the Roman villa, or at least its remains: discovered by a local estate agent, who was also an enthusiastic amateur archaeologist, in 1942, it has yielded coins, other objects, and a fine geometrical mosaic laid over an older floor of chalk.

Martin, NW of Rockbourne and just off the A354 (Salisbury–Blandford Forum) was in 1978 voted Hampshire's best-kept village – and that was after having been runner-up on four occasions. Contributing factors must have been a neat mixture of cottages in brick and thatch, stone and tile – plus a green complete with parish pump. Martin Down, a rare stretch of unploughed chalkland, is a nature reserve.

Breamore, 2m N of Fordingbridge in the Avon Valley, has a particularly fine Saxon church. It lies in the grounds of Breamore House (Elizabethan, but largely rebuilt after a fire in 1856), home of a Southampton merchant who must have been the town's first businessman to have a place in the country. His descendant has opened a carriage museum in his 17th-c stables – part of a countryside museum which shows among other things the development of agricultural implements and machinery.

SELBORNE, *Hants.*, is rare among world-famous villages in appearing almost unaware of its fame. Somehow it has kept to a minimum the selling of antiques, bric-à-brac and rubbish to the visitors who come from all over the globe to see the home of Gilbert White, whose *Natural History of Selborne* has run through more editions than any other book in English apart from the Bible.

Born in 1729, White was the grandson of a vicar of Selborne; he himself became curate of the parish, and his home from the age of nine was Wakes, a house in the main street named after the farmer to whom it had once belonged. Much extended (and wrongly renamed The Wakes) the original house was – like so many others in the pleasantly winding street – built of the local chalky sandstone and faced with brick. A private house until 1953, it is now the Gilbert White Museum, run in conjunction with a Field Study Centre for Hampshire schoolchildren, and visitors may see where the parson-naturalist wrote the letters which later became his *Natural History*. His scene-setting is still valid:

'The parish of Selborne lies in the extreme eastern corner of the county of Hampshire ... is about 50 miles from London ... and near midway between the towns of Alton and Petersfield ... The high part to the southeast consists of a vast hill of chalk rising 300ft above the village; and is divided into a sheep down, the high wood, and a long hanging wood called the Hanger ... The village consists of one single straggling street which divides two very incongruous soils: rank clay ... and a warm forward crumbling mould called black malm ... Nore Hill is remarkable for sending two streams into two different seas. The one to the south becomes a branch of the Arun, falling into the British Channel: the other to the north ... makes one branch of the Wey, passes to Guildford, and so into the Thames and thus into the German Ocean. In the centre of the village, and near the church, is a square piece of ground surrounded by houses, and vulgarly called the Plestor ... Among the singularities of this place are two rocky hollow lanes by the traffic of ages and the fretting of the water worn down in many places 16 or 18 feet beneath the level of the fields ... These rugged gloomy scenes affright the ladies but delight the naturalist with their various botany.'

Between the Hanger – a later resident of Selborne, the poet Anthony Rye, likened it to a stranded whale – and White's home is his garden. Also the object of careful restoration, it is notable in its own right as a modest example of how formal gardens were beginning to give way to 'romantic' landscaping with vistas of distant countryside. Like its statelier counterparts it had a haha, or walled ditch, which kept out the cattle without interrupting the view – possibly the first example to be dug for a small private garden.

Selborne is lucky in having a specialist country bookshop founded next to Wakes in 1968. Numerous editions of the three 'local' authors – Gilbert White, Jane Austen and Edward Thomas – are among volumes on country matters of all kinds; there is a special corner for the publications of the National Trust, including a guide to the land it owns in the village; and the shop intermittently plays host to craftsmen demonstrating their skills as hurdle-makers, thatchers, woodcarvers, besommakers and wheelwrights.

Less peaceable demonstrations at Selborne are recalled by a heavy leather collar displayed in the parish church. It was worn by a mastiff which in the 1830s the Rev. William Cobbold bought (somewhat belatedly) to protect him from 'the Selborne Mob' – agricultural rioters who 'persuaded' him to take a cut in tithes and went on to ransack the workhouse which symbolized the degradation to which low wages had brought them. Also in the church are some 13th-c encaustic tiles from Selborne Priory, founded in 1232 1m E and suppressed in 1486 by Pope Innocent VIII.

Behind Wakes a path which White frequently trod, The Zigzag, leads up to Selborne Hanger. From the summit the view stretches away to the South Downs: and in the opposite direction lies Shoulder of Mutton Hill.

Steep is a good name for the village at the bottom of the slope. The poet, Edward Thomas had a cottage here and a memorial to him stands on the hill in the form of a sarsen stone. In the parish church below a memorial window designed by Laurence Whistler was dedicated in 1978 – the centenary of Thomas's birth – by the Welsh parson-poet R. S. Thomas. Nearby is Bedales, where Edward's children went to school in its pioneering days before World War I – in which their father was to lose his life during the Battle of Arras in 1917. A third memorial may be found in the form of a plaque in what is now the Edward Thomas Bar of the White Horse, an isolated but deservedly popular pub on the high ground near Colemore (W of Steep): it is mentioned in his first published poem, 'Up in the Wind'.

Chawton is at the other end of Selborne's literary axis, a small village sadly bisected by the Alton by-pass but retaining some attractive corners. Chawton House was left to Jane Austen's brother in 1794: the 16th-c house stands on rising ground on the Fareham side of the village, ½m from the modest building of red brick in which Jane herself lived between 1809 and 1816. Visitors may now see the home where she wrote *Mansfield Park*, *Emma*, and *Persuasion*, for the years when the two-storey house was divided into separate cottages are happily past.

SHORWELL, *Isle of Wight* (5m SE of Newport), is a village which has survived the tourist invasion better than most – drawing a kind of strength, perhaps, from the downs which shelter it and the three manors which still seem to promise some kind of protection. West Court and Wolverton are on the outskirts and North Court next to the (mostly) 14th-c church. Here the early 19th-c primitive altar-piece of the Last Supper is a replica of an Icelandic craftsman's work: the original, sold to the owner of North Court at the turn of the 20th c when the church authorities at Thingvellir replaced it by a modern painting, was returned by Shorwell to its original home after the help of Magnus Magnusson had been enlisted to trace its whereabouts. The road into the village from the N winds downhill between high banks and under a rustic footbridge: do not let it lead you out the other side without giving you a chance to look round.

Brighstone (another show village) and **Mottistone,** both W of Shorwell, suffer from heavy summer traffic: the latter, with its church-and-manor nucleus, usually keeps its calm but there are moments when Brighstone suffers from seeming to consist of a square of lanes with a coach park in the middle. Consolation may be found on the high ground to the N where Brighstone Forest – a forest in scale with the rest of the island – and Mottistone Down offer some of the best walks and views in the Wight.

SINDLESHAM, *Berks.*, midway between Wokingham and Reading, has a long, arched, three-storey mill in plain brick, which contrasts with the stucco finish given to the brickwork of Sindlesham House with its imposing pediment and seven bays. The village is, however, chiefly of sociological interest, one side of Sindlesham Green being occupied by houses of the Bearwood Estate. This was laid out in the 1860s and 1870s in a Victorian version of Jacobean, with red brick and gables manufactured from clay and timber on the 17,500-acre estate, to go with Bear Wood – the vast mansion constructed for John Walter III of *The Times*. Robert Kerr's plans for the big house included such contemporary necessities as gaming room, brushing room, deed room and butler's corridor; while the estate village had its own pub, church and one of several schools in the neighbourhood for which the philanthropic John Walter footed the bill.

SINGLETON, *W. Sussex*, would be worth a visit even without the wholly admirable Weald and Downland Open Museum, where neglected or endangered buildings from S and SE England have been re-erected on a sloping grassy site topped with woodland. Visitors may also see such reconstructions as a charcoal-burner's hut – put up with the help and advice of an old lady who remembered living in one with her family as a child – a pottery and a smithy. On occasion craftsmen and craftswomen demonstrate their skills *in situ*: spinning by a log fire of which only some of the smoke finds its way out through a hole in the roof must require considerable dedication in the 20th c. It is a treat to be able to look round such buildings as a Wealden farmhouse or the market hall from Titchfield (q.v.) from the inside as well as admiring their fine exteriors.

In Singleton village flint cottages spread back from the Chichester–Midhurst road into a modest block of lanes, their plots recalling Cobbett's comment that the cottage gardens in these parts included some of the very best he had ever seen in England. The Norman church has a memorial to Honest Tom Johnson, huntsman of the Charlton Hunt, who died in 1744, with this intimation of mortality:

Unpleasing Truth – Death hunts us from our Birth
In view; and Men, like Foxes, take to Earth.

Charlton itself, and **East Dean** further on, lie due E of Singleton in the upper stretch of the River Lavant.

SLINDON, *W. Sussex*, lies 4m W of Arundel at the hub of a picturesque wheel. The most clearly defined section of the rim forms part of the A29 (Bognor–Dorking road); this takes through-traffic over Slindon Common and away from the village, which is connected to the main road by a series of lanes radiating like irregular spokes. The circular hub contains a square of little streets: before restoration the 11th-c church in the NE corner must have fitted even more naturally into its surroundings, and even today it is enhanced by a little open space. Not that there is any sense of constriction – 'open' is in fact an adjective which may justly apply to much of Slindon, and the view S from this village on the slope of the Downs stretches as far as the sea.

Slindon belonged to the Archbishops of Canterbury from Saxon to Tudor times, apart from a hundred-year break after the Conquest: a tablet in the church records that Stephen Langton, 'upholder of English liberties in Magna Carta', died in the parish in 1228 – and the brief remains of a tower from the 13th-c palace of the archbishops are in the kitchen garden of Slindon House. There was an Elizabethan manor here with a secret chapel where Mass is believed to have been celebrated for 500 years – including the period during which it was illegal. In the 18th c the manor passed to the Earls of Newburgh: the last Countess died in 1861 and a series of lawsuits ensued over both title and property. The house

was, says Pevsner, 'gratuitously messed about' in 1921: after World War II it became a school, but the entire estate of over 3000 acres, including much of the village, was bequeathed in 1948 to the National Trust.

Flint is the predominant building material in the village but there is some brick and of course the two appear in combination. With its traditional cottages, duckpond and background of beechwoods Slindon in many ways epitomizes the Sussex village. Hilaire Belloc spent his childhood here, and though it was as an exile that he recalled 'the great hills of the South Country' he found Slindon when he returned as an adult even more delightful than he had remembered.

Eartham, 2m NW of Slindon, is another lovely village of flint and brick that has benefited from a policy of preservation: it was, however, applied too late to save the parish church, though the interior has survived. Memorials include a tablet to William Huskisson of Eartham House: as MP for Chichester he attended the celebrations for the opening of the Liverpool and Manchester Railway and, to quote a contemporary account, 'from some cause not clearly ascertained fell under the engine': thus achieving distinction as one of the first victims of a railway accident.

Stane Street runs 1m W of Eartham on its course from Noviomagus (Chichester) to Londinium: various stretches remain in use, and staging posts have been discovered, but the line is lost for a while on its N descent from the South Downs.

Bignor is near this point, some 5m NE of Slindon. It looks back to the Downs from a square of lanes, one side of which boasts a splendidly untitivated 15th-c half-timbered thatched cottage with Kentish-looking upper-storey overhang, and separate infillings of flint, brick and plaster. Eastward is a well-excavated Roman villa.

SONNING, *Berks.*, has a Thames Street winding up from the river – and its 18th-c brick bridge into Oxfordshire – between walls of mellow brick. One shelters a house designed by Lutyens and topped by a bold trio of chimney-stacks. Brick is also the building material for Georgian houses and Victorian alms-cottages in the other two, rather quieter, streets at the centre of the village; while there is timber-framing in the handsome pub and a number of earlier cottages. Little evidence remains, except in Tudor brickwork in the churchyard wall, of a palace which belonged to the Bishops of Salisbury.

STRATFORD-SUB-CASTLE, *Wilts.*, is in the Avon valley 3m N of Salisbury – the 'castle' being Old Sarum on the ridge above the village. This was successively an Iron Age hill fort, the Roman town of Sorviodunum, and a medieval city with castle and cathedral: when church and state fell out in the 12th c the clergy moved downhill where there was more room – and water. Their 'City of New Sarum' is still the correct name for Salisbury. Old Sarum seen from below is a background of earthworks rather than a dominating skyline and, like other Avon villages, Stratford is an unhurried place retaining much of the 17th- and 18th-c calm implicit in the appearance of the houses dating from that period. Main roads N from Salisbury stick to the high ground on either side of the valley, and it is not until an E–W route crosses the valley at Amesbury that the rural quiet is rather hideously lost.

Durnford, upstream from Stratford with stone church and brick manor, is the only village E of the river on this stretch: the elegant stone front of Little Durnford Manor faces a lane which zigzags up Camp Down on the Salisbury–Devizes road and continues by way of a once tree-lined avenue towards Wilton.

The Woodfords – Lower, Middle and Upper – lie on the W bank of the Avon, hugging the stream without contributing much to the embrace: it is the widening water-meadows with their waving lines of pollard willows which are the main attraction here.

Wilsford and **Lake** hide among trees and though there is a classic example at the former of a cruck cottage it is only with a short stretch of houses and cottages confusingly known as **West Amesbury** that this length of the Wiltshire Avon shows any style. N of the jumble of Amesbury the valley shows, alas, little but evidence of armed occupation: rows of married quarters and barrack-blocks look as though some NCO has told them to get fell in with total disregard of existing village layouts, building styles, or natural features of the landscape.

Ablington, S of Figheldean, has a hint of past attractions with a row of timber-framed cottages; **Fittleton** has fared comparatively well, with church, rectory and manor still providing the nucleus for a group of non-military buildings; but **Enford**'s church and thatched cottages in the water-meadows are dominated by a modern estate marching stridently along the skyline.

Stonehenge is 2½m W of Amesbury. An apparently serious suggestion by a local councillor that visitors might be diverted to, and presumably by, a plastic replica, has not so far been adopted. As the top pop monument of the Department of the Environment it has however begun at last to show such signs of wear and tear that it is now roped off from its coachloads of admirers by wire fencing: a pity, because it is only from inside the circle that one feels any sense of grandeur. Against the impressive open landscape the mighty stones are, unless strong sunlight throws them into silhouette, almost incidental.

TISBURY, *Wilts.* (12m W of Wilton, midway between the A30 and the B3089), grew up at the confluence of the Nadder, flowing NE from Tollard Royal (q.v.) and Donhead, and its tributary stream flowing S from Fonthill. This extensive village has overflowed into the fields around but is worth a visit for its vast thatched barn at Place Farm on the E outskirts. Originally a grange in the widespread estates ruled over by the Abbess of Shaftesbury, it is 190ft long and has 13 bays, which by some people's reckoning makes it the biggest in the country. Built – like most of the older houses and cottages in Tisbury – of stone from local quarries, it has survived as part of a group of 15th-c buildings which included an inner and outer gatehouse.

Fonthill Gifford (2m NW of Tisbury) is a little more than a cross-roads with cottages grouped happily round a church. On the road to Fonthill Bishop is a triumphal-looking gateway optimistically but understandably attributed to Inigo Jones. This led originally to a Jacobean mansion and, when it burned down, to Fonthill Splendens, a Palladian mansion built on the site by Alderman William Beckford, a Lord Mayor of London who had inherited a vast fortune founded on West Indies sugar-plantations. It passed to his son, also William, an eccentric who played out his less scandalous fantasies by writing the early Gothic novel, *Vathek,* and getting James Wyatt to replace Splendens – one wing remains as a pair of cottages – with Fonthill Abbey, a Gothic fantasy in stone. It was his home for 15 years but his impatience had meant over-hasty construction and in 1825, three years after he had moved to Bath and sold the building to a speculator for literally a knock-down price, the 300ft tower collapsed. Today little remains but a smaller tower and one end of the elaborate and costly oddity of architecture.

Chilmark, 3m E of Fonthill Bishop, provided stone from its quarries for houses up and down the Nadder and Ebble valleys, for Salisbury Cathedral and Wilton House, and for buildings all over the South Country. The vaults and tunnels are now used for storing *matériel de guerre,* which means that few see anything of the underground network – first excavated during the Roman occupation – but wire fences and warning notices.

Teffont Magna and **Teffont Evias,** further E, are both pretty villages – in stone, naturally – which follow the line of a stream joining the Nadder 5m E of Tisbury.

Dinton is downstream but separated from the river by a railway running through the water-meadows. The village has groups of stone houses and cottages (some National Trust property) with mullioned windows.

TITCHFIELD, *Hants.,* is in essence the largest and farthest downstream of a whole series of Meon Valley villages. It grew in importance until the 17th c, when the building of a sea-wall at the mouth of the river cut its links with the Solent; then the increase in E–W traffic – once through the village, later to the N along the re-routed A27 and now M27 – began to block its geographical and historical connections with Hants. hinterland.

Early Jutish settlers in the Meon Valley were converted to Christianity by St Wilfrid, and the parish church (standing at the end of a side-street from the old market square) contains in its 8th- or 9th-c porch – now the base of the tower – some of the oldest Saxon masonry in the county. The next social and architectural phase in the life of the village is typified by the zigzag Norman decoration over the arch between the tower and the nave, while the N aisle is a remarkable exercise in the Perp style: but many visitors to the church are drawn straight to the family tomb of the Wriothesleys in the 14th-c S chapel.

Thomas Wriothesley, 1st Earl of Southampton, was Chancellor to Henry VIII. Granted Titchfield Abbey, which had been founded in 1232, at the Dissolution he built on its site his magnificent Place House – Tudor in time but earlier in mood. His grandson, the 3rd Earl, was Shakespeare's patron, and there are stories to the effect that many of the sonnets were written at Titchfield while the poet was his youthful patron's guest: and even that several of his plays – *Love's Labour's Lost, Romeo and Juliet, Midsummer Night's Dream*, and *Twelfth Night* – were first performed at Place House. The 4th Earl, who gave temporary shelter to Charles I *en route* to captivity at Carisbrooke on the Isle of Wight, died childless and the estate passed in 1781 to the Delme family. They demolished almost all of it, but for the spectacular three-storey gatehouse, to enlarge their own mansion a few miles away – Cams Hall, Fareham.

The Square at Titchfield – boats must have tied up at wharves hereabouts in its heyday as a port – is predominantly Georgian in appearance; but many of the façades conceal brickwork and timber of the two preceding centuries, examples of which may be seen in streets radiating from The Square. During the Georgian improvements the 17th-c market hall – with its lock-up jail in one corner – was moved round the corner out of sight and allowed to deteriorate. By 1971 the local authorities, Fareham Urban Council and Hampshire County Council, seemed happy for it to be demolished – and this despite the fact that Titchfield had become the first entire village to be defined as a Conservation Area under the Civic Amenities Act. At the last moment, however, agreement was reached and the money found for the building to be dismantled, re-erected and restored at the Weald and Downland Open Air Museum at Singleton, W. Sussex (q.v.).

The Meon enters the Solent about as romantically as a sewage outfall, through what is little more than a culvert under the winding shore road. This is only the most recent of a series of efforts to reduce flooding along the final stretch of the river. The 1st Earl of Southampton is usually credited with having appointed a marine engineer, Richard Taulbotte or Talbot, and a team of Dutch specialists to dam, divert and widen the Meon. This ruined the fishing, and indignant villagers burned the Earl in effigy: the origin, some say, of the Titchfield Bonfire Carnival which now attracts thousands of visitors each November. What was once a busy estuary is now a stretch of fields and marshland offering sanctuary to waterfowl and other forms of wildlife. Its survival is something of a miracle under the threat of increasing pressure of population from E and W, the most frightening indication of which was a monstrous plan to link the conurbations of Portsmouth and Southampton into a vast Solent City.

Wickham, the largest of the other Meon Valley villages, lies upstream: birthplace of William of Wykeham, founder of Winchester College, it is built round an otherwise attractive rectangle which has become a car park first and a market square afterwards. The great majority of the buildings on the two longer sides, N and S, are modest but attractive variations in Georgian brick: recently efforts have been made to retain existing façades even when wholesale reconstruction has been carried out on the buildings themselves. W of the Square a new development almost succeeds in echoing the earlier constructions but its courtyard-style blocks of flats are on far too big a scale. At its E end the Square dips round into Bridge Street, which curves past some older timber-framed cottages down to Chesapeake Mill – built in 1820 with timbers from the American man-o'-war *Chesapeake* captured seven years earlier. It was the now defunct Meon Valley railway on the far bank of the river, rather than the river itself, which cut off Wickham from its (brutally restored) parish church – and put an end to any natural growth E of the village.

Droxford, upstream again, has some attractive groups of buildings along its sloping, winding main street. They include the church (Norman nave with many later additions), 17th-c manor house, and former rectory – an imposing Georgian building where Izaak Walton was a regular visitor. The abandoned railway station was the setting in May 1944 for a conference between Churchill, Eisenhower, Smuts, Mackenzie King, de Gaulle, Eden and Bevin – the meeting, it is believed locally, at which the decision was taken to postpone the D-Day landings on the beaches of Normandy because of bad weather.

TOLLARD ROYAL, *Wilts.*, on B3081, Shaftesbury–Ringwood road, 5m W of its junction with A354. From Shaftesbury in Dorset the Ringwood road climbs Zigzag Hill into a corner of Wiltshire and runs along Charlton Ridge: with the ground falling spectacularly away to the N the prospect still gives some indication of how high turf downland used to look before artificial fertilizers meant it was worth ploughing and seeding. From Woodley Down further along the road a steady descent means that drivers may find themselves beyond Tollard Royal with hardly a glimpse of the village: but there is room, and there should be time, to stop at the bottom of the hill and look – better still, turn – back. The (partly rebuilt) medieval church is up the hill on the left; the pub is on the right; and the village's connection with royalty is in King John's House, a hunting lodge dating from the 13th c. It was owned at one time by General Pitt-Rivers – an early, enlightened, practical and philanthropic archaeologist. He also owned land over the Dorset border at Rushmoor, where he lived, and **Farnham.** Here most of the exhibits at the museum he started were dispersed after his death in 1910 but his pioneering work is commemorated in the name of Farnham's pub – The Museum. Outside it,

Sir Stanley Spencer, r.a. (1891–1959): Swan-upping at Cookham. Oils, 1915 (*Tate Gallery, London*). For all his preoccupation with religious symbolism, Stanley Spencer's work never moved far from Cookham on the Thames, in Berkshire, where he lived for most of his life. Swan-upping is an annual event organized by the Vintners Company, when the Queen's swans are rounded up to have their wings clipped.

JOHN BRETT, A.R.A. (1830–1902): February in the Isle of Wight. Watercolour, 1866
(*By courtesy of Birmingham Museums and Art Gallery*). One of the early Pre-Raphaelites,
Brett later specialized in coastal scenes expressing his great interest in rocks and trees.
The scene of this watercolour drawing has not been positively identified.

sheltered by a sort of wooden platform, are the remains of the village stocks. Nearby, new houses as well as old are thatched and whitewashed so the village – unlike Tollard Royal – obviously enjoys organic growth: though both suffer here and there from outbreaks of corrugated sheeting.

TOLPUDDLE, *Dorset* (5m W of Bere Regis on A35), has a row of cottages and a shelter near the church which both commemorate the Tolpuddle Martyrs, whose early attempts to secure reasonable wages and conditions by banding together into a trade union led to their deportation to Australia as convicts. This makes it the best known, though not the most compact or attractive, of the settlements in the valley of the stream known variously as the Piddle, Puddle, or Trent.

Puddletown (3m W), is the largest: unlike Tolpuddle, it survives as a village with a proper focus since the highway runs to the S of its square. Piddlehinton and Piddletrethide line B3143 which runs along the E bank of the rivulet.

Affpuddle, downstream from Tolpuddle, begins with thatched cottages and has a fine church on the corner where the Weymouth road comes in from its junction, 1m N, with the A35. **Briantspuddle** has not only thatched cottages of similar vintage but some 20th-c additions which fit in reasonably well. Between the two, Bladen Valley is not yet another attempt to find an alternative name for the Piddle but a small combe devoted, less successfully, to a further attempt at twenties Rustic. The War Memorial, also from this latter period, is by Eric Gill.

WHERWELL, *Hants*. (3m SE of Andover in the valley of the Test), is approached from the NW by a zigzag road which takes in its steep stride a bridge over a dismantled branch railway. Where the old track broadens out into what was a goods yard behind the station, houses have been built with even better views over the water-meadows than the older buildings at road level. Here a big block of old people's flats might have been expected to obtrude but, with white walls and a grey roof, doesn't. Below the railway track and above the meadows, heavy thatch on timber-framed cottages is echoed by hanging woodland on the ridge behind, from which the ground sweeps away N into Harewood Forest. On the river is Priory Park, where an early 19th-c house has been built on the site of a nunnery founded in AD 986: this flourished in the 13th c under a redoubtable abbess named Euphemia. She had advanced ideas on sanitation, though her schemes included the use of the river in a way which would considerably lessen its later reputation as one of the world's most famous – and expensive – trout streams. Wherwell is usually pronounced 'Werral'.

Chilbolton lies on the river bank on lanes leading to the Andover–Stockbridge and Andover–Winchester roads; but it may also be approached by a 10-minute walk from Wherwell across the water-meadows (a wooden footbridge makes the ideal place for feeding ducks or playing Pooh-

sticks) and on to Chilbolton Common. Here two thatched cottages – the larger was an inn until some 50 years ago – mark the end of an abandoned lane leading to the village. The buildings which lined it are said to have been destroyed in a fire and never rebuilt though their contemporaries, together with recent interlopers, survive in the main village street.

Leckford is on the main road which follows the Test S; **Longstock** is on the more attractive alternative route on the W bank of the river. It is very much a working village with a farm at either end and a friendly pub, the Peat Spade, in the middle. The thatched cottages are long pre-dated by the remains behind Charity Farm (a private house) of a wide artificial channel in the water-meadows believed to have been a dock used by Danish longships. Over 300ft long, it runs parallel with the river and is wide enough to have taken the invaders' flat-bottomed boats.

Stockbridge is at the end of the lane from Longstock: go straight over the main road and on the right you will see another private house which used to be an inn. This one recalls the pre-railway days when Welsh cattle were driven across the breadth of England to the great fairs and markets at Farnham and Maidstone. Part of the landlord's message to passing drovers is still legible: 'Gwair Tymherus, Porfa Flasus, Cwrw Da, A Cwal Cysurus' ('Worthwhile grass, pleasant pasture, good beer, and comfortable shelter'). These last two Stockbridge still provides at various points along its wide but undistinguished main – only, in fact – street, a section of the main road from Winchester to Salisbury. Two of the hostelries date from the early 19th c: the White Hart is at the E end and the Grosvenor, where an entire room projects over an impressive porch, in the centre.

Broughton, 5m WSW of Stockbridge and just off the B3084, winds attractively along the Wallop Brook with scarcely a gap between the buildings. The brook gives its name to three settlements – Upper, Middle and Nether Wallop – before passing through Broughton and joining the Test at Bossington.

Mottisfont, 2m S of Bossington between the A3057 and the B3084, is famous for its so-called Abbey (now a National Trust property): this incorporates the nave of a 13th-c priory church, an 18th-c brick frontage, and a 20th-c Gothic drawing-room decor designed by Rex Whistler. The gardens are no less notable, their chief attractions include a collection of pre-1900 European shrub roses and a double plane-tree 100ft high.

WIELD, *Hants*. (7m NE of Alresford), is in name a variation of 'weald' and in fact a village slightly S of the middle of the Basingstoke–Alton–Winchester triangle which forms the greater part of the Hampshire uplands. In all directions there stretches away a gently undulating landscape of copses and fields: nothing dramatic, but satisfying at all seasons. The remoteness of the village has saved it from almost every wind of change but the blast of Victorian church restoration. It was particularly violent in this part of Hampshire and in Wield few signs remain of the original 12th-c building, though the houses and cottages emphasize in their compact layout how the church was often in every sense – social and topographical as well as religious – the centre of village life.

Bentworth, somewhat posher than Wield with a number of bigger houses standing slightly aloof from the village, is 5m W under the silent wings of gliders from Lasham Airfield (2m farther on beyond the Basingstoke–Alton road). The pub looks out at fields over a minute village green – one tree, two posts. Nearby, in a cul-de-sac with flint-walled school alongside, the 13th-c church has survived attempts at improvement. This is more than can be said of those in the string of settlements 1m W where a road follows the course of the Candover Brook.

Preston Candover, the most northerly of these villages, offers glimpses of Georgian elegance beyond the thatched cottages which line the road. By the time of the Enclosure Act in 1830 over three-quarters of the parish had fallen into the hands of three landowners and, as Philip Sheail records in his parish history, *A Downland Village* (1979), a traveller of 1839 thought that the most noteworthy features were three 'respectable gentlemen's houses' – North Hall, South Hall, and Preston House. All of the 17th-c church but the chancel was destroyed in Victorian times to provide building material for its successor, thus Preston Candover has two St Marys. In front of the 'new' is a triangle of grass – all that remains of a 2½-acre village green with pond and pound – on which stand a war memorial and a parish pump dating from 1870.

Chilton Candover has an 'underground church', actually the crypt (rediscovered by an enterprising incumbent in 1925) of a Norman church.

A straighter lane than that which follows the line of the Candover Brook cuts off the latter's curve down the valley: the two are connected by an impressive avenue of yews highly commended by William Cobbett but which are today marked at either end with the warning 'Private Road'.

WINTERBORNE MARTIN, or Martinstown, *Dorset*, is halfway along B3159, which connects **Winterbourne Abbas** on the A35 (Dorchester–Bridport) with Upwey on A354 (Dorchester–Weymouth). Many of the villages which lie along the courses of these winterbornes or bournes exemplify a natural ribbon development enforced by narrow valleys between chalk ridges: often there is just room for a lane and a single row of cottages, with the stream or ditch – as in part of Winterbourne Abbas – separating the two, so that each building is provided with its own little bridge between its front door and the road. Winterborne Martin, however, boasts a green once considered wide enough for an annual fair.

Between this village and **Winterborne Monkton** downstream the valley is dominated by the giant earthworks of Maiden Castle. High as the chalk shoulder is, they can be appreciated almost in groundplan from the ridge N which takes A35 W from Dorchester. This still provides something of a legionary's eye-view of the complex Celtic hill fort – a gathering-place for people and their stock, something between an encampment and a cathedral – finally stormed by the Romans.

From Winterborne Monkton the stream flows down to the River Frome by way of **Winterborne Herringston** and **Winterborne Came,** where the dialect poet and parson William Barnes died in the thatched rectory. The other Dorset Winterborne ('this unreliable stream', Ralph Whitlock calls it) has its main source at **Winterborne Houghton** and flows (intermittently) E to **Winterborne Stickland** before turning due S by way of **Winterborne Clenston** and **Winterborne Whitchurch** – the best known, because of its position on A354 from Salisbury and Blandford, but not the most attractive of this second string; **Winterborne Kingston; Winterborne Tomson** (or Thomson or even Thompson); and, to end the alphabet, **Winterborne Zelstone,** before finally it joins the Stour.

WISBOROUGH GREEN, *W. Sussex* (3m W of Billingshurst), is more Green than Wisborough: no modest triangle here, but a generous rectangle lined by trees and echoed by more grassy patches all round. On the S side the A272 takes traffic between Petworth and Billingshurst, and from the N side three lanes fan out among undulating farmland and woodland. Weatherboarding and brick, timber and tile, appear in combination and permutation in this delightfully open village.

Kirdford (3m WNW) has like Wisborough a happy combination of trees and grass; but here the green is a modest background to a short avenue rather than a tree-lined square. The 12th-c church and many of the tile-hung cottages lean (stylistically, that is) to the E and the Weald of Kent, but there is some stone in evidence as well. Looking at Kirdford and other equally unsullied hamlets and villages in the area it is difficult to grasp that this part of Sussex was a sort of industrial belt in the 16th c, with ironfounders, glassmakers and shipbuilders competing for timber supplies as either fuel or material. Kirdford took to forges and foundries after its glass industry collapsed following legislation – promoted by the ironmasters' lobby – which banned the use of timber as fuel for glassworks.

Loxwood, on the Surrey border 4m N of Wisborough Green, is an impromptu sort of village with what Pevsner calls 'an oddly urban row of shops': like the brick chapel, they are a legacy from a 19th-c sect known formally as the Society of Dependents (*sic*) and locally as the Cokelers, apparently from their preference for cocoa over alcohol. Their cooperative venture established its own shops: Dennis Hardy says in *Alternative Communities in Nineteenth Century England* (1979) that this was partly to overcome the restrictions on adherents who might otherwise, as servants, be forbidden to attend weekday services. Like the three Sunday ones, these were regarded by the Establishment as subversive activities.

Mid-Anglia

NORTH BUCKINGHAMSHIRE   NORTHAMPTONSHIRE
BEDFORDSHIRE   NORTH OXFORDSHIRE

Richard Muir

This region, which comprises Northamptonshire, Bedfordshire, the northern half of Buckinghamshire and the eastern side of Oxfordshire, loosely corresponds to the Dark Age territory of Middel Engle which in the fifth to seventh centuries lay between the lands of the Mercians and those of the East Anglians. In terms of geology the area is a diverse one, and this diversity is clearly mirrored in the different building styles that can be seen in the many pleasant villages of the four counties. Northamptonshire aligns itself along the belt of oolitic limestone which then sweeps northwards into Lincolnshire and extends from Northamptonshire to the south-west to provide building stone for the superb villages of the Cotswolds. It can be argued that only Northamptonshire can begin to rival the Cotswolds for beauty of stone village buildings. The buildings are of pale grey limestone with very high-pitched roofs. In the regions of ironstone mining a reddish staining appears in the stone, and the effect is often emphasized with the laying of stone in alternate rust and golden courses. In some places, notably near the famous quarries at Collyweston, the roofs are of stone slates; in others roofs of stone give way to roofs of neat straw thatch.

In striking contrast, the three counties to the south are poor in building stone, and the village landscapes are composed of brick, brick and timber-framing, pantiles and thatch. Buckinghamshire has a countryside of chalk downs and misty valleys and is endowed with a rich legacy of buildings in which the studs of the timber frame are infilled with brick, a style of building shown to perfection in the Moot Hall at Elstow in the neighbouring county of Bedfordshire. In the area around Aylesbury a local recipe for cob produces buildings in 'wichert', a mixture of chalk and clay which is often finished off with a coat of plaster and colour wash. The brickwork of Buckinghamshire and Bedfordshire is usually of a high quality, and modern brickworks exploit the deep beds of brick clay in many places. The old locally made bricks come in a wide variety of hues: rich reds, silvery greys, burnt blues, and some are brindled. If the stone village buildings of Northamptonshire have the edge in terms of nobility, those to the south are homely, snug and sound.

Although this region is not large, it has a truly remarkable heritage of churches. There are a number of Saxon and partly Saxon buildings; there is the beautiful Saxon apse at Wing in Buckinghamshire, the seventh-century church at Brixworth, the round tower at Brigstock, and probably the finest Saxon tower of all at Earls Barton, all in Northamptonshire. This latter county, traditionally famed for its spires and squires, has a skyline pierced by a profusion of glorious church spires, and at Titchmarsh there is perhaps the best parish church tower in the Perpendicular style that can be seen outside Somerset.

In enthusing over the stony splendours of Northamptonshire, it would be easy to undervalue the more homely charms of the three other counties of the region which have their own lovely villages like John Bunyan's village of Elstow and Willington in Bedfordshire or Quainton and Whitchurch in Buckinghamshire. All these villages, and several others around, accord well with the typical conception of the English village as a place of gentle charm and beauty. Northamptonshire, however, is particularly interesting because it has recently been the subject of an intensive investigation by the Royal Commission on Historic Monuments which has shown that the traditional view of the medieval village as a place of slow, unplanned growth and stability is quite wrong. Most of the villages studied yielded evidence of a lively medieval history during which new streets were pushed out, other streets were abandoned and in a number of cases whole villages died, or were removed.

There has always been a place for industry in the English village, ever since the first bronze-smith set up his workshop in a Bronze Age hut, and the villages of the region are richly endowed with the products of old industries. In Northamptonshire stone quarrying has a long history and has left a distinguished endowment in buildings both within and beyond the county. For centuries quarries like those at Weldon have provided beautiful building stone, and the stone roofing slates from Collyweston are unsurpassed. The warm mellow hues of villages in Bedfordshire and Buckinghamshire testify to the skills of past generations of the village brickmakers. The old duck-breeding industry of the area around Aylesbury has provided shady ponds in many of the villages, while the famous Bedfordshire industry of lace-making is still represented in the old cottages of the lacemakers and lace market buildings like the market house at Harrold.

Relics of bygone ways of life abound in the village landscapes of the region; there are sombre

relics like the hanging tree at Maids' Moreton (Bucks.), the numerous village lock-ups, which survive in villages like Harrold (Beds.) and Gretton (Northants.). This last village also retains stocks and whipping post, and a set of stocks can be seen at Aynho in the same county. Northamptonshire has at Hardingstone and Geddington two of our three beautiful surviving Eleanor crosses, set up at the resting places of the funeral cortège of the Queen who died in 1290. Several village crosses also survive, at Harringworth or Brigstock for example.

The works of the rich and the mighty are numerous in the region; there are many stately homes like Woburn Abbey (Beds.), Wotton House and Waddesdon Manor in Bucks, and Rushton Hall

(Northants.), and castles, like the old royal castle at Rockingham (Northants.) or the motte and bailey stronghold at Castlethorpe (Bucks.). In some cases the influences of the rich were benign, as with the provision of almshouses in villages like Quainton (Bucks.) or attractive estate cottages, such as the Whitbreads built at Southill (Beds.), or in the remodelling of villages like Cardington (Beds.) which was redesigned by the Whitbread and Howard families. Stewartby (Beds.) is a recent model village, created for the workers of the London Brick Company in 1936. In other cases, the villagers had cause to regret the intrusions of the mighty; Higham Gobion (Beds.) was laid waste by the lords of the manor, the Butler family, at the start of the sixteenth century in order to clear the way for sheep, while Horton (Northants.) was devastated in the seventeenth century to create a fashionable park for the local hall.

In terms of village architecture, history, landscape and relics the old region of Mid-Anglia has a great deal to show to the visitor. Diversity is one of its greatest gifts, and the transition from the brick, timber and thatch of the downs and lowlands of Buckinghamshire and Bedfordshire to the imposing stonework of Northamptonshire is sure to impress the traveller.

GAZETTEER

ALDWINKLE, *Northants.* (2½m N of Thrapston), displays traces of many of the ancient occupants of the English landscape. Moreover, it is one of the few villages with a tower to rival the one at Titchmarsh, for the church of St Peter is said to have the best broach spire in the county. There are two churches here, pointing to a period of medieval prosperity and growth, although the church of All Saints has fallen into disuse. On top of all this, the quaintly named village has good stone cottages and a pleasantly curving street. The old rectory opposite All Saints is thatched and though partly built in the 18th c, it incorporates walls of the 14th c. It was the birthplace of John Dryden. Thomas Fuller, author of *A Church History of Britain* and other works, was also born in Aldwinkle.

Neolithic occupation at Aldwinkle is evidenced by the discovery of a burial area and a circular ditched enclosure. During the Bronze Age two ancient residents were buried in boat-shaped coffins under round barrows (now levelled by quarry work) and during the Iron Age a large round hut stood here surrounded by a defensive ditched enclosure and approached by a causeway and gate. The Roman road from Huntingdon to Leicester passed nearby and a timber bridge was constructed and renovated by the Romans. The present bridge at Aldwinkle dates from 1760. The church of St Peter contains 13th-c building and 14th-c glass, while All Saints has a 15th-c exterior, so the story of man in the English countryside from Neolithic times to the present can be read at Aldwinkle with very few chapters missing.

ASHTON, *Northants.* (9m due S of Northampton), has something to tell us about the ways of society. Most people will find much modern village building both unexciting and incongruous: Ashton is the product of a building venture which took place as recently as 1900, using traditional vernacular styles of Northamptonshire building and employing the local materials of stone and thatch. It has some pretty corners and is in harmony with its surroundings and with other villages in the region, and we may wonder why it is no longer the custom to perpetuate those regional styles of building which so enhance the countryside. The answer is, of course, that we have neither the money nor the craftsmen; afficionados of the modern styles may scoff at Ashton and brand it as contrived and picturesque, but there is nothing wrong in the notion of a village being picturesque.

Geographers who study rural settlement build models based on social and economic forces which are seen to mould the pattern of villages. Ashton is a warning that the theory-maker must always allow for the unique cases which arise from human whims. Ashton owes its location not to considerations of economics of transport, but to a butterfly, the Chequered Skipper, to be precise. Charles de Rothschild was a fervent entomologist, and the village was built in the habitat of this rare insect and presented as a wedding present to his bride. Huckvale, who had made designs for the Rothschilds on their estates in Bucks. and Herts., was the architect, and while traditional features like the inn, the thatched cottage and the green featured largely in his designs, allowance was made for the incorporation of the best features of the model world; the cottages had the novel addition of modern bathrooms, and the wiring was all laid underground. This latter feature would be welcome in old wire-festooned villages such as Geddington (Northants.) and Barnack (Cambridgeshire).

AYNHO, *Northants.* (on the A403 8m SW of Brackley), stands out in a county which is noted for its beautiful villages. Some guidebooks refer to Aynho as a defensive hill village which was once surrounded by a wall, but such villages are un-English and there is not reliable evidence of such a wall. The church of St Michael is certainly unusual, for although the medieval tower remains, the rest of the building resembles a Georgian country house or town hall. It was rebuilt by Edward Wing, a local architect, in 1723 to harmonize with Aynho Park. The great house was bought by the Cartwright family in 1616; in 1645 it was burnt by Royalist troops retreating from the Civil War battlefield at Naseby. The house was rebuilt, using money awarded as compensation, in the late 17th and early 18th c and further extensions were made in the early 19th c. The park was landscaped by Capability Brown in 1761–3. Following the death of the last of the Cartwrights of Aynho, the big house was converted into flats.

The grammar school at Aynho was built in 1671 and now serves as a private residence. To the N of the school can be seen a group of two-storeyed stone almshouses, built in 1822 and near the road to Deddington are the old village stocks.

While the oral tradition is notoriously unreliable, there are a couple of local legends which are worth repeating. Pesthouse Wood to the E of the village is said to take its name from the custom of isolating plague victims here, but since the

Black Death was almost invariably swiftly fatal, the story seems a little dubious. A pun on the village name is said to have been made when two rival 17th-c candidates for the post of Rector preached competing sermons. When asked of the result, the victor said that it was divided – he got the Ay, and his rival the No. A pleasant feature of the village is the number of peach trees trained against cottage walls, provided originally, it is said, by the Cartwright family.

BRIGSTOCK, *Northants.* (7m SE of Corby), is a large village of good stone-built cottages, but the most notable feature must be the oldest building in the village – the Saxon church tower with its unusual semi-circular extension. Although the church has medieval additions and the tower was heightened during the 14th c, the original Saxon building will have been quite a large one of its kind. Experts are unable to understand the tower extension, or to agree whether some of the work belongs to an early stage in the Saxon era.

The market cross, which stands in the village square, was erected in the reign of Elizabeth I, and its head may have been reworked from a medieval cross. The manor house stands to the W of the church; a Tudor or medieval hall range comprises its core and there are Jacobean extensions to the N and S and the old moated manor received further additions during the 19th c.

4m E is **Wadenhoe**, a picturesque village which runs down towards the River Nene where there is a mill, millpond and pond race; it is a place of thatch and stone. At the top of the street which runs to the church is a house with an unusual polygonal end which may have been a toll house and there is no mistaking the circular dovecote which stands at the start of the road to Pilton. Manor House Farm, which dates from the 17th c, looks over the green but the church of St Michael stands on the hill outside the village. The church tower is Norman and most of the remainder of the building belongs to the 13th c.

BRILL, *Bucks.* This village, with its imposing hilltop site (6m NW of Thame), is steeped in history. The Saxon king Edward the Confessor is believed to have had a palace here, although exactly where we cannot be sure; William the Conqueror is thought to have hunted here and Henry II signed a charter at Brill, with Thomas à Becket as his witness; Henry VIII also hunted in the area. The village had a pottery industry which dated back to the medieval period. During the Civil War Royalist troops guarding the approaches to Oxford threw up ramparts and after their withdrawal Parliamentary troops were stationed here. A tramway which was built by the Duke of Buckingham to link his estates to the railway network terminated at Brill. Opened in 1872, the Wotton Tramway is commemorated in the name Tram Hill.

The church of All Saints has a 13th- and 14th-c nucleus but was largely rebuilt in 1888. Norman work can be seen in the chancel and doorways.

The stumpy tower belongs to the 15th c and is topped by a small leaded spire while the splendid chancel roof is Jacobean. The N and S aisles respectively date from 1839 and 1888, and this is clearly a church of many ages. The green lies to the S of the church and some attractive brick houses can be seen here, and in the square to the W. At the end of the square on the edge of the village stands the handsome red brick gabled Elizabethan manor house. The most notable building in the village however is the post-mill which stands on the highest ground overlooking the plains of Oxfordshire; it is a very old example of its kind, dating from the 1680s.

Two National Trust properties can be seen within 6m of Brill; to the NE is **Wotton House**, built at the start of the 18th c and restored following a fire in 1820; ENE is **Waddesdon Manor**, a fanciful mansion built for the Rothschild family which made such a mark on the county in the 1870s. It contains a wonderful collection of works of art, especially French furniture and carpets. It now belongs to the National Trust. 4m SSE of Brill is the picturesque village of **Chilton,** which is notable for a Georgian manor house.

BRIXWORTH, *Northants.* (7m N of Northampton), is famous for its remarkably old Anglo-Saxon church. Writing in the 12th c, Hugh Candidus of Peterborough records that a monastery was founded at Brixworth around AD 675. With dimensions of 140ft by 30ft, the Anglo-Saxon church is the largest to survive from this period and consisted of a lofty nave with aisles, a presbytery, a polygonal apse and a two-storeyed porch. The nave remains with four arches containing Roman bricks from an unknown building which the Saxon masons reused. The flanking aisles have disappeared and the monastic function seems to have ended with Danish invasion in 870. The apse was reconstructed in tufa some decades before the Norman Conquest, and the Normans provided a new S doorway; the S chapel was added around 1300 and a little later, the Saxon tower was heightened (*see illustration on page 13*).

A Roman villa stood about $\frac{1}{2}$m N of the present village in the 2nd c while the base and shaft of a 14th-c village cross can be found in the village. The kennels of the Pytchley Hunt lie 1m W of the village, but the actual village of **Pytchley** lies 6m NE; here there is an early medieval church, the 16th-c Pytchley Hall and the 17th-c Manor House. A complex of hummocks in the fields nearby show how the medieval village advanced across its own open fields before contracting and retreating.

CLIFTON HAMPDEN, *Oxfordshire.* Situated at a loop of the Thames, between Abingdon and Dorchester, this is one of the prettiest villages in a region of beautiful villages. Facing the village from across the river in Berkshire is the thatched riverside inn, The Barley Mow, famous since its visit by the *Three Men in a Boat.* The river is crossed by a brick-built bridge of seven four-centred arches which was reconstructed by G. G.

Richard Muir

The free-standing bell tower in Elstow churchyard where John Bunyan rang the bells

Scott in 1864. There are many picturesque timber-framed and thatched cottages which date from the 16th and 17th c and the inn employs the cruck-frame construction which is most common in N and W England.

A fine view of the village which lies beneath can be obtained from the church of St Michael and All Saints which is perched atop a steep river bluff and reached by a flight of stone steps. The nucleus of the church is formed by the 12th-c S arcade and the 14th-c N arcade and chapel. An interesting feature of the older part of the church is the 12th-c relief of a boar hunt built into the N wall with the boar under attack by a hound while the hunter approaches. It may have formed the lintel of an earlier doorway. The church was heavily restored by the 1st Lord Aldenham, whose father made his fortune in banking; Scott was the designer and the work was carried out in the middle years of the 19th c, with the lychgate of 1844 marking the beginning of the process. Scott also designed the village school standing on the facing slope and the Manor House, which began in 1843 as a parsonage.

COLLYWESTON, *Northants.,* 6m SW of Stamford. This large and attractive village of stone cottages is renowned for its quarries which produce the Collyweston stone roofing tiles. The stone has been quarried here for centuries and is split by the action of water which freezes in the fissures of the bedding planes. In Collyweston Great Wood, to the SE of the village, a strange group of buildings was excavated in 1954 and is thought by some to form a Roman sanctuary. Three of the buildings were round, one hexagonal and one octagonal. The oldest building in the village itself is the church of St Andrew, where the S wall of the chancel appears to be Saxon. The rest of the church, which has a fine tower and overlooks the village, belongs to the 15th and 16th c.

Lord Cromwell who was treasurer to Henry VI had a mansion which stood to the W of the church, but only the barn and the adjoining dovecote, dated 1578, remain. On the road to the SW of the church stands a manor house bearing the date 1696 while the village bridge dates from 1620.

Collyweston stone is displayed in several of the good stone houses at **Easton-on-the-Hill,** 2m NE, a hill village with views over into Lincolnshire. The church of All Saints has one Norman window and the medieval church was largely rebuilt in the 18th and 19th c. The tower is in the Perp manner and reminiscent of the tower at Collyweston. A Priest's House can be seen to the W of the church and dates from the late 15th c. Formerly used as a stable, it has been restored and now serves as a museum and meeting room. A little to the N is the Georgian Rectory.

EARLS BARTON, *Northants.,* 4m SW of Wellingborough. There can be little doubt that the village has our grandest surviving Saxon tower. It belongs to the late-Saxon period and is built of packed rubble which has been plastered and decorated with long and short work and blank arcading and with raised flat bands which form X-shaped patterns. Some believe that such Saxon work imitates timber building, at which the Saxons were so adept. The battlements were added during the 15th c; meanwhile the church experienced considerable Norman rebuilding and an elaborate frieze was provided around the S doorway and new additions were made in the 13th and 14th c.

Directly N of the church, the visitor will recognize the dominating Norman castle motte which intrudes upon the churchyard and is protected by a ditch behind. The church stands within the bailey of the castle, and it may well be that the Norman lord intended to dismantle the church but never got round to it before the castle itself was redundant. The large surrounding village is characterized by the brick-built homes of workers in the shoe industry. It is seldom admired, but is not without charm and whether looking down or up the village, the view from the churchyard is a commanding one.

ELSTOW, *Beds.,* just S of Bedford. While best remembered as John Bunyan's village, Elstow has much more of historical interest to offer to the visitor. A Benedictine nunnery was founded at Elstow *c.* 1075, probably by Countess Judith, a niece of the Conqueror. Only fragments of the nunnery remain standing but they include the

13th-c vaulted room known as the 'chapter house' which opens out of the church. The property was bought by Thomas Hillersdon in 1616 and much of the abbey masonry was re-used in the construction of Hillersdon Hall, although excavations have revealed the cloister buttresses, chancel, apse and Lady Chapel. A portion of the abbey buildings was converted into the parish church of St Mary and St Helen following the Dissolution, and although parts of the building were heavily restored during the Victorian era, the work of Norman and 13th-c masons can be seen in the stark and lofty interior. There is a beautiful brass to Margaret Argentine, who died in 1427, and another to the former abbess of Elstow, Elizabeth Herwy, who died in 1527, as well as monuments to members of the Radclif and Hillersdon family. John Bunyan once rang the bells in the freestanding 15th-c tower, and the visitor can see the large octagonal Perp font in which the great religious writer was baptized. The pulpit from Bunyan's church is now on display in the Moot Hall, which stands in the field to the N of the church.

This building, of timber with brick infillings with an overhanging upper storey and tiebeam roof, was built around 1500 and carefully restored in 1951. A meeting room was housed in the upper floor while at ground level there were six small shops. A reconstruction of a working room of Bunyan's time, with oaken seating and writing table, can be seen on the ground floor while a collection of early editions of Bunyan's works is housed above.

Bunyan came from humble origins, a tinker like his father before him, and the modest family home was outside the village and has long since disappeared. A stone beside the footpath leading out from the village marks its site. With its ancient church and abbey ruins, Moot Hall and the timber framed cottages which line the village street to the E of the church, it will not be difficult to imagine the Elstow of Bunyan's childhood.

GEDDINGTON, *Northants.* Here (4m N of Kettering), we have one of the most widely admired village squares in England, with our best preserved Eleanor Cross as its focus. Queen Eleanor died at Harby in Notts. in 1290, and the king caused decorated crosses to be set up at every place where the funeral cortège had rested for the night: Lincoln, Grantham, Stamford, Geddington, Hardingstone, Stony Stratford, Dunstable, St Albans, Waltham, Cheapside and Charing Cross. Only the crosses at Hardingstone, Geddington and Waltham now survive, and the Geddington cross probably commemorates a night spent by the funeral party at Delapré Abbey. It was probably erected about 1295; it is less flamboyant than the other crosses but finely preserved. The shaft is triangular and carries three figures of the Queen in three niches and is crowned with pinnacles.

The church of St Mary Magdalene looks over the square and contains evidence of Saxon

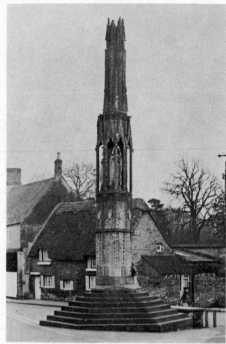

The Eleanor Cross at Geddington

origins in the arcading of the nave although most of the building belongs to the early 14th c. A priory was built to the SE of the church, an L-shaped building dating from the latter parts of the 16th and 17th c. Beyond the stone and thatched cottages there is the beautiful medieval bridge over the Ise; it was built in the 13th c, but much altered and repaired in the 18th c.

HANSLOPE, *Bucks.,* 5m N of Stony Stratford. Pevsner is in no doubt: 'The church' he tells us, 'has the finest steeple in Buckinghamshire.' More characteristic of the Midlands than of Buckinghamshire, the spire of the church of St James zooms upwards for 186ft; originally it went on for a further 15ft but it had to be rebuilt and lowered. The spire was built in the 15th c, but there was a church here long before that for the chancel is Late Norman and the aisles belong to the 13th c. The historian of the county, John Camp, has drawn attention to the interesting characters who lie in the churchyard. There is Joseph Cox who was 92 and his wife who lived to be 101 and an epitaph to the Scottish prizefighter Alex McKay who died at Hanslope in 1830 following 47 bare-knuckled rounds with the Irishman Simon Byrne. Doubtless the pair were fighting at Hanslope in order to be able to nip over the county boundary into Northamptonshire in the event of the authorities arriving, for fights of this kind were banned in England. A number of 17th-c gabled cottages and handsome Georgian buildings line the village street and there are chapels for both the Baptists and the Wesleyans, dating from 1809 and 1826.

The village of **Castlethorpe** 1m to the S probably takes its name from the motte and bailey castle which William Maudit built here in defiance of King John. It will have been quite a stronghold for the inner bailey covered 4 acres and the mound rises to a height of 36ft. The church of St Simon and St Jude stands in a corner of the well-preserved castle earthworks and was rebuilt from a Norman church in the 14th c. The tower dates from the 18th c and was built after the original tower collapsed in 1729. Inside is a tomb in marble and alabaster to Chief Justice Sir Thomas Tyrell who died in 1671 and included both the supposed assassin of William Rufus and Sir James Tyrell, who was implicated in the murder of the princes in the Tower, among his ancestors.

HARRINGWORTH, *Northants.* This village in the N of the county (8m N of Corby), offers much of historical interest and it is also one of the villages studied by the masterly landscape historian Christopher Taylor, who has done so much to prove the lively and mobile nature of the medieval village. The present village has the form of an inverted T, with the greater part of the settlement lying along the E–W bar of the T. S of the village however among the tracks and hollows can be seen the unmistakable earthworks which show the former S extension of the village and suggest that the original village ran NW to SE from a point near the church and river crossing to another which was 250ft up the hillside. By the late 18th c the village had taken on its present form, but a map of the 1630s shows that the village had the remains of its S extension while its W–E expansion was then less. This is one of many examples of a village that has realigned itself.

The church of St John Baptist has a tower which must date back to the 12th c although the rest of the church contains 13th-, 14th- and 15th-c work and while the chancel arch and doorway date from the early 14th c, the chancel itself is in the Perp style. The pulpit was brought from Barrowden in Rutland and is known to date from 1605. The helmet displayed in the N aisle belonged to Lord George Zouche and was brought from the family chapel which stood between the church and the manor house. The Old Manor House is the shrunken remains of the Zouche Manor while the manor house between the church and the Swan Inn belongs to the late 17th c. The Inn, with its blocked double centred archway is an old one, pre-dating the nearby manor by almost two centuries. Northamptonshire is noted for its village crosses, and Harringworth has one with a shaft of columns of alternate greater and lesser width; the top dates from 1837 although the shaft may date from 1387. The Welland viaduct with its 82 arches dominated the western vista of the village from its construction in 1874.

HARROLD, *Beds.*, 10m NW of Bedford. First noted for its priory, Harrold has faced rising and falling prospects, developing a flourishing lace industry during the 17th and early 18th c, and then seeing the decline of the industry and market later in the 18th c. The Great Ouse is crossed by a long narrow bridge of 11 arches, part of which dates from the 14th c. Near the bridge and beside the river stood the Augustinian priory; it does not seem to have flourished and the abandoned site was taken over to build Harrold Hall for Thomas and Ann Boteler in 1608. The Hall in its turn was demolished, in 1961, and recent homes now stand on the site.

The church of St Peter belongs mainly to the 13th c when the N and S arcades and aisles were built. The N chapel and tower are in the Dec style; the spire, clerestory and pulpit and benches are in the later Perp manner. There are two buildings of note on the pleasant tree-lined green: the early 18th-c market house which was used for the assembly and marketing of the products of the local lace industry and for the distribution of thread and patterns, and the lock-up. This was built in 1824 to a circular design and provided a little more space for the unfortunate inmates than did many contemporary lock-ups. A number of old houses and cottages can be seen on High Street, including Old Manor, a stone house with mullioned and transomed windows which dates from about 1600. Although Harrold has lost its priory, lace market and also the row of six 18th-c almshouses, some of its recent buildings have been praised, such as the houses by John Gedge seen to the E of the church.

The village of **Odell**, 2m NE is well worth a visit, with its pleasant stone-built cottages signalling the approach to Northamptonshire. On a hill overlooking the Ouse valley Walter de Wahull set up his motte and bailey castle after the Norman Conquest. A stone keep was added later, and it remained in occupation until the 17th c though a modern stone house now occupies the castle site. Like Harrold, Odell was a focus for the Bedfordshire lace industry and it too suffered from the mechanization of the industry during the 19th c. The church of All Saints is built almost completely in the Perp style and contains a Jacobean pulpit and panels and screen of the same period.

HIGHAM FERRERS, *Northants.* This was a town of considerable importance during the Middle Ages, and monuments of its former glory abound. The area was occupied during the Roman period; numerous Roman finds have been made and during the 2nd, 3rd and 4th c a small stone building lay to the W of the present settlement. A Norman castle stood N of the church, built in the 11th c by the Pereval family; it passed to the Ferrers, from which the village takes its name. In 1266, Henry III granted the castle to his son Edmund Crouchback and it was a Lancaster possession until returning to the crown under Henry IV. In 1523 the castle was quarried for stone for the building of Kimbolton House.

The association with the House of Lancaster greatly contributed to the former importance of

Higham Ferrers. The church of St Mary is a splendid example of mid-13th and mid-14th-c church building on the scale of a small cathedral. It is full of interest and superb decoration, with the sculptured reliefs above the W doorway being especially engaging and taking the form of ten medallions which depict scenes from the life of Christ. The interior has medieval screens, misericords, carved stalls and one of England's finest church brasses depicting the priest Laurence St Maur who died in 1337.

Archbishop Chichele, the founder of All Souls, Oxford, was born at Higham Ferrers and did much to enhance what was, in his lifetime, a thriving town. He refounded the school, a building of three bays with three-light and five-light windows to the NW of the church. In 1428 he also refounded the Bede House as a hospital for 12 old men and a nurse. It stands S of the church, a striped building of alternating red and grey stone courses. The living space for the aged residents was divided into cubicles with beds and lockers and a chapel stood at the E end. The gatehouse and chapel of Archbishop Chichele's college, which was founded in 1431, can be seen in College Street.

The triangular market place and market cross give further evidence to the past importance of Higham Ferrers and the town returned a Member of Parliament until the Reform Bill and there was some renewed growth in relation to the 19th-c shoe industry.

HIGHAM GOBION, *Beds.,* 1½m E of the A6, 8m N of Luton. Although only a hamlet today, Higham Gobion will interest any visitor with a sense of history, for it is the site of a lost medieval village. Until relatively modern times, lost villages were thought to be quite exceptional, but a count of known medieval lost village sites made in 1978 brought the tally to a remarkable 7000. Following the track which leads N from the church the historian with a practised eye may be able to discern the outlines of tenement sites and the medieval fishpond.

The village takes its name from the Norman Gobion family, the old lords of the manor which, in due course, passed to the Butler family. The modernized Manor Farm incorporates parts of the old Butler manor house, including a wooden Elizabethan chimney-piece. Like many Tudor landlords, the Butlers cannot have cared much for their tenants for they put their estates over to sheep and in 1518 only one parishioner is said to have remained. The church of St Margaret was built *c.* 1300 and extensively restored in 1879; it contains brasses to women of the Butler family.

Barton Le Clay, 2m SW, is a much more thriving village with a very long history; an Iron Age hillfort and an adjacent oval enclosure stand on Galley Hill. In the Middle Ages the village lands were a property of the great abbey at Ramsey (Hunts.) and later the manor passed to the Willes family whose manor house can be seen at the bend of Manor Road. The EE church of St

Nicholas has a fine roof with angels and carved bosses and an early 16th-c painting of St Nicholas, which may have come from S Germany.

HILLESDEN, *Bucks.,* at the end of a gated road across farmland and meadows, enjoys a rare seclusion. It lies but 4m S of Buckingham and can be reached by the winding backroad that comes via Gawcott. The village has lost the mansion of the Denton family and consists of a small cluster of cottages, although the unusually ornate medieval church suggests former glories. The church of All Saints is built entirely in the Perp style of the end of the 15th c. It has a long association with the Denton family who held the former mansion, and their monuments range in age from the alabaster memorial to Thomas Denton who died in 1560 to the marble sarcophagus of Sir Alexander and Lady Denton of 1733. Some of the stained glass, notably the scenes from the story of St Nicholas in the S transept windows, belongs to the early 16th c. The family pew dates from the latter part of the 17th c and the benches display linenfold panelling. A fine view of the embattled building with its splendid windows can be obtained from the N.

Several miles away by road, but little over 1m SE as the crow flies, is the village of **Steeple Claydon,** with some very attractive timber-framed and thatched cottages. An unusual feature is the public library building, which originated in 1656 as a school built by Sir Thomas Chaloner.

HORTON, *Northants.* (7m SE of Northampton), is a village which almost isn't, and it exemplifies the fate which has befallen many English villages. We may begin with the Hall, for before the Hall itself was pulled down in 1936, it played a large part in the undoing of Horton. Two Victorian lodges and the red-brick 18th-c stables remain and the land between was built upon in the 1960s. Some of the elaborate 18th-c garden furnishings of the old hall survive in the grounds in the form of a menagerie and temple, as do the remains of the old village. In the mid-17th c the village of Horton stretched E from the hall, along the river valley, but at some time before 1676 this village was completely destroyed in the creation of the hall park. In fact, the history of Horton is more complicated than this, for stretching directly S of the site of the hall are the remains of a medieval village which ascended the gentle slope for a distance of ¼m. Christopher Taylor's search for pottery on this site suggests that this village of Horton was abandoned during the 14th c. Probably the villagers chose to move to the village which was set up across the river and in its turn, destroyed by the lord of the hall.

The church of St Mary stands 600ft NW of the hall and boasts a 13th-c tower capped by early-18th-c work and a grand weather-vane. The church was largely rebuilt in 1862 although some of the old monuments remain in the form of a brass to Roger Salisbury, who died in 1491, and the figures of Lord and Lady Parr, uncle and aunt to Catherine Parr, wife of Henry VIII. There are also monuments to members of the Lane and Montagu families.

Denton, 2m NE is a delightful village with a pocket-sized 13th-c church, a small pub, a circular dove house and a charming well-thatched cottage of ironstone, breached by a pathway which ascends to the higher village level from the main street. Beside the main street there is a narrow green and a copious horse trough.

ISLIP, *Oxfordshire* (5m N of Oxford), will always be remembered as the birthplace of the saintly king, Edward the Confessor, the last Saxon king to die in bed. The problem of Edward's death concerned his choice of successor, but at least his intentions concerning Islip are clear, for in his will he stated, 'I have given to Christ and to (the monks of) St Peter in Westminster the little town of Islippe wherein I was born.'

Whether or not the village existed, the area was well farmed 700 or more years before the Confessor's time, for a Roman villa has been discovered ½m SE of the village. While few villages can claim a king among their offspring, Islip has some other noteworthy associations. Abbot John Islip, the builder of Henry VIII's chapel at Westminster spent his childhood here; Dean Buckland the geologist was rector and was buried in the churchyard in 1856, and his son who became a naturalist gained some local fame by sharing the rectory with a tame bear, while the pioneer balloonist James Sadler landed here on his first flight in the course of which he travelled 5m from his ascent at Oxford. Another famous rector Dr Robert South built the village rectory in 1689 and the school house some years later.

It is difficult to imagine that a church did not stand at Islip in the time of the Confessor, but the oldest portion of the church of St Nicholas is the N arcade which dates from *c.* 1200. The building was remodelled in 1680 and 1861 although the tower is *c.* 1450. Under canopies in the recent oak reredos are the figures of the Confessor, Abbot John, St Peter and St Nicholas.

5m SE beside the road to Wheatley, **Stanton St John** is another village with famous associations. This was the home of John Milton's father, who was disinherited when as a student at Christ Church, Oxford, he turned to the Protestant faith. John White was born here in 1575; a fellow of New College, Oxford, he became a rector in Dorchester where he gained a reputation for his concern for the weak and infirm. In 1624 he arranged the migration of many members of his Dorset congregation to Massachusetts, where he is remembered as the chief founder of the New England colony. An L-shaped 16th- and 17th-c house in the village bears his name. The church of St John the Baptist overlooks the village, and the chancel *c.* 1300 is said to be one of our finest examples of the transition from the EE to the Dec building styles. Some of the windows contain part of their original medieval glass and double poppy-heads decorate bench ends in the chancel.

KIRTLINGTON, *Oxfordshire* (5m NE of Woodstock), seems to have had some importance in the ancient transport system of the Midlands, with Akeman Street running from the village in Saxon Mercia. Port Way runs N from the village towards Souldern and its southern portion was used by a local Roman road running from Oxford into Northants. The Aves Ditch which runs NNE from Kirtlington is undated and may be Roman.

Before the church of St Mary had reached its centenary, it was rebuilt in the late 12th c, and then gave seven centuries of use before another rebuilding by G. G. Scott in 1877. Fragments of the early-12th-c church survive in the tower arches and an exploration of the foundations during the last rebuilding show it to have had an apsidal chancel. The church has experienced many modifications and by 1770 the tower had become unsafe and was demolished with the Victorian Norman tower being added in 1853. With a little good fortune, the church might have been improved by the greatest of English architects, for buried here in 1658 was Christopher Wren, chaplain to Charles I, variously bishop of Hereford, Norwich and Ely, and father of the rebuilder of London.

The Palladian mansion of Kirtlington Park was built for Sir James Dashwood in the 1740s by the architects William Smith and John Sanderson, under the influence of James Gibbs. The original decoration of the dining-room now graces the New York Metropolitan Museum. The park was landscaped by Capability Brown following the completion of the house. In the village, the Manor House dates from the 16th c and Portway House from the late 17th c while Northbrook House which stood 1m NW was demolished in the 18th c and only a brick dovecote and a part of the garden wall remain.

3m E on the A43, is **Weston-on-the-Green,** a village of scattered thatched cottages which can boast stocks on the village green. The church of St Mary has a lovely tree-shaded setting and a violent history, being rebuilt in 1743 following a disastrous fire. Only the splendid tower survived, with its different stages marking phases in the construction of the church, the lowest stage dating from *c.* 1200, the middle section belonging to the 13th c and the top to the 15th c. While parts of the interior of the Weston Manor House Hotel date from the time of the completion of the church tower, the façade is less Tudor than it appears to be; the medieval frontage was remodelled in the 16th c and the present façade is the result of a Tudorization effort of *c.* 1820. The original house belonged to the abbots of Olney and their moat now serves as a swimming pool.

LONG CRENDON, *Bucks.* This large village of thatch and timbered buildings (2m N of Thame), has a long association with woollen and lace-making industries. The most notable building in the village is the Court House, a jettied timber-and-brick building which stands on a stone base. It is now owned by the National Trust and may have been built in the 14th or 15th c as a store house used by wool merchants; later it became a meeting place for the scholars of All Souls College who were granted the income from the village. Four of the five bays of the building form one vast chamber and curving beams support the roof. Immediately E is the church of St Mary, a large church which has Norman masonry in the walls and is built in EE and Dec styles, with a lofty crossing tower in the Perp style added in the 15th c. John Cannon, who died in 1460, his wife and their 11 children are commemorated in a brass portrait and there is an imposing tomb for the armoured figure of Sir John Dormer who died in 1626 and is buried with his wife beside him.

The village contains a number of interesting buildings: the Manor House SE of the church is a fine building of the 17th c; Madges on the High Street has an 18th-c front of chequered brickwork; while Long Crendon Manor lies S of the square along Frogmore Lane. The Manor and its stone gatehouses have 15th-c cores and additions were made to the hall in the 16th c and, in sympathetic manner, in the 1920s. 1m E of the village is Notley Abbey, established for the Augustinians in 1162. The large church was built in the 12th and 13th c, but only the foundations remain and the house that still stands was built in the 15th and 16th c as the Abbot's Lodging. The medieval roof remains and the building became a private house after the Dissolution. A 14th-c square stone dovecote stands N of the church ruins.

MARSTON MORETAINE, *Beds.,* 8m SW of Bedford. Some visitors will find the surrounding forests of brickwork chimneys oppressive, but the industry here can trace its pedigree back to the production of hand-made bricks in the 16th c. Marston Moretaine was also one of the several Bedfordshire villages which were involved in the making of pillow lace. The strange name has come down from the Morteyne family who held a manor in the medieval period. A number of manors shared the parish; Wroxhill Manor, Beancroft Manor and Shelton Manor are all remembered in local farm names while Moat Farm retains its Elizabethan Manor frontage and was the home of the Snagge family who followed the Reynes as Lords of the Manor, the Reynes having taken over when the Morteyne family became extinct in 1428.

The church of St Mary is notable, for like the church at Elstow (q.v.) it has a detached tower. The tower, like the oldest parts of the church, is in 14th-c Dec style, but during the 15th c the church was virtually rebuilt by the Reynes family in the Perp style. The old lords of the village are commemorated in the church where alabaster monuments of Thomas Snagge, his wife and children date from c. 1600, while Thomas Reynes and his wife, sponsors of the church rebuilding, are represented on a brass. A restored doom painting above the chancel arch dates from the early 16th c while the stained glass in the chancel S window is by Burne-Jones and dates from 1893.

Wootton, 3m N is another village with a long association with the Bedfordshire brick-making industry. It also had, between 1715 and the closure of the foundry in 1789, a bell-making industry where the bells for a number of neighbouring churches were cast. If the spirit does not warm to the landscape of brick-making then a journey to Stagsden 3m NW of Wootton is advised, for here there is a secluded bird garden. The spacious enclosures house a large collection of birds of many kinds, some ferocious, some exotic, though the collection of old English poultry may be most interesting to lovers of rural history.

MELCHBOURNE, *Beds.,* 5m E of Rushden. Although a small village today, Melchbourne formerly had a medieval market and fair. The Knights Hospitallers had a preceptory here during the Middle Ages; the stone building was still standing, but in a bad condition when it was bought by Lord St John in 1608, and it was demolished during the construction of Melchbourne Park the following year. The St John family moved here from Bletsoe, where their moated castle with its early-14th-c crenellations had probably become outmoded and uncomfortable. The house at Melchbourne Park was remodelled in 1741 and given a brick façade with two projecting wings with large canted bay windows.

The church of St Mary Magdalene stands along the row of thatched estate cottages which date from the 18th c. Only the tower and fragments of the chancel are medieval, the remainder of the church is Georgian and dates from a rebuilding in 1779. An interesting feature is the private fireplace to warm the area of the St John family pew.

2m NW is **Yielden** where old thatched cottages are mixed with modern housing. The earthworks of the motte and bailey castle with its dominating rectangular motte mound standing 40ft above the ground remain a striking feature. The castle was the base of the Norman overlords, the Trailly family, and excavations have revealed the traces of round stone towers which will have helped to make the castle a formidable defence work.

MIXBURY, *Oxfordshire,* lying just N of the Buckingham to Deddington road, stands in a salient of Oxfordshire which is surrounded by Northants. to the W and Bucks. to the N and E. It is interesting as a model village which was created in 1874 by order of the Court of Chancery and resulted in the replacement of the old village cottages by the ones which can be seen today, built of stone rubble with brick dressings. Some of the older village features survived the change; across the road NE of the church, the green banks and hollows mark the site of a moated Norman castle, built c. 1100, and known as Beaumont. The church of All Saints is almost equally old, with the nave and chancel dating from the 12th c. Much of the rest of the church belongs to the 14th c, including the fine tower, but a substantial rebuilding took place in the 1840s. The outstanding feature of the church is the beautifully carved Norman doorway with its deeply incised bands of chevrons and double chevrons. 1m from the village, on the border with Northants, a farmhouse marks the site of the home of Monk, Cromwell's famous General.

NUNEHAM COURTENAY, *Oxfordshire,*

flanking the road to Oxford, which lies 6m N, is thought to have provided Oliver Goldsmith with the inspiration for his famous poem 'The Deserted Village'. George Simon Harcourt, son of the village's founder, was the patron of a number of contemporary artists and writers, including Reynolds, Gilpin and William Whitehead. The last-mentioned writer, who rose from being the son of a Cambridge baker to poet laureate certainly produced a poem in 1771 on 'The Removal of the Village at Nuneham'. What is surprising about Goldsmith's poem is the way in which a deserted village is made to appear a thing of mystery, for in his time dozens of old villages were being removed in the course of grandiose schemes for 'landscape improvement' by the owners of the great houses. During the 18th c this process had less of the iniquity of the wretched Tudor sheep enclosures; landlords were less able to ride roughshod over the rights of their tenants, and in many cases the villagers emerged far better housed than they ever were in the original village.

Nuneham Courtenay has become something of a classic in the annals of improved, removed and model villages, and its case is well documented. Both the inspiration and the execution of the grand plan for Nuneham Courtenay derived from the local magnate, Simon, 1st Earl Harcourt, antiquarian, designer and a leading light at the royal court. During the 1760s he began to implement the grand design for his park – and since the original village intruded upon his vision of a classical landscape, a vista to be enjoyed from the big house, it was swept away. Had the next village of Nuneham Courtenay been built a few decades later, it would have probably been constructed in a picturesque manner with the help of a celebrated architect or using designs from a fashionable manual. In the event the plans seem to be the creation of the Earl assisted no doubt by a local master builder. The cottages are designed according to a Georgian variant of the local vernacular style with pairs of plain semi-detached cottages set on either side of the Oxford road in ribbon fashion. Chequer brick and grassy verges featured in the design and provision was made for a curate's house, forge and inn.

The old village stood on a hill behind the Palladian mansion which was still only partly built when the removal of the village began; the village street became an open avenue through the landscaped setting, a classical temple appeared near the site of the old village church and even the village name did not escape the transformation as Newnham became Nuneham. Much sentimentality was attached to the one old lady whose cottage survived the clearance, though whether she preferred her old neighbours to the contrived setting which replaced them, we do not know. Goldsmith disapproved; gossip cast the Earl as an ogre who built edifices from the bones of massacred villagers; Whitehead's poem was a rejoinder; and meanwhile the new village became a minor landmark and probably the inspiration for several later exercises in landscape manipulation. What had been done was in no way exceptional, even if it slightly anticipated the full flood of eviction and rebuilding; sometimes the villagers were severely inconvenienced but as often as not they moved from the semi-dereliction of the old villages into homes which were serviceable, more spacious and sound, even if their opinions were never invited.

The church of All Saints on the hill in the park was built in 1764 to the Earl's designs which included both Greek and Roman influences, with Ionic columns, a marble floor and a certain austerity of atmosphere. A second church of All Saints was provided in 1872 to relieve the villagers of the uphill trek to the original. In this case, a more traditional 13th-c design was employed, with a S chapel in the Perp style being added in 1890. Nuneham Park was set up on a site selected for its landscape capabilities and its prospect of distant Oxford, and incorporates various 18th- and early-19th-c features. In 1780 the gardens were described by Horace Walpole as being the most beautiful in the world, but they were not improved by army occupation during World War II, and the construction of an unsightly line of pylons. Efforts at rehabilitation were made when the park passed to Culham College of Education.

OLD WARDEN, *Beds.* (4m E of Biggleswade),

has many associations with the distant past; an Iron Age earth bank ran from Old Warden Hill in the direction of Luton to cross the Icknield Way, while a bronze mirror, dating from around the lifetime of Christ, was discovered at Old Warden and is one of the finest treasures in the Bedford museum. 1m W of the village, Warden Abbey was established by Walter Espec in 1135 as a house for the Cistercians, who travelled down from Rievaulx. The Abbey was quite a large one (and was renowned for its crop of Warden pears), although none of the buildings now remain. A small Tudor brick house was built on the site after the abbey was dissolved, and a part of this house still stands. N of the church can be seen the overgrown remains of an Iron Age earthwork, partly destroyed when Old Warden Park was set out.

The village has a long association with the Ongley family who arrived in the village as linen drapers involved in the India trade at the end of the 17th c. The church is rich in endowments from the Ongley family and during the Victorian era the park was created and a measure of planning was imposed upon the village. The present Old Warden Park was built for the new purchaser, Joseph Shuttleworth in 1872. Following the death of the last Shuttleworth in a flying disaster the home became an agricultural college and the Shuttleworth collection of early aircraft was established.

The brown cobblestone church has a Norman tower arch and was largely built at the close of the 12th c, and after the plain exterior, the interior with its profusion of Belgian 16th-, 17th-, and 18th-c wood carving will come as quite a shock. The woodwork was collected by Robert Henley, Lord Ongley, in the mid-19th c and according to Pevsner, 'It oppresses you from all sides; it is utterly disjointed . . .' Even so the visitor may pick a way among the collection and find several pleasing items. There are also several monuments to the Ongleys, including one of the Lords looking rather ridiculous in Roman costume.

2m SE is **Southill**, which pleased Pevsner more for he found the big house there to be 'one of the most exquisite English understatements'. The famous Whitbread brewing family employed Henry Holland to remodel the mid-18th-c Southill House which they had bought, and by 1801 £53,000 had been spent on the project. The Byng arms can be seen on the gates of the N terrace, and it was John Byng who was cruelly executed when he refused to risk his ill-equipped ships against a stronger French fleet in 1756. Before the house passed to the Whitbreads, the grounds were landscaped by Capability Brown. The Whitbreads, whose good taste is evidenced in Southill, were, unlike the archetypal 19th-c industrialists, great patrons of the arts and theatre and supporters of democratic freedom. A group of golden thatched estate cottages dates from the period when Southill was remodelled.

PASSENHAM, *Northants.* Located in a southward salient of the county, 1m SW of Stony Stratford, Passenham is a small tree-shaded village with an attractive church and manor and some ancient historical associations. King Edward the Elder camped here, close to the Ouse meadows in AD 921 when Towcester fortifications were being restored following a Danish attack. The church is dedicated to St Guthlac who founded Crowland Abbey and whose sister, St Pega, had a cell at Peakirk. It belongs largely to the 13th c although the upper part of the late 13th-c tower was rebuilt during a restoration of *c.* 1626. This restoration was sponsored by Sir Robert Banastre who provided the barrel roof for the chancel, the richly carved stalls with misericords and the Venetian styled wall paintings of Biblical figures. He died in 1649, and his monument can be seen in the chancel.

The manor probably belongs to the time of Sir Robert although it was considerably remodelled in the 19th c. Two fine barns stand at right angles to the manor building; one is an early Tudor tithe barn, a full 110ft long, the other a manorial barn dating from 1626.

The building styles of Northamptonshire and Buckinghamshire meet and mix at **Cosgrove**, situated on the county border 2m N of Passenham. It was here that the two halves of the Grand Junction Canal met and there is an attractive canal bridge in the Gothic style which dates from 1800. Cosgrove Hall is an early 18th-c building of seven bays and two storeys. In front of the Hall and beside the canal, the remains of a Roman bath house were discovered in 1958; one of the baths had been tiled, the other, lined with lead. The Priory was always a private dwelling, but stands on land that was owned by Snelshall Priory. It contains an elaborately carved Tudor screen. The church of St Peter and St Paul is a 13th-c building which was altered in the Georgian period and heavily restored in 1864, though the attractive gilded copper weathercock may be genuine 14th-c work.

PRESTON CAPES, *Northants.*, 6m S of Daventry. Two important events in the life of the village occurred during the 11th c; a small Cluniac priory of but four monks was established here in 1090 and survived for less than 20 years before being transferred to Daventry. A little E of the present church, a castle was also built here in the 11th c and its mound can still be seen although the full extent of the defence works is difficult to trace. The church of St Peter overlooks the pleasant countryside which lies N of the village and belongs to various periods of medieval building; it has a battlemented tower in the Perp style. Some of the original benches with traceried panels survive inside; the font is 15th-c and the Ten Commandments appear in the chancel.

The village is built of ironstone with cottages in the traditional Northamptonshire manner, but the two rows of red brick cottages, the castellated archway and battlements seem strangely out-of-place. In fact the cottage group was built as an eye-catcher to be viewed from Fawsley Hall.

3m E is **Farthingstone** which can also boast castle ruins, with the extensive bailey earthworks to be seen at Castle Dykes, 1m N of the church. The church of St Mary is an unpretentious building which belongs largely to the 13th c and its greatest treasure is the beautiful carving of the poppyhead pews. This is another village which is predominantly of ironstone and exceptions include the strange brick and plaster cottages of Pension Row, S of the church, and the King's Arms, a Victorian 'Tudor' building which was rebuilt after being destroyed by fire in 1870, 25 years after being built.

QUAINTON, *Bucks.*, 7m NW of Aylesbury. With its green, pond, cross and a wealth of old cottages, Quainton has all that the visitor would hope to find in an English village. The large triangular green is spacious, tussocky and sloping. At the head of the green stands the base and shaft of a 15th-c market cross which may have been erected by the Knights Hospitallers who had a hospice in the village and are thought to have built the church.

The church of St Mary and Holy Cross is built in the medieval Dec and Perp styles and is noted for the wealth of monuments which it contains. It is one of the few Buckinghamshire churches with

Gillian Darley

Cottages ornés at Old Warden, Bedfordshire

paintings, and four saints are represented in the N aisle. There are a number of brasses of which the oldest is of Joan Plessi and dates from around 1350. Rector of Quainton Richard Brett, one of the translators of the Authorized Version of the Bible, and his wife are portrayed in painted alabaster figures. Several members of the Dormer family are represented, from Fleetwood Dormer, who died in 1638 to Mr Justice Dormer whose tomb dates from 1730. Also represented is Richard Winwood, who died in 1689 and who provided the Winwood Almshouses which date from 1687 and stand at the entrance to the churchyard. The rectory lies on the other side of the churchyard gate, a Georgian building in homely red brick. Buried in the churchyard is James Lipscomb, surgeon and sailor who lived in the Magpie cottage which stands by the green and was the father of George Lipscomb who devoted his life to writing a history of the county and died a pauper.

A number of attractive 17th- and 18th-c cottages in timber framing and in brick can be seen around the green and above Cross Farmhouse stands the tower of a windmill which was built in 1830. The mansion of the powerful Dormer family stood at Grange Farm, 1m NW of the village; it was destroyed in the 18th c although its ancient barn survived. Denham Lodge stands a little way NE of the village, a moated house of stone and brick dating from the 17th c. Quainton became something of a railway focus in the late 19th c, a meeting of the Metropolitan and Great Central railways, and more recently Quainton Road station was taken over by the local railway society as the nucleus of a collection of steam locomotives and rolling stock.

ROCKINGHAM, *Northants.,* 1½m NW of Corby. The 17th- and 18th-c stone cottages of this attractive village follow the main road at the foot of the hill. The outstanding feature of the village is the former royal castle of Rockingham; William the Conqueror chose its site well, for guarded by steep land to the W and N, it commands the Welland valley, its crossing and the early iron workings of the neighbourhood. Iron Age and Roman remains have been discovered in the locality, and the Saxons may have had their own fortifications here. The Norman castle consisted of a bailey with curtain walls which guarded the great hall and chapel while the motte in due course gained a keep and stood in the position of the modern rose garden. King John used the castle regularly and extended the fortifications, as did Henry III, while a large-scale rebuilding was ordered by Edward I in the late 13th c. He was responsible for adding the two semi-circular towers to the gatehouse. During the Middle Ages the castle was a defensive and administrative focus and a favourite royal hunting lodge, but during the Tudor period it began to fall into decay. In 1553 it was leased from the crown by Edward Watson and converted into a domestic residence. While the alterations were in progress, Walker's House, N of the gatehouse, accommodated the family. Continuing building work was interrupted and considerable damage was done during the Civil War and a new phase of alterations was undertaken in the 19th c. Dickens was a regular visitor to Rockingham, and he dedicated David Copperfield to the Watson family.

The church of St Leonard was considerably damaged when the Roundheads took Rockingham and most of what can be seen dates from a

19th-c rebuilding. The font dates from 1669 and the pulpit is Jacobean and there are numerous monuments to the Watson family.

At the stone village of **Gretton,** 3m NE, the visitor can see the old village stocks and whipping-post standing on the green S of the church. **Weldon,** a similar distance to the SE of Rockingham, displays another facet of the rough justice of the 18th and 19th c in the form of a circular conical-roofed village lock-up which also stands on a green. There is much else of interest at Weldon for an important Roman villa site was discovered in Chapel Field N of the Brook on the site of earlier buildings of the 1st and 2nd c. It was equipped with an iron furnace, bath suite, barn and had two mosaic decorated rooms. The important limestone quarries have re-opened at Weldon; first worked by the Romans, Weldon limestone was exported far and wide and is said to have been used to build Old St Paul's. The church tower has a lantern which according to legend was donated by a traveller who had been lost in the surrounding forest and spotted the church tower as a saving landmark.

STEVINGTON, *Beds.,* 5m NW of Bedford. The village contains most of the things one would hope to find in an English village: a church, a couple of pubs, a market cross, a holy well; and its most distinctive feature is the beautifully restored post mill which stands on the SE outskirts of the village on the road to Oakley. Stevington occupies a cross-roads site close to the River Ouse and 5m NE of Bedford. Although the village stands on heavy clay, the lands were clearly being intensively farmed by the time of Domesday Book when village lands supported only around 30 acres of woodland. There was obviously a well-established church at Stevington by this time for the church of St Mary contains Saxon work in its plain square tower. Inside, a brass commemorates the early 15th-c knight Sir Thomas Salle while the carved wooden bench ends of 16th-c pews have been preserved. Just opposite the church there is a holy well which, according to legend, attracted pilgrims during the medieval period. The village also has a religious association with the Nonconformist supporters of Bunyan in nearby Bedford, and a Baptist Meeting was established here more than 70 years before the construction of the present Baptist church on a site NW of the village in 1720. The 'Act of Parliament' clock inside is decorated with a portrait of the Marquess of Granby and was made in the middle of the 18th c by William Covington of Harrold (q.v.). The village school is found between the church and the cross-roads and stands on land provided by Alston, the lord of the manor, and the building and teacher's house were donated by the Duke of Bedford in 1863. Opposite the school and S of the church is the site of the original manor house.

The post mill is the only one of Bedfordshire's 12 still standing windmills which retains its sails. It dates from *c.* 1770 though the name Miller's Piece elsewhere in the parish may denote an earlier

mill. It continued to operate until 1936. It was rebuilt in 1921, and 30 years later it was acquired by the County Council and a very comprehensive restoration was carried out, making it one of the most beautifully preserved examples in the country, being in full working order. Milling was not the only industry formerly found in the village for, as in many others in Bedfordshire, lace-making was practised here, while matmakers were settled by the river to work the rushes which it provided.

Bedfordshire is less generously endowed with beautiful villages than some other counties, but it makes the very best of what it has and the local authority's conservation efforts at Stevington and at lovely Elstow, S of Bedford, merit the highest praise. A pleasant day could be spent visiting these two villages.

THORNBOROUGH, *Bucks.,* 3½m E of Buckingham. The only surviving medieval bridge in the county spans Claydon Brook at Thornborough. It is a splendid construction, 165ft long, but only 12ft in width with six pointed arches and three breakwaters on the S side. The church displays Norman herringbone rubble work in the S wall and has a 13th-c N arcade and chancel; nave arches and clerestory of the following century and a 15th-c porch with stone benches and the original roof above. Just beyond the bridge are a pair of Roman burial mounds and the excavation of one of them in 1839 yielded bronze jugs, a lamp and amphorae dating from the 2nd c.

Maids' Moreton, 3m W has the county's finest 15th-c church. Tradition tells that the church was the gift of the two maids commemorated in the village name, maiden sisters of the Peover family. Their portrait brasses are kept in the church and replace the original brasses lost long ago. The sisters' masons may have pulled down an early Norman church in order to build the present one, and the font is certainly Norman. With a magnificent tower with moulded battlements, vast Perp windows and a wealth of carving in wood and oak, the church also contains a more sombre relic for an oak door shattered by the bullets of Cromwell's soldiers is preserved in the tower. The sombre theme is retained by the Hangman's Oak outside, where sheep stealers were hanged.

TITCHMARSH, *Northants.,* 2m E of Thrapston. The church of St Mary has what some writers regard as being the finest parish church tower in England outside Somerset. It is built in the Perp style, with setback buttresses, a decorative frieze around the base, a pair of niches flanking the doorway and it is crowned by pinnacles. Although the tower is later than the nave, it cannot be dated exactly and the donor is unknown. During the 17th and 18th c, the Pickering family had their manor close by the church but it was demolished when the family became extinct at the end of the 18th c. The family also had their private pew in a room above the S porch although their wooden staircase has disappeared and the entrance is now blocked. The church is built of good

Richard Muir

The churchyard at Titchmarsh

Northamptonshire limestone from Great Weldon (q.v. *under* Rockingham). A group of almshouses with dormer windows in the thatched roofs stands to the S of the church and green. They were provided by the Pickerings in 1756.

SW of the village is the site of a moated and fortified manor house. The fortifications were licensed in 1304, but appear to have rapidly fallen into decay.

TOTTERNHOE, *Beds.,* 2m W of Dunstable. There is much here to interest the prehistorian or the industrial archaeologist. About ¾m E of the castle mound in the Late Bronze Age and Early Iron Age there was a village which was surrounded by an enclosure ditch, while the outlines of the fields which the prehistoric villagers worked can be traced on the slopes of a nearby ridge. A Roman villa is thought to have stood in a field opposite the church, while the dominating site of the castle mound contained a Norman motte and bailey castle. The quarries in the surrounding downlands were worked at least from medieval times, and although the stone is but a clunch, it was exported for use in neighbouring churches and some even went to Windsor and to Woburn Abbey.

The village is divided into sections known as Lower End, Middle End and Church End. Until recently a moat could be discerned at Lower End, probably marking the site of a medieval manor; Lancotbury in Middle End is a timber-framed manor house dating from the 16th c. The local quarry stone is displayed in the large church of St Giles, a spacious building in the Perp style. Perhaps the most striking features are the very fine roof to the nave and the E window, which was designed by John Piper.

2m S is the famous **Whipsnade** Zoo on a site selected in 1931 as a country retreat for the London Zoo overspill population. The village of Whipsnade is not exceptional although the church of St Mary Magdalene is attractive. By the

standards of E England, the church with its 16th-c brick tower and 18th-c brick nave is but an infant, though the combination is charming. The visitor returning from Whipsnade may find the downland village of **Kensworth** of interest. Like several villages in the S of the county, during the 17th c Kensworth developed a straw-plaiting industry, a trade which seems to have been pioneered by the villagers of nearby Studham. It received a temporary setback in 1689 when the Government passed an act to promote the wearing of hats of wool. Kensworth was the site of one of the chain of national beacons set up to warn of a Napoleonic invasion.

WHITCHURCH, *Bucks.,* 5m N of Aylesbury. This picturesque village of the Vale of Aylesbury has many attractive old houses. The Priory to the SW of the church is one of the finest, built on a stone base with brick infilling the spaces between the framing timbers and an overhanging upper storey. Houses of similar construction stand on High Street with the herringbone pattern of brick nogging being quite a feature of the landscape of old Buckinghamshire. Hugh de Bolebec had his medieval castle beside the stone-fronted house which faces the church and Bolebec House a little further along was the home of the painter Rex Whistler who painted the Vale from the vantage point of his garden for a famous Shell poster.

The church of St John Evangelist dates from the 13th and 14th c and the original medieval glass is preserved in the sanctuary window. A 15th-c painting of St Margaret and her dragon is opposed by an incongruous early-19th-c relief of a local farmer John Westcar who profited by discovering the advantage of using the Grand Union Canal to convey livestock to Smithfield Market.

1m NE of Whitchurch, the oldest house in the county is the manor house at **Creslow**, which was built in the early 14th c. A Norman castle once stood here and before the Dissolution, the manor belonged to the Knights Hospitallers. Their chapel became a stable and the vaulted crypt a cellar but the plan of the original house has been obscured by 17th-c and recent alteration.

WILLINGTON, *Beds.,* 5m E of Bedford. The most appealing buildings in Willington – the church and the manor outbuildings – were provided by John Gostwick who rose from being a yeoman farmer to the Master of the Horse to Cardinal Wolsey and then Treasurer of the First Fruits and Tenths to Henry VIII. He purchased the manor at Willington in 1529 and in 1541 he entertained his king here. The great manor house has gone and all that remain today are the Tudor minor buildings of stone with stepped gables which are now in the care of the National Trust. These are the dovecote and stable. The dovecote is an impressive building which provides roosting niches for 1400 birds, a valuable addition to the winter larder of the lord of the manor. An oak staircase has recently been inserted in the stables, giving the visitor access to the old loft.

An inscription above Sir John's tomb tells that he caused 'this work' to be done, but it is not clear whether it refers to the chapel or the rebuilding of the whole church. In any case, the church is entirely built in the late Perp style and, as Sir John was involved in the Dissolution of the local religious houses, these may have provided stone for his buildings. The church contains two helmets, one was worn by Sir John at the Field of the Cloth of Gold, the other belonged to Sir William Gostwick who died in 1615. Although Sir John prayed for heirs, on his death the estate passed to a brother. The Gostwick house was destroyed by fire and the family wealth was wasted in contesting Parliamentary elections and the Gostwicks sold the remainder of their property in 1731.

The village contains a number of yellow brick estate cottages while at the cross-roads the timber-framed house and the cottage opposite were formerly the White Hart Inn and the village smithy respectively. The earthworks near the former railway station are thought by some to represent a former Danish boat repair yard.

The village of **Cardington,** 2m SW, has some more recent associations of interest. Samuel Whitbread left the village in 1734 to learn the trade of brewing in London; he returned a rich man, and together with his relative John Howard, remodelled much of Cardington. The five-arch bridge into Cardington was designed for Whitbread by John Smeaton in 1778. The planned green encircles the church and is surrounded by John Howard's estate cottages and his own 18th-c house stands N of the church. When he became sheriff of Bedfordshire in 1773 Howard was shocked by the conditions which he discovered in Bedford jail and began a campaign for prison reform which took him to the continent to expose conditions there, and he died in Russia in 1790. The church of St Mary was largely rebuilt in 1900 although fragments of medieval masonry can be seen. There are several brasses including a splendid one to Sir Jarrate Harvye, who died in 1638.

In 1917, Short Brothers set up a works at Cardington and in 1924 the site was taken over by the Government and the great R 101 airship was built in the vast sheds. A monument in the churchyard commemorates the 46 people killed when the airship crashed at Beauvais. Shortsdown close by is a garden village built by the Short Brothers. The RAF came to Cardington in 1936.

WING, *Bucks.* (4m SW of Leighton Buzzard), is noted for its Saxon church, one of the finest 10th-c churches in the country. The church of All Saints is large for its period; the seven-sided apse is perfectly preserved, apart from the ground-storey windows which belong to the 15th c, and two of the original window openings can be seen above. The crypt was discovered in the 19th c and is of a rare and well preserved type; it was probably lost during the 15th-c alterations which provided the tower and the decorative roof for the Saxon nave. The church also has the largest Saxon chancel arch in the country while the discovery of two high doorways at the end of the nave in 1954 suggests that originally there was a gallery there for an important person. In all probability that person was Lady Aelfgifu, the widow of King Edwy, as she held the nearby manor. The church contains a number of monuments to the Dormer family, and that to Sir Robert Dormer dates from 1552 and is said to be the finest monument of the period in England. The church has the distinction that one of its 18th-c incumbents, William Dodd, was hanged at Tyburn for forgery.

¼m N of the church can be seen the remains of a Norman castle mound, and it is strange to think that when this mound was built, the church appeared much as it does today, and had already celebrated its centenary. The influence of the Dormer family is still evident in the village as in the church, and the dormers of the almshouses echo the family name. The houses were provided by the great family in 1569 and can be seen beside the main road. 1m along the Leighton road, Ascott House was built in 1606 on the site of the Dormer manor. It was bought by the Rothschild family in 1874 and is now owned by the National Trust. It contains a fine collection of oriental pottery and Dutch paintings. A curious custom exists at the hilltop Norman church at **Wingrave** 3m SW of Wing; ½ acre of land was bequeathed to the church and on a particular Sunday in June, hay from this meadow is strewn on the floor of the church.

3m SE of Wing stands the lonely mansion **Mentmore House,** built in palatial style for Baron Meyer Amschel de Rothschild by Sir Joseph Paxton and G. H. Stokes. It was inspired by Wollaton Hall and built of the same Ancaster stone. In 1858 Stokes carried out an over-ambitious restoration of the church of St Mary which dates from the 12th and 14th c. Paxton provided a model village arranged in a picturesque manner around a large green, completing the scheme at around the time that the great house was ready for occupation in 1854.

The Heart of England

WARWICKSHIRE WEST MIDLANDS

Charles Lines

In writing of the 'Heart of England', it is Warwickshire that first comes to mind, but the region of which I treat extends beyond its bounds. Writing of the – old – county early this century, Dr J. Charles Cox said: 'the general aspect . . . though undulating and picturesque, with its numerous streams in most directions, is fairly diversified . . . Almost everywhere, it can claim to be well wooded, and from its luxurious hedgerows and the number of its well-grown trees, it has acquired the distinctive title of "Leafy Warwickshire".' Sadly, since his day, like other areas, it has suffered severely from the Dutch elm disease, and the skeletons of once noble elms have become only too melancholy a feature of the late twentieth-century landscape. The loss of the 'Warwickshire Weed' would deeply grieve the topographers of yesterday, but the decimation can be exaggerated. To take instances at random, one thinks of Ufton Wood, Whichford Wood, Hampton Coppice, Spernall Park, the woods near Weston under Wetherley and Princethorpe, or beside the road from Meriden to Fillongley. It is comforting, moreover, to find that extensive tree-planting is under way, though farmers tend to prefer small groups in a corner of a field, rather than single specimens in hedges.

Even that indefatigable cyclist and naturalist, Edith Holden, author of *The Country Diary of an Edwardian Lady*, would find much to please her, although she would scarcely be able to repeat that astonishing list of wild flowers and birds she found near her Olton home, or watch a kingfisher beside her local station! One must remember, too, that the Edge Hills, whose plantations are visible from afar, were as bare as part of the outlying Burton Dassett Hills when the great battle of the Civil War was fought on the land below, 'with the harvest scarcely in'. And what a debt, if too often unacknowledged, we owe to landowners and creators of magnificent parks whose Arcadian beauty is still with us, if diminished. Though much parkland has been taken over at Stoneleigh for the permanent Royal Show ground, great care has been taken to retain trees. Sutton Park, at Sutton Coldfield, can remind us of earlier centuries in its comparative wildness, and must be jealously guarded by conservationists!

The Heart of England boasts no mountains. The Edge Hills escarpment has been mentioned; other natural landmarks include Ilmington Down, Corley, Barr Beacon, Napton on the Hill and Sedgley Beacon. A trifle arrogantly we speak of the 'Warwickshire Avon', though it has to be admitted that it rises in Northamptonshire, and traverses Worcestershire before reaching the Severn at Tewkesbury. Alne, Arrow, Stour, Itchen and Blythe – among those 'numerous streams' – still boast rural charm; the Tame is less polluted than for many a year; and, if the fabulous lake of Kenilworth Castle no longer shimmers in the sun, we have the new, and far larger, expanse of Draycote Water, near Rugby.

A huge slice of the old county of Warwick has been carved out to form part of the new county of West Midlands, which also embraces the enormous industrial conurbations of Birmingham and the Black Country; something of Staffordshire that does not call itself Black Country; includes Coventry; and extends into Worcestershire. What is now Warwickshire in the administrative sense is predominantly rural, although too often perhaps we tend to ignore the area long dedicated to coal-mining.

Dairying, the growing of cereals, poultry-rearing, and in the south-west, horticulture, are carried on extensively. Units have tended to become larger; the owner-occupier has often succeeded the tenant farmer, although large estates exist. The heavier clay of the south-west responds better to modern farming methods than it did to the horse. It is a matter for regret that some of the most fertile land – at Maxstoke, near Coleshill, for example – has disappeared under a motorway.

Architecturally, despite the intrusion of alien materials, and some – not all – of the planners, the region has a wealth of interest to offer. Remains of Saxon buildings are very scanty, apart from a good example at Wootton Wawen. The Normans are well represented in the grand, if mutilated, keep at Kenilworth, at Berkswell and Beaudesert churches, and in the crypt of St Mary's, Warwick. The later medieval churches – Brailes, Solihull, Knowle, Monks Kirby, Astley, Holy Trinity in Coventry, St Peter's at Wolverhampton, to mention but a few – present a wide spectrum, and there is the glorious Beauchamp Chapel at Warwick. The post-Reformation period is distinguished by the late seventeenth-century church at Compton Wynyates, Honiley's enchanting little church of 1723, and the later Georgian beauties of St John's, Wolverhampton, and the (possibly Robert Adam) church at Binley.

Apart from Kenilworth – ruined by seventeenth-century vandals – there are important castles.

Warwick's fourteenth-century towers loom dramatically above the Avon, providing one of the world's great views. Moated Maxstoke, with fourteenth-century outer walls, corner towers and gatehouse, is still in private and ancestral occupation. Compton Wynyates, chiefly in Tudor brick, must rank among England's most beautiful houses, and Baddesley Clinton – partly in grey sandstone – is as splendid a moated manor house as Ightham Mote in Kent or Oxburgh in Norfolk. The noble Tudor gatehouse of Coughton must be mentioned, as well as an exquisite little gatehouse of Elizabethan brick at Charlecote. Jacobean brickwork is seen superbly at Aston Hall, and late Stuart brick at Honington.

Ragley Hall was designed by Dr Robert Hooke about 1680, though its magnificent interiors are later, and Francis Smith's early eighteenth-century west wing at Stoneleigh Abbey is outstanding, and perhaps his masterpiece. Stoneleigh,

too, has monastic work, like Coombe, but the Heart of England has no Tintern or Fountains, despite the former existence of over fifty religious houses in Warwickshire alone.

The motorways are bringing drastic change to the landscape, although it has already seen so many changes; the Roman Fosse has been revived as a highway. The West Midlands county has the only sizeable new main-line railway station (Birmingham International) to be built in the present century. But rural stations and useful little lines, as elsewhere, have vanished, though the line from Tyseley to Stratford-upon-Avon survives miraculously, and that from Leamington to Coventry has been re-opened for passenger traffic. Rural bus services have suffered decline. Pleasure boats have almost entirely taken over the canals: the lower section of the Stratford Canal, with its fine aqueduct near Bearley, is now National Trust.

GAZETTEER

ARROW, *Warwickshire* (1m SW of Alcester), is a very small village of quietly attractive houses in brick, timber and stucco. A former toll-house, at the junction of the road to Worcester, has Gothick windows. The village takes its name from the River Arrow running close to a deserted railway track. The church of Holy Trinity is of ancient origin, but much restored, and has a W tower reputedly designed by that entertaining gossip, Horace Walpole. Among the monuments is a recumbent effigy in white marble to General Sir Francis Seymour, of the Ragley Hall family, who died in 1870. It is by his son-in-law, Count Gleichen (Prince Victor of Hohenlohe-Langenburg) an admiral of the Royal Navy.

Almost opposite the drive to Arrow Mill (now a restaurant) are the lodges of Ragley Hall. This great house, home of the Seymours, Marquises of Hertford, stands splendidly in a former deer park, commanding glorious views. Designed by Robert Hooke, the eccentric curator and secretary of the Royal Society, it dates from about 1680, but the interior decoration is later, much apparently by James Gibbs, and some certainly by James Wyatt who added the entrance portico. The breathtaking great hall is over 40ft high, and adorned with baroque and rococo stuccowork of a very high order, with Aurora (some say Britannia) riding in a chariot across the ceiling. A vast mural, 'The Temptation', by Graham Rust, now occupies the S staircase hall. The Prince Regent's Room contains a canopied bed with Chinese silk hangings and the Prince of Wales's feathers. It was the Prince who suggested to his host that the latter should build a 'castle' on Oversley Hill beyond the Arrow, and a folly, or 'eye-catcher', accordingly arose. The little village of **Wixford**, below the 'castle', has a restored church of 12th-c origin, with the rare dedication of St Milburga and a magnificent early 15th-c brass to Thomas de Cruwe, attorney to the Earl of Warwick, and his wife, Juliana. In the churchyard is a huge yew tree. The village has some timbered houses and the very pleasant Fish Inn beside the river.

ASTLEY, *Warwickshire,* 4m SW of Nuneaton. The bustle and pageantry have long departed from tiny Astley, which lies in rural surroundings often a surprise to strangers because of the proximity of industry and large populations. Its small, moated castle is, at the time of writing, in a state of ruin after a fire, before which it had served as a hotel. There are a few old cottages, several new dwellings, farm buildings and a shop; but Astley's glory is in its imposing church of St Mary, though this is only a shadow of its medieval self. In 1343 Sir Thomas Astley founded a college of priests here, and the great church had a central steeple known as the 'Lanthorn of Arden', owing to its prominence. After the dissolution of the

Edwin Smith

Gothick interior at Arbury Hall

college the magnificent edifice was allowed to decay, with much help from the avaricious Adrian Stokes (second husband of Lady Jane Grey's mother, the Duchess of Suffolk) who sold the lead. A drastic renovation was put in hand early in the 17th c by Richard Chamberlayne of Astley Castle. No trace remains now of the great nave; the original chancel serves that purpose.

Inscriptions in typical Jacobean 'frames' adorn the walls of the present nave. The very important Perp stalls of the priests survive, and there are alabaster effigies of members of the Grey family and memorials of the Newdigates or Newdegates of Arbury Park. The church has changed little since George Eliot described it as 'Knebley Church' in *Mr Gilfil's Love Story*, with Lady Felicia Oldinport and her husband walking down the aisle 'diffusing as they went a delicate odour of Indian roses on the unsusceptible nostrils of the congregation'.

Lady Jane Grey's father, the Duke of Suffolk, was captured in the vicinity after the Wyatt Rebellion, and subsequently executed, and the castle has greatly changed since his day. Close by, swans inhabit a large pool and there is one of the lodges of Arbury Park, home today of the Fitz-Roy Newdegates, with its quite outstanding Gothick embellishments, many treasures and the remains of a private 18th-c canal system.

ASTON CANTLOW, *Warwickshire* (5m NW of Stratford-upon-Avon), amid the lanes of the

Alne Valley, with the Alne Hills nearby, is distinguished as the only Warwickshire village to have had an incumbent who became – officially – a saint. This was St Thomas Cantelupe, the last Englishman canonized before the Reformation. His family gave the village the second part of its pleasant name, traditionally built a castle here – now vanished – and certainly obtained a charter for a market in 1204. Thomas was also Chancellor of England and Bishop of Hereford, and died in 1282 in Italy on his way to see the Pope. The present church of St John the Baptist – its chancel is rightly praised by Pevsner – is chiefly late 13th- and late 14th-c. Over the N door is a carving of the Nativity with the Virgin in bed. A NW stair-turret, now reduced in height, may have been intended to carry a beacon to guide people over the water-meadows to the castle. There is a Guild Chapel in the N aisle, and the church is notable for its ancient woodwork. Sedilia and piscina, a little old glass and a 15th-c font remain.

Aston Cantlow – where once paper-making and needle-scouring were pursued – has another possible claim to fame. It is thought that John Shakespeare and Mary Arden, the parents of William, were married here in 1557. Most unfortunately the register does not begin until 1560. The 'picture-book' King's Head Inn has been suggested as the scene of the wedding-feast; but the building, with its square timbering, is too late. A possible candidate would be the Guild House, which is 15th- or early 16th-c, with close-studding; after serving as cottages and subsequent restoration it has become part of a village hall.

The Victorian architect William Butterfield designed a school and Master's House here, and he was active to the SE at **Wilmcote**. There a school – unfortunately altered – and a vicarage are by him, but doubt has been expressed about the architect of St Andrew's Church, built under the influence of the Oxford Movement. Many more visitors are attracted to the timbered house believed to have been the home of Mary Arden. Now belonging to the Shakespeare Birthplace Trust, this is simply and charmingly furnished, and its little garden, with roses and box hedges, is a delight. Old stone barns house a museum of by-gones. Much stone was formerly quarried here.

Billesley, also pleasantly reached by lanes from Aston Cantlow and Wilmcote, has no village now, but there is a handsome early 17th-c mansion in lias, much restored, and with later additions, including a wing by Detmar Blow. Billesley belonged for generations to the Trussells, one of whom was Speaker of the House of Commons in Edward II's day. The present house, now a hotel and restaurant, was begun by Sir Robert Lee, son of a wealthy London merchant; it was later the home of Thomas Sherlock, successively Bishop of Bangor, Salisbury and London. The small William and Mary church of All Saints – easily missed – incorporates something of a predecessor where Shakespeare's granddaughter, Elizabeth Nash, was married to John (later Sir John) Barnard.

BARFORD, *Warwickshire* (3m SW of Warwick), lies on the A429, but those who know it only from the main road will have missed much of the charm and individuality of this tree-embowered village beside the Avon, though they will have caught a glimpse of the Regency Barford House. Church Street, its continuation, High Street, and the side roads have a wide range of architecture, extending from 17th-c brick and timber to numerous 'executive' houses dating from after World War II. Ivy House, with Venetian windows and stucco façade, should be noted. So should Watchbury House, with carvings of musicians on the porch, and the thatched cottage neighbouring the humble birthplace of Joseph Arch, M.P. for NW Norfolk, 1882–1900, and champion of the farm labourer.

Arch was visited at Barford by Edward VII as Prince of Wales, accompanied by Frances, Countess of Warwick, but the tea-party was not an unqualified success. On the main road the former Red Lion now bears his portrait in caricature. A Georgian rectory is now the Glebe Hotel, and a house called Dragonyard has been well converted from a brick and timber barn. The parish church, in a setting of old tombstones and clipped bushes, was rebuilt in 1844, and has several 'storied urns' among its memorials and a rather bad E window to the chancel. In the recreation ground is a survival (minus its cap) of the iron pumps once used locally to water roads and traction engines.

Across the Avon, beside the early 18th-c mansion of Sherbourne Park, is the very small village of **Sherbourne**, containing Tudor-style estate cottages of last century behind a yew hedge. Church Farm House has an attractive garden and a mixture of styles, but the surprise is the grand Victorian church, the fourth on the site, and its lofty spire a landmark. Sir Gilbert Scott was the architect and it was built at the expense of Miss Louisa Ann Ryland, also a great benefactress of Birmingham. It is replete with marble, stone carvings of flowers, foliage and birds, and stained glass. The pulpit stair is of brass by Skidmore of Coventry and Meriden, whose metalwork is found on the Albert Memorial in Hyde Park, in Lichfield Cathedral and in many churches.

BERKSWELL, *West Midlands,* retains much rural charm, despite its proximity to Coventry, 5m to the E. Five-holed stocks (five holes, it is said, because they were made especially for a one-legged pensioner and his two boon companions) stand on the tiny green; there is a solitary shop with Georgian windows, some thatch and timber-framing, and the celebrated well believed to have been the scene of early Christian baptisms. The Bear Inn (in 1874 described as the Bear and Ragged Staff Commercial Hotel, a reminder that the Earls of Warwick were once lords of Berkswell) occupies a terrace with a Crimean cannon, fired years ago at some local festivity with devastating results to property.

All this is a delightful prelude to the exceptional

church of St John the Baptist, flanked by the Dutch gables of a former rectory, and with many fine trees as a backcloth. The approach to the church through a beautifully kept churchyard is unforgettable. The church has a clock and sundial on the tower, and incorporates work from Norman times to the 17th c. The red and grey sandstone is an admirable foil to the timbered S porch.

Below the nave and chancel are remarkable Norman crypts, one octagonal, the other oblong. These can be approached by small stairs on either side of the chancel arch, which may have been used for the ingress and egress of pilgrims. It is thought that the church once contained relics of a saint, and the 16th-c traveller, John Leland, mentions the former presence of the bones of a St Milred. There are monuments by John Bacon, R.A., and Sir Richard Westmacott, R.A., relating to the family of Sir John Eardley-Wilmot, Bt, M.P., Governor of Van Diemen's Land, who is also commemorated. There are Thompson of Kilburn mice on excellent modern woodwork, heraldic hatchments and, in the porch vestry, pegs for top-hats and a curious hobby-horse used in the pulpit by a hunting rector, as 'eloquence only came to him on horseback'.

Nailcote Hall, former home of the Lants, 1¾m SE, is a timber-framed house of the 16th or 17th c, enlarged and altered. Ram Hall, ½m SSE, is of Elizabethan date, in red sandstone, and it was probably built as the country home of a Coventry merchant.

Balsall Common, on the A452, has much modern development. The George-in-the-Tree Inn is said to derive its name from a visit to the neighbourhood by George IV, and from his portrait in a tree; the name is, in fact, far older. The White Horse Inn displays both white and black horses.

BICKENHILL, *West Midlands* (1½m NW of Hampton-in-Arden), is included because it is a curious survival close to Birmingham Airport, the National Exhibition Centre and ceaseless traffic on the old London–Holyhead Road (A45) and the M42. A very small scattered village – which strictly should be called Church Bickenhill – is by-passed, no doubt to the relief of inhabitants. Stucco or brick hides the antiquity of several houses. A former vicarage looks Regency, and is spacious and quite imposing. There are modern villas in Church Lane and elsewhere, and a residential block in a farmyard just W of the church. The only inn is on the A45.

The church of St Peter – its attractive spire rebuilt after being struck by lightning in 1876 – has one of the few single-handed clocks on any ecclesiastical building in the country. Inside, a N arcade is Norman and quite striking, and a rare stone screen incorporates a doorway with heads of a king and queen, as well as niches for vanished figures of saints. A wide arch from the chancel to the Perp N chapel bears unpleasant mythical figures, one a harpy with a woman's head in a high head-dress, the feet and claws of a bird and

dragon's wings. Heads of a king and queen are again found on a blocked doorway at the W end of the aisle. This may have led to a priest's dwelling, though Pevsner argues convincingly that this could have been part of the stone screen if the original position of this was across the chancel and fronting a possible relic chamber or sacristy. There is a 15th-c font with angels holding books. The neatly kept churchyard contains a big 'teacaddy' tomb of the Thornleys, a family formerly of local note. Bickenhill is associated manorially with the medieval Ardens, Queen Henrietta Maria, the Fishers of Packington and their descendants the Earls of Aylesford.

BRAILES, UPPER and **LOWER,** *Warwickshire* (3m SE of Shipston-on-Stour), are twin villages in hilly countryside with lovely views. Brailes Hill is some 760ft high. Lower Brailes is justly famed for its church of St George. Often termed the 'Cathedral of the Feldon' (Feldon, or open country, as opposed to Arden NW of the Avon) this has a magnificent Perp W tower, 120ft in height, and forming a conspicuous landmark. The church is said to have traces of 12th-c origin, but grew to its present size during the 14th c, when the stately chancel was built, the nave remodelled and probably extended, and the clerestory added. (A bellcote on the E gable of the clerestory is much later.) There is a sundial on the Perp S porch. A good deal of rebuilding seems to have occurred to the N of the building as a result of Civil War damage, but a too-drastic restoration of 1879 destroyed much evidence.

A monument to Richard Davies (1639) is surmounted by sculptured books, spines to the rear. A table tomb has a sadly defaced effigy, probably representing a priest in mass vestments. The Dec font patterns are reminiscent of window tracery. Slabs in the floor are to members of the Bishop family, one of whose members was the revered William Bishop, Bishop of Chalcedon, who, after enduring long imprisonment in England as the result of an earlier mission, was sent back to this country by the Holy See and 'so modestly behaved himself that he was by all, both Clergy and Senators, dearly beloved and honoured', dying 'in peace near London' in 1624. Through the churchyard you reach a simple Roman Catholic chapel, originally built by one of his family in 1726, and approached by an outside stair.

Despite some modern development, Lower Brailes still evinces a good deal of its old character with brownstone dwellings and the George Hotel (probably dating back to Elizabethan days) beside the main street. Brailes House, in spacious grounds with many trees, was a home of the Sheldons, descendants of the William Sheldon who introduced tapestry-weaving to the area in the 16th c.

Upper Brailes has a Gate Inn, now lacking the sign and rhyme usual with hostelries of that name. The 'old stone houses', says Lyndon Cave (*Warwickshire Villages*, 1976) look 'slightly lost among the Victorian red brick cottages and groups of modern bungalows.' Earthworks on Castle Hill may indicate a residence of the de Newburghs, Earls of Warwick.

A road N, between the villages, leads to **Compton Wynyates**, the famous Tudor mansion of the Marquis of Northampton, 'dropped into its grassy hollow as an ancient jewel is deposited upon a cushion', to quote Henry James. There is now only very limited public access. The little parish church (dedication unknown) was almost entirely rebuilt after severe Civil War damage. It retains box pews, Laudian altar rails and a fine array of heraldic hatchments.

CHARLECOTE, *Warwickshire* (4m E of Stratford-upon-Avon), has estate cottages of the 19th c and houses of brick and timber, in a tiny village on the edge of a fine park. The great feature here, of course, is the ancestral mansion of the Lucys and Fairfax-Lucys, now a property of the National Trust, but there is also the elaborate Victorian church of St Leonard, beside the deer fence, and built by Mary Elizabeth Lucy in memory of her husband. Richly furnished with oak and stained glass, it contains impressive tombs from an earlier, and simpler edifice. That of Sir Thomas Lucy, who died in 1640, incorporates marble books, including volumes of Homer, Virgil and Cato, and a panel showing the squire riding round his estate; he died as a result of a fall from his horse. His house was begun by his grandfather of the same name, who is supposed to have prosecuted William Shakespeare for deer-stealing, and was host to Queen Elizabeth I on her visit of 1572.

Sadly, the Grand Avenue (of elms) has been a victim of disease, but there is a replacement leading to a perfect Elizabethan gatehouse, which has turrets, an oriel window and a vaulted passageway. In it is a small family museum, where the long table from the great hall is on view. The house, so much altered in the first half of last century, when it was greatly enlarged, possesses a fine collection of family portraits, including examples of the work of Gainsborough and Batoni. In the dining-room is an astonishing sideboard made by Willcox of Warwick as a present for Queen Victoria, but not accepted by her, on a point of etiquette. The library is one of the most important in any National Trust property, and there are fascinating 19th-c wallpapers and fabrics, much armorial glass by Thomas Willement, period utensils in the kitchen quarters and a good collection of carriages in the stable block. Capability Brown landscaped grounds and park, and the latter contains red and fallow deer and Spanish sheep.

Terraces beside the Avon give a distant view of **Hampton Lucy** church, built on a splendid scale in 1822–6 by the Rev. John Lucy, to the designs of Thomas Rickman and Hutchinson, with an apse added by Sir Gilbert Scott. The former rectory, now Hampton Lucy House, is by Francis Smith of Warwick. A cast-iron bridge of 1829, another gift of the Rev. John Lucy, came from the Horseley Ironworks in Shropshire. The church has cast-iron window tracery.

CHESTERTON, *Warwickshire* (5m SE of Warwick), has been called eerie and haunted, and the historian, Mary Dormer Harris, asks, 'What is it that makes the place so sad?' Set amid undulating open fields, with the Fosse Way and a Roman encampment near at hand, it has few houses today, and has lost its splendid manor house, reputedly (if incorrectly) designed by the inevitable Inigo Jones. This stood within sight of the church. Garden walls and a striking gateway of brick remain. The house was demolished in 1802 after the Verneys of Compton Verney had succeeded to the estate. They were the heirs of the Peytos, the great people here for centuries, one of whom became a cardinal under Mary Tudor, after years in exile. In 1443 Sir William Peyto had been taken prisoner at Dieppe, and his wife had licence to mortgage Chesterton towards the payment of his ransom.

Sir Edward Peyto, the Parliamentarian famed for his defiance of the Royalists while governor of Warwick Castle, built the stone-arched windmill (lovingly restored in recent year) but it may have been an observatory originally. The suggestion has been made that Benedict Arnold, born in Leamington in 1613, based the Old Stone Mill, or Round Tower, at Newport, Rhode Island, on the Chesterton example. A nearby watermill, rather later in date, has a classical touch.

The lonely, embattled church of St Giles, overlooking a modern lake, is mostly 14th and 15th c. Over the S porch is part of a carving, perhaps from a reredos, and probably representing the Three Magi. There are three interesting monuments to the Peytos. That to the Elizabethan Humphrey Peyto and his wife has alabaster effigies, she with a tiny dog (reminding one of the Greville tomb at Alcester) as well as figures of ten children and much heraldry. William Peyto's memorial, with busts of himself and his spouse, was made by Nicholas Stone in 1639. That to Sir Edward and his wife was apparently the work of Nicholas's son, John, who may well have designed much of the vanished mansion.

Perhaps one cause for Chesterton's feeling of sadness, apart from medieval depopulation, is that in 1415 the vicar hid a noted fugitive, the Lollard, Sir John Oldcastle, Lord Cobham. The cleric was pardoned for sheltering 'a heretick . . . holding opinions contrary to the Catholick Faith', but Oldcastle was caught in the Welsh Marches and hanged in London.

CLIFFORD CHAMBERS, *Warwickshire*, 2m S of Stratford-upon-Avon, on the A46. This pleasing village has hawthorns and houses of widely varying dates bordering a long street that ends in a charming manor house, and one of two old watermills in the parish. Several timbered houses are a delight, and there is a little thatch. The rectory is a Tudor building of the hall type, with some Georgian windows, and is claimed by some as the possible birthplace of William Shake-spear. Certainly, plague visited Stratford in 1564, the year of the poet's birth, and the rectory – perhaps as a temporary refuge – was occupied by a John Shakespeare at this time. Walter Roche, who drew up legal documents in connection with the Henley Street property of William's father, John, was master of Stratford's grammar school, and for a few years incumbent of Clifford Chambers. The Hollies, opposite the rectory, with square framing and brick infilling of the 17th c, is a most attractive house.

The manor house has a somewhat unusual history. This was a 16th-c structure, but about 1700 Henry Dighton, whose family had followed the Rainsfords there, remodelled it externally. Fire destroyed the old interior in 1918, and Sir Edwin Lutyens reconstructed it. Lutyens also rebuilt a timber-framed monastic grange at the rear, but this has been demolished. Altogether, about 26 rooms have been demolished. For centuries the manor belonged to the Benedictine abbey of Gloucester, its revenues being devoted to clothing the monks and keeping the abbot's chamber and the guests' chamber in order. This was the responsibility of the chamberlain – hence the second part of the village name.

The beautifully kept church of St Helen has Norman doorways (the N blocked) and EE features. One authority suggests Saxon work in the W tower. There is a Norman pillar piscina in the much-restored chancel, which has carved heads of saints and angels, Rainsford brasses of Elizabethan date and a wall monument to Sir Henry Rainsford, 1622, showing him kneeling opposite his wife, with three children below, one in swaddling clothes. A glass super-screen in the tower arch is an excellent piece of modern work, and the war memorial just outside the churchyard has artistic merit: more than can be said of many.

COUGHTON, *Warwickshire*, 2m N of Alcester. The motorist passing through chiefly notes the broad front of Coughton Court, and perhaps the two attendant churches on the edge of a small park. But the little village is pleasing, with some timber-framing, particularly good thatched cottages and a post office whose Georgian façade gives way to timber and brick at the rear. The Court, now a National Trust property, is the outstanding feature. Some part is said to predate the arrival of the Throckmortons in 1409, when Sir John, Under Treasurer of England, married the heiress of the Spineys; and the formerly moated house is an amalgam of various periods.

Stone, timber-framing, with beautifully carved barge-boards, brick and stucco, all figure in the building, which encloses three sides of a deep courtyard. The towering gatehouse, said to have been erected by Sir George Throckmorton in Henry VIII's reign, though part seems to be earlier, is flanked by stuccoed and embattled walls with several 18th-c Gothick windows. There was a fourth side to the courtyard, but this was

Edwin Smith
The monument to Sir Thomas Lucy (died 1640) at Charlecote

damaged by a mob from Alcester when James II fled from this country; and later the rubble was used to fill up the moat.

Earlier damage had occurred during the Civil War, and for a time the Court was uninhabitable. There are recusant and Gunpowder Plot associations, and the house contains a grand array of family pictures, as well as documents, tapestries and historic relics.

St Peter's church, adjoining, was built principally at the behest of Sir Robert Throckmorton who died 'beyond the seas' in 1518, while attempting a pilgrimage to the Holy Land. It possesses a faceless clock, fish weathervanes, and a good deal of the ancient glass. There are family tombs, among them the one prepared for Sir Robert in the centre aisle, hatchments, and excellent woodwork including a dole cupboard from which wheaten loaves were distributed to the poor. The nearby Roman Catholic church dates from 1857.

DUNCHURCH, *Warwickshire* (on A45, 3m SW of Rugby), was extremely busy in coaching days, its inns accommodating numerous visitors and horses at the confluence of roads to London, Holyhead, Oxford and Leicester. It lost most of its importance after the railway came to Rugby, although that town, with its school and a better market, 'had already outpaced it', according to the *Victoria County History*. The prominent porch of the Dun Cow Inn, 'a large and good house' (*White's Directory*, 1874) has been described as Early Victorian, but it appears that the Marquess of Anglesey reviewed troops from it in 1815 after their return from Waterloo, where he lost a leg. Dominating the green is the Portland stone statue (by J. Durham and erected by grateful tenantry in 1867) of Lord John Scott of the Duke of Buccleuch's family, who were formerly extensive local landowners. 'Wroth Silver', said to be a payment to the lord for rights of cattle-way from one village to another, is still paid at sunrise on 11 November at Knightlow Hill, Ryton-on-Dunsmore.

There are the remains of a market cross and what the 1874 directory calls the 'detestable stocks'. The former Lion Inn, with close studding and overhang, was the scene of the oft-described gathering of Gunpowder conspirators in 1605. There are excellent thatched cottages and a brick School House of 1607. The parish church of St Peter has a Perp W tower and N arcade; the S arcade has Dec piers on earlier bases. It contains an unusual tablet, with marble doors, to Thomas Newcombe, Court Printer to Charles II, and a native of Dunchurch.

Thurlaston, 1m W of Dunchurch, beside the great expanse of Draycote reservoir, has a windmill converted into a house, and seems to have been noted for the longevity of its inhabitants; the 1874 directory tells us that William Barnwell 'is in the 93rd year of his age, but is quite childish', and William Barnett lived until his 96th year and his father was 102 when he died, 'and very active up to a short time prior to his death'. Bilton Grange, ½m NE of Dunchurch was designed by A. W. N. Pugin for a brother-in-law of the Earl of Shrewsbury, but received additions when it became a school.

FARNBOROUGH, *Warwickshire* (6m N of Banbury), is a very pleasing village with old stone houses and cottages close to the gates of Farnborough Hall, now a National Trust property. The church of St Botolph, enlarged in 1875 by Sir Gilbert Scott, who gave it the small spire, has a Dec chancel, a Norman doorway to the S, and Norman stones in a rebuilt chancel arch. A monument to Jeremiah Hall (1711) includes an open book, 'an unusual motif', says Pevsner; and there is a verse, beginning 'Ten children of their mother are bereft' on the tablet to Mrs Wagstaffe, 1667. There are also memorials to the Holbeches of Farnborough Hall, including a S window with Roman warriors. The Holbech home is late 17th- and 18th-c, in a particularly lovely setting of trees, lawns and water. Around the entrance hall are busts of Roman emperors, and a fine ceiling 'reflects' the pattern of the floor. The plasterwork is a feature, that in the old dining-room forming rich and permanent frames for copies of paintings by Canaletto and Pannini; the originals were sold years ago, before the Trust acquired the property.

A great mown terrace made by William Holbech (whose father bought the manor in 1684) ascends from the house to a distant obelisk, and is bordered by 'temples', one an oval casket set on Tuscan columns. Miller, in his *Rambles round the Edge Hills* (1900), tells us that William's brother inherited the nearby Mollington estate, and 'there was a charming love and affection between these

two brothers'. William constructed the terrace 'so that he might walk to the end of it each morning at a stated hour, and at the same time his brother of Mollington arrived at the end of his property, a few hundred yards off, when, having exchanged greetings, they returned to their respective homes and duties.'

HAMPTON-IN-ARDEN, *West Midlands* (4m NE of Solihull), in pleasantly wooded country by the River Blythe, retains a good deal of the character bestowed upon it in the last century by Sir Frederick Peel, M.P. An autocratic and benevolent squire, he was a son of the Prime Minister, Sir Robert Peel, who previously held the manor, once the property of Robert Dudley, Earl of Leicester, and leased to Queen Elizabeth I's trumpeter, 'a soldier of some distinction'.

Sir Frederick built the 'Tudor' stone manor house to the design of W. Eden Nesfield, as well as many picturesque houses and cottages in the village, including some with jettied upper storey and pargeting, the latter being a very unusual feature in this part of the country. A Georgian vicarage has unfortunately gone in recent years; so has a gazebo overlooking the High Street, but the stuccoed White Lion Inn, now minus its hanging lamp, is pleasant in its mild way.

Immediately W of the church of SS Mary and Bartholomew is the Moat House, chiefly 15th- and 16th-c, and displaying close-studding and herringbone work, as well as later brick. The prominent W tower is 15th-c and said to have once borne a light to guide folk through the surrounding countryside. It was once crowned by a spire, demolished 'by the extraordinary violence of lightning and thunder happening on St Andrew's Day at night, in the year 1643', in the words of the historian Sir William Dugdale. A Norman chancel has been partly rebuilt, and has a heart-shrine. The E window is to the first Lady (Frederick) Peel. She was a niece of the poet Shelley who, with other literary figures, is depicted in the window designed to express 'Te Deum Laudamus', sung by poets and prophets. The S arcade of the nave is 12th-c, the N rather later. The aisles have long stone benches, reminding one of the saying 'the weakest go to the wall' and the scarcity of seating in the medieval church. Instruments from a former church band are in a case, and there is a large painted panel with the Royal Arms of 1799. A clock escapement, removed from the tower, may be 17th-c, and the work of Nicholas Paris of Warwick.

An ancient packhorse bridge SE of the village spans the River Blythe. At **Eastcote,** between Hampton-in-Arden and Knowle is the moated Eastcote Hall, with a 15th-c great hall, the black-and-white Eastcote Manor, and two good brick houses known as Wharley Hall and Eastcote House, both dated 1669. **Barston,** 2½m S from Hampton-in-Arden, retains timbered cottages and the Georgian Barston Hall, together with a brick church which was built in 1721 and subsequently altered.

Edwin Smith

Sir Henry Parker's late-seventeenth-century mansion at Honington

HONILEY, *Warwickshire* (5m NNW of Warwick, on the A4177), has lost its village, but the
small church of St John the Baptist of pale sandstone, in a unique setting amid the fields and trees,
should not be missed. Built in 1723, at the expense
of John Sanders, the lord of the manor, it is sometimes ascribed to Sir Christopher Wren, but was
most probably designed by Francis Smith of
Warwick. As one approaches, the scene is greatly
enhanced by ornamental gate-piers with heraldic
elephants' heads and the brick outbuildings of
John Sanders' vanished mansion on either side
of a forecourt. The building to the S formed a
lodge to the modern Honiley Hall, now used for
educational purposes. The ruins of Kenilworth
Castle are visible from the churchyard, which has
Irish yews. There is a decorative W steeple in the
baroque manner, round-headed windows, and a
tiny apsidal chancel with marble paving and
pilasters. High pews have extending – and uncomfortable – benches running on rollers. The
modern glass in the apse is striking, if not entirely
appropriate.

The attribution of the church to Wren probably
arises from the fact that in old age the famous
architect purchased the neighbouring Wroxall
estate, with a house, now replaced, embodying
remains of a Benedictine nunnery. A garden
wall there, in a series of curves, is also ascribed to
him, and his funeral hatchment is preserved in a
medieval lady chapel. Some garden gates were
designed by Sir Clough Williams-Ellis.

Haseley church (just off the A41, 3½m WNW of
Warwick), should be visited. Medieval and later,
it has a wagon ceiling, box pews and candles, and
a palimpsest brass on the tomb of Clement
Throckmorton, cupbearer to Queen Katherine
Parr, and father of the Puritan Job Throckmorton
who was concerned in the issue of the illegal

'Martin Marprelate' tracts, but somehow escaped
punishment when others were fined, imprisoned
or hanged.

The church of Holy Trinity at **Hatton,** on the
main road, retains the Perp W tower and memorials of its predecessor, where Dr Samuel
Parr, eccentric and chaplain to Queen Caroline,
the unfortunate wife of George IV, made his
congregation wait while he retired to the vestry
to smoke a pipe. In sight of the church is the former
parsonage where he housed an immense library
and took in pupils.

HONINGTON, *Warwickshire* (1m NE of
Shipston-on-Stour, just E of the A34), is an
exceptionally pretty village, approached from the
main road through gate-piers with 'pineapples',
and over the Stour by an old stone bridge set with
small globes. There is a village green and many
trees, but no inn or shop; houses are in brick or
stone with one good 'magpie' example, known, in
fact, as Magpie House. A rather grand baroque
gateway marks the entrance to the grounds of
Honington Hall, a late 17th-c mansion built by Sir
Henry Parker, and subsequently noted with
admiration by the diarist John Byng. Its elegant
red brick is punctuated by busts of Roman
emperors and white-painted sash windows, and
there are stone quoins and a prominent cornice
below the hipped roof. Over the main door the
Townsend arms replace those of Parker, and to
this succeeding family is owed the splendid
Georgian plasterwork within and the insertion of
the domed and octagonal saloon, one of the most
beautiful rooms of mid-18th-c date in the country.
Stables and a dovecote with revolving ladder belonged to an earlier house.

The church of All Saints is just across the lawn.
Apart from most of the W tower, this is a Parker

rebuilding of much the same date as Honington Hall. Monuments include that to Sir Henry and his son, Hugh, their standing figures in togas displaying a rather haughty air. One to Joseph Townsend, who did so much for the interior of the house, has an extraordinary cherub.

The road continues to **Idlicote**, about 2m distant, where there is a very small church with Norman work, a W gallery, and – somewhat surprisingly – the Underhill Chapel divided from the chancel by classic arches with a Tuscan column. **Tredington**, 1m from Honington, nearer Stratford, has an outstanding church with evidence of Saxon origin and a lofty steeple rising above old stone houses and less happy modern development.

ILMINGTON, *Warwickshire* (3m WNW of Shipston-on-Stour), is one of the 'show villages' of the county. It has Cotswold-type houses, delightful gardens, wide views over delectable countryside and intersecting lanes and footpaths. The cruciform church of St Mary, reached only by footpaths, is internally spectacular, with Norman arches to the tower and the 13th-c chancel with its puzzling recesses N and S. A special feature is the modern woodwork with the mouse sign-manual of Thompson of Kilburn, Yorkshire. There are the remains of a holy-water stoup in the deep S porch, and in the churchyard an odd tomb in the form of a Gothic church with a spire and apparently chancels at both ends! A nearby stone now only faintly commemorates a parishioner who achieved the age of 106 years, 9 months and 11 days.

A gabled manor house is 16th-c, but much restored and enlarged in recent times, after partial occupation as a post office and by squatters. A former schoolhouse has been converted into a Roman Catholic chapel, replacing one at the mansion of Foxcote, 1¼m SW. This handsome house, former home of the Cannings and Howards, is of the early 18th c, and probably built by Edward Woodward of Chipping Campden. Ilmington, for a while, had some reputation as a spa. The chalybeate spring remains. White's *Directory*, 1874, says 'the water is not often used by the parishioners, but frequently by visitors'. In the neighbourhood of the village are remains of the horse tramway, opened in 1826 between Stratford-upon-Avon and Moreton-in-Marsh, and later extended to Shipston-on-Stour. It was eventually converted to steam between Shipston and Moreton, but regular passenger traffic ceased many years ago.

KNOWLE, *West Midlands* (4m SW from Hampton-in-Arden, on the A41, and merging into modern Dorridge), was formerly a hamlet of Hampton and did not become a separate parish until 1850. What is now the parish church of St John the Baptist, St Lawrence and St Anne, was the chapel of a guild founded by Canon Walter Cook, a native of Knowle, and saved after the guild's dissolution by the petition of local people because of the distance from Hampton-in-Arden

and the dangerous flooding of the River Blythe. It is a grand example of the Perp style, the pinnacled S side forming a delightful picture with a blue cedar and the adjacent Guild House. Traces exist of a passageway leading under the E end of the chancel (as at Walsall) but when this was removed, the floor was lowered, with the result that piscina and sedilia are at a height often puzzling to the visitor. The wooden chancel screen – there is no arch – is outstanding, though it was at one time proposed to abandon it. An hour-glass on the pulpit, intended to time the sermon, has been described as 'running for a merciful twenty minutes'.

The Red Lion Inn, opposite the church (probably early 17th-c but heavily restored) has the fine wrought-iron sign bracket of the earlier, timber-framed White Swan, now unhappily demolished. Medieval Chester House, a focal point of the gently curving High Street, has been handsomely restored, thanks to the local authority. Grimshaw Hall, ½m N of the church, on the road from Knowle to Hampton-in-Arden, is an Elizabethan mansion with rich timbering, formerly the home of the Grimshaw family.

The A4023 to **Temple Balsall** (5½m SE of Hampton-in-Arden) winds past the Victorian Knowle Hall, and its belt of trees, and the red-brick Springfield House, and suddenly reveals the late 13th-c church of St Mary, built by the Knights Templars. This edifice, beside the water-meadows of the Blythe, was rescued from ruin by Lady Anne Holbourne, granddaughter of Robert Dudley, Earl of Leicester, and restored in the last century by Sir Gilbert Scott. The adjoining Old Hall, dating back to the 13th c, and later altered and extended, was part of the extensive domestic buildings of the Templars and their successors the Hospitallers. It contains the hatchment of Lady Anne's sister, Lady Katherine Leveson, founder of the hospital, or almshouses for aged women, bearing her name and still functioning. The buildings, and the deep courtyard with stone paths intersecting lawns, are of a charming, reticent design, mostly in red brick. They were reconstructed extensively by Francis Smith of Warwick from 1725 to 1727 and have been judiciously modernized. Until recent years the 'Dames' of the hospital wore picturesque shawls and bonnets, but the custom is no longer maintained.

LAPWORTH, *Warwickshire,* in pleasant, undulating country, is just off the A34 and 4m NE of Henley-in-Arden, if one is referring to the church of St Mary the Virgin and the 'executive' houses adjoining it. The exceptional church possesses a medieval steeple originally detached from the main structure and situated – unusually – to the N. To the W is a curious Perp 'porch', with a processional way beneath it. Until recent years this had no direct communication with the main building, and the presence of two small staircases leading to the upper chamber suggests that some holy relic was venerated here and provision was made for one-way traffic. A Norman window survives above the N arcade of the nave, but most of the building dates from the 13th to the 15th c, the latter the date of the noble clerestory. There is an Elizabethan altar table with bulbous legs, heraldic glass in the W window of the nave, and a memorial with lettering by Eric Gill.

Another and larger settlement exists on the Old Warwick Road, B4439, near Lapworth (formerly Kingswood) Station. Here is the junction of the Grand Union and Stratford canals. The latter, from Lapworth to Stratford-upon-Avon, belongs to the National Trust, and has barrel-vaulted lockside cottages and 'split' bridges; the horses or donkeys did not pass under the bridge, but the tow-rope was dropped through the centre. The manor of Lapworth belonged to the Gunpowder conspirator, Robert Catesby, and later to the Holtes of Aston Hall.

Now included in Lapworth parish is **Packwood House**, 1m E of Hockley Heath, given to the National Trust in 1941 by Mr Graham Baron Ash. Its 16th-c timber-framing is entirely concealed, but Carolean additions in brick, with large painted sundials, are delightful. The famous yew garden, said to symbolize the Sermon on the Mount, is often held to date from Charles II's time, and to have been planted by John Fetherston, but the 'Multitude' below the Mount is Victorian. Gazebos, old and new, stand at each corner of a walled garden. The house, much restored between the wars, contains a fine collection of tapestries, needlework and furniture. Packwood church (St Giles) about ¾m NW was the scene of the marriage of Dr Samuel Johnson's parents in 1706, and has a Perp tower built by Nicholas Brome of Baddesley Clinton, as one of his acts of expiation after the killing of a parish priest whom he found 'chocking his wife under the chin'.

LONG COMPTON, *Warwickshire* (6m SE of Shipston-on-Stour on the A34), lies between the woods of Weston Park and chequered fields rising to the Rollright Stones of ancient legend on the Oxfordshire border. Writing in 1934, the historian John Burman called it 'an attractive village, with a history nearly as long as its main street', a history that includes manorial associations with the Mohuns, Stanleys and Comptons. In 1976 Lyndon Cave (*Warwickshire Villages*) found Long Compton 'a disappointing place'. Nonetheless, despite recent development, it still has its charms, even if the warm stone houses and cottages of the 17th and 18th c admittedly display some air of unrustic sophistication. The village straggles rather sadly towards the Little Compton turn.

A curiosity is the lychgate to the churchyard, which is really a cottage with the lower storey removed save for the side walls. It has been carefully restored in recent years, after sad neglect. Almost opposite, and now converted into a garage, is a building erected in the last century by Sir George Philips of Weston, who was accustomed to attending church in considerable state, 'to accommodate the equipage during services'.

Monumental clipped yews guard the path to the large church of SS Peter and Paul, which is of the 13th c, and later, but heavily restored in Victorian times, when the chancel was virtually rebuilt. The most engaging features are the carved corbels below the Perp clerestory (angels' heads and those of a bishop and a priest with chalice and book among them) and an appealing little 15th-c chapel S of the chancel. It measures only 8½ft by 6ft.

The 16th-c Weston House, NE of the village, a seat of the Sheldons of tapestry-weaving fame, was replaced about 1830, after Sir George Philips's acquisition of the estate, but its successor has also gone, although 'baronial' lodges remain. A widespread belief in witchcraft persisted in the neighbourhood until well into last century.

At **Little Compton** (2m SW of Long Compton on the A44) is an ancient stone-built manor house remodelled about 1620, and again after a fire between the wars. This was the home during the Commonwealth of William Juxon, Bishop of London (and eventually Archbishop of Canterbury), who attended Charles I on the scaffold. It is said that he brought the execution block with him and that it was destroyed in the fire. The house has an exceptionally beautiful garden, with a small herd of deer in a paddock. Adjoining is the church of St Denis, rebuilt in the last century, except for its saddleback tower (there is another at Barton-on-the-Heath, not far distant) and notable today for its glass depicting the last hours of the 'Martyr King' and his funeral at Windsor in a snowstorm.

LONG ITCHINGTON, *Warwickshire* (2m N of Southam on the A423) has grown appreciably in recent times, not always to its visual advantage. Noble poplars fringe a pool and one of several inns has the pretty name of the Buck and Bell. There are some houses of distinction, with notable examples of timber-framing. Tudor House, beside the main road, belonged for many years to the Sitwell family; it is mentioned in Osbert Sitwell's autobiography and in his brother Sacheverell's *British Architects and Craftsmen*. Their eccentric father spent many years, and much money, restoring this 16th- and early 17th-c house, which was once an inn called the Flower de Luce. Legend has it that Robert Dudley, Earl of Leicester, lord of the manor, entertained Queen Elizabeth I there in 1572, but the honour really fell to the village of Bishop's Itchington. The queen was here, however, in 1575, on her way to the gorgeous festivities at Kenilworth Castle, and Dudley provided for her reception 'a tent, which for number and shift of large and goodlye rooms might be comparable with a beautiful palace'.

The fine church of Holy Trinity lost most of its spire during a thunderstorm of 1762, but a small portion is still visible above the tower. The S aisle is early 13th-c. The chancel, with a particularly beautiful sedilia, nave and W tower are about 1300, and there is a Perp clerestory. The chancel bears a strong resemblance to that at Solihull, built by Sir William de Odingsells about 1280. Both places were in the hands of Christina, sister of Edgar the Atheling, and later passed to the de Limesis and de Odingsells families whose arms appear in a window at Long Itchington. Close by, another panel commemorates St Wulfstan, a native here, who was Bishop of Worcester in 1066; he alone of the bishops then in office submitted to William the Conqueror. He assisted with the compilation of Domesday Book and King John was to regard him as his patron saint.

There is a wall monument in the chancel to John Bosworth, 1674; he left money to provide twopenny loaves every week for the poor and for a schoolmaster to teach their sons and daughters. An armorial board with skull and hour-glass border relates to Lady Anne Holbourne, granddaughter of Robert Dudley and restorer of the church at Temple Balsall. At Stockton Locks, about 1m E of Long Itchington, the Blue Lias Inn beside the canal has a sign depicting a dinosaur, 'the dominant life form 180 million years ago when the Lower Lias was deposited' (Vivian Bird, *Warwickshire*, 1973).

MANCETTER, *Warwickshire* (beside the A5, Watling Street), is now joined to the town of Atherstone. There are modern houses and flats, but the core of the erstwhile village is of special interest, if scarcely in tourist country. Church, manor house and two rows of almshouses flank a small, sloping green, with a view of Witherley church (Leicestershire) across the Roman road. The Roman settlement of Manduessedum was here, and it is suggested that the defeat of Queen Boadicea and her army occurred in the vicinity. However, apart from the architecture, Mancetter's chief claim to the visitor's attention may be in its association with the Marian martyrs, Robert Glover and Joyce Lewis, both of whom were burnt at the stake for their faith: Robert in Coventry in 1555, Mrs Lewis at Lichfield in 1557. Robert's two brothers escaped arrest, but died of hunger and exposure. Mrs Lewis lived at Manor Farm, the Glovers at the black-and-white manor house, which stands handsomely above the green with twin gazebos and gate-piers of the 18th c. Part of the house is medieval, but it has been altered and extended.

The martyrs are commemorated on wooden tablets in the fine church of St Peter which is of early 13th-c origin, with notable Dec and Perp work, the latter including the W tower. A 17th-c S porch is mainly in brick with a sundial. The glory of the building is the rich glass in the E window of the chancel, most of it 14th-c, and probably of Coventry workmanship. Part of a Tree of Jesse from nearby Merevale Abbey is incorporated. Chained books remain. Vivian Bird (*Warwickshire*, 1973) calls the churchyard with its many epitaphs and Swithland slate tombstones 'possibly the most attractive in Warwick-

shire'. It is certainly enhanced by the almshouses founded in 1728 by James Gramer, a London goldsmith, and 'capable of entertaining six persons'. The other almshouses, with a very pretty iron veranda, are just across the road, and date from 1822.

There are remains of the Cistercian Merevale Abbey 1½m to the NW, founded by Robert, Earl Ferrers in 1184, with the early Victorian Merevale Hall superbly placed on the wooded hill above. Through a 'medieval' gatehouse of last century you reach a small parish church with a chancel larger than the nave. This was once the chapel at the abbey gate to which pilgrims came in great numbers to pray before a statue of the Virgin, many being 'brought near to the point of death' in the resulting crush and confusion. There is some important 14th-c glass and, among the monuments, the tomb of another Robert, Earl Ferrers, 1412, with fine brasses of himself and his wife. This, like the glass, was no doubt brought from the vanished abbey church.

MERIDEN, *West Midlands,* is now by-passed by a new stretch of the A45, and is about 6m WNW of Coventry. Although there has been much growth since World War II, (which has added little to its architectural merit) the village still possesses something of its ancient character, with several mansions near at hand. One of about 13 places said to mark the Centre of England, it retains a celebrated cross of indeterminable age on a pleasant green flanked by modern shops and thatched cottages. A prominent obelisk is the Cyclists' War Memorial.

Sir William Dugdale, the 17th-c historian, wrote: 'This place, situated upon London-road, having from some Inns and Alehouses built for the receipt of Passengers grown of late times to the credit of a Village, doth now utterly eclipse the name of Alspath, by which and none other, the Town itself (cf. where the Church standeth) was known even from the Saxon times till about King Henry the sixths reign.' One of the later inns, the Bull's Head, was called 'the Handsomest Inn in England', but the diarist Byng had hard things to say of its hospitality. Other guests included the future Queen Victoria and William Cobbett. It eventually became a private residence (as it is said to have been earlier) but like the belfry in the garden, once noted for its sweet set of chimes, has been demolished. The early 18th-c manor house, next door, has become part of a large hotel complex, having served in the last century as the co-educational Meriden Academy and centre of Weslyanism.

Meriden Hall, designed by Francis Smith of Warwick, and well documented, has been converted into flats; its fine pillared drawing-room has later, Adam-style decoration. It is possible that the grounds were laid out by Capability Brown, when working at nearby Packington Hall. The parish church of St Lawrence, on the high ground towards Coventry, with work of every century from the 12th to the 16th, has two

Kenneth Scowen

Meriden – claimed to be 'the centre of England'

medieval tombs with effigies in armour, and a notable modern window in the S aisle from the Camm studio at Smethwick. There are superb views from the churchyard, which contains the tomb of General George Whichcote, who died in 1891, and was the last surviving British officer of the Peninsula and last but one of those who fought at Waterloo. Off the road to Fillongley is the restored Walsh Hall, a 15th-c timber-framed hall house, altered somewhat later, and enlarged in 1938. On the road towards Stonebridge is the Forest Hall, the older part designed by Joseph Bonomi, also linked with Packington Hall and Great Packington church. It is the headquarters of the exclusive archery club, the Woodmen of Arden.

NAPTON-ON-THE-HILL, *Warwickshire* (3m E of Southam, beside the A425), is a surprisingly long and large village climbing up to the fine church of St Lawrence, with houses flanking a green and on the main road. L. T. C. Rolt in *Narrow Boat* (2nd edition, 1948) thought it 'surely the strangest . . . in all Warwickshire', and found close resemblance to a Cotswold village. Stone and brick are intermingled. Thatch survives here and there and a few houses go back to the 16th c. Modern additions are not always inappropriate, though there has been criticism and mention of 'over-restoration' of existing properties. The remains of a windmill (about to be restored?) are a landmark on high ground that commands views over a wide area.

The church – its position something of a test for the devout – is chiefly EE, with Norman work that includes windows on the N side of the chancel. Pevsner rightly calls the transepts of about 1275 impressive; they have tomb recesses, and that to the N a mutilated double piscina and one of two stone altar slabs. The W tower was largely, or even entirely, rebuilt in the 18th c, but includes medieval material. The 16th-c or early 17th-c S porch has some much older stonework that may

have been added when J. Croft (not 'wild', as he was at Lower Shuckburgh, q.v.) carried out the inevitable Victorian restoration. (It is worth noting that the contractor on this occasion was a local man, William Watson, who was extensively employed on churches in the neighbourhood; he and his father served the Shuckburgh estate 'for upwards of a century', says White's *Directory* of 1874.) A brass to John Shuckburgh, 1625, is a reminder of the long manorial connection of his family and their maternal ancestors, the de Naptons. A chest was 'the gift of Thomas Garit and Isabel his wife 1642'.

The Oxford Canal, one of the most attractive of man-made waterways, sweeps 'round the base of the hill in a horseshoe curve like a moat about a castle mound', says Rolt. His description of an evening at the Bull and Butcher Inn should be read.

PRESTON - ON - STOUR, *Warwickshire,* reached by a lane skirting Alscot Park, about 3m S from Stratford-upon-Avon off the A34. This secluded and quietly enchanting village is separated by the River Stour from the mansion of James West, the bibliophile, connoisseur and Joint Secretary to the Treasury, who bought the estate in 1749. Feudal Victorian cottages with attendant Irish yews line the approach to a sloping green neighboured by a gabled and timbered house of about 1600 and other interesting dwellings. A path beyond a dignified gateway with stone piers leads up, with agreeable melancholy, to the church of St Mary, remodelled or rebuilt by James West with the aid of Edward Woodward of Chipping Campden. The Rev. J. Charles Cox, in his *Little Guide* to Gloucestershire (in which county Preston was formerly situated) says it is 'of singularly poor work throughout', and quotes a fellow cleric who declared that the chancel reminded him of 'a railway carriage upon a good company's line!'

These views are by no means endorsed today; we can now regard the church as a fascinating period piece. James completely rebuilt the chancel, retaining the skeleton of the ancient nave, including a low-pitched roof. He also inserted a good deal of notable English and Continental glass and provided a Georgian screen of wood and iron and other features. Characteristically, Cox only mentions the monument to Sir Nicholas Kemp (1624) and his two wives, but there are examples of the art of Sir Richard Westmacott and R. Westmacott, Jun. among the West memorials. There is another handsome gateway at the tower end, where 'the family' used to arrive in some state in a carriage with liveried footmen.

West remodelled and extended his home which stands in a beautiful deer park, and, like Arbury Hall, near Nuneaton, is a grand example of the Gothick taste, but with some Victorian decoration within. At Atherstone Hill, ½m NW, is an early 18th-c brick house bought by Dr William Thomas, editor of an important edition of Dugdale's *Antiquities of Warwickshire*. The district is scenically rewarding, and along the main road will be found traces of the horse tramway from Stratford to Moreton-in-Marsh, opened in 1826. A sole surviving wagon from the line is preserved near the Clopton Bridge in Stratford.

RADWAY, *Warwickshire,* about 3½m SE from Kineton, off the B4086. This charming stone village, with some thatched cottages, and the new blending well with the old, lies below the richly wooded Edge Hills. Radway Tower, now part of an inn, stands on the high ground and marks the site of Charles I's standard at the Battle of Edgehill in 1642. It was built by the Georgian amateur architect Sanderson Miller, who lived at Radway Grange, a house which he altered, adding Gothick features. There, Fielding read the manuscript of *Tom Jones* to an assembled company that included William Pitt, Earl of Chatham, who planted trees in the park. In the present century, Field-Marshal Earl Haig (as he became) lived at the Grange, and his name appears on the village war memorial.

An ancient parish church was demolished last century, although – as pictures in the present building reveal – it had been extensively restored by Charles Chambers, Miller's son-in-law, not very many years before. The stones, however, were used in the construction of the Victorian church of St Peter, which has a broach spire and stands on a different site. It contains some interesting features from its predecessor, among them elegant wall tablets, one to Chambers, who was Surgeon Extraordinary to the Duke of Clarence, later William IV. As a naval surgeon he was present at an engagement in the Gulf of Finland in 1809, subject of a relief on the tablet. A mutilated effigy is of Captain Henry Kingsmill, who fell at the Battle of Edgehill; his white horse, it is said, was an easy target. In a S aisle window is some rather beautiful Netherlandish glass of the 17th c, with Biblical scenes; it came from Radway Tower, and earlier, we are told, from a house in Dorset.

Ratley, on the Oxfordshire border, and just over 1m NE of the A422, by a lane starting near Upton House, is another village of warm brown stone. The undulating setting is most attractive, though one may agree with Lyndon Cave (*Warwickshire Villages*) that 'a number of new houses on top of the hill between the original buildings and Edge Hill ... are foreign to the existing character of Ratley.' The Rose and Crown Inn is partly 16th-c, but the old manor house has gone. Five steps lead down from a 17th-c N porch into the pleasing church of St Peter ad Vincula. (St Peter in Chains, an unusual dedication reminding us of the legend that the saint was held in chains by Herod in Jerusalem and imprisoned by Nero in Rome before crucifixion.) The building has much Dec work, but goes back to the 12th c. A S arcade has no capitals to its pillars, and the lofty nave is reminiscent of a Dutch church. A pretty marble tablet commemorates one of the Earls of Jersey. His family owned Upton House within the parish.

This fine mansion may have been designed originally by Francis Smith of Warwick. Later altered by Sanderson Miller, it was remodelled by Morley Horder for the 2nd Viscount Bearsted, who gave it to the National Trust in 1948. Reached by a drive from the A422, near the summit of Sun Rising Hill, it is notable for its collection of European paintings, porcelain and furniture, and has lovely terraced gardens.

SHUCKBURGH, UPPER and LOWER, *Warwickshire,* on the A425, E of Southam. 'A sad village, we could have no entertainment', wrote the diarist and traveller, Celia Fiennes, when she and her companions were overtaken by nightfall at Lower Shuckburgh (Southam 4m) or 'Nether Shugar', as she calls it, on their way from Warwick to Daventry. There is no inn today, and some of the house names, Cabul, Nowshera, Joaki and Gandamuck (inspired by the participation of a member of the ancient Shuckburgh family in the Second Afghan War) would certainly astonish the diarist of 300 years ago.

So would the Victorian church of St John the Baptist, designed by J. Croft, and externally, 'lively, rich, and enterprising', in Pevsner's words; the interior, he says, 'knocks you out with the contrast of stone and particularly flaming brick with white joints.' (The 'brick' is painted on.) Fragments of a predecessor are to be found at Upper Shuckburgh in the gardens of Shuckburgh Hall (the lodge gate about 1m towards Daventry). The house has undergone extensive rebuilding since Celia and her friends found hospitality there, after their initial disappointment, at the hands of Sir Charles Shuckburgh and his wife. Still the family home, much of it is of 1844, lying in a curve of rising and thickly wooded grounds with peacocks, antique cannon and a church of medieval origin. The last possesses a wealth of family memorials, including brasses, works by Flaxman and one with a notable bust by Peter Bennier to Sir Richard Shuckburgh, who was knighted on the battlefield of Edgehill, afterwards suffering for his loyalty by imprisonment in Kenilworth Castle.

A few miles distant, and best approached from the A45, near Braunston (Northants.) is **Wolf-hamcote,** or Wolfhampcote. Its village has disappeared, but the ancient church of St Peter has been carefully repaired, after years of dereliction and abuse, thanks to the Friends of Friendless Churches. **Priors Marston,** 5½m ESE from Southam, off the A425, is 'one of the most rewarding villages in this part of the country', says Pevsner, and has some excellent stone houses, especially High House of the late 17th c. Unfortunately, a small yard producing hand-made bricks has closed. Chairs made by Priors Marston craftsmen are much prized.

STONELEIGH, *Warwickshire* (3m NE of Kenilworth on A444), lies picturesquely beside the River Sowe, which is crossed by Rennie's 19th-c bridge and joins the Avon near the village.

Approaching from Leamington – the road skirting two parks of Stoneleigh Abbey, and bypassing the medieval Stare Bridge – you are conscious of modern development across the valley. The old village, however, is remarkably untouched, with much brick and timber, a black-and-white manor house, some excellent thatching and two sets of almshouses. A cruck house dates from the early 16th c, but has been carefully extended. The Old Almshouses, just N of the church, are of red sandstone and display striking chimneys. They were built at the cost of Sir Thomas Leigh, Lord Mayor of London, and his wife, Alice, the former having acquired the old estate of Cistercian monks who were here from Henry II's reign until the Dissolution.

The church of St Mary is particularly notable for its Norman work. The W tower is largely of that period and the tympanum of the N doorway into the church has dragons and snakes biting their own tails. There is a magnificent Norman arch to the chancel, and much-restored Trans arcading beyond, as well as a grand monument to Duchess Dudley, who lived to be 90, with trumpeting cherubs holding marble curtains and recumbent effigies of herself and her daughter Alicia. A S chapel is of 1667; that to the N is early 19th-c, and monuments to the Leighs, who are still at Stoneleigh, are a conspicuous feature. High pews with candle-holders and a Hanoverian Royal Arms in cast iron add a period note.

A tablet with ambiguous wording and evidently a sly dig at a deceased porter 'at Stoneleigh's Gates', who 'dealt Large Almes out of his Lord's store', is outside on the S wall. The 'Gates' may refer to the altered and extended abbey gatehouse built by Abbot de Hockele in the 14th c; it now forms an entrance to the grounds of the great house of the Leighs, which incorporates Norman and other monastic remains and is a considerable distance from the village. It boasts a superb W front built by Francis Smith of Warwick and completed in 1726. Although badly damaged by fire this still contains fine plasterwork of somewhat later date. The house has interesting associations with Queen Victoria and with Jane Austen, whose mother was a Leigh. Much of the parkland is now the permanent home for the annual Royal Show.

TANWORTH-IN-ARDEN, *Warwickshire,* is 10m S of Birmingham, on high ground with a landmark of a church spire and a wide-reaching prospect from the churchyard. It was simply called Tanworth until 19th-c, when an attempt was made to distinguish it for postal reasons from Tamworth, Staffs, not with entire success. The commuter long ago discovered it, but there are old houses in a variety of styles, and a small green overlooked by the Bell Inn. The dignified Aspley House, with Doric porch, was built in 1808 by John Burman, owner of the local bank.

The (largely) early 14th-c parish church of St Mary Magdalene is a noble building, if over-restored in Victorian times: it was brought 'up-to-

date' by the Rev. Philip Wren, great-grandson of the famous architect. The N arcade was rebuilt during the restoration. Among interesting features surviving are the image brackets in the chancel, a delightful little brass with a kneeling figure to Margaret Archer, 1614, and another to Ann, wife of John Chambers, 1650. A stately monument commemorates Thomas Archer, 1685, his wife and daughter-in-law. This was probably designed by Thomas's son, also named Thomas, who was Groom-Porter to Queen Anne (an office giving him control of gaming establishments throughout the kingdom) and architect of what is now Birmingham's Anglican cathedral, of part of Chatsworth, and of St John's Church, Westminster. He did not, however, design Umberslade Hall, 1½m NE, for his brother Andrew. Almost certainly, this was the work of Francis Smith of Warwick. Somewhat altered, and recently converted into luxury flats, it stands on land that belonged to the family in the male line from Henry II's reign until the death of the 2nd Lord Archer in 1778. The house has associations with Florence Nightingale and the poet Tennyson. The well-known Umberslade Obelisk was built by the 1st Lord Archer in 1749. A windmill at Danzey Green, 1m SE of Tanworth village, has been removed to the Avoncroft Museum near Bromsgrove and carefully restored.

Tanworth still has its Association for the Prosecution of Felons; founded in 1784 before the establishment of a regular police force for the apprehension of malefactors, it paid rewards to that end. Its activities are now chiefly of a social nature, the annual dinner being an occasion of some hilarity. Similar associations survive at Berkswell (q.v.) and Knowle (q.v.).

WARMINGTON, *Warwickshire* (5½m NE of Banbury on A41), is still undoubtedly one of Warwickshire's most beautiful villages, with houses of Hornton stone disposed around a very large green in a setting of wooded countryside beside the once notorious Warmington Hill. The gabled manor house near the Town Pool (once used for sheep-washing) is a hall house of Elizabethan date, with mullioned windows, moulded beams and queen-posts. A former rectory seems to be early 18th-c (curiously, an insurance document still uses the term 'new' considerably later in the century) with pilasters and sash windows and some older work. There is good panelling and a pleasing staircase.

The church of St Michael (or St Nicholas) stands aloof, and is reached from the village by many steps. Work of each century from the 12th to the 15th is evident, with some excellent Norman arcading in the nave and a Dec two-storeyed projection (somewhat reminiscent of the upper and lower chapels at Solihull): the upstairs room was obviously used for residential purposes. In fact, there is a record of the Vicar of Holy Trinity, Coventry, paying rent for this in 1570, and the room has a fireplace and garderobe. The churchyard was the burial-place of soldiers killed in the

Battle of Edgehill in 1642, but the name of only one, a Scotsman, Alexander Gourden, or Gourdin, is recorded. The manor of Warmington belonged to the very rich 18th-c banker, Robert Child, who owned Upton House (now a National Trust property) a few miles distant, and Osterley Park, Isleworth. The manor later passed to his daughter, Sarah, who made a runaway match with the Earl of Westmorland.

The hamlet of **Arlescote** in the W of the parish, beyond the main road, has a fine manor house, a late Stuart remodelling of an Elizabethan building, with summer houses in the garden.

WHICHFORD, *Warwickshire* (2m NE of Long Compton, off A34, and 5m SE of Shipston-on-Stour), is in an area rich in interesting villages, although all have not escaped the attention of the modern builder. Set in quiet, undulating countryside, rising to 800ft, with Whichford Wood to the SW, stone cottages, a school and the Norman Knight Inn border an extensive well-kept green. The church of St Michael stands a short distance away to the W, and, like Brailes (q.v.), retains a sanctus bellcote. Rearranged tombstones lining the churchyard path look as if they awaited a procession. There is Norman, 13th-c and 14th-c and later work including a Perp clerestory to the nave. In the S chapel a stone coffin lid bears the arms of Mohun, a reminder that William de Mohun gave the church to Bridlington Priory, which his father-in-law, Walter de Gand, had founded. The Mohuns afterwards became lords of the manor here. Window glass in the chancel also bears the family arms, and there are monuments to John Merton and Nicholas Asheton, 16th-c rectors, the former with an incised effigy on alabaster, showing him in mass vestments, the other with a brass figure in a Geneva gown. (Both were chaplains to the Stanleys, also associated manorially with Whichford.) The pulpit is reached by modern steps through the wall. There is a lectern with an aloof-looking eagle in wood, and the church has both candles and electric light. A former rectory close by has been heroically rescued from dereliction. It is partly of the early 17th c, with charming Queen Anne additions, although two – obviously intended – balancing bays to the W were never built. Its garden shows evidence of much thought and care.

Sutton-under-Brailes (1¾m NW of Whichford) possesses another large village green and is remarkably unspoilt, with old stone dwellings, some beautiful trees and a remarkable air of seclusion. The site of a moated manor house is visible, but this would be presumably the residence of a bailiff, as Sutton belonged for centuries to the monks of Westminster. Earlier, it was owned by Deerhurst Priory in Gloucestershire, and until 1840 stood on a detached 'island' of that county. The church of St Thomas à Becket stands in a scrupulously kept churchyard set with weathered tombstones that are a reproach to many a modern mason and his clients. There is Norman work in the N and S walls of the nave, and a N

doorway of the period was discovered during a restoration in 1879 when, unfortunately, the Victorian 'scraper' got to work on the interior, a fate that Whichford escaped. The 13th-c chancel has a fine E window, and N and S windows are decorated with memorable carvings of heads, including those of two ladies of the period, and of a fox and an ape. A curious feature is that the S porch and ground floor of the tower is also the ringing-chamber: with seats for the ringers and some inconvenience to church-goers.

WOOTTON WAWEN, *Warwickshire*, on A34, 2m S of Henley-in-Arden, formerly in Wootton parish. Anglo-Saxon (strictly Anglo-Danish here) work is rare in the county, but it can be seen with quite striking emphasis here in the church of St Peter, and the very narrow arches of the central tower (the upper part of the structure is later) are a fascinating, if inconvenient, feature. The arch to the chancel is only 4ft 8in wide. The church is in sight of the village, but separated from it by fields. It is a kind of manual of church architecture, and almost three churches in one. Other impressive features are the 15th-c clerestory of the nave, and the chancel's big E window of similar date. Woodwork includes beautiful chantry screens, and Wootton Wawen has the only chained library in Warwickshire.

A chancel tomb with an effigy in armour is believed to be that of John Harewell, who died in 1428. In the S chapel is the figure of Francis Smith, a later lord of Wootton, 'looking rather like an old gentleman reclining on a park bench', and an urn-topped cenotaph of 1744 is to Robert Knight, absconding cashier of the South Sea Company. His son, the unpleasant Earl of Catherlough, is also commemorated, together with others of the family. But there is no memorial here to his wife whom he 'banished', for some misdemeanour, to Barrells Hall a few miles away. There she engaged in landscape gardening and formed a literary coterie that included the poets Somervile, Shenstone, Jago and Graves. Originally interred at Wootton, her present, and third, resting-place is in the partly demolished Ullenhall Chapel, 2½m WNW from Henley-in-Arden.

E of the church are the wooded grounds of Wootton Hall, with a large caravan park. Part of this fine house is earlier, but most of it dates from 1687, and was built by Francis Smith, 2nd Viscount Carington. At the rear is a former Roman Catholic chapel; its fittings, including a marble altar, were transferred to a new building (now beyond the railway) in 1906. The River Alne flows close to the mansion, forming a double cascade, well seen from a balustraded bridge on the main road. Close by is a former paper mill of brick and an aqueduct of the Stratford Canal of much interest to the industrial archaeologist. The village contains modern almshouses of good design, the 16th-c Bull's Head Inn, and attractive old houses and cottages, including a farmhouse with an overdoor decorated with carved fruit, flowers and acanthus.

The North Midlands

LEICESTERSHIRE DERBYSHIRE NOTTINGHAM STAFFORDSHIRE

M. W. Barley

In the long history of our countryside villages have come and gone; some have grown into towns and then dwindled again to villages; new owners or conquerors have descended on peasant communities, built their castles, palaces or monasteries and then gone down into tombs in their churches or even vanished into oblivion. Compared with churches and mansions, the homes of peasants had to be rebuilt time and again. The most recent changes are naturally the most easily noticed, but the art of looking at villages – and it is an art – is to read from their appearance and buildings as much as possible of

their long history and to trace the changes. This way of looking at places is a branch of archaeology – field archaeology, which stops short of uncovering buried remains. This group of North Midland counties is as rewarding as any part of England if looked at in this way.

The landscape and fields are the setting. Few visitors seeing these parts for the first time would regard them as scenically exciting, except of course for northern Derbyshire and Staffordshire, the southern end of the Pennines. Nevertheless, a distinct pattern of landscape can be picked out. The grain of the Midlands runs from

north-east to south-west. So the sandstone of Rutland (*see* Lyddington), rust-coloured from the iron in it, can be followed into Northampton-shire and Oxfordshire; the grey lias limestone of Nottinghamshire (*see* Collingham) can be picked up again in Gloucestershire; the sandstone of Nottingham is the same as at Kinver in south Staffordshire. Ridges of high ground follow the same direction, as is very evident at Burrough on the Hill (Leics.). The oldest and hardest rocks are those in the north-west corner of the region, in upland Derbyshire and Staffordshire, apart from those of the Charnwood area of Leicestershire, where the granites of Mountsorrel and the slates of Swithland have been pushed up to the surface. All four counties depend for their drainage on the River Trent and its tributaries; they have formed their valleys and deposited their sands and gravels across the older shape of the landscape.

To think of country villages as dependent now on farming is very wide of the mark and has rarely been wholly true in the past. Buried minerals, especially lead and iron, attracted settlers; in-dustries have helped to shape villages in one age or another and even if a particular industry has died, as has lead-mining at Brassington (Derby-shire) or nail-making at Kinver (Staffs.), the village as it is cannot be understood if the trades cannot be discerned. The textile industry is a thing of the past at Tean (Staffs.) and Woodborough (Notts.) and the traffic in lime through Buxworth (Derby-shire) has ceased; the warehouses on the Trent and Mersey canal at Shardlow (Derbyshire) are empty and the slate quarries at Swithland (Leics.) are overgrown, but industry gave those places their visual and their social character.

The countryside has had its rich and its poor, its lords and priests as well as its peasants, ever since prehistoric man built Arbor Low (*see* Hartington, Derbyshire). The homes of such early settlers have not been found, but over the past 1000 years many villages have become what they are through the initiative and expenditure of the wealthy and powerful. Under the walls of the Norman castles of Bolsover and Castleton there grew up the homes of those who served their lords. Saxon monasteries generated the villages of Breedon, Repton and Southwell. After a Nor-man baron founded Blyth a village grew up to serve the inmates and travellers who passed that way. Bishops of Carlisle had a palace at Mel-bourne and bishops of Lincoln a manor house at Lyddington; the abbots of Burton upon Trent owned and developed Abbot's Bromley.

Rich and powerful individuals and institutions could afford the most durable (and expensive) materials, and their castles, cathedrals and mansions had the best chance of survival. The village church represents the collective endeavour of village people to ensure that their place of worship kept time and change at bay; they could usually afford only local materials, however good or bad they were, and so one fascination of looking at churches is to notice the kinds of stone used. This pattern reflects the local geology – slate at

Swithland (Leics.), gritstone in parts of north Derbyshire and Staffordshire; softer sandstone in much of the rest of the region until one reaches the grey lias limestone, the rust-coloured iron-stone and the golden oolitic limestone of the south-eastern part of the area.

When we come to the homes of ordinary people – the farmhouses and cottages – we find ourselves looking at buildings rarely more than 300 years old and often much less. Timber-framed buildings are rare except in the western part of the region (*see* Abbot's Bromley and Long Whatton), and even there belong mainly to the end of that tradi-tion; elsewhere, good oak was never plentiful and cheap enough to create a rich and elaborate crafts-manship in oak such as one finds in Hereford-shire. Sometimes the inside of a house is older than the outside because decaying walls of timber or even of mud have been renewed or cased in brick, but the ordinary traveller, able only to stroll down a village street rather than poking about inside houses and hunting for ancient timbers, must be content to enjoy the qualities of modern materials. That means brick and tile in the main, though where stone was readily avail-able it continued to be used. It is fascinating to notice, if one crosses Nottinghamshire from west to east, where stone slates give way to flat clay tiles and then to the pantiles of eastern England. Midland bricks are astonishingly rich in their range of colour and texture, if one chooses to compare Betley (Staffs.) with Bunny or Thrump-ton (Notts.) and Bottesford (Leics.).

We are all conscious nowadays of the part that planning plays in the life of a community. This is nothing new, except in the scale of modern plan-ning controls. Research has recently shown that in medieval England a landowner might plan to turn a village into a town by getting a market and a fair for it, and by laying out streets and making building sites available. Whether we call this planning or speculation, it seems to account for the wide main street of Abbot's Bromley and the traces of a grid of lanes there and at Bottesford. Some of the most distinctive villages of the region, such as Gringley on the Hill (Notts.) and Hallaton (Leics.), were once market towns and seem to have grown in an unplanned way. In modern times, total control by one landowner has given some villages a homogeneity that cannot be called planning but remains a unique quality. For that reason such places as Buckminster (Leics.) with its row of labourers' cottages, Milford with its housing for textile workers, Bunny, Sudbury and Thrumpton have been included.

At the end of such a review as this one is bound to ask how villages are faring today. A generation ago we were conscious that their historic char-acter was threatened by the continuing flight from the land and changes in agricultural tech-niques. In Britain as elsewhere in western Europe the consequence was the disappearance of man-sions, the decay of farmhouses and the dereliction of farm buildings and cottages. In recent years, increasing ownership of cars has reversed this

Janet and Colin Bord

The Horn Dance at Abbot's Bromley

process and has brought new blood, and new money, to villages. At the end of the working day, the people using the back lanes of the countryside are not farmworkers leaving the fields but commuters who have worked out the shortest route from their jobs in a town to their country homes. One of the results is that old houses are if anything more at risk from new owners with too much money than from those with too little. Hedges to village gardens are replaced by fancy walling; good stone and brick houses are whitened for show. Owners with limited means find that mass-produced windows and doors are cheaper than getting a carpenter to copy exactly fittings

that have to be renewed. And finding tradesmen who will make a good job of pointing brickwork becomes even more difficult.

Even in the villages here selected, the visitor will sometimes find new houses that strike a jarring note and old houses that have been made too smart. These Midland villages provide a chance to look, and to look hard, both at grand houses and at cottages, both great churches and modest ones. Their quality resides in the combination of the grand and the ordinary. It is the ordinary – or traditional, or vernacular, call it what you will – which presents the greater challenge to the perceptive traveller.

GAZETTER

ABBOT'S BROMLEY, *Staffs.* (4m NE of Rugeley), once belonged to the abbey of Burton upon Trent. The little market town promoted by the abbots has long since decayed; now it is a village with a very long street and nothing of age behind. The street curves enough to show the houses to advantage. The market place is grassed over; the 17th-c market house or butter cross still stands – a hexagon of big posts and a pyramid roof – but behind it is an 18th-c cottage. Gaps between houses were entrances to farmyards and there are glimpses of barns, now disused; malting was once carried on here.

The best part of the church is its W tower, rebuilt in 1688 after its predecessor collapsed; it is classical in style, with quoins and pilasters and is topped by a balustrade and urns instead of battlements. This is a good village for timber-framing: Church House (1619 and 1659) and the Goats Head Inn with typical West Midland decorative panelling. Elsewhere, framing may well be concealed by later brickwork; notice the gable end of Crofts' Cottage and a house at the S end of the village. At the top of Schoolhouse Lane stands the school founded in 1606: timber-framed with a storeyed porch. Part of the framing is still visible, rather hidden behind a Victorian school planted in the front garden. By 1705, when the original part of the Bagot almshouses was built, brick had be-

come the normal material. At the S end of the village the girls' public school (St Mary and St Anne, founded 1874) has purpose-built buildings and has taken over some houses. The chapel built in 1881 is lofty and majestic.

Blithfield Hall, 2m W and in the valley of the River Blithe, has long been the home of the Bagots (notice **Bagots Bromley**, 1m NW), and long ownership has meant much addition and alteration; the overall impression is of Georgian Gothick. The church of Blithfield is rich in Jacobean fittings. Whatever village there was has vanished.

The Horn Dance at Abbots Bromley, performed early in September each year, is a picturesque folk survival. Dancers in medieval dress, some of them bearing huge reindeer antlers, assemble on the village green and dance round the village bounds, performing set 'figures' at Blithfield Hall and other stopping places. There is a jester, an archer representing Robin Hood and a man dressed as Maid Marian, and there are musicians playing a melodeon and a triangle. The dance symbolizes the rites of the chase and establishes the villagers' privilege of hunting in Needwood Forest, which was the hunting ground of John of Gaunt.

ALREWAS, *Staffs.*, alongside A38 and 5m NE of Lichfield, is pronounced to rhyme with *walrus.* The village took its name from an alder swamp by the Trent, and the river has always dominated its history. Like Barton under Needwood (q.v.), it must have been an early Anglo-Saxon settlement and a springboard for the later colonization of Needwood Forest. To judge from the church, the 13th c was a time of prosperity – notice the fine EE chancel. The village must have flourished in the 17th c too: it has more timber-framed cottages of that period than most others in Staffs. They have walls composed of square panels, and a number are still thatched. The pattern of the village was transformed in the 1770s when the Trent and Mersey Canal was cut round what was then the edge of the place. Fradley Junction (2m SW) came into existence when James Brindley in 1768 started to construct a canal from there, first to Coventry and later to Oxford. Although England's canals are nowadays quiet and picturesque, if not overgrown, we who have seen motorways come into existence ought to appreciate how this new system of communications transformed industry in Georgian times. There is no trace now of the camps of the 'navvies' (navigators) who dug the canals, and the few boats carry not cheese, coal, pottery or iron, only people at leisure; but you can still appreciate here that Staffs. was the pivot of England's waterway system and that Alrewas was an essential element in it. North of the church is a tall Victorian mill, built for cotton.

Yoxall, 3m NW, represents an ancient settlement on the edge of Needwood. The Forest was first nibbled into, and eventually devoured, over a period of 1000 years. If you go out NW towards Hadley End, the lane is lined by cottages of every age; the oldest, with timber-framing still visible, show how peasants were squatting from at least the 17th c on the edge of waste land and carving out small holdings. In the centre of the village there are homes of wealthier people. Birmingham House, N of the church, is a small timber-framed house of *c.*1675, its square panels filled with brick; it is quite unaltered except for the inserted shop windows. S of the church the Grange, just visible over its garden walls, has curved gables (? *c.* 1750) and still further is a remarkably tall late Georgian house called The Rookery. There are pleasant dormered cottages in Victoria Street.

ALTON, *Staffs.,* in the Churnet Valley between Cheadle and Ashbourne, offers some of the most romantic prospects in England. Come in from the N along lanes from Ellastone or Oakamoor and it is easy to forget that there is heavy industry, started long ago (*see* Longnor), at Oakamoor and Froghall. At the brink of the valley, by the entrance to Alton Towers, you see the roofs of the village on the further crest, but the view is dominated by a towering castle that might be on the Rhine: on a sandstone cliff strong walls rise to be topped by turrets, gables and a little copper spire.

The village was always dominated by the castle, which had belonged to the Talbots, Earls of Shrewsbury, from the 15th c. The 15th and 16th earls (1787–1852) made Alton what it is. The village got new stone houses, an inn (the three-storey Talbot Arms), a railway station (now closed), and a curious circular stone lock-up, with a dome. All this was a spin-off from turning a small lodge on the N side into the earls' principal residence, and also rebuilding the castle, with alongside it a hospital intended for retired Roman Catholic priests. Among several architects, A. W. N. Pugin put the most distinctive mark on the buildings. Now the castle houses a Roman Catholic prep school and the house has become a ruin since the estate was sold in 1924. But the company which then bought it has kept the gardens of Alton Towers in immaculate condition. While children enjoy endless amusements specially introduced for them, adults can enjoy the earls' gardens, crowded and overpowering with their terraces, conservatories, fountains and pagodas: a unique monument to the romantic tastes of the English aristocracy.

For a great contrast, go E towards **Hollington.** To the left stand the ruins of Croxden Abbey, a Cistercian monastery now an ancient monument, and open free. The lane cuts right through the complex and EE ruins stand on both sides. They are built of local sandstone, and it is worth while to go on to Hollington where the quarries that produced the red and white sandstone for the new Coventry Cathedral are still working. You may visit the masons' yard and watch them carving capitals, mullions and the like for the repair of historic buildings all over England.

APPLEBY, *Leics.,* lies close to A453 just S of Measham. The two Applebys, Magna and Parva, and the other village of **Stretton en le Field** on the other side of A453, are a reminder of how village names are sometimes in forms fixed by medieval clerks who spoke Norman French and kept their records in Latin.

There is not much to **Appleby Parva** except the school, and what a surprise that is! No one expects a village primary school to look like a country house, but that is precisely what this one was intended to do. The explanation is that a local boy, John Moore, went to London and made a fortune in the East India Trade. He contributed to the rebuilding of St Paul's – providing much of the lead and the cost of all the gilding – and so was in a position to consult his friend Sir Christopher Wren about the design for a school in his home village. Wren's designs for the Free School were actually carried out, and altered, by Sir William Wilson in 1693–7. When it was finished Wilson had a job to get his money out of Sir John Moore, especially for the founder's statue, made for a niche in the hall. The hall or grammar school room occupies the main range; the room over it with round windows was to be the dormitory for boarders. The left-hand wing was for the English and Writing School, the right-hand wing the headmaster's house. The building stands back from the road, as a country house should, with entrance gates and ironwork, and has a garden behind (*see illustration on page 25*).

Appleby Magna, too, has its surprises. The church is large, mainly Dec, with reticulated tracery in the aisle windows. They originally had stained glass, and a few figures survive. The inside was given a new look in 1827 by an elaborate plaster vault, which tries to look 14th-c; there are box pews in Gothick style. A few years later a W gallery was inserted. The medieval moated manor house has gone, but its stone gatehouse was rebuilt in Elizabethan times and a new timber-framed range added to it. At the same time a square dovecote was built nearer the church.

Other buildings in the village demonstrate the transition from timber-framed to brick houses. There is a timber-framed inn at the corner of Mawby's Lane and Top Street, and, opposite, a brick house with stone quoins and mullioned windows. Further along Top Street is Eastgate House, dated 1720, entirely in brick.

ASHFORD-IN-THE-WATER, *Derbyshire*

(2m NW of Bakewell), depends for its popularity on its setting. This means inevitably that its houses have been smartened up by wealthy newcomers but the overall character and the setting are unspoiled. The traffic on A6 has always passed on the other side of the river; so the village is still entered by three bridges over the Wye. Sheepwash Bridge has a sheep pen alongside, and near it is a well which is dressed on Ascension Day. Ashford is a cluster of grey walled houses surrounded by smooth grassy slopes and narrow wooded valleys. None of the houses is particularly notable, though it is a surprise to see evidence of weaving: one tall house has a top storey with a long window intended to light the work of a weaver or a framework knitter (*see* Woodborough). There was once more industry here, for quarries in Kirk Dale produced that black marble so popular in Georgian days for making a chequer-patterned floor in a fashionable house. From A6 there is a glimpse of Ashford Hall, built *c.* 1785, and on the road towards Buxton are two cottages designed by Paxton (*c.* 1859) for the Chatsworth estate.

To see a hamlet apparently untouched by commuters or weekenders, go 1m SW, up the wooded Kirk Dale, to **Sheldon.** The street climbs gently, with wide grassy verges, between unpretentious farmhouses and cottages of limestone. Beyond Sheldon, on the limestone uplands, are prehistoric tombs and barrows (Rick Low, Ringham Low), invariably damaged and hard to locate. More plentiful are the traces of lead-mining. Magpie Mine is worth finding, because the ruins of a Cornish engine house with chimneys and other mining gear have been conserved by the Peak District Mines Historical Society. Less than ½m S of the village, go further up Kirk Dale and turn W for the mine.

W of Ashford, the Wye loops round Fin Cop, rising 1070ft above the wooded Monsal Dale. On the windy and open top is an Iron Age hillfort of about 10 acres with double defences. It was presumably only a place of refuge, not regularly inhabited. Settlements of the earliest inhabitants remain largely undiscovered in this landscape with so many traces of the prehistoric dead.

BARTON UNDER NEEDWOOD, *Staffs.,*

is only 4m SW of Burton upon Trent, and so inevitably swollen by recent development; but the nucleus of the village is still intact and attractive. It stands on the edge of the Trent valley, and of the medieval royal forest of Needwood. Archaeologists have recently excavated a Saxon village 1m away at Catholme, showing that early settlers must have found the Trent a convenient highway; from it they established such villages as Barton, which in turn served as bases for colonization of the higher ground of the Forest. The Trent highway was improved in 1766–77 when the Trent-Mersey Canal was constructed, on the initiative of Josiah Wedgwood, to serve as an outlet for the pottery, coal and iron industries of Staffs. Its humped-backed bridges can still be spotted alongside A38. More recently, the demand for gravel has created strings of lagoons along the valley, as it will do at Catholme when the archaeologists have finished.

The main street of Barton has pleasant cottages, some still timber-framed, but round the church there are more fashionable houses, including the vicarage, SW of the church, with its unusual porch. Along the road to Dunstall there are other quality houses of the Georgian period and the very simple but attractive Hall. The parish church, in spite of being low and spreading, dominates the centre. It spreads partly because the aisles were widened in 1864; otherwise the church is exactly as built in 1517 by a local man who made good. John Taylor became a churchman and obtained lucrative employment under Henry VIII: hence his benefaction to his birthplace.

N of Barton you enter what was once Needwood Forest. **Tatenhill** has a medieval church and a handsome early Georgian former rectory, but **Dunstall** seems entirely 19th-c – Victorian church, hall, school, vicarage. The Jacobean poet Michael Drayton wrote regretfully about 'those fallow deer and huge-haunched stags that grazed' upon Needwood's shaggy heaths being 'by vile gain devoured'. He observed the beginning of the re-replacement of natural forest by rolling parkland and pasture farming.

BETLEY, *Staffs.,* has a long main street on the road from Crewe to Newcastle under Lyme, but there is not enough traffic to spoil it. The village has strong affinities with Cheshire and Salop. For one thing it has a timber church, standing above the village on a back lane; only the tower and aisle walls are of the local pinkish-brown sandstone. Timber churches were once common but there are only a few left now, nearly all in the West Midland counties. Betley has octagonal timber piers: arched braces instead of arches; heavy and cambered tie-beams; a wooden clerestory. The chancel was rebuilt, still in timber, in 1610; notice the turned pendants, similar to those on Jacobean staircases and court cupboards.

Edwin Smith

Barlborough Hall

The village street has a fascinating mixture of materials and styles. The Old Hall (1621) at the N end is timber-framed with close studding; notice the big sandstone chimney stacks. Timber-framed cottages look 17th-c, with square panelling and straight braces. But brick-making must have started by about 1700 or even earlier; there are several brick cottages with original dormer windows, the upstairs rooms being half in the roof space. Notice that the bricks are very dark – no doubt the clays came from the coal measures. But the most remarkable group comprises Betley Court, with its large stable yard, an octagonal dovecote (or pavilion!) and hundreds of yards of walling alongside the road. The Court is said to date from about 1720. All the brickwork has a chequer pattern, achieved by using purple bricks as stretchers and red bricks as headers. The purple bricks must have been so fired intentionally, with at least one purple side, and it would be remarkable if they were not made on the estate. The whole group serves as a testimonial to the technological skills of country brick-makers. The group has been saved by conversion into flats.

As you drive through **Wrinehill**, on the Cheshire border, notice on the E side of the road the Summerhouse; was it a Georgian weekend cottage for some industrialist? It has brick walls with giant stone pilasters and a big pediment, making a very eccentric design. There is also a range of Victorian farm buildings – built of dark bricks with round pitching holes for the hay loft.

BLYTH, *Notts.,* has seen many vicissitudes. A thousand years ago the 'great way of the north', from Nottingham to York, came through here. In 1088 a Benedictine priory was founded and a little town grew up at its gates; travellers passing through Sherwood Forest had Rufford Abbey (*see* Wellow) and Blyth Priory to give them hospitality. After the Priory was dissolved (1536) the market ceased and the town declined. The Priory had come to the Saundersons, who built a mansion on the site, and then to the Mellish family. William Mellish revived the village in the 1770s in response to growth in road traffic. There are still several inns but the village is now by-passed by A1 and can be viewed in peace and quiet.

The W half of the Priory church survives as the parish church, and 'there is nothing like Blyth to get a feeling for early Norman grimness' (Pevsner). The nave was finished by about 1100. Two centuries later the S aisle was rebuilt and widened, possibly for the use of the townspeople;

did they also contribute to building the Perp W tower? The nave ends in a blank wall, and there is nothing beyond; the site of the conventual buildings (and the mansion) to N and E is now covered with recent houses.

The village owes its character to the Georgian buildings of William Mellish, all recognizable by their Gothic window casements. There is the former rectory close to the church, a row of three cottages on the green with its back to the churchyard and another row on the E side of the green. Going S the road widens to form another green with a long row on the left-hand side. It has a tall carriage entrance in the centre, but nearly half the row has been rebuilt in a sadly nondescript style. Further S there is an older house, possibly about 1700, with stone quoins and doorway; beyond it more of Mellish's work in a pretty octagonal cottage. This was the end of ancient Blyth. Across the road is a stone building on a knoll, now a house; it was originally the Hospital of St John the Evangelist, founded early in Blyth's history for travellers reaching the town exhausted or sick.

Going S from **Barnby Moor** (2½m SE of Blyth) a minor road represents an old line of the Great North Road, before it was switched (c. 1770) to go through Retford. Several houses on the old road were once inns, such as Jockey House. Elkesley had one called Eel Pie House.

BOLSOVER, *Derbyshire* (5m E of Chesterfield), catches the eye of motorists, standing as it does on a commanding ridge E of M1. Leaving the motorway by exit 29 and turning N along the ridge through Glapwell, you come first to the village which grew up outside the gates of the Norman castle. It eventually became a market town, but the market died long ago. There is nothing distinguished about the centre and there has been much clearance in favour of car parks.

The castle fulfils all the expectations of the distant view, if in an unexpected way. The medieval castle gave way from 1610 onwards to a new building by the 1st Duke of Newcastle (1593–1676) who also rebuilt Nottingham Castle; he was a grandson of Bess of Hardwick; so Bolsover is one of the group of great houses built by Bess and her descendants – Hardwick (also visible from M1, further S), Chatsworth and Welbeck among them. The new building was designed by John Smythson and thus is linked with his father's work at Wollaton, Notts. Since Bolsover became an ancient monument in 1945, the buildings round the outer court have been restored, particularly the Riding School. (The Duke of Newcastle wrote a famous book on horsemanship.) The pleasures of what is called the Little Castle can only be savoured from outside. To quote the excellent Department of the Environment guidebook 'it has dreamlike qualities: a romantic folly with vaulted chambers, frescoed walls and battlemented turrets'. The interior decoration is remarkably complete. At a more mundane level, the enquiring visitor can find traces of the 17th-c water supply – a conduit house NE of the castle,

roofless, but the spring flowing through it, and a series of others, like stone sentry boxes, to the S.

At the foot of the slope lies New Bolsover, a model mining village of 1888–93; it is worth a visit, especially as the Coal Board has kept the houses in good order. Terraces surround three sides of a large green, and semi-detached managers' houses are on the road N. Sad to say, the large school on the fourth side of the green is derelict, as are the Co-operative Society's 'Stores'.

Among nearby villages, **Barlborough** is exceptional for having kept its rural character, with Georgian houses and Victorian estate cottages. The Elizabethan Barlborough Hall – another design of the Smythson family – is now a prep school; visitors may see it in late August.

BOTTESFORD, *Leics.* (7m W of Grantham), grew up where a N–S road from Belvoir Castle crossed the Nottingham–Grantham road. It was always under the sway of the lords of Belvoir – first the Roos, then the Manners family – and they not only promoted it as a market town but also gave it a grid layout, as you will see if you explore back lanes. The market has been long dead, but there is the stump of a market cross and a Market Street. The River Devon winds its way through the village, and there are two old footbridges over it: Fleming's Bridge, S of the churchyard, has two stone arches (c. 1600); Devon Lane has a charming bridge, probably Georgian, alongside a ford. There is a lot of new housing, both as infilling and as enlargement, but a variety of older houses survive from the 17th c onwards; a few of ironstone but mostly of a very dark red brick.

There is a great contrast between the little chapel of the Particular Baptists (1832), tucked away at the end of Chapel Lane, and the grandeur of the parish church. The latter's slender spire is a landmark in the flat expanse of the Vale of Belvoir. Inside, the church seems spacious and lofty, but the visitor's eye is soon drawn to the chancel, which is crowded with monuments of the lords of Belvoir. There are 11 of them, with 20 life-size effigies (counting wives) and innumerable children kneeling round their parents. They range in date from a recumbent Roos lady (c. 1320) to a standing Earl of Rutland of 1679. There is also a magnificent brass to a rector of 1404, Henry de Codyngton, who was born in a village near Newark and became a canon of Southwell. This was a rich living and the rectory is the grandest house in the place, with a large garden next to the church.

If you go SE from Bottesford, through Easthorpe and past Muston, you cross the Grantham Canal – still holding water and good for fishing but not for boats; the locks are derelict. While it flourished it carried not only coal from Nottingham and agricultural produce, but also Welsh slate for headstones and the building material for Harlaxton Manor (Lincs.) and Belvoir Castle. **Woolsthorpe by Belvoir** (*not* Newton's birthplace) is a pleasant estate village. By some quirk of parish history, there are no graves round the Victorian church; the Woolsthorpe dead were carried up the hill to the S, where there is an ancient grave-yard carved out of a wood. Going from Wools-thorpe provides the best view of Belvoir Castle, the perfect romantic castle. There is something for the taste of every visitor: the park and gardens with statues; a late Georgian rebuilding of the castle in medieval styles; inside, a maze of pas-sages, staircases and galleries and some grand rooms; lastly, collections made by successive dukes, of prehistoric pottery, medieval floor tiles, Georgian insurance plaques and military relics.

BRADLEY, *Staffs.*, lies 4m SW of Stafford, S of the Newport road. It should be pronounced Bradeley. It can be taken to represent many mid-Staffordshire villages not overwhelmed by recent growth. The church stands on a slight ridge, with views W over the valley of the Church Eaton Brook and the course chosen for the Shropshire Union Canal, which we also encounter at Brewood (q.v.) and Norbury (q.v.). The country round has a thin scattering of brick farmhouses and cottages, mostly of 19-c date, and near the church there is a Georgian farmhouse and a modest Victorian school (now, of course, closed). Has the village shrunk? It managed to build quite a grand church in the 13th and 14th c, and the impression one gets of the nave with its elegant and lofty arcade to the N aisle is dramatized by the light from the tall Perp windows in the S wall. There is a simple Norman font – just a stone drum covered with chip-carved ornament. The medieval stair to the rood loft has survived, with a new screen of 1908 (but no loft). There are fragments of medieval glass in a S window. There is a sombre tomb to Thomas Browne and his wife (1633), facing one another and dressed in black.

The ground rises still further to the E. On the slope of Butter Hill (502ft) stands a manor house, Littywood, within a round moat or ringwork which may be Norman in date. The brick exterior of the house conceals a hall of *c.* 1400. On another isolated hill, 2m away towards Stafford and just N of the Stafford road, there is a small prehistoric hillfort, Berry Ring. Still further towards Stafford is the Norman motte and bailey known as Stafford Castle. NE of Bradley is another small settlement on its own hill, **Coppenhall.** It has a perfect small church, built in the 13th c when Coppenhall was allowed to break away from Bradley. The Ord-nance Survey map marks several medieval moated sites on this high ground. Such places were evi-dently preferred in ancient times; the low ground was only drained and settled in recent centuries. The map also marks a number of ponds; they were marl pits, usually in the corners of fields, from which marl was dug to spread on the soil to improve it.

BRASSINGTON, *Derbyshire,* is 5m SW of Matlock. The village and its neighbourhood are dense with evidence of man over nearly 5000 years. Inevitably the activity of later generations has made some traces of earlier times difficult or im-possible to find. There was a Stone Age tomb

above Harborough Rocks (1m NE); it is now only a mound. Harborough Cave must have been in-habited then, as it still was in the 1720s when Daniel Defoe found a poor lead miner and his family in it and wrote, in his *Tour through England and Wales,* a very moving account of his visit. The Neolithic tomb at Minninglow (2½m NW) is still recognizable. The Roman road from Derby to Buxton passed very near Minninglow and Brass-ington, and the Romano-British village at Rain-ster Rocks (1m NW) must have depended in part on lead-mining. Now the popularity of such places with climbers, picnickers and treasure-hunters threatens to spoil them.

Lead-mining started in Roman times; if it ceased in AD 400 when the Roman Empire col-lapsed it soon began again: hence Brassington. There is no trace of it in the village, except in the age and size of the Norman church, but the fields around are riddled with old lead mines; now just grassy mounds over abandoned shafts. The miners exploited the mainly vertical veins of ore known as rakes; to see the buildings in which ore was processed go to Magpie Mine at Sheldon (*see* Ashford in the Water). **Wirksworth,** the little market town 3m E, was from Saxon times the centre of this industry; in the Barmoot Court there the miners managed their affairs.

Brassington stands at about 750 ft on a S facing slope: a cluster of light grey houses with the church in the centre and surrounded by meadows defined by pale grey walls. Good quality stone and money from lead-mining made for a fine church with ash-lar walling; by 1200 it already had an unusual W tower (notice the buttresses), a fine S arcade and even a S aisle to the chancel. There are some good houses. Tudor House, Town Street, is dated 1615 and the Gate Inn 1616; both are built of fawn-coloured dolomitized limestone like the church tower and in contrast to most of the village.

Of nearby villages, **Hopton** (2m SE) and **Kirk Ireton** (3½m SE) are equally rich in stone houses.

BREEDON ON THE HILL, *Leics.,* is 5m NE of Ashby de la Zouch. Escape from the traffic on A453 by taking, at the S end of the village, the turning signed 'motorway to church', and you will see the pleasantest part of the village. You will have to go on towards Nottingham to see the vil-lage lock-up: circular, with a conical roof, rather like what is called a Butter Cross at Hallaton. It is built of limestone, and this is the key to Breedon's long history. The isolated hill has no rival in north Leics.; it is at once a landmark, a viewpoint and a source of road material. Not surprisingly, Iron Age settlers chose to make a hillfort of it, the Bul-warks, and as you follow the road to the top you trace the ancient rampart on your right. At the top, from the viewing platform by the church, there is an immense distant panorama, and sad destruction at your feet. More than half the hill has gone, for the limestone makes road metalling that we cannot do without. Archaeologists, busy in ad-vance of quarrying, found not only prehistoric and Roman material but also burials belonging to a monastery founded about AD 675. It was meant to bring Christian teaching and baptism to the Anglo-Saxons of the surrounding country; that work collapsed with the Danish invasions two centuries later. How impressive the church must have been can only be deduced from fragments of Anglo-Saxon sculpture rescued later and built into the church. About 1120 the monastic tradition was revived; an Augustinian Priory (not *Augustian* as on the board outside the church) was founded. Its residential buildings have totally vanished.

What is left is a parish church whose architectural history is very puzzling, but its sculpture and fittings are of great interest. First the Saxon sculpture: nearly 30 fragments carved before AD 800 – friezes and panels with birds, beasts, humans, naturalistic and geometrical ornament; larger figures of the Virgin Mary and angels. Scattered through the church, they are worth hunting out; nowhere else in England can you see such skilful and vigorous artistry of that distant age.

The church also has the Shirley pew, an elaborate Jacobean affair (1627) and alabaster tombs of the same family. They lived at **Staunton Harold,** 2m SW, where there is no village, but Sir Robert Shirley rebuilt the church as a private chapel in 1653. For spending money on a church rather than raising a regiment Cromwell sent him to the Tower, where he died in 1656. The church is unique and unaltered; the National Trust maintains it. The Hall is 1763 in front (brick with stone quoins) and Jacobean behind. Becoming a Cheshire Home saved it from demolition; the interior may be seen on application. Church, Hall and lakes form a superb monument to an ancient family.

BREWOOD, *Staffs.,* is 6m W of Cannock and only 1m S of Watling Street, near the sites of a Roman fort, the town of Pennocrucium and a Roman villa. There is no trace of them in the meadows alongside the little River Penk. Like much of Staffs., Brewood grew up inside royal forest, with woodland to harbour the royal deer. Narrow winding lanes link the small hamlets and isolated farms which developed as the woodland was cleared. Brewood once had a market promoted by the Bishop of Lichfield: hence the tight pattern of streets round the church and market place. People with means and taste must have built the handsome Georgian houses in Dean Street, but here, as elsewhere in Staffs. there is often medieval timber-work behind a later façade. In the market place, Speedwell House is a splendid exercise in Georgian Gothic, built with advanced taste for its time (1753) and with money won by a local apothecary on a horse named Speedwell. Although Wolverhampton exerts much pressure on the village for new houses and infilling, the centre is still intact.

The Shropshire Union Canal skirts the village but in such a deep cutting that it is not noticed. Just across the canal from the village is a Roman Catholic church designed by Pugin in 1843; he also built the Priest's House and a school which now serves as a nunnery. The existence of a Cath-

olic congregation must have been partly due to the Gifford family of nearby Chillington; although Catholics, and persecuted for it, they have monuments in the parish church. They were naturally on Charles I's side in the Civil War, and his son Charles sheltered for three days in 1651 at their hunting lodge (Boscobel House), 3m W of Brewood. There Charles, as everyone knows, had to hide one day (6 September) in an oak tree. Boscobel House (an ancient monument) and a tree descended from the Royal Oak are by a few yards in Salop.

Chillington Hall is about 2m SW, and is approached by the Upper Avenue; Telford designed a classical bridge where his canal cut the line of the Lower Avenue. Capability Brown, about 1770, formed the great lake and a winding canal, and the romantic landscape he created was then embellished with the temples, arches and a sham bridge that such taste required. If M54 is constructed, it will curtail the S edge of this Georgian landscape. As for the Hall, John Gifford (d. 1556) built a house round a courtyard. It was enlarged in 1724, and remodelled again in the 1780s; the grandest rooms were created in these later phases.

BUCKMINSTER, *Leics.,* stands on the highest point of the limestone tableland in the E of Leics., and 7m S of Grantham. Its name suggests its ancient importance, for 'minster' shows that while Christian missionaries were converting the Anglo-Saxon peasants they chose this site for a minster church (like Southwell, q.v.) with a band of priests to preach and baptize in these parts. There is no trace of a Saxon church; perhaps it was a wooden building, rebuilt later in stone as was every other wooden church of Saxon date (except Greensted in Essex, q.v.).

Apart from the church and a few stone cottages on a back lane, the village now bears the mark of its modern landowners, even though the Georgian great house has gone. Coming up from Sproxton (pronounced 'Sproson'), the road is lined with chestnut trees like a private drive. As you enter the village, on the right stands a row of 16 estate cottages built about 1850, each with a small latticed porch and one dormer window. The village centre is a large green with grand trees, including two evergreen holm oaks. Facing its E end are the stables of the Hall (now a private house): an imposing range with pediments and pilasters. To the N is the long unbroken wall of the kitchen garden. In the churchyard is the mausoleum of the Dysart family, c. 1875, looking like an enormous stone box, gabled.

½m E is Sewstern Lane, a prehistoric trackway which ran from the Welland Valley at Stamford to the Trent Valley at Newark. SE of Buckminster it is a metalled road (some of it now lost under Cottesmore airfield), but on the road from Buckminster to A1 it takes off to the left (by a water-tower) as a green track. It is not for motorists but for walkers or horse-riders, imagining that they are Iron Age or Anglo-Saxon peasants or even medieval travellers, for this was once part of the

Great North Road. Villages to the S such as **Sewstern** (which gave its name to the lane), **Market Overton, Cottesmore** and **Greetham** are worth exploring for fine churches with elegant spires and for stone farmhouses and cottages.

BUNNY, *Notts.* (6m S of Nottingham on A60), is still the village of Sir Thomas Parkyns (d. 1741), though the church was already a grand one before his time. It is mostly 14th-c, with a nave of five bays, aisles, a long chancel and a W tower and spire. The Parkyns monuments span two centuries, and that of Sir Thomas is unique: a portly effigy in wrestling posture, a miniature representation of him thrown by Father Time (he was a wrestling enthusiast) and underneath, an inscription of 20 lines which tells all. He was a lawyer, a physician and amateur architect. The school (1700) on the edge of the churchyard is his; it combined accommodation for four widows with a schoolroom and schoolhouse. Standing by it, you can glimpse the Hall, certainly of his own design; it has a brick tower above a huge pediment and coat of arms. From the tower he could survey his park, surrounded by 5m of brick wall which can still be followed. He must have kept his brickmakers busy; he had kilns, where bricks are still made, at the foot of the hill going S.

Some of his buildings have gone, such as Home Farm with a cottage row across the street N of the church; a new school stands back, leaving only a gap. To the right of the gap is one of his houses with mullioned windows. The Rancliffe Arms was his, for a village had to have its inn (compare Sudbury, q.v.); it is now whitened. In its car park is Park Farm, saved recently from demolition and to be restored; its gable is corbelled out for a dovecote. He probably built Ivy Cottage, S of the church, with coped gables and ball finials. There are other pleasant 18th-c farmhouses and cottages, including The Grange, but commuters have ringed the village with new houses.

Bradmore (1m N) also belonged to Parkyns. When the church was burnt in 1706 he must have decided not to spend his money there; only the tower and spire are left. The small village contains little but his half dozen farmhouses with their enormous barns. He built no cottages here, and his tenants must have expected workers to walk from Bunny. **Costock** and **Rempstone**, to the S, are worth visiting for characteristic building. **East Leake**, 3m S and W, is suburbanized but still has good brick houses round the church.

BURROUGH ON THE HILL, *Leics.* (5m due S of Melton Mowbray), lies on the edge of the broken country of E Leics., overlooking the more open ground to the W. The ridge on which it stands rises N to Burrow Hill, the prehistoric hillfort which gave a name to the modern village. Iron Age hillforts are not common in these Midland counties, and they are smaller than such gigantic enclosures as Maiden Castle in Dorset; so for its rarity and completeness Burrow Hill is worth a visit. It was a stronghold of the tribe called

the Coritani, whom the Romans easily conquered; whether the village sheltered by its ramparts was then abandoned we do not know, for as yet there has been no large-scale excavation. Imagine the ramparts topped with a timber palisade and the entrance defended by a gate tower; a hollow at the left side of the entrance must have been a guardhouse.

Prehistoric settlers discovered that iron ore could be got from the band of ironstone that runs from NW Lincs. (Scunthorpe, Humberside) through Rutland and E Leics. to N Oxfordshire. Iron-working created settlements, and settlements (whether villages or isolated farmsteads) then as always generated traffic. Without the barriers of fields and private ownership of land that we take for granted, long-distance travellers made their own way, along ridges and high ground, and what was in effect a main road in prehistoric Britain could have more than one line. One from Lincs. to Somerset (the Jurassic Way) passed by the Burrough hillfort; today most of its line is represented only by very minor roads or footpaths.

The modern village grew up on the line of that trackway but on somewhat lower ground. Ironstone made not only tools but also building material for the 13th-c church and cottages of the 18th c. The church has a W tower and the village evidently felt it had to have a spire, but could afford no more than a little one. The masons who put it up also felt that the spire had to have spire lights (lucarnes) but put in only one tier, disproportionately large. The post office was built as a farmhouse in about 1750; a deep zone above the bedroom windows must represent lofty attics, but they were originally lighted only from the gable ends. Midland carpenters avoided the difficulty and expense of making dormer windows. There is now a row of skylights, and a large extension (a restaurant) has been done in suitable stone. By 1781, when the Manor House (nearly opposite the church) was built, ironstone was giving way to brick, very red owing to the iron in the local clay. At the S end of the village, with its tiny green, there are Victorian stone houses and cottages, and even a group of post-1945 prefabs, still looking neat. They are on the site of the other manor house. At Burrough Court, a hunting lodge out towards Twyford, the then Prince of Wales and Mrs Simpson met in 1930 for the first time.

BUXWORTH, *Derbyshire* (7m NW of Buxton), was Bugsworth until some vicar decided that Bux- sounded more refined than Bug-; villagers still know it colloquially as Buggy. The village is entirely a creation of the Industrial Revolution. The little church, on the N slope of a steep-sided valley of the Black Brook, was built in 1874. Only Bugsworth Hall, dated 1627, survives from an earlier, pastoral age. Make for the Navigation Inn, and do not be misled by the sign of a galleon; it should be a narrow boat. Near it you can trace the canal basin, created in 1800 and in use till about 1914; today the basin is silted up and wharves and walls are decaying, but there is hope that new interest in inland waterways and industrial monuments will restore them.

To link Manchester with sources of heavy minerals in the Peakland, the Ashton canal was constructed to Whaley Bridge by 1796, and then as far as Buxworth. The Peak Forest Canal Company employed Benjamin Outram (1764–1805), Derbyshire by birth and godson of Benjamin Franklin, to construct a tramway (for horse-drawn wagons) to the quarries at Doveholes, N of Buxton, since gradients made a canal impossible. Soon Buxworth was a thriving inland canal port with up to twenty long boats in the basin, which was surrounded by tramway lines, lime-kilns and wharves. Coal and general provisions came up; down went lime for tanneries, limestone and gritstone for building, lead and ore. The tramway was disused by 1926; relics have found their way into museums at York and Buxton; parts of the line and buildings can be traced by the enthusiast through Chinley and Chapel-en-le-Frith towards Dove Holes. Down the canal, at Whaley Bridge, a trans-shipment warehouse serves now as a centre for converting canal boats for leisure use; there is a museum and literature about inland waterways.

At **Chapel Milton**, 2m up the valley, there is a large Independent Chapel of 1711. The steam railway line which came in 1867 required two massive stone viaducts which tower over the chapel; another viaduct nearer Buxworth is built of blue bricks which no doubt came by canal. Going on through Barmoor Clough you reach Dove Holes; just E of the road is the Bull Ring. It is a henge monument of the Bronze Age: first cousin to Stonehenge and Arbor Low near Youlgrave. Its stones have disappeared, but the embanked circle with opposed entrances and a ditch *inside* the bank is impressive.

CASTLETON, *Derbyshire,* is best approached from Bakewell (10m) or Sheffield (16m) since the road from Buxton below Mam Tor is closed indefinitely. Castleton has attracted visitors for more than 200 years and there are many reasons for visiting it: superb and varied natural scenery; the caves; the garlanding ceremony (29 May). Let us concentrate on the village.

A Bronze Age community fortified Mam Tor, to the W; a Norman lord, William Peveril, chose another and even stronger site for his castle. The siting will remind you of Bolsover (q.v.) built by William's son, but here William I not only built a stone circuit wall; he also constructed an outer bailey, below the village, and within it gathered his retainers, along with lead miners and peasant farmers. The Peveril estates and castles became Crown property in 1155, and Henry II built a new keep here in 1175–7. It was then one of the strongest fortresses in Derbyshire and the centre of Peak Forest, but by 1400 it had lost both administrative and military importance; its buildings began to decay. It has been a scheduled Ancient Monument since 1932. No doubt lead-mining kept the village going. The church still has a Norman chancel arch, but you will notice particularly the box pews, carved with the names of pew holders and dates from 1661 onwards. Castleton Hall (Youth Hostel Association) is 17th-c, and some cottages such as Causey House have cruck construction.

Peak Cavern is part of this story of the village in a special way. The river which emerges from it supplied the village. There is still a cluster of cottages outside its mouth and alongside the stream. The cave opening – the largest natural entrance of any cave in Britain – was taken over centuries ago by ropemakers. Commercial rope-making has now ceased, but the ropewalks and gear survive, and rope-making is still demonstrated for visitors; the cottages have gone but the soot from their chimneys still blackens the cave roof. The other caves open to the public are man-made to one degree or another; you can see both their natural beauty and the industry and daring involved in mining for lead, Blue John and other minerals.

Peak Park Information Centre near the church provides literature and attractive displays, and Losehill Hall is a residential study centre.

CLIFTON CAMPVILLE, *Staffs.,* 5m W of Measham and N of A453. You are in the Midland plain here, as you can see from the big arable fields with hedgerow trees, and the big barns of scattered farmhouses. It was always an important village; now it is a big one with a lot of new housing to the E. The nucleus of the village is intact: an impressive church, an equally impressive rectory alongside (perhaps 17th-c ?) and some old cottages. Sadly, Manor Farm across the road looks on its last legs: farm buildings unroofed; the very tall brick dovecote at the back and the little gazebo or summerhouse in the front corner of the garden seriously in need of repair. With the brick farmhouse, they were probably built about 1700. The local clays make a dark red brick. There is another sad story in the fields E of the village: isolated wings of what was to have been a great house, Clifton Hall. It was started about 1720 but money ran out before it was completed.

Back to the church: the tall slender spire with its flying buttresses dominates this open landscape. The tower is remarkable from inside: the big W window throws a flood of light into the church through the unusually lofty tower arch. The tower is vaulted and so is the chapel of the N aisle. The chapel is unique in having a chamber over it with a fireplace and a garderobe. A chantry priest was intended to sleep there. There are misericords in the chancel; they go in date with the oak screen between chancel and aisle, and it has quatrefoil openings cut through. Both the fabric and these fittings belong to the time of Hugh Hopwas, who became rector in 1361 and must have had both grandiose ideas and money. The squire who appointed him and perhaps helped to pay for the building, Sir Richard Stafford (d. 1381), is buried in a tomb recess in the S aisle; a painting over his tomb showing the coronation of the Virgin was uncovered in 1933. There are grand monuments to later Lords of the Manor. Sir John Vernon (d.

1545) lies on an alabaster table tomb, with an inscription extolling his hospitality – a quality every Tudor gentleman was expected to show. There are wall monuments by Rysbrack, the famous Georgian monumental sculptor, to 18th-c landowners. There is a brass to a woman of c. 1360, made from a secondhand sheet; the back has part of an earlier knight in chain mail. It has been copied on another sheet so that enthusiasts can rub both.

COLLINGHAM, *Notts*. (5m N of Newark on Trent), is a double village like Laneham; it lies on the old road down the Trent valley from Newark northwards. Collingham, like its neighbours, was planted as close as possible to an ancient course of the Trent, now a tiny stream called the Fleet. Fishermen make their way across the Fleet, over the floodbank which now protects the villages, and then by a lane crossing 2m of meadows they reach the river and face Sutton on the other side. Further N at Besthorpe there are now extensive lagoons made by extracting sand and gravel deposited by the river.

There are traces of an older pattern of settlement. There was a little Roman town (Crocacalana) at Brough on the Foss Way, 2m SE; there is no trace of it on the surface, though it attracts treasure seekers with metal detectors, to the dismay of archaeologists. There was a Roman villa on the high ground 2m E and a road passing S of Collingham made for a Trent crossing where there was a Roman bridge, found when Cromwell Lock was built. Since Saxon times the Trent has been both a magnet and a hazard; if the river bank was breached by floods, there was nothing to prevent the waters reaching Lincoln, as they did in 1795. Notice the records of flood levels on stones in North Collingham churchyard.

The main street must have started as a by-pass, for the two churches and the best houses are on Low Street nearer the Fleet. But why two churches, one near each end of the long village? The Collinghams belonged to Peterborough, first the abbey and then the bishop, and the Anglo-Saxon abbots must have provided both churches, perhaps in the 7th c, though both were rebuilt in Norman times. The first churches could well have been of wood, for houses here still have more traces of timberframing than elsewhere in the area. Now the dominant building materials are red pantiles for roofs, grey lias limestone for garden walls and for replacing timber in ground floor walls (and occasionally whole houses) and, most recently, brick. One farmhouse and a nearby granary on Low Street have gables with brick tumbling, that Dutch device adopted in eastern counties; it scarcely penetrated W of the Trent. Altogether, a village of handsome houses and attractive cottages; the Council for the Preservation of Rural England rates it the best-kept Notts. village. Infilling is confined to lanes linking the two streets.

At **Langford**, 2m S, a field alongside the road is the site of the deserted village. The Hall by the church and three identical farmhouses by the road, built of limestone and brick, represent a 17th-c revival.

COSSALL, *Notts.*, lies 6m W of Nottingham, in a small triangle of unspoilt countryside surrounded by industry and towns. It provides a chance to enjoy the landscape that D. H. Lawrence knew as a young man. Church Cottage, Cossall, was the home of Louie Burrows to whom he was once engaged. It is unchanged, and all the details of its appearance are worth examining for an appreciation of cottage style hereabouts in say 1750. Others in the village are exactly like it. One of them, School House, differs in having windows with a lozenge pattern of glazing. So has the Manor House, though it is Victorian in date. The explanation lies in the story of landownership; Cossall became part of the estates of the Willoughby family of Wollaton Hall. Manor Farm, on the right as you enter the village from Nottingham, retains one brick bay window of their Elizabethan house there. In 1685 they built the almshouses, a splendid row of dark brick, and quite unaltered. A double wall in front encloses the footpath along the narrow street. In the centre, a taller block was schoolroom and schoolhouse; to either side are the almshouses, each with its tall dormer window. All the windows have lattice glazing. The Victorian Willoughbys (by then Lords Middleton) imitated the almshouse in their new building and renovations: hence the Victorian lattice windows. Opposite the almshouses, in the grounds of the Manor House, is one relic of an earlier style: a cottage with timberframing still visible in its back wall.

Cossall stands on a ridge overlooking the Erewash valley, which by 1792 was flanked by two canals, to help the exploitation of a rich coalfield. As you go S from Cossall, the road goes alongside the Nottingham canal, now disused. Turn E and skirt Nottingham and you come to **Strelley**, absolutely unspoilt because two families who have owned it – the Strelleys and the Edges – since the 12th c have kept time and change at bay. The church was rebuilt by Samson de Strelley (c. 1356); the Edges rebuilt the Hall in 1792, but some medieval walling survives in the extensive outbuildings. The inn (Broad Oak) and the cottages are Georgian and Victorian.

ECCLESHALL, *Staffs.* (7m NW of Stafford on A5013), owes its being and character entirely to Christianity and the bishops of Lichfield. The name, which derives from the Latin word for a church (*ecclesia*), shows that there was already a church there when the Saxons arrived, and soon after Augustine's missionaries re-established Christianity a large estate centred on Eccleshall was acquired by the bishop of Lichfield. A Norman bishop built himself a castle close to the River Sow, where the stream could provide some defence, and then proceeded to lay out and promote a town with a market and fairs.

Today the market and fairs have ceased; Eccleshall is a large village, so handy for Stoke on Trent and Stafford that some of the recent infilling consists of blocks of flats. How much of its past can be observed or deduced? The castle, besieged and destroyed in the Civil War, was rebuilt as a grand country house by Bishop Lloyd (1695); now his successors have only Lloyd's equally fashionable but smaller palace in Lichfield. That a Norman bishop planned the town is evident from the straight and unusually wide main street and two tiny cross lanes, relics of a grid plan. The medieval bishops gave the town one of the most perfect 13th-c churches in Staffs. The nave and aisles are wide; the arcades of five bays have round piers with stiff-leaved foliage on the capitals. The W tower, open to the aisles as well as the nave, is of the same character. The tower was heightened and the large clerestory added later in the middle ages. Several bishops were buried here, including Overton (1609) who has an alabaster effigy with his two wives kneeling behind.

The High Street is now lined with buildings of the 18th and 19th c. Three of the inns encroach on the wide pavement so as to provide a covered arcade.

EMPINGHAM, *Leics.* (between Stamford and Oakham), is the place to make for to see Rutland Water, the largest man-made lake in England, nearly the size of Windermere. The large and impressive church is a landmark, and especially the lofty 14th-c W tower with its tall pinnacles and short spire. As elsewhere in Rutland, masons with the best stone in England to use must, from the carved decoration, have enjoyed the contract. The rest of the church is 13th-c with 15th-c clerestory and nave roof. There are traces inside of masonry joints and flowers painted in red on the plaster. N of the church there are stone houses of the 17th c and onwards, roofed either with thatch or with Collyweston stone slates. Prebendal House, SE of the church, is c. 1700. How to preserve the grand stone barns of these parts is a major problem. One N of the church dated 1634 is converted to a house.

Rutland Water has filled the valley of the River Gwash (*see* Great Casterton). The landscaping and amenities have been carefully planned by the Anglian Water Authority and good maps and leaflets are available at the Sykes Lane Information Centre near Empingham (open at weekends in the summer). If you decide to do a clockwise circuit, notice first the 17th-c bridge over the Gwash, just S of the church, with three round arches and cutwaters between. Turn right and a new road along the S side gives you a good view of the horseshoe-shaped lake, with Upper Hambleton on the peninsula between the arms. From the Normanton Picnic Area you can see Normanton Church, surrounded by water. The Sailing Club is based at **Edith Weston**, the next village. There is a glimpse of Lyndon Hall, built in 1671–3, and further W is a Nature Reserve. Completing the circuit (via Oakham) takes you along a new road (A606) with a view of Burley on the Hill, a mansion built for an Earl of Nottingham about 1700, and comparable with Chatsworth or Petworth.

At **Whitwell** with its tiny church and only a bellcote instead of a spire, there is another Picnic Area, a Sailing Centre and the Fishing Lodge. The best views of all are from the peninsula. Middle Hambleton Old Hall (1611) now stands by the water. It and Normanton church are a reminder that 3100 acres of good farming land, houses, roads and footpaths disappeared under the water.

FORTON, *Staffs.* (1m out of Newport, Salop, on A519), is a small village with some houses of sandstone, but most of them are of Victorian brick, with a Tudor–Jacobean flavour. They were meant to resemble the style of Forton Old Hall, which stands alongside the church, E of the main road. The Old Hall is most impressive, with its sandstone basement, brick walls, mullioned windows, gabled dormers and towering chimney-stacks. It may look Tudor, but is dated 1665, and documents tell that it cost only £100 to build. That figure did not include the cost of transporting the stone and bricks, which were quarried or made locally.

The Hall was built by owners of the Aqualate Estate which lies just out of sight across the canal: the park, landscaped by Repton, the great Aqualate Mere, and a Hall built only in 1927 after its predecessor was burnt down. One of the 17th-c owners, Sir Thomas Skrymsher (1633), is buried in Forton church on a table tomb with rows of kneeling children, and it was Gerard Skrymsher who built the Hall as a dower house. The nave of the church was rebuilt in 1723 and has an elegant arcade of Tuscan columns. The medieval N aisle has a very handsome roof.

Not much more than 2m to the NE we enter another world – that of the Staffordshire canal system. **Norbury** village has some pleasant brick and timber-framed cottages and a very impressive church – a Dec nave and chancel with Georgian brick tower. Nave and chancel both have fine roofs of early form. The monuments include two of the Skrymsher family. Down the hill is Norbury Junction, where a branch canal from Telford's Shropshire Union Canal went off towards Newport. Unhappily the fantastic flight of 17 locks (in 1½m) is now derelict, and on lanes towards Forton bridges rear up over a filled-in course. But you can still admire the way Telford in 1830 carried his canal on an immense embankment and built two tunnels under it for a country lane. The basin at the junction is of course full of pleasure boats.

GADDESBY, *Leics.* (5m SW of Melton Mowbray), has grown recently, but the new houses are discreetly placed and do not spoil it. Two lanes lead off B674, the road from Rearsby into the unspoilt heart of upland Leics. At the end of one of them is the Cheney Arms, a purpose-built inn of c. 1750 and quite unaltered: brick, three storeys high, and typical of the county. This lane leads up to the church, one of the most attractive in Leicestershire not only for what medieval builders accomplished but even more because it has not

Eighteenth-century 'Norman', Tickencote

been 'restored'. It is best to walk round the outside first. The walling is partly local ironstone, partly Northants. oolite (S aisle and broach spire). The S aisle is the showpiece, and indicates major remodelling in 1300–50; it has lavish decoration especially in its W doorway and the gable over it. On the S side there are matching buttresses with niches and a battlemented frieze. Inside, one notices the simple brick paving and slightly decayed (but sound) bench ends. There are medieval monuments such as a knight's effigy in limestone, and an incised alabaster slab of 1498. In the chancel is an unexpected monument, to Col. E. H. Cheney (d. 1848) who fought at Waterloo: he is shown with one of the horses shot under him that day – all in white marble and nearly life size.

The monument is said to have come from Gaddesby Hall, which stands W of the church, an attractive house of c. 1740. It can be glimpsed from a footpath W of the church which runs through what must once have been park, for there are fine trees – cedars, pines – on both sides. The footpath brings you to the main street, with pleasant cottages. There are more in Chapel Lane, including one with timber-framing in the gables and brick dormers of c. 1700.

1m SE is the hamlet of **Barsby**. It too has largely retained its character. Three houses show the virtuosity of country builders when brick was a novel material. One of them has the date 1701 picked out in dark headers. Another, dated 1691, is remarkable for its use of vitrified bricks to emphasize the Flemish bond of the lower walls and to make a diaper pattern higher up, above a moulded string course. The third, dated 1707, is distinguished only by having stone quoins. In

Baggrave End there are framed cottages, over-restored, and in Chapel Lane, Godson's Folly (c. 1860) which was intended to be a mortuary chapel but has been converted into a house.

GREAT CASTERTON, *Leics.,* is far older than Stamford (2m SE) for here was a Roman town on Ermine Street, which is still the village main street. It was a tiny place, but had substantial stone walls. The church lies just inside the SE corner of the town. Coming down the hill from Stamford, and after crossing the bridge over the little River Gwash, one can imagine the Roman gate astride the road; and, instead of the church, a *mansio* or hostelry where official travellers could get a bed and a change of horses for the next day. The Crown Inn on the right is a pleasant modern substitute. Less than ¼m N, turn right at a crossroads (just outside the site of the Roman N gate) and stop opposite College Close. In the field to the S is the best view of the wide ditch of the Roman town; the bank beyond it marks the line of the wall. There is nothing Roman above ground, and excavations have shown that the wall, with square towers at intervals, was robbed long ago. No doubt the church and the stone houses that line the village street contain much re-used Roman limestone.

An aerial photograph taken in the very dry summer of 1959 showed from crop marks that there had been a timber-built Roman fort in the field to the E of the town. The Roman garrison was there for about 40 years early in the conquest, but long enough for a native settlement outside its gates to become the nucleus of a town which lasted until c. AD 400. Archaeologists also found a Roman villa, with buildings round a large courtyard about ¼m further on towards Ryhall. All the finds are in Oakham Museum, along with agricultural bygones originally collected by a headmaster of Great Casterton school.

Tickencote, 1m N, has an astonishing church, its chancel most elaborate Norman work, vaulted and with a large but badly constructed chancel arch. The rest of the church was rebuilt in 1792 in what was then thought to be Norman style.

GRINGLEY ON THE HILL, *Notts.,* stands on A631, 5m E of Bawtry. It has the longest views in the county from Beacon Hill, at the E end of the village; E across the Trent to Lincs., with Scunthorpe steelworks in the distance, S up the Idle towards Retford, W to the Pennines. To the N the ground drops away steeply to the Isle of Axholme. The Iron Age settlers who are said to have built a little hillfort on Beacon Hill (it is almost impossible to trace) chose a commanding situation. The Chesterfield Canal (1775) winds round the foot of the hill on its way to the Trent at Stockwith; the traffic in coal and lead has given way to pleasure boats. Beyond the canal is a regular pattern of fields of the 'carr' lands; from the time of the Dutchman Vermuyden (1626–9) onwards generations of drainage engineers created new waterways and then a grid pattern of smaller drains to carry upland water to the Trent without drowning the Isle of Axholme. The rich soil still has a dark tint from the peat.

Gringley grew up on the ancient road skirting the S edge of the Isle, from Gainsborough to Bawtry and the N. Its little grid plan of streets has an urban quality; the shaft of the market cross at a cross-roads in the centre show that it was once a market town. The church stands above High Street; it has EE arcades but was mostly rebuilt in the 15th c. There are good farmhouses and cottages, in the dark brown brick common all the way from here to York. The bricks must have been made down by the canal; new houses round the edge of the village are also of brick, intended to be in keeping but too red to match the old. As in all the villages of N Notts., dovecotes are noticeable among the farm buildings, often with crow-stepped gables (there is one near the cross). At the W end of the village there is a tower mill with the skeleton only of an ogee cap. Between Gringley and Everton the canal loops round Cuckoo Hill, and where road and canal cross at Drakeholes stands the White Swan Inn, built to serve both road and canal traffic; opposite are two tiny (and derelict) lodges at a disused drive to Wiseton Hall. **Wiseton** is an unspoilt village. The Hall (demolished), the White Swan and several farmhouses were built by an enlightened landowner, Jonathan Acklom, from 1771 onwards. Mattersey Priory stands just across the River Idle, the remains of a small monastery of the Gilbertine order. It is about 1m E of **Mattersey** village.

HALLATON, *Leics.* (5m SW of Uppingham, off B664), lies away from main roads but five local roads converge on it, for it was once a market town. It was never planned, for its tight pattern of streets is quite irregular. Its remoteness has preserved it from modern pressures, but there is a price to be paid; a few cottages are run down. Nevertheless at every age Hallaton has had money and a strong sense of community, so there is a rich variety of buildings. The Norman motte and bailey castle ½m W has no trace of stonework; because its earth and timber defences were never remodelled, it is an unusually fine example.

The vigour of the community is evident in the church, the tiny Congregational chapel and the almshouses; in the 17th-c water conduit (near a telephone box, and spoiled by it); in the curious Butter Cross, round with a conical roof, and in the new notice about Hallaton's traditional game. Choosing the Hallaton Bottle King involves kicking small wooden barrels (harvest bottles) from the Fox Inn to Hare Pie Hill and scrambling for bits of hare pie.

The church we see is probably the third; the Saxon one has gone without trace, except for a tombstone. From the Norman one there is a splendid carving (now in the porch) of St Michael and the dragon; it once formed a doorhead or tympanum. The aisled Norman church was largely rebuilt in the 13th and 14th c, and there was money enough for limestone (from Nor-

thants?) instead of local ironstone. The masons carved flowing tracery with plenty of cusping, and a turret at the NE corner (nearest the village) with crocketed niches and a tall pinnacle. Perhaps they came from Northants. where such craftsmanship is common. The older houses are of ironstone with mullioned windows in Northants. limestone. By about 1700 bricks were being made locally and the purple bricks that come from the hottest part of the kiln were used to make a chequer pattern. Notice it in the upstairs wall of the Bedehouse N of the churchyard (1747) and elsewhere.

By the time the Congregational chapel was built (1822) and more almshouses in Hog Lane (1842), the brickyards produced only red bricks. The Fox Inn at the N end of the village was rebuilt about 1830; notice that like all older country inns it stands back from the road so that carriages and wagons could halt in front.

HARTINGTON, *Derbyshire* (2m W of the Ashbourne-Buxton road), attracts those who wish to walk Dovedale or to fish the Dove. 3000 or 4000 years ago the limestone uplands attracted Neolithic man, and the moors E of the Dove are dotted with prehistoric tombs, now marked by names like Carder Low, Lean Low, and End Low – all shown on the Ordnance Survey map. Archaeologists remember best the barrow at Benty Grange, just E of the Buxton road and 2½m N of Hartington. From it came an Anglo-Saxon helmet, now in Sheffield Museum; it has a bronze boar as a crest. Arbor Low, Derbyshire's grandest henge monument, is only ½m further E from Benty Grange, towards Youlgreave.

This is lead-mining country, and lead must have been the foundation of Hartington's ancient growth. The splendid church, on the N side of the dale coming in from the E, is mostly of gritstone – plain but substantial. It has plenty of wall monuments which make interesting reading, but its most attractive feature is a set of 12 painted panels representing the tribes of Israel. Recently cleaned, they are *c.* 18th-c. Hartington evidently prospered in the last century to judge from dates on houses, and there was an attempt to revive the market. The little town hall (1836) is now a general store. The Dukes of Devonshire, whose eldest son has the title of Marquis of Hartington, must have promoted the place.

It is difficult now to imagine how busy the place once was, for so much industry has ceased. In the enormous parish, there was by the 19th c mining and quarrying for lead, limestone, gritstone, silica and even coal. Until 1830 packhorses carried lead ore to the hilltop smelts; they crossed the Dove at Crowdecote (3m up the Dove from Hartington) so that their drivers could have a drink at the Packhorse Inn. Then came the Cromford and High Peak Railway (1830–1); it became part of the London and North West Railway in 1861, but the line was closed in 1967. Now a length of it forms the Tissington Trail, a pleasant and level walk or bicycle ride.

Dairy and sheep farming endure longer; exploring the moorlands, you may find an ancient sheep-fold, usually circular in form. The Hartington Cheese Factory, W of the village, makes a variety of cheeses, including Stilton (*see* Langar). There are still trout and grayling in the Dove, and in Beresford Dale, S of the village, the little fishing lodge built by Charles Cotton, and used by him and Isaak Walton, still stands.

ILAM, *Staffs.*, lies 4m NW of Ashbourne in the Manifold valley. If you approach it from Ashbourne, you pass first through **Mapleton** (Derbyshire) and can enjoy an unusual Georgian church with a tiny dome crowning the tower, and two handsome buildings: Manor Farm and the Clergymen's Widows Almshouses (1727). All were built by the Okeovers who still reside at Okeover Hall, just across the Dove, which is here the county boundary. The Hall itself, just visible from the road to Ilam, is mid-Georgian; the church is Dec, and there is no village. You may prefer to go through **Thorpe**, a pleasant village of limestone cottages, set in front of green hills (Thorpe Cloud and Bunster Hill) with the limestone peeping through.

Just as Mapleton was made by the Okeover family, Ilam was created, or re-created, by a wealthy manufacturer, Jesse Watts Russell, who bought it early in the 19th c. He first rebuilt the Hall (1821); it was demolished in the 1930s except for parts used as a Youth Hostel and for a National Trust shop. In the middle of the village Russell put up a memorial to his wife in the form of an Eleanor Cross (cf. Geddington, Northants.). Facing the cross is a group of cottages *ornées*, with the school and schoolhouse behind. Russell's architect chose for them a style never seen in Derbyshire before or since: he must have been a Londoner, familiar with the home counties, for the cottages have very steep roofs with shaped tiles, gables hung with the same dark red tiles and finished with openwork barge boards. The gables of the school (1854) have a lattice pattern in timber. The church was Russell's last enterprise; he had built a large memorial chapel in 1831 and then in 1855–6 employed Gilbert Scott to restore the medieval part. Altogether, Ilam is a completely homogenous example of a Victorian estate village in a most romantic setting.

The bottom of the Manifold valley may in summer seem sheltered and idyllic but if you go NW across the Manifold and climb to Throwley Hall you can appreciate the enterprise and endurance required to colonize this high moorland. The first Throwley Hall (early Tudor) is a ruin, replaced by a farmhouse of about 1830. At this altitude cattle had to be kept long under cover, so there is a remarkable farm building, known jocularly as Throwley Barracks. It must have been built in the early 17th c, with cattle below and a long hay loft above.

IPSTONES, *Staffs.* (off the Leek-Ashbourne Road, A523), is a large village, though it was never even a market town. It stands on high and rising ground, with the wooded Churnet Valley to the S. There, at Froghall, a large factory spoils the valley. To the N the road along Ipstones Edge must have started as a prehistoric trackway and there are fine views from it, even if the enormous quarries at Cauldon seem a disfigurement.

The village has recently seen a lot of new building, but handsome houses survive, such as the Grange, at the S end of the village: a tall Georgian farmhouse of sandstone with mullioned windows. In the back lane Meadows Place Farm, its fields filled with new houses, is long and low, typical of the Jacobean period. Near the church is a fashionable early Georgian house, The Grove, with a pedimented doorway and a Venetian window above it. It is surprising to find that with such good stone available, brick-making must have started here in the 18th c. The bricks are dark – purplish or brown – made from the clays of the coal measures and typical of N Staffs.

The soil round here is poor, with gritstone crags peeping out of bracken-covered slopes. The task of colonizing and draining must have started in the 17th c, for if you explore (on foot) the lanes of the parish you will find historic houses such as Whiteclough (¼m N) built in two stages, 1620 and 1724. Halfway up the hill to Ipstones Edge, New House Farm on the left is dated 1711. In a wooded valley W of the village, near Belmont Hall, is Chapel House. It looks like a converted church, and indeed it was intended (*c*. 1790) to be one, but the owner of Belmont Hall changed his mind and rebuilt the parish church instead. It looks Gothic but is really 1792, with a later chancel. It has interesting paintings. None of these farmhouses is open to the public, and some, such as the 17th-c Sharpcliffe Hall, can only be viewed from some distance, but even at that range they tell their own story.

At **Cheddleton**, 2m W, the Victorian railway station, in picturesque Tudor Style (1849) has been saved, and railway enthusiasts are restoring steam locomotives. The Flint Mills, grinding flint for pottery, are open as a museum.

KIBWORTH, *Leics.* (halfway between Leicester and Market Harborough on A6), consists of two villages, Kibworth Beauchamp and Kibworth Harcourt; they are separated by the busy road from Leicester to Market Harborough. Since Leicester is only 9m away there is much new development on the fringes of both villages, but both centres are worth seeing. Kibworth Beauchamp has pleasant cottages, some as old as the 16th c. Kibworth Harcourt has the church and was the smarter place. The W tower of the church first strikes the eye, for its smooth ashlar walling. At a second look you realize that although in medieval (Dec) style, like the rest of the church, it is actually a rebuilding of 1832–6, and presumably a copy of its predecessor. Both aisle and chancel windows have flowing tracery.

At the E end of Kibworth Harcourt is The Old House, well worth lingering over. It was built in

Kenneth Scowen

Hartington

1678 by a country builder, trying his hand at a fashionable style. It is square on plan; what a contemporary architect, Sir Roger Pratt, called a 'double pile': that is two rooms deep. The roof is hipped, with dormer windows; the walling is brick with all the details, such as quoins and openings, in limestone. The windows have moulded frames and plain mullions and transoms. You may contrast it with Manor Farm, across the road, built 24 years later, and still in the vernacular tradition: a long range, one room deep, with brick walling in a chequer pattern. Notice the date and initials on incised brick plaques. Paddocks Farm, towards Leicester, has the date 1704 in dark headers in the gable. It is somewhat more fashionable in detail, with a wooden cornice, but the plan is fairly traditional, with a hall range and a cross wing. No. 53 Leicester Road must be of similar date; it is a long range with a moulded brick cornice. All these variations in the plans of houses, and in the way materials and especially bricks were used, show the response of country builders to the demands made about 1670 to 1720 by owners of substantial farms.

A grammar school was founded in 1725, not so grand as Appleby Magna but like it still in use. It consisted simply of a long school room with the master's house attached to it. The house was later enlarged. At the Leicester end of the village is a Congregational chapel of 1759. A house next to it, presumably for the minister, is derelict.

KINVER, *Staffs.*, lies 4m N of Kidderminster and W of Stourbridge. It would be hard to find a more striking setting for a village, or a landscape which has seen more changes at the hand of man. W of the village is Kinver Edge, a dramatic sandstone ridge now National Trust property and offering views of distant hills such as the Clees, the Malverns and even the Cotswolds. Prehistoric man built a hillfort on the Edge, and in this densely wooded country Britons no doubt survived the tide of Anglo-Saxon invasion, for Kinver is a Celtic name. Pagan temples often stood on hilltops and the site chosen for Kinver church, alone on a hill commanding the village and the Stour valley, was meant to give it the same dominance. It is a fine medieval church; its size reflects the fact that Kinver was once a market town. The N aisle collapsed recently and was rebuilt in an unusual and attractive way.

It is hard to imagine now that through the 18th and 19th c the iron industry flourished here. There were five slitting mills (for nail making) powered by the Stour. The oldest and largest was at the Hyde (1627), with a work force of 250 or more in 1800. There is no trace of it now. The mills came to depend on the Staffordshire-Worcestershire Canal (1772), designed by Brindley to link the Severn and Trent. At Gothersley, the Round House was the wharf manager's residence. At Kinver Mill the building complex survives but the wheel has been removed and the tailrace filled in. There is a circular weir at Stourton. The village street reflects the prosperity of Kinver in the 17th–19th c. A few timber-framed buildings survive and have had a face-lift; notice the Old Grammar School House on Dark Lane. By 1660 or so, only brick was being used, and that is the date of the gabled Old White Hart. Church Hill House is elegant early Georgian.

At the other end of the social scale, pressure for working-class housing led to the contrivance of homes, half houses and half cave-dwellings, in every exposed rock face in the valley and on Kinver Edge. At Gibraltar Rock, just beyond Kinver Lock (by the Vine Inn) there were tiers of such dwellings, now inaccessible and unsafe. Several outcrops of rock on the Edge became cottages – Astle's Rock, Vale's Rock, Nanny's Rock, and best of all, Holy Austin Rock. They were dry and warm, but what was no doubt called slum clearance has emptied them all, and nature aided by vandalism is destroying their remains. It is sad that the local authorities and the National Trust together cannot protect them. Rooms, staircases and chimneys can be discerned, and old photographs exist to fill the openings with doors and windows, to furnish the interiors with their lime-washed walls and to re-create the tidy gardens.

By 1900 Kinver was dead as an industrial village and began to flourish as a beauty spot, 'the Switzerland of the Midlands'. An electric tramway was opened in 1901, linking Kinver with Stourbridge by a line down the Stour valley. For a time it brought many thousands of Black Country people to Kinver, but it closed in 1930, killed by the motor car. Some of the rock cottages used to provide afternoon teas, but now the motorist brings his own picnic.

Across the river from Kinver, the Whittington Inn is a 16th-c timber-framed building which started as the Hall. At **Stourton**, upstream, the Hall was originally a Royal Hunting Lodge in Kinver Forest and still has a medieval embattled gateway. Enville Hall, 2m NW, is a fine Georgian house in glorious grounds. They are not open, but a public footpath crosses the park.

Literature about Kinver and the neighbourhood may be consulted at the branch of the County Library.

LANEHAM, *Notts.,* lies about 1m N of A57, 10m W of Lincoln. Riding, fishing and water-skiing now bring many visitors to the two parts of this village on the lower Trent. Starting 1m from the river, the village street has good farmhouses and cottages, especially Binge's Farm, a tall early Georgian house on the S side, with a barn dated 1819. Notice in the gables of houses those triangular wedges of brickwork laid at an angle called tumbling; this device came from Holland about 1700 and is common in the Trent valley.

Nearer the river a flood-bank keeps the Trent within bounds. Then comes **Church Laneham** on a slight knoll and always above danger. We are just beyond the reach of tides, so that at any time the river is a broad sweep of blue or grey water sliding smoothly but powerfully N to the Humber. Its course is now marked by power stations – Marnham a few miles upstream, Cottam just N of Laneham and beyond that West Burton. Their scale and simplicity of form make them immense and attractive features in the landscape, dwarfed only by the wide skies, and in winter the steam from cooling towers turns into fleecy clouds.

The river has carried boats for thousands of years: the dug-out canoes (there are two in Nottingham Castle Museum) of prehistoric settlers; Roman barges carrying Derbyshire lead to Brough on Humber (*Petuaria*) and abroad; wool from medieval monasteries to Flanders. Its busiest time was no doubt from about 1775 onwards; now you will see only a few petrol or gravel barges and pleasure boats. At Church Laneham, across from the church is a handsome granary of about 1820, now turned into a house, and ½m N past the manor house (now spoiled by a new brick front) is a malt kiln right on the waterside. Corn, malt, butter and cheese went down river to feed London and the industrial towns of W. Yorks.

But the river had to be crossed as well. The Roman road from Lincoln to Doncaster crossed it by a ford at **Littleborough**, 4m further N; that village now has a tiny Norman church and not much else – certainly no trace of this buried Roman town of *Segelocum*. Laneham's own ferry has ceased and the Ferry Boat Inn now depends on the holidaymakers in their caravans. The little church, mainly Norman, has a fine monument to the Markhams (1638).

LANGAR, *Notts.,* lies in the Vale of Belvoir (*see* Bottesford), to the E of A46 and 3m S of Bingham. The Vale is the prospective location for England's newest and deepest coal mine. The Vale is a landscape of regular fields and neat hedges; gently undulating country defined to the E by a scarp with Belvoir Castle at its N end. The Nottingham-Grantham canal winds round the Vale, in parts overgrown and in parts cleared by enthusiastic volunteers. Dairies here specialize in making Stilton cheese.

Tombs in Langar church perpetuate the distinguished families once resident here. The Scropes and Howes of Langar are in the S transept; note particularly the splendid four-poster in which Thomas Lord Scrope (d. 1609) and his wife repose. His ancestors must have built the grand cruciform church, of yellow limestone from Lincolnshire. One of the Howes in the 17th c made a park 'well stored with Deer' in 1677, and the village dwindled. Scrope Viscount Howe in George I's time built it up again, with bricks from his own yards: notice the Unicorn Inn (1717) and Bottom Farm of similar date. Notice also the wall round a paddock S of the church, with a monumental gateway; it was once a garden for the Hall. The church was virtually annexed as a private chapel to the Hall, which was built up to it. The present Hall (1828) is discreetly separated.

There are good cottages E of the church, well restored, and the Victorian-Tudor school is charming. In front of it the children play on the recumbent trunk of an elm planted to commemorate the 'Glorious First of June' (1794), the naval victory of Earl Howe who is buried (without any monument) in the S aisle of the church. Bricks from the estate brickyards may well have gone into the elegant rectory and its garden walls. It was the birthplace of Samuel Butler who in *The Way of All Flesh* (1903) painted a grim picture of his youth here.

The Chaworths whose tombs are in the N transept of Langar church lived at **Wiverton** (pronounced Werton), 1m NW. The village has totally vanished, and so has their manor house which was fortified during the Civil War as an outpost for the Royalist garrison of Newark. All that remains is the 15th-c gatehouse, enlarged in 1825 in Regency-Gothic style.

The churchyards in this area are full of Swithland slate headstones (*see* Swithland); craftsmen working in the Vale of Belvoir *c.* 1700–50 specialized in stones with an angel's head above the inscription. Later on, Welsh slate, to be distinguished by the smooth back, reached here by the canal system.

LAXTON, *Notts.,* is mentioned in many a school history book as the only place in England with a medieval open field system, visible and working. It will not disappoint visitors, whether adults or school children, provided they realize that history does not stand still. The village has changed, even in recent years, but its past can still be read. The best approach is from Kneesall (on the Ollerton-Newark road, A616); stop after driving past Kneesall Wood and from the high point there the tightly clustered village and two of the fields are spread out: South Field to the right, Mill Field to the left. The Common, at the W end of the village was enclosed in 1940, because motorists failed to shut gates on the road through it. At some earlier time ring-fence farms were carved out of the margins of the medieval field system, but three open fields have survived in reduced form.

The essence of the system was that farmers had land scattered in the fields, in strips of varying width. The fields were divided into blocks of strips (furlongs), and access was by grassy ways, called *sykes* or *sicks.* They are shown on the Ordnance Survey map and you can still use them to walk through the fields. The individual strips or *lands* were once demarcated by posts or stones (*landmarks*) but they are no longer to be seen; nor does modern ploughing give arable that pronounced corrugation of ridge and furrow that identifies former open fields in so much of the Midlands. Nevertheless Laxton presents a faithful picture of medieval fields – large expanses under the same crop, without hedges or trees. Admittedly, you have to know the history of the village to distinguish its fields from the prairies created by those farmers who have recently ripped out hedges.

The medieval lords of Laxton brought to it wealth from widespread estates. Soon after the Norman Conquest they built a grand castle N of the village; a footpath going N opposite the churchyard leads to the finest motte and bailey castle in the county. Go first to the motte itself and see how it dominates the countryside. Turn back and notice the embanked bailey; its timber palisade must have been replaced by stone, but little masonry is now visible. Then you will see the added outer bailey. Within it, bumps and hollows show the site of a grand 16th-c manor house, known only from a tiny drawing on a 17th-c estate map.

The church tells a similar story of wealth derived from elsewhere; its impressive clerestory was built about 1490 by Thomas Rotherham, Archbishop of York, who was Lord of the Manor for a short time.

The manor house was demolished and the church neglected: hence in 1859 a church too large for its congregation was reduced – shortened nave, narrower aisles and a rebuilt W tower. The church still tells a long story with EE nave, Dec chancel, Perp clerestory and high-handed Victorian restoration; fittings (Easter sepulchre, sedilia, screens) and monuments of the Everingham family, including a woman's effigy in oak.

The fields have preserved their medieval form partly because the soil was not rich enough to offer much return to improving landlords. So, the buildings of this village – farmhouses, cottages, barns – are modest, and all rebuilt after about 1700. The oldest is Bar Farm (1703) on the way out to Egmanton, at a point where there was a gate or bar to keep livestock on the open fields out of the village. Since farmers moving crops or livestock might have to go to any of the fields, a yard on the street enclosed by barn and cowsheds and house is still typical. It would be nice to visit Laxton soon, since the Minister of Agriculture (the landlord) proposes to sell the estate. The field system is kept going voluntarily, so its future is uncertain.

LONGNOR, *Staffs.* (5m S of Buxton), thinks itself a market town, and the little town hall of 1873 still displays the old list of tolls payable at markets and fairs; the market place is marked out for tourists' cars, not for stalls. The church was rebuilt in 1780 and galleries added in 1812; now, with fewer worshippers, only the W gallery remains and a lowered ceiling spoils the interior. But the place is unspoilt: houses in gritstone, many of them with three storeys, mark its former prosperity. Only the Crewe and Harpur Arms is different, being built of brick with stone quoins.

This is pastoral farming country. On the Ordnance Survey map is a scatter of solid dots in the fields; they must be distinguished from the tiny open circles by which the Ordnance Survey marks old lead mines on the other side of the Dove. The dots are small field-barns, in which cattle could shelter in hard weather, and be fed with hay from the loft overhead. It was once cheese-making country, and in many a farmyard the weights from cheese-presses lie about, unused; now the milk goes away by tanker to distant chocolate and cheese factories. Roads radiate out to the high moorland NW of Longnor. Follow them and you come to **Hollinsclough,** where the little church of 1840 has a house attached to it, and further on is **Flash,** standing at 1518ft and calling itself the highest village in England. There the Methodist chapel of 1821 is the oldest building. The older farmhouses are on the lower ground; there is a handsome one N of the village at Glutton Bridge with a datestone of 1675.

Going S from Longnor to Sheen, the road follows the crest of the narrow ridge between the Dove and the Manifold, with fine views across to limestone Derbyshire (the White Peak). 4m S of Longnor is **Ecton,** where the Manifold flows in a narrow gorge. There is a road on each side of the river. That on the W was a light railway, from Hulme End, just N of Ecton, right down to Waterhouses; it is now a footpath. Behind this oddity lies industrial history. The 18th-c Dukes of Devonshire had a copper mine under Ecton Hill which was the deepest in England and a marvel to visitors; it provided capital for the development of the Spa at Buxton. The light railway was opened in 1904 to carry milk and holidaymakers, and to help to revive the copper mine. The line closed in 1934, and there is now no trace of the copper mine.

LONG WHATTON, *Leics.*, is 4m NW of Loughborough, just off A6. The village street is certainly long, as the name implies, but is worth walking for the variety of houses to be seen. Starting at the church (over-restored), one moves on to Whatton Hall, late Georgian and square. Going W, one comes to Keeper's Lodge on the right, timber-framed with close studding and probably Tudor. Further on (on the left) is Ivy House Farm, square in plan and tall with gables; over each window is a sort of brick eyebrow, characteristic of N Leics. and the Soar valley in particular. This expresses the exuberance of country builders using a new material (brick) in a novel style. Going on, a long timber-framed house on the left stands on a plinth of Mountsorrel granite. Further still, Uplands Farm on the left is tall early Georgian. Beyond it is a smaller brick house with no ornament but a tiny window which lit the hearth or inglenook. Opposite, a brick house with balancing gables is perhaps *c.* 1660. The village thus displays what farmers on good soil could afford to build for themselves, over a period of more than two centuries. There is inevitably some recent infilling, but not enough to spoil the pleasure of a close look.

Diseworth, 1m W, offers as rich a variety, with a somewhat different mixture. Here again it is worth while to walk, avoiding the W half of the village where the new houses are. All the older houses stand on stone footings; perhaps the village roads were already cut down into the clay soil. There is rather more timber-framed building, most of it 17th-c, with panelled walls and straight braces. In Hall Gate one is dated 1692. Perhaps brick-making did not start quite as early here as in Whatton. At the junction of Lady Gate with Hall Gate stands Lilly's Cottage, the main range close studded, and so earlier. Here was born William Lilly (1602–81) the astrologer. Across the road and in a corner of the churchyard is a tall and gabled brick house *c.* 1700; here again one feels that, once they started, bricklayers found it difficult to restrain their enthusiasm. At the N end of the village is Old Hall Farm, the grandest farmhouse of this age, tall, brick with stone quoins. The builder knew that symmetry was now the fashion, but used an old-fashioned plan. Notice that the farm-buildings, presumably contemporary, are still timber-framed.

The church was rebuilt, including its tower and broach spire, in the 13th c, but a N porch was added in 1661.

LYDDINGTON, *Leics.* (2m S of Uppingham), is the most harmonious village in what was the smallest county in England: Rutland. The single street contains ¾m of building in which the only discordant note is a pair of new and pretentious bungalows set back from the road instead of keeping to the frontage line. All the older houses are of ironstone, used with the greatest ingenuity and skill. Lyndon House even has mullioned windows of ironstone: very unusual. In the 18th c masons chose varying tones of stone – rusty brown used with bands of mottled purple – and laid large facing blocks with the finest possible joints. Notice the house on the W side with an inscription RDA MDCCLXIII.

Lyddington owed its ancient importance to the fact that the bishops of Lincoln had a manor house there from about 1200. In an age when the greatest in the land expected to keep several residences going, bishops of Lincoln had three castles (Banbury, Newark and Sleaford), a palace at Buckden (Hunts.) and several manor houses. The house in Lyddington was rebuilt by Bishop Russell in 1480–95 at the same time as he rebuilt the nave of the church. The manor house has lost its outbuildings (kitchen, stables, etc.) but the range alongside the churchyard shows what a bishop of his importance needed in such a place, where local clergy and others had to meet him. The ground-floor rooms were then used only for storage; kings and dignitaries preferred to have principal rooms on the first floor. So, at the head of the staircase are two doorways, the one on the left to the room in which suitors waited, the one on the right to the grand room, with a superb panelled ceiling and a carved cornice, where the bishop gave audience. Beyond were his private rooms. Russell's new nave to the church is very elegant, with tall slender columns; traces of painting have been exposed on the screen (figures and cornflowers), on a wall behind the pulpit (a king in ermine) and between the clerestory windows. The rood screen has lost its loft but the staircase survives.

In 1547 the manor house became Henry VIII's, and his daughter Elizabeth passed it to the Cecils. With Burghley House (Northants.) they did not need another manor house, so Thomas Cecil, 1st Earl of Exeter, converted it into a bedehouse for 10 poor men. Tiny rooms, like cells, were contrived for them downstairs, with a kitchen in the middle. Now it is an Ancient Monument (open May to October) and has been superbly restored.

MELBOURNE, *Derbyshire* (7m S of Derby), is a large and spacious place, with exceptional qualities stemming from its history. First, the manor belonged to the bishops of Carlisle and what is now the Hall started as their favourite residence, more peaceful than living on the Scottish border. Fragments of the palace survive in the courtyard and outbuildings N of the Hall. The first bishop built the church *c.* 1150; only a parish church, it must have been intended for a monastery. It is surrounded by buildings and one feels one might be in France. The graveyard is nearby. Outside, the church is rather disappointing; the W towers have been reduced and the crossing tower rebuilt; if the E arm had not lost its three apses it would look even more continental. Nevertheless, the interior is remarkable: the nave has round piers set close together with stilted arches, and there is a unique western gallery.

N of the church is Castle Square; only that name, and Castle Farm and Castle Mills, recall what was a great building as recently as 1733.

The bishops of Carlisle disposed of their palace to the Coke family; between 1628 and 1744 they enlarged and rebuilt the house, and (in the 1690s) had the gardens laid out by London and Wise, gardeners to Royalty. Some visitors are attracted by the gardens, the best of their age in England; others by the house and its contents – the paintings and furnishings, and especially the room of Lord Melbourne, Queen Victoria's Prime Minister, whose father (Peniston Lamb) acquired the Hall through marriage with a Coke heiress.

Superior buildings cluster round the Hall: the vicarage (1863), Close House (dower house to the Hall) and Chantry House (early 18th-c). Further away there is a mixture of urban and rural. The Athenaeum and Savings Bank in Potter Street was opened in 1854 by Lord Palmerston; almost next door is a timber-framed cottage. On the way out of the market square there is a thatched cottage with the remains of a cruck truss exposed in the gable end – perhaps 17th-c. The textile industry has left its monument in an unusual row of cottages in Blanchcroft (off High Street), built perhaps for framework knitters (*see* Woodborough, Notts.). A slate panel on the garden side is inscribed 'Sick Club Buildings No. VIII 1795'. Further along High Street you come to a group of cottages and a General Baptist Mission Hall commemorating Thomas Cook, a native of Melbourne. Every tourist should look for them, perhaps to puzzle over the inscription ('Memorial House of Call for Mr Cook and Invited Friends, 1891'), or else to salute the father of the cheap railway excursion.

MILFORD, *Derbyshire* (on A6, 5m N. of Derby), was once an industrial village, founded by Jedediah Strutt, who built a cotton mill here in 1780. The mills have gone, but the workers' housing still stands, and so Milford is an essential complement to Cromford, 8m N, where mills built by Richard Arkwright (for a time Strutt's partner) can still be seen. William Strutt, Jedediah's son, designed fireproof mills, using cast-iron columns, and his foundry also turned out hardware for the houses. On the E side of the Derwood are two long rows on Hopping Hill and Shaw Lane built in the 1790s; the upper row consists of back-to-backs, very ingeniously designed with interlocking plans. After the Strutt estate sold the houses new owners inserted new windows and the original uniformity has been diluted. The Strutt School on the W side of the river (Chevin Road) is still in use. Higher up Sunny Hill is another row of back-to-backs (The Barracks) and

Janet and Colin Bord
The Norman church at Melbourne

No. 4 Sunny Hill still has cast-iron window frames (the bull's-eye panes are new!). A keen eye may spot other Strutt products such as cast-iron gutter brackets, door numbers and drain covers. The Strutts, before they abandoned Milford House and turned country gentlemen (*see* Sutton Bonington) gave thought to most aspects of the life of their communities (Belper and Milford), from starting a village band to laying drains. The tiny Primitive Methodist Chapel (Shaw Hill, 1823) and the Baptist Chapel (Chevin Road, 1849) were none of their work, for they built a Unitarian Chapel at Belper. There too, the oldest mills have gone except for North Mill (1804), linked to a military-looking archway over the road (*c.* 1795). The arch has genuine gunports, for use in case of industrial unrest.

NORBURY, *Derbyshire,* between Ashbourne and Uttoxeter, is only a tiny village, with cottages high on the banks above the road dropping down to the River Dove. The combination of manor house and church is one of the most beautiful and peaceful imaginable. As you approach, the church is partly hidden by an enormous yew; as you stare at it, you realize that the only sound comes from a weir on the Dove. From a nearer view, the church is unusual as well as beautiful. For one thing, the tower is over the porch. Then you notice how large the chancel is. In the Middle Ages the rector was responsible for the chancel of his church, and here one of them in the 14th c built the chancel and filled its windows with heraldic glass; another in the 15th c provided a new roof and more stained glass. The architectural details are unusual; notice the wavy cresting instead of square battlements, and the rosettes at the intersections of tracery bars. The tombs of Fitzherbert Lords of the Manor are most impressive. Sir Henry (d. 1315) is in chain mail, cross legged; he is carved in gritstone. Nicholas (d. 1473) and Sir Ralph (d. 1483) each lie with their wives beside them on table tombs of Derbyshire alabaster; the tables have rows of weepers in nearly perfect condition. The glass, attacked by lichen, is being restored, and every visitor should contribute to the cost.

The Manor has recently been lovingly restored by a new owner descended from the Fitzherberts. The oldest part is the stone range closest to the church; it was the solar wing to a hall which has gone. In its place is a trim brick house of about 1680, symmetrical and with a hipped roof and dormer windows.

You cross the Dove by a handsome bridge (1777) to Ellastone, which itself has not much to offer. Take a lane from the village going W and you pass Wootton Lodge, a new hunting lodge built just after 1600 and designed by Robert Smythson, the Nottinghamshire architect. The present owner guards the privacy of his home and its park with miles of formidable steel fencing, but through gateways there are glimpses of the house, its lawns, its newly introduced deer and even a few llamas. Further W, the improving hand of man has dammed streams to make lakes flanked by wooded slopes. Soon you are on the edge of another park, Alton (q.v.), and this is the best approach to that village.

REPTON, *Derbyshire* (6m SW of Derby), has a long-recorded history centring on an Anglo-Saxon monastery, a Norman priory and (since 1557) a school. Within a century of the arrival of St Augustine and his mission (597), monasteries became part of the Christian life of England. Peterborough established several colonies, for instance at Brixworth (Northants.) and at near-by Breedon-on-the-Hill (q.v.) and at Repton a monastery for both men and women, as was common. The rulers of the Midland kingdom of Mercia occasionally stayed in it, and two of them were buried here. Recent excavations round the crypt under the chancel of the parish church have shown that it started as a mausoleum, for the two kings (Aethelbald and Wiglaf) about 757. Later the mausoleum became a tower and the vault was inserted, and two staircases were cut so that pilgrims could descend by one to pay their respects to the remains lying in each recess and return by the other.

The Danish attacks put an end to this. A Danish army wintered here in 874. At Ingleby (3m to the E) archaeologists have found a small group of Viking barrows, but the pagans must soon have adopted Christianity, for a Viking axe found near the crypt in 1923 must have come from a burial. But the sanctity of the place was not forgotten, and

in 1174 an Augustinian priory was founded here. What remained of the Saxon church was presumably already being used as the parish church, so the priory was established further E. The church was rebuilt, the nave in the early 14th c with tall octagonal piers; the tower with its very slender spire in 1340; the 15th c raised the clerestory, built the new roof and the two-storey porch (in which there are architectural fragments including two Anglo-Saxon columns). There are monuments to the Thacker family, including an exuberantly Baroque wall tablet to a bewigged Francis Thacker (1710).

The Priory buildings were acquired in 1557 by Sir John Port and converted into Repton School. The school has now spread throughout the village into buildings of various ages, but visitors may see the older buildings within the precinct, entering by the medieval gateway alongside the church. There are some 13th-c remains of the church. What was the W range of the cloister has an undercroft (now School Museum) with the prior's hall over it (*c.* 1400); this became the school after 1557 and had mullioned and transomed windows inserted. In the 15th c many monastic heads built themselves new lodgings; Prior Overton (1437) did it here, and his tower survives on the river front. Built of brick with corbelled out angle turrets, it recalls secular buildings such as Kirby Muxloe near Desford (Leics.) or even Buckden and Tattershall. Repton Hall, a private house of about 1680, was built against it.

The long village street has two timber-framed houses, including Tudor Lodge with a storeyed porch; the Grange is a brick house of 1703.

Foremark lies 1½m to the E; its Georgian Hall is now the preparatory department of Repton School. The church, in effect a chapel for the hall since there is no village, is a fascinating and unaltered building dated 1662, with box pews, three-decker pulpit, a rich rood screen and iron altar rails by Robert Bakewell, a famous local blacksmith.

RISLEY, *Derbyshire,* is 7m E of Derby. Apart from ribbon-building along the former main road from Nottingham to Derby, it consists of no more than a small group of old buildings, but they are unique. Risley was yet another property of the Willoughby family (*see* Cossall). The Hall on the S side of the road is a community school but its setting and character have been safeguarded. Risley Lodge Farm, 1m N of the road, must have started as a hunting lodge in Risley Park. In 1593 Michael Willoughby started to rebuild the church; the style is Gothic, with a hint of Renaissance – notice the round heads of the aisle windows. Katherine Willoughby founded a school in 1593, but the existing buildings were erected in 1706 and onwards by the trust founded by the family. The first building (now Latin House, 1706) was both school and school house; the boarders slept in the garrets. It is text-book Queen Anne, with symmetrical front, hipped roof, brick walls and generous stone trim. Immediately E two identical buildings for boys, the Latin School (1724) and the English School (1753), and another School House (1771) show a flourishing concern with unusually enlightened control of new building. Happily the trustees still keep the buildings unaltered. The English and Latin Schools are tall with lofty windows.

At **Ockbrook**, 2m W, another historic institution has kept a corner of the village unchanged. In 1750 the Moravians, a Protestant sect which influenced John Wesley early in his life, established a settlement here. Its buildings surround a green. On the W side the chapel with its white cupola is flanked by tall Georgian houses now occupied by the girls' school (founded 1799) which still flourishes. On the S side of the green is a row of brick cottages (Nos. 9–15) for humble members of the settlement.

Avoiding the main road (A52) between Risley and Ockbrook involves going N to **Stanton by Dale**, a small and tidy village built of a mixture of gritstone and brick. There is a slender village cross, a row of almshouses and fine cast-iron pump and horse-trough, given by women of Stanton to mark Victoria's Diamond Jubilee (1897). Further W, Dale has much of interest. A post-mill (Cat and Fiddle Mill) stands on the ridge N of the village. The remains of the Premonstratensian Abbey stand in the valley bottom and on the S slope is the Hermit's Cave, carved out of the cliff by a Derby baker turned hermit.

SHARDLOW, *Derbyshire,* is 6m SE of Derby. It should not be missed, though it will provoke mixed feelings if only because there is rarely a gap in the traffic on A6 through it. The old nucleus of the village is marked by the church (rebuilt 1838) and by the Hall. Shardlow Hall has been saved by becoming the headquarters of the Advisory Service of the Ministry of Agriculture, Fisheries and Food, which means temporary buildings and car parks in the grounds, but changes have been fairly discreet, and the Hall itself is unaltered externally. Like Sudbury, it faced N when the central block was built in 1684, with a stone face; it was later turned round and presents a brick face to the visiting public. Later still, single-storey wings were added leading to two-storey pavilions; the further pavilion housed a new kitchen, the one nearer the road a library. The latter has been enlarged.

After 1777, when the Trent and Mersey Canal was opened, a canal port grew up further E, one of two recognizable examples in England, the other being Stourport. Liverpool, Hull and Bristol were now linked by water, and the warehouses at Shardlow quickly filled with heavy goods of all sorts carried at half the cost of road transport and (especially for Staffs. pottery) more safely. The homes of the canal carriers and their warehouses are therefore a precious survival. There is a modern marina linked to the Trent but the canal basin is filled now with painted boats, a charming and appropriate foreground to a warehouse (1780) with a pediment, a clock and inscription 'Navigation from the Trent to the Mersey', and a boat inlet. It has been converted to dwellings. Wandering around you will see other warehouses characterized by half-moon openings. One now called the Old Brewhouse was built in 1791. One canal carrier built Broughton House on the main road (later Stevens, Corn Miller), a handsome stone house of about 1800 having a curved verandah over the porch from which he could look down on his yard, its buildings and the basin. Round the corner is Shardlow Lodge (Lady in Grey Restaurant), another carriers' house. There are several inns, including the Navigation on London Road.

SOUTHWELL, *Notts.* (7m W of Newark on Trent), is the one village in England with a cathedral. It has only had a bishop's throne since 1884, but the minster church, founded about 956, had something of the status, and from the 12th c the appearance, of a cathedral. The first settlement here was a Roman villa – a country house which stood E of the minster. After the settlement of pagan Danes in the 870s, Christianity had to be re-established. In 956 King Eadwig gave to Oscytel, Archbishop of York and himself a Dane, land in Southwell and in 11 Nottinghamshire villages, to endow a minster church with a group of canons to preach and baptize. The canons were never supplanted by monks, and so the collegiate church has lasted for more than 1000 years. Its buildings tell a story of that length.

The minster was rebuilt from 1108 onwards; only fragments survive from its predecessor – a carved doorhead in the N transept with St Michael and David, and some tessellated paving in the S transept (*not* Roman). The Norman Choir was rebuilt in 1234 onwards in EE style, and a new chapter house in 1288 onwards. Each part has its own distinctive glory. Archbishops of York continued to foster the minster, for they had a palace alongside. The ruins of the large courtyard house are 15th-c, with a house of 1909 built into the W end for the bishop.

The canons or prebendaries each had a house in their village (*see* Woodborough) and another at Southwell, so there are fine houses N and W of the minster, each of which can be identified as a former prebendal mansion. As wealthy men with several livings, the canons were rarely seen at Southwell (*see* Bottesford); their houses were leased off and eventually sold. Canons took it in turn to occupy the residence (1689, refronted in 1772), now the home of the modern Provost. The vicars choral who did the duties of absentee canons were housed in Vicars' Court; it was rebuilt in 1781 as four houses flanking the residence, E of the minster.

The village which grew up round the minster never achieved urban status; its former market place (in King Street) was built over. Its Tudor and timber-framed inn, the Saracen's Head, still survives; here Charles I spent his last hours (on 5 May 1646) as a free man before surrendering to the Scots. The brewery company has spoilt the interior. The former Assembly Rooms next door have been absorbed as the hotel dining-room. Up King Street is Burgage Green, with Georgian houses which include Burgage Manor, once the home of Byron's mother and now a Youth Hostel.

Hallougton, 1½m S, belonged to the minster, and the 14th-c stone tower of the Manor House must have been the prebendal house.

SUDBURY, *Derbyshire,* is 5m E of Uttoxeter. Now that a by-pass has diverted the traffic on A56, the character of the village can be savoured. The monuments in the church provide a key: there are two wimpled effigies of women of the Montgomery family which held the manor for more than 400 years until in 1513 Ellen Montgomery married Sir Henry Vernon of Haddon. The later tombs are of the Vernon family, which became synonymous with Sudbury. George Vernon, who built the Hall, is commemorated by a wall monument (1710). The 10th Lord Vernon transferred the Hall to the National Trust in 1967.

When George Vernon inherited in 1659 he resolved to build something more imposing than the small manor house already there. Who designed the house we do not know, but bricks were made on the estate (as they usually were). The house faces N, for that was then thought to be the healthier aspect. Though the front never sees the sun, it is most satisfying to the eye, and the garden side shows best the combination of sandstone with dark bricks forming a diaper pattern in the red brickwork. The house is somewhat old-fashioned for its date, with an E plan and a long gallery but in 1670, when the carcass was finished, Vernon employed famous London artists and craftsmen to carve the gorgeous staircase (Edward Pierce) and woodwork in the drawing-room (Grinling Gibbons), and to make the plaster ceilings. Louis Laguerre arrived in 1691 to paint ceilings. The formal garden can now be seen only in the painting hanging in the entrance hall. The range of fish-ponds in the foreground became a romantic lake in the 19th c; the tree-lined avenues stretching into the distance are now no more than marks visible on aerial photographs. The house was also enlarged, and the big servants' wing has been turned by the Trust into a fascinating museum of childhood.

Landowners like George Vernon felt free to remove a village if it interfered with a new design; it happened at Castle Howard (Yorks.), at Houghton (Norfolk), and at Oliver Goldsmith's 'sweet village of the plain' (Nuneham Courtenay, Oxfordshire). Some built new-planned villages (Houghton and Nuneham Courtenay). Vernon demolished the cottages strung across the front of the Hall, and built along the curving street further E. The village had to have a suitable inn, so the old one was rebuilt in 1671 as the Vernon Arms, in stone and brick like the hall but with gables in the vernacular manner. The oldest cottages along the street with chequer brickwork are also evidently his work. His enlightened enterprise was sustained by his descendants, so the

M. W. Barley
Headstone in Swithland slate at Tithby, Notts.

village in the 19th c got a school, new houses and cottages and even a gasworks.

SUTTON BONINGTON, *Notts.* (4m N of Loughborough), is a double village: two churches less than ¼m apart and two communities fused together. Bonington as the parent village has the grander church with a tall 15th-c tower and spire. No doubt it attracted more of the wealth and ambition of this community, but Sutton has had its own church for about as long. The right to appoint the rector was given to Leicestershire monasteries, first Calke, then Repton; this must explain why not much village money was spent on St Anne's after the 14th c. It still has only a bell-cote instead of a tower or spire. Repton's interest can also be seen in the square stone house S of the old village called locally Hobgoblins. It is of stone, with gables topped by ball finials and was evidently rebuilt in the 17th c with material from a medieval grange of Repton Priory.

The village stands just above the flood plain of the Soar; alongside the road across to Kegworth a raised wooden causeway can carry pedestrians across even when the road is flooded. The ridge behind is Keuper Marl (compare Thrumpton q.v.) with the railway line cut into its flank. S of the village terra cotta, beloved of late Victorian and Edwardian architects, was made; now the works produces glazed earthenware pipes. The village winds along at the foot of the slope, with gentle curves that show off houses at their best – some with gables to the street, some fronting it. The oldest, still timber-framed, are two with gables to the street; the one at the N end (Soar Lane) is well preserved, dated 1661, with a stone plinth and brick-nogging. The grandest house is the Georgian Hall with its brick walls and Swithland slate roof just glimpsed over its garden wall. But the street has kept its traditional character. A distinctive pair of facing houses near the N end, both c. 1700, have gables and ornamental string courses. Unhappily one of them has discarded tradition and become White House. Several cottages are of three storeys in the south Notts. manner (compare Costock, 4m E). The village has not, however, escaped recent pressures: witness the bungalows near Sutton church, on the site of the old manor house.

The University of Nottingham's Faculty of Agriculture occupies the ridge above going N. Beyond it, **Kingston on Soar** is a tiny estate village dependent on the Hall, built in 1840 for Edward Strutt, the cotton magnate who became Lord Belper (*see* Milford). It is now divided into flats. A big Anglo-Saxon cemetery was found in laying out its garden. It is worth while to cross the Soar to **Kegworth** to see its grand church, entirely rebuilt c. 1325 except for the tower.

SWITHLAND, *Leics.*, lies between Loughborough and Leicester. Observant motorists travelling on M1 as it passes W of those places notice that the motorway sweeps magnificently through outcrops of rock. This is Charnwood Forest, an area of poor soil rising in places to over 800ft and broken by outcrops of granite and other ancient and hard rocks. There are still places like Beacon Hill, near Woodhouse Eaves, where the public can enjoy the natural landscape of oak and silver birch rising out of bracken. The aristocracy long ago managed to annexe parts of the royal forest for their own hunting lodges and parks. One such is Bradgate Park, between Swithland and Newtown Linford; it belongs to the local authorities and is open.

The villages of Swithland and **Woodhouse Eaves** (3–4m S of Loughborough) flourished most in the 18th and 19th c, when the demand for Swithland slate for roofing, and for graveyard headstones, was at its height. All the older houses, and the best of the recent ones as well as garden and some field walls, are built of slate slabs, undressed; roofs can be identified by their thick and greenish slates. The churchyard is a good place to see the oldest headstones, dated in the 1680s: small and crudely lettered. During the Georgian period masons decorated their products with elegant lettering of great variety and even scenes in low relief. There is a superb wall monument of c. 1750 in Swithland church. Slates for headstones, and for roofing, went all over Leicestershire and into adjacent counties (*see* Langar), until ousted by c. 1800 by Welsh slate, carried on the new canal system. Swithland headstones can be distinguished by their rough backs. At The Brand,

between Swithland and Woodhouse Eaves, there are old quarries on both sides of the road. Quarry workers must have lived mainly at Woodhouse Eaves; Swithland looks like an estate village, belonging to the owners of Swithland Hall (1834). The local granite, pinkish in colour and irregular in shape, was quarried in the Middle Ages. Being too hard to dress, granite lent itself to round turrets; notice the little tower with a conical roof in the main street; was it a dovecote? Rothley Church, and the country house which is now Rothley Court Hotel, are also of granite. The quarries for it were at Mountsorrel, NE of Swithland, and are still worked. The main street there is too busy for anyone to stand and stare, but if you dare do so you will notice ordinary houses with granite walls. The skill of past generations of village craftsmen in quarrying and working the hardest of materials – slate and granite – is a thing of wonder.

TEAN, *Staffs.* (on the A50 between Stoke on Trent and Uttoxeter), has suffered from the vicissitudes of the textile industry and the growth of road traffic but is still a fascinating, if slightly grim, village. In 1748 the Philips family promoted tape weaving, and in 1830 the manufacture of tape here was said to be the most extensive in Europe, employing several hundred people in the mills and in the bleaching grounds. Tean Hall Mills dominate the centre of Upper Tean; they were enlarged in 1823 and 1885, as the looms were shifted from the weavers' cottages into the mills and as the business grew. The manager's house is a smart addition, in brick with giant pilasters, to a timber-framed house of 1613. Alas, the buildings now look shabby since the enterprise has been broken up and various new uses found for the buildings. The Philips family in 1836 built Heath House for themselves, on high ground N of Lower Tean. They also built cottages for their workers. The oldest and most interesting have gone; they consisted of a terrace of interlocking back-to-back houses. Now the most curious evidence of a benevolent employer are a couple of groups of earth privies, both in the last stages of decay, behind cottages in New Road and Old Road. Each octagon has eight privies with a stench pipe like a chimney from the conical roof. They deserve to be listed as of historic and architectural interest! The Philips are said to have provided schools, which have also gone. Did they contribute to the Providence Chapel of 1882 and the Wesleyan Chapel of 1843? It is more likely that they engaged the architect to rebuild the parish church, also in 1843 – one more of Staffordshire's innumerable Victorian churches. It is a pity that some people, now that they own their cottages, have stuck synthetic stone on to brick fronts. It destroys the homogeneity of the rows. It would have been better to wash the brickwork and repoint.

Going E from Upper Tean you pass a classical temple; its columns came from the Georgian predecessor of Heath House. You are soon at Hollington (*see* Alton).

THRUMPTON, *Notts.,* lies 7m SW of Nottingham. The approach road (A648) which now feeds M1 is evidently older than Thrumpton and Barton in Fabis (1½m to the N), for it leaves them to one side. It started as a prehistoric trackway along the higher ground S of the Trent. The ridge to the S of Thrumpton is Keuper marl which makes the soil dark red; it contains gypsum, mined for plaster-board at Gotham. The same mineral, calcium carbonate, is alabaster when the seams are hard and thick enough. The alabaster columns at Kedleston Hall, Derbyshire, came from quarries on Red Hill, 1m W of Thrumpton and overlooking the junction of the Soar with the Trent. Some travellers on A648 in ancient times were on their way to a Roman shrine on Red Hill. The ridge hides from view the power station at Ratcliffe on Soar, one of the biggest in the Trent valley; a familiar sight from M1.

Fishermen know Thrumpton well as they make their way to the Trent bank: another world, of locks and weirs, low meadows; of flood banks protecting villages; of broken lengths of older courses of the Trent forming lakes. Downstream and across the river are the Attenborough gravel lagoons, now a nature reserve.

The old village – disregarding the recent development along the lane approaching – still bears the imprint of a succession of benevolent landlords, particularly John Emerton (d. 1745) and the 8th Lord Byron (the poet's cousin) who inherited in 1843. John Emerton rebuilt the houses, no doubt inspired by his near neighbour, Sir Thomas Parkyns (*see* Bunny). His work is marked by the use of brown and purple bricks, made locally, in a chequer pattern; there is no discordant note in the length of street from the church to Lord Byron's battlemented gateway to the Hall. Lord Byron also built a row of seven cottages on the approach lane (notice their red and blue bricks in window heads) and put new roofs on a few cottages; they have overhanging eaves with elaborate large boards instead of high copings. Three cottages near the Hall gateway have John Emerton's initials and dates in the 1730s.

Happily the Hall, from which this paternalism was exercised, survives and is open to parties of the public. Built in 1609–17 by Gervase Pigot, it remains essentially Jacobean: brick walls with stone dressings and, inside, timber-framed party walls. Gervase Pigot II (d. 1669) gave the gables their fashionable Flemish outline by adding the wavy cresting, and he put in the splendid new staircase with acanthus scrolls instead of balusters.

WELLOW, *Notts.* (on A616 between Newark and Ollerton), is the only village in the county with a green as distinct from a grassed-over market-place. Most English villages are mentioned in the Domesday Book (1086), but not Wellow because it did not then exist. The nearest villages were Grimston (perpetuated in Grimston Hill, less than 1m E) and Rufford to the SW. When Cistercian monks arrived at Rufford in 1145 they proceeded to create the kind of rural seclusion they desired by buying out the villagers of Rufford. The displaced peasants planned a new fortified village for themselves, Wellow, with a bank and ditch (called George Dyke) all round and a triangular green in the centre, now dominated by the maypole. On the S and W the defence is natural, a stream cutting its course deep into the Keuper marl, like a dumble (*see* Woodborough). You can walk some way along it at the S end of the village. The rest of the circuit is a man-made bank and ditch. It crosses the road to Newark (A616) at the E end of the village, opposite the pinfold.

The green has remained intact except that the Primitive Methodists were allowed in 1847 to build their chapel on it. Houses surround the green in a pleasantly unselfconscious way. All are brick, except for one with exposed timbers, and facing the N end of the green is another evidently timber-framed under its white rendering, for it has a jetty or overhang. It is a pity that some of the brick houses have been painted white. Wellow Hall, on the left as you come in from Ollerton, has recently been restored; its Georgian wing alongside the road now looks very elegant. Towards Newark there are three simple farmhouses of the kind fashionable here in Georgian times: central doorway, one window either side, three windows upstairs, chimneys at the gable end – like a child's drawing of a house. The church, off the green to the E, is small; it was started in the 12th c by the villagers themselves without any squire's help. The track going N from the pinfold leads to Jordan Castle Farm. It takes its name from an earthwork in the field beyond, nearly ploughed out now. Archaeologists recognize it as a ring work, and it must have belonged to a 13th-c Jordan Foliot, lord of Grimston.

There is much to see at **Rufford,** 1½m to the SW. The great house built by the Saviles on the site of the Cistercian Abbey is an Ancient Monument, the medieval portions (the lay brothers' range) and part of the later house being conserved. It is not yet open to the public. The environs are a country park, with recreational facilities for the public. Landscaping by the Saviles, such as a new lake and the Broad Ride, can be seen. There is a good exhibition in the mill, at the N end of the lake; it is soon to be moved to the Victorian stables, S of the house. The exhibition shows the many changes in the landscape at the hands first of the Cistercians and then of wealthy landowners.

WILLOUGHBY WATERLESS, *Leics.,* lies 7m S of Leicester on what was once a through road to Rugby; so it consists of one street only, and traffic eventually moved to other routes saving the village from being overwhelmed. It lies between two streams, and well-watered meadows (water leys) must have been the source of wealth for farmer-graziers who built several good houses from the 17th c onwards. The Old Hall at the S end of the village still has one wall of exposed timber framing; the rest is cased in brick and in the 18th c a grand garden wall was put up, its piers topped with urns. The Limes, standing back from the street, is a farmhouse of 1702, built in chequer pattern brickwork; it too has a walled garden with piers and vases. In the middle of the village, Manor Farm is dated 1693; a tall brick farmhouse with prominent chimney-stacks, and the usual garden wall with vases. In front of the church The Leys, hidden by trees but just visible from the path to the church, is a handsome house of c. 1740. Needless to say, its garden wall has four vases.

Compared with such wealth and display, the church is an anticlimax. It is worth noticing that, as in other churches of South Leics., rounded boulders from the boulder clays (deposited during the Ice Age) were used for walling, in default of better local material.

The villages nearer Leicester, such as **Countesthorpe**, have been overwhelmed by urban pressures, but if you go S towards upland Leics. and keep away from main roads there are pleasant villages. They give an impression of Victorian prosperity, both in the character of the houses and the money then spent on restoring churches such as **Gilmorton**.

WINSTER, *Derbyshire* (3m W of Matlock), is a good centre from which to sample two kinds of Derbyshire scenery: the limestone uplands (what the signposts call the White Peak) and the gritstone moorland. Winster was once a market town. The Market Hall (National Trust) is stone below, the arches of its open ground floor now filled in; the hall above, originally timber-framed, was rebuilt in brick (strangely enough) about 1675. There are no farmhouses in the main street but grander residences – the Hall, cube-shaped with a flat lead roof, and Stanley House with Venetian windows. Cottages of former lead-miners are piled on the steep slope to the S, and surrounding fields are pock-marked with tip heaps and filled-in shafts. All the houses are of dark gritstone, except for the Dower House at the W end. Going out that way, Elton is 1m further; it has even better houses, several dated to the 17th c, in the main street. One on the N side of the street, dated 1717, shows the striking contrast between near-white limestone for the walling and dark gritstone for quoins and openings. The Old Hall, now a Youth Hostel, is of gritstone and dated 1668 and 1715. Here too narrow and winding lanes lead through a dense cluster of miners' cottages – now mostly weekend cottages.

Birchover, 1m N, is set in a totally different scenery of gritstone crags such as Eagle Tor. At the bottom of the village street is Row Tor, and near it the Druid Inn, a relic of the craze for Druids in the 18th c. Across the valley to the W is Hermit's Cave and the little Jesus Chapel, both 18th-c. The village street of simple houses climbs up to Stanton Moor. Quarries still extract enormous blocks of pinkish gritstone – not any more for millstones but still for grindstones and for special building purposes.

Early man colonized central Derbyshire intensively from Neolithic times onwards. The richest finds have come from Anglo-Saxon burials, when tombs were re-used. To see the best you must go to Sheffield Museum, where finds made by the Derbyshire antiquary, Thomas Bateman (buried 1861 at Middleton by Youlgreave), are on show. But Stanton Moor has a stone circle (Nine Ladies), a standing stone (King's Stone) and many Bronze Age barrows. The urns and other finds from here are in the Heathcote Museum in the village and may be seen on application.

WOODBOROUGH, *Notts.*, 6m NE of Nottingham. Two parallel valleys fall E into the Dover Beck and Woodborough lies in the N one. The earliest settlers preferred the high ground between, for Plains Road, Mapperley, was a prehistoric trackway on a ridge, and from it two minor tracks turned E. N of Woodborough, the ridgeway (a public footpath) goes alongside Fox Wood, and in it a small Iron Age hillfort can just be picked out. Its inhabitants stayed there under Roman rule, to judge from pottery found.

The Anglo-Saxon settlers preferred the valley bottom. The Norman church was rebuilt as the village prospered and the chancel (c. 1350) is on a generous scale. It must have been done by a canon of Southwell (q.v.), Woodborough church being part of the endowment of the minster there, and he employed masons, possibly from Lincs., who carved some of the wildest of flowing tracery for the E window.

The Hall, hidden in trees at the W end of the village, is Carolean, enlarged in Victorian times. On the N side of the village street is Hall Farm, hidden by ivy but a nice gabled house of 1710. Further E, Manor Farm presents to the road a monumental range, of two storeys with gabled entrance (1878), built as racing stables. Still further E is a typical farm group round a yard, with an elaborate stable, granary and dovecote at the back. For the rest, Woodborough is a village of cottages (with inevitably, some recent infilling). Their occupants had two means of livelihood. One was knitting stockings, for this was one of the villages in which framework knitting, on the stocking frame invented by William Lee of Calverton in 1589, eventually established itself. Stockingers' cottages can be identified by the long downstairs window to the room where the frames were. The row at the E end of High Street must be early 19th-c. The cottagers may also have started market gardening commercially, for that is now the valley's specialization.

The best group of stockingers' cottages is at **Calverton**, over the ridge to the N: Windles Square, recently restored. **Lambley**, 1½m over the ridge to the S has a fine church, rebuilt in c. 1470 out of a bequest by Ralph Cromwell, the builder of Tattershall Castle (Lincs.) and S Wingfield Manor (Derbyshire). On the ridge between Lambley and the Trent what looks like a moat round Lodge Farm is really another Iron Age hillfort. You may walk up Lampley Dumble W to Mapperley Plains; a dumble is a miniature gorge cut by a stream into the Keuper marl.

The Cotswolds

GLOUCESTERSHIRE NORTH WILTSHIRE NORTH AVON
WEST OXFORDSHIRE

David Verey

We know we are in or near the Cotswolds when the houses are built of limestone and the fields are divided by drystone walls rather than hedges; fields which are smooth and sculptured, and stone which catches every change of light, and grows mosses green as cress, and lichens varying from bright rust to black that turn yellow–green to an intricately textured white; good country for sheep and barley.

Viewed from the Severn Vale, the Cotswold escarpment is impressive not for its height, since at its highest point at Cleeve Hill it is only 1083ft, but for its length. For about 50 miles, from Dyrham to Dover's Hill near Chipping Campden, the great cliff presents a virtually unbroken skyline. It is the western edge of a limestone plateau, which dipping always gently to the east or south-east merges finally into the clay plains of Oxford.

The limestone of the Cotswolds is composed of small rounded grains of calcium carbonate packed together like the roe of a fish. From this resemblance the stone is called oolite, meaning egg-stone. The Inferior Oolite, so called because it is the lower and older stratum of this limestone, is tilted upwards at its western edge. There it forms the escarpment which includes all the highest points. Further east it dips under the Great Oolite, the newer rock which extends across into Oxfordshire. Some beds of Great Oolite provide fine-grained stone, called free-stone, or ashlar, which can be cut or carved very easily when freshly quarried, but hardens on exposure. Others provide thin layers of rock which can be split by exposure to frost, thus producing the stone tiles which have always till now been used for roofing and are called Cotswold slates, though they are not slate in the geological sense. The correct term should be 'tilestone', for it is in fact a sandy limestone which splits nicely into thin layers. When used they are carefully graduated, and the huge tilestones at the bottom of the roofs often weigh 50lb or more, requiring enormous oak beams. Their weight is one of the reasons for the decline of the stone-tile industry, and the only way to obtain them now is to buy them off some old unwanted barn. The supply, of course, is uncertain and it is so expensive that new roofs are now made with reconstructed stones with trade names like Bradstone and Hardrow. The walls of the houses are also made of a reconstituted material which the planning authorities consider most resembles stone.

The Cotswold plateau is cut by small rivers which all run east and are picked up by the Upper Thames. It is in the valleys formed by these rivers that the villages mostly shelter. The rivers are called Churn, Dunt, Coln, Leach, Windrush, Dikler, Eye, Sherborne Brook, Evenlode, and Ampney Brook. If it was not for these valleys the Cotswolds would be bleak indeed.

Besides the Cotswold plateau of Gloucestershire, this section of the book also takes in some neighbouring areas which can be considered Cotswold in character, particularly in North Wiltshire, Avon north of Bristol, and the north-west part of Oxfordshire which is traversed by the Windrush river. We have also included some northern places such as Bloxham where the iron content of the limestone has deepened its colour to a golden brown more like Northamptonshire. And from Worcestershire we have plucked the most typical Cotswold village, Broadway.

The Cotswolds were not always fashionable. William Cobbett, on riding out of Cirencester in the 1820s, wrote 'I came up hill into a country, apparently formerly a down or common, but now divided into large fields by stone walls. Anything so ugly I have never seen before.' It was not till he got to the escarpment at Birdlip and plunged down into the fertile Severn valley that he felt at home. The Cotswolds only became famous in the last quarter of the nineteenth century, when the spaciousness of the wolds, the charm of the wooded river valleys and the distinctive vernacular architecture came to be widely appreciated. Not that the Cotswolds in the nineteenth century were remote. They had their share of railway development, and of those semi-private country stations required by local aristocrats like the Duke of Beaufort at Badminton or peers on the boards of railway companies such as Lord Northwick at Paxford or Lord Leigh at Adlestrop where, in Edward Thomas's poem:

> . . . one afternoon
> Of heat the express train drew up there
> Unwontedly.

Nor were they positively unfashionable. Mary Anderson, the celebrated American actress, who brought distinction to Broadway – just as Princess Grace has brought some elegance to Monte Carlo – found to her surprise when she settled there that she knew many people in the neighbourhood, the Elchos at Stanway, the Redesdales at Batsford. It

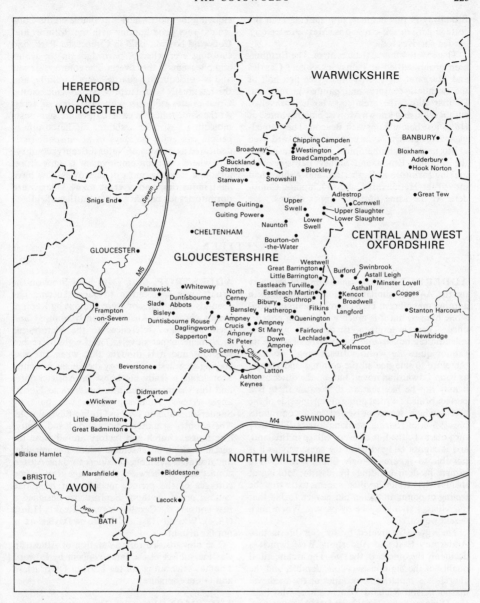

was just that hitherto people had not found the Cotswolds specially attractive. For instance – when the third generation of a Yorkshire business family had made sufficient money in about 1870 to think life in the South would be more desirable, they bought an estate in the Vale near Gloucester, not on the Cotswolds. However, by 1928 the next generation moved up on to the Cotswolds converting a large farmhouse in the arts and crafts manner. The Cotswolds were nearer London, more convenient and had now become more fashionable than the Severn Vale.

The cult of the Cotswolds began in the mid-1880s, though Morris and Rossetti at Kelmscott in 1871 were the first enthusiasts for the 'little grey manor house' way of life. Morris interested himself in the conservation of Broadway. He wrote the letter which founded the Society for the Protection of Ancient Buildings from Broadway Tower because he was concerned about Scott's intention of scraping Tewkesbury Abbey. At Broadway gentrification of the old farms and cottages followed the arrival of the American artists Edwin Austen Abbey and Frank D. Millet. Another artist, Alfred Parsons, who specialized in landscape and flower painting, lived in Broadway. He was a firm adherent of the English cottage garden school, and designed two large gardens in

Broadway in this manner, thus making even the cottage garden self-conscious. Mary Anderson's garden survives today.

There were other artistic centres. The Birmingham group settled at Painswick, where Charles and Margaret Gere lived during the first half of the twentieth century, and painted in tempera. Detmar Blow, the architect who had travelled with Ruskin and known Morris, built his house at Hilles just below Painswick Beacon. The stained-glass artist Henry Payne and his son Edward lived at Box near Minchinhampton. Ernest Gimson and the brothers Ernest and Sidney Barnsley were making furniture at Sapperton, and Ashbee had moved the Handicraft Guild to Chipping Campden. At the same time the upper classes were enjoying the sport which is available on the Cotswolds; very good hunting with the Beaufort and Cotswold hounds, polo in Cirencester Park, and shooting everywhere – partridges on the wolds and pheasants in the coverts. The countryside was and is consequently guarded very carefully, and this has greatly helped to preserve its scenic beauty. Great estates still exist with thousands of acres. At the same time everywhere there are sign-posts indicating paths for walking, so that ordinary people can enjoy holidays in an unspoilt (it is dedicated as an Area of Natural Beauty) countryside where the main employment is agriculture, although it is true most of the towns now have light industries, and a great many villages are dormitories for people working further afield.

GAZETTEER

ADDERBURY, *Oxfordshire* (3m S of Banbury on the A41), is similar to Bloxham (q.v.), with another magnificent Perp church, and many ironstone houses, but it is much wealthier in appearance. There is a green, surrounded by rather splendid big houses into the gardens of which we cannot quite see without trespassing. We have therefore to imagine all the comings and goings, as in an Edwardian novel; but, on the other hand it may not be like that at all because there is a perfect brute of a road going along one side of the green, which seems possessed by a continuous procession of roaring, stinking lorries. This may turn out to be the fate of every village in England, and it cannot be ignored in the same way as it is possible to ignore an ugly filling station, or a bizarre modern building, by just not looking at them. Heavy traffic in villages seems to destroy the feeling of community life, but heaven forbid that our villages should all be by-passed. Where then would we walk?

The village is divided by the Sor brook into Adderbury East and Adderbury West, which is decidedly the quieter of the two. The architectural quality of the big houses is considerable, and the church is a remarkable product of the medieval master mason Richard Winchcombe, who built the Divinity School in Oxford; but it was neglected, and had to be restored in the 19th c by J. C. Buckler, which leaves a big question mark in the mind of the student who is studying the style of Richard Winchcombe. Did the restorers know what they were replacing, or did they just copy what had survived so much better at Bloxham?

Adderbury now provides work for more than 500 people in manufacturing industry. The location of a large firm producing prefabricated concrete garages and garden furniture is due to the fact that the site was scheduled for industrial development, actually for ironstone working which has now ceased. **Hook Norton,** another former ironstone quarry, has also become a self-help industrial estate.

ADLESTROP, *Glos.* (3½m E of Stow-on-the Wold), was well-known to Jane Austen. The grounds of the mansion were laid out by Repton, a man whom Jane Austen fervently admired, and there are many references to the Picturesque movement in her novels. The Leighs were her relations and it is thought that when she was staying at Adlestrop Rectory the Leighs inherited Stoneleigh, a really big house in Warwickshire, and this she introduced into her work as Northanger Abbey. Adlestrop House was built by Sanderson Miller in 1762 in Gothic-Revival style. The country is undulating, wooded, and pretty. The house, church and rectory are all close together making an ensemble which is agreeable, and nostalgic when one considers the Jane Austen connection. Otherwise the village has some cottages of the period, including at least one cottage *ornée*. Anthony Sanford has designed a new house in the Caroline manner, Reality House (1974). Warren Hastings' house at **Daylesford** is not far distant.

The now disused railway station of Adlestrop was the subject of the famous poem by Edward Thomas celebrating 'all the birds of Oxfordshire and Gloucestershire'.

THE AMPNEYS, *Glos.* The prettiest of these four villages is **Ampney St Peter,** although it is on a very small scale and slightly self-conscious, situated either side of a turning which leads nowhere from the A417 4m E of Cirencester. On the right is the Pack Horse Inn, genuine enough. Facing a small green, closing the view, is a house with a sundial dated 1703. Here the road bends to the right past the small Saxon church with its gabled tower, and on to a Cotswold-style house built in 1908 by architect Sidney Gambier-Parry.

Only ¼m away in the fields is the church of **Ampney St Mary,** a 12th-c church, deserted after the Black Death so there are no cottages anywhere near it and its village has moved to the hamlet of Ashbrook. The church is near to the Ampney

STAINED GLASS: Detail from the east window of the Corpus Christi Chapel of the church of St Mary, Fairford, Gloucestershire; fifteenth-century. This detail represents Peter, James and John witnessing the Transfiguration of Jesus. (*Photograph by Birkin Haward*)

FREDERICK LANDSEER GRIGGS, R.A. (1876–1938): Almshouses at Chipping Campden.
Watercolour, 1907 (*Cheltenham Art Gallery and Museum*). Griggs was a noted etcher, engraver and
book-illustrator, who had a keen architectural sense and was connected with the Society for the
Protection of Ancient Buildings. He did much to preserve the amenities of Chipping Campden,
where he lived for many years.

Brook and there must have been a medieval village there.

Another church higher up the Brook is that of **Ampney Crucis**. This also has Saxon features, and is well-known for its churchyard cross. The mansion of Ampney Park sits close to its W end, and there is an old mill and vicarage. The village itself has been tightly infilled, so it is a mixture of old and new, owner-occupied and council tenanted. A flourishing modernized pub on the main road is called The Crown of Crucis.

The fourth village, **Down Ampney**, is set further apart, almost over the Wiltshire border, with an old vicarage (19th-c) famous as the birthplace of the composer Vaughan-Williams. Here the village street has a higher percentage of modern houses and bungalows than old or 19th-c cottages, and it appears to be lacking in shops and amenities, or even a centre. The church is some little distance away, almost in the grounds of Down Ampney House, that beautiful 15th-c hall house of the Hungerfords, with alterations by the great architect Sir John Soane. It is flat country here, and the church spire is glimpsed from the village through trees; but how beautiful the churchyard and church are when we get there!

ASHTON KEYNES, *Wilts.* (4m W of Cricklade), is an example of a village which was, till recently, extremely attractive and desirable. However, it has been spoilt by three factors, the death of the elm trees, the proximity of the new gravel pits, and unsuitable development.

The village is spread out, and what is still very charming is the way in which the houses at the Ashton House end are all approached by bridges over the stream, which here resembles a moat. Ashton House itself projects fortresslike up to its moat with a gazebo oriel window commanding a view along the straight flat road the other side of and parallel to the water. There are four old preaching crosses; at almost every cross-roads in the village there is one, such as the one opposite Gosditch and the one at Church Walk. The church and the manor house are slightly apart from the village and from each other, though the gateposts leading to the manor are near the church, which was altered by Butterfield in 1876–7. The noticeable feature of the church from the outside is the clerestory which has alternately upright and diagonal quatrefoils in circles. Inside it is easy to see Butterfield's decorations in the Norman chancel which he enlarged by widening and raising it. The font appears to be upside-down; it is tall enough for adult baptism. There is a monument by Flaxman and a window by Christopher Webb.

BADMINTON, *Avon*, 6m E of Chipping Sodbury. Great Badminton is a ducal village situated by the side of the mansion of the Duke of Beaufort. It has a long street with quite large 17th-c houses either side, which have rendered façades, and coats of arms dating back to the first Duchess who was a Capel and consequently a very good gardener, like the rest of her family. Essex House is nearest to the gateway to the mansion and opposite the Estate Office. At the other end is the residence of the heir and his wife, Lady Caroline Somerset, who have a beautiful garden set back behind their house. This is a grand village on a spacious scale. Once every year it becomes the hub of the sporting world, when everyone interested in horses, from the Queen downwards, spends three days here to watch the Event, and when the park looks like a tented city.

Thomas Wright, the 18th-c architect, is now known to have lived here under Beaufort patronage, and he was responsible for most of the fantastic Gothic cottages *ornées*, castellated barns, log cabins, and ragged castles, not to mention the classical church.

Little Badminton is quite different. It is unspoilt vernacular, with a large green surrounded by cottages, a tiny church and a dovecote.

BARNSLEY, *Glos.*, 4m NE of Cirencester. The *Architectural Review* as long ago as December 1956, in an item called 'Counter-Attack', probably written by Ian Nairn, had this to say about the village: 'Here is a village which has made itself into one of the most memorable places in Britain, simply by doing everything in a country way and by resisting all efforts to import alien elements . . . everything is in the right place with the right treatment . . . yet there are no outstanding buildings, no set-pieces.'

The explanation is simply that until recently it has belonged to one family, so that commercial developments, like tea-shops, never happened. Furthermore, there are no council houses, because the local authority never forced them on to a reluctant landlord; and because for a long time there was only a private water supply, and there still is no public sewerage, and the subsoil is not suitable for many septic tanks. Another reason is that the road through the village – a turnpike road dating only from the late 18th c – has sharp bends at either end, thus putting a definite stop to the village developing further in either direction. A little agricultural building has broadened it slightly, but generally it is lined up along the main A433, a road so much used as to prove somewhat uncongenial to ordinary village life. Dogs and cats and children are all in danger of being run over; even adults on the footpath cannot be sure they are completely safe.

The church and pub are rightly situated in the centre of the village; so is the village hall. The church is set slightly back on a rise, and its Elizabethan tower is visible among trees for a long way along the approaching road from Cirencester. There is no shop, however; nor post office nor school. All these, which existed once, have disappeared. The estate, now owned by a charitable trust which keeps selling cottages, is still farmed by one tenant farmer; but the occupants of the cottages are no longer all farmworkers, and are mainly newcomers, with various employments outside the village, who have bought their homes from the estate. As it is a conservation area any alterations, additions and improvements are carefully scrutinized by the planning authority; but even so, reconstituted materials are allowed for additions at the rear of the houses, and a few poles carrying electric cables have been introduced where once all wires were buried underground.

There are Roman tracks running either side of the turnpike road through the village, connecting a large Roman farming complex in Barnsley Park with the markets in Cirencester, and the old Bath–Oxford coach road is green on the E of the village. The mansion in the park may have been designed by Hawksmoor. The gardens at Barnsley House in the village are normally open to the public on Wednesdays. Most of the houses are built of locally quarried golden limestone, which has the quality of reflecting light, thus enhancing the mood of the day. Barnsley House (the former Rectory) is one of these, and there are two 18th-c summer houses, one classical and the other Gothic, in the garden.

THE BARRINGTONS, *Glos.*, 3m W of Burford. Some of England's best known national buildings were partly built of Cotswold stone from the Barringtons, such as the interior of St Paul's Cathedral, the City churches of London, and the Sheldonian Theatre and Colleges in Oxford. The Strongs and the Kempsters owned quarries at Little Barrington, Taynton and Burford, producing in various qualities of hardness the attractively coloured and easily worked oolitic limestone. From 1667 they increased their fortunes rapidly, owing to the enormous demand for stone and masons for the rebuilding of the City of London. Wren regarded Thomas Strong as the leading builder of his day, and appointed him

Arlington Row, Bibury

J. Allan Cash

principal contractor for St Paul's. He laid the foundation stone, but died in 1681, leaving money, 'to make a way between the Barrington bridges in Gloucestershire that two men may go a front to carry a corpse in safety'. It is still known as Strong's Causeway. His brother Edward Strong laid the last stone on the lantern of St Paul's in 1708.

The quarries at Barrington were worked from the 14th c and were closed before the end of the 19th c. Barges could easily float down the Windrush and Thames to St Paul's Wharf. On the N side of Little Barrington village lies a spot near the Fox Inn known as The Wharf, where the stone must have been loaded, and several hundred yards lower down on the Windrush there still exist the remains of a sloping weir where the water level could be raised to enable the stone-laden barges to float over to avoid the mill-race below. It is not surprising therefore to find some of the village houses beautifully built of finest ashlar.

Little Barrington is specially attractive, with its triangular green open space in the middle, and houses in terraces on two sides. On the NW the houses are set out on a slight rise in a convex line, like the back of a crescent. Each house is different, but they are naturally associated in scale and texture. It is one of the most appealing village scenes in the Cotswolds.

Great Barrington, on the N side of the river, consists of a compact double row of houses and outbuildings along a village street with the park of the big house and the War Memorial Cross closing the W end. The houses are all of stone, and date from the 17th, 18th and 19th c and they are unspoilt in a way that only a feudal village can be; but the process may have been allowed to go too far, as happened at Great Tew before the rescue operation began. Glimpses of park buildings can be seen through wrought-iron gates.

Both the Barringtons have interesting churches; but Great Barrington has the larger and with splendid monuments. It is almost in the pocket of the mansion and is approached along a path parallel to the drive of the house. Besides dead elms, the Cotswold stone walls are often to be seen fallen down since the havoc which the cold winter of 1978–9 caused them. Several houses in Great Barrington appear to be empty.

BEVERSTONE, *Glos.*, 2m W of Tetbury. Gillian Darley in *Villages of Vision* has this to say about Beverstone: 'There were numerous estates where landowners seem to have heeded Loudon's strictures against the "many formal and disagreeable villages designed purposely to be ornamental".' In Gloucestershire R. S. Holford, a notable Victorian connoisseur of the Italian Renaissance period, had rebuilt the villages of Westonbirt and Beverstone, using as his consultant architect Lewis Vulliamy, who had also built his mansion at Westonbirt and his London palace Dorchester House. The housing is an excellent example of the best combination of good design with improved standards; the terraced cottages, lodges and model farms are carried out in a warm golden limestone and are sparingly decorated with bargeboards, finials and Gothic porches, though never obtrusively so. Westonbirt was a late product of emparking, which means that Holford removed all the cottages that would be in the view of his mansion and rebuilt them at a little distance, so that only the church remains close to the house.

At Beverstone there was no need for emparking because the occupants of a rather derelict castle were in no position to demand a park. The new cottages were therefore mainly strung along the side of the road which goes straight through the village. A side road leads to the castle, which is now partly inhabitable, past an ancient barn, and beyond is a medieval church, which has a mutilated but beautiful pre-Conquest sculpture of the Resurrection on the tower. Beverstone was occupied by Earl Godwin (the father of King Harold) in 1051, so there is a good long history, and it is a combination of farm, church, castle, rectory and Victorian model housing.

BIBURY, *Glos.* In the winter Bibury is empty. The wind whistles across the trout farm, and few people are about. The A433 crosses the Coln on a bridge so well built in 1777 that it can take a 20-ton lorry. However, there is an acute bend the other side which needs skilful negotiating by large lorries, or at worst they will land up in the Swan Hotel, at best knock some of the parapet down. The road then runs along parallel to the river with Arlington Row, the National Trust's cottages, at right angles.

These cottages are pretty, set very low into the water meadow, with the smoke from their chimneys rising against a backdrop of trees. The building was originally a 14th-c sheephouse converted into cottages for weavers in the 17th c when Arlington Mill was used for fulling cloth as well as grinding corn. The mill is now an attractive museum with 16 well-set-out rooms, and open to the public every day, as is the trout farm. These are the two main attractions of the village, which certainly is not commercialized or spoilt like Bourton-on-the-Water. However, there are a lot of visitors in the summer, who would come to Bibury anyway to see the river and its ducks, the Saxon church, and to flavour the atmosphere of what William Morris called the 'prettiest village in England'. People, of course, do present problems, and the village badly needs a car park, which no doubt will come.

In the Arlington Mill Museum there are photographs, all taken before 1900, showing the village has not altered greatly since then. The cottages, built of stone and stone roofed, are still there, intact, and almost unaltered. Public water supply and sewerage there now is, so people no longer have to dip buckets into the river as they were doing well after World War II. There are also before and after watercolours of inside Bibury church at the time of the Gilbert Scott restoration. These show that he replaced the Perp roof in the chancel with the pointed Gothic one there now, besides removing the box pews, hatchments, com-

P. D. Turner

Beverstone Castle

mandment boards, and Laudian altar rails, as one might expect. The church is, however, of extreme interest and beauty, with a most peaceful churchyard, much admired by Alec Clifton-Taylor who wrote: 'As for Bibury, I cannot say more – nor less – than that this is perhaps the most enchanting churchyard in England. (Painswick is of course more spectacular.) Some of the numerous Georgian tombstones are gorgeously carved and in excellent preservation. There is a wide expanse of grass, all faultlessly mown, and a few standard roses, which look exactly right. It would postulate a very perverse mentality, or so it seems to me, to go fault-finding here.'

There has been a sporting side to Bibury life in the past. The turf near Aldsworth was very good for racing, and there was a Bibury Race Club from the time of Charles II. Sartorius painted the horses in the stables at Bibury Court. However, Newmarket took over in the end. Aldsworth still retains a slightly sophisticated look, as if its racing days had not quite worn off, and the Bibury stables are now occupied by hunters in the winter and Argentinian polo ponies in the summer. The house is an hotel and has a perfect setting by the side of the broad River Coln and against a bank of hanging trees. The site was chosen by the Romans for a villa, then the Saxons had a minster here, and the Norman abbot of Oseney a grange. The existing house was built after the Reformation by a favourite of James I, and altered in the 20th c by a cousin of President Roosevelt.

BIDDESTONE, *Wilts.* (4m W of Chippenham), is a very handsome village round a green which has a sizable duck pond. It is handsome because the houses are handsome, more especially a house dated 1730, with segment-headed windows and a central pediment, and a formal garden in front with wrought-iron work. The farm house nearest the pond is older, with gables and mullioned windows. It has a Georgian gazebo in the garden overlooking the green in which people could wait for the arrival of the coach at the nearby inn, or idly watch the white geese splashing in and out of the pond.

The Manor House itself is built outside the village. It has gables and symmetrically set mullioned windows, and a large walled garden, again with a gazebo on the road to keep an eye out for the approaching coach. The houses are built of a grey stone, duller than on the Cotswolds proper, and the countryside is rather flat.

BISLEY, *Glos.* (3m E of Stroud), is redolent of 19th-c church history. When Thomas Keble, who had matriculated at Corpus Christi College, Oxford, in 1808, aged 14, entered on his duties as vicar of Bisley in 1827, he found the church in a ruinous state. The roof of the nave was propped up with a fir tree, and the windows were used as private entrances to the galleries, which made it like a theatre. He soon secured a succession of Tractarian curates, and with their ready assistance he brought about such a revival of church life as the parish had not known since the Reformation. Bisley was a prototype for what went on in many other parishes all over England in those stirring days of personal religious revival.

The vicarage was built in 1832, and it was the home of the Keble family till 1903, as Thomas Keble was succeeded by his son. Through all this time there were daily services in church. It was the centre of an enormous parish, but gradually the Kebles built new churches in distant parts to care for the needs of the industrial populations, and Bisley remained a village. Today, sadly, the vicarage has been abandoned by the vicars, through no fault of their own. The church authorities are not historically minded, and they can no longer afford a house of that size. The school, designed by Bodley, is however still used, and the dressing of the seven wells on Ascension Day, a custom invented by Thomas Keble in 1863, is still attended by a large number of spectators.

Bisley is a high place, 784ft above sea level. A saying at Stow-on-the-Wold, many miles away across the Cotswolds, is, 'These poor sheep have nothing to shelter them but Bisley spire'; or when the wind blows, 'Bisley gates are open'. 'Beggarly Bisley' is a curious mixture of rather seedy-looking houses, and others of distinct architectural merit, sited round a sloping churchyard, and more dramatically in a steep cleft with narrow streets, so narrow it is almost difficult for two motor cars to pass. An unexpected notice says *Defense de stationner. Sortie de voitures*, perhaps a civilized way of saying 'No Parking'. The top side of the village has the inevitable collection of rock-faced houses with ill-proportioned windows, low pitched roofs and hideous drainpipes. They are put to shame by the smooth stone walls and steeply gabled stone roofs of the older houses.

BLAISE HAMLET, *Avon,* on the N outskirts of Bristol. A group of nine cottages can hardly be described as a village but it lay behind the planning and form of almost every subsequent Picturesque village. For this reason it perhaps merits inclusion in this book. 'By bringing together', Miss Darley writes, 'the qualities of cliché, nostalgia and escapism and expressing them in architectural form', John Harford and his architects, John Nash and George Repton, made their 'gesture of confidence in the Picturesque' (*see colour plate facing page 64*).

It is now owned by the National Trust and visitors are invited to walk on the green, but not into the houses. The cottages were built in 1809 to house Blaise estate pensioners. The green is pretty and undulating, with ornamental trees. The cottages are stone built, some with stone roofs and some elaborately thatched, with thatched verandahs with seats, and all with ornamental brick chimneys of considerable height. They are cottages *ornées par excellence*. Great care was taken in making enormous projections of thatched roof over a window, and the exact dimensions of that window. The front doors face in different directions, and the gardens enjoy some privacy owing to the planting of hedges and some are backed by the outside wall of Blaise Castle grounds. On the green, but not in the centre, is a pump-cum-sundial and weather vane, so that the pensioners could get water, guess the time, and see which way the wind was blowing. From the beginning Blaise Hamlet provided a favourite excursion from Clifton and Bristol. Now it is surrounded by modern developments, but is more than ever worth visiting.

BLOCKLEY, *Glos.* The bishops of Worcester were Lords of the Manor for a thousand years and once had a palace here. The industrial history is an eye-opener to those who think of the Cotswolds only in terms of the wool trade. The Domesday Book records 12 mill wheels on the brook which later powered silk mills (making thread for Coventry ribbon weavers), an iron foundry, piano, collar and soap factories and finally gave Blockley its claim to be one of the first villages to be lit by electricity. The reason for all this was the great number of springs which fed the Blockley Brook with a never-failing head of water. No one looking today at this tranquil and unspoilt village, tucked away in its secluded valley, would guess at its industrial past. However, the Rev. F. E. Witts (*Diary of a Cotswold Parson*, edited by David Verey, 1978) writing on 17 August 1836, says, 'Blockley is a most enjoyable village, situated in a deep valley accessible on most sides only by steep hills and embowered in woods. The village itself has a handsome ancient church in its centre, standing on a knoll. Adjacent to the church is the residence of one of the silk throwsters of the place, and there are other comfortable and respectable dwellings evidently occupied by persons in easy circumstances, the whole being built of an excellent freestone from the adjoining quarries on Bourton Hill. There is an air of prosperity about the place, and a new Dissenting Meeting House. The produce of the mills is sold at Coventry chiefly, some of it in London. Bengal and Turkey silk are here manufactured into silk thread. The process seems simple and the operatives chiefly young females and boys from 8 to 10 years of age.' No longer is there exploitation of child labour in silk mills; otherwise little has changed, and the silk mills make very desirable residences.

BLOXHAM, *Oxfordshire,* was prettier when there was less traffic on the A361, which bisects it. Coming from Banbury the road descends into a dip with Bloxham School's 19th-c buildings on the left. At the bottom there is a tall bridge over a stream and the road ascends again to the awe-inspiring church with its splendid spire. This is a dramatic view, with alder trees and willows by the stream, and brown ironstone houses, some still with thatched roofs, climbing up the hill to the church. The Marlborough trophy sign says it was the best-kept village in Oxfordshire in 1978.

The vicarage, designed by G. E. Street, stands almost opposite the church, with its garden forming an acute triangle between the road and a converging lane, one of several lanes or narrow streets with names like Hawke Lane, Frog Lane and The Gogs, all closely built up and old, so there is not so much room for infilling here as there is the other side of the ravine. The church was unfortunately scraped inside by Mr Street, but it is of great magnificence.

This was a large agricultural village which has seen days of great poverty in the past, and now has a slightly seedy air about it, combined with a prim tidiness which betokens everlasting afternoon. Further to the W is a new housing estate. People living there complain of the long distance they have to walk to shops, schools, and post office; but the shops have more to offer, for instance, the former baker's is now selling fashion fabrics. This is a reflection of the changing life style. The increase in jobs in Banbury and elsewhere has made the Bloxham district attractive for residential purposes, and so farming villages have become transformed into commuter villages.

BOURTON-ON-THE-WATER, *Glos.,* is famous as a tourist attraction. The village approached from the Stow road is ugly until we reach the church, which has an 18th-c Georgian tower complete with cupola. There is then a wide green traversed by the Windrush river which is crossed by a series of low pedestrian bridges. It is these bridges which give the village its appeal, combined with the green and the trees and the clear running water. There is nothing else except that the houses are built of a warm-coloured stone, brown to grey in tone, and the back streets have some good houses architecturally, particularly Harrington House which is built of a beautiful ashlar with classical pediment and dome. There

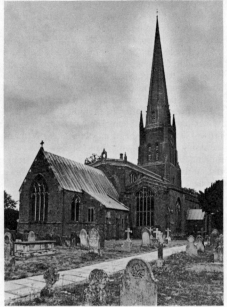

P. D. Turner

The 190-feet spire of Bloxham church

is an air of excitement and expectancy generated by the festive crowds. Nearly all the houses round the green are shops and it does seem that the British public on holiday enjoy shopping for souvenirs more than doing anything else.

There is a model village of the village which of course intrigues everybody, and Birdland is a large collection of foreign birds, including penguins, macaws, and flamingoes, owned by a man who has made a serious study of the subject and a great reputation in this field. He even maintains a tropical house with tropical birds.

It is not a peaceful place but many find it invigorating.

BROADWAY, *Worcs.* Like nearby Chipping Campden, Broadway has the inestimable advantages of being built in a beautiful golden limestone and having houses spread out along a broad main street, so that their architectural merit can be properly appreciated by anyone. The length of the Broadway street is quite considerable so that the excitement mounts as we proceed along it. Broadway is at the bottom of Fish Hill, and it has decidedly a more salubrious climate than Campden. The stone is still there, but it is in the Evesham vale of fruit blossom and is at its best in the spring.

It never was so prosperous as Campden till the 19th c, and there is no back history comparable. In fact the old church is some distance away on the road to Snowshill so it would seem that the village has moved, and taken up its position on another road. Broadway is now somewhat self-conscious. There are a great many antique dealers and shops for tourists. One attraction and cause of its popularity may be the Lygon Arms Hotel. This famous inn is a beautiful, romantic, gabled, and genuinely old house, and it has an atmosphere which is easily appreciated. Here the local hunt balls take place in the ballroom and it is therefore as useful to the neighbouring squires as it is to the American tourists. Sir Gordon Russell has also added dignity and fame to the village with his modern furniture workshops and excellent taste.

Broadway can hardly be thought to have solved its car-parking problems, and cars do not improve the appearance of an old village. Without harassing shoppers and visitors, however, it is difficult to say exactly what ought to be done. Before there were all these cars, Broadway was a favourite place for artists and intellectuals. Round about 1890 and 1900 there was a coterie of friends centred on the American actress Mary Anderson and her husband Antonio de Navarro, who made a beautiful home at Court Farm. Their house was really two old houses. Bell Farm had a medieval room, with crucks, converted into two floors with a splendid ceiling carved with angels in the 16th c, and it was joined to the other by a music room designed by the architect A. N. Prentice. Here, the artists Sargent, Millet and Abbey and the garden designer Alfred Parsons, who all had houses in the village, could meet for chamber music. Parsons designed the garden so that it should be seen from the house, and seldom has there been such a beautiful composition of house and garden together. The uninterrupted view up the Fish Hill escarpment is unmatched. The two old farmhouses have quality. Court Farm was bought by the de Navarros in 1895 and Bell Farm by Valerie Maud White, the composer, at about the same time. Bell Farm had been a Society for the Protection of Ancient Buildings subject in 1892, and William Morris was interested in it. He had written his letter founding the Society for the Protection of Ancient Buildings from Broadway Tower in 1876 and he was very much responsible for the conservation and cult of Broadway in the 1880s, a cult which led to the gentrification of most of the cottages.

Henry James, writing in *Harpers Magazine*, New York, in 1889 in an article entitled 'Our Artists in Europe', says of Broadway, 'The place has so much character that it rubs off on the visitor, and if in an old garden with old gates and old walls, and old summer-houses, he lies down on the old grass it is ten to one he will be converted. It is delicious to be at Broadway . . .' This article probably made the reputation of Broadway among Americans. The artist Edwin Abbey commented that it 'did not much help the privacy of the place'.

BROADWELL, *Oxfordshire* (4m NE of Lechlade), forms with Kencot part of the group of charming stone-built villages situated in the low-lying country between the Thames and the Cotswolds. In general character they closely resemble the villages of the Cotswolds proper, and all their ancient churches have considerable

interest and beauty. Broadwell is very small and has a surprisingly large church with a magnificent tower and spire which can be seen for miles around in this flat country. The 13th-c spire is octagonal and is linked with the corner pinnacles by small flying buttresses, a neat method of connecting an octagon to a square. The interior is very light because the big Perp windows are filled with clear glass; but the walls were disastrously scraped in 1873 by E. G. Bruton. That is the only thing one can say against Broadwell.

Immediately NW of the church is the Manor Farmhouse designed by Richard Pace, an architect-builder from Lechlade, in 1804. The central bay breaks forward under a pediment which has concave sides and a semi-circular lunette. On the side facing the church the windows have Gothick glazing. There is a pond, farm buildings and a very grand pair of stone gate piers on the lane, now drive-less. The lane leads straight on into Kencot past a thatched cottage, big chestnut tree, preaching cross, table tombs in the churchyard and the Five Bells Inn.

Kencot is a little larger than Broadwell and in 1978 won the Marlborough trophy for the best-kept small village in Oxfordshire. Again the church is a delight, with a Norman sculpture over the door of Sagittarius shooting a monster, and a plastered interior with a monument to a Colchester from Westbury Court, Gloucestershire. Kencot House is charming, early 18th-c, with windows with arched keystoned heads, close to the main road at the far end of the village.

BUCKLAND, *Glos*. Writing his diary on 1 December 1840, the Cotswold Parson, Rev. F. E. Witts says, 'Buckland is a retired village in a dell under the hills extending from Stanway towards Broadway, looking at this season as little to advantage as possible; but it must have great attractions in summer among fine timber trees, and surrounded by rich meadows and pastures. The church is on a bank, where the valley is contracted between two wooded hills. The church porch is on the north. A very striking feature occurs on opening the door, viz. on the L formed out of the wall, a holy water stoup'.

In the intervening 140 years nothing has changed except that the elm trees are dead, and many people have come and gone. It is a tiny village, but it has a timeless air. People still ride their horses through the village and up the track to **Snowshill** – the steep banks are very good for horses' wind. Others, with antiquarian interests, come to see the little church which has much to offer. William Morris was so thrilled with it that he paid for the restoration of the 15th-c glass E window. A generation later Detmar Blow restored the rectory which also has a window with 15th-c stained glass – products of the Malvern Priory school of glass workers. Some say it is the oldest rectory in England: it has a medieval hall with carved angels on the hammerbeams.

There is a table tomb in the churchyard, just E of the church, to Col. Bernard Granville who

P. D. Turner

The Lamb Inn, Burford

died in 1727 and his wife. They were the parents of the celebrated Mrs Delany, who in her autobiography makes one or two slight references to the village of her childhood. There is also the grave of a lady-in-waiting to Queen Mary. When George V died everyone in the village wore black.

BURFORD, *Oxfordshire*. This is a genuinely old wool place, and it has much more history than a village like Broadway. It also has very considerable architectural merit. To begin with there is a splendid large church with a spire which is right in the village, and visible up and down the Windrush valley as well as from the hills either side.

The main street is rather steep, dipping down from the Cotswold gateway to the river and bridge at the bottom. If, on the other hand, the village is approached from Shipton-under-Wychwood we enter past Compton Mackenzie's old house with twin Flemish gables, over the narrow bridge controlled by traffic lights, and we are immediately in an impressive enclave of ashlar-fronted houses. The feeling is more Georgian than Tudor, though there are plenty of Tudor houses, with gables and mullioned windows. However, the wonderful baroque Methodist Chapel sets the very high standard, and there is a somewhat similar house called The Mansion in a side street. Another good early 18th- or late 17th-c house is Roger Warner's, with its *piano nobile* windows on the first floor.

Part of the attraction of Burford today is indeed Roger Warner himself, the fabulous Quaker antique dealer, who has provided most of the furniture for Williamsburg in Virginia (and that is saying something), and many other places. Antique dealers think that the large number of them in the High Street does their business more

good than harm; but there is none whose taste is as impeccable as Roger Warner's, albeit Frank Williams's must run it pretty close.

In Sheep Street there are two famous hotels The Lamb and The Baytree, and opposite are the headquarters of the *Countryman* magazine.

CASTLE COMBE, *Wilts.* There is a car park outside the village; in fact it is quite a little walk down a rather narrow lane. The streets in the village have double yellow lines everywhere so that people are obliged to put their cars in the car park whether they like it or not. The reason for this is of course that Castle Combe is remarkably picturesque and unspoilt even if a bit self-conscious. It also has real beauty. The church is magnificent with an example of EE, Dec, and Perp windows, one in each of the three E gables facing the entrance from the village and thus providing a complete lesson in Gothic architecture at one glance. Rising behind this is a terrific Perp tower with a crocketed pinnacle and diagonal buttresses like the Cotswold churches. In front is the central Market Cross with its hipped roof.

The village is on a hillside, and the main street narrowly descends with stone-built gabled cottages tightly packed either side to a perfectly picturesque river at the bottom. On the other side is the manor house, now an hotel. This is a large low-gabled 16th-c mansion which was Victorianized, and looks a comfortable hotel again in the most beautiful setting, complete with lawns, river and a huge wellingtonia.

THE CERNEYS, *Glos.* **South Cerney** (3m SE of Cirencester), is a large fairly compact village; but whether it can still be thought of as attractive is another matter. Its proximity to large gravel pits and lakes has altered its sleepy afternoons. Lorries full of gravel rush through the village, or leisure seekers come to sail or race their boats on the water. There are bridges over the Churn, gazebos, manor houses and a street called Bow Wow. The church is notable for its splendid Norman carved S doorway, like the ones at Quenington (q.v.). There are clasping beak heads continuing down the jamb shafts, like those at Mesland near Blois. Another great work of art is the wooden Head of Christ and His Foot from a Crucifix, perhaps Spanish, and brought back from Compostela by a pilgrim.

North Cerney, which is higher up the Churn, 4m N of Cirencester, also has a very beautiful church, full of interesting things including a rood screen by F. C. Eden. The village is on the opposite side of the main road to the church and is rather ordinary; but visually all is redeemed by the church and two lovely classical houses, one near the church and the other in the village opposite.

CHIPPING CAMPDEN, *Glos.,* is probably now the most famous village in the Cotswolds and it still is a village though in the past it was evidently easier to call it a small town. The *Shell Guide* in 1970 said: 'till the coming of the motor the town remained remote and peaceful'. The Cotswold Parson (Rev. F. E. Witts), in 1836, said 'Campden is a dull, clean, disused market town. In former times of greater prosperity it was the seat of an active trade in woollen cloths; but those days and that trade have long since passed away. The only remaining indications are the ancient market house situate in the fine wide street, with many good houses of a century or more standing and others boasting a much higher antiquity with gable ends, fine oriel windows and other remains of the domestic architecture of by-gone centuries.' This description, although 140 years old, is accurate enough to quote today, because Campden has not lost those old houses. They are still there. Could this perhaps be something to do with C. R. Ashbee who in 1902 moved his Guild of Handicrafts here, bringing a community of over 100 people from London? He restored a quantity of the houses in the main street. Then in 1929 F. L. Griggs formed the Campden Trust which since then has worked closely with the National Trust, so that conservation is constantly in people's thoughts. (*See colour plate facing page 225.*)

In the 17th c Campden was well-served by Sir Baptist Hicks who built the beautiful almshouses in the shape of the letter J for James I. Close by are the Renaissance lodges of his great house, built in 1613 but destroyed by Cromwell. And all in the same unforgettable picture is the complete late Perp church in all its glory with an exquisite tower based on that of Gloucester Cathedral. The surroundings of such architectural delights must not be spoilt by us or our descendants.

Westington is a hamlet of Campden on the SW with an old farmhouse restored and enlarged. There are other residences here, all beautifully maintained behind a broad grass verge to the road. On Westington Hill, which leads to the quarry, is a little Jacobean conduit house made by Sir Baptist for the inmates of his almshouses. Another road goes to **Broad Campden** where Ashbee made a Norman chapel into a house for the Indian philosopher Dr Coomaraswamy. The secret of so much beauty is the stone, which is a golden ashlar very good for building.

COGGES, *Oxfordshire,* was a medieval village on the SW outskirts of Witney. Owing to the action of the Oxfordshire County Council in making the Manor Farm into a museum Cogges can be viewed probably in a more rustic condition than most villages. After we have paid and got past the turnstile we are in a farmyard which would not have altered greatly through the ages except that there are pieces of 19th-c farm equipment on show. The manor of Cogges was settled when the Domesday Book was written. The first manor stood on the banks of the Windrush, surrounded by moats fed from the river. These moats still survive though dry. In the 13th c a new house was built to which major alterations were made in the 16th and 17th c. A new wing was added on the E. The external appearance of the house has altered little since then. A village grew up farming the fields round the manor. Later there was a priory with fish ponds; deserted earthworks and field systems can still be seen. Remains of the priory exist in the vicarage, and the tithe barn is now the school. The church is set in a pleasant churchyard with Irish yews, and it has an unusual tower placed diagonally across the W end of the N aisle. It is a 12th-c building enlarged in the 14th c. There is a rather stunning monument to a William and Sara Blake and their 22-year-old son (died between 1681 and 1701) with three busts, the lady *décolleté* and the gentlemen be-wigged.

CORNWELL, *Oxfordshire,* 3½m W of Chipping Norton. The village and manor house are the creation of Clough Williams-Ellis in 1939. The house is beautifully situated on a small hill overlooking an elaborate formal garden laid out by him. He terraced the valley S of the house and canalized the stream into an artificial pool. From a gateway on the road there is a vista directly in line with the front of the house. The ballroom on the NE was added by Clough Williams-Ellis, who also entirely rebuilt the tiny village, and, I expect, planted the pleached lime avenues.

The cottages, stone-built and stone-roofed, are on a hillside sloping down to a stream and the village hall (once the school) has been remodelled in neo-Georgian style. The village green, which has been enclosed by stone walls ending in piers with ball finials, is furnished as a children's playground. The group has the stamp of Portmeirion upon it, and is charming in consequence, contrived though it may be. For instance, the village hall has a bowed end with a hipped Stonesfield roof, tall Queen Anne-like windows with glazing bars, and an elaborate bellcote-cum-chimney-stack. In front there are cobblestones, and cars

Gillian Darley

*The village hall at Cornwell, built in
the 1930s*

have to cross the stream through the splash of a
ford. It all makes a very pretty scene.

DAGLINGWORTH, *Glos.* (3m NW of Cirencester), is on the Dunt together with the Duntisbourne villages in a delectable valley, which runs
almost parallel to the Gloucester–Cirencester
Roman road, Ermine Street, now part of the link
between the M4 and the M5. But it is completely
rural, in fact the lane passes not only through the
river but along its course for some distance, a
convenience for washing cart wheels in the past.

Daglingworth possesses Anglo-Saxon sculptures in the church, making an unforgettable
impact on the visitor, so well preserved are they
and so poignant in their simple fervour. It is
indeed one of the shrines of art in England. Near
the church is a rather gaunt square Georgian
house which stands up without much shelter, but
below it the village looks comfortable and attractive. There is a large Victorian former rectory on
the stream, village hall, and cottages which belong to the Duchy of Cornwall, all spread out with
nice gardens, and all built of oolitic limestone.

The Duntisbourne villages are further upstream: **Duntisbourne Rouse** has a well-known
little church, and **Duntisbourne Abbots** is charmingly situated, with some pretty cottages.

DIDMARTON, *Glos.* (7m NE of Chipping
Sodbury), is a pretty Georgian-looking village
quite near William Kent's Worcester Lodge
entrance to Badminton Park. There are stone-
built houses with stone roofs and regular fronts
punctuated with sash windows; others have
rendered or even painted façades. Kingsmead
House, which is larger than the rest, has an octagonal gazebo strategically placed on the highway
to see the coach coming from Bath, as it may

have been with Jane Austen inside, on her way to
Northanger Abbey after stopping at Petty France.
It also has a Gothick yew house in the garden,
suitable for a hermit.

On the other side of the road is one of the two
churches, and the most interesting, although it is
declared redundant and at present has a notice
to this effect on its open door. It is to be hoped that
it will be taken over by the Redundant Churches
Fund so that its 18th-c look and simple Georgian
furnishings can be preserved for the future. It
was unrestored in the 19th c because a new church
was then built which is not nearly so pretty as
little St Lawrence's, and if one was thinking only
in architectural terms the Victorian church is the
one which ought to have been made redundant,
unless St Lawrence can be looked after by the
Fund. Between the two churches is the Manor, a
house which has seen grander days.

EASTLEACH, *Glos.* (4m N of Lechlade),
would be in the top category of villages if it depended solely on the scenic quality and the fact
that it has two medieval churches almost within
a stone's throw and separated by the River Leach.
Architecturally however most of the cottages are
19th-c estate workers' homes formerly owned by
Sir Thomas Bazley and not cottages of an earlier
period. Originally there were two different
manors held by different lords. **Eastleach Martin**,
or Bouthrop (pronounced Butherop), was founded by a Norman called Fitzpons. The church has
the atmosphere of an unrestored building, completely countrified with its oil lamps, medieval
oak benches and 17th-c pews, and its marvellous
Dec windows. The other church, of **Eastleach
Turville**, is even more beautiful with a S doorway
in the same vibrant style as the Quenington (q.v.)
doorways though not so elaborate: both were de
Lacy properties. Inside it has a spacious EE
chancel. It would be difficult to find a village with
two such lovely churches. The Keble family
were Lords of the Manor in the 16th c and in 1815
John Keble, author of *The Christian Year* became
curate. He was also in charge of the other church,
and the flat stone bridge over the river is called
Keble's Bridge to this day.

The village is mostly situated on the Turville
side and is built on a bank. Greenbury House was
incredibly romantic until it was over-restored.
It was earlier than the date-stone 1738, and had
a Chinese wallpaper (now most probably in
America), and a 19th-c Gothic wing with a
traceried window overlooking the valley. Next
door was the home, until she died, of Nadia
Benois, Peter Ustinov's mother.

FAIRFORD, *Glos.*, is on the eastern edge of the
county, where it is flatter, and near where the
Coln runs into the Upper Thames. In medieval
times it was a manor of the Earls of Warwick,
which fell to the Crown, so that when the wool
merchant John Tame paid for rebuilding the
church after *c.* 1480 the manor belonged to
Henry VII. This may account for the superior

quality of the stained glass which has survived in every window of the church and forms one of the most complete collections in England. There is a theory that it is a memorial to Prince Arthur of Wales, and certainly after the divorce of Henry VIII the manor was given to the Princess of Wales (Catherine of Aragon). The glass is designed by different artists, Flemish and English, and shows background scenes derived from both countries. The architecture is Perp of the most elegant kind, and the church is set in the middle of the village in a large churchyard with the river on one side and a village square on the other. Fairford is a large village; in fact, it is a bustling place, with a wide street having a disproportionately narrow entrance.

The houses are stone-built without showing any outstanding architectural qualities except for the former big house in the park which was unfortunately demolished after World War II. The park buildings have also gone, but the river is artificially broader in the park before it flows out in a cascade by the old mill. This was achieved by Eames, a follower of Capability Brown.

Croft House garden is walled and has a gazebo, strategically placed for departures by coach. In the same back lane is the cottage hospital and new vicarage. When John Keble wrote *The Christian Year* he was living at home with his father and family in what became known as Keble House. It had a large orchard which is still a private sanctuary in the village. Neither he nor his father were ever vicars of Fairford; but his great-grand-nephew Canon Edward Keble was vicar. He died in 1978.

The aerodrome used to be a home of Concorde, and now it is the Americans who are there in the role of strategical defence. The aerodrome cuts off Fairford from the country on that side. Kempsford church has a splendid Perp tower and at Whelford the tiny church is designed by G. E. Street. They are either side of the aerodrome.

FILKINS, *Oxfordshire* (5m S of Burford on the A361), is now quite a sizable village but it was originally only a hamlet of Broadwell. The Roman road called Akeman Street running from Verulamium (St Albans) to Corinium (Cirencester) crosses the northern portion of the medieval parish of Broadwell which extended from about 2m S of Burford to the Thames at Kelmscott, a distance of about 8m. There is no evidence of a church at Filkins before the middle of the 19th c when in 1857 the church was built by the distinguished Victorian architect G. E. Street, with a hexagonal E end, French Gothic windows and a steeply-pitched tile roof. This building is not exactly out of key but it is quite different to the rest of the village, which is strictly Cotswold in feeling with stone-roofed stone-built cottages and houses. Even the council houses are built of stone with natural stone roofs.

The village lane winds about between the garden walls and some big stone fences, made of large flat stones which can also be used for hoods for cottage porches. It is quite unspoilt but definitely cared-for. There are stone barns, huge chestnut trees which were in full flower on 1 June, together with wistaria climbing up the houses, or montana clematis almost onto the roofs; one garden with an umbrella cedar, another with a great topiary yew hedge, and at the end of the village, Pear Tree Farm, dated 1688 and the cottage next door 1804. There is also a post office shop. The big house is difficult to see, but it was rebuilt in 1914, in Jacobean style, we read in Miss Sherwood's Pevsner, and the stables are by Richard Pace of Lechlade, 1809. Its presence is felt more than seen, and no doubt Filkins would not be what it is if it were not there.

FRAMPTON-ON-SEVERN, *Glos.* (1½m W of the A38, 8m S of Gloucester), is in the vale between the Severn and the Cotswold escarpment, and is therefore flat. The village green is divided in the middle by the road and must be about ¾m long and 1500ft wide. Approaching from the N we can see the mountains of distant Wales. At this end there are brick Georgian houses with sash windows enriched with voussoirs and keystones below an enormous skyscape. Then on the E is William Halfpenny's Orangery designed in Gothic with a tower and ogee windows, and this shows we are near to Frampton Court visible but partly screened by ilex trees and chestnuts. This wonderful house, built 1731–3, probably by the Bristol architect John Strachan, with large Vanbrugh-inspired chimneys, has very fine masonry and is raised up steps with low wings either side. It is the seat of the Clifford family, and opposite on the other side of the green is their original manor house built in the 15th c and partly timber-framed. There is a rectangular canal in front of the Orangery but this cannot be seen from the green.

As we continue to the S we pass the duck pond on our right, and houses and cottages with thatched roofs and gables. Here the houses are closer together and there are some small 19th-c shops. The road then bends, and we are out of the green in a village street with houses close together, and following the now winding road past later building more spread out we arrive at the church, which is set apart close to the Berkeley-Gloucester Canal, and in view of the Canal Keepers' little classical Doric house. The church tower has an open parapet with pinnacles. A Judas tree hangs over the churchyard wall. Inside this beautiful church it is light and airy with mostly clear glass windows but some medieval glass. Note the Romanesque lead font. Also note the tablet by John Pearce who calls himself a Statuary and Diagraphist; this is also a memorial to his two youngish brothers one of whom he describes as an Accomptant and Professor of Music. His style is also to be found on a gravestone in the churchyard which is carved with a weeping willow.

GREAT TEW, *Oxfordshire* (6m E of Chipping Norton), has recently been designated an Outstanding Conservation Area. The outstanding part of the title means that it should get grants from the Historic Buildings Council; and just about time too. Its present decay had become a cause for national concern. With the cooperation of the landlord, and enlightened planning committees, it should now be preserved as a unique example of 18th-c landscape improvement. The village, parkland, church, big house and farms were planned by J. C. Loudon in 1808 as an agricultural improvement scheme combined with landscape gardening, which he called 'landscape husbandry'. Loudon was only 25 at the time, and his work here was a wonderful experience for a man who later became a pioneer in town and country planning. General Stratton gave him complete control over 132 workers, and the planning of roads, drainage, fences, buildings and plantations. Loudon's 'Theories of Beauty with Utility' took shape at Great Tew, where he was able to demonstrate that, in spite of Repton and Gilpin, utility and the picturesque were not incompatible. He decried the practice of removing villages out of sight from the park, maintaining that vernacular cottages with $\frac{1}{4}$-acre gardens at the back, and neat small gardens opening on to the road, greatly contributed to the visual amenity of the landlord's estate. In fact many of the cottages at Great Tew had been built in the 17th c by Lord Falkland, and they survive today. One cottage is dated 1636, and is distinguished by a coat of arms and buttresses. The Falkland Arms Inn has a newly re-thatched roof. Some improvements to living conditions were made in the 18th c and elegant touches like the oval niche dated 1728. General Stratton began picturesque improvements in the Loudon era but it was probably Thomas Rickman, architect for the new owner, Matthew Boulton, in the 1820s, who gave many of the cottages picturesque porches and other features which reinforced the village's rusticity. Its oolitic-limestone buildings tinged golden brown with iron content, and roofed with gabled thatch, present a wholly contrived picture of the traditional English village, complete with church and mansion set somewhat apart, vicarage, post office, shop, school, stocks, and terraced cottages with front gardens edged by quickset hedges, cedars and monkey-puzzles.

THE GUITINGS, *Glos.* (7m W of Stow-on-the-Wold), are two villages in the North Cotswold which is the original Cotswold country, derived from the Old English 'Cod's forest'.

Guiting Power can be approached by a gated road through rolling wooded wolds from Hawling, but more normally the way to it is past the park of Guiting Grange where the mansion has been demolished but the Victorian lodge and many pretty trees survive – chestnuts, sycamores, beeches and limes. From there it is $\frac{1}{2}$m to the stone-built village which has a green with a War Memorial Cross, and many neat stone cottages, with gables, stone roofs, mullioned windows and well-cared-for blue doors. The post office has hanging flower baskets in summer. Everything is simple and perfectly well-kept, even to the mowing of the village green. The pub is appropriately called The Farmers' Arms. By the green there is a well-lettered inscription to Mrs Cochrane who died in 1977 and who it says 'gave much to Guiting Power'. Some of the new housing consists of terraces. This has a good appearance. The churchyard is also well-mown and surrounds a somewhat solid-looking square castellated tower.

Temple Guiting is further up the Windrush river. There is a good church and Georgian house, well-sited on the banks of the river. It was considered delectable by the Templars who founded a preceptory here in the mid-12th c, and in the early 19th c. Parson Witts could not understand how it was that the owners of the Georgian house could leave it for a London season, and then a Spa season, when their own home was so beautiful. There is not so much village as at Guiting Power.

HATHEROP, *Glos.,* 9m E of Cirencester. This is a model village built in the 1860s. Here is an atmosphere of firm proprietorship and restrained grandeur, with deer in Williamstrip Park opposite Hatherop Castle, now a girls' school. The two mansions stand near together, with their land spreading away in opposite directions, and the River Coln passing close by. Cottage No. 10 has the datestone 1868, and was built for Sir Thomas Bazley who bought the Hatherop estate in 1867. It is typical of the others. They are stone-built with modest Gothic features.

The church, which is in the pocket of the castle, is approached from the village by a long path running behind the cottages on the edge of the park. It is well worth a visit if you are a Victorian enthusiast as it contains the mortuary chapel of Barbara Lady de Maulay by William Burges. It was built when Burges was in partnership with Henry Clutton, who rebuilt the castle, 1850–6. The loss of the elm trees is very noticeable; but the gardens at Hatherop are good.

KELMSCOT, *Oxfordshire,* is situated in the flat deeply rural area of the Upper Thames, $2\frac{1}{2}$m E of Lechlade. Famous for Kelmscott Manor, the country home of William Morris, its total unpretentiousness comes as a slight shock to the visitor. Now that most of the old trees seem to be dead the house is possibly not so attractive as it was when Rossetti was flirting with Janey Morris; but even then the village bored Rossetti, who complained that it was 'the doziest dump of old grey beehives'. The village is spread out and the Manor House where Morris lived is not near the church where he is buried. There are, however, some sophisticated buildings in between, which were not there in Morris's time: the village hall by Ernest Gimson, and cottages by Philip Webb and Gimson. The village hall has a relief of Morris carved by George Jack from a sketch by Webb. The cottages are all impeccably designed and built in stone. Some of the garden fences are built of large, upright stones as they are at Filkins, and it must be a local characteristic. The Manor House, half hidden by its garden wall, and next to a farmyard, has its well-known charm. The roof has many gables and ball finials and some of the mullioned windows have small triangular pediments, Renaissance details which have somehow penetrated here. In fact, the village was obviously prosperous *c.* 1700, and there is a group of large farmhouses at the other end of the village, all examples of the change from traditional gables to the classical square box.

Morris delighted in the roof of his house with its graduated stone tiles and wrote, 'It gives me the same sort of pleasure in their orderly beauty as a fish's scales or a bird's feather.' Inside, the house has been restored by the Society of Antiquaries and is sometimes open to the public. It contains furniture and textiles designed by Morris. The medieval church is also well worth looking at.

Rather puzzlingly, the name of the village is spelt with one 't', but that of the Manor House with two.

LACOCK, *Wilts.,* is one of the very best villages in the county. It is compact, without any loss of scale anywhere, and built in a square of streets. The houses are stone-built with mostly stone roofs, but several are timber-framed. There are architectural features everywhere. The Carpenters Arms has Georgian windows with moulded stone architraves. The church is quite large with a spire, Perp N chapel, and transepts which have pitched roofs and look almost domestic. One house, built of ashlar, has a set of classical capitals. Nearby a brick house has white shutters to the windows. Older picturesque buildings have gables, with timber framing jettied out or oriel windows.

However, I suppose for me the real reason why Lacock is so unutterably precious is the Abbey and its setting. At one end of the village there is this house, Lacock Abbey. As we walk past the museum of early photography (very interesting, with many examples of photographs taken by William Henry Fox Talbot as early as 1839 and afterwards) and enter the drive, we can see across the cow-grazed park a Strawberry Hill Gothic mansion by Sanderson Miller against an unspoilt background of English countryside. But

it is in fact a 13th-c Augustinian Nunnery, and has a hidden Perp cloister. Imposed upon this, in a most tactful way, is the house of the 16th-c Sharingtons and then the Talbots, all now very well shown by the National Trust. The interior has tremendous charm and atmosphere, and must have been a most livable house with a beautiful outlook. Even if you are expecting something like this, it comes as a surprise, such is the improbable juxtaposition of a well-preserved Nunnery and the house of the earliest Victorian photographer.

LANGFORD, *Oxfordshire* (6m NW of Faringdon), is celebrated for its quite exceptional church, which incorporates the most important Saxon remains in Oxfordshire. The parish was listed in the Domesday survey as among the royal estates, and this could account for the high quality of the work which shows a knowledge of development in the chief centres of art in England in the 10th and 11th c and is certainly not by local craftsmen. The tower is entirely Saxon, and there are two pieces of sculpture reset on the porch, a Saxon relief of the Crucifixion, and a headless figure of Christ triumphant. The church is just out of the village which has winding lanes and several fairly large houses; but there is no squire or particularly big house. All are stone-built and the village belongs to the Broadwell group of stone villages in the low-lying country between Thames and Cotswold which resembles in general character the villages on the wolds. Lockey House has windows with 18th-c moulded stone surrounds in five bays and a gazebo in the garden. Another house has the datestone 1655 in one of its tall gables.

The village is alive with activity, and some 20 gardens are open for viewing on one day in aid of funds for the new village hall appeal.

LATTON, *Wilts.,* is on the A419, 1m N of Cricklade. This is flat Upper Thames country. The Cricklade by-pass starts at Latton and there is a most rewarding view of the old Wharfinger's house with its large classical pediment on a disused canal. It is very easy to imagine that it is the Brenta

Lacock Abbey

Iris Fresson: Spectrum

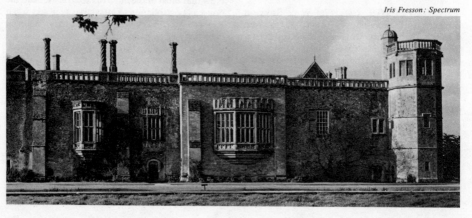

Canal, and that we are seeing a small Paladian villa, somewhere near Venice. If nothing else this puts Latton on the map. The water-meadows here grow wild fritillaries. The rest of Latton, however, does not look at all Italian. It is extremely modest with some largish Victorian-looking houses and a Norman church splendidly restored by that most forceful Victorian architect William Butterfield, who rebuilt the chancel, and was accustomed to provide pews more comfortable for kneeling than sitting. There are also some charming 17th-c Cotswold stone houses scattered along the A419.

Originally Latton was part of the estate of the Earl of St Germans which is now owned by the Cooperative Wholesale Society. The community comprises farmworkers, business people, and retired folk, with a small council estate, and a block of flats for the elderly.

LECHLADE, *Glos.* (6m NW of Faringdon), is on the Oxfordshire–Berkshire–Wiltshire border where the Thames forms the boundary. The tall church spire can be seen from the flat water-meadows where the river meanders through on its way past Buscot Rectory towards Oxford. There is a bridge known as St John's Bridge, near a lock, which is good for picnicking, just as the river is good for boating.

Lechlade had an enterprising late-Georgian architect called Pace who designed several houses such as the old vicarage, but Lechlade's most delightful feature is the gazebo, a fashionable adjunct repeated at the end of every respectable garden. A good example is the garden of Church House which is next to the churchyard in which Shelley wrote: 'Here could I hope . . . that death did hide from human sight sweet secrets . . .'

Lechlade is a busy place, and takes quite a lot of traffic on its way to Swindon from the Midlands. The street is wide and the houses and shops look attractive, particularly in the Market Place. The river is crossed here by the Halfpenny Bridge, a fine 18th-c semicircular stone arch.

MARSHFIELD, *Avon* (6m N of Bath), has a long High Street lined with grey stone houses, some with brown pantile roofs, or Welsh slates. The houses are mostly Georgian, or look so, with their sash windows and smart doorcases. There is rather a lot of dark coloured pointing to the rubble walls; but some have ashlar fronts, and a great many of them have bay or bow windows which enable the occupants to see and enjoy what is going on in the street, without getting wet or even being seen too much. It is a distinctly stylish street architecturally, and perhaps the best building is an old coaching inn called The Catherine Wheel, which must be early 18th-c and by some Bath architect-builder. Today there survive a quantity of unsophisticated shops, the grocer, the draper, all with Victorian shop fronts. Quite rightly it is listed as a Conservation Area. At one end is the church with its splendid Perp tower and a spectacular open parapet pierced with trefoils alternately upside-down. At the other end are the

P. D. Turner

The Saxon church at Langford

Almshouses surrounded by a monastic-looking wall. In between, the street is more or less straight, and provides the visitor with a nostalgic feeling of earlier times. However, on the outskirts there are developments to the N; but on the S side of the churchyard the land falls away delightfully with a view of wooded valleys towards Bath.

MINSTER LOVELL, *Oxfordshire* (2½m W of Witney), is one of the prettiest places on the Windrush, set well off the beaten track. The river here is quite wide as it flows past the modern-style buildings of the Mill Conference Centre, a better site for which could hardly be imagined. Opposite is the Swan Inn, which is partly timber-framed and has a very steeply pitched stone roof. Some of the cottages are thatched. A brook flows in front of them crossed by flat stone-slab bridges. The village street is picturesque as it ascends slightly up hill, and the houses become more 19th-c, till we come to a place where vehicles can go no further, and everyone has to walk to Minster Lovell Hall, which is an Ancient Monument. It was formerly one of the great houses of Oxfordshire, in a memorable setting in the unspoilt Windrush valley, still lush and pastoral with grazing cows in the water-meadows. The remains, although zealously tidied by the Department of the Environment, are still the most picturesque ruins. The house was built *c.* 1431–42. The Lovells were Yorkists, and after the defeat of Richard III at Bosworth in 1485 their estates were confiscated. The name Minster derives from the church. It was served by a small priory which in the late 12th c passed to the Benedictine Abbey of Ivry in Normandy. It was dissolved in 1414. The church was rebuilt by Lord Lovell in the 15th c.

NAUNTON, *Glos.* (6m W of Stow-on-the-Wold), was called Naunton-super-Cotswold in

1570 and it certainly could not be more Cotswold in character. It is situated near a great stone quarry in a cleft of the hills, and all its buildings are of stone. Like so many of these high-up places it is known for the different varieties of wild flowers which grow there. It has been quite a large village for a long time. In the early 19th c it was usually possible to obtain a fly from the coaching inn on the Stow-Cheltenham road. This was like catching a taxi if you missed the bus. The road descends into the village by the church where there are copper beeches at the lychgate. The church was rebuilt in Perp but the windows have since lost their tracery. There is a Perp tower and a Perp pulpit. Under the brass inscription in the chancel to Clement Barksdale, the 17th-c poet, is another to Charles Barksdale with these lines:

Young man lay to Thy heart this sacred truth
Remember thy Creator in thy youth.
Old man, if pious, do not thy death fear,
Having good hope of better things so near.

The churchyard has some good gravestones with lettering deeply cut in the age of taste – they compare most favourably with the rows of modern Nabrasina headstones. Leaving the church we cross the Windrush over a stone bridge and proceed along the village street. Several cottages and houses are set at right angles to the road and have stone walls and orchards. Everywhere in early July the elder trees are in flower – what tastes more delicious than an infusion of elder flowers? Some of the houses are very pretty 17th-c examples with old gables and mullion windows. Others, however, are faced in ashlar like the Black Horse Inn.

PAINSWICK, *Glos.* The stone of Painswick was quarried on the Beacon. It is a white limestone which goes grey and is such good building stone that it was used in Gloucester Cathedral. In the 17th and 18th c the many masons living in the village formed a 'school' of sculptors who created the imaginative tombstones in the churchyard intersected by lines of clipped yews.

The tall spire of the church can be seen on every approach, downhill on the Cheltenham road, or uphill from Stroud. The best view of all is from Bull's Cross over the valley, a view immortalized by Thomas Robins in his rococo painting from Pan's Lodge. He also painted the wooded gardens of Painswick House. Everything at Painswick is picturesque and dramatic owing to the steep hills. Any view from the village shows hills towering above the roof tops in a rather unEnglish way more reminiscent of Italy. This is perhaps what the early 20th-c architect Temple Moore had in mind when he designed the Italianate loggia and garden for a large house just S of the churchyard. A small boy who lived there can remember the decorations put up after World War I, and wondered why the barber's pole in Bisley Street was left up when the rest was taken down. Then in World War II a bomb fell in Friday Street creating one of the few open spaces among the narrow streets. Tibbiwell descended from here to a pin mill on the brook at the bottom of the valley, and Greenhouse Lane went up the other side and over Bull's Cross to **Slad** when Laurie Lee was having cider with Rosie.

Nowadays Painswick is more residential. All the gardens are infilled with new houses. Above the village towards the Beacon there are new housing estates before we get to the Arts and Crafts Almshouses and the hanging beech woods.

QUENINGTON, *Glos.* is a village on the Coln. The name means 'The women's farmstead'. Approached on the lane from Fairford (q.v.; 2½m S) past the tall Column in what was Fairford Park, we come to a bend in the road and suddenly look down on the village. The river and the millstream run almost parallel under two bridges, with the old Rectory and Knights' Mill on the bank of the millstream. Close by is the church, a small Norman building restored by the Gloucester Cathedral architect F. S. Waller in 1882, when he built on the vestry and bellcote, and porches N and S to protect the precious tympana which had hitherto been subjected to the weather. On the N the subject is the Harrowing of Hell witnessed by the face in the sun, and surrounded by very rich Norman carving: limpet shells, jacks-on-the-green, symbols of fertility, chevrons, and huge marguerites. On the S there is what is considered to be one of the first representations of the Coronation of the Virgin, close to a Heavenly Mansion, and surrounded by beak-heads and pellets as large as apples. These are a *tour de force* unequalled in the Cotswolds; the date is *c.* 1150. Soon afterwards the place became a Preceptory of the Knights Hospitaller, and the churchyard almost merges into the garden of the Knights' Mill. In the yard there is one unusual chest tomb in that it has a bale top combined with lyre ends. Otherwise the churchyard is cleared and has mown lawn, clipped yews and Florence Court yews. Nearby is the Knight's Gatehouse, opposite some cottages built new in 1974 in natural stone.

The village has several streets with mostly restored cottages and high garden walls and stone garages. The most stylish house is Quenington House, with an ashlar façade on the street and an ilex tree dropping its leaves in the middle of summer, a curious anachronism in high June. The pubs are called The Keepers Arms, with a very Victorian-looking gamekeeper painted on the sign reminding us we are near Earl St Aldwyn's estate, and The Earl Grey which also has a political sound. There is a pair of stone gateposts which look as if this once led somewhere important. Now, this end of the village has a light industry, Godwin's Pumps, and some new housing development round a green with newly planted trees.

SAPPERTON, *Glos.*, is situated between Cirencester and Stroud, on the edge of a most beautiful steep valley with hanging beech woods, and backed by Lord Bathurst's park and its broad 10-m ride squeezing the village into a narrow strip of cottages precariously balanced. There is something of a green, on the E side of which are spectacular examples of topiary in a cottage garden, which must have been clipped with pride for many a long day. Here the artist-craftsman, architect and furniture designer Ernest Gimson found many wheelwrights living in 1900. These he turned into cabinet-makers in a short-lived Utopia which collapsed with World War I.

Now many of the houses are let to Argentinian polo players. The beautiful Queen Anne church is one of seven, looked after by one clergyman, who is also Chaplain to the Royal Agricultural College at Cirencester. The 1st Lord Bathurst destroyed the manor house which was sited overlooking the valley on a green platform and which cries out to be excavated. The stones from Sapperton Manor were re-used in the park to build follies, and the woodwork went into the church so that the pews end in Jacobean Atlases. The good Lady Bathurst of the 19th c built another church for tenants at Frampton Mansell; but this is declared redundant, so whether the users of the old Great Western Railway will see its soaring Italianate campanile for much longer is doubtful.

THE SLAUGHTERS, *Glos.*, are a couple of villages between Bourton-on-the-Water and Stow-on-the-Wold. **Lower Slaughter** seems to catch the visitor who cannot find room in, or does not enjoy, the attractions of Bourton. It is picturesque and has the immediate effect of causing everyone to produce his camera. Even on fairly dark days people rush about clicking madly at river, trees and cottages, for that is what Lower Slaughter consists of. It could be peaceful, because, tourists apart, it seems to be quiet. The river is very clear and runs through the main street of the village, from a large brick-built mill, past some grey stone cottages, and the village hall, dated 1887 but remarkably Arts and Crafts looking for so early a date, and on, taking a bend to avoid the church. It is difficult to be very enthusiastic about the church, by Benjamin Ferry, 1867, with a fibre-glass tip to the spire. The Manor House was once an interesting building but it has been 'mucked about' and is now an hotel.

Upper Slaughter is quite different, and to me as attractive as Lower Slaughter is unattractive, and this is not wholly because it was the home of the Cotswold Parson who wrote *The Diary* – the Rev. F. E. Witts (1783–1854) – although the literary association is very strong. To start with, the River Eye, tributary of the Windrush, is more unsophisticated in Upper Slaughter village until it bursts into a lake in front of the old Rectory, now the Lords of the Manor Hotel. The square in the village has quality, which is not surprising as the cottage group was designed by Sir Edwin Lutyens, with some six-light windows and no dripmoulds; and the church in many ways is a beauty. It contains the splendid mortuary chapel of the Cotswold Parson designed by his friend Francis Niblett, and as it says, 'This monument was erected in testimony of the regard and esteem of many persons who possessed his friendship and who admired his character'. It resembles a medieval Founders' Tomb with a carved ogee-arched canopy covered in crockets, and cinquefoiled but with trefoils inside each foil; underneath is a chest tomb with a cross and text in its matrix. The chapel floor has good Victorian tiles, and the small window is dedicated to the parson's wife Margaret by their son Edward, who was the next rector, as indeed was his son after him; most of the windows and tablets are Witts memorials. A notice says that the *Diary of a Cotswold Parson* can be bought at the Lords of the Manor Hotel, which indeed is featured on the dust jacket. However, the house was very considerably altered by his son Edward, and has lost its Georgian appearance in favour of comfortable Victorian, but the pleasure ground remains recognizably the same and one expects to see Mrs Backhouse taking a walk therein. Surprisingly close to the pleasure ground and its tall trees is the old manor house, that ancient mansion which in Parson Witts's time was occupied by a farmer tenant of Lord Sherborne. On the other side are the rectory stables from where Parson Witts so often set off on horse-back, or in his carriage, and always uphill in almost every direction.

SNIGS END, *Glos.*, 7m N of Gloucester on the A417. Situated between the old villages of Staunton and Corse, this is a Chartist land colony, founded in 1847, but it had failed by 1853. Lowbands, also in Staunton parish, was another such colony, bought in 1846, and sold in 1858. The settlement was founded by Fergus O'Connor. Today there are 16 of these houses S of the road between Swan Inn and the church at Staunton, and nine others adjacent to Brook Farm. The smallholding communities were intended to be self-supporting and education was considered of great importance. The Snigs End School is the largest and most impressive of their buildings with a tall two-bay house surmounted by an open pediment in the centre, intended for the schoolmaster and mistress and school-rooms for boys and girls either side. It is now the Prince of Wales Inn.

The haphazard finances and muddled conception of the Chartist schemes doomed them from the start. O'Connor chose areas with bad soil and no accessible markets for his goods, and was faced with groups of patently unsuitable town people, while he himself lacked the necessary mental stability for his task. The villages, on the other hand, were well-built. Snigs End is laid out in a crescent form with sturdy stone-walled cottages which are still attractive today and in spite of later additions and alterations their simple classical design is apparent.

SOUTHROP, *Glos.*, is an attractive and well-cared for village in spite of some modern development on the approach from Fairford (3½m SW). It is in the flat country on the E edge of the Cotswolds merging into the Oxford plain. There is no development on the approach from Oxford-shire because the Manor House is situated at that end of the village, with its distinguished gateposts and magnificent barns, and opposite a restored millhouse on the River Leach. In the Manor farmyard is the very precious church, precious because of its Norman architecture and font, and its association with John Keble, who lived in the Old Vicarage, 1823–5, and there sowed the seeds of the Oxford Movement with Wilberforce, Isaac Williams and Hurrell Froude.

In the village attractive stone ball-finials seem fashionable everywhere. There is a magnificent barn profusely decorated with these ball-finials being converted into a house, in such a way it is hoped that the columbaria will not be disturbed. Stone cottages with stone roofs along the winding lanes all have well-kept gardens. A Georgian house with a rendered front, and a montana clematis climbing up to the television aerial, is opposite the new village hall which is untraditional but redeemed by being rendered like the house. There is a small green by the Swan Inn, chestnut trees, an old-fashioned post-office shop window, sheep grazing in the fields, and a very elegant Queen Anne house built of ashlar with quoins, called Fyfield Manor, just beyond the dovecote of the former manor of the old Keble family of which little else now remains.

STANTON and **STANWAY**, *Glos.*, are two Cotswold villages nestling under the wooded edge of the escarpment. **Stanton** (½m E of A46, 2½m SW of Broadway, q.v.), has been described as a perfectly preserved village without blemish. This is partly due to the sympathetic restorations of its former owner, the architect Sir Philip Stott, who lived here 1906–37. His good example has been followed by the local authority whose council houses are built here in traditional style and natural stone. The church has a spire which often seems the case with churches situated just in the vale. It is also distinguished for its Perp S aisle and porch, added when a possession of Winch-combe Abbey, and for its 20th-c furnishings and stained glass by Sir Ninian Comper, who signs his windows with a wild strawberry. The E window, however, contains medieval glass from nearby Hailes Abbey.

Stanway (1½m SW), Stanton's aristocratic neighbour, consists of a delightful group of golden coloured buildings, mansion, and gate-house with memorable curvilinear gables surmounted by stone scallop shells, medieval church and tithe barn. High up in the gardens on the E is a pyramid from which in the 18th c came a formal waterfall and canal. In the days of country-house cricket and political hostesses Sir James Barrie designed a cricket pavilion for the Countess of Wemyss. Earlier in the 19th c Parson Witts, who was a non-resident vicar, describes on one of his rare visits from Upper Slaughter how the Wemyss family 'kick up' a dance with their servants in the evening.

Stanway War Memorial has a bronze St George by Alexander Fisher, with names by Eric Gill, and the Memorial Hall is neo-classical and designed by Detmar Blow.

STANTON HARCOURT, *Oxfordshire,* is rather difficult to find in the flat country W of Oxford. It is probably best to approach from Eynsham (3m to the N), rather than by crossing the river at **Newbridge** to the S attractive though that bridge is with its six pointed arches of 14th- or 15th-c date. The village really consists, apart from several attractive thatched cottages and some new housing, of the buildings of the Manor House, which are indeed surprising, in a group with the church, and near the Parsonage House, all of which are of extreme interest. The church is a mausoleum of the ancient and distinguished family of Harcourt. The chancel is very stylish work of *c.* 1250. The Harcourt chapel is *c.* 1470 and has Perp architecture with super-mullions in the windows and quatrefoils in the parapet, and a fabulous collection of effigies, statues and monuments of all dates. Near to the Norman Perp tower is another tower called Pope's tower, but actually *c.* 1460–71, and possibly by the same mason as the Harcourt chapel, none other than William Orchard of Magdalen College and the Divinity School. Another separate building is the Great Kitchen, one of the most complete medieval kitchens in England, and certainly the most spectacular, with its octagonal pyramid roof surmounted by a lead griffin. These two buildings are inside the garden walls of the manor which has a garden, with walks, and lake, and seems to surround the churchyard. The Parsonage is a perfect example of an unaltered house of *c.* 1675 situated by a chain of medieval fish ponds, E of the church.

Stanton Harcourt was too flat to suit the tastes of the 1st Earl Harcourt after his grand tour in the 18th c. Nuneham Courtenay (q.v.) provided a more picturesque and classical landscape nearer Oxford, so he decided to leave his old home and build another house, church and village at Nuneham, where he proceeded to destroy the existing church and cottages to improve his view. It is said that the inhabitants did not so much object to being re-housed as that their ancestors' bones were no longer protected in a churchyard, and they were not altogether surprised when poor Lord Harcourt, trying to rescue his dog from a disused well in the former village, now his park, fell in himself and was suffocated.

THE SWELLS, *Glos.*, consist of two villages, Upper and Lower (or Nether) Swell, situated on the Dikler in a delectable valley 1m N and W of high-up Stow-on-the-Wold. **Upper Swell** has a charming manor house which has recently been restored. It contains a 16th-c upper room with a modelled plaster ceiling with a frieze of sphinxes. The two-storey porch is *c.* 1625, and again shows Renaissance details. However, the most interesting feature from the point of view of the village is that it was landscaped in the 18th c. Behind the house there is a landscape containing a classical

J. Allan Cash

Stanton

bridge of two arches and a lake, hill, and appropriate trees. Next to the house stands a fascinating little church, with ashlar nave, bellcote, and very good Perp windows. The river flows round it reappearing at the Mill where there is an enlarged mill pond, and continuing under the road by an 18th-c bridge.

Lower Swell is slightly larger. In 1294 the Earl of Cornwall gave to the Abbot of Hailes 40 acres of pasture in this parish of good sheep-rearing country. Today there are some new houses besides an interesting church and a War Memorial designed by Sir Edwin Lutyens with a stone cenotaph. The buildings in the village, even the new ones, are all of stone and mostly still have stone roofs. The oldest houses are 17th-c including the Golden Ball Inn. The large house called Abbotswood was designed by Lutyens in 1902. He also laid out the gardens with a characteristic water garden connected to the side of the house.

In the 19th c, to be precise from 1850 to 1902, there was a remarkable rector with a passion for antiquarian pursuits. He made a collection of 4500 flint arrowheads, nearly all from a few square miles of his parish.

SWINBROOK and **ASTHALL**, *Oxfordshire*, are set in mild countryside where the modest hills of the E Cotswolds come down to the wide Windrush valley between Burford and Witney. Willow trees grow along the river. Swinbrook is a small village with 17th- and 18th-c farmhouses and

some early Victorian cottages in Tudor style which was then the rage. The former mill is now an inn and it is a popular place in summer near where the road crosses the river. S of the church was the mansion of the Fettiplace family built *c.* 1490, one of the great houses of Oxfordshire. In 1805 the last Fettiplace died and the house was demolished. No record of its appearance seems to remain. In the church the Perp E window, filled with clear glass coming down low, floods with light the remarkable Fettiplace monuments which consist of two fascinating trios of reclining gentlemen, one lot Tudor the other Stuart. A German land mine blew out the E window in 1940. In the churchyard are the graves of Hitler's friend Unity Mitford and of her sister the authoress Nancy Mitford.

Asthall is further along the valley and has another interesting church. In the churchyard there is a bale tomb which appears to be a unique survival as it is more explicitly carved to resemble a hearse and the addition of finials may represent the candle sockets of the hearse. It is the grave of Harman Fletcher, 1729–30, and should be guarded with more care than it evidently is. A large manor house overlooks the churchyard. The small village has stone-built cottages, an inn called Maytime, acacias and roses.

At **Asthall Leigh,** which is on higher ground away from the valley, and rather bare now that the elm trees are dead, there is a redundant church converted into a house. The church was built in

1861 and has no aisle with chancel and nave under one roof and was obviously a good subject for conversion; but it is a little disconcerting to find the font still *in situ* in the entrance passage when it was clearly the intention of the Church Commissioners that fonts should be removed from churches not in use. However, the stained-glass windows can be seen to advantage on the staircase.

WESTWELL, *Oxfordshire* (2m SW of Burford), has escaped 'the calculated cultivation and prettification now usual with anything so picturesque', wrote Miss Sherwood, though it must be admitted there is now a rather calculatedly pretty new house and garden near the church, and no harm done. Its charm consists of the church, rectory, manor and barns grouped around a small green with a duck pond. The War Memorial is a monolithic stone which incorporates a brass numeral from the clock of the Cloth Hall at Ypres, dedicated to the brave. It stands by the pond which is surrounded by wild yellow irises and is the home of moorhen. The cottages are all stone built with steeply pitched stone roofs, and the tall walls of the manor garden have a gateway with stone sphinxes on the gateposts. Pond Cottage has a post office collecting box set into its wall. The cottage next door has a spectacular clipped mixed golden and green privet archway over its porch, and a garden with a row of Irish yews. Then there is a William and Mary house faced in dressed freestone with cross mullion and transom windows and leaded lights, and Albertine roses introduced in 1921. Nothing could be more charming.

At the entrance to the churchyard there is a seat situated exactly right, overlooking the pond, placed here to commemorate the Queen's Silver Jubilee in 1977 and next a newly planted oak tree. The adjacent cow byres are incorporated into the new garden and have roses climbing up the pillars. An exquisitely pretty churchyard has a varied collection of chest tombs, some with 17th-c bale tops, a fashion emanating from nearby Burford. A path leads from the S door to the old rectory which is a large Queen Anne house faced in ashlar and with a hipped stone roof and modillion eaves cornice. Inside the church porch is a niche on the E wall with an ogee-shaped trefoil opening and embattled head which the visitor in July would probably find filled with sweet peas. The inside of the church is truly rewarding, with surprising rustic monuments, stained glass, and a magnificent roof.

WHITEWAY, *Glos.*, 6m NE of Stroud. 'Long after the Chartist land colonies had faded from public view, one practical attempt was made to set up a community based on a similar brand of self-sufficiency supported by home-based industry', writes Gillian Darley in *Villages of Vision.* This is the Whiteway village near Miserden in Gloucestershire. It was founded in 1898 by a group of Tolstoyan anarchists, who built their own houses, wooden shacks for the most part. The colony lasted, while many other such experiments failed, and exists today, in some respects still intact. The inhabitants still hold their land in common and support some small workshops. In the past they had a reputation as a bunch of eccentrics and were said to walk about with no clothes on, to the disappointment of at least one expectant adolescent who never caught the slightest glimpse of a nudist when passing through the village; but then it is situated on the cold, high-up Cotswold plateau.

The centre is an iron-fronted building, the Colony Hall, and each cottage is surrounded by a considerable area of ground. In spite of suburban incursions, of which there are many, such as house names inscribed in rustic boards, there still exists in the opinion of Miss Darley, 'an extraordinary air of an enclave and a historic continuity with the original founding members who laid out the network of earth footpaths which still link one house to the next.' This network of footpaths obviously, in the minds of the neighbouring villagers, facilitated the wife-swapping which they imagined went on.

If some of the theories of the small group who bought the original house with its 40 acres were not carried out, aspects of their communitarian principles still flourish and it continues to exist alone amid the wreckage of many other schemes. Community ideals have rarely proved translatable into reality, but utopias of course are a continuing currency.

WICKWAR. *Avon* (4m N of Chipping Sodbury), is rather like Marshfield, its not too distant neighbour, but on a somewhat smaller scale. Again there is a long straight High Street with Georgian houses either side, built of grey stone rubble, often with rendered elevations, pantile or Welsh slate roofs and brick chimneys. The windows are mostly sash, and there are several doorcases with classical hoods and elegant entrances with steps up and wrought-iron hand rails. As at Marshfield many houses have bay windows, and there are the small shops of the draper and others. More or less in the middle there is a clock tower on a town hall *c.* 1795, restored for the Queen's Silver Jubilee in 1977. At the far end of the village stands the church on a slight eminence and secluded by an avenue of beech trees which passes the air vent of the railway tunnel. From here we can see the chimneys of Devey's rectory, with their emphatic outline, on one side with the Duchess's trees beyond, and a nursery garden on the other. The churchyard contains table tombs and inside the porch are two well-lettered War Memorials; but the church is locked, and it requires quite a walk to fetch the key. If we did get in we would find that many of the memorials show Wickwar to have been a centre of the clothing industry; in fact John Leland described it in 1553 as a 'prayte clothinge tounlet', and there was a Weavers' Chapel used by the weavers and dyers for their Guild activities, restored in 1969.

The West Country

SOMERSET DEVON CORNWALL

Roger Kain

With contributions by Sally Dench, Jane Havers, Harriet Holt,
John Manterfield, Minda Phillips and Michael Turner

Many of the unifying traits of the SW peninsula counties (Somerset, Devon, Cornwall) stem from the proximity of land to the sea. No place even in inland Somerset is much more than 30 miles from the coast, while at its narrowest point near Penzance only four miles of land separate the Atlantic Ocean and the English Channel. The scenery of the West Country is one of its most valuable assets (two National Parks and eleven Areas of Outstanding Natural Beauty) and the scenic splendour of the coastline is undoubtedly the main attraction for tourists.

The influence of the sea is felt inland as well as on the coast, not least for the moderating effect it has on the climate. Winter rarely lasts long and spring arrives early. 'Mild' is an oft-used adjective in tourist guides; St Mawes on the tip of the Roseland peninsula in Cornwall claims to be the warmest wintering place in the British Isles, with average temperatures on a par with those on the French Riviera. By contrast, parts of the north coast are open to the full force of Atlantic gales, and at about 2000ft on Dartmoor blizzards have been known to drift snow to the level of upstairs windows.

Within the peninsula, the facts of geology, relief and settlement history interact to produce diversity within an overall unity: as varied a range of landscapes, in fact, as is to be found within a similar small compass anywhere in England. On the Lizard in the far west there are Precambrian rocks, among the oldest in the British Isles, while the appearance of quite young rocks like the chalk in the east help to define the marchland between the south-west peninsula and 'mainland' England.

There are also great contrasts in relief; Dartmoor boasts the highest land in England south of the Peak District, while parts of Somerset lie below the level of the sea. The present appearance, though, of the high open moorlands of Devon and Cornwall is in fact no more 'natural' than the lush pasture fields of the Somerset Levels. The latter were made by Man in the seventeenth and eighteenth centuries, when drainage schemes were masterminded by Continental reclamation experts; Dartmoor and Exmoor only remain as open moorland because of careful management of their grazing.

Thus the appearance of the present landscape is a product of a complicated interaction between the facts of its physical geography and the history of human occupation. This duality of influence is reflected in microcosm in the villages of the West Country. Part of their character stems from the physical environment, notably the nature of site and building materials, while their arrangement and style are deeply rooted in human tradition, custom and culture. Certainly to understand and appreciate the variety of villages in this part of the country one must know a little about the rocks and the form of the land as well as the sequences of occupation of its soil.

The physical structure of south-west England was profoundly affected by great mountain-building upheavals of so-called Armorican age (about 290 million years ago) during which the five granite bosses of Dartmoor, Bodmin, Hensbarrow, Carnmenellis, and Penwith were intruded through the older sandstones and shaly rocks which make up the plateaux of most of the rest of Cornwall and West and Mid-Devon. The granites give rise to a distinctive upland moorland landscape with their principal heights topped with castle-like tors while the incredible temperatures and pressures involved in the movement of the granite upward from deep within the crust of the earth mineralized the surrounding rocks with ores of metals like tin, lead, copper and silver. Although now largely defunct, the metal-mining industry has left a considerable landscape legacy of spoil heaps and engine houses (*see* Mary Tavy) but quarrying for stone and china clay is still very active. In West Somerset and North Devon an outcrop of very resistant sedimentary rock stands out as the heathery highland of Exmoor. The famous red rocks of Devon, responsible for the characteristic red soil which when freshly ploughed in autumn contrasts so effectively with the deep green of lush permanent pastures, are, in fact, confined to just the eastern third of Devon. The gold of the greensand and the white of the chalk can be seen capping the tops of hills and cliffs in this part of the country. The outcrop of all these relatively young red, yellow and white sedimentary rocks marks the boundary between Highland Britain on the west and Lowland Britain to the east. South and East Somerset and East Devon are really a continuation of the scarp and vale scenery which runs across the whole of southern England. Some of these rocks, like the limestone of the Mendips, give rise to their own distinctive landscape: in this case one of dry valleys, gorges and caves produced by the particular combination of physical strength and water solubility that this rock possesses.

The myriad of local variations in scenery can, however, be explained only in part by reference to the nature of the underlying rocks. Much of the landscape of the West Country is a relic fossilized from the Ice Age, formed not by erosive ice sheets or glaciers, which did not reach quite this far south, but simply by erosion and deposition in an Arctic-like climate. For example, groundwater in the usually porous chalk was frozen solid all the year, so that streams could flow and erode valleys during the short summers. Today we can see the valleys these streams cut in South-East Devon but water no longer runs through them. Similarly, a rise of sea-level long ago at the end of the Ice Age was responsible for producing the intricate, indented coastline of South Cornwall as the sea invaded and drowned the lower parts of river valleys to produce hundreds of inlets and in the process created ideal sites for dozens of coastal villages and a handful of major ports.

However, perhaps the most fundamental contrast in the scenery of the West Country is not a function of the rocks at all but is that major distinction already alluded to between the coast and the inland country. Much of inland Devon and Cornwall, particularly the old plateaux of North-East Cornwall and North Devon, is a rather monotonous landscape neither wild and picturesque wilderness like the moors, nor with the intimate, pastoral variety of Quantock Somerset, East Devon or the South Hams. In fact, travelling in a car along by-ways in parts of Devon can be very tedious, incarcerated as one is in a sunken lane with hedgebanks rising up above, more like a corridor than a road and affording only tantalizing glimpses of the landscape through gateways. Any suggestion of boredom, though, is dispelled where the plateaux meet the sea in thrilling coastal scenery.

Imprinted upon this natural landscape is a pattern of human occupation of even greater complexity. As with the rocks, some of the best relics of earliest, prehistoric settlement survive in the West; the Penwith peninsula must have been a very populous place in the Iron Age. Human occupation of caves in South Devon is known in the Stone Age, and Dartmoor is particularly rich in evidence of Bronze Age settlements which thrived when climate was drier than now. It is now known that the Romans went on west beyond Exeter, as did the later Saxons, though the number of Saxon place names diminishes abruptly across the Cornish border where one enters a realm of Celtic continuity with the *tre-* (farmstead) prefix replacing the Saxon *-ton* (homestead) suffix on place names.

Except on the very highest moors there is a complicated patchwork of field boundaries testifying to various periods and purposes of enclosure. Cornwall was a country of early enclosure and its pattern of small 'Celtic' fields bounded by banks of earth and stone (*see* Zennor) is reminiscent of the *bocage* of Western France or Ireland. In East Devon and Somerset the medieval agrarian system was more akin to the communal three-field system of the Midlands of England, so that there were intermixed strips to consolidate and enclose by Parliamentary act in the eighteenth century (vestiges today at Braunton and Forrabury, Devon). At this time there was also active enclosure and reclamation of wasteland throughout the peninsula from the Newtakes of Dartmoor (see around Princetown, Postbridge and Two Bridges) to the drainage of the marshland of the Somerset Levels (*see* Weston Zoyland).

Isolated farmsteads, hamlet groups of two or three farms and nucleated villages occur widely throughout the West Country. Hamlets with characteristic Celtish names are most common in Cornwall while the nucleated village is more usual in Somerset. Devon has examples of both types, together with villages 'planted' during the prosperous years of the Middle Ages when wool and tin brought wealth to landowners and encouraged them to speculate and attract new colonists (*see* Newton Poppleford and South Zeal).

Many of the older village buildings are built of local materials in the true vernacular tradition; apart from colour-washes and some all too frequently applied picturesque *chic*, they must look much as they did when built. These are our touch-stones to the past, and confirm the close link between vernacular architecture and the physical environment. The red rocks and shaly rocks of East and mid-Devon do not make satisfactory building stone, and here cob (a mixture of mud and straw with perhaps river pebbles, horse hair and dung added) was used for walls. Today the cob has usually been rendered and colour-washed for protection but cob cottages can be recognized by the rounded corners and massive thickness of their walls. A similar lack of slate or easily split stone led to the use of primitive thatch roofs. Today the presence of cob and thatch cottages adds greatly to the charm of many East Devon villages (*see* Broadhembury, Otterton, Sidbury). Elsewhere, the traditional building material in the West Country is stone, which itself varies enormously, from the harsh granites of many Cornish cottages, often slate-hung for further protection

against the elements (*see* Mousehole, Port Isaac) to the mellow warmth of South Somerset sandstone from the Hamdon Hill quarries between Yeovil and Taunton (*see* East Coker), to the grey stone of the Quantocks (*see* East Quantoxhead) and the limestone of the Mendip villages. Slate for roofs came from quarries in South Devon and at Delabole near Tintagel in North Cornwall or was brought across from South Wales. For important buildings like churches a village would often bring in a special stone. Luxulyanite is an attractive porphyritic granite quarried from the village which gave it its name, while the freely worked stone from the quarries at Polyphant near Altarnun was used in churches all over the county of Cornwall.

Almost all the villages described in this section of the gazetteer have a church that is unspoilt or sensitively restored. The church is still a dominant feature of the village landscape, even if it is no longer the only focus of English village life. The churches of Somerset and Devon are by and large grander than those of Cornwall, reflecting the greater wealth of those counties during the main

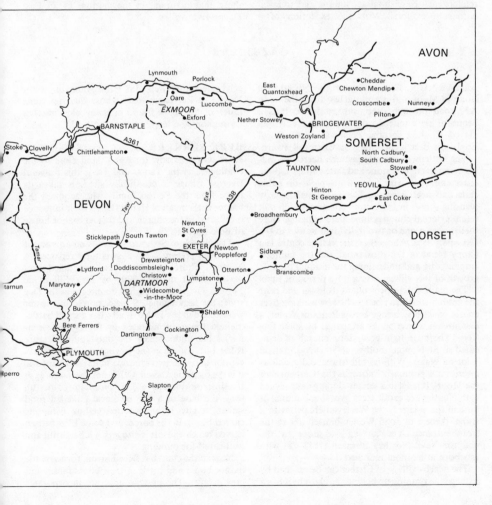

phase of church endowment and rebuilding in the late Middle Ages. Somerset churches are most notable for their towers, which really do dominate the homes of mere mortals as they rise up over a lowland landscape. Many interiors of Devon churches have rich wood-carving, and some in isolated districts escaped from the purges of the Civil War with their stained glass intact. Many churches in the poorer, remoter Cornish villages were rather crudely restored in the late nineteenth century, their hand-carved barrel-roof timbers replaced with mechanically cut planks. With their short, squat towers and low naves it is tempting to suggest a correlation between the solidity of the architecture and the Atlantic gales which sweep across the peninsula in winter.

Many coastal village sites are restricted in size, with harbour buildings squeezed in at the bottom, cottages piled tier upon tier up the cliff sides, and then a church like a beacon on top; other villages are set in protective hollows where houses cluster tightly around the church. The range is infinite; it is the particular relationship between human occupation and the natural landscape which renders each English village unique and so fascinating to explore. With the exception of a relatively small number of planned settlements, growth was accommodated by adding new buildings as and when they were wanted. Buildings for which there was no longer a need just fell into ruin or were plundered to build anew. The direction of growth was a reasoned adaptation to the site, the precise nature of building was a function of the local vernacular. Always the end result is a happy marriage of Man's buildings and Nature's physical environment which together produce a village landscape.

The villages described in the following gazetteer have not been chosen solely for their beauty. In fact many traditional beauty spots are notably absent. Picturesque appeal was certainly an important consideration in the selection of places for description but they have also been chosen to illustrate the variety of types found in the South-West of England. Each place illustrates a particular theme in the wide spectrum of South-West villages, a spectrum which runs from places that dominate a flat landscape in Somerset to those that sit boldly on a moorland edge, from those that huddle protectively in a Cornish declivity to those that luxuriate in the verdure of an East Devon river valley.

GAZETTEER

ALTARNUN, *Cornwall,* is on the NE edge of Bodmin Moor and is approached from the main A30 road through deep, sunken lanes. It is a beautiful place indeed worthy of its proudly displayed Council for the Preservation of Rural England's Best Kept Village in Cornwall award.

The settlement is really just one narrow, winding street lined with stone and slate cottages, these latter enlivened with some white paint on gable ends and neat gardens. There is a particularly pleasing group in the centre, some of which still retain external chimneys and slate-hanging. Here there are also one or two individual houses in the Georgian style. Altogether, the village centre is a happy blend of the substantial and the humble, emphasizing and underlining the gradual organic growth of this village over a long period of time.

The main street opens out at its lower end near the church which can be reached by walking over an old packhorse bridge across Penpont Water, a fast stream whose banks are edged by some fine trees. The huge light-grey stone church is dedicated to St Nonna, mother of St David, patron saint of Wales. With its tall tower and spacious interior it is popularly known as the 'Cathedral of the Moor'. It is set in a steeply sloping churchyard with plantings of exotic trees. Another building of note in the village is the Wesleyan chapel, with a stone likeness of John Wesley himself above the front entrance. The carving was done by the sculptor Nevil Northey Burnard (1818–78) who was born at Penpont mill next door.

The nearby village of **Clether** can be reached by a steep lane running up behind the church; it has a celebrated holy well. 3m E of Altarnun is the hamlet of **Polyphant** from whose quarries came much of the stone found in many old churches throughout the length and breadth of Cornwall.

BERE FERRERS, *Devon,* 9m SSW of Tavistock. On a narrow tongue of land close to the confluence of the Tamar and Tavy, this peaceful riverine village is beautifully sited. It takes its name from the Ferrers family who acquired the manor in the reign of Henry II, and their influence is reflected in the church and former manor house of Bere Barton.

The church of St Andrew stands on an ancient site. The present 13th-c structure replaced a Norman church but was itself modified and partly rebuilt in the 1330s by Sir William de Ferrers. Originally a perfect cruciform in the Dec style, the lady chapel, S aisle, porch and tower were added in the 15th c. It also has a small battlemented tower surmounted by four granite pinnacles but undoubtedly the outstanding feature is the 14th-c glass in the E window. With the exception of one or two windows in Exeter Cathedral it is the oldest in Devon. Other notable features of the interior include a late Norman girdle-tub font, the base of a late medieval panelled rood screen, a late 15th-c wooden ceiling with fine carved bosses in the porch, and some Elizabethan carved bench ends. It is altogether a beautiful and well-cared-for building.

Near to the church is Bere Barton, formerly the manor house and castle of the Ferrers family but now a farm. The present structure incorporates

A typical cottage at Boscastle,
with wavy roof and crooked chimney-stack

British Tourist Authority

one wall of the 14th-c castle but is generally a much altered medieval house of irregular plan and elevation. The frontage with narrow projecting wings on N and S is 18th-c. The house is not open to the public.

The most attractive village cottages of whitewashed stone and cob are to be found in Silver Street (formerly Duck Alley) and along the short main street where there is an inn and post office. This area marks the heart of the medieval village, and, although renovated and redesigned, many properties can be dated to the late 16th or early 17th c. Close to the church is a small square with a massive stone well erected for the use of the poor by Lady Frances Shelley in 1852.

There is also much of interest in the surrounding area. **Buckland Monachorum** is a pleasant village and Buckland Abbey is close by. Converted to an Elizabethan towered house after the Dissolution of the Monasteries, it was sold in 1581 to Sir Francis Drake and is now owned by the National Trust. Along the banks of the Tamar deserted quays and leaning chimneys are relics of a once extensive mining industry. The outstanding site is at Morwellham Quay.

BLISLAND, *Cornwall,* is on the W fringe of Bodmin Moor not far from one of the principal heights, Hawks Tor. There is some modern development on the outskirts but this is well away from the central village green, one of only a few in Cornwall. Many of the majestic ash and sycamore trees which once adorned the green have recently been felled but it is still a very pleasant

area, with well-built stone cottages arranged in a semi-circle on the N. The green drops away quite steeply to the S where the church is situated; this is almost hidden from view by the fall of the land.

The church has a somewhat unprepossessing basically Norman granite exterior but inside it is truly breathtaking. There is richly carved woodwork on the barrel roof and a magnificent rood screen erected in 1896 when the church was being restored. This is painted in the dazzling medieval style and the gold, red, green and blue of its panels are still quite vivid today. Blisland is worth a long detour if only to see this screen which evokes the splendour of the medieval ecclesiastical past.

Also of interest are a number of old manor houses in the area. There is one newly restored on the edge of the village green, with a fine gabled entrance from its courtyard. Others are now farmhouses but their exteriors can be glimpsed from the road. For example, Lavethan lies almost hidden by trees on a slope on the W edge of Blisland village. Helligan across the River Camel is a part 17th-c house with some older buildings.

At **Bradford**, 3m NE, there is a well-preserved clapper bridge over the De Lank river.

BOSCASTLE, *Cornwall.* The main village occupies a steep site on the side of a small valley which runs down to join the larger Valency Valley on the N coast about 5m N of Camelford. There is a secondary settlement (with a car park) near the harbour which may then be reached on foot.

Built at the point where fresh and tidal waters meet, the harbour nestles back from the sea within a rocky cleft and is necessarily tiny but is most attractive for its simplicity. Beyond it the narrow, twisting estuary between high masses of dark, slaty rock is dramatic even on a sunny day, and in storms is quite spectacular. This was formerly a much busier place, the harbour receiving most of the coal and other supplies for the region. Now the old watermill nearby houses craft workshops and there are several tourist-orientated activities in the vicinity.

Walking back from the harbour up the smaller valley one finds the main part of the village unspoilt and charming. Below the solidly-built villas which cling to the edge of a precipitous drop beside the approach road from the S and W, a minor road starts upward again. It threads its way between the pleasant stone houses and variously shaped cottages (some with wavy roofs and crooked chimney-stacks) of the old village where boundary walls are often built of diagonally-set slate. The way is steep, but it is worth persevering to the top and turning to look over the tree-filled valley with the cliffs and sea beyond.

In contrast to the thrill of danger sensed at the estuary the village in the valley has a delightfully sheltered and secluded feeling. It contains the grassy site of the castle which belonged to the Bottreaux family; the village takes its name in fact from the 13th-c Cornish word for dwelling – *bos* – and from this castle. The growth of the settlement was given impetus in the 14th c by the granting of the right to hold a fair at the castle.

Boscastle lies in two parishes – those of **Forra-bury** and Minster. Forrabury church can be seen on the cliffs W of the harbour. It is partly Norman, and the remains of an ancient strip or 'stitch' field system are visible beyond the N boundary of the churchyard on Forrabury Common.

Many of Thomas Hardy's poems were set in Boscastle or on its cliffs. Boscastle is 'Castle Boterel' in his novel, *A Pair of Blue Eyes* (1873). The Valency Valley provides a lovely walk through woods to the church of St Juliot where Hardy as architect supervised restoration work in 1870. He met his first wife, Emma, at St Juliot Vicarage and St Juliot is 'West Endelstow' in *A Pair of Blue Eyes*.

BRANSCOMBE, *Devon* (4m E of Sidmouth), is a beautiful village in a superb setting. Much of its character stems from the presence of numerous thatched farms and cottages of flint and stone from the chalk quarries at Beer (2m E). Two steep wooded valleys cut through the chalk and green-sand into the softer red marl beneath before the streams meet the sea. The chalk forms almost vertical cliffs which have retreated through great landslips such as that of March 1790, when a great fissure opened up on the cliff top and a whole mass of chalk some 750ft wide and over 1800ft long slipped into the sea, breaking into columns of chalk known as the Pinnacles. Between these and the present cliff, and running parallel to the coast, there is a narrow valley, along which the visitor may walk and which was once the clifftop. The present cliffs rise to over 500ft W of Brans-combe at Coxe's and Berry Cliffs, where there are Bronze Age barrows and a large rectangular earthwork of unknown date.

The road from Sidmouth runs along the N side of the valley. Across the road and opposite the medieval church living is the church, which will delight any ecclesiologist. It is dedicated to St Winifred, a Welsh saint, and there is late Saxon work on the inner base of the tower stair-turret although the rest of this massive square crossing tower is Norman. Part of the nave is also Norman, but the transepts just W of the crossing tower were built in the mid-13th c by Bishop Walter Branscombe (1258–80), a native of the village. The nave was lengthened by Bishop Branscombe but the chancel was rebuilt in the next century and its Perp E window added by Bishop Neville (1458–64). The fittings too are of many dates; the octagonal font is 15th-c, the wooden three-decker pulpit is late 18th-c and there is an Elizabethan gallery with external stairs. Among the monuments is one to Joan Tregarthen who died in 1583. It is dedicated to her two husbands who are shown kneeling opposite each other with twelve children behind one and five behind the other.

The visitor should explore the scattered farms in the valleys on foot and see the homes of some of the descendants of those whose monuments lie in the church. Past the thatched smithy, a road leads up to Edge Barton about 1m N of the church.

This was the home of the Branscombes, whose family produced three sheriffs of Devon as well as Bishop Walter. The present house is mostly 16th-c with some evidence of earlier work. The Brans-combes sold it to the judge Sir John Wadham in the late 14th c, and it is from him that Nicholas, the founder of Wadham College, was descended. Just SE is Hole, another late 16th-c house, home of the Holcombes and later the Bartletts. 1m E is the Elizabethan Bovey House, now a hotel. The summerhouse is flanked by 13th-c statues, probably from Forde Abbey, of an abbot holding a model of a church and a king holding a sceptre and charter.

BROADHEMBURY, *Devon,* lies in the small but open valley that feeds the River Tale. About 4m NW of Honiton a flat country road leaves the A373 and heads E, where it joins with four others to form Broad Street at the village centre. This road is lined along the N side with a curving terrace of simple cottages with thick cob walls painted in cream with a mellow brown for the doors and window frames. Their roofs of close-cut thatch are characteristic of this and similar tidy E Devon villages. Across the road is an interesting Tudor building whose small mullioned windows are slightly askew as the foundations have settled over the centuries.

St Andrew's Church stands impressively on a gentle rise, its tower overlooking the rest of the village. The finely vaulted N porch leads directly into the nave where the wagon roof still has 15th-c scroll paintings on the beams although much of the church was restored in the 1830s. On the S chancel wall a memorial tablet commemorates the Rev. Augustus Toplady – famed for the hymn 'Rock of Ages'. He spent his last years here as vicar from 1768 to 1778.

The main street leads down from the church to the river where a stone bridge crosses it next to a shallow ford. This is the lowest part of Broadhem-bury, but less than 1m SE a towering wooded spur rises to over 400ft and partly hides the deeply incised banks and ditches of Hembury Hillfort. Perched on the southernmost end of the spur, it was first occupied some 6000 years ago by Neolithic peoples although most of the remaining fortifications – steep-sided sinuous ditches and complicated entranceways to keep out unwanted intruders – were constructed during the Iron Age period when it was reoccupied until *c.* AD 70.

BUCKLAND-IN-THE-MOOR, *Devon,* sits on Dartmoor's S edge 3½m NW of Ashburton. Although surrounded by the bleak and exposed landscape of Rippon Tor and Haytor, Buckland itself is enveloped by woods where sheltered conditions provide an ideal habitat for a rich variety of flora and fauna.

The village, void of any definite plan, spreads lazily across a small valley that drains S into the River Dart. On its E side the first of the three small groups of buildings that make up this settlement includes a granite farm and several converted cottages. The road then dips down to the centre of the village; here there is a delightful cluster of granite and thatch cottages grouped on either side of a rocky stream which is culverted under the road.

Passing another small stream and a waterfall, the road, now walled on either side by huge rough-cut granite blocks, climbs up towards the over-grown driveway of Buckland Court. Once a splendid Georgian mansion, with a mansard roof added, it has gradually fallen into decay behind the high granite walls of its grounds.

W on a valley spur is St Peter's – a little church mostly of the 13th and 15th c, with a sturdy W tower. Its external stair turret is a characteristic feature of Devon towers. The clock has an unusual face and a beautiful chime. Inside the early 20th-c restoration is apparent but thankfully not too excessive. There is an attractive rood screen, the lower panels of which are painted on both sides, and the twisting rood stairs still lead out onto the roof of the screen. An unusual feature is a display of the Ten Commandments, Lord's Prayer and Apostles' Creed carved out of slate slabs rather than painted on wood. There is more slate, probably from the S Devon coast, on the floor.

Outside, to the S, Church Cottage is tucked in below the churchyard. It is a strong granite building with a heavy thatched roof and marks the end of the village.

The road S from the church leads down through the wooded Webbern Valley to the River Dart. Nearby is the village of **Holne** where the novelist and social reformer Charles Kingsley was born in 1819. Widecombe-in-the-Moor (q.v.) is 2m N of Buckland, approached by steeply winding moorland roads.

CHEDDAR, *Somerset*, is famed for its gorge, caves and, of course, cheeses. Cheddar is a large village spreading away from the foothills of the Mendips across the flat valley of the River Axe. It has a great mixture of houses incorporating many ages and styles.

The village centre is marked by a 15th-c preaching cross surrounded by a 16th-c colonnade of six arches. This is set in a spacious area, once the market place, from which several roads radiate. According to the Church Warden's accounts, travelling merchants paid rent for the use of this cross. A short distance S is the church of St Andrew, occupying an historic site in the village; the foundations of a Roman villa were excavated in the grounds of the neighbouring vicarage. The present church is the fourth on this site. Built in the late 14th and 15th c it is Perp in style with a few reminders of earlier periods. It is an imposing building with its open parapets and graceful Somerset-style tower reaching a height of 110ft. The interior is rich in dark oak woodwork. Many pre-Reformation bench ends survive; the N aisle contains some of particular note depicting sin in contemporary fashion. Other features include a fine moulded oak ceiling in the nave, the lierne vaulting of the belfry roof, and a 15th-c

Kenneth Scowen

St Peter's, Buckland-in-the-Moor: the clock face is lettered 'My Dear Mother' in place of numbers.

stone pulpit. Under a sycamore tree in the churchyard William Chatterton Dix (1837–98) is buried. He is the author of many hymns including a well-known favourite, 'As with gladness men of old'.

The Mendips were one of the great Royal forests used for hunting by the Saxon kings. Turning left from the church a path leads to the Kings of Wessex School. Here a series of Saxon palaces surrounding a chapel dedicated to St Columbanus have been discovered. The chapel ruins are preserved; the palaces disappeared long ago, but their positions can still be seen marked by concrete posts. Returning towards the village centre it is worth turning left up Lower North Street to view an oblong, whitewashed cottage which was the home of Hannah More, one of the great 18th-c philanthropists. She did much for the welfare of Mendip people and founded Cheddar's first day school in 1789.

Cheddar Gorge, well-signposted from the village, stretches for 1m NE through which a narrow road winds like a meandering river. On either side wooded cliffs rise steeply. It is an awe-inspiring scene but spoilt perhaps by the sheer number of visitors in high summer and some over-commercialization. Much more pleasing, if maybe not matching Cheddar in grandness, and much less visited, is Burrington Coombe, another gorge N of Cheddar. It was in a cleft here that a curate from Blagdon, Augustus Toplady, sheltered during a storm and wrote the famous hymn 'Rock of ages cleft for me' on the rock face.

Kenneth Scowen

*The village square at Chittlehampton
seen through the lychgate of the church*

Equally impressive scenery has been created within the cliffs. In the caves the earliest records of occupation in Mendip have been found. The skeleton of a man who lived between 12,000 and 13,000 years ago was discovered in 1903. This and many other artifacts can be seen in a museum by Gough's cave.

Priddy (E of Cheddar), once an important lead-mining centre, is famed for its Bronze Age remains. S are the Priddy nine barrows, some of the many ancient burial chambers in this area.

CHEWTON MENDIP, *Somerset* (NE of Wells on the A39), is a grey-stone, former lead-mining village huddled in a dip on the NE slopes of the Mendip Hills at the source of the River Chew. Its history goes back to at least AD 901 as King Alfred mentioned it in his will. Now Mendip stone houses line the main road and a smell of wood smoke pervades the air. The whole village is dominated by the magnificent tower of the church of St Mary Magdalene.

This church has a long history of which fairly continuous records exist; the building and land have changed hands a number of times since the Norman Conquest. In 1420 they passed to the Prior of a new Carthusian Monastery, known as the Bethlehem House of Sheen. The monks lived in an ancient Benedictine religious house SE of the church. A relatively modern building, Chewton Priory, now occupies this site. It is the seat of the Earl of Waldegrave and was once home of the Countess Waldegrave, a friend of Edward Lear. Originally a simple Saxon structure, the church itself has changed in form in the course of time

under the influence of the Normans, the monks, and 19th-c restorers. The distinctive tower was built by the Carthusian monks: one of the finest in Somerset, it reaches a height of more than 126ft. The decorative carving is beautifully executed and includes traditional Somerset tracery. Started in about 1441 it took over 100 years to complete. When the topographer Leland saw it a century later he remarked on the 'goodly new tourrid stepl of Chewton Mendip'. Inside the church there are many interesting and beautiful treasures. A first edition of the Authorized Version of the Bible published in 1611 is contained in a glass case. It is known as a 'he' Bible due to a misprint in the third chapter of Ruth at verse 15. The Lady Chapel contains a striking 15th-c tomb with the carved figures of a Knight and Lady. Below a window in the chancel is a seat, considered to be a 'fryd' stool or sanctuary. A criminal could run to such a place and be immune from arrest. The fan vaulting in the roof of the tower is very fine. Outside the church porch there is a 14th-c churchyard cross, one of only four canopied crosses which survive in Somerset.

CHITTLEHAMPTON, *Devon.* Lying 7½m SE of Barnstaple and reached by lanes from the B3227 between South Molton and Umberleigh, Chittlehampton dates from the time of the Saxon colonization of this area in the 8th c. It was the 'farm of the dwellers in the hollow (or *cietel*)', and is set in a dip among gentle hills. The village is linear in plan, its dwellings lining both sides of a long, undulating main street, but there is also a steeply-sloping square which may have been the 'town place' of the original Saxon settlement. The atmosphere is peaceful, to which the sounds of sheep in the surrounding pastures and the songs of birds contribute.

Chittlehampton is worth a visit merely to wander around on foot and absorb the air of quiet country life, but it has some claim to renown too in its church. This is next to the village school, on the highest side of the square, the other sides being occupied by thatched and slate-roofed cottages facing onto cobbled pavements. The tower of the church dominates the view of the village on approach from the E or W. Rising in four stages to a height of 114ft this early 16th-c masterpiece is described by W. G. Hoskins as 'unquestionably the finest church tower in Devon'. The grey stone is warmed with orange lichen, while its double bell openings are large and beautifully ornamented.

The church itself was rebuilt in the late 15th and early 16th c and attractively restored in 1871–2. It is on the site of an earlier structure over the burial place of St Urith, or Hieritha, to whom it is dedicated. This Celtic maiden, born at East Stowford nearby, was slain by the people of Chittlehampton with their scythes, probably early in the 8th c. The traditional place of the saint's martyrdom is St Urith's Well (now known as St Teara's, or Taddy, Well) at the E end of the village, where a pump is now to be found. A carved figure of St Urith is on the N side of the pulpit (*c.* 1500) in the church; here she is holding the palm branch of martyrdom and what is possibly the book of her acts.

Some new development has taken place at the W end of Chittlehampton but is not obtrusive, while the square has been well laid out to accommodate parked cars and also contains a smartly painted pump. Nearer the E end of the village the restored, cobbled site of the old Pound may be seen. There are a couple of shops, a post office and a pub. This is a village, one feels, where country people live – pleasant just because of this quiet impression.

CHRISTOW, *Devon* (9½m SW of Exeter), is one of several delightful villages lying in the upper Teign Valley. It displays a considerable variation in housing both in age and style, and has some 16th-c thatched cottages with gnarled exterior chimney-stacks as well as modern detached brick houses. This mixture of old and new enriches the community atmosphere of a place that has remained alive as a village without becoming grossly overdeveloped.

On the NW the village clings to the hillside. Here is the steep Dry Lane with its twin Wet Lane below, more gently sloping and liable to flooding in earlier times. In the lower part of the village the Perp granite church of St James dates mostly from the 15th c. It is dominated by a fine ashlar-faced tower. At the entrance to the S porch is a granite slab commemorating Nicholas Bussell, a clerk of the parish for 46 years. Local tradition says he died at the hands of the Parliamentarians for refusing to hand over the keys to the church, but his death in 1631 was 11 years before the Civil Wars began.

The inside of the church is light and simple, although the Perp rood screen is richly painted. Along the aisles are several 17th- and 18th-c tombstones, simply but boldly carved, as are the surrounding granite pillars supporting the wooden wagon roofs over the nave and N aisle. There are also several monuments to the Pellew family who became Viscounts Exmouth in the 19th c. They lived 1½m S at **Canonteign Barton**. Here the original stone Elizabethan house on an E plan was abandoned in 1820, but it has now been well restored, while in the grounds next to the road stand the chimneys of a now derelict lead-mine. The central engine house is ivy-covered.

On the E side of the Teign is the hamlet of **Lower Ashton**, entered over a simple early 17th-c bridge near a thatched mill and leat. Further up the hill is **Higher Ashton**, a string of rough-walled cottages. The church of St John the Baptist is worth a detour as it contains some beautiful woodwork. Behind the simple Jacobean pulpit are the rood stairs and deeply carved rood screen *c.* 1476 with some fine panel paintings. The arch-braced roof and pews are also late 15th-c.

CLOVELLY, *Devon* (12m W of Bideford), is situated in a narrow valley which runs steeply down to the coast. It is one of the most picturesque villages in Devon, with its stepped and cobbled streets lined with quaint little cottages bedecked with window boxes and wooden balconies full of flowers. Much of the woodland on the surrounding hillsides was planted by Sir James Hamlyn in the early 19th c. This adds greatly to the charm of the place. It was just a peaceful herring fishing village until Charles Kingsley, whose father was rector here, made it more widely known in *Westward Ho!* (*See colour plate facing page 257.*)

All cars must be left in a car park above the village, from which there is a footpath to the top of the main street. The open grassy area here is known as Mount Pleasant and now belongs to the National Trust. From here there are fine views across the bay to Lundy Island. In the main street sleds used for carrying loads can be seen tied to some cottages. Most of the houses are white-washed and many have on them the initials of Christine Hamlyn, who lived at Clovelly Court and who in the first 20 years of the 20th c did much to restore the cottages. Narrow, winding, cobbled streets lead off either side of the main one. At the lower end of the main street is a lime kiln, which was well placed to burn limestone brought by boat to the harbour. Just beyond this is the quay itself, dating from the 14th c.

The church and Clovelly Court are situated close together about ¾m above the village. The church of All Saints dates from several architectural periods; the N porch is rebuilt Norman, the tower probably EE, and the remainder of the church Perp. Inside, the pews at the back of the church have small seats projecting from their ends which were used by children and apprentices. There is a Norman font, Jacobean pulpit and 18th-c hour-glass.

Clovelly Court was built by Zachary Hamlyn in 1740, with Gothic detail, but in 1795 Sir James Hamlyn gave it a classical appearance. On the lodge at the entrance to the court is the inscription 'Go North, Go South, Go East, Go West; Home's Best', yet another reminder of the 'folksy' taste of Christine Hamlyn.

The Hobby Drive, which was designed by Sir James Hamlyn in the early 19th c to wind through the newly planted slopes of his estate overlooking the sea, is an example of the prevailing taste for wild, romantic nature. In summer it is open to cars, which must enter from the Bideford–Bude road. Clovelly Dykes, possibly a Roman encampment, 1½m S of Clovelly on the hilltop, is also of interest.

COCKINGTON, *Devon,* on the SW of the sprawling resort of Torquay, has, apart from a little unfortunate ribbon-development to the E, escaped intrusion by snugly nestling in a protected valley. It is now owned by Torquay Corporation which is very conscious of its attractiveness. Cockington succeeds in providing an image at least of 'Olde Worlde'; it abounds in rustic thatch cottages and tidy well-kept gardens, with the village forge as its focal point.

The village may look very old, yet in fact around

1800 most of the original buildings were pulled down and new ones built on a fresh site in the Picturesque style. Cockington was an estate village serving Cockington Court and the houses were moved to prevent spoiling the view from the big house.

The Court dates from the 16th c, with extensive Georgian alterations, and sits comfortably at the head of a valley which opens out into a bowl of grassy slopes dotted with trees and shrubs. Nearby is the church dedicated to St George and St Mary, in fine red sandstone with a low and broad tower which was probably added by the monks of Torre Abbey who acquired the church in 1236. Inside there is an early Renaissance pulpit.

Footpaths to the S meander through flowery gardens and alongside lakes and eventually lead out by the Gothick gatehouse of Lower Lodge. This was built in 1838 and its tiny windows and crenellated arch over the road are especially interesting. Further N there is another lodge with larger Gothick windows and a thatched roof supported by a rustic verandah.

Nearby, hidden by the winding main street of the village, are the remains of a 19th-c mill. Gravelled courtyards lead to the derelict water wheel, which was cast in iron by a Newton Abbot firm in 1878. It no longer turns to grind corn but the mill leat still drains over the wheel from the duckpond above. Behind is the Drum Inn, built in 1934. The steeply pitched thatch roofs and overhanging eaves are well-designed to be in keeping with the rest of the village. Sir Edwin Lutyens was the architect. He also designed Castle Drogo, some 20m NW (*see* Drewsteignton).

There are, however, other interesting villages closer at hand. **Berry Pomeroy**, 5m SW, contains a delightful 15th-c church, and 1m from it to the N are the broken remains of a Norman castle still with its gatehouse of *c.* 1300. Compton Castle is 2m NW of Cockington. This is a fortified manor house built in three phases from 1320 to 1520 and is one of the best examples of its kind in the country. It was the home of Humphrey Gilbert, the 16th-c explorer who discovered Newfoundland. The two attractive coastal villages of **Shaldon** and **Ringmore** are 6m NE on the S side of the Teign Estuary.

CROSCOMBE, *Somerset* (between Wells and Shepton Mallet on the A371), is an attractive, linear village climbing the N slopes of the Sheppey valley which is very narrow at this point. The church of St Mary with its tall steeple dominates the village. Clustered around it and along the main road there are many stone and pantile cottages, some of which still have their 15th-c lintel doorways. The Old Manor House at the E end is an early Tudor building now sadly in a dilapidated state and supported by wooden buttresses. Recent local authority and private housing on the outskirts does not mar the village atmosphere.

Along the main road there is much evidence of past industrial activity to explore. Sheep roaming over the Mendips were the basis for a prosperous woollen industry bringing wealth to this small village. The River Sheppey was diverted to form leats providing power for at least three mills S of the road. All are now disused or converted to other uses. The site of one is particularly obvious, being marked by a brick chimney – a sign of advancing technology in the rural SW.

A 14th-c cross with an eventful history marks the village centre. Proposals to demolish it in the 18th c were greeted with uproar as the villagers rallied round to defend it. No further attempts were made at demoliton and the cross remains in its original position. Turning uphill, the church of St Mary the Virgin is reached. This magnificent building dates from the 15th c although evidence of earlier work is present. The spire is considered to be among the finest in Somerset. After being struck by lightning during a violent storm in 1936 it had to be taken down and rebuilt. Stone from the original quarries and excellent craftsmanship have been skilfully combined so that today the new and the 15th-c stonework are indistinguishable. The interior of St Mary's is dominated by its Jacobean woodwork, some of the finest in Britain. It is in dark oak, with the original colours, rediscovered in the early 1900s, highlighting its decorative designs. Much was given by the Fortescue family, once Lords of the Manor. The superb pulpit was a gift of Bishop Lake in 1616. Highlighted in red, white and gold, it has an elaborate canopy crowned with a golden pelican. So much wood, although majestic, gives a dark, sombre appearance to the church. The wagon roof of the nave has three bosses which testify to the importance of the woollen industry here.

N of the church is a mustard-yellow building with mixed history. Once a chapel of the Fortescue manor house, it became a Baptist chapel and is now owned by the Landmark Trust for use by visiting groups. A plain oblong building, it has the appearance of a religious house, with the E end retaining large Perp windows.

Nearby **Dinder** (1m W), is a charming village, set in the grounds of Dinder House, a fine Georgian manor, just off A371. The village has several attractive houses. Wistaria House, opposite the church, has a fine Georgian shell porch. The church of St Michael and All Angels is built in 15th-c Perp style, but over the centuries its interior has been often changed to conform with contemporary fashion.

DARTINGTON, *Devon* (2m NNW of Totnes), is set on a small hill around which the River Dart meanders. Village life is centred on the Dartington Hall complex managed by a Trust responsible for the College of Arts. Crafts such as textiles, woodworking, forestry and gardening are taught as well as the arts. The Trust possesses some 4000 acres of land of which about half is forested and a quarter farmland. The associated Dartington Glassworks lie at Great Torrington in N Devon; over 100 young people are trained there. Visitors are welcome at both Dartington and Torrington and there is much to see. The Dartington Trust was founded in 1925 by Dr and Mrs Leonard Elmhirst, who bought the ruined buildings of the medieval hall and some 820 acres, for use as a vehicle for experiments in rural reconstruction and education. The Middle School, a symmetrical modern Tudor stone building, was built in 1931 and the neo-Georgian Senior School was completed the following year. Other modern residences and ancillary buildings soon followed.

The Hall, which has been extensively restored, was built between 1388 and 1400 by John Holland, Earl of Huntingdon and later Duke of Exeter, half-brother and adviser of Richard II. Visitors may walk into the large central quadrangle with the hall block facing them at the W end. The E block, part of the earlier manor, was cut through by the present gateway. To the N of this lies the 14th-c barn which connects to the Hall block by a two-storeyed range of servants' buildings. The rooms above are reached by external staircases. The Hall measures some 80ft by 40ft and has a cross-passage through which access to the kitchen and buttery is obtained. The boss in the roof of the porch is the White Hart, emblem of Richard II. The hammer-beam roof and the glazing of the Hall are restored but the atmosphere of this and the college is medieval. Outside is a tilting yard, now an open-air theatre with tiers cut into the banks. The gardens and garden centre are open to the public. N of the hall is the tower of the old church. The new church of St Mary stands alone, 1¼m W of the Hall; it was built in 1878–80 and its interior fittings, including the screen and pulpit, as well as the S porch, came from the old church.

SE of the Hall, at Shinners Bridge, is a nature trail through a pretty wood, and at the nearby Cider Press Centre, visitors can eat in the restaurant, watch craftsmen at work and buy Dartington produce.

Beyond Shinners Bridge is the busy village of **Cott** which caters for the tourist as well as the farmworker or commuter to Totnes and Torbay, 6m E. The Dart below Totnes is tidal and the beautiful valley can be explored by boat or railway.

DODDISCOMBSLEIGH, *Devon*. Perched beside the Shippen Brook 5m N of Chudleigh this village is surrounded by a colourful maze of sloping hedged fields indicating the heavy dependence upon agriculture in the region. At the centre of this dispersed settlement where three roads meet stands the Nobody Inn, a low building with a large and inviting granite fireplace in winter.

To the E can be seen the tower of St Michael's Church which incorporates an unusual arrangement of central buttresses on the N and S sides. Of sturdy granite, the church mostly dates from the 15th c but does contain some 12th-c remains. Inside, the walls are simply whitewashed and contrast with the fine furnishings, which are mostly provided out of profits from the wool trade. Some of the 16th-c bench-ends are well carved,

but the pride of this church is the magnificent 15th-c glass preserved in five N aisle windows. It is reputedly some of the finest in the country. During the Civil Wars the religious fanaticism of the Roundheads caused much destruction inside many parish churches but the isolation of Doddiscombsleigh spared the beautiful bright yellow, green and blue windows. The seven sacraments are depicted in the easternmost window while elsewhere are portrayed some of the saints, including the rarely depicted St Jacobus Major.

Beside the church to the E is Town Barton, manor house of Ralph de Doddescumbe in the 13th c, from whom the village takes its name. It has a later porch and crest above the door and an early 17th-c extension to the W.

The rambling village of **Bridford** is 2m NW where there are granite houses by the Teign and the attractive granite church of St Thomas à Becket containing rood stairs and an interesting early 16th-c carved screen with traces of ancient colouring.

DREWSTEIGNTON, *Devon*, 1m S of A30 Exeter–Okehampton road. It is approached via steep country lanes enclosed by hedgerows over which there are glimpses of the rolling arable farmland and the forests that plunge down the sides of the deep gorge-like valley of the River Teign.

This quiet hill-top village on the N boundary of Dartmoor National Park is hidden by trees almost until the last road bend when the open square comes into view. It is dominated at its E end by the sturdy buttressed Perp tower of Holy Trinity Church. Although the carved base of the font is Norman, much of this moorland granite church was built in the 15th c, financed from the profits of the two major local occupations at the time – wool and tin. There is a well-preserved coat of arms of Elizabeth I above the S door on which the usual unicorn is replaced by the Welsh dragon. Two old tombstones carved with incised crosses are set in the floor, one in the S aisle by the entrance and another by the lectern.

Around the village square are two other buildings important in any village community – a post office cum general store and a pub, the Drewe Arms, that has been neatly re-thatched. Travellers noted the 'fine alehouses' of Drewsteignton in the middle of the 19th c. A Gospel Hall reminds one of the importance of 19th-c Nonconformity. Beside this is the Victorian village school. The rest of the village consists mostly of small workers' cottages serving the outlying farms.

Contrasting with the quiet simplicity of this agricultural community is Castle Drogo, 1m W. It is perched on the extreme edge of a high ridge commanding extensive views over the deeply incised valley of the Teign, indeed an excellent site for a 20th-c mock-castle. Julius Drewe bought the land in 1910 and chose Sir Edwin Lutyens as architect. Lutyens was a master of architectural grandeur and the ideal man for the commission, although it took 20 years of effort, revision and compromise before the castle was finished in 1930. Everything is designed according to a romantic medieval ideal that the two men shared. The harsh granite walls seem to grow out of the rough moorland that the castle dominates. It is entered through the heavy W entrance, complete with an heraldic lion and a working portcullis. Rigid corridors of granite ashlar contrast with and are softened by rich furnishings that give the house a warm, lived-in look of the 1930s. An impressive staircase links what are essentially two buildings set at an angle to each other. Early plans included walls 6ft thick, but eventually Drewe could only afford to build the Chapel on such a grand scale. Nevertheless, Drogo was built to impress, and Lutyens succeeded in producing a truly overwhelming effect.

From the castle it is a pleasant walk along the river to the narrow 17th-c Fingle Bridge. This spans the Teign and is built of coarse granite blocks, while high above is Prestonbury Castle, a multiple enclosure hill fort dating back to the Iron Age. Over the river is Whiddon Park which was formerly an Elizabethan deer park and still retains part of its original wall.

EAST COKER, *Somerset* (3m S of Yeovil), is a quiet village whose buildings exude great warmth. They are of amber-coloured stone brought from Ham Hill, which is about 5m NW. The streets lead to a small village green planted with daffodils and bluebells. To the S is the row of 12 Helyar Almshouses, founded *c.* 1640, with gabled dormers and mullioned windows. Further S the visitor may follow a row of yews on one side to the church and on the other to the manor. The manor, known as Coker Court, is private but can be viewed from the drive sufficiently to note the central 15th-c hall with Perp windows and solid porch. The E range is late 18th-c and has two Venetian windows.

Just NE of the house lies the church of St Michael. Although remodelled by the Victorians, it is essentially Perp despite the 13th-c S arcade and the Norman font. Two worthies are buried here. The first is William Dampier (1651–1715), born at Hymerford House by the mill stream. Dampier was a mariner and explorer. At 16 he went to Newfoundland and then the Dutch East Indies, became a privateer, and at 40 he wrote his *Voyage Round the World* and a *Discourse on Winds, Tides and Currents* which Nelson bade his midshipmen to study and Alexander von Humboldt praised. In 1699 he explored the South Seas in a government ship and was the first Englishman to see Australia, which he thought barren and inhospitable. In his career he was shipwrecked, but survived to bring Alexander Selkirk, the prototype of Robinson Crusoe, home to England.

The other worthy was buried on 4 January 1965. He was the American-born poet, T. S. Eliot, who commemorates his adopted village of East Coker in the second of his *Four Quartets*. It is easy to see why Eliot chose East Coker. It has several pretty cottages such as the thatched St Roch cottage, the

17th-c Bubspool House and the Helyar Arms, originally 1491 and rebuilt 1834, but above all its character has not been lost by discordant modern buildings. The new houses of East Coker are generally of stone and blend with the rest of the village. Of the other Cokers, **North Coker** has been spoilt by essential industrial buildings and **West Coker** lies along the busy A35. The 'exquisitely beautiful small manor house' (Pevsner) at West Coker was rebuilt after a fire in 1457 and the church tower turret has two original windows glazed with horn. The Cokers, however, remain essentially a pleasant group of S Somerset villages.

EAST QUANTOXHEAD, *Somerset* (5m E of Watchet), is an ancient, picturesque village on the edge of the Quantocks where they slope gently to meet the N Somerset coast. The focus of the village is a duckpond, neatly edged with stone blocks. Beyond this the ground rises slightly to a farm, a small grey-stone church and a grand, but equally grey, Court House. The whole village was built about 500 years ago but the land has been owned by the Luttrell family even longer. It is said to be the only piece of Somerset not sold since the days of William the Conqueror.

The church of St Mary, although small and unimposing beside the Court House and farm, has a charm all of its own. It can be viewed to its best advantage by approaching through fields from the car park. The tower is short and battlemented and the interior is of dark oak and stone. It contains some fine stone and wood carvings. The Elizabethan pulpit and bench-ends have decorative foliage designs. Beside the altar is Hugh Luttrell's tomb, a large stone monument carved by 16th-c craftsmen. This is perhaps a little incongruous in a church so small. Leaving the church, a path returns to the village past the Court House, a sombre, Jacobean building with a contrastingly colourful garden. Between the duckponds and cottages a track offers a pleasant walk to the N Somerset coast and the sea.

Kilve, a short distance E of East Quantoxhead, can be reached on foot along the coast or by returning to A39. Larger and more dispersed than its neighbour, it was once a haunt of smugglers, and is mentioned in Wordsworth's poetry. Wordsworth and his sister lived 1m S, at Alfoxton Park, for a short time. The church of St Mary at Kilve, nearer the sea than the main village, is a small grey stone building with a short tower. It was greatly restored in 1861 and incorporates a mixture of styles. A small window lighting the pulpit probably dates from the original 13th-c structure. Beyond is a ruined chantry but little of its stonework is now visible beneath the mass of ivy.

EXFORD, *Somerset* (10m S of Porlock), is in the sheltered valley of the River Exe. Around the village are pasture enclosures, but above these is the bleak, open moorland, formerly a Royal Forest, which is used as sheep walks. The centre of the village is its green which is now used as a football pitch and recreation ground, but this has

Kenneth Scowen

The duck pond at East Quantoxhead

detracted little from its appearance. Around the green are small Georgian and Victorian cottages and shops. Individually they are of no great architectural interest but collectively they form a pleasing feature.

The River Exe is of a fair size by the time it reaches Exford. The present stone bridge spans the river just outside the White Horse Inn. In the time when Leland was writing (1540) it was, like most other bridges on Exmoor, made of timber.

On some of the minor roads these timber bridges were not replaced by stone ones until the 19th c.

The Methodist Chapel which adjoins the village green is of note because it contains two stained-glass windows made in 1890 by Sir Edward Burne-Jones in the workshops of his Oxford friend and contemporary William Morris. The Anglican church of St Mary Magdalen is situated ½m E of the village at the top of a steep hill. The present church dates from the mid-15th c, the oldest parts being the plain W tower and the S aisle. The nave and chancel were almost wholly rebuilt in the 19th c. The arcade of clustered pillars with carved capitals dividing the S aisle from the nave is typical of churches in W Somerset. The much restored rood screen was originally in the medieval church of St Audries at West Quantoxhead. After that church was pulled down in 1858 the screen was restored in London and later brought to Exford. In the churchyard is the broken shaft of an ancient cross and $\frac{1}{2}$m N of the church are the ruins of a prescott (a cottage formerly used by priests).

From the church there is a good view across the Exe valley to hills along the crest of which runs the prehistoric trackway from Bridgwater to Barnstaple. This track can be traced to Court Farm at Exford. In prehistoric times the valley would have been filled with dense oak woods, and so lines of communication developed on the hills. The Iron Age spur fort on Staddon Hill between Exford and Winsford and the clapper bridge at Tarr Steps spanning the River Barle below Winsford Hill are both worth visiting.

HELFORD, *Cornwall* (7m E of the one-time stannary – or tin-mining – town of Helston, home of the Furry Dance), is on the estuary of the Helford river, a beautiful waterway with wooded banks and many side inlets. One of these shelters the village of Helford which can either be approached from Gweek in the W by a tiny lane which crosses and recrosses the heads of inlets, or by a more open road over Goonhilly Down.

Helford village itself is closed to daytime holiday traffic from 1 June–30 September, but just above it there is a large car park and picnic area with lovely views over the Helford river. From here it is only a short, if rather steep, walk down to the centre of the village. The road crosses the head of the inlet by means of a ford but there is a wooden footbridge for pedestrians. Facing each other across the creek are a couple of rows of neat cottages. It is well worth walking along the road on the W side of the inlet to see some tiny thatched cottages like over-sized dolls' houses and then to go on by way of a footpath to the pedestrian ferry which crosses the river to Helford Passage. Looking out and back from here it is quite obvious that Helford has been appropriated by the yachting fraternity.

Another of the side inlets of the Helford River is Frenchman's Creek, which provided the title and created the setting for one of Daphne du Maurier's best-known novels. It lies just $\frac{1}{2}$m W of Helford but the only practicable way to approach it is by boat.

HINTON ST GEORGE, *Somerset* (3m NW of Crewkerne), is best approached from the E. The road, which passes some undistinguished modern houses, widens out into High Street with its fine stone buildings including the Poulett Arms behind which is a high stone wall known as the Fives Court. At the end of High Street stands the 15th-c Preaching Cross one side of which has the figure of St John the Baptist. The Priory, formerly Priory Farm, once belonged to St Bartholomew's Hospital in London and dates from the 14th c. NW of the Cross is the Perp church of St George. The tower dates from *c.* 1470 and is surmounted by a gilded weather-cock dated 1756.

In what was the N transept is the Poulett family pew, which can be examined on application to the rector. In the family pew and Poulett chapel are the numerous monuments to the family. The earliest, *c.* 1475, is a knight in armour on a tomb chest. That of Sir Amyas Poulett (I) (d. 1537) has figures of his children kneeling at a desk. He once put the young Thomas Wolsey in the stocks at Loper but the Cardinal later had the pleasure of arresting Sir Amyas in London. On the W wall is the tomb of Sir Amyas (II) who died in 1588. He was once the guardian of Mary Queen of Scots at Fotheringhay and was first interred at St Martin's in the Fields, in London, before being brought to Hinton in 1728. The monuments continue to the 19th c. The last countess, who died in 1962, is commemorated by a new window in the S side which depicts St Francis of Assisi and her household pets. In 1973 the 8th Earl died and the title is now extinct. There are also small 15th-c brasses of John Thudderle, his wife and 11 children. These brasses were returned to the church in 1948, having been found in Warwickshire.

The Pouletts lived at Hinton House, which is set in a 1000 acres of park just S of the village. The house is not open to visitors but may be seen from a distance. The S front dates from *c.* 1700. The clock tower and main gateway by Inigo Jones were rebuilt at Hinton after the demolition of Clifton Maybank near Yeovil in the late 18th c. The parks contain a stand of cedars brought back from the Holy Land by Susan, Countess of Pembroke, daughter of the 1st Earl Poulett, in 1684.

Visitors to the village on the last Thursday in October will experience Punky Night. Children carrying mangolds containing lighted candles commemorate the search by village wives for their overdue husbands returning from Chiselborough Fair, and cry, 'Gie us a candle, gie us a light, It's Punky Night tonight'.

LUCCOMBE, *Somerset* (4m SE of Porlock), is owned by the National Trust. It is a quiet and peaceful place reached only by steep and narrow winding roads. It is in a hollow, bounded on the W and S by the wooded slopes of Dunkery Hill, and to the N and E by more gently inclined land which is used as sheep pasture in the winter. A stream which rises on Dunkery Hill flows through the village just outside many of the cottages and is crossed by a low sandstone bridge at the N end of the village. The picturesque cottages are a main reason why this village attracts so many visitors. Although some new houses have been built, they are mostly tucked away in large gardens behind trees and so do not detract from the rustic charm of the cottages, some of which date from the 17th c and are thatched. On a few of them the roofs

JOHN WHITE ABBOTT (1763-1851): View near Canonteign, Devon. Watercolour, 1803 (*Victoria and Albert Museum, London*). Abbott, who spent all his life in Devon, was a pupil of Francis Towne, but although he exhibited regularly at the Royal Academy it was always as 'an honorary exhibitor', and he considered himself a country gentleman rather than a professional artist. He did not consider his watercolour drawings (now so highly prized) as being of much account, and many of them, such as this, were drawn and painted on small pieces of paper joined together.

Clovelly on the Coast of North Devon.

WILLIAM DANIELL (1769–1837): Mevagissy, and Clovelly. Coloured lithographs, 1814, 1825 (*The London Library*). Two of the illustrations to *A Voyage round Great Britain*, by Richard Ayton.

Mevagissey, Cornwall.

have been tiled, and dormer windows, not wholly in keeping with the style of the rest of the building, have been added. At one corner of some of the cottages the rounded projection of a bread oven can be seen. Most of the cottages have a cream colourwash and a skirting around the base painted black. Perhaps the most delightful row is along the lane which runs SW by the side of the church.

The church of St Mary the Virgin dates from the 13th c. The chancel is EE and the rest of the building Perp. The pillars of the S aisle have carved capitals such as are found in many of the churches in this area. The roof of the nave is 13th-c and of very fine construction, with large bosses. The 15th-c roof of the S aisle is in the same style and typical of work in this part of the country. In the churchyard are the remains of an old cross destroyed during the Civil War.

Dunkery Beacon, 1705ft above sea-level and offering fine views of the county, is 4m S of Luccombe. The last 450ft to the viewpoint must be climbed on foot. **Selworthy,** a village 2m N, has a very fine church and a tithe barn.

LUXULYAN, *Cornwall.* This unassuming little village lies some 6m SSW of Bodmin. It is in quiet countryside threaded by winding lanes, with occasional signs of extractive industry. Prosperity for Luxulyan in the past came from quarrying, but today only one local quarry is working. The village itself is pleasant: the older cottages are stone-built and very sturdy and although there are some newer buildings, the place remains small. The main attractions for the visitor are the church with an interesting history and the lovely Luxulyan Valley nearby.

The name of the village is pronounced locally as 'Lucksillian' and probably means 'the place of St Sulian'. In medieval times the Chapel of St Sulian was a shrine on the route between two religious houses – Tywardreath Priory near St Blazey and St Benet's Abbey at Lanivet. One of the stone crosses which marked this route has been moved to the gate of Luxulyan Church, where it can now be seen. Associated with the ancient shrine was a Holy Well, dedicated to the Celtic St Cyors, and this still exists in the village: it is downhill from the post office stores, in the grounds of a cottage on the other side of the road.

The church dates mainly from the 15th c and is built of great blocks of locally quarried granite; those in the base of the tower are particularly large. The tower has a turret at one corner in which the seal, charter and records of the Cornish Stannary Court of the Tinners' Parliament were kept until the Civil War, when they were removed to Lostwithiel and disappeared.

The solid, square porch of the church is embattled and has a small niche for the statue of St Sulian over the door. The niche is now empty, but St Sulian is depicted in the W window of the tower where the remaining 15th- and 16th-c glass has been gathered together. The colours of this glass are especially well seen against the evening sun. The oldest work in the church is the Norman font

of 1150, on which are carved animals symbolizing evil driven out by regeneration through baptism.

Immediately SE of Luxulyan is the enchanting valley of the same name. Here a very narrow lane twists among moss-softened woodland, with trees clothed in bearded lichens overhanging a rushing stream. Scattered about on the ground are enormous boulders of the porphyritic granite to which the parish has given the name 'luxulianite'. Most impressive too is the Treffry Viaduct (which is also an aqueduct), built in 1839 by Joseph Treffry to carry a railway to his quarry. It rises up out of the trees and soars above the road in the valley.

LYDFORD, *Devon,* is 7m N of Tavistock on the W edge of Dartmoor, and the slopes of the open moor rising immediately above the village give the place a fresh, airy feeling. The small size of the present settlement and its unpretentious brown-grey stone cottages with slate roofs belie the significance of Lydford in the past. For Lydford, commanding a promontory above the valley of the River Lyd, was probably the site of a Saxon outpost against the Celts of Cornwall and certainly was one of Alfred the Great's four burghs of Devon, founded for defence against the Danes. Remains of an earth rampart can still be seen on either side of the road at the NE end of the village, but the Saxon castle was destroyed in a Danish raid in 997. Lydford also served as a royal mint during the 10th and 11th c. Several metals were mined and smelted nearby and Lydford is mentioned as a borough in Domesday Book.

An impressive square stone keep standing on a mound is all that remains of a second castle built in 1195 as a prison for offenders against the Stannary, or Tinners', Law. The building served this purpose until the 17th c and the Stannary Courts continued to sit here until 1800. Lydford Castle acquired a fearsome reputation throughout Dartmoor: legend has it that men were hanged in the morning and tried in the afternoon! The ruins of this notorious place are open to the public.

Next to the old prison is the charming little parish church of St Petrock. Much of the present building is 15th-c but there has probably been a church on this site since *c.* 600. In medieval times the dead from outlying parts of the very extensive parish of Lydford were brought to its graveyard by the 'lych way' from near Lydford Tor on the moor. The church contains some fine early 20th-c wood carving – an intricate rood screen and a series of fascinating bench ends. On the latter are depicted the figures of saints, martyrs, prophets and others within borders of local flora and fauna. Just outside the S porch of the church is the tomb of George Routleigh, watchmaker, on which an amusing epitaph is couched in horological terms. Near the gate is a wheelwright stone, used locally before 1920.

The visitor to Lydford should not miss the gorge immediately SSW of the village, through which the River Lyd flows. This extremely deep, tree-filled ravine, lined with mosses and ferns, is most beautiful. The river, 'boiling' along in the bottom, has formed potholes in its rapid descent from Dartmoor, of which the largest is known as the Devil's Cauldron. There is also a 90ft waterfall – the White Lady Waterfall. The gorge is in the custody of the National Trust, and visitors may walk a path which runs in the depths of the chasm for the whole of its mile-long length, although the less adventurous may obtain a good view from the road bridge near Lydford village.

LYMPSTONE, *Devon* (7m SE of Exeter), nestles between two low red sandstone cliffs on the E shore of the Exe estuary. The village of Lympstone runs inland along the valley of the Watton Brook. The coastal railway line from Exeter to Exmouth (2½m SSE) divides the harbour and fishing cottages along the shoreline from the church and the rest of the village and the agricultural parish which extends E up on to Woodbury Common at 500ft. N of the harbour at the foot of the cliffs which are owned by the National Trust lies Darling's Rock, which has been eroded to a low stump scarcely visible at high tide. It is said that cock-fighting and even bonfires took place on the rock. The Watton Brook has formed a channel subsidiary to the main Exe channel, which lies hard on the W shore against Powderham and Starcross, and is known as Lympstone Lake. Between the two channels lies a ridge of sand and mud exposed at low tide. Here in the 17th and 18th c Newfoundland 'bankers' and Greenland whalers were laid up in winter. Shipbuilding was an important activity in the 18th c, but competition from Topsham's yards closed the Lympstone industry in about 1815. The principal occupation in the 19th c was fishing for oysters and mussels which were dispatched by rail to the London markets and for herring and mackerel for consumption locally. Even today, fresh seafood is a speciality at local inns.

At the kilns near the harbour imported limestone was burnt to make lime which was then spread on the Devon clay soils. The white-painted fishermen's cottages lie almost on the foreshore, with narrow jetties and alleys which lead from the Strand to the boats and nets behind. Overlooking the harbour is a brick clock tower with spire. This was built in 1885 at a cost of £1000 by W. H. Peters of nearby Harefield House as a memorial to his wife Mary Jane to commemorate her kindness and sympathy for the poor of the village. Much of Lower Lympstone was rebuilt after a disastrous fire in 1833 when 58 houses were destroyed. Further inland, beyond the railway bridge and halt, a number of well-built Georgian brick houses and villas line the winding road which leads to the church of St Mary. The Perp tower, chancel arch and N arcading were part of a newly built church consecrated in 1409. The rest of the present church is the result of extensive rebuilding in 1864 to which an extension to the chancel was added in 1928.

N of the village, in Woodbury parish, is Nutwell Court and Park, overlooking the estuary. The Court, once in the hands of descendants of Sir Francis Drake, is a square, stuccoed, Georgian mansion of five by five bays rebuilt in 1810. Further up the estuary coast is the Royal Marines Training Centre at Lympstone Barracks. **Woodbury** (2½m NE) is a large nucleated settlement adjacent to the Iron Age hill fort of Woodbury Castle. Today Woodbury is increasingly a dormitory suburb for the University and City of Exeter.

LYNMOUTH, *Devon,* on the N Devon coast ½m N of Lynton. From the mid-16th c to the 19th c the village depended on its herring fishing industry, and it was only at the beginning of the 19th c that it began to become popular as a holiday place. English tourists at this time were no longer able to visit the Continent because of the Napoleonic Wars and turned their attention to places like Lynmouth. Robert Southey and Samuel Taylor Coleridge likened it to a Swiss village, and in 1812 Shelley took a cottage at Lynmouth. They found in Lynmouth and the surrounding area a landscape similar in many ways to that which they had seen in Germany and Switzerland – the thickly wooded gorges of the East and West Lyn and footpaths through the coniferous woods on the hillsides.

Today, Lynmouth is remembered because of the terrible 1952 flood which resulted from heavy rain inland causing the swollen River Lyn to burst its banks. Thirty-one people were drowned and many houses, including the cottage which had belonged to Shelley, were destroyed.

Much of Lynmouth dates from the Victorian period, when it became really popular as a holiday resort. There are, however, a few pre-Victorian buildings left; to the E of the River Lyn near the gardens, Rock House and Manor House; and near Mars Hill, a picturesque row of thatched whitewashed cottages. Along the Esplanade is a row of mainly Victorian houses, shops and cafés with imitation Gothic detail. A number of larger boarding houses and hotels were also built at this time. On the quay is a replica of the Rhenish Tower which was built by General Rawdon in 1860 and used for storing saltwater for baths. The original was destroyed in the 1952 flood. The church of St John is only about 100 years old.

From the Esplanade it is possible to take the cliff railway up to Lynton town hall. There are two parallel sets of rails and the two cars are moved by emptying a tank of water in the bottom car while a similar tank in the top car is filled. Thus one car moves up while the other comes down.

Glen Lyn, the steep gorge down which the West Lyn plunges, is just to the S of the village and can be visited at a small charge. 1m W of Lynmouth by the sea is the Valley of the Rocks. This is a spectacular barren valley strewn with rock debris. 2m E of the village is Watersmeet, a beauty spot situated at the confluence of the East Lyn and Farley Water.

MARY TAVY, *Devon,* takes its name from the parish church of St Mary and the River Tavy. A small scattered village, 4m N of Tavistock, A386 passes through one section, while to the E lies the older core, close to the church.

The village played a dominant role in the mining boom of the 19th c. The remains of abandoned tin and copper mines abound, mute evidence of the once prosperous industry. The two most important mines were Wheal Friendship, just N of the village and lying between it and the Tavy, and Wheal Betsy, below Kingsett Down. The former was a copper, arsenic, lead and iron mine worked from 1796–7 to 1925 and was one of the largest copper producers in the district. Skilfully exploited and developed by the engineer and land surveyor, John Taylor, the mine was an early success. The nearby hamlet of Horndon, known as Miners Town, was built for Wheal Friendship workers. A few old stone cottages and an inn remain. Wheal Betsy mine exploited a lead lode which it followed for over $\frac{3}{4}$m and worked from 14 levels to a depth of 170 fathoms. Wheal Betsy engine house, built in the 1860s, has been preserved. Owned by the National Trust, it is clearly visible from the main road a short distance N of the village.

The A386 bisects the later extension of the village, which is a straggling line of undistinguished buildings. The Methodist Chapel erected in 1836 reflects the religious convictions of a mining community. In more pleasant surroundings lie the church of St Mary, a few scattered cottages and the school. The church, rebuilt in granite in the 15th c in Perp style, replaced a smaller Norman building. It consists of chancel, nave, lady chapel, S aisle and tower. The interior was extensively restored in 1878–9 by the architect P. S. Aubyn. At about the same time the churchyard was extended W, embracing a large part of the former village green and including a 15th-c preaching cross.

The surrounding moorland has fine rugged scenery and Tavy Cleave is particularly attractive. However, the proximity of army firing ranges restricts public access, and care and caution must be exercised. A wealth of prehistoric sites abound and at Standon Down the hut circles of an unenclosed Bronze Age village can be found. Coxtor, Collacombe Manor and Wringworthy Mansion are among the interesting and ancient dwellings in the area. **Morwellham**, a former riverside port, has been restored by the Dartington Amenity Trust and recreates most effectively the halcyon days of mining prosperity.

MEVAGISSEY, *Cornwall*, lies on the bay of the same name, 5m S of St Austell. It is a solidly built little fishing port, first recorded as such in 1410. Facing E, Mevagissey had the advantage in the old days that boats could be launched when the weather closed harbours facing S or SW. The village enjoyed prosperity in the 18th c, the great days of pilchard fishing, when many millions of pilchards were exported each year, mostly to Italy. Mevagissey was also at times much involved in smuggling. In the fishing trade it was

strongly rivalled by the tiny village of Gorran Haven, some 3m S.

The larger, Georgian, houses in Mevagissey bear witness to its past success, but fishing (including shark fishing), although still carried on today, is now much less important and more reliance is placed on tourism. The outward signs of this are sadly evident, and there is also a great deal of unsightly modern development around Mevagissey. If to this extent the village has been spoilt, the place still has a 'saltiness' and an attractive maritime atmosphere.

It is probably the double harbour and the fine coastline which make Mevagissey most worth visiting. The inner harbour is full of boats, and nets hang over the wall to dry. One can still see examples of the old fish 'cellars' or 'palaces' – ground floors of houses or courtyards with lean-tos where fish were smoked, pressed and pickled – though some have been converted to other uses. The fishermen of Mevagissey now run a co-operative, and locally caught fish can be bought.

There is usually a tangle of traffic in the twisting, congested streets around the Market Square and it is quieter walking among the old cottages which line the steep lanes on the N side of the harbour: many of these are three-storeyed and have slate- or plank-hung walls. At the end of the N quay is an 18th-c boat-builder's shed which houses a small museum of fishing gear and implements of the china clay industry, while on the other side of harbour in the old lifeboat shed is an aquarium.

The name 'Mevagissey' is a combination of two saints' names – the Welsh St Meven, or Mewan, and the Irish St Itha, or Issey. The church, however, is dedicated to St Peter. It was built in 1259 and much restored in the 19th c, but it stands on the site of churches going back to 550.

Gazing out from Mevagissey, with fishing smells and the cries of gulls carried on the breeze, the sea looks quite blue even on a dull day. The coastline here is rocky and, especially to the S, very beautiful. (*See colour plate facing page 257.*)

MOUSEHOLE (pronounced 'Mowzell'), *Cornwall,* is a substantial village on Mount's Bay, 1m S of Newlyn, and is a complete contrast to the rusting corrugated iron of the latter's fish wharves. It too is a fishing village, with a port facing E and so quite protected from the prevailing SW gales. Once W Cornwall's most important fishery, it is now but a shadow of its former self. Mousehole is perhaps not as quaint as some other Cornish coastal villages but it has not been as much affected by the intrusion of tourist paraphernalia and picturesque chic. It is still very much a working village with few frills; its stone cottages, some painted and some pebble-dash rendered, cluster around the medieval harbour which drains completely at low tide so that it is possible for the more intrepid to walk right through the harbour entrance and around on to the rocky shore. Modern development is mostly on the outskirts of the village on the Newlyn side, where there is also a large car park. In summer especially it is advisable to park here and explore the village on foot; there is an easy path from the car park along the foreshore to the harbour. In the village itself there is little that is really ancient, as Mousehole was raided by four Spanish galleys in 1595. Little other than the Harbour Cottage (1261) and the Manor House survived the raid.

The parish church is up the hill in the separate settlement of **Paul.** It was rebuilt after the 1595 raid and its barrel roof and very tall tower are noteworthy. **Raginnis,** ½m S, is also worth a visit. At its Wild Birds' Hospital there is usually a wide range of land and sea birds in care which offers a chance to see close-up views of gannets and cormorants. Lamorna Cove can be reached on foot by a path leading from the top of Raginnis Hill along cliffs with breathtaking views. The road route is also signposted from Mousehole and runs down a narrow winding valley sheltered by steep, wooded slopes which unfold to reveal a tiny harbour encircled by rugged cliffs.

NETHER STOWEY, *Somerset* (7½m NW of Bridgwater), is the largest village on the E slopes of the Quantocks. It has important literary and historical connections and also a charm of its own.

Turning left off the A39 from Bridgwater opposite the village church and manor house, the centre of the village is reached along the original, winding Bridgwater–Minehead road. A great variety of houses is encountered along this road, giving the impression of organic growth and development over a long period of time. Among these are a small toll house in the Gothic style with arched windows and doorway, many stone and colour-washed cottages, and a few late Georgian and early Victorian houses. The centre of the village is marked by a Clock Tower (1897) and a T-junction from which another road climbs up over the Quantocks. On one side houses crowd onto the street, on the other they are set back behind a small stream flowing from the hills, creating a feeling of spaciousness. Small new housing estates are appearing around the village but do not affect the essential village atmosphere.

The literary associations of Nether Stowey owe much to the activities of one local man – Thomas Poole. He was an ambitious and determined person, teaching himself Latin, French and Italian and winning the friendship of many of the literary figures of his day. In 1795 he inherited a tanning business from his father, enabling him in 1797 to house his friend Samuel Taylor Coleridge in one of the cottages. This is now owned by the National Trust and open to the public. This marked the beginning of the 'Nether Stowey Brotherhood'; Coleridge moved to Nether Stowey after the failure of his periodical *The Watchman*, and took a great interest in the garden: 'I hope to live on it with a pig or two, for I would rather be a self-maintained gardener than a Milton if I could not be both.' Although he lived in the village for only three years, his literary achievements reached their apogee during this time. William Words-

worth and his sister Dorothy became his close companions after their move to Alfoxton Park, near Holford. Coleridge received great inspiration from their friendship. During 1798 the two poets published *Lyrical Ballads*, including 'The Ancient Mariner'. Many local places can be recognized in its lines – the port of Watchet and Nether Stowey Church are two examples.

Castle Hill leads from the Clock Tower to a mound encircled by earthworks marking the site of a Norman castle. It is worth climbing for the tremendous view it gives over Bridgwater Bay and the drained marshlands of the Somerset Levels. The castle itself was dismantled during the 15th c to provide material for the manor house by the church at the E end of the village. Before he could complete the house the builder was beheaded on Tower Hill for joining the Cornish men marching to London in protest against new taxation laws. The house, almost obscured from view by a wall and overhanging yew hedge, has a somewhat neglected appearance. On a corner of the wall is an 18th-c gazebo, an attractive building with Venetian windows and ogee roof.

The small stone church has an over-all pleasing appearance. Over the years it has been much renewed and interest in it really stems from its connections both literary and historical. Thomas Poole is buried in the churchyard and Coleridge preached from its pulpit on several occasions.

NEWTON POPPLEFORD, *Devon*, 3m NW of Sidmouth. The history and topography of this linear village is very interesting, for as the name suggests, Newton was founded as a new town at a time of increasing population in the 13th c. It was developed by the Lord of the Manor of **Aylesbeare,** some 3m NW across the common. In order to improve the income from his lands, William Brewer was granted the right to hold a market in 1226 and he sited this not in Aylesbeare village, but on the road out from Exeter to Sidmouth. By 1331 a chantry chapel had been to serve the growing community of Newton Poppleford.

The speculation evidently paid off since the settlement has survived as a village. The layout of the village is of plots of land, termed burgages, which front the main road. Each plot contained a toft, or house, and a croft or garden beyond. To the N where they slope to a stream which drains E to the Otter the burgages are about 132ft long and can be clearly seen. S where more land is available they are longer. The village street is narrower at both ends where it is lower, but in the middle near St Luke's Church, built in 1897, it is wider and noticeably higher. This was the site of the market.

The medieval settlement aimed at agricultural self-sufficiency, so Newton Poppleford and the neighbouring older villages of **Colaton Raleigh** to the S and **Venn Ottery** and **Harpford** to the N all took a share of the rich meadows alongside the Otter. This is reflected in the pattern of parish boundaries. All these villages lying to the W of the Otter are overlooked by the steep scarp slope of the greensand plateau which outcrops at Beacon

Hill (752ft) and Bulverton Hill (693ft), on either side of the gap through which the Exeter–Dorchester road climbs on its way to Sidmouth.

The village today has a pleasant mixture of cob and thatch cottages of 17th- and 18th-c date interspersed with more modern buildings. At the W end there is a fine cottage and garden at which Devonshire cream teas may be obtained.

NEWTON ST CYRES, *Devon,* is in the lower valley of the River Creedy, 4½m NW of Exeter, and is surrounded by pleasant countryside, rich agricultural land and some fine woods. A variety of buildings adjoin the A377 road, among them some attractive cob and thatch cottages and a group of carefully designed modern houses.

The church of St Cyr and St Julitta overlooks the village and the distant Exe valley. Most of the present stone structure was rebuilt in the 15th c but the small, crenellated tower is reputedly much older. Carefully restored and refurbished in the 1920s, the interior is light and spacious. Of particular interest are a stone arcade, the fine wagon roof with plastered panels and carved bosses, the mahogany pulpit and canopy, and a piscina in the Lady Chapel.

Among the many monuments in the church are several belonging to the Quicke family who settled here in the reign of Elizabeth I. The family owned extensive estates in the neighbourhood, were Lords of the Manor, and lived in nearby Newton House (the present property replaces one destroyed by fire early in the 20th c). The house and the churchyard are linked by a footbridge over a cutting for the main road. The bridge was constructed by the turnpike trust to provide access to the church and family arboretum.

The nearby villages of **Thorverton** and **Bramford Speke** as well as Cadbury and Bickleigh castles are worth a visit while in the neighbourhood.

NORTH CADBURY, *Somerset* (7m W of Wincanton), is larger than its neighbour South Cadbury (q.v.) and an attractive compact village of stone houses and colourful gardens. The inn is named after the Hundred of Catash in which North Cadbury is situated. North Cadbury Court and the church standing side by side form an impressive sight when viewed across the valley of the River Cam. From the village they can be approached along an avenue of beech trees. Straight ahead is the Court which is basically an Elizabethan structure. The N side retains its original gables with mullioned windows, but the S was given a new front during the 18th c. The 15th-c church of St Michael is well worth a visit. Carved on the bench-ends are many interesting 16th-c designs; some are symbolic and others portray aspects of everyday life. In the S aisle the Tudor cat and mousetrap is thought to be the only such representation in existence. The interior is high and light with a beautiful tie-beam roof. A school was once held here; painted on the vestry wall remnants of the alphabet are visible.

The landscape of this part of Somerset is very beautiful; its topography is varied and it abounds in warm stone villages each having its own beauty and attraction. **Templecombe**, the home of the Knights Templars, **North Cheriton** and **Horsington** are three that deserve mention.

NUNNEY, *Somerset* (3m SW of Frome), has been described by Maxwell Fraser as a village which is 'perfection, having everything which the heart could desire to make it both lovely and interesting'. The village, clustered along a street parallel to a stream, contains a number of dated 17th- and 18th-c Mendip stone houses and earlier thatched cottages. The sign-board of the George Inn spans the street, on one side of which lies the castle and on the other the church.

The partly ruined castle is of simple design; its strength was concentrated in a four-storey keep of rectangular plan rising straight from the moat. The present terrace is a later addition. There are cylindrical towers at the four corners, surmounted by further turrets offset from centre. At roof level the castle bears evidence of the projecting gallery through which missiles could be dropped, but is remarkable for the lack of gunports. It was in 1373 that Sir John Delamare, later sheriff of Somerset, was given licence to fortify and crenellate his manse at Nunney. He apparently made his fortune during the Hundred Years' War. On the inside he had three upper floors built above the kitchens whose fireplace and oven are visible today in the S wall. The Great Hall on the second floor was reached by a staircase in the NE tower and was lit by deeply splayed windows. Above was a solar and guardroom; the lavish decoration of the upper floors can still be discerned despite all the ruination. The castle passed from the Delamare family to Sir John Poulet (d. 1436), whose tomb lies in the church, and eventually to the Prater family in 1577. Their descendants included Colonel Richard Prater, a Royalist and Catholic who was besieged in the castle by the Roundheads in 1645. The N wall was breached and weakened by gun-fire in this inglorious siege which ended on 18 September in surrender to Fairfax. The castle, rendered defenceless, decayed until 1910, when the whole N wall and entrance front fell out. It is now in the care of the Department of the Environment.

All Saints Church is probably on the site of a Saxo-Norman church, for a Saxon Cross fragment may be seen in the N wall of the chancel and a circular Norman font with coarse spiral fluting lies at the W end. The chancel, rebuilt in a series of Victorian 'restorations', is of 13th-c origin and the transepts were added in the second quarter of the 14th c. The wagon roof of the nave, the S porch, the tower and the fine wooden chancel screen were all built by c. 1525. The N transept contains five recumbent effigies; the earliest, c. 1390, probably of Sir John Delamare, lies next to the table tomb of Sir John Poulet and Constance his wife. Next to this is the tomb of Richard Prater and wife, grandparents of the Richard Prater of the Civil War.

OARE, *Somerset,* is 6m E of Lynton, just S of A39. The tiny village, consisting of a small church, the manor house, and a few farm houses, is situated in a deep and narrow valley. Immediately around the village is a patchwork of arable and pasture fields, some with such a steep slope that they seem impossible to plough. Above these fields the hills are capped with open moorland. Many people visit Oare and the surrounding district in an effort to trace places described in *Lorna Doone.*

The church of St Mary the Virgin is one such place, for it was here that Jan Ridd married Lorna Doone and it was through one of the single-light windows of the old chancel that she was shot. Although the nave and inner chancel are of EE period, the church is not now as R. D. Blackmore envisaged it when he wrote *Lorna Doone.* The W tower was rebuilt in the 19th c and at this time the chancel was lengthened and the altar moved to the E. On the S side of the old chancel is a piscina indicating the earlier position of the altar. The pulpit, reading desk and box pews are Georgian and so would not have been in the nave in the 17th c when Lorna Doone was supposed to have lived. Instead, the pews would have been simple benches like those at Culbone Church. The roofs of the old chancel and nave are of the wagon type and date from the 15th c, but the ribs and bosses are now preserved only under the chancel arch. Among the memorials is one to R. D. Blackmore, whose father was Rector of Oare from 1809 to 1842, and one to Nicholas Snow whose family lived for many centuries at Oare Manor, close by the church.

It is not possible to trace the 'Plover Barrows Farm' of *Lorna Doone.* It is sometimes identified with Malmesmead, sometimes with Oareford, but R. D. Blackmore probably based it on the farmhouse at Oare which was demolished when the present Oare House was built. 1m W of Oare at Malmesmead the Badgworthy Water flows into the East Lyn. Here an elegant stone bridge with two arches spans Badgworthy Water and just below it is a ford. A footpath leads up the wooded valley through which the river flows, to Hoccombe Combe, which is more commonly known as the Doone Valley. The tiny Robber's Bridge at Oareford is a reminder of the way the Doones made their living.

OTTERTON, *Devon,* lies in the Otter valley 2m N of Budleigh Salterton, where the Otter meets the sea. Nevertheless Otterton is very much an inland village. Approaching from East Budleigh, which lies to the W, the traveller bridges first a disused railway line, and then the Otter. Facing him is Otterton Mill which used to grind corn as long ago as Domesday, but is now a craft centre. Beyond the mill on the right is a row of nine cob and thatch cottages whitewashed and with black trimmings which frame one side of the green. The wide village street leads E and its course is accompanied by a stream first on the left and then on the right. Numerous farms and cottages front this street. Cob, local red sandstone and

flint are the chief building materials, together with thatch and some Welsh slate. The exterior chimney-stacks of some houses are evidence of their 17th-c date, and one is dated 1627.

The church of St Michael stands on a bluff behind the mill and overlooks the Otter. The old red sandstone tower is 15th c, but the rest was rebuilt in 1871 by Benjamin Ferrey. It is typical late-Victorian with much marble; Pevsner says it is 'insensitive' and Hoskins calls it 'a suburban edifice'. It does however contain several relics of the earlier church, including two early 17th-c brasses of the Duke family. Richard Duke was Clerk of the Court of Augmentations, the body Henry VIII empowered to handle the disposal of monastic property at the Dissolution. Duke prospered; when the Priory of Syon, Middlesex, was dissolved in 1539, he bought the manor of Otterton which was part of the endowments of Otterton Priory. Richard Duke, using masonry from the priory erected the house, now in separate flats, standing to the N of the Church.

Outside the village the parish extends S and E to the coast, which has cliffs of 500ft near Sidmouth. Ladram and Chislebury Bays are particularly attractive. To the N, the road to Newton Poppleford leads through five or six farms on the edge of the Otter flood plain. W of the Otter lie the pleasant parishes of **Colaton Raleigh** and **East Budleigh.** Brick Cross, on the boundary of these parishes, is a brick pillar surmounted by a stone cross with the four faces of its base inscribed with verses from scripture and directions are written on plaques set into the brick. **Bicton** is noted for its garden and an avenue of monkey puzzles. Bicton House, which belonged to the Rolle family, is now an agricultural college. The house itself is brick and neo-Georgian and overlooks a pretty lake and park open to the public.

PILTON, *Somerset* (2½m SE of Shepton Mallet), is a small, attractive, grey stone village. Huddled in a hollow in the hills, it has many pleasant houses surrounded by trees and flower-decked gardens.

Overlooking the valley and across to Glastonbury Tor is a magnificent stone tithe barn. This once belonged to the Abbots of Glastonbury and has medallions of the four evangelists on its gables.

The church of St John the Baptist is a *mélange* of architecture from Norman to Perp styles; it is an impressive sight with its pinnacled tower heightened by a stair turret. The interior is rich in treasures; a superbly carved 15th-c tie-beam roof dominates the nave. It is of the traditional Somerset style and is supported by angel busts.

SW of the church is the manor house, an attractive building with a plain Georgian front. Some aspects of its structure hint at a medieval origin and support the popular tradition that Pilton was once a summer house of the Abbots of Glastonbury.

POLPERRO, *Cornwall,* is a charming fishing village on the coast 5½m E of Fowey, approached

Kenneth Scowen

The church at Oare in which Jan Ridd married Lorna Doone

by road down a narrow valley. If coming by car, one is well advised to park in the car park where the road reaches the valley bottom as space is very restricted further on and in summer only permit holders are allowed to drive right into the village. From the car park continue on foot beside the stream, passing the old watermill whose site is mentioned in Domesday Book and, once past some rather unattractive newer development on the outskirts, the heart of Polperro is reached in the tangle of tiny lanes and the harbour itself.

It is best to visit Polperro out of season and, if you ignore the commercialization, you will find that this is a real fishing village with fascinating little streets and a jumble of whitewashed and colour-washed stone cottages with slate roofs. The cries of the gulls seem always to be in the air. Simple Georgian houses stand beside the harbour and other houses climb the steep sides of the estuary and are reflected in the water. The mouth of the estuary is guarded by strikingly jagged rocks, while the entrance to the actual harbour is so narrow that in rough weather it can be closed with timber booms.

Kenneth Scowen

Polperro

Recorded as a fishing village as early as 1303, pilchards are still caught from Polperro, although the fishermen now spend some time taking tourists out to see the caves. The cliffs each side of the estuary are in the hands of the National Trust and there are terraced walks here giving views of a forest submerged by the sea. Part of Chapel Cliff, W of the harbour, has been given over by the Trust for use by village people as allotments as land is so scarce in the valley.

The village has a colourful history of smuggling activity and Polperro is believed to have been the first station of the Preventive Men. There is a museum of smuggling in the cellar of a house near the centre of the village. In the same area is the late 16th-c house of Dr Jonathan Couch (grandfather of Sir Arthur Quiller Couch) who lived here for 60 years in the 19th c as village doctor, naturalist, and collector of fossils. There are also a number of shops and a variety of arts and crafts are represented.

Polperro is in Lansallos parish and has no parish church of its own, but a chapel of ease dedicated to St John the Baptist was built here in 1838. It is a pleasant walk, however, to see the wood carvings of either **Lansallos** church 2½m W or of **Talland** church, 1½m E.

PORLOCK, *Somerset* (on A39, 8m W of Minehead), is a large village which is now well-known because of the exceedingly steep and winding road which descends to it from the SW and 'the person from Porlock' who interrupted Samuel Taylor Coleridge when he was writing *Kubla Khan*. Porlock means 'the enclosure by the harbour' but the sea has retreated to such an extent that up to a mile of fields now divide the village from the sea. To the W, S, and E the village is surrounded by high hills and steep valleys.

The main street is narrow and winding. Some of the houses lining it are medieval and have thatched roofs and tall, sturdily built chimneys typical of W Somerset cottages. Others are much more recent and have roofs with overhanging eaves and imitation Tudor façades. The latest development in the village are a housing estate, situated off a side road to the N of the main street, and a camping site towards the beach. These are unobtrusive, but the increased population may put pressure on the village's facilities in peak seasons. The original Doverhay Manor House was 15th-c but it was restored in 1883 and only a fragment of the old house remains. It is now the County Library Reading Room. The village hall, a low, plain, pebble-dashed building with buttressed walls which peers out from under an overhanging roof was designed by Charles Voysey. One of the leaders of the Modern Movement, he worked extensively on the estate of Lord Lovelace to the W of Porlock Weir, building Lilycombe House and several estate cottages, and altering Worthy Manor.

The church, dedicated to St Dubricius, a Welsh saint, dates from the EE period, but the oldest object in the church is a fragment of a pre-Norman cross which is affixed to the W wall of the S aisle. The 13th-c tower is topped by an unusual spire of wooden shingles. Inside, the church was largely reconstructed during the 15th c; Perp windows replaced EE ones, and a wagon roof took the place of a lean-to roof. There is a fine alabaster monument of John Harrington and his wife and in the sanctuary a tomb which was possibly used as the base of the Easter Sepulchre.

2m W of Porlock is **Porlock Weir**, a hamlet of thatched colour-washed houses clustered around the harbour. The Ship Inn here was once a haunt of smugglers and wreckers. **Culbone** Church, the smallest complete church in England, can be reached from here by a path through the woods.

PORT ISAAC, *Cornwall,* is a much-visited fishing village on the spectacular N coast between Tintagel and the Camel estuary. It is a piece of pure Cornwall, with exceedingly steep, narrow streets lined with thick-walled cottages arranged tier upon tier down the slope to the harbour with its lobster pots and fishing boats. Although there is some modern development at the top of the old village, the heart remains unspoilt except, of course, for the almost inevitable tourist shops.

The only effective way to appreciate this place and to take in its detail is to park in the car park at the top and walk down to the harbour. Almost every building and geranium-filled alleyway has something to fascinate: bulging walls abound, there are flights of time-worn steps up to doorways, crooked roofs, upper storeys overhang or even completely bridge some narrow lanes. At sea-level the reward is a picturesque harbour with a long finely worked stone building at its side. This is the headquarters of the local shell fishermen; Port Isaac is still an active fishing port.

Passing up the W side of the harbour is a road from which a coast path leads on to the clifftop fields by way of Varley Head and Reedy Cliff and down again into the almost deserted village of

Port Quin at the head of a narrow inlet which empties with the tides. (For the motorist, there is a signposted road inland with a junction swinging back seaward to Port Quin). As the remaining cottages and the ruined fish cellar testify, there was once a bustling little fishing village here but now, alas, devoid of permanent population. Legend has it that one day all the men of the village put out to sea as usual and rode into such a terrible storm that none of them came back. There is, however, no historic basis for this tale, and it is just as likely that economic decline brought about a less spectacular, but none the less effective, demise. Some of Port Quin's houses have been converted into holiday cottages but along the lane leading into the village and at the seaward end of the old quay there are a number of quite ruined properties.

Doyden Castle on the headland overlooking Port Quin is a red-brick Victorian folly (National Trust). Its architecture can certainly be faulted but the magnificent view which its builder appropriated cannot but be admired. Beyond the castle there is evidence of the old Cornish mining industry which was last worked in this area in the late 19th c. There is an adit right by the footpath.

ST JUST-IN-ROSELAND, *Cornwall,* lies on and to the W of B3289 about 7m S of Truro via King Harry Ferry. The parish contains two villages, St Just and **St Mawes**, which are set on the E side of Falmouth estuary, with magnificent views of Falmouth harbour right down to the dreaded Manacle Rocks. St Mawes is now the main settlement and in summer is a busy, bustling tourist centre for the verdant Roseland peninsula.

St Just has the old parish church, a simple structure set in what must be one of the most beautiful churchyards in the country. It is sited at the head of a side inlet of the sea and the churchyard is in effect the sheltered cliff-face. It is entered on its uphill side by a lychgate leading from the road. Protected still further from high winds by some massive pine trees, it is a 'sub-tropical' garden, with azaleas, hydrangeas, camellias and all sorts of exotic palms and shrubs providing a riot of colour among the sombre headstones. It is particularly attractive in spring, a season which occurs very early here. It is possible to walk a path through the churchyard to see the boats on Carrick Roads.

There is also much else of interest in Roseland. St Mawes' Castle, a twin of Pendennis Castle, was built by Henry VIII in 1542 to protect the entrance to this valuable harbour. It is open to the public. A little further afield there are a number of delightful villages to explore. On the E side of the peninsula and reached by quiet lanes, are Gerrans and Portscatho. Only 5 minutes apart, they each retain their individual charm, though some recent development is tending to merge them. **Gerrans** is a bright little village with a smart white-painted rectory on the crest of a hill. The rebuilt medieval spire of the church, one of only a few in Cornwall, has been a trusted landmark for generations of local sailors. Below the hill, **Portscatho** spreads along the base of the cliffs and although it has received a number of small blocks of modern holiday flats these have been fitted in sensitively to its existing fabric. Indeed, it can be argued that they add to its attraction by providing yet another variation of form and colour to add to the mosaic of the past.

Veryan nearby has a real picture-postcard centre but a lot of rather obvious new development on its outskirts. A visit here, though, is worth while if only to see the Round Houses which guard the main entrances to the village. Legend has it that these were built long ago by a parson, one for each of his daughters, and built in a round shape so that the devil would find no place to hide. For good measure they are topped with crosses.

If approaching St Just from W Cornwall or if leaving Roseland for that part of the county, a trip on the King Harry car ferry is not to be missed and it will save many miles of driving. It crosses the Fal river 1m above Turnaware Point where beautiful National Trust woodlands run down to the water's edge. The ferry is well signposted but operating hours do vary according to the time of the year.

SHALDON, *Devon,* sits on the S bank of the Teign Estuary while its larger neighbour, Teignmouth, spreads across the N. There has been a ferry linking the two at least from the 13th c, but today travellers can use a road bridge. Shaldon, however, still retains its individual atmosphere and has escaped much of the commercialization characteristic of the other side.

The street plan of the village has been dictated by the curving coastline to the N and the red sandstone promontory of the Ness which rises up on the S side. The village was being developed during the 17th c, but it suffered a setback in 1690 when the French sailed into the estuary and set fire to over 100 houses here. Today, the architecture is predominantly a free type of Regency and many houses are decorated with colourful window-boxes. Around the Square are some delightful early 19th-c low terraced cottages, and a handful of modern houses at the N end of Albion Street have been carefully designed in a neo-Regency style to blend in well with the existing housing. Look out also for Victorian Gothic which is well represented; see especially the rusticated Hunter's Lodge in Fore Street complete with leaded windows, pointed frames and a row of foxhead mouldings above. Ringmore Towers on the Ringmore Road was extravagantly enlarged in the 19th c.

There is also an old centre at Shaldon which is less frequently seen. Stray down the narrow alleyways off the Strand and Middle Street where you will find Crown Square, a misnomer really, for it isn't a square at all but leads on into other small lanes. Here are some of the oldest houses in the village; Teign Cot for example, has thick cob walls and a heavy thatch roof.

Marine Parade leads out to the S past the boats dotted on the beach, and on up the hill to the Ness, where there is a tunnel leading to another beach otherwise cut off at high-tide. There are two tunnels although only one is now open. Romantic legends of smugglers are associated with these but the main tunnel was only cut in the early 19th c by Lord Clifford to give access to his own private stretch of sand.

Leaving Shaldon W by the high Commons Lane, or back along the coast, the neighbouring village of **Ringmore** is reached. This is mostly Georgian and much smaller. Ringmore and Shaldon form one parish and here, tucked away behind the main Ringmore Road, is the original chapel of St Nicholas dating back to the 13th c but with much later rebuilding. Simple unrendered stone inside, it is still in use and lovingly cared for.

A string of thatched cottages with heavy buttressed walls line Higher Ringmore Road leading out of the village to the S while a further 2m along the estuary is the tiny village of **Coombe Cellars.** Formerly a notorious smuggling centre it was made the scene of one of Baring-Gould's West Country novels, *Kitty Alone,* published in 1895. Today the attractive inn is still the centre of much of the village activity as it must have been in the smuggling days of long ago.

SIDBURY, *Devon* (3m N of Sidmouth), lies deep in the valley of the River Sid, surrounded by the wooded spurs of the greensand plateau into which the river has cut its course. The village, lying at the centre of a very extensive parish which includes **Sidford** (1m S), has grown up around the spired church of St Giles which W. G. Hoskins reckons one of the most interesting in Devon. A Saxon crypt, which can be seen every Thursday afternoon in summer, was found under the chancel in 1898. It is one of only six in the country.

Around the church there are a number of white-painted cottages roofed with thatch or attractive blue slate; Court House is partly Elizabethan but largely early 18th-c. There is a pleasant walk by the river and alongside the mill leet. W of the village is Sidbury Castle, an Iron Age hill fort (600ft). This pear-shaped enclosure, some 1300ft long and nearly 400ft wide, is surrounded by a double rampart and ditch. Elsewhere in the parish there are a number of 16th-c farmhouses such as Lincombe Farm and Sand Barton. The late-Victorian Sidbury Manor is set in a park with two lakes.

SLAPTON, *Devon,* is a South Hams village lying 5m SW of Dartmouth in a steep valley. Houses hug the hillside, their fronts built against the steep narrow streets that wind around the contours. Roofs are mostly of slate, and many of the walls are now rendered; a reminder that in 1943 Slapton and the adjoining villages were taken over by U.S. troops and used as a practice ground for D Day. The place was pitted with shells but time has healed the scars and, although parking is difficult, it is well worth walking through the village to admire its character.

Visually the most dominant landmark is the late 14th-c chantry tower to the N, once part of St Mary's College of Chantry Priests. This was founded in 1372 by Sir Guy de Brien who was formerly a standard-bearer to Edward III. The nave and rest of the College no longer exist and all that remains is the tower constructed of local slate and rising 80ft above the ground. The carved stone corbels and squat spire above the external stair turret appear silhouetted against the skyline. The large W window is now blocked up but on the E is the gaping hole where the nave once projected.

To the S is a rambling late Georgian house called The Priory rising way above the road, which is hollowed out of the hillside at this point. Entered on one side through a winding tunnel it is encased by shaky verandahs and climbing wistarias which evoke a rather French atmosphere. W is what was probably the Church House; sharing a fate common with many others, it is now an inn.

Nearby is the parish church of St James the Great, with a low tower topped by a broach spire. The surrounding graveyard is raised up several feet and there are many early 19th-c tombstones of Devonian slate. Above the extended N porch of the church are the two small windows of the Parvis Chamber – probably a priest's room – approached by a steep staircase in the N aisle near the Jacobean cover of the font. Further towards the rood screen are the altered remains of the rood stairs with an outside turret. The 15th-c screen has been heavily restored and leads into the oldest 14th-c part of the church.

The village also houses Slapton Field Studies Centre which manages Slapton Ley to the S. The Ley is a large freshwater lake protected from the sea by Slapton Sands, a raised shingle bank over 2m long. It lies in the centre of Start Bay, which is notorious for its severe storms. In 1917 the village of Hallsands to the S was completely swept away, while in January 1979 damage was widespread at Torcross on the S of the Ley.

The quiet village of **Sherford** straddles its own small valley 3m to the W. It incorporates several Domesday manors and there are some fine examples of vernacular architecture around St Martin's Church. This contains some mid-14th-c workmanship, and, like Slapton's chantry tower, is built of local slate from Charleton near Kingsbridge. S is Kennedon Farm, originally a manor house built around a courtyard. Much of it is 15th-c, and the thick-walled porch may once have been a tower.

SOUTH CADBURY, *Somerset* (7m W of Wincanton, S of A303), is one of many delightful villages in an area of Somerset made beautiful by its colour and distinctive topography. South Cadbury nestles at the foot of Cadbury Castle, one of Britain's finest natural forts, surrounded in legend from the days of King Arthur.

The oldest buildings are clustered directly below the castle and near the church. Only a small amount of recent development has taken place but the red bricks used are rather out of place beside the original yellow stone. This is in contrast to the sensitive development at **Compton Pauncefoot** (1m E). The present structure of the church of St Thomas à Becket at South Cadbury dates mainly from the 14th and 15th c, and is Perp in style. The tower has not the height of many Somerset church towers but is still an impressive sight, with its stair turret and pinnacles, corner buttresses, and gargoyles. The interior, although much renovated, has a pleasing appearance. Its walls are whitewashed and the windows and arches retain their natural stone surrounds. In the splay of one S-facing window is a faint wall painting of a bishop in his cope and mitre, believed to be a representation of St Thomas à Becket.

The old rectory faces the church gate; it is an 18th-c house in the Georgian style. To the left is a building with a bell on its roof; this is the schoolhouse of days gone by. Further along the road is Castle Farm house, a fine building with a thatched roof and mullioned windows, dating from 1687. Opposite, a stony track, once known as Arthur's Lane, leads to the castle.

Mystery has long surrounded the history of this castle, especially in its connections with the legends of King Arthur. Extensive excavations during the late 1960s have shed light on many questions, but whatever facts are established, the romance of the Arthurian legends will surely live on. Cadbury Castle is an oval, flat-topped hill covering 18 acres. Its fortifications are immense; four banks with their dividing ditches reach a depth of 40ft in places. After a climb to the uppermost bank it is easy to appreciate the strategic importance of such a site, with its commanding view across Somerset. The earliest evidence of occupation on Cadbury dates from Neolithic times. This settlement thrived until soon after the Roman Conquest when there was a forced evacuation. Probably during the 5th c it was reoccupied by the legendary King Arthur. Arthur was almost definitely not a king but a military leader using Cadbury Castle as a base for raids on the barbarian invaders. Archaeological evidence provides support for the reoccupation, but for those of romantic inclination there is other evidence to link Cadbury with the Arthurian legend. Two wells – Arthur's Well and St Anne's Wishing Well – are now drinking places for cattle, and parts of Arthur's hunting path to Glastonbury survive.

SOUTH TAWTON, *Devon.* About 4m E of Okehampton and 1m or so N of A30 lies the tiny, pleasant village of South Tawton. Its site is hilly and even its miniature square slopes steeply. Some of the older dwellings are whitewashed cottages with thatched roofs, some are more solid-looking houses built of dark granite enlivened by touches of white paintwork. There are also a few newer buildings tucked into the edges of the village.

The main focus of interest, however, is the little square. Here, set slightly back within its graveyard, is a 15th-c granite church with an attractively light and spacious interior, while next to the church, but built directly on to the square, stands the Church House which dates from the 16th c. In the centre of the square a tree has grown since the days of Elizabeth I, and there is one here now – the Cross Tree.

The few lanes of this village form a compact and intricate knot. This result of organic settlement growth contrasts strongly with the long, straight main street of South Tawton's 'offspring', the purpose-planned new town of the 13th c, which is now the village of **South Zeal**, ½m to the S. This is one of the many towns which were deliberately created during an intense spate of economic development and interior colonization which occurred in Devon in the 12th and 13th c.

South Zeal dates from c. 1264 and occupies a strategic site on the then high road from Exeter to Okehampton. Its old market place can be found in the middle of the village where the houses are set back further from the road. The small chapel in the centre of the market place is a 1713 rebuilding of the original medieval chapel.

STICKLEPATH, *Devon*, on the N edge of Dartmoor, 4m E of Okehampton, lies astride the main A30 and beside the River Taw. A typical one-street Devon village, its layout virtually unchanged for centuries, it now awaits the blessing of a by-pass and the threat of prospective residential development.

The road and river provide the twin elements of historical continuity, the latter having been harnessed for centuries to drive a variety of mills. The Finch Foundry stands in the centre of the village as a testimony to this tradition. Restored and renovated, this outstanding example of a 19th-c water-powered factory is in working order and daily operation throughout the summer months. The wooden launder and water wheels have been rebuilt and once again the trip and drop hammers, shears and forges have been brought to life. Part of the building has been converted into a museum of rural industry and waterpower.

Behind the foundry lies a former Quaker burial ground. A peaceful place, close to the murmuring River Taw, it is evidence of the long and interesting association of this place with Dissent. In the reign of Charles II there were reputedly 200 Quakers here – the majority of the population. In 1682 a strong contingent of Friends from Sticklepath were among the party which sailed with William Penn to America. A further reminder of the tradition of Nonconformity is the Methodist church. Erected in 1816, this attractive and well-proportioned building with a small bell turret reminds us of the village's earlier association with the Wesleys. Sticklepath was a frequent halt on their journeys to Cornwall.

Most properties in the village predate the established church, which was not built until 1875. The cottages spreading out along the axis of the road are probably late 16th- or early 17th-c. Attractive thatched dwellings of plastered rubble and cob predominate. The Devonshire and Taw River Inns are typical of these picturesque structures. The latter was probably one of the most important houses in the village and may have been the old manor house.

At the W end of the village is the Lady Well, with the charming inscription 'drink and be thankful', and a boundary or standing stone. Nearby a narrow minor road gives access to attractive woods and impressive moorland scenery. Cawsand Beacon, Belston Cleave, Belston Tor and the pretty village of that name may be visited.

STOKE, *Devon*, 2m W of Hartland and 1m E of Hartland Quay, is a small settlement now mainly agricultural. The village is surrounded by farmland and contains several farmworkers' cottages. During the Middle Ages, however, the church at Stoke and the Abbey ½m NE would have featured prominently in the lives of the local population. The original church was built in 1055 but this was replaced by the present church in 1360. Hartland Abbey was first founded in the mid-11th c as a college for secular canons. At this time the Church House, on the S side of the square outside the churchyard, was used by priests serving the church and the upper rooms of the house by parishioners for meetings. This room was reached by outside stairs which can still be seen. Later, during the reign of Henry II (1154–89), Hartland Abbey was refounded as an Augustinian abbey by Geoffrey de Dinant, and the Church House was used as the Abbot's lodging. The close ties between the abbey and Stoke remained until Henry VIII dissolved the abbey in 1535 and five years later gave the Abbot's lodging to his chief butler.

Hartland Abbey is now a private house approached through a pretty wooded glen. Little of the old abbey remains, however. The present house was built in 1779 in the imitation Gothic style incorporating some portions of the old cloisters. In 1860 when fashions in architecture had changed it was made to look thicker and more solid.

The church of St Nectan at Stoke can be seen for miles around because its tower stands 128ft high and is in fact the tallest in Devon. On the E wall of the tower there is a figure of St Nectan. The church is of the late Perp period and has been altered little. It contains fine wagon roofs typical of N Devon churches and a 15th-c rood screen which is in excellent condition. Above the N porch is the Pope's Chamber where the priest in charge of the church would have slept. This now houses a small museum.

Leaving the village by the road to Hartland Quay a coastguard station is passed on the right. 1m further and the clifftops are reached. From here there is an excellent view of the contorted synclines and anticlines in the rocks of the cliffs, and on a fine day Lundy Island is easily visible. Below is **Hartland Quay**, first built in Elizabeth

I's reign but abandoned in 1893. Little of it now remains but there are still a few houses there. The harbour buildings have been converted into an hotel.

TINTAGEL, *Cornwall,* sits in a high, windy position on the N coast, 5m NW of Camelford. It is chiefly distinguished as the legendary birthplace of King Arthur and, except for a few very old cottages, the village has been rather spoilt by tourism and insensitive development since Victorian days.

It is Tintagel Castle, on the headland just NW of the village, which is most strongly connected with King Arthur. The present ruins are of a castle built about 1145 by Reginald, Earl of Cornwall, on a huge rock called 'The Island'. Joined to the mainland by a mere neck of rock and towering high above the sea, the site is so impressive and romantic that only a little imagination is required for the ruins to become King Arthur's castle. When visiting 'The Island', the site of a Celtic monastery founded here *c.* 500 should not be overlooked. It was abandoned by 1086 but the ground plan is still visible.

Immediately W of the village is Tintagel Church, standing in an outsized graveyard, isolated and exposed on the cliff top. Although parts of the church are Anglo-Saxon, most of it is Norman work and there is a five-legged Norman font.

In the village proper the Old Post Office is certainly worth a visit. Maintained by the National Trust and open to the public, this low building of well-weathered local stone with uneven, heavy slate roof and tiny windows is a rare surviving example of a probable small manor house of the 14th c. Certain features of the exterior, such as the chimney-pots made of four slates set on edge, were typical of N Cornwall and can be seen on other old houses in the village. Inside it feels 'lived in' and smells of wood smoke – one can easily picture it as a family home. From 1844 to 1892 a room in this house served as the post office for Tintagel and surrounding district and the building retained this name even after the post office business was removed elsewhere. The Post Room is now once again furnished as a Victorian village post office.

The cliff-bound coastline N and W of Tintagel is superb, and much is in the care of the National Trust. It is also worth making a diversion of a mile or two on the route to or from Camelford to the mining village of **Delabole** to see one of the quarries for the slate which was so important in the history of Cornwall. It is still being worked, from what is probably the largest hole in the ground that many people will ever have seen.

WESTON ZOYLAND, *Somerset* (4m SE of Bridgwater on A372), is one of three villages whose church towers dominate Sowy Island, an area of some 2000 acres of silty land on the edge of King's Sedgemoor, which was the site of the Battle of Sedgemoor.

The land is extremely flat, but the village does not sprawl haphazardly over it. The church is a focal point around which the older buildings cluster, forming a mixture of small cottages and narrow roads. The narrow main street is lined with a few inns, shops and a post office; interspersed among the cottages are many farms and patches of open ground creating the feeling that this is still very much a working village. Around the edge modern houses indicate its new function as a dormitory for Bridgwater.

The characteristic features of Somerset churches are their fine towers and tie-beam roofs, and the church of St Mary the Virgin at Weston Zoyland has magnificent examples of both. The yellow-grey stone tower forms a landmark in the flat landscape. Reaching a height of over 100ft, it includes elements of Somerset tracery among the delicate stone carving. The present church was built mostly during the 14th and 15th c, incorporating aspects of the Dec and Perp styles. On entering the church the most striking feature is the tie-beam roof of the nave. The angel busts supporting both tie-beam braces and king posts add an extra dimension to the characteristic Somerset style. This interior, with its light, open appearance, is probably little changed since the days of Sedgemoor. One major addition was made in the 1930s when a rood loft was sensitively erected over an existing screen and the newel stairway rebuilt.

A plan in the church porch shows the route to the Battlefield of Sedgemoor. This begins as a footpath beside the inn leading among houses and gardens to the outskirts of the village. Turning left, one follows the road through modern housing to Bussex Farm whence a drove road leads to the battlefield and its monument. 'Ye Last Battle on English Soil' was fought early one morning in July 1685. Monmouth and his rebellious forces found themselves halted at Bridgwater by detachments of James I's troops stationed at the three Sowy villages. An ill-planned attempt at a surprise attack ended in battle, with disastrous consequences for the rebel forces. The Royal troops suffered very few losses but treated their opponents harshly. Many were shot or hanged on the spot, and 500 were locked in Weston Zoyland Church overnight, before being marched to Bridgwater. Some months later Judge Jeffreys set out on the Western Assize to deal with these prisoners. Sentences were harsh; many were executed or transported. The only evidence of battle now on this quiet open fenland is a granite memorial erected by public subscription in 1928.

WIDECOMBE-IN-THE-MOOR, *Devon.* Situated in the heart of Dartmoor National Park, the village is well signposted. It lies in the valley of the East Webburn river, surrounded by high granite-strewn ridges and tors. These landscape features, together with the granite buildings in the village, reflect much of the essential character of the area.

While farming is a central feature of the local economy, the area was once important for tin

mining. The church tower is reputed to have been built with tinners' money. This church of St Pancras, known as the 'cathedral of the moor' is a most imposing granite building. Standing on the site of a 13th-c church, it is a cruciform structure, reconstructed and enlarged in the late 15th or early 16th c in Perp style. The lofty tower, 120ft high, is the outstanding feature, providing a beacon-like guide to the village. It is one of the finest towers in the West of England and is of characteristic Dartmoor design. The tower is battlemented and crowned with fine crocketed pinnacles holding up crosses; the pinnacles are repeated in stages down the tower. There was some restoration and rebuilding in the 17th c, following a severe storm. On Sunday 21 October 1638, one of the pinnacles was struck by lightning and fell into the church below, killing four and injuring 62 persons. Verses commemorate this tragic event. Notable features of the interior include the original 16th-c wagon roof, with some interesting bosses. One of these depicts a rabbit, emblem of the tinners. The remains of a 15th-c rood screen with painted figures of saints and apostles may also be seen.

Leaving the churchyard by the lychgate we find a tiny village square surrounded by a group of interesting buildings and containing a yew and lime tree. Foremost among these buildings is the Church House, an early 16th-c granite structure with a portico. A fine example of a moorstone building, it served in the past as an almshouse and school. It is now owned by the National Trust. On the opposite side of the square is the Glebe House, a plain granite building reputedly erected in 1575 (now a gift shop). Completing the square is the 17th-c, but possibly earlier, Old Inn. This is a granite building with slate roof and an open courtyard bounded by two wings, one of which boasts an external stair. A recent extension to a gift shop has narrowed this courtyard.

The old name for the village green – Butte Park – reveals its past use for archery practice. This was also the setting for the famous Widecomb Fair, held on the second Tuesday in September and popularized by the ballad of that name. A monument commemorating the characters of the song stands on the green close to the church. The fair was important for sales of cattle, sheep and ponies, but is now grossly commercialized. Former houses around the green have been similarly spoilt.

There is much to see in the surrounding area. In addition to the attractive villages of Buckland-in-the-Moor (q.v.) and **North Bovey**, there are interesting prehistoric sites at Foales Arrishes and Grimspound. There are also a number of fine old moorland farmhouses like Venton, Corndon and Lower Tor. The privately owned Rugglestone Inn is close to an interesting logan-stone. Hay Tor, Wind Tor and others provide good views.

ZENNOR, *Cornwall,* is set in a hollow on the windswept Land's End or Penwith peninsula; 'Penwith' is an old Cornish word meaning 'farthest extremity'. The village comprises a number of farms which cluster tightly around the church and inn. The landscape around is a piece of pure Penwith, with small, irregular pasture fields bounded by dry-stone walls and dotted with gorse bushes. It has that treeless, upland flavour.

Extensive renovations were carried out to the little church around 1890 but some of the S wall near the door and part of the porch probably belong to the original structure. It has a typical Cornish barrel roof but its most interesting feature is the so-called Mermaid Chair which sits in a side chapel. The sides of this chair are made from two bench-ends preserved during the 1890 restoration. One of these shows a mermaid with a glass in one hand and a comb in the other; legend has it that she was entranced by the singing of the squire's son and lured him down to the sea with her.

The cliff scenery of this part of Cornwall is awe-inspiring, and a magnificent stretch can be reached by taking the easy, level path left of the church and behind the Tinners' Arms past the coastguard station to Zennor Head (National Trust). The great cliffs are magnificent, particularly on a rough day when at high-tide huge Atlantic rollers boil through a blow-hole at the base of the cliffs. 1½m NE along the cliffs is the little hamlet of **Tregerthen** where during World War I D. H. Lawrence and his German-born wife Frieda spent a pretty miserable time with everyone convinced they were spies.

During the Stone and Iron Ages, Penwith was a very populous area and there is plenty of evidence of this on the Ordnance Survey map and on the ground. Among the more remarkable of the relics is a number of quoits (cromlechs or chambered burial tombs) formed by raising boulders on end and then laying a vast slab of stone over these to form a roof. The sides of the chamber would then have been walled-in with turf or stones. Zennor quoit, reached by a track running S from the 'Eagles Nest' on B3306 (Zennor–St Ives road) has one of the largest roof slabs in all England and is also probably unique because it contained two chambers covered by one great stone. W of Zennor the five lines of fortifications of Treryn Dinas fort are still clearly visible on Gurnard's Head. Some 3m S is the impressive 1st-c BC–AD 3rd-c village of Chysauster. The houses no longer have their roofs; much of the walling is also in utter ruin, but nevertheless it is known apocryphally as the 'oldest village street in England'. All these monuments in Penwith are real touch-stones to the distant past of human civilization; they are more evocative than any museum exhibit ever can be. Just to see them in the rudeness of this landscape conveys the harsh reality of our ancestors' existence.

The Welsh Marches

Sir Jasper More

SALOP HEREFORD AND WORCESTER

Apart from some small peripheral areas of Shropshire – or Salop as it is now called – the whole of the area covered by this section of the book is drained by the main streams and tributaries of the great rivers Severn and Wye. A western wall is formed by the Welsh mountains, some of whose foothills are within the Salop and Herefordshire borders; otherwise with one exception there are no mountains. There are, however, large areas of countryside that are high or hilly or rolling. Though there are some areas of flat valley land there is nothing remotely comparable with the fen landscapes of the Eastern Counties; and in the middle or further distance there is always some natural feature in the view.

The most dramatic of the hills, thanks less to their height than to the flatness of the surrounding plains, are the Wrekin in Salop and the Malvern Hills on the Worcestershire-Herefordshire border. As to the mountains, the exception is provided by the South Shropshire Hills (so called) – Clun Forest, Long Mountain, Stiperstones, Longmynd, Caradoc, Wenlock Edge, Brown Clee, Titterstone Clee – which spread themselves from the Welsh border to the Severn, and most of which include sizeable areas of true mountain scenery.

The county capitals are on the great rivers, and many of the other towns are riverside towns. From all this it would seem to follow that a selection of villages from the counties would include a high proportion of hill villages and riverside villages. Sadly this is not so. From the area of the South Shropshire Hills have been selected Chirbury, Lydbury North, Little Stretton and Munslow, but three of these stand in the wide valleys which divide the successive mountain masses and only Little Stretton, closely hemmed in between Longmynd and Caradoc, gives any suggestion of an upland character.

The Severn does not always make itself as attractive as one might hope, and of the selected villages Arley is the only one that can truly be called Severn-side. Eardisland in Herefordshire on the little River Arrow is really the most at home with its river. Sadly the Wye, most gracious of English rivers, does not appear to attract villages to its banks; even Fownhope, which looks so Wye-side on the map, resolutely turns its back on the river and is simply a village of the Herefordshire countryside.

The villages selected for their beauty are thus generally villages of the valleys or the rolling plains. Geographically they are not well spread over the area and this fact must reflect the economic backgrounds of the different zones. Worcestershire has always been richer than Herefordshire, Herefordshire richer than Salop; and this was particularly true of the pre-industrial ages during which the beauty of our villages was created. Before the industrial era the wealth of the Marches, as of other parts of England, was primarily in its agriculture, and the richest agricultural areas produced the finest villages.

The two greatest concentrations are in Worcestershire and Herefordshire; in Worcestershire in the area round Evesham and Pershore, which is watered by the Avon and is called the Vale of Evesham; in Herefordshire in that small triangle west of Leominster of which the points are Kingsland, Pembridge and Weobley. But beautiful villages do not always have beautiful churches or manor houses, and the converse is equally true. In Herefordshire in particular there appears always to have been a fashion for building churches away from their villages or even in total isolation; and it must be a matter for reproach that no mention is made in this gazetteer of Herefordshire's most exquisite Norman church, Kilpeck, or of that splendidly preserved relic of the monastic age, Abbey Dore, neither supported by a village.

Notwithstanding such hard facts of topography, there are included in the village descriptions a series of churches in which both Worcestershire and Herefordshire can take a pride. One must not lose proportion to the extent of comparing them with those of Lincolnshire, Somerset or the Cotswolds; nevertheless it is no exaggeration to describe some of them as little cathedrals. Coming from Shropshire one is constantly astounded by the size and scale of churches south of the border.

Shropshire, as a poor county, was indebted for her major buildings to outsiders; to the religious orders who arrived with religious wealth to build their monasteries; and in later ages to new arrivals who came, already monied, to build their country mansions, though a few, it is true, were built of money made in Shrewsbury or Ludlow. Only in special circumstances did money go on great village churches, and seldom were there conscious efforts to build up or beautify the villages themselves. Thus Shropshire in this context is the poor relation.

The building materials of the Welsh Marches are stone, brick and black-and-white, and the

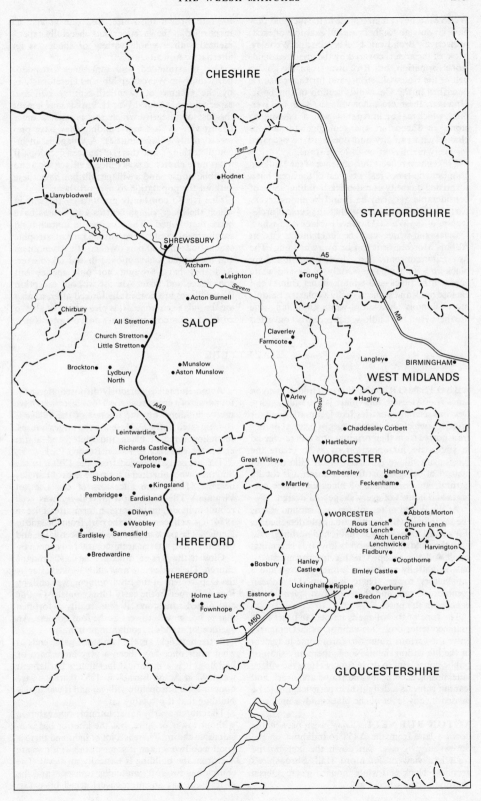

Welsh Marches can take pride in the fact that they have an outstandingly beautiful example of each: respectively Broadway, Feckenham and Weobley. Most of the area is covered by the great red sandstone formation, but Broadway is in the golden belt of the Cotswold stone, and for that reason is described in the Cotswolds section of this book. However, there are other villages, such as Overbury, which make a brave show with not dissimilar stone. In Shropshire the geological formations change with rapidity and one must be prepared for every manifestation of local stone.

Feckenham reflects the influence of the Midland counties and is not really typical of the area, but a surprising quantity of red-brick building, some of considerable age, can be found in almost every part. Yet the fact remains that the typical architecture of the Welsh Marches is black-and-white.

Black-and-white can be enchanting, as at Abbots Morton, or it can be overwhelming! The two major concentrations already mentioned are black-and-white villages. Oddly, black-and-white need not be black-and-white; timber frames can enclose brick and stone as easily as plaster. Salop's most famous black-and-white building, the Feathers Hotel at Ludlow, has recently converted itself to brown-and-white; and one village, as mentioned in the gazetteer, has cheerfully experimented with a whole variety of shades as an alternative to white.

One is astounded, and sometimes distressed, particularly in Worcestershire and Herefordshire, by the volume of twentieth-century building, especially since World War II. Purists may lament the loss of integrity which this entails; a more robust view is that new building may have preserved many village entities. A village is an incomplete thing – and this is often seen in Salop – if it has not a church, a post office, a village shop and a public house; and a village will not have these without the population to support them.

One is also constantly gratified by the way in which the older village centres and houses have been maintained. The decline in agricultural employment could have entailed a catastrophic evacuation; instead new owners – the commuters and the retired – have moved in and taken over. And they have brought not only money but conscience and taste. Almost without exception these villages are beautifully looked after, as also are the village churches. It is pleasant to be able to conclude these comments on a note of optimism.

GAZETTEER

ABBOTS MORTON, *Worcs.* Hidden away in lanes W of Alcester, this village is like a fairy story. One has seen in countries like Denmark open-air museums which are assemblages of peasant houses transported from their original sites and re-erected in suggestive juxtaposition so as to create the illusion of a village. Abbots Morton is like this, but instead of being an artificial creation it is totally natural, an assemblage of black-and-white cottages and houses of every shape and design.

At the W end of the village on a mound stands the stone-built village church; a little detached, as if it wished to make clear that it had nothing to do with the childish goings-on below. It is charming, small and has escaped 19th-c improvements; it has delightfully eccentric Gothic windows and a satisfactory tower. There is a good Jacobean communion rail, and there are two splendid old benches in the porch.

The tone of the village is immediately set by a thatched letter box. One cannot, as in Denmark, enter the various houses to form some judgment of the life within them. Nor is there any shop or public house. But to drive slowly along the village lane, noting each beam and frame and cruck and leaning gable, is a delightful experience, not to be missed by any lover of the black-and-white.

ACTON BURNELL, *Salop*, is approachable down a lane from the A458 roundabout on the Shrewsbury by-pass. 5m down the lane on the right is a view of Pitchford Hall, Shropshire's grandest black-and-white house, where Queen Victoria stayed when a girl.

Acton Burnell is curiously disposed along the four arms of a cross-roads. All four directions have pretty buildings but the interest of the village is concentrated in the E. Here are the larger houses, including three of black-and-white; and at the end is the entrance to Acton Burnell Park.

The property belonged from the 17th c to the Smythes, who inherited it from the Lees of Langley nearby. (They were ancestors of the Lees of Virginia.) The Hall, now a college, was well rebuilt in its original Georgian form after a fire in 1914; it is well seen across the park from the lane to Kenley. The park must once have been large and romantic, and a large architectural folly survives.

Close to the park entrance are the Castle and the church. The castle ruin, now tidily looked after by the Department of the Environment, was built by Bishop Burnell in the early 14th c; mostly Gothic and of red sandstone, it is in reality a fortified manor house with towers at the four corners. An aged cedar stands in romantic proximity.

In the next field are the two stone gable ends of what must once have been a very large barn or building. It is a historical fact that a Parliament was held in Acton Burnell in 1283 (surely a rare honour for a Shropshire village) and it was in this building that it probably sat.

The church nearby has an unimpressive exterior, without tower or spire, but the interior has considerable charm. There is a lot of light and there is good woodwork; and if some of the windows are Victorian the building is basically medieval. The church has two lofty matching transepts and the N transept has an impressive Burnell brass (AD

Kenneth Scowen

The ruins of the castle at Acton Burnell

1382) and some elaborate Smythe memorials (though they were Roman Catholics) and a very impressive tomb of Richard Lee dated 1591.

About 2m S are the remains of the gatehouse of **Langley**, also the remarkable Langley chapel, which stands isolated in a field. This is of the late 16th or early 17th c and it is worth seeking out the key, for all the original woodwork is still in place, including the free-standing altar and the pulpit.

ARLEY, *Worcs.* (sometimes called Upper Arley), is a village for river lovers. For 15m, from Bridg-north to Bewdley, there is no bridge for motor vehicles across the swiftly flowing Severn. Arley used to have a ferry; this has now been replaced by a bridge, strictly marked 'Pedestrians Only', by which one can cross to the miniscule Harbour Inn (when was there last a harbour at Arley?) and to the Railway Station. The Railway Station is part of that enterprising venture the Severn Valley Railway, which on most days of the week will transport you hence by steam haulage to Bridg-north or Bewdley. These two buildings apart, the W bank is populated only by fishermen.

Seen from the west bank, Arley is very pic-turesque. Red-brick cottages and houses line the waterfront. The village centre is made a little further on by the Valentia Arms, an ambitious construction, part Victorian-Tudor, part Geor-gian and part Scottish Baronial. A village lane then climbs steeply upwards to the church en-trance whence there is a steep path to the church.

Arley church is not very agreeably constructed, both inside and out, of a mixture of pink and grey sandstone blocks. On the exterior under the E window is inscribed the sinister date 1885 but there

are older things in the church, notably some memorials to the local proprietors, the Valentia family. But the most unexpected object is the tomb of Sir Robert de Balun who in 1270 went to Southampton to meet Henry III for the Eighth Crusade, and shortly afterwards died there. There is a good nave-roof and some nice clerestory windows. From the churchyard is a pretty view of the grounds of Arley Castle.

ATCHAM, *Salop* (4m E of Shrewsbury), is a beauty spot but is also a danger point, and those arriving by the A5 road from London would do well to turn straight into the lane leading to village or church, park the car, and do the village on foot, for the distances are small.

Half the village is new. There is a daunting yellow-brick Victorian School house, but there are also some pretty houses, notably a plastered house with a Gothic bow window, a malt house transformed into a village hall, and an attractive vicarage almost in the churchyard. The very satisfactory red-brick Georgian façade of the Mytton and Mermaid Hotel looks out from a decent distance upon the main road.

Atcham avoids the horrors of the traffic by the simple expedient of being built wholly on the S side of the A5. We are here in the flat centre of Salop where Tern and Severn unite; both rivers have noble 18th-c bridges, the Tern by Mylne, the Severn by Gwynne. From the Tern bridge is a splendid view of the long façade of Attingham.

Originally called Tern Hall, this house was rebuilt by Steuart about 1785 into the much grander Attingham, and the 8th Lord Berwick presented it to the National Trust, by whom it is opened to the public. The park lies all along the N side of the A5 and opposite the Mytton and Mermaid is the splendid entrance inscribed *'Cui uti scit ei bona'* ('Wealth should belong to him who knows how to use it').

The house was not improved by Nash, but it is worth seeing, for in several of the rooms the decoration is very fine. There are ceiling paintings possibly by Angelica Kauffman and some very delicate plaster work. The contents are less good than the decoration, but there is a beautiful set of drawing-room furniture from Naples bought by Lord Berwick from the selling-up of King Joachim Murat after 1815. The grounds were laid out by Repton, whose Red Book survives.

Behind the Mytton and Mermaid is the church of St Eata (a unique dedication). It is built of red sandstone. The interior is too dark for comfort partly due to medieval glass brought here from Herefordshire. There is good woodwork and there are some beautiful Berwick hatchments.

A final delight at Atcham is to walk across Gwynne's bridge up the Cross Houses road and view the tranquil scene – bridge, hotel, village, church and river, which might be a hundred miles from the A5. 1m on is a Nash house called Cronkhill. 2m SE is the Roman Uriconium, with relics of the Baths and a small museum.

BOSBURY, *Herefordshire* (4m N of Ledbury), lies in flat fruit- and hop-growing country within sight of the Malvern Hills. Herefordshire can boast few prettier village scenes than the view of the village street from the churchyard, the wide extent of which means that for two hundred yards the village street is built upon on one side only. There is a fair variety of building but overwhelmingly what makes the charm of the village is its black-and-white. A prominent black-and-white building opposite the church is the Bell Inn.

Not the least remarkable feature of the scene is the church tower. This is detached from the church and stands isolated in the churchyard halfway between church and street. The church, notwithstanding the absence of an attached tower, has a dignified exterior. Even more dignified is the interior. A high nave is borne on 12 Gothic arches with clerestory windows above; there are excellent wooden pews and not too much stained glass. A remarkable font, early medieval, is supported on five stone pillars. Above all, there is splendid carved woodwork, some forming the screen and some the surround to the vestry.

The chancel contains two remarkable tombs. On the S wall a tomb dated 1573, and attributed to Guido of Hereford, is a very civilized composition. Opposite is a grand but much cruder affair dated a few years later. On the SE corner of the nave is the attractive Morton chapel in Perp style with fan vaulting.

In the surrounding countryside one is seeing the best of Herefordshire; lush flat fields with their hedges, trees and lanes; a middle distance of gently rolling country; and the very satisfactory background of the Malvern Hills.

BREDON, *Worcs.*, gave its name presumably to Bredon Hill, that great hump of land that makes such an impression in the flat scenery of E Worcestershire. But the village is in fact at some distance SW from the hill and is really a riverside element in the Avon Valley.

Its charms have clearly been noted for it has accumulated round it a quite remarkable volume of modern housing, particularly on the main road from Tewkesbury to Cheltenham; but the village lane was built up in previous ages and retains great character. A remarkable feature of the village houses is old red brick, apparently of pre-Georgian times. The village is an admirable mixture of red-brick, stone and black-and-white, and there is an excellent proportion of thatch. Hospitality is provided by the Royal Oak on the main road and by the Fox and Hounds in the village lane.

The village lane leads past the church to the Avon, and the houses built along the river, though they are within sight and noise of the great bridge carrying the M5, have a very satisfactory view of uncluttered water-meadows on the far bank.

The presence of the village is announced from afar by the church spire, an unusual feature in Worcestershire. The church is immensely grand for a village and it would take long to catalogue all its features. One is immediately impressed on arrival by not one, but three, very grand Norman entrance arches. Inside the building is Gothic and well lit by high windows; the plan is curious on account of two side additions which are neither aisles nor transepts. In the southern addition is an enormous and impressive monument of the early 17th c with the figures carved in alabaster. Much older monuments are in the chancel.

There are a number of distinguished houses round the church, including the former vicarage, a Georgian building which has been given a 'Cotswold' centrepiece, with a good red-brick stable range. But the great pride of Bredon is its tithe barn, which stands to the W of the church but which has to be approached from the main road near an obelisk milepost. This is a building of such quality as to have been accepted by the National Trust, who keep it open to the public during daylight hours but who sensibly allow it still to be used for storage of hay and straw. Stone-built and stone-tiled, it is of impressive height and width and must embody an enormous weight of timber. There is said to be another similar tithe barn at Middle Littleton some 15m NE; both have been dated to the mid-14th c.

John Moore, some of whose delightful books are thinly disguised studies of life in this neighbourhood 50 years ago, lived in the nearby village of Kemerton. His *Brensham Village* is obviously a composite of Bredon and the riverside Strensham.

BROADWAY, *Worcs. See under* 'The Cotswolds', page 229.

CHADDESLEY CORBETT, *Worcs.* The tower and spire (said to be 18th-c) of the village church overlook the main road from Kidder-

Jeffrey W. Whitelaw, Spectrum
The doorway and steps of the great tithe barn at Bredon

minster to Bromsgrove but the village sensibly leads backwards from the main road and so avoids the horrors of the traffic. Unlike many Worcestershire villages, it has a regular village street.

At the far (N) end is an area of by no means unpleasing red-brick building; then the road drops to cross the Hockley Brook, and one enters the old village.

Chaddesley Corbett is the perfect mixture of old red brick and black-and-white. On the right, as one proceeds S, is the Swan Inn, painted black-and-white; opposite, the Georgian House, red-brick as its name implies. Then on each side of the street very attractive black-and-white cottages. Then, on the left, the timber-framed Talbot Hotel.

The place seems to have been very school-conscious. A red-brick house on the left was built for the school-master in 1785; and a red-brick building by the churchyard (now apparently the school kitchen) was enlarged by a local benefactor as a school in 1809. The modern school, discreetly set back from the street, is next door. A very handsome narrow red-brick early Georgian house with stone quoins adjoins the lychgate entrance to the churchyard.

Chaddesley Corbett has a very grand church. The visitor is immediately struck by the two rows of splendid circular columns in the nave, surmounted by noble capitals and round and transitional arches; these must clearly be Norman. The chancel is an ambitious effort of the Dec period with an elaborate E window.

The church has a number of treasures: a finely carved font of the 12th c; an ancient stone tomb; some ancient brasses; and some fine memorial tablets to the Pakington family. Also a modern copy of the famous Ardebil carpet now in the Victoria and Albert Museum, made in the 16th c in Kashan, with 32,037,200 knots.

Back on the main road, next to the church, is a large ancient house, part timbered and part painted brick.

1–2m NW is **Harvington Hall**, Elizabethan and full of priest holes, once the property of the Pakingtons, now of the Roman Catholics and often open to the public.

Mrs Chaddesley Corbett was the name given by Nancy Mitford to a colourful character in her famous novel, *Love in a Cold Climate*. A pity Miss Mitford did not incorporate some other local names: examples – Mrs Stretton Grandison, Mrs Upton Snodsbury or Mrs Tedstone Delamere.

CHIRBURY, *Salop* (3m NE of Montgomery), is a splendidly compact village close to the Welsh border amid the splendidly unspoilt hill and valley scenery of SW Salop. It is on two minor main roads but avoids traffic horrors by the ingenious layout of the village street, a sequence of right angles.

The name of Chirbury has a small place in history thanks to Lord Herbert of Cherbury, a colourful character of the early 17th c, a poet who wrote his own life and played a somewhat equivocal part in the Civil War. His beautiful house nearby, the black-and-white Lymore, had to be demolished in the 1930s and the principal memorial of the family now is the tomb of his parents in Montgomery church just over the border.

Chirbury has a rather severe village hall (red brick of 1912) but, this apart, the village is a delightful compound of plaster fronts, red brick, black-and-white and local stone. SE of the church is the school with a pretty black-and-white house added on it; NE is a fine stone farm house with a beautiful red-brick octagonal dovecote.

The church is too big for the village. This is because it is the nave, with its aisle, of a former priory church of Augustinian Canons. The massive stone-built tower is an impressive sight as one approaches from Welshpool, and the entrance under the tower, with its stone paving and good hatchments, is excellent. Inside the great pillars which support the Gothic arches of the nave should be noticed if only for the fact that they lean markedly outwards.

The church is the end of the village. Opposite and facing the Welshpool road is the good black-and-white façade of the Herbert Arms Hotel.

The very fine carved rood screen and choir stalls which once stood in the church have been removed to Montgomery 3m away where (together with the Herbert tomb) they can be well seen.

CLAVERLEY, *Salop*, is, as the crow flies, only 7m SW from the town centre of Wolverhampton, but it is hidden in a maze of narrow country lanes, driven sometimes through deep cuttings of the soft red sandstone which is the local geology. It is worth making the effort to find, for Claverley is a rare example of a village which has been developed without losing its essential character.

Wolverhampton and the Black Country discovered it in the 20th c, and the result has been, along the various approach lanes, a sequence of villa residences and housing estates, some unpleasing but mostly pleasing, leading up to the village street.

The parish is a large one and includes some distinguished country houses. Not to be missed, on a side lane from the Wolverhampton approach, is Ludstone Hall, a house which has had many ownerships but clearly of a responsible kind for it has been well cared for and is a most distinguished example of a red-brick Jacobean manor house. Another ancient house, not so well visible, and alas now falling into ruin, is Gatacre Hall, the property of the ancient family of Gatacre. The SW approach has some excellent red-brick Georgian houses at **Farmcote**; then the unfortunate Victorian error of Sandford; a beautiful black-and-white farmhouse; and finally a sensational view of Claverley Church. What is really the village street is the approach from the SE, a most agreeable mixture of period red-brick and black-and-white. The church presides over the small but distinguished village centre. Here the Kings Arms, closely flanked by The Plough, dispenses village hospitality; both are of brick pleasingly painted white. Opposite and flanking the churchyard is a most imposing black-and-white building once the vicarage, on the side of which a black-and-white lychgate leads to the church. This is, for a Salop village, a considerable building; built, as one would expect, of the local sandstone with a massive and imposing tower.

The very venerable interior with its nave and two aisles has four Norman pillars supporting three Norman arches; everything else is Gothic including windows that are Gothic of every period. Two small transepts are built out near the E end, that on the S side being the chapel of the Gatacre family. Here is a most imposing 16th-c alabaster tomb commemorating Sir Robert Brooke, his two wives and ten children, its position here due, presumably, to the fact that his second wife was a Gatacre. Transepts, aisles and nave are furnished with memorials, inscriptions and hatchments.

The ultimate distinction of this church is a series of wall paintings above the Norman arches of the nave; these have been dated to approximately 1200 BC and represent five sets of contests between mounted gladiators – a most exceptional embellishment for a Salop village church. Not to be missed, finally, are the two very early stone fonts.

CROPTHORNE and FLADBURY, *Worcs.*,

are two attractive villages disposed on each side of the River Avon a little downstream from Evesham. Starting down the lane from the main A44 road the beginning of **Cropthorne** is heralded by gardens literally pouring over the surrounding walls of the village houses: houses mostly black-and-white, with a generous sprinkling of thatched roofs and some stone tiles.

The church is that excellent combination, Gothic outside and Norman within. It is built of a pretty pale stone and with an attractive tower in an attractive churchyard. Within are two remarkable 17th-c tombs to the Dineley family. Even more remarkable is a stone 'Cross-head', said to be of Anglo-Saxon art, and to date back to the 9th c, which stands on a window-sill. All this in a beautifully light church lit with clerestory windows of clear glass.

The village lane continues to a small green where the lane to Fladbury divides. After 1m you will see the bridge over the Avon; then **Fladbury** begins with an impressive red-brick mill house which apparently was in use until 1930.

Fladbury has a large village centre disposed round a beautifully kept green on which the Anchor Inn looks out. Almost opposite is Fladbury church, which is more pretentious than that of Cropthorne, and perhaps for that reason suffered the full Victorian treatment of scraped walls, glazed tiles, pitch pine and stained windows. But the exterior of the church can be admired, particularly the tower over the entrance porch. And inside under the tower is a very fine 15th-c tomb chest with two brasses.

Fladbury is remarkable for some very good early Georgian (or Queen Anne) red-brick houses, including the Manor House, the former rectory and another house W of the church. After the church, brick and plaster fronts predominate, and the lane then continues beneath some fine chestnut trees until it joins the other Evesham–Worcester main road (B4084).

DILWYN, *Herefordshire*, 6m SW of Leominster, once on the main Brecon road, is now mercifully by-passed, and lives a peaceful life below the new road. It possesses a feature unusual in Herefordshire, a village green; small, triangular and charming, surrounded by some admirable ranges of black-and-white building. The Crown Inn demurely presides over one of its sides. There has been new building but this has been on the lanes leading away from the centre.

On a mound towards the N end of the village rises the very impressive church. Stone-built and clearly medieval, it presides like a small cathedral over the village. Its spire is in fact said to be 18th-c, but it surmounts a tower which is clearly Norman. Inside is a majestic nave, with an incoherent W end, due no doubt to changes in the building plan. There is a very fine royal hatchment of George III. The nave is of three aisles carried on noble Gothic arches rising from circular columns; above are clerestory windows and a very fine wooden roof. On the N side is a high and wide transept with windows that are almost Perp and fill the church with a flood of light.

The chancel with its finely moulded E window is preceded by a carved screen of the utmost distinction, datable doubtless to the 16th or 17th c.

The church possesses a good font (with its Norman predecessor attractively perched behind it), some interesting tomb slabs and some attractive Georgian monuments. The entrance porch is a small work of art on its own.

Opposite the E end of the church are the school buildings in pale mauve sandstone, by no means devoid of a certain Victorian Gothic charm.

EARDISLAND, *Herefordshire*, 5m W of Leominster. There can be few more romantic spots in Herefordshire than the point where the River Arrow and its mill race are crossed by the stone bridges of the village street. Alas that the village street is also the A44 road from London to Aberystwyth and that buses and lorries disturb the harmony of the scene.

The actual mill has disappeared but the wide opening formed by the two parallel streams has been formed into an idyllic vision of lawns and houses. Looking upstream, there is first, on the right, a black-and-white gable, then some white-painted brick houses, then Georgian red-brick, then a plaster front, then two more charming bits of black-and-white, the restored Georgian stone mill house and finally the timber-framed manor house. In the middle of all this a splendid red-brick dovecote, crying out to be adapted for human habitation. E of the bridge there is more splendid black-and-white, some of it Dickensian in its dilapidation.

Eardisland is one of a trio (with Pembridge and Kingsland, q.v.) of pretty black-and-white villages, and is the most compact of the three. Most of the village lies W of the bridge, and here the Cross Inn and the White Swan hang out their welcoming signs. An attractive and unusual feature is a combined post office, filling station and stores all in black-and-white.

The church is hidden away on the S side of the village. A satisfactory exterior in what is presumably local stone, with a square squat tower. But the interior is disappointing. There is a good stone floor, but in 1864 the Incorporated Society for Church Building did its worst, and both nave and chancel are a sea of pitch-pine pews. The windows on the N side are slits admitting hardly any light and it seems astonishing that all the other windows should be filled with stained or tinted glass. An interesting drawing of the church before its restoration hangs opposite the entrance door.

2m S of Eardisland is Burton Court, a private house open to the public on certain afternoons through the summer. It contains a medieval great hall and a remarkable collection of costumes.

EARDISLEY, *Herefordshire*, 7m NE of Hay-on-Wye. Two licensed houses greet the visitor on the N approach; on the left the Mountie in stark red-brick, on the right the Tram Inn in black-and-white. Names not easily accounted for, since Eardisley to all appearances has neither mounties nor trams. What it does have – and this is sufficiently rare in Herefordshire to be remarked – is a regular village street; the more surprising in that this is a western outpost of the county within a few miles of Wales. Nor is there anything Welsh about the village; in this respect it is unlike Shropshire.

The village houses are a satisfactory mixture. A degree of plaster-fronts, but often with Georgian windows; rows of pretty black-and-white cottages, old stone houses, new stone houses, occasional Victorian red-brick, 20th-c bungalows and very satisfactory displays of stone tiles.

At the S end of the village on the right are some highly commendable conversions of old black-and-white barns into modern living accommodation; then on the left the rather daunting red-brick school of 1867; and on the right the church.

The church, much surrounded by trees, deserves to be better shown for it is a large and fine building of local stone with a good square tower. It is not without the inconsequences and characteristics of Herefordshire, for the tower is built on to the NW corner; the interior is full of pitch pine; and haphazard building additions have made nonsense of any plan. But it is beautifully light, there is good stone paving and the nave with its lofty roof borne on pillars and arches, some pointed, some rounded, makes a fine impression.

The organ was given by John Coke 'in grateful remembrance of the protection of Almighty God in many dangers but especially at Delhi 14 Sept 1857.' Another memorial tablet begins: 'Bubbles broken; but Death's the Gate to Life . . . .'

The great treasure of the church is the font, called by Pevsner 'the most exciting piece of the Norman school in Herefordshire'. Dating apparently from AD 1150, it is deeply carved with ornamental motifs which enclose spirited scenes of human combat accompanied by a large lion.

4m S of Eardisley is **Bredwardine**, where the Rev. Francis Kilvert spent the last two years of his life, and was buried.

EASTNOR, *Herefordshire*, on the E edge of the county, is a feudal village which has been much under the influence of the family of Somers, builders of Eastnor Castle. There is no village street and no real village centre but near the church is an attractive triangular village green with a well under a pyramid roof erected, it is said, by Lady Henry Somerset. The inscription reads: 'If any man thirst let him come unto me and drink'; but there is nothing to suggest that there are any longer any water-drinkers in Eastnor. Conversely there appears to be no village pub; the fleshpots of Ledbury are, however, only 1m away.

There are some modern houses which have neither added to nor detracted from the beauty of the village scene. Also one or two stone houses. Also some black-and-white houses including the post office, which has a very fine thatched roof.

The church tower is old, but the main part of the building is the work of Gilbert Scott of 1852, mostly in red sandstone and with Gothic windows. The windows are so full of stained glass as to make it difficult to appreciate the Victorian woodwork and glazed tiles below.

W of the church is an estate office in black-and-red brick; NW a former rectory by Scott; E the village school by Sir Robert Smirke. Smirke was also responsible for the castle, which is open to the public on occasional afternoons through the summer months. It was inspired by grand ideas

The main street of Elmley Castle

Geoffrey N. Wright

and could be called Norman Revival, though some might call it the Horrific Style. There are a number of large rooms, one said to be designed by Pugin; the *pièce de résistance* is the Great Hall, 60ft long and 65ft high. Whether one admires or dislikes the architecture of Eastnor Castle one must admire the beauty of its grounds, which have been skilfully planted over the years with a variety of splendid and exotic forest trees.

ELMLEY CASTLE, *Worcs*. An interesting model of the castle which gave the village its name is to be seen in the parish church. Already ruinous by 1300, the castle has now virtually disappeared.

The village lies at the foot of the N slope of Bredon Hill and is among the most distinguished of Worcestershire villages. Lanes lead off in four or five directions and all of them have two or more attractive houses. But the impressive part of the village is the wide street which runs due S to the village church.

There is modern building and infilling but not such as to spoil the village character, which is made up of occasional red brick and a good deal of stone building, but overwhelmingly of black-and-white. Additional character is provided by a few roofs of thatch.

At the foot of the main street is the Plough Inn whence a lane leads E to the Old Mill Inn. Higher up the main street on the right is a proud sign announcing the Queen Elizabeth, with a date commemorating a visit paid by her to the village. W of the church is an estate of new houses in an attractive setting of grass lawns.

The church is at the upper end of the village and to the approaching visitor it presents a very satisfactory sequence of Perp windows and at the W

end a good square tower. The architecture is all stone. What is immediately charming in the interior is that in the nave the ancient woodwork has been meticulously preserved in the pews. Thanks to the absence of stained glass the nave is beautifully light and the treasures of the church can be well seen. These include a font heavily carved with dragons, on a base which is clearly medieval; also a number of monuments two of which are outstanding. First, the Savage monument, one of Worcestershire's greatest works of art. Father, son, daughter-in-law and four sons are commemorated in a magnificently carved alabaster group surmounting a massive tomb; this must be mid-17th-c. Secondly, the black-and-white marble monument of the 1st Earl of Coventry and his second wife, placed here, it is said, because the 2nd Earl, disapproving of his stepmother's mean ancestry, would not admit it to the family church at Croome. The chancel has suffered from Victorian woodwork and glass but the church as a whole with its robust Gothic arches is a fine thing.

FECKENHAM, *Worcs*. Worcestershire is thrice blessed in its village architecture. It has the glorious stone of Broadway; it has the sequence of black-and-white in the Vale of Avon and round Evesham; and now at Feckenham it has red brick.

Red brick can be an emotive topic, ranging as it does from the garish hideousness of Ruabon brick to the arty-crafty products favoured by some modern builders. But Feckenham is an honest-to-goodness red brick, datable doubtless to the 18th c but creditably matched in the centuries following and even in our own day.

The motorist on the Droitwich-Alcester road comes, from whichever direction, over a slight hump and sees before him the long village street, and a very satisfactory view it is. Occasional plaster fronts, occasional black-and-white, but overwhelmingly red-brick. Halfway along the street the Lygon Arms marks the turn-off of a side road which leads to the church.

The church follows the almost invariable Worcestershire rule that whatever the architecture of the village, the church must be of stone. It is not the most beautiful of village churches but there is an effective square tower with pretty fanciful Gothic windows. Inside, too much trouble has been taken to paint the roof and the arches but the church is full of light and it contains good wood-work, two splendid oak tables, a fine ancient chest and a very good collection of memorial tablets.

The chief delight of the visit to the church is the drive back and forth down the village road from the Lygon Arms. Here are the grandest houses of Feckenham, nameless alas, so that it is difficult to identify them in a description; but splendid with their symmetrical Georgian fronts and Georgian details, notably their fanlights.

Halfway along one comes to a village green near the Rose and Crown. The green is beautifully planted with chestnuts and is itself surrounded by most alluring cottages and houses. Fortunate Feckenham!

4m W of Feckenham is **Hanbury Hall**, a Wren period house containing Thornhill paintings, now vested in the National Trust. The house is open to the public on certain afternoons throughout the summer months.

FOWNHOPE, *Herefordshire*, 6m SE of Hereford. 'The Little Cathedral' has been the name given to Fownhope church, and after walking round it or viewing the interior, one must agree that the title is justified, for it is a beautiful and dignified building. Historically it must have begun with the tower, which is still visibly Norman; and the chief pride of the church, now separately displayed inside, is a tympanum of the Virgin and Child which is clearly of that date.

There is an impressive round chancel arch but, this apart, the architecture is Trans or later. The sea of glazed tiles and pitch pine which are one's first impression must have brought a glow to the hearts of the Victorian improvers, but even they do not seriously detract from the rest of the interior, the four-bay nave, the extensive chancel and the large S aisle. There is an E window of pretty coloured fragments set in a background of plain glass and there is a sequence of dignified monuments to the local family of Lechmere. Above the tower rises an attractive spire, slightly twisted and roofed with wooden tiles.

Fownhope must be called a Wye valley village for undoubtedly it is in the Wye valley. Disappointingly, it is not a riverside village, and its main village street could be miles from a river. One is astounded, as so often in Herefordshire villages, by the sheer volume of modern housing, but this does not detract from the village character, which is the informal, unplanned, charming series of non-sequiturs which is the true English village genius. The best house, probably, is the Georgian rectory near the church, and there are excellent stone houses in the village; much of the red-brick has a 19th-c look but there is also good black-and-white. The visitor is catered for by the New Inn and the black-and-white Green Man Hotel; also by the Forge and Ferry Inn, but even this does not get one to the riverside.

2m across the Wye is **Holme Lacy**. There is not much of a village, but Holme Lacy House, the ancient seat of the Scudamores, survives. It was the greatest private house in Herefordshire and still preserves its impeccable architecture of the 1670s. It now serves as a hospital.

HAGLEY, *Worcs.*, is only 10m from the centre of Birmingham and has become in effect an outer suburb of the city. It is also an ancestral estate redolent with history and architecture. The two do not mix very happily, but Hagley should none the less be seen.

The estate came in the mid-16th c into the ownership of the Lyttelton family (now Lord Cobham). It was greatly developed by the 1st Lord Lyttelton, poet and 'Man of Taste', in the mid-18th c, who not only built himself a new house but laid out the surrounding parkland as an early example of English landscape gardening.

Arriving along the main road from Birmingham and topping the rise above the village, the first impression is of a sea of suburban villa residences. Then in the surrounding scenery unexpected objects appear, including an obelisk and a Greek temple.

Hagley is now in effect two villages. West Hagley is entirely given over to modern development. Hagley proper can be reached as one descends the hill by turning left down School Street or Hall Street which lead into an intimate mixture of old and new building. Then one can turn N along the lane which leads to the church.

Hagley church is an unashamed piece of Victoriana, having been built by Street as a memorial church in the 1850s. From it a splendid view can be obtained of Hagley Hall. This is a very large house, totally symmetrical and strictly Palladian in style, built in the 1750s by Sanderson Miller. It suffers, like many Palladian houses, the practical disadvantage of having no back; instead it has four fronts, eleven bays by five.

Hagley Hall is now open once more to the public, and should be visited for it has distinguished interiors, some of which, surprisingly, were accurately re-instated after a fire in 1926. The rococo ceilings and plasterwork in particular should be noticed, also reliefs by Vasalli and medallions by 'Athenian' Stuart.

Those interested in landscape architecture may pick out in the surrounding parkland not only the obelisk and the Greek temple but also the Rotunda and the Ruined Castle. Much of this work was done in friendly competition with the poet Shenstone who lived not far away at the Leasowes, near Halesowen, where he built a number of garden features in what has now become a golf course.

Coming down from Hagley church one passes a large red-brick stable block and a charming Georgian rectory. The old village lane then descends past houses to the Lyttelton Arms.

HANLEY CASTLE, *Worcs.* A charming little enclave down a lane off the road from Worcester to Upton on Severn. On the main road northern approach is a magnificent black-and-white farm house, then a delicious miniature thatched black-and-white cottage, and other interesting-looking houses half hidden by trees.

The village lane passes an enormous school, half Victorian and half modern, but has on its other side a sequence of pretty cottages which lead to the village green, which is tiny but charming. It lies immediately N of the churchyard and church, and a large cedar tree dominates it. It is surrounded by delicious small houses, some red-brick, some black-and-white, among them the red-brick Three Kings Inn attached to another black-and-white cottage. Altogether an idyllic spot. A splendidly leaning black-and-white house is just N of the green. More good black-and-white houses on the N and E sides of the churchyard are not improved by a large recent construction in modern red-brick.

The church has a feature most unusual in Worcestershire, a red-brick tower and a red-brick chancel (in fact two red-brick chancels). The architecture and internal planning make a most curious muddle, due apparently to the addition of the red-brick constructions in the Restoration period. The end result is two churches side by side made into one, with the tower rising out of the southern church where nave meets chancel. The naves of both churches are so filled with stained glass that it is difficult to see anything, but the N chancel is beautifully light and one can admire the large windows, square or rectangular, but with little round arches at the top. This chancel is largely a memorial chapel for the local family of Lechmere; it has good altar rails and the church generally has interesting woodwork and pieces of old furniture.

HARTLEBURY, *Worcs.* It is a discouraging approach to Hartlebury from the dual carriageway on the Worcester-Kidderminster road, but it is worth persisting down the hill, for the village is full of character and unexpected interest. The old village begins with red-brick houses, some white-painted; a village centre is provided by the attractive white-painted White Hart, clearly Georgian in origin. Above this towers Hartlebury church, on a considerable elevation above the Inn. The church is built rather forbiddingly of large blocks of the local red sandstone and is a work of the 1830s by Rickman, who also built Ombersley. An ambitious interior with nave and two aisles (not quite symmetrical) and side galleries and pews engraved with the coats of arms of the bishops of the diocese. Notice in the churchyard N of the church a large tomb chest to a bishop's nephew

with a carved stone bishop's mitre thrown negligently on the top of it.

E of the churchyard are some attractive white painted houses. Further down the street is the pretty black-and-white Church Cottage and a delightful garden, apparently private, though not fenced from the road, opposite the school.

Hartlebury possesses a major attraction in Hartlebury Castle, situated in a small park immediately N of the village. The Castle has been for centuries the residence of the Bishop of Worcester. Though some of the building is medieval, the Castle was largely destroyed at the end of the Civil War and most of what one sees is 17th- and 18th-c work. Built mostly of red sandstone but also partly of red brick, the Castle throws out two large projecting wings which are connected by the main body of the building. The E wing has recently been adapted by the County Council as a museum of old Worcestershire; open to the public six afternoons a week, it is a model of how such things should be done. The W wing of the building is the Chapel. The central block contains the Bishop's state rooms which are on view to the public on occasional Sunday and Bank Holiday afternoons.

HARVINGTON, *Worcs.,* is a pretty village in the flat Avon Valley scenery between Evesham and Stratford-on-Avon, and now mercifully bypassed. As one enters the village from off the main road there is a positively dazzling display of black-and-white houses, stone walls and thatched roofs. The village lane winds on amid more black-and-white and reaches a sort of summit where facing each other are the Coach and Horses Inn and the village church.

The church is conspicuous for a copper spire, an unusual feature in Worcestershire, and added in fact in 1855. Below it is a fine stone Norman tower with small round-headed windows. The interior was very severely dealt with by Preedy in 1855 and could almost be a 19th-c church. A fine high roof over the nave and a few interesting memorial tablets. There is a fine spreading black-and-white house immediately S of the church.

The village lane then evaporates into a not unattractive 20th-c suburb but there are some good Georgian fronts in the 'Village Street' at the back and more black-and-white and thatch. The suburb continues on the far side of the Evesham-Alcester road, but becomes steadily less attractive.

HODNET, *Salop,* is a largish village which suffers from being on two main roads. A first impression is that one is no longer in the Welsh Marches but in the W. Midlands, for there are considerable sequences of houses and cottages built in that darkish – some might say 'dirtyish' – red brick that is characteristic of Staffordshire. Salop, however, asserts itself, for against this red-brick background there are at intervals very fine displays of black-and-white and the wide street, traffic permitting, offers the opportunity for very effective village views.

The focal point is the Bear Hotel where the

Whitchurch and Market Drayton roads divide. This is itself a very fine spread of black-and-white; it looks across the road to the entrance to the church. Here again we are back in the W. Midlands with that dull red sandstone so characteristic of Staffordshire, which after all is only 6m away.

Hodnet Church is very extraordinary, being in fact two complete churches, nave and chancel, placed side by side and made into one. There is an octagonal stone tower, not large enough for the building, against the W end of the northerly church. The windows are Gothic and sometimes Victorian and the two adjacent churches are supported on lofty Gothic arches.

Hodnet has belonged successively, but always through inheritance, to Vernons, Hebers and Percys and a chapel at the NE corner contains their memorials, including one to the famous Bishop Heber. It produces the curious effect externally that the E end of the church is three large gables with Gothic windows.

Beyond the church is the entrance to the gardens of Hodnet Hall which are open to the public on afternoons throughout the summer. May and June are the most recommended months when there are magnificent displays of rhododendrons and azaleas. The house, which is not open, is an 1870 reproduction of Condover (Elizabethan) near Shrewsbury and owes its present appearance to the removal of its upper floors in the 1970s. The gardens which were always large were greatly planted up and extended by the late Brigadier Algernon Heber Percy, D.S.O.; the columns and pediment opposite the front entrance were removed by him from Apley Castle near Wellington and have been re-erected here as his memorial.

KINGSLAND, *Herefordshire*, 4m NW of Leominster. We are here in the country of the Mortimers, the great family who ruled this part of the Marches almost as sovereigns through the Middle Ages. 2m NW is Mortimer's Cross (with an inn of that name) where the decisive battle was fought in 1461 between the Yorkists and Lancastrians which finally fixed Edward IV on the throne of England. An interesting commemorative monument was set up in 1799 at the W end of the village in the grounds of what is now the Monument Inn.

Kingsland is close to the River Lugg and forms with nearby Eardisland and Pembridge a most attractive trio of Herefordshire black-and-white villages. But one is constantly surprised in Herefordshire villages by what has happened in the present century, and starting from the Monument there are a number of modern houses before we reach the village proper.

The village street is long and its houses are spaced, thus providing many opportunities for infilling. The first landmark is the black-and-white Corners Inn, so called presumably from its location at a cross-roads; the road to the right has a beautiful Georgian red-brick farmhouse, some black-and-white houses and the 20th-c village hall. Following the main street, we have houses of a large variety: Georgian stone, plaster fronts,

red-brick and black-and-white of several varieties; but primarily it is black-and-white.

The next landmark is a second cross-roads on the corner of which are the black-and-white post office and the black-and-white Angel Hotel. Beyond this the village abandons its black-and-white character in favour of 19th-c red-brick, and the houses space themselves out until we find ourselves in open country.

S from the post office a road leads to the modern Georgian rectory (red-brick) and to the very grand stone-built parish church. One glance at the exterior is sufficient to suggest a very complicated architectural history. There is an imposing W tower with corner buttresses; a vestry curiously added onto the chancel; and two porches. A curious feature immediately to the left of the present entrance porch is the tiny Volka chapel.

Inside, the church surprisingly makes an impression of great regularity. Two rows of lofty Gothic arches carry the nave; above them a series of clerestory sexfoil circular windows. The church is set in a beautiful churchyard looking over the open country to the S of the village.

LEIGHTON, *Salop*, traditionally Salop's most beautiful village, is situated in the Severn Valley on the minor main road from Shrewsbury to Ironbridge. Its reputation it must owe to its natural features rather than to its buildings for there is not much in the way of houses nor a regular village street. Mary Webb, author of *Precious Bane* and other stories of Shropshire life, was born at Leighton in 1881.

The gaps in the old village have been largely filled with modern bungalows and houses, on the principles of in-filling beloved by planning officers; they are built of a pleasing red brick. More traditional are the older brick buildings built of that mauvish-yellowish brick which one associates with the Ironbridge Gorge; among these is the Kynnersley Arms which presides over the village's W approach.

The beauty of the village derives largely from the fine trees which border both sides of its main street. On the S side these are the trees in the park of Leighton Hall which regrettably cuts off the village from its view of the river valley.

This was long the seat of the Leightons of Leighton; they married into the Kinnersleys, with whose descendants the ownership remained until recent years. The church is in the park and visitors to it can see the outlines of the hall, originally a brick building of the late 18th c with stone dressings but considerably added to in later times. Nearer the village a stable block with attractive 18th-c cupola is well seen from the main road.

The church is also of brick and is also described as being 18th-c. Its somewhat nondescript exterior does not prepare one for the interior, full of character and originality. There is much that is older than the 18th c, including good woodwork, an effigy of a cross-legged knight probably of the 13th c, a tomb chest of the 16th c and two curious floor tombstones of the 17th c.

The windows are remarkable for their totally uninhibited modern stained glass. But the most remarkable feature is the chancel which, almost literally, is panelled with memorials both in marble and in brass to members of the Leighton and Kinnersley families.

Back in the village there are a few individual houses to admire, some in brick and some in black-and-white. And out of the village at its E side is a lay-by from which the view can be seen – the water-meadows, the great windings of the river and in the distance the great cooling towers of the Iron-bridge Power Station.

E along the main road is Buildwas, with the Edwardian bridge replacing Telford's original cast-iron bridge of 1796, and beyond it the remains of the beautiful 12th-c Norman abbey. 1m further on is the beginning of Coalbrookdale and Iron-bridge, the home of Britain's most imaginative venture into industrial archaeology, the Iron-bridge Gorge Museum.

LEINTWARDINE, *Herefordshire*, midway between Ludlow and Knighton. As in so many Herefordshire villages, a lot of recent building has occurred, both Victorian and 20th-c, but Leint-wardine has absorbed this successfully and in its lower reaches it preserves very satisfactorily the sense and atmosphere of old-world village charm. This is so particularly as one descends the main village street with its high raised pavement and its attractive trees. The descent is to the impressive stone bridge over the River Teme.

Leintwardine has the Sun Inn and the Swan Inn but in terms of situation primacy must be given to the Lion Inn, whose grassy meadow slopes down to the river and the bridge. The Teme, so turbulent in its upper and its lower reaches, achieves here a certain poise; it receives the waters of the Clun, to form the Leintwardine Fishery, a name to conjure with among the trout-fishermen of the Borders. The Lion Inn, at the foot of the main street, makes a most attractive scene. There are some surprising pieces of architecture in the village, including the Nonconformist chapel, stone-built but with doors and windows vividly outlined in blue and yellow brick.

The church is to be found in the dead centre. Arriving over the Salop border, one is astounded, as so often, by the size and scale of Herefordshire village churches. Here one finds a lofty nave interior of pillars, Gothic arches and clerestory windows, at first sight a symmetrical composition leading into a large symmetrical chancel. Then one discovers a transept made into a chapel and then a second large chancel leading into a much larger chapel. Finally there is a large tower, added on, quite inconsequentially, to the SW corner of the building.

The nave interior has had the full Victorian treatment of stained glass and pitch pine, but in the chancel some attractive old pews survive, and sections of choir-stall panelling with finely carved arm-rests between the seats. (Pevsner says these may have come from Wigmore Abbey.) The nave

and chancels have fine wooden roofs. Against the E wall of the chancel are what may be relics of a medieval stone reredos.

Leintwardine is not a large place, but in this thinly populated area it is a notable centre and one in which one can pleasantly drink in the true charm of this corner of the Welsh Marches. It was once a Roman settlement called Bravinium.

LITTLE STRETTON, *Salop*. In the middle of South Salop rises that extraordinary geographical feature, the Longmynd. An elevated heather-covered plateau rising to nearly 1700ft and extend-ing to thousands of acres, it has been acquired by the National Trust and the public can roam at will. (It is wise nevertheless to stick to the paths.) Its rocks are said to be the oldest in the world.

The W side is a steep escarpment but on the E the Longmynd throws out huge outcrops divided from each other by steep and narrow valleys. At the base of these ran the A49 main road and on it, going from N to S, were the three Strettons: **All Stretton, Church Stretton** and Little Stretton. In in 1930s the three Strettons were bypassed.

Both approaches to Little Stretton have been ribbon developed and the bounds of the old village street are marked by the two licensed houses, the Ragleth Inn to the N and the Green Dragon to the S. Between them is a charming village street, tranquil and well-to-do, so that one might imagine oneself in some well-heeled settlement in the prosperous Home Counties.

There has been some modern building but tastefully done in red-brick Georgian. The charac-ter of the village derives from black-and-white. The Malt House, the Town House, the Old House, the Manor House all have their individual charm, particularly the Manor House. A benefactress who lived in the Manor House decided in 1905 that Little Stretton ought to have its own church. The result is a delightful Edwardian essay in black-and-white, its interior entirely panelled in pitch pine and its roof covered with thatch.

The charm of Little Stretton is that in a matter of minutes one can by taking one of the back lanes remove oneself from this cosy environment into the totally wild scenery of the Longmynd, perhaps walking for hours without seeing a person.

LLANYBLODWELL, *Salop*, is approachable from the Shrewsbury-Lake Vyrnwy B4396 road which leaves the A5 beyond Nescliff and crosses the Welshpool-Oswestry A483 road at Llanclys. It is buried in the idyllic scenery of the foothills of the Welsh mountains; 'the hills above the village' wrote Samuel Bagshaw in 1857, 'command a scene of sublimity perhaps unsurpassed in any part of Wales.' The clue to all this is the River Tanat which 2m further on flows into the Vyrnwy.

An idyllic moment is provided where the village lane crosses the river by an ancient narrow bridge in three arches built of red sandstone. Here is the charming black-and-white Horseshoe Inn said to date in part from the 16th c, which dispenses local hospitality.

There is no village in the sophisticated sense of the term but on the surrounding hillsides can be seen the farmhouses responsible for the flocks of sheep which make such effective features in the middle distance.

Llanyblodwell, if not a formal village, was a typical hamlet of the Welsh border and might have continued indefinitely as such but for an accident of history. In the year 1845 there arrived at Llanyblodwell a new vicar, the Rev. John Parker.

Parker was a man of means, imagination and initiative and clearly fancied himself in the arts and in architecture. (A large collection of his watercolours, mostly of Welsh scenery, can be seen in the Library of the University of Wales at Aberystwyth). At Llanyblodwell the first sign of his handiwork, as one approaches the village, is the former school and schoolhouse, an astonishing skyline of gables, chimneys and spire, all in largish blocks of reddish sandstone. The schoolhouse is now the post office and the school is a private house, but still inscribed over its Gothic entrance door with the warning words: 'That the soul be without knowledge it is not good. Even a child is known by his doings whether his work be pure.' The buildings are surrounded by a splendidly crenellated wall.

On the way to the church is an attractive five-bay Georgian house. The church could hardly be a greater architectural contrast. Here again John Parker has taken hold, and though parts of the church are clearly medieval the whole effect is of a glorious essay in Early Victorian Gothic. An astonishing bulbous spire is the most prominent landmark; this is attached to the church only by a Gothic brick arch bearing the inscription: '1855 & 1856. From Lightning and Tempest from Earthquake and Fire Good Lord deliver us.'

The interior is a maze and forest of inscriptions, painted decorations and carvings. Carved organ case, carved galleries, carved screen, carved bench pews, carved pulpit dominate the interior scene, which is oddly made up of two bays of equal width. Desecrated after Parker's death, the parish to its eternal credit effected in 1960 an almost complete restoration of his work.

LYDBURY NORTH, *Salop*, is on the B4385 road from Craven Arms to Bishop's Castle, amid the unspoilt hill and valley scenery of SW Salop. The parish is a large one and includes a number of hamlets and also country houses. To the E is Plowden Hall, home of the Roman Catholic family of Plowden since the early Middle Ages. Walcot Park to the S was the ancient home of the Walcots; sold in the 18th c to the great Lord Clive, it became, until World War I, the residence of his descendants, the Earls of Powis.

The arriving motorist is struck immediately by the splendid vision of the parish church with its massive 13th-c tower. The main road houses are mostly plaster-fronted but the bulk of the village which lies on the lane to the N includes black-and-white, red brick and a great preponderance of local stone. The large Georgian stone building at the

W end of the village is the Powis Arms, marking the present drive entrance to Walcot Park.

The church is largely 12th-c. A glorious impression is made as one enters; it is not often that one sees a large village church nave still completely furnished with ancient woodwork. The pews here are Jacobean, beautifully carved and well restored about 1900. More excellent woodwork in the pulpit (Jacobean) and the screen. More still in the magnificent roof, collar beams on arched braces.

The two transepts are a curious feature. N is the Plowden chapel, built it is said as a thank-offering for a safe return from the Crusades; S is the Walcot chapel built or rebuilt by a Walcot about 1660 with a room overhead as a village school. The chancel contains two very rare wooden candlesticks thought to be mid-17th c.

Lydbury was well restored by Micklethwait at the turn of the 20th c. It also owes much to the Rev. Gerald Gardner-Brown, vicar from 1948 to 1977, who organized the restoration of the tower, achieved the re-opening of the Plowden chapel (closed since the Reformation) and also the conversion of the Walcot chapel into a side chapel for the church.

In the valley below the village is the stone-built hamlet of **Brockton**. Higher up is the stone farmhouse curiously called Lower Down.

MARTLEY, *Worcs.*, is a pleasant, unassuming village in the pleasant, unassuming country of the Teme Valley 7m NW of Worcester. This is scenery very unlike the black-and-white villages of the Avon Valley; red sandstone and red soil predominate, and hills are all around.

The village is at a cross-roads and the centre is the red-brick Crown Inn. There is no dominating architectural style. Pretty black-and-white cottages alternate with enormous red-brick farm buildings and there are a number of red-brick houses that must date from Georgian times. Architecturally interesting according to Pevsner is the rectory, which is centred round a 14th-c hall with trusses that are vaguely reminiscent of cruck construction.

The church is on the S side of the village and looks out pleasantly over the open countryside. It is a building of distinction, originally Norman, and reflects the highest credit on Sir Charles Nicholson who is said to have restored it in 1909. Good woodwork and good tiled and wooden floor; a very fine wooden roof; pulpit and two screens at tower and chancel ends which could be medieval, so good are the design and the carving. In the chancel an astonishing display of flat tomb slabs. Some good pieces of old furniture, good wall tablets and a 15th-c carved alabaster tomb of one of the Mortimers killed in the War of the Roses. Altogether a church to be proud of.

4m N of Martley is **Great Witley**. Witley Court was successively the home of the Foleys, the dower house of Queen Adelaide, the immensely grand residence of the Dudleys, and the property of Sir Herbert Smith, during whose ownership in the 1930s it was gutted by fire. What remain are ruins on a Piranesian scale which can be seen from the main road or nearer at hand from the church.

The church should be visited. Much of it was brought from Canons in Middlesex and re-installed here. It is the grandest baroque church interior in Britain and contains one of the grandest baroque monuments, the memorial by Rysbrack to the 1st Lord Foley.

MUNSLOW, *Salop*. Situated on the main roads from Bridgnorth and Much Wenlock to Craven Arms and Ludlow in the centre of the very attractive area of Salop known as Corvedale; to the N the reverse slope of Wenlock Edge, to the SE some attractive views of Brown Clee Hill. In spite of modern intrusions of red brick Munslow is basically a stone-built village, mostly random stone but also a few houses in cut stone. An effective centre piece on the main road is provided by the village school, an impressive stone building in Jacobean style said to have originated as the home of the Littleton family, including Lord Keeper Littleton who played a leading part in the political troubles of the reign of Charles I.

To find the church and former rectory one must take the lane N past some impressive stone farm-houses still with their good stone buildings and good stone walls. The church, also of stone, has tower, nave and chancel; the tower originally Norman, the rest of the church medieval with later alterations. Some original features are provided by the stained glass, among which one may find examples of almost every century from the 13th to the 20th c. The interior woodwork is very redolent of the 19th and 20th c but some older work survives; notice also the excellent medieval carving on the exterior of the entrance porch on the S side. The living was remarkable for being for two centuries in the hands of the Powell family who during this period provided all the rectors; their attractive stone rectory with pillared entrance survives beside the yew-fringed churchyard.

1m E along the main road to Bridgnorth is Millichope Park, a house built by Haycock of Shrewsbury in 1840 and praised by Pevsner in the 1950s as being 'of high architectural value, full of character and original ideas'; but it has since been modified and reduced in size. 1m N is Upper Millichope Farm said to date from the 14th c; built in stone and much written up in Victorian times as an example of early medieval domestic architecture in Shropshire.

As one leaves Munslow the Crown Hotel presides in a dignified way over the W exit whence the main road to Craven Arms takes one in less than 1m to the satellite village of **Aston Munslow**. Here is the attractive black-and-white Swan Inn, from which a lane leads N through the hamlet to the White House. This claims to be a 12th-c homestead, and in the summer months is open to the public for whom are displayed a cruck hall, a dovecote and a country life museum.

OMBERSLEY, *Worcs*., is a distinguished village on the main Worcester-Kidderminster road, mercifully relieved by a by-pass from the worst of the traffic.

The Sandys family have been at Ombersley since 1560 and the village breathes much family history. The centre is the roundabout where the Droitwich-Tenbury road crosses, and from it the village radiates in three directions. N are two distinguished black-and-white buildings of very early date, their crucks distinctly visible. W are a very attractive black-and-white Dower House and a series of lesser houses still attractive, though of later date.

The best part of the village is S towards Worcester. First, on the left, some good Georgian red-brick houses. Then begins the black-and-white, first on both sides of the road and continued on the E side, while the park trees of Ombersley Court provide the scenery opposite. The southern landmark is the Crown and Sandys, white-fronted and with picturesque curved gables which appear to be purely ornamental. Close to it is the Kings Arms, timber-framed and said to be partly pre-Reformation; N of the roundabout is another hostelry, with the proud sign 'Free House'. The quality of the village may be judged by the fact that it has 20 listed buildings of special historic or architectural interest. Two buildings specially worth seeking out are the Georgian rectory and the Charity School built in 1729.

The village church is entered through a small churchyard, well kept, on the W of the village street. There was an older church dedicated to St Ambrose, pulled down doubtless when the present church was built. The present church is early 19th-c, decorated with an imposing W tower and spire.

Churches of the 1830s are not everybody's cup of tea, and Ombersley with its lofty interior, regular high Gothic windows and tinted glass produces an effect which is chilly, if stately. But the church has a wonderful redeeming feature, its woodwork; a complete nave-ful of box-pews in the original 1830 woodwork. Notice in the corner the charming private box-pew with fireplace for the great house.

S of the present church a portion of the old church does duty as the mausoleum of the Sandys family. It has recently been restored for worship.

ORLETON, *Herefordshire*, lies in the flattish country between the two main roads from Ludlow to Leominster. On the W road the landmark is the Maidenhead Arms from which the village street immediately begins. For a short distance one is in the 20th c, a riot of modern bungalows in no way suggestive of Herefordshire; then one reaches cross-roads and the village proper starts on the left arm.

It is a pretty winding village street containing some particularly attractive black-and-white houses with overhanging upper storeys. Georgian red-brick is also to be seen and inevitably some intrusions of more recent date. An emphatic centre is provided by the Boot Inn.

Orleton is fortunate in having an impressive

Kenneth Scowen

Looking towards Overbury Court and its stable block

church, not situated as so often in this county a mile away, but in the village itself. Built of attractive grey stone, lofty and with a dominating spire. The building originated clearly in Norman times and a good Norman arch survives in the W entrance. The present entrance is by a porch and venerable doorway on the N side where the windows, as in the church generally, are Gothic. A very impressive timber roof surmounts the whole.

The church possesses a number of treasures. In the vestry are two remarkable 'dug-out' chests, dated by Pevsner to the 13th c. A finely carved Jacobean pulpit dominates the nave; at the back of the nave a very impressive stone font, deeply carved with standing figures under arches; this must belong to the Norman period, of which one sees examples elsewhere in Herefordshire. A small tablet touchingly records that the whole church was restored in 1956 by Mr Rodney Proctor of Cincinnati, Ohio, whose great-grandfather and great-great-grandfather were both vicars in the 18th c. Do not miss the charming tombstones in the churchyard.

3m S of Orleton are two very notable Herefordshire houses. Eye Manor, open to the public every afternoon from July to September, is a late Jacobean manor house with sensational plaster ceilings in the rooms. Berrington Hall, open on many afternoons through the summer months, is a park and house of 1780 in the grand manner by Capability Brown and his son-in-law Henry Holland, with beautiful interiors still in their original state.

OVERBURY, *Worcs.*, on the S slope of Bredon Hill, is a banker's village, and looks it. This is intended not as a sneer but as a compliment, for the most superficial examination will reveal that its development and present state must be the result, not only of the expenditure of much money but also of the exercise of much loving care and much good taste.

The Martin family (of Martin's Bank) have been here at least as far back as the early 18th c, and it is satisfactory that they should live here still. Their house, Overbury Court, is not open to the public but the fine stone pillars of the entrance gates face on to one of the village lanes, and beyond can be clearly seen the character and outlines of the house, which is still more strikingly visible from the churchyard. It is a beautiful early Georgian composition in yellow stone, with three storeys and seven bays, with a stone Georgian wing and beyond it a stone stable block with elegant cupola.

The village is a total contrast to so much of Worcestershire for it is almost totally of stone. Not the least impressive features are the beautifully built and maintained stone walls which surround so many of the village houses. The houses themselves, though of stone, are of stone of different kinds, but mostly are clearly akin to the stone of the Cotswolds. Of different styles too is the architecture, though Georgian predominates.

Driving through by car one could be almost unaware of the most substantial part of the village which is on the N–S lane running uphill at right angles to the usual approach road. This is a sequence of charming stone houses, with one surprise – a handsome red-brick Georgian house of three storeys and five bays with Gothic Venetian windows, now called Red House School.

The churchyard is planted with pollarded

Overhanging first floors in Pembridge

Kenneth Scowen

cherries; below it is a charming memorial garden. The church with its square tower and Gothic windows is everything that one would expect. But inside there is a dramatic surprise for the whole structure is carried on robust circular columns with very fine Norman arches above them. Observe also the somewhat later rib vaulting of the chancel, and a goblet-shaped Norman font, the sides carved with two standing figures, one holding a church.

Back in the village the initials RM provide the clue (and sometimes the date) to stone buildings, including the village school. A large stone village hall standing on the N–S lane is attributed to Norman Shaw.

The village proper has no licensed house but the Star Inn lies only a little way to the E.

PEMBRIDGE, *Herefordshire* (7m E of Kington), is a charming place in the valley of the Arrow and makes with nearby Eardisland and Kingsland a charming Herefordshire trio. To include it among Herefordshire's most beautiful villages is perhaps unkind, for it claims to be a town, but its population is now only 820 and it is difficult to identify anything resembling a town hall.

The focus is the point where the road coming S from Shobdon (called Bridge Street) makes a T-junction with the main street, divided here into East and West Streets. The village street is also the main road from London to Aberystwyth but traffic is less of a menace than one might expect.

Bridge Street, as its name implies, leads down to the bridge over the pretty River Arrow and beside

the river are seats thoughtfully provided for the visitor. On the way are samples of Pembridge's black-and-white, including that much favoured local feature, the overhanging first floor. Notice immediately on the left the pretty row of 17th-c almshouses. West Street has at its W end some particularly attractive houses, including one called Brick House, for it is of 'black' and red brick. Walking back towards the centre one sees on the right the picturesque New Inn, black-and-white-painted-brick on a massive stone base.

Behind this is the miniature market square, retaining still a Market House carried on eight wooden pillars. Further along the main street is the Red Lion and then the focal point of the village at the T junction, the Olde Steppes with the village store next door.

The best of the black-and-white scenery is in East Street, beginning with the beautiful Greyhound Inn. Notice on the right the Old Forge which appears literally to be falling into the garden. Also a pretty façade with the cryptic inscription in Latin: 'St George restored me 1926'.

From the Olde Steppes one can climb up to the pretty churchyard (made into a Garden of Rest) and the village church. Here there seems to be something missing, and this is true, for it has neither tower nor spire. Instead it has beside it in the churchyard that unusual and impressive feature, a detached bell tower, tall, truncated, weatherboarded and stone-tiled. It is an impressive experience to explore the inside of the base and to view the eight massive oak pillars and the forest of structural timber above.

The church is Gothic, almost entirely of the 14th c. It has a fine interior, with two transepts and lofty Gothic windows in all parts. The nave is carried on five lofty Gothic arches with clerestories above. There is too much stained and tinted glass but much of the paving is stone and the seating, most unusually for Herefordshire, is not Victorian pews but modern chairs. Treasures of the church include a finely carved lectern, pulpit and altar rails, and some very ancient stone tombs in the chancel.

3m N of Pembridge is **Shobdon**, with a church that is a remarkable contrast, a Georgian-Gothic extravaganza, furnished and decorated with every imaginative elaboration of the 1750s.

RICHARD'S CASTLE, *Herefordshire and Salop*, has three peculiarities. It extends into two counties; it has two parish churches; and both churches are 1m from the village.

Following the lesser main road from Ludlow to Leominster, the village centre is announced by the Castle Inn which, like a number of other houses in Richard's Castle, is built of an agreeable pale squared stone. There is also some red-brick and black-and-white but the bulk of the village is along the lane to the W. The best house is the brick Georgian rectory.

The village lies at the foot of a steep slope and it is 1m up this steep slope that the original church is to be found. Coming along the road from Ludlow one passes through the fine beech woods of Moor Park, the ancient home of the Salweys, a family still prominent in the area. In the 19th c Moor Park was purchased by Johnston J. Foster and on his death his daughters decided as a memorial to build a more convenient church. Oddly they chose a site 1m away on the Ludlow road.

The new church (built *c*. 1890) is a very grand affair. Gothic and of pale squared stones and with great Gothic windows and arches, it gives the impression, as one mounts the imposing entrance stairway and faces the well scrubbed and brightly lit interior, that one is arriving for morning prayers at the school chapel of a minor public school. The architect was Norman Shaw, and clearly no expense was spared. Sadly the church tower is placed beside the nave and does not grow out of it and thus fails to make its proper impression.

Back in the village one turns up the lane away from the main road to find oneself in the middle of a new red-brick housing estate which however does no damage to the village. Thereafter the vernacular reasserts itself and there is a succession of very attractive black-and-white houses up the climb to the old church.

The excursion to the old church is very recommendable to all who like the unusual. The church stands next to the relics of the castle which give the village its name and commands a splendid view. There is an attractive detached bell tower and in the church a wide S aisle and a big N transept and as there is no stained glass before the E window the church is full of light. One is immediately struck by the stone-flagged floor and by the magnificent box pews, still intact, as well as a matching gallery and pulpit. The church is a veritable mausoleum of the Salweys, and the effect is completed by a splendid set of family hatchments now sadly mouldering away. The stonework has been dated to the 12th, 13th and 14th c.

RIPPLE, *Worcs.*, is a small village hidden away on the Severn Valley and reached from the Worcester-Tewkesbury road just S of Upton-on-Severn. Though Ripple has had its share of modern building, the kernel of the village is charming and relatively unspoilt. There is no formal village street, but pretty red-brick and black-and-white houses and cottages with splendid gardens line the winding village road which opens eventually into a small triangle containing an ancient pillar on steps which one associates with churchyards. The churchyard is in fact immediately behind and has some excellent tombstones. Next to it is an admirable Georgian red-brick rectory, five bays by six.

Ripple Church is very grand for the present size of the village. Transitional in date, it has a large nave with Gothic arches and clerestory windows and a large W window which looks Perp. But it was unkindly dealt with by the Victorians in terms of woodwork and scraping.

There are two considerable transepts but the real glory of the church is the chancel, which must be later in date. The large E window is Victorian glass but lofty Gothic side windows let in a flood of light and there is much to admire. Good panelling, good altar rails and an attractive sequence of memorial tablets. The great distinction is provided by the choir stalls, the 12 seats of which have carved misericords representing the months of the year. Note particularly November – killing the pig – and December – huddling round the fire.

Ripple once had a railway station on an improbable line from Ashchurch to Great Malvern, and this is still commemorated by the Railway Inn. Beyond this one can proceed to the sister hamlet of **Uckinghall**, which also has pretty houses, and thence over a bumpy road to the waterside to gaze at the unromantic Severn.

ROUS LENCH, *Worcs.* We are here in the country known to the road signs as 'The Lenches': flattish country, full of fruit trees and market gardens and near, though not in, the Avon Valley. N of Evesham are **Lenchwick** and **Sherriff's Lench**; the lanes lead on to **Atch Lench**, to **Church Lench**, to **Abbot's Lench** (generally called Ab Lench) and finally to **Rous Lench**.

Of these last four none are without character. Atch Lench is full of delightful black-and-white cottages. Church Lench has a Main Street ending as one might expect with a church; opposite the church a Victorian red-brick school heavily carved with the prayer: 'From all false doctrine heresy and schism Good Lord deliver us'. The stone-built church stands very attractively with its clerestory windows and square tower capped with four little spires. It is hard to believe externally

Edwin Smith

Weobley: the capital of black-and-white

that this is 1855 but internally it is all too true. Ab Lench is predominantly Victorian red-brick. And so to Rous Lench.

Rous Lench owes its name to a family who long ruled it and who called themselves successively Rous, Rouse, and Rouse-Boughton. They clearly were of masterful character, and their handiwork is strikingly evident round the village green, flanked as it is on one side with a house inscribed RB 1872 and on another by the elaborate school building of 1864; this is a riot of black-and-white barge-boards surmounting a composition of red, white and blue brick. Another red-brick house is dated 1890. The green has a village letter box mounted in an elaborate architectural frame and flanked with houses of 1861 and 1862. The Old Rectory is dated 1866. One wonders what the village was before the 1860s, for clearly this was an ancient place.

Earlier generations of the Rous family have memorials in a small chapel added onto the village church and it is a pity it is not better lighted for clearly some of them are of quality and of interest. They include a big tomb chest of 1611 and an interesting marble monument of 1719 to Lady Rous, daughter of the architect Thomas Archer. The church is basically Norman, with some excellent Norman features including a remarkable piece of sculpture over the entrance door. In the interior imaginations have run riot in several epochs. Tinted glass abounds and the decoration and furnishing includes two Elizabethan pulpits, a curious set of black-and-gold carved chairs in the chancel (?19th c) and an ornate apse at the end of

the N aisle suggestive of the Byzantine-Norman style of S Italy.

The Rouse-Boughtons sold out in the 1870s, but their house still stands at the top of the hill outside the village and one can admire its most astonishing feature, the topiary garden made up of huge yew hedges at different levels down the slope.

TONG, *Salop*, 3m E of Shifnal. The pride of Tong is its church, generally accepted as the most magnificent village church in Shropshire.

The village is divided not very logically between Tong proper and Tong Norton, about ½m to the N. Tong proper, although not actually on the main A41 road, suffers from being within very audible distance of it; Tong Norton is slightly more remote. A preliminary look at them suggests that Tong Norton was the working, and Tong proper the residential section of the community. Tong Norton still has its unsophisticated farmhouses and buildings in the vernacular red brick of Shropshire, but vivid surprises are provided by more recent structures – expensive essays in modern Georgian red brick perfectly expressing the ethos of anyone preferring life in a Shropshire village to Wolverhampton or the Black Country.

Tong proper is without such intrusions and is the agreeable and inconsequent mixture of red brick and black-and-white which is so familiar in Salop. The village has no public house but there are a village hall and village almshouses and an agreeable former vicarage; and the elevation is just sufficient for very satisfactory views over the agricultural and wooded countryside.

The church by contrast is of stone. One of the tombs which we shall visit gives the clue to its foundation: 1410 by Lady Elizabeth de Pembrugge. The architecture, correctly for its date, is Perp out of Dec. Noble Gothic arches support a very handsome wooden roof over the nave and two symmetrical aisles; similarly over crossing and chancel; and the church begins and ends with large Perp windows. The pews of the nave are undistinguished and the peculiar glory of the church begins with two screens towards the E end of each aisle. Within and outside their enclosures are the tombs which are so remarkable a feature of the interior: tombs of late medieval and Tudor ages which deserve a prolonged examination. Another remarkable feature is the small extension of the S aisle; this now forms a little chapel roofed by a most distinguished essay in fan-vaulting.

No less satisfactory is the chancel, divided from the nave by a splendid rood screen. This forms part of a most distinguished scheme of panelling which includes the carved choir stalls and even carved sedilia.

The landmark here then is the noble 15th-c spire which rises from the centre of the building. The landmark for Tong Norton, however, is the Bell Inn on the main road where the lane leads off to the village.

Until recent times Tong had a sensational folly in the form of Tong Castle, an 18th-c eccentricity in the Moorish Gothic taste attributed to Capability Brown and built for the Durrant family who are profusely listed in memorials in the church. This was pulled down in 1954 and all that now remains is some landscape gardening, including water, in the former grounds.

4m E of Tong are White Ladies and Boscobel. White Ladies is the ruin of a nunnery, probably Augustinian, of which not much remains. Boscobel, which is regularly open to the public, is famous as the house of the Penderells where Charles II was successfully hidden after the battle of Worcester and where his oak tree (or its successor) may still be seen.

3m N of Tong (and in Staffs.) is Weston Park, a stately home where on most afternoons through the summer months many thousands of visitors are welcomed to both house and grounds.

WEOBLEY, *Herefordshire*, 9m SW of Leominster, is undoubtedly one of the most beautiful of Herefordshire villages; yet to say this is insulting, for Weobley was once a borough and it returned two Members to Parliament until 1832. However, it is now of village size (population of the whole parish is only 1035); a state due partly to its last 'proprietor', the Marquess of Bath, who, it is alleged, in the 19th c had at least 40 buildings taken down.

Weobley lost more of its buildings as a result of a fire in the 20th c in Broad Street. The destroyed area has been walled in as a garden and provided with a bus shelter in what has thus become a disproportionately wide street. So far as the place has a centre, this is it.

There are some attractive Georgian façades in Weobley, but overwhelmingly this is the capital of the black-and-white. Timber frames, crucks, cross-wings, angle posts, cross braces, bargeboards – these are the vernacular of Weobley and those who cannot do with black-and-white should give it a wide berth.

The inhabitants are not unaware of its attractions. Guest houses, a café and licensed houses welcome the visitor; among the last are the Salutation Inn and two hotels ranking two stars, the Unicorn and the Red Lion.

Upon all this the village church, situated a little to the N, looks down with a distant superior air for it is built of stone and is provided – most unusually for the Welsh Marches – with a lofty spire supported by flying buttresses from the tower beneath. The tower ought to be, but apparently is not, the oldest part, and the church (which is the size of a town church) or an extension of it, has been built onto it at an angle which makes no external or internal sense. The church is overwhelmingly Gothic, and one breathes the spirit of the Middle Ages, somewhat Victorianized, until one is brought up sharp by the tremendous marble monument of 1691 in honour of Col. Birch, a Parliamentary Commander who established himself in the vicinity after the Civil Wars.

Near the church admire the Red Lion Hotel, admire the black-and-white in Bell Square; diverge into Back Lane and Meadow Street; come back into Broad Street to get the full panorama of the scene; then diverge to High Street to admire the Unicorn Hotel; and finally a little way up Hereford Road to see the Old Grammar School and the house called The Throne.

A curious tailpiece to Weobley is the Workhouse of 1837, later used as Council offices.

3m W is the lonely church of **Sarnesfield**, late Norman and very charming.

WHITTINGTON, *Salop* (3m NE of Oswestry), is a largish village, and its outlying quarters contain breath-taking visions of that well-known local product, Ruabon brick. At the time of writing it groans under all the passing traffic of the main A5 road but hopes are being held out of a bypass which will leave the village in peace.

The distinction of Whittington is its centre, where another breath-taking vision of an earlier period greets the traveller on the main road. This is Whittington Castle beautifully set in a weed-grown moat which comes right up to the roadside.

Whittington Castle is a building of venerable antiquity which has suffered some strange vicissitudes. Some of what remains has been dated to the very early 13th c; some of what does not remain was dismantled in the 18th c to provide material for repairing the road to Ellesmere. Originally royal, it is now in a private ownership dating back to the 16th c and is looked after by the Council.

What principally remains is the very imposing entrance gateway with its two circular stone towers. Between these the entrance door admits to what must once have been a courtyard surrounded with other considerable buildings. It provides now a large, green and agreeable recreation area for the village; in the S part another large block of building up to first-floor level survives with the remains of a third tower.

The main village street boasts two hostelries, one on each side of the castle, the White Lion and Ye Olde Boote Inn. Close to the latter is the village church, an architectural curiosity rather than a work of art.

Approaching it from the castle and looking at its agreeable dark red-brick outlines and the campanile with its pyramidal roof, all surrounded by the dark cypresses of the churchyard, one would be inclined to say a modernized church in a small town of N Italy. This may in fact have been the effect that it was intended to produce, for the church, built originally in the late 18th c, was 'reopened' after restoration in 1894. Nothing could be less suggestive of a Shropshire village church than the interior, but in its way it is a *tour de force* – a totally symmetrical design of vivid brown woodwork dominated by the Lombardic arches of the windows and an impressive flat wooden roof.

Opposite the church a former churchyard has been charmingly laid out as a garden surrounding a memorial cross in honour of William Walsham How, long a vicar of this parish and later Bishop of Wakefield.

YARPOLE, *Herefordshire*. There has been, as in so many Herefordshire villages, a good deal of modern building here but the village has main-tained, notwithstanding, a delightfully unsophisticated charm. It is buried in lanes 4m to the NW of Leominster.

Yarpole has that very appealing feature, a clear open brook running down the side of the village street. The principal landmark beside it is the Manor House, now white-fronted with an attractive stone gatehouse in front of it.

There is some good black-and-white, particularly a house immediately W of the church. The inhabitants of Yarpole have imagination in their colour schemes and in addition to black-and-white one may see black-and-pink, black-and-orange and brown-and-yellow. Notice at the N approach the Bell Inn.

The church has that attractive Herefordshire feature, a detached bell tower (*see* Pembridge). It has some good Gothic arches and a fine lofty roof.

2m NW of Yarpole is Croft Castle in a large park with very fine trees. This was in ancient times the seat of the Croft family: in the 18th c it belonged to the Knights of Downton and the Johneses of Hafod; in the mid-20th c the Croft family made the heroic financial effort necessary to vest it in the National Trust by whom on certain afternoons through the summer months it is opened to the public.

Opposite the castle entrance is the charming little church, still retaining its box pews. The castle still has the castle air and inside has some good panelled rooms; but Gothick windows betray its 18th-c owners, and much of the interior is in fact decorated in charming Georgian styles. There are some quite excellent contents.

The old bake-house in Yarpole

Kenneth Scowen

Cheshire

Charles Lines

Travellers heading by train towards Liverpool or Chester receive a good, if limited, impression of Cheshire. They might be forgiven for believing that, with the exception of Crewe, the small county consisted mainly of lush fields dotted with splendid cattle, mercifully surviving hedges, views of woods and distant hills. The stranger may think vaguely of Nantwich salt, mined over centuries, Macclesfield silk – though man-made fibres are the great stock-in-trade today – Cheshire cheese (and Cheshire cats!) or the fine taste of Dee salmon. But Cheshire has so much more to offer than casual acquaintance would suggest. There is spectacular contrast in its countryside, with wooded, gentle lanes in the Wirral – that part of it remaining after boundary changes many still deplore – and the wild, glorious uplands of Macclesfield Forest and adjoining areas, and the lovely meres of Rostherne, Tatton, Tabley, Combermere, which are such a surprise.

It is a county, too, of fine homes and surviving estates, old mills and canals, and stately churches – if not renowned for the earlier ecclesiastical work – and, though unfortunate materials and poor planning may sometimes jar, there is still a positive wealth of architectural interest to explore at leisure. And, in using that word 'leisure', it is impossible not to reflect on the poor state of public transport in many a rural, and not so rural, district, though there are those useful little stations on the often delightful railway line between Chester and Knutsford – birches and bracken and views over Delamere Forest – whatever one may think of Altrincham.

Grand old names occur in Cheshire, even if their owners may have vanished: Grosvenor pre-eminently, though somewhat obscured by the Westminster title, Warburton, Stanley, de Tabley, Legh, Mainwaring, the oddly pronounced Cholmondeley. One can hardly fail to notice the Grosvenor influence in the vicinity of Chester. But, naturally, there are less aristocratic, yet worthy, figures in Cheshire history. Mrs Gaskell (not a native) is linked inextricably with Knutsford which, as everyone knows, is her *Cranford*. Bishop Heber, whose hymns echo around many a church ('From Greenland's Icy Mountains' and 'Holy, Holy, Holy, Lord God Almighty' are two) was born at Malpas; the saintly Bishop Wilson at Burton in the Wirral; Dean Stanley at Alderley. Too often overlooked is Ralph Holinshed, whose *Chronicles* were so extensively used by Shake-speare; he hailed from Sutton. John Gerard, surgeon, naturalist and gardener (his famous *Herball* of 1597 contains what is said to be the first picture of a potato) was a native of Nantwich.

Turning to architecture, black-and-white – not necessarily of any real antiquity – is insepar-able from Cheshire, which is the home of some of the grandest timbered houses anywhere in England. Little Moreton Hall, which can still make one gasp after many visits, is perhaps the finest; but there is Bramall Hall, Churche's Mansion at Nantwich, where there is so much else to see, Adlington Hall, with its curious, effective blending of magnificent timber-framing with classical work (to say nothing of the famous organ), and two timbered treasures at Gaws-worth. Cheshire is, indeed, rich in grand homes, although, as elsewhere, there have been regret-table losses, such as High Legh Hall, and Dun-ham Massey has gone to Greater Manchester. It would be impossible to list them all, and some receive due mention under the village entries. One important example is Lyme Hall (where Leghs lived for 600 years), allied closely to the Italian architect, Leoni, also with earlier work and red deer in an enormous park. Lyme is the Vyne Park of Phyllis Elinor Sandeman's *Treasure on Earth*. At the time of writing, however, one wonders what will be the fate of Salvin's Peckfor-ton Castle, so splendidly placed, with its towers mocking the ruins of Beeston not far distant.

There are timbered churches – Marton, Lower Peover, Rostherne – of much importance, and who can ever forget the first sight of St Michael's, Macclesfield, on emerging from the railway station, and subsequently the first glimpse of Earl Rivers' monument therein? Or the wonderful screen at Mobberley, the Perp roofs of Malpas and Astbury, the wood carvings of Chester Cathedral, and the strange elaborate pulpit at Daresbury?

It is impossible to forget the impact of the motorways, if it is not as great in Cheshire as else-where. Jodrell Bank, with its radio telescope, excites wonder. The Saxon crosses of Sandbach draw the archaeologist. But when, from afar, one dreams of Cheshire, it is perhaps of marching Romans at Chester, rather than its Civil War siege; the heights on the Derbyshire border; the black-and-white; ghostly Parkgate – not on Saturday night!; Great Budworth; the cattle in those quiet fields – and Mrs Gaskell.

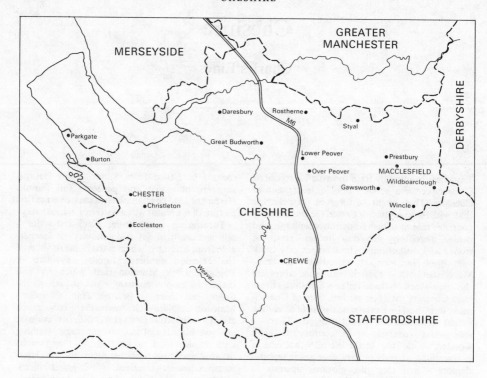

GAZETTEER

BURTON, *Wirral*, about 7m NW of Chester, off
A540. A medieval port of importance, this is now
a charming old village, not spoilt by modern
development as yet, with a grand screen of trees as
a backcloth and views over the Dee to the hills of
Wales. The architecture is decidedly mixed in style,
date and material, but none the worse for it. Stone,
some of it painted, black-and-white, brick, thatch,
are all there, and there are some interesting estate
dwellings by H. S. Goodhart-Rendel. Burton
Manor, now a college, is associated with the Congreve family, long prominent here, but was much
enlarged and remodelled for a member of the
Gladstone family early in this century, with Sir
Charles Nicholson as architect. It is a classical
house with some good interior decoration, a pretty
clock tower, and delightful formal gardens designed by T. H. Mawson, with clipped hedges.

The church of St Nicholas – with a baluster
sundial and a modern memorial to St John Ples-
sington, one of the victims of Titus Oates, in the
churchyard – stands above the main street. It is of
ancient foundation, but there was a rebuilding in
1721, 'at an estimated cost of £1548 – 19 shillings –
and upwards'. The W tower has that rarity, a
single-handed church clock, one of only two, it is
said, in the county. There is a 13th-c coffin lid in
the porch, and medieval work remains in the
Massey Chapel in the NW corner of the church. A
W window by C. E. Kempe depicts St Nicholas
with the money-bags he threw into the house of a
destitute nobleman to provide dowries for three
unfortunate daughters who would otherwise have
been put upon the streets. Altar rails are said to be
the oldest in the Wirral. A hatchment has the arms
of Congreve and Birch. One Congreve built the
chancel in 1870, though the family's claim to fame
is a military one. General Walter Congreve won
the V.C. in 1899, as also did his son in World
War I. The General rescued the son of Lord
Roberts who, like his father, also won the V.C.
Burton was the birthplace of Thomas Wilson,
Bishop of Sodor and Man, called by Dean Farrar
'the last survivor of the saints of the English
church'. He founded a school at Burton, and after
serving as bishop for nearly 60 years died in the
Isle of Man in 1755, being buried in a coffin made
from an elm that he had planted.

A short drive from Burton, towards Neston and
Parkgate (q.v.), are the Ness Gardens of Liverpool
University. These are regularly open to the public,
and comprise wild herb, heather and rose gardens,
herbaceous borders and lawns, with many and
varied trees.

CHRISTLETON, 2m SE of Chester. A canal
bridge and good Georgian houses are the prelude
to this pleasing village with its shingled well-house
like that at Eccleston (q.v.), not far distant. This
pretty little structure was presumably designed by
John Douglas, who was much employed in the
last century on the Eaton Hall estate of the
Grosvenor (Westminster) family. Trees shade a
tiny little green, and there are 19th-c and earlier

cottages, the Old Hall and the Ring o' Bells. Picturesque Victorian almshouses, in black-and-white, designed by J. Oldrid Scott, are reflected in a pool; and recent development does not spoil the older village. A Regency villa E of the church has a classical porch, Gothic window tracery, and an embattled gazebo.

The church of St James, in red and white stone, occupies a prominent position, and has W tower, clerestory, chancel, and N and S aisles. Much of the tower is 15th-c, but is surmounted by Victorian work of which the architect, H. S. Goodhart-Rendel wrote: 'Top stage of the old tower most quaint and original – almost suggesting Douglas – a sort of square-headed pigeon house with a spire roof set inside the battlements.' He thought the church of 1875–8 'exceptionally interesting'; it is a rebuilding by William Butterfield, and the only one in Cheshire designed by him, although he was responsible for restoration work at Marton and the chapel of High Legh Hall. The rather dark interior has a tympanum between nave and chancel, and the sanctuary roof is handsomely decorated. There is glass by C. E. Kempe – whose work is always worth looking at – and an iron memorial screen of 1954. In the churchyard are table tombs and a pillar sundial.

An old milestone survives in the village, which was a Royalist outpost in the Civil War, and at nearby Rowton Moor the forces of Charles I were defeated in 1645, the battle watched by the King from the walls of Chester.

DARESBURY (4m E of Runcorn, off A56), may not have much to offer in contrast to, say, Great Budworth (q.v.), but it must be included for a very special reason. It was the birthplace in 1832 of Charles Lutwidge Dodgson, better-known to us as Lewis Carroll. Most unfortunately the vicarage where he was born no longer exists, but in the church of All Saints, largely rebuilt in the early 1870s, is a window by Geoffrey Webb commemorating him and given by admirers from far and wide. It shows the author of *Alice in Wonderland* in surplice and hood, with Alice by his side. The window also includes the Infant Christ in a cradle, with the Virgin Mary, St Joseph and the shepherds. Below the cradle are the Mad Hatter and March Hare holding lines from Carroll's *Christmas Greetings*. Other Tenniel figures from *Alice in Wonderland* and *Alice through the Looking Glass* are depicted, among them the Dormouse (in the teapot) and the White Rabbit, and there are also the arms of Rugby School and Christ Church where Carroll was educated.

Restoration of the ancient tower was undertaken by Sir Gilbert Greenall as a memorial to his nurse, who left him her life savings. The pulpit appears to be Jacobean, and there is much handsome woodwork of last century, including font cover, reredos and screen. A monument from the old church is signed 'Gibson, Roma', and is to Sarah Byrom, 1833, with figures of herself on a couch, her sorrowing husband bending over her and an attendant angel. (The sculptor was presumably the John Gibson of 'The Tinted Venus', who died in Rome in 1866, where he is buried in the English cemetery). Daresbury Hall, ½m E of the village, is of 1759, and in brick. Sadly, as Pevsner and Hubbard remind us, the 'Scottish baronial' mansion of Oaklands has been demolished.

ECCLESTON, 3m S of Chester. There is a fine, feudal air about this village amid many and varied trees, which gives its name to a London street and square. And well there might be, for – largely Victorian, and with much work by John Douglas of Chester – it is one of the estate villages of Eaton Hall, seat of the princely Dukes of Westminster. Rhododendrons, wistaria and laburnum bloom; the school boasts a spire; steps lead up to a little rural post-office-cum-shop. You find white-painted gates, black-and-white, Dutch gables, pargeting, twisted chimneys, a touch of Regency Gothic. The Paddocks is a small French château, built for the agent. The ducal chef had his home nearby, and there is a prominent shingled well-house in the centre of the village.

But Eccleston's glory is the church of St Mary the Virgin, built in 1899, regardless of cost but with restrained grandeur, for the first Duke of Westminster, with G. F. Bodley as architect. The 'small cathedral' which, it is said, the Duke stipulated, is approached today through magnificent gates by the Davies brothers of Wrexham, which were originally at Emral Hall, Flintshire. They now form a memorial to the 2nd Duke, the legendary 'Bend Or'. Beyond is an avenue of pleached limes leading to a S porch with statues in niches. The lofty red sandstone church has a W tower, a very fine peal of bells, flying buttresses, and clerestory to nave and chancel. The original furnishings are intact. Reredos and screen, carved bench-ends, oak pulpit with sounding-board and resting on a marble base – all add to the beauty, as do the angels in the clerestory windows holding a scroll of the Magnificat. The 1st Duke's monument bears an effigy in alabaster by Chavalliaud. The surroundings of the church, with terraced lawns and clipped yew, are beautifully kept; easily overlooked is the graveyard of the previous church. This forms a peaceful burial-place for the Grosvenor family.

To the S, watered by the Dee, lies the huge park of Eaton Hall. Sadly, if inevitably, the Victorian Gothic palace by J. F. Waterhouse, incorporating earlier work, has been demolished, save for the soaring clock tower, private chapel, stables and various auxiliary buildings forming a curious contrast to the new, white mansion. The famous Golden Gates, partly by the Davies brothers, and partly by Francis Skidmore of Coventry and Meriden, survive. So does G. F. Watts' equestrian statue of Hugh Lupus, the Norman Earl of Chester, a Grosvenor ancestor. Extensive formal gardens remain, and are occasionally on view, like the chapel and family carriages.

GAWSWORTH, 4m SW of Macclesfield, off A536. From the Warren cross-roads and a corner

The church of St Oswald, Lower Peover

J. Allan Cash

shop you pass a former school of 1832 (now privately occupied), a wayside cross, many modern houses and Maggoty's, or Maggoty Johnson's, Wood, a National Trust property with the grave of the last professional jester in England. Johnson, who achieved brief London fame with an extraordinary opera, *Hurlothrumbo*, lived at Gawsworth Hall, once the home of the Fittons, and died in 1773. This house, ½m from the main road, is among the features of a village unique in Cheshire. There are, in fact, two halls, as well as a fine church, a rectory and an old rectory, all of much architectural interest in a setting of pools, swans, many trees and an avenue leading to the Harrington Arms.

The church of St James, with its battlements and pinnacles, dates from the 15th and 16th c. A S porch has curious weathered gargoyles; indeed all the exterior carvings are worthy of inspection. There is a striking W tower. The wide nave has no chancel arch and no aisles, though a S aisle may have been merged into it. The screen is copied from one in Elvaston Church, Derbyshire, and is by J. Oldrid Scott. (The Earls of Harrington lived both at Gawsworth and Elvaston Castle for many years.) The Fitton monuments are of great interest. One commemorates Francis Fitton, buried here in 1608, and bears his effigy, with a skeleton below and notable heraldry. N of the altar is the tomb of Sir Edward (d. 1606) with kneeling figures of children beside it; their mother, seated, looks very melancholy. One daughter was supposedly the Dark Lady of the Sonnets.

The Fittons were at Gawsworth for about three and a half centuries, and built the richly timbered hall. This was reduced in size by the Earl of Macclesfield, whose death in 1701 was followed,

some years later, by the most famous duel in British history, in which both the Duke of Hamilton and Lord Mohun lost their lives in a dispute over the property. The internal timbering is superb. Other features include a panel on the N front, carved, with the Fitton arms, in Galway by Richard Rany in 1570, and actually signed; the three-decker window overlooking the garden court; Pugin bookcases from Scarisbrick Hall, Lancs., in the library; fine pictures and sculpture. There is a very long Tudor wall to the park and tilting-ground. The 'new' hall was begun in 1707 and never completed. The black-and-white old rectory is 15th-c; its successor, of Queen Anne's day, was a school and has a handsome Georgian doorway from a demolished house in Knutsford.

GREAT BUDWORTH, 2½m N of Northwich, off A559. This is an almost unbelievable storybook village of brownish brick, gables, brick and stone mullions, pargeting, angled chimneys, and a mixture of Victorian and restored older work, with pretty little gardens. Near the church and the remains of the stocks is the George and Dragon Inn of 1875, by John Douglas, with a wrought-iron sign that might belong to Germany or Switzerland. Just N of the church is the former schoolhouse built by John Deane in Shakespeare's time, and the black-and-white cottages of Church Lane.

The magnificent, heavily-embattled church of St Mary and All Saints is beautifully placed at the head of the main street. It is largely Perp, with a clerestory. Above the chancel arch is the entrance to the rood-loft, but there is no sign of stairs and it is assumed that it was reached – unusually – by means of a ladder. The building of the nave seems to have been spread over a number of years; one pier bears a carving of a lion and what seems to be Eve and the Serpent. A roof corbel represents a man playing bagpipes; indeed all the carvings are a delight. The 15th-c font has emblems of the Passion. The Lady Chapel is the burial-place of Sir Peter Leycester, the Cheshire historian, who tells us that it was called Lady Mary's Chapel and contained a wooden statue of the Virgin 'burnt in the Vicar's oven about 1559 by command of Queen Elizabeth'. The chapel windows were designed in Expressionist style by M. Fourmaintreaux in 1965, and made at the Whitefriars Glass Studios. The S aisle is adjoined by the Warburton Chapel, which contains a medieval altar-slab and the sadly-mutilated effigy of Sir John Warburton, d. 1575, in fine armour. Oak stalls are said to be 13th-c. The W tower is early 16th-c and apparently had the same master mason, Thomas Hunter, as that at Northwich. It bears paterae and the arms of the local families of Dutton and Warburton, and those of Norton Priory. The tithes and patronage of Great Budworth belonged to the Augustinian Canons of Norton, but passed under Henry VIII to the new College of Christ Church, Oxford.

LOWER PEOVER, also called Peover Inferior, 3m S of Knutsford, has been described as 'a lovely village, its churchyard bordered by rhododendrons, its meadows running down to an old watermill, a coaching inn and a quaint school-house', the 'timbered church among the fields as enchanting as one could wish.' So wrote Arthur Mee, who is really an invaluable guide to the counties of England, even if sad changes have occurred in many places since his time. The church of St Oswald is of much importance, if greatly restored by Salvin in the last century. A stone W tower is said to be late 16th-c; the body of the church is richly timbered, and ascribed to the 14th c, though the arcades are possibly older. There are beautiful Jacobean screens, lectern and pulpit, and curious box pews 'with odd little doors which begin halfway up so that striding into them is like going over a stile.' A wooden hand, nailed to the wall, may have been hung outside the church to indicate that buying and selling were allowed at fair-time; and there is a massive dug-out chest of great antiquity. Memorials are to the de Tabley, Cholmondeley, and Shakerley families; one is to the Shakerley who, at Rowton Moor, crossed the river in a tub, his horse swimming beside him, to carry orders from King Charles I. Here is buried John Byrne Leicester Warren, last Lord de Tabley, born in 1835, poet, diplomat, botanist and barrister, of Tabley House. One fears that few read his verses today, though they have some merit.

At **Over Peover,** or Peover Superior, 2m SE, is Peover Hall, situated in lonely, wooded countryside and charming gardens. The house is curious and very interesting, being either what is left of a larger structure of Elizabethan date, or one that was never completed. It has lost a Georgian wing following a fire, but has been admirably restored and furnished. There are extraordinary stables of the 17th c, with Tuscan columns and other decorative woodwork, as well as an ornamental plaster

The old Rectory at Gawsworth

F. Leonard Jackson

The Norman chapel at Prestbury

ceiling. Near the house is the church of St Laurence, largely an early 19th-c rebuilding, but with older chapels; that to the S is delightful. There are monuments of the Mainwarings; that to John Mainwaring, 1410, and his wife, is 'uncommonly good', as Pevsner and Hubbard say. A modern screen to the N chapel is by F. H. Crossley.

PARKGATE, 12m WNW of Chester, off A450. You expect – and find – fresh shrimps and ships in bottles and a faintly ghostly air about the place, once an important departure point for Ireland. It has memories of Handel (who left here for Dublin and the first performance of *Messiah*), John Wesley, Nelson, Lady Hamilton, Mrs Delany and Mrs Fitzherbert. William III embarked at Parkgate before the Battle of the Boyne. In the 18th c it replaced Chester as a busy port where Irish linen and Spanish wines were unloaded and Cheshire cheese and salt and Macclesfield silk were dispatched overseas, but in the early 19th c, owing to silting of the Dee, Liverpool began to take its trade. Now the sea has retreated from the stone quay, and one looks over melancholy, yet somehow attractive, marshes to the Dee estuary and the Welsh coast. Old houses along the straggling Promenade or Parade and Station Road reflect days when Parkgate was a fashionable resort, with a theatre. It is still very pleasant to spend a holiday there. There are comely modern houses, and the small mid-19th-c church of St Thomas, beside the Square, was, one is told, originally a Nonconformist chapel. Wirral Way replaces the railway line.

A tiny but remarkably informative local guidebook tells us proudly that Ken Cranston, former England and Lancashire cricketer, was a member of Parkgate Cricket Club. But the old port has another claim to fame. On the Promenade is Mostyn House School, a remodelling and enlargement of the inn where Handel stayed. Here in 1865 was born Sir Wilfred Grenfell, the doctor and medical missionary who was chosen by the Royal National Mission for Deep Sea Fishermen to start a pioneer service on the stark Labrador coast, where in two months he treated 900 patients. The sea has claimed its inevitable victims. Nearby, Milton's friend, Edward King ('Lycidas is dead, dead ere his prime') was drowned; and 106 folk lost their lives when the *George* sank in 1806.

PRESTBURY (3m N of Macclesfield), has been called a town, which it is not, although numerous modern houses – and fortunately many trees – embrace the old village with its fine church, white-painted buildings and good restaurants that suggest a Mancunian clientele. The village street has become somewhat sophisticated, and inevitably the pseudo-Georgian window has made its appearance. Nonetheless, the general aspect is pleasing, with some real Georgian doorways, the long, low Legh Arms and Black Boy, the Admiral Rodney, and the handsomely timbered Priest's House. This last, which seems to be later than the date given to it in more than one account, retains a small balcony from which, it is said, an ejected incumbent preached during the Commonwealth. At the head of the village street is the early Victorian Prestbury Hall, with pretty fan decoration and figures of two fierce-looking lions guarding the principal doorway. A little schoolhouse has some black-and-white and a spirelet, and Prestbury can boast a garage that is not the eyesore these structures so often are.

The church of St Peter, near the River Bollin, shares its churchyard (entered through a pinnacled stone gateway) with a remarkable little chapel. This is of Norman origin, but largely rebuilt in 1747; its W doorway, with beak and zig-zag ornament, has a badly weathered tympanum, apparently of Christ in Majesty and, above, what were presumably figures of saints. Close by, in a glass case – most peculiar – are the remains of an Anglo-Danish cross discovered here in the last century. The church has a W tower of the late 15th c, built with the financial help of Richard Legh, whose memorial remains. There are 13th-c arcades to the dignified nave, with early 18th-c paintings of the Apostles, 'gay and reminiscent of Continental rather than English churches', say Pevsner and Hubbard. The S aisle windows are 17th-c, and there was restoration last century by Sir Gilbert Scott and J. O. Scott. The Jacobean and Georgian screens are a feature and, as in other Cheshire churches, one finds good chandeliers and benchends. Incised monuments have portraits of men in armour. Altogether a most satisfying church.

ROSTHERNE (3m N of Knutsford), is a small village with one shop in the main street, and is admittedly something of an appendage to Tatton Park nearby. It is included here because of its beautiful and unusual situation, though there is attraction, too, in the brownish-brick cottages with such names as Lilac, Rose, Virginia, and Apple Tree. St Mary's Square has estate housing of 1910 with a nice touch of heraldry, and a delightful thatched house stands high above the roadway on its green bank. Close to the village is undulating, wooded landscape and Rostherne Mere, Cheshire's largest lake and over 100 acres in extent, now a very private nature reserve. During World War II it was extensively used in training parachutists to descend on water under cover of darkness.

The delightful church of St Mary stands above the mere, and one may sit and admire the view. The main entrance to the churchyard is through a curious gate of 1640, which swings on a central beam. There are plenty of large tombstones laid flat, with the good lettering that is a reproach to so many latter-day monumental masons. A large monument rather like a miniature · Albert Memorial may lead the unsuspecting to assume that it is connected with the Egertons of Tatton rather than the Simpson family. That interesting family, however, has notable memorials inside the church, as do the Langford Brookes of Mere Hall; and Rostherne Church receives six entries in Rupert Gunnis's *Dictionary of British Sculptors*. A poorly preserved 13th-c effigy of a knight may be that of Sir Hugh Venables. Outstanding is the memorial to Lady Charlotte Egerton, 1845. She was accidentally drowned just before her marriage, and Richard Westmacott, Jun., depicts her as sleeping, her hands folded over lilies, with a watching angel. The church itself has EE, Dec, and Perp work, an imposing W tower of the 18th c, and a Victorian chancel and vestry by Blomfield.

A horse-drawn conveyance – also used for carrying game for shooting-parties – used to bring servants to services from Tatton Park, now a National Trust property, financed and administered by Cheshire County Council. There is a gate ½m S of Rostherne. The classical mansion is largely by Samuel and Lewis Wyatt (uncle and nephew) and dates from the late 18th and 19th c. The splendid interior retains no less than 120 pieces of furniture by Gillow of Lancaster, as well as important pictures, silver and other treasures. Domestic regions recall spacious days, and in the Tenants' Hall, apart from the servants' 'bus', are wildlife trophies, an estate fire engine, and the first motor car registered in Cheshire. It was owned by the last Lord Egerton of Tatton, who bequeathed house, gardens, and park to the Trust in 1954.

STYAL, 1½m N of Wilmslow, off B516. In 1784 Samuel Greg from Belfast founded a cotton mill in the beautiful wooded valley of the River Bollin, not far from the hamlet of Styal. His employees came from a distance, and at first he used existing buildings, converted from other uses, to house them, as well as purchasing scattered cottages. As the business expanded, he built additional houses. A strange feature to modern eyes is the Apprentice House, dating from 1790. Here, at one time, 100 boys and girls were housed in conditions that were spartan, but good for the period. From 1833 onwards, the children spent four hours per day in the mill and four at the school that Greg built, and where their elders could attend evening classes. Today, the National Trust owns, in addition to 225 acres of land, the cottages that Greg built and the former mill, a fine piece of industrial architecture now being developed as a textile museum. An excellent little guide, with map and illustrations, is provided for visitors to aid their walk from Quarry Bank Mill and Quarry Bank House, Greg's own residence of 1797, past the Apprentice House and round the village. There one may see Cruck Cottage, Unitarian and Methodist chapels, the Oak Cottages built for the work people (small rents were deducted from wages) and the attractive, timbered Oak Farm, partly of 15th-c date. Samuel Greg bought the farm so that the workers could be supplied with fresh meat and dairy produce. The whole is a remarkable survival, but it should be emphasized that the Styal houses are homes, and privacy should be respected.

WILDBOARCLOUGH, 5m SE of Macclesfield, off A54 (this involves a long detour). A local guide describes this remote spot as 'one of the most beautifully sited of all Cheshire villages . . . standing in a fold of the Peak moors, sheltered by, yet close to some of the wildest and loveliest hills of the Peak Park.' The situation is, indeed, of surpassing beauty, with stream, numerous trees and the heights. The village consists of little more than a small, charmingly set church, a row of cottages with Gothic windows, an inn, and a former mill that dates from 1770. This last resembles a country house at first sight and, until not long ago, was used in part as the post office. The mill manager lived at Crag Hall, built early in the 19th c.

The small church of St Saviour was built in Edwardian days by the 16th Earl of Derby, a local landowner, as a thankoffering for the safe return of his sons from the South African War, the Countess attending the consecration in 1909. It was built by estate craftsmen, largely with local materials, but it is attractive in its quiet way, rather than of any special architectural merit. It is curious to read now that silk, cotton, and carpets – including carpets used at the opening of the Crystal Palace – were manufactured at Wildboarclough. The only wild boar, incidentally, is to be found on the sign of an inn in the vicinity.

Wincle, 2m SW, 'reached by steep roads', has a church of St Michael, chiefly of 1882, with an earlier tower. The Ship Inn has a sign depicting the *Nimrod*, the vessel in which the local Sir Philip Brocklehurst accompanied Shackleton to the Antarctic. Within the parish is the Post Office Tower, 225ft high, as well as the boulder called the Hanging Stone. The medieval Wincle Grange belonged to the monks of Combermere Abbey.

The North-West

CUMBRIA LANCASHIRE MERSEYSIDE GREATER MANCHESTER

Christopher Hanson-Smith

The boundary changes of April 1974 both extinguished the historical counties of Cumberland and Westmorland and removed from Lancashire the contrasting extremities of Furness, across Morecambe Bay in the north, and the great conurbations of Manchester and Liverpool in the south. In terms of population the net loss to the old Lancashire was about three million. As a consolation both the new county of Cumbria and the new Lancashire were given some rural and very attractive areas of Yorkshire west of the Pennines. But in this book all four new counties in the North-West are covered, a region of 130 miles north to south and 35 miles wide at one point.

The M6 motorway winds like an impersonal ribbon of concrete from top to bottom of this region, an excellent way for those who wish to pass quickly through it with eyes fixed on the highlands of Scotland or the warmer south. Other motorway spurs and links to east and west make access to the surrounding country that much easier, so much so that this North-West country is probably blessed with better road communications than any other. To the explorer of villages and quiet countryside it is a boon to have such swift access to counties of such diversity.

South and mid-Lancashire are all moorland and mill town; north Lancashire has even more moorland. The truth is that the new county is a very rural one – climb out of the steep valleys where the industrial towns are sited and the open moors stretch from one dark skyline to another. Even around Merseyside and Greater Manchester quiet oases of green are found within a few minutes of the city centres – the six villages within the Saddleworth conservation area are all within half-an-hour's drive from Manchester's Piccadilly. North of the Kent estuary and into the 'new' Cumbria are fells and drystone walls which give a foretaste of the central massif of the Lake District, a hub from which the dales spread out like the spokes of a wheel. The barrier of the Pennines on the east is continuous and at Cross Fell rises to over 3000ft. Along the length of its foothills are old settlements, their names taken from the nearest conical hill or pike. Then north up the fertile Eden valley, where all the buildings are of warm sandstone, to the undulating border lands chosen by Emperor Hadrian 1900 years ago for his protective wall. North of this is bleaker, 'debatable' land which was fought over for centuries until the Act of Union with Scotland in 1707.

The buildings and layouts of villages faithfully reflect the historical events and social changes that have gone before. Likewise the older houses and cottages are really extensions of the land on which they are built; the stone won from the communal quarry nearby and used for walls and riven roofing tiles, resulting in a village that today is dubbed attractive or pretty. The North-West abounds in such villages – Downham under Pendle Hill in mid-Lancashire and Morland south-east of Penrith in Cumbria are examples.

For centuries the rural settlements within striking distance of the Scots marauders lived under the threat of attack. They therefore grouped their houses around a central 'green' on which the stock could be driven for safety when the alarm was raised. Narrow alleys, easily barred, lead to enclosed courtyards – Hawkshead is an excellent example of this communal defensive system. Many of the present mansion houses in Cumbria began as fortified pele towers built in the thirteenth and fourteenth centuries as an impregnable defence against marauders. Animals were safe within a stockade around the base of the tower and the family sheltered in the top two floors. At Great Salkeld the church tower is an old pele, thoughtfully provided with a fireplace on the first floor. At Beetham the pele and adjacent Great Hall are now ruinous farm buildings, but outside Ravenglass the pele fits well into Salvin's grand design for Muncaster Castle.

By the fourteenth century most of the important villages were already established as self-contained communities and linked by tenuous tracks over enormous stretches of bog and through thick forests. At that time cattle farming was first allowed and the monastic houses such as Furness, Whalley and Cartmel imposed their efficient farming systems over their enormous domains. The name today of the grey sheep of the Lake District is that given by the monks of Furness to the 'runs' of their sheep farms – the herdwicks.

Beacons set on prominent landmarks – Rivington, Parbold and Black Combe in Cumbria – flashed news within hours over rugged countryside that would have taken weeks to traverse by horse. Turnpiking the first roads only started in the early eighteenth century, but by 1760 regular stage coach services were running between the main towns. Lancashire had the earliest canal, the Sankey Canal of 1755, quickly followed by others which now wind their placid ways throughout the

county, and as far north as Kendal in Cumbria. Railways came in 1830 and the main line to Scotland was completed in 1847. Today the motorways bring twenty-two million people within reach of the Lake District for an easy day's outing and, of more importance for village communities, enable the people to live many miles away from their place of work in the neighbouring towns. A significant sight in a village today is a converted cottage, once the home of a frugal miner or weaver, that becomes an extension of the erstwhile suburban surroundings of the proud owner. Strict planning requirements over fenestration, porches and extensions exist in National Parks, but these are hard to enforce; they need to be applied as protection for what remains unspoilt in so many of the lovely villages.

When communications were so poor the weekly market and seasonal fairs were the means of trading produce and finding out about the world beyond the parish boundaries. Borough charters granted by the monarch were the key to growth in medieval times – Liverpool and Lancaster started to grow apace as the traders sought the protection of the town walls. Market charters were also much prized – Kirkham, near Preston, was granted one in 1269 and in 1208 King John authorized a Saturday market in Ravenglass on the Cumbrian coast. The market cross, or more often its pedestal, survives in most villages, beside the stocks on the village green.

The preachers of Christianity, like the later Vikings, came into the North-West from Ireland and the Isle of Man. St Patrick (c. 389–461) has a ruined chapel dedicated to him at Heysham, south of Morecambe Bay, and St Kentigern was the leader of a crusade down the coast from Cumbria in c. 470. A glance at the map shows how the oldest churches are in the river valleys or at the heads of sea inlets. The Lune valley is particularly rich in ecclesiastical relics of the ninth and tenth centuries – churches such as Tunstall, Hornby and Gressingham, the former one of fifteen mentioned in Domesday Book in Lancashire. The word 'ecles', indicating a church, appears in several place-names.

The plain church tower, with embattled top and small pinnacles, remains as the focal point of most villages in the North-West. The body of the church will very likely have been altered and enlarged, the Perpendicular style predominating. The older buildings are history lessons in stone;

the clues in the shape of arches, hatchments and piscinas, as to how the congregation thought and lived over the centuries. Churchyards, approached through lychgates, are places to linger in. The preaching cross stands beside the south porch, marking the spot where the faithful worshipped before the church was built, and the grave headstones, their inscriptions in the lee of the prevailing winds, tell of suffering and endeavour that can but be imagined.

Lancashire has always been one of the strongest Roman Catholic counties and many are the halls where the recusant and unrepentant families had their priests hidden away in secret 'holes' which are now obvious attractions for the visitor. The slender spires of Catholic churches built in Victorian times often share the skyline with the older towers of the Anglican churches. Nonconformism has always found strong support in the North-West as well. The Quakers first preached their simple brand of faith in north Lancashire and many 'Friends' languished for years in Lancaster Castle's dank cells. Their Meeting Houses, with single naves and whitewashed walls, continue to be used. Presbyterian and Unitarian chapels – that at Rivington was built in the reign of Queen Anne – appear in nearly all the villages.

The region is well endowed with building stone, and brick is therefore little used except for the stark mills and factories. Yellow and red sandstones predominate in Lancashire, with millstone grit all down the west side of the Pennines. Limestone appears from the Ribble valley northwards and forms a ring round the Lake District with its distinctive grey stone and slate. The Cumbrian farmhouses and cottages have thick walls of grey stone, roughcast and then whitewashed. The roofs are of carefully graded slates, sealed beneath by 'torching' made of plaster strengthened with horsehair.

The diversity of colour in walls and roofs reflects the fascinating contrasts to be discovered and enjoyed throughout the villages of the North-West. The appearance of a line of stone-built cottages around the green may seem austere to a visitor accustomed to dripping thatch entwined with honeysuckle and fragrant roses, but the warmth of welcome that awaits within leaves nothing to be desired. The villagers bring the community alive and it is they whom the enquiring and sympathetic traveller must approach to appreciate all that has gone before.

GAZETTEER

AINSDALE, *Merseyside.* Sand dunes, rows of new houses, and a large holiday camp – this is the first unrewarding impression of Ainsdale-on-Sea, 4m down the coast from Southport. But there remains a strong village community, centred on the shopping centre by the railway station and around the triangular green with the War Memorial. Some early cottages, probably once

belonging to fishermen, still survive here. The church is of 1867, red-brick, and with a pleasing atmosphere. Behind the RAF airfield of Woodvale are 1216 acres of heath, dune and saltmarsh, preserved by the Nature Conservancy and rich in flora and fauna. This reserve was created in 1971 and acts as a vital lung for the encroaching dormitory estates that line the main road.

4m inland from Ainsdale is the village of **Halsall** which boasts a church of rare distinction and beauty. A 15th-c Perp spire rises from an octagonal tower, and the 14th-c nave and chancel are buttressed and pinnacled. In the N wall is a fine Dec doorway with original panelled oak door; the misericords and bench-ends in the choir stalls are of equally high standard and there is a mutilated effigy of a priest carved from alabaster in a recess that dates from the 13th c.

ASKHAM, *Cumbria,* 4m S of Penrith. Turning off the A6 at Eamont Bridge towards Ullswater there is on the corner an ancient circular earthwork which is known as King Arthur's Table. 2m further on is Askham, a village overshadowed by Lowther Park. At the centre of the park are the spectacular ruins of Lowther Castle, built 1806–11, that manage to look impressive even without the roofs which were taken off in 1957. Through the park and near the A6 is an interesting example of a model village which was constructed between the years 1765–73 to a design by J. Adam. The effect of the rose-coloured stone and the clean, classic lines of the two-storeyed houses in this park-like setting is very pleasant. To the W is a row of estate houses with hipped roofs, which include the estate office, dating from 1684. An area within the park has been set aside for rare birds and animals.

The 7th Earl of Lonsdale, whose family trusts own the Lowther estates, lives at Askham Hall at the bottom end of the village. This semi-fortified house, commanding a magnificent view of the river below and the park, is of 14th-c construction, with extensive Tudor additions. In April and early May the grounds of the Hall are a yellow sea of daffodils. The village itself stretches along either side of a broad green, Yorkshire-style, with 17th-c cottages, many colour-washed. There is an outdoor swimming pool and a new council house development that compares unfavourably with the older cottages.

BARBON, *Cumbria,* 3m N of Kirkby Lonsdale. The setting of this quiet, straggling village is the attraction, against a bare backdrop of Middleton fell, cleft by the steep dale through which winds the road to Dent. The Barbon beck is spanned by an old packhorse bridge before joining the River Lune. The church of St Michael is a late 18th-c example of Austin and Paley's work in Perp style built on the site of a 12th-c chapel. Much of the wooden carving was executed by village craftsmen and there are fine examples of older 17th-c work on a chest, cupboard and chair preserved in the church. Nearby, **Casterton** Church, 1½m S, was built in 1821–3 for the girls' school that continues to flourish in the village, and contains large wall paintings and stained glass in Pre-Raphaelite style by Henry Holiday. Whelprigg Hall, between the two villages, is of 1834 in Tudor-style and superbly sited at the end of a long drive.

BEETHAM, *Cumbria* (7m N of Carnforth), is a delightful cluster of houses, built from grey limestone, beside the A6 and commanding a stretch of the Bela river whose waters were here both fordable and able to be harnessed for driving machinery in two mills. One mill is now a thriving factory making specialist papers, but the other, now called Heron Mill, on the left bank, has been restored to appear and work very much as it would have done in about 1750 when it was built. The waterwheel, 14ft in diameter, drives four pairs of millstones which were grinding 80–90 tons of corn each week as late as 1930. A charitable trust has restored the mill which is open daily throughout the season.

The church of St Michael proves that Beetham is long established; its tower rests on Saxon foundations and there are several Norman arches within. Over the centuries the fabric has been enlarged but the result is a sturdy building with a fine timbered medieval roof. Masons' marks are visible everywhere. A hoard of coins dating back to Norman times was found under a pillar in the nave in Victorian times. A tomb in the chancel is surmounted by two mutilated effigies of Sir Thomas Beetham and his wife, who lived over 500 years ago at Beetham Tower, a fortified farmhouse that was once surrounded by a 15ft curtain wall, part of which remains. The pele tower and great hall adjoining are well preserved. The farmhouse is late 17th-c and in a field just N of it is a huge boulder on which the tenants paid their rents. Morris dancers regularly perform in the courtyard in front of the Wheatsheaf Hotel, the old coaching inn.

1m SW is Hazelslack, a 15th-c pele tower, just inland from Arnside Knott, from whose summit there is a magnificent view of the Kent Estuary and the S fells of the Lake District. A guide is available for a nature walk around the Knott.

Leighton Hall, 4m down the A6 and just W of Yealand Conyers, has superb views of the Furness fells across the sparkling sands of Morecambe Bay. For centuries the most direct route to S Lakeland lay across the sands, and, at Cartmel Priory on the N of the bay, a 'carter' was retained as a guide to travellers. Between the house and the shore is Leighton Moss, a wilderness of bog and salting, now a bird reserve where bitterns 'boom' and ospreys can halt *en route* to and from their Scottish nesting grounds.

In the centre of a green amphitheatre the present Leighton Hall stands out white against the backdrop of fells: a confection of Gothick turrets, battlements and pointed window arches. A house has stood in the same position since medieval times; the land was granted to Adam d'Avranches in 1173 by William de Lancaster and a fortified manor was built by him not long afterwards. Since then there have been 24 owners and only twice has ownership passed by sale. In 1786 the estate was sold to a Lancaster banker, Alexander Worswick, whose mother was Alice Gillow, and it was he who gave the Georgian house a Gothick façade.

In 1822 Richard Gillow acquired Leighton and thus established the connection of that famous cabinet-making business with the Hall. Richard's father founded the business at Lancaster and furnished the Hall with many outstanding examples of Gillow craftsmanship. In the dining-room are two sets of early Georgian walnut chairs and the prototype expanding table which Gillow patented in 1800. Of more recent interest is the music room on the ground floor of the tower, added in 1870 to the SW corner. Here Kathleen Ferrier gave her last performance in a private house before her death.

During the summer, hawks are flown in the park and teas are served in the old brewhouse of the Hall.

BEWCASTLE, *Cumbria,* 10m N of Brampton. Tucked away in the far NE corner of Cumbria is a wind-swept hamlet that boasts some remarkable links with the past. Pride of place goes to the famous cross in the shadow of St Cuthbert's Church, itself 13th-c, with a Georgian tower. The cross was probably carved in AD 680 and stands 14ft 6in high on its pedestal – with the cross-head, tragically lost, it would have been higher. The quality of the intricate vine scrolls, the knot patterns and runes is matched only by the Ruthwell Cross across the Scottish border. It is worth the long drive simply to stand in front of this exquisite relic of art as practised in the so-called Dark Ages. If, however, there is only time to visit Carlisle, an excellent reproduction of the cross stands in the Tullie House Museum there. Within a 6-acre area once bounded by Roman fortifications are now found the church, the ruins of a square castle, a massive fortified farm-house, and the rectory. Nearby are several of the pele towers which were essential for survival during the Border warfare that racked the 'debatable lands' until the Act of Union with Scotland finally brought peace in 1707.

BOLTON-BY-BOWLAND, *Lancs.* 6m NE of Clitheroe. This unspoilt village is best approached from the A59 at Gisburn. The road winds down to the Ribble through a deep cutting overhung by beech trees. There are two village greens and the houses beside them are of grey stone, some whitewashed, others with only the mortar picked out in white. A line of trees graces the top green but on the lower one are the base and shaft of an old market cross with the stocks close by. The Kirk Beck flows above this green, its course altered by embankments to give the appearance of a mill stream which flows into the larger Skirden Beck on whose banks a bobbin mill once stood.

Opposite the church, set on the slope between the two greens, is a fine avenue of trees which lead to the site of Bolton Hall, now demolished and once the seat of the Pudsay family who were Lords of the Manor from 1349 until 1771. Sir Ralph Pudsay rebuilt the church in the same year, 1464, that he entertained Henry VI after the Battle of Hexham. His limestone memorial is unusual both for its size and the carved effigies of his three wives and their 25 children. A direct descendant was William Pudsay, who made the famous leap on his horse from Rainsber Scar on the Ribble while escaping from officers of the law who had discovered his private mint. The oak door of the church, studded with nails and secured by a stout wooden bar, is worthy of note as is a small, Saxon carved stone let into the west inner wall of the porch. Several of the late 17th-c pews remain, carved with the initials of their original owners.

BRINDLE, *Lancs.,* 6m SW of Blackburn. The tall church tower has watched over this simple village for hundreds of years and tradition has it that Cromwellian soldiers fired at the Cavaliers from its battlements. Today the factories of Central Lancashire New Town to the W can be espied from the same tower and the villagers, who have a great community spirit, hope that they will not be swallowed up by a new conurbation. Meanwhile, the church, the school and the white-walled cottages all make for a village which is well worth visiting. The Lodge is early 19th-c and has an imposing front elevation of stone. Inside there is elaborate plaster work and, in the grounds, a red sandstone folly in the shape of a tower.

Down in the valley to the E runs the Leeds-Liverpool canal, constructed about 200 years ago, and on the E bank is the delightful small village of **Withnell Fold,** grown up around the paper mill established on the canal banks in 1840. Everything here is well cared for and a model of how a small industrial community can appear. The well-preserved stocks are from an earlier age.

3m NE on the W slope of Darwen Hill is the split-level and breezy village of **Tockholes.** The stone cottages that once belonged to the hand-loomers in the lower part of the straggling village are now much in demand for suitable 'improvement' by newcomers. The inns on the higher road cater for those from Preston and Blackburn who like to drive out for a drink in such fresh surroundings and admire the distant views. Up behind is Darwen Tower, a stumpy memorial to Queen Victoria's Jubilee.

In Lower Hill is the school of 1834, built in the churchyard and unusual in having an outdoor pulpit of stone. Also to be seen nearby are several early 17th-c farmhouses that belonged to the 'statesmen' or yeoman farmers.

On St Bartholomew's Day, 1662, the Act of Uniformity was passed which resulted in nearly a fifth of all the English clergy being driven from their parishes. At Tockholes the parishioners refused to accept the Act and thus became one of the first 'nonconformist' congregations in the country.

Also Nonconformist were the Hoghtons of **Hoghton** Tower, a family that has lived in their hill-top mansion since the 14th c. The fortress-like building stands on a 560ft-high conical hill within easy view of Tockholes and N of A675. From the ramparts of the Tower on a clear day can be seen the summit of Snowdon in Wales; the modern towers of Preston in the foreground; Blackpool tower on the Fylde coast to the NW; and the Lake District fells to the N. A 14th-c pele tower first stood on this hill and there remains a complete arch from its vaulted basement in the present NW corner of the inner courtyard. Since 1565 little change has been made to the buildings, which remain an impressive example of Jacobean architecture. The family owns a mid-18th-c painting by Arthur Devis which is a pictorial view of the mansion looking much the same as today, but perched on a treeless hill. All the timber had been sold off to pay the bills for entertaining James I and his court in 1617. The King was on his way back from Scotland and Sir Richard Hoghton invited him to spend three days with him which were taken up with feasting and hunting. At one banquet the King was so taken with the excellence of the beef that he dubbed the roasted loin with his sword so that it became 'Sir Loin' – a name that has remained in use for that particular cut ever since.

The massive table around which the King and his courtiers sat can be seen today in the Great Hall, as can a long-case clock that runs for 400 days without requiring to be wound: the weight needs two men to lift it! The Tower is open to the public in season, usually on a Sunday.

BROUGHTON-IN-FURNESS, Cumbria.

The spacious main square, surrounded by grey terraced houses and with an obelisk on a massive plinth set importantly in the centre, gives Broughton the appearance of a small town, but in reality it is but a large village. The site is a strategic one where the River Duddon broadens into an estuary up which a succession of invaders and settlers have sailed to tame the rugged hinterland – Romans, Celts, and Norse Vikings. The name Broughton derives from an Old English word for 'stronghold'. In 1322 a pele tower was built, following punitive forays by the Scots, and from this grew the present Manor House, called Broughton Tower, that dominates the village. From 1487 until 1920 only two families held the Lordship of the Manor of Broughton – the Earls of Derby until 1651, and then the Sawreys, who were responsible for building the Square and town hall in 1760.

Unusually the church is sited to the S, outside the village, and in April the churchyard is a carpet of daffodils, among which old gravestones bear grey witness to the longevity of many of Broughton's inhabitants. Stones in the beautiful Norman porch are marked where 14th-c arrows were sharpened on them. Inside the church are displayed an Elizabethan Bible and a 15th-c bell which rang out after the defeat of the Spanish Armada. The present building is a reconstruction by Austin and Paley, Lancaster architects responsible for many Cumbrian buildings in Victorian times.

Many and varied are the bridges that carry the roads to and from Broughton. To the E is the great causeway over Wreaks Moss, and at the far end is an early 18th-c bridge that bears an interesting assortment of inscriptions. Further up the Lickle Valley are several arched packhorse bridges, spanning the tumbling beck, and field walls made from huge slate slabs.

In Elizabethan times a charter was granted to hold a market in Broughton and fairs were held thrice yearly. The Proclamation of this Charter is read every year on the first day of August, and coins are distributed.

CALDBECK, Cumbria (7m SE of Wigton),

is an old community that for centuries was self-sufficient, with many trades followed by the inhabitants, who numbered no fewer than 1795 in 1780. The waters of the Caldew beck were harnessed to drive mills of which there were once 13 and several of the water-wheels with their machinery still survive. The 19th-c bobbin mill was powered by a 42ft-diameter wheel which was once the second largest in the world. Below the 15th-c packhorse bridge on the right bank is the church's own corn mill built in 1740.

Other interesting buildings that served useful purposes include the old wash-house, the forerunner of the modern 'laundromat'; the old brewery that supplied 16 inns in the village; a mill that is now used by a clogger; and the original schoolhouse, which stands shuttered and forlorn on the approach from Uldale.

½m up-stream is a wooded dell called the Howk which can only be approached on foot. A waterfall and unusual 'fairey-hole', hollowed out of the limestone, make the excursion very worthwhile.

The church of St Kentigern had Norman beginnings, as witness the entrance to the S porch. Rebuilding in 1512 and 1727 is recorded within the church, and as late as 1932 a piscina and stoup were uncovered in the S aisle. Two graves in the churchyard are much visited – those of John Peel, the huntsman who died in 1854, and Mary Robinson, the Buttermere Beauty, whose seduction by the notorious John Hatfield in 1802 is recorded in song and verse. Overlooking the churchyard is a fine rectory of 1785, whose tri-partite Gothick windows on the E front are particularly elegant.

Taking the road S and E out of Caldbeck the next village is **Hesket Newmarket**, a delightful cluster of 18th-c houses around a green and market cross with, at the W end, an unusual square house with gabled wings. A big chimney projects from the centre of the pyramid roof.

Further S down the narrow road is **Mungrisdale** where the simple, white church has a three-decker pulpit and box pews.

CARTMEL, Cumbria. In about AD 680 the

district of 'Cartmel and all the Burtons with it' was granted to St Cuthbert by Ecgfrith, King of Northumbria, for the purpose of establishing a monastery. No trace of any building from that period remains, but the present village of Cartmel, on a peninsula thrusting out into the sands of Morecambe Bay, has much of historical interest to commend it. It is dominated by the great medieval church, part of a long-vanished priory established by the Earl of Pembroke in 1190 for

The square and the medieval gatehouse at Cartmel

the Augustinian or Black Friars. His insistence that the church should also serve the parish, whose inhabitants were predominantly cocklers and fishermen, ensured that, when all other traces of the priory were swept away at the Dissolution, the church was allowed to remain. The slate and limestone 12th-c walls were pierced by Perp windows of the 15th c when the diagonally set upper stage of the central tower was also added – a unique solution to the great stresses caused by tower and lantern. The magnificent Renaissance screen and stall canopies in the choir surround misericord seats with poignant carvings. In the vestry is one of the oldest surviving umbrellas, having a leather canopy. A first edition of Spenser's *Faerie Queen* is another of the treasures.

The Eea brook, tamed by limestone embankments, meanders through the village. There is a small square surrounded by several hotels and inns, and one road enters from the N under the arch of the medieval gatehouse, built in 1330, and used successively as a grammar school, a lock-up, an artist's studio, and now as a craft shop. This unique building, restored and given to the National Trust in 1946, has one large room approached by a circular staircase. To the W, Cartmel is bounded by the racecourse where four meetings a year are held during bank holiday weekends.

Cartmel has for centuries been the N terminus of the route across the sands of the Bay, and an old milestone in the village records the distance to Lancaster and Ulverston by that way. **Grange-**

over-Sands, beyond the limestone ridge to the SE, was once the 'grange' or granary for the priory. It is now a quiet place of retirement and a holiday centre, endowed with a large sea-water swimming pool, and a fine climate.

Holker, 2m W, offers the visitor much of interest. The Hall itself has a friendly air about it and the Cavendish family, the owners, live in the older part. During the season a series of events take place on the rolling green acres of the deer park – horse trials, horticultural shows, parachuting and regular ascents of the blue Holker hot air balloon that is often seen floating gracefully over the Lakeland fells. The first Hall was built by the Preston family in the 16th c and they also acquired the ruins of Furness Abbey after the Dissolution. In 1756, there being no male heir, Holker was bequeathed to a cousin, Lord George Augustus Cavendish, the second son of the 3rd Duke of Devonshire. The present owner is a direct descendant of Lord George and close relative of the present Duke of Devonshire.

In 1871 the W wing of the Hall was destroyed by fire and with it many priceless family treasures and portraits. Undaunted, the 7th Duke commissioned the architectural firm of Paley and Austin, of Lancaster, to build an entirely new wing and it is this striking Victorian mansion with a strong Elizabethan motif that is seen and can be visited today. Around the Hall the distinguished gardener and architect, Joseph Paxton, laid out a Victorian park for his patron and employer, the 6th Duke. His grand design here makes possible the inclusion of banks of rhododendrons and azaleas; formal beds filled with fragrant old-fashioned roses; clumps of scented eucryphias and magnolias, and 'wild' glades full of daffodils and wild hyacinths.

CHIPPING, *Lancs.,* is tucked into the S flank of Fair Snape Fell (1675ft) on the edge of the Forest of Bowland, 8m from Garstang on the A6. The approach to this ancient market town is along delightful, winding lanes – whether the main street is called Windy because of this is uncertain! It is understandably the favourite village of many Lancashire folk because it contrives to remain a working community despite the temptation to pander to the visitors who flock to admire the cobbled courtyards, the alleyways, and the traditional cottages with stone porches and mullioned windows. A larger building with these windows is the old grammar school founded in 1683 by a village lad who made good, John Brabbin. In the portico of the almshouses nearby his benefaction is summed up by the inscription, 'Let Him that loveth God, Love his brotherhood'.

By the bridge the old corn mill, complete with waterwheel and mill stones, has been converted, tastefully, into a restaurant. In a hollow off the main street and beside another old stone bridge are the works of Berry & Sons, 'chairmakers for a century', where waterpower once turned the machinery, as it did the old saw mill opposite. The wheel still stands within this building.

The Sun Inn, on the corner of Windy Street, is remarkable for the stone steps that rise to the doorways high above. Although the church of St Bartholomew looks Victorian the interior is of the Perp period, with arcades and capitals adorned by heads of 14th-c locals and even the ass which worked beside them. The modern chancel screens were hammered out by craftsmen at Tweedies' foundry in the village.

Chipping was, and is, the centre for the surrounding hamlets and villages. Fairs were held to mark the passing seasons – Candlemas in the spring for servants' hirings, and the great fair in October. In such an isolated community old customs linger, and fortunately they are now well documented.

At **Hesketh End**, 1½m SSW, is a 16th-c farmhouse built by one Richard Alston who recorded history as he knew it by a façade of inscriptions in the form of a frieze across the walls.

CONDER GREEN, *Lancs.* (4m S of Lancaster), is at the centre of unspoilt scenery which is known to few of those speeding up and down the nearby A6 and M6. Hostelries and a council picnic area serve as good bases for exploring it.

The Lune estuary was formed about 5000 years ago but silting has always hindered navigation to the port of Lancaster. In 1787, therefore, a wet dock big enough to hold 25 merchantmen was opened at Glasson, a small fishing village at the estuary's mouth. In 1826 a canal with six locks to link the dock with the Lancaster canal was cut, and finally came the railway in 1883 which operated until 1964. It is along the route of this old railway that the walker can now reach Glasson and have an excellent opportunity to study *en route* the saltmarsh and spot the many varieties of wildfowl and wading birds.

Glasson Dock is now used by pleasure craft and the canal kept open by the Waterways Board. Across the estuary is Sunderland Point, a haven for countless sea birds, and looming over all is the huge silhouette of the nuclear power station at Heysham.

A winding minor road that snakes across the reclaimed marshland S of Glasson ends on the coast where stand forlorn piles of red sandstone that were once part of the 13th-c abbey of Cockersands. A wooden cross, symbolically askew, tops a roofed relic of an aisle, and the nearby, derelict farmhouse has stone corbels supporting the guttering and carved stones lying all around. This stretch of coast is under threat and may be chosen as the natural-gas terminal for the developing fields off the NW coast.

On the first piece of high ground to the E is the village of **Thurnham**. The mill was bought by the canal company, rebuilt, and only ceased to grind corn in 1960. Today dried milk is blended for animal feedstuffs. Thurnham Hall stands on a wooded knoll, a Gothick façade of 1823 hiding the much older building behind it. There is a good collection of pictures and the Hall is open to the public at certain times.

CROSBY RAVENSWORTH, *Cumbria.* Approached either E from Shap on the A6, or W from Appleby via B6260, the valley of the Lyvennet beck has attracted settlement along its delightful banks since earliest times. This village, that nearly merges downstream with **Maulds Meaburn**, is surrounded by bare, low fells on which prehistoric man built his circles, tumuli and hamlets, protected by high walls and ditches. There is the line of a Roman road to the SW and in the churchyard stands the shaft of a cross around which 7th-c Christians, led by St Paulinus, once worshipped. The Vikings settled in this fertile valley and the name of the village denotes a Danish origin. The Saxons built a wooden church, followed by the Normans with one in stone, which the Scots destroyed in the 12th c. The present church of St Lawrence stands beside the beck, some say like a miniature cathedral, and in its stones and monuments can be traced the history of this secluded corner of the old county of Westmorland.

Meaburn Hall to the N, built in 1610, was the home of the 1st Earl of Lonsdale, who had the body of his second wife embalmed in a coffin with a glass lid and kept in a cupboard. Two square summer houses remain at the corner of what was once a walled pleasure garden, and at the base of each gate pillar at the front of the Hall are ancient stones with sun whorls carved upon them.

Several single-arched bridges span the beck on whose banks stands Flass House, a Victorian building set in lovely grounds.

Due S, past the head of Crosby Gill where the Lyvennet rises and Charles II once halted with his army in the summer of 1651, on the bare uplands, is the village of **Orton**. The church stands on a

The stall canopies in the church at Cartmel

knoll by the N approach and its musical bells chime every quarter. A massive frame of three other bells, one dated 1513, stands by the N door in the nave; and beside the 17th-c porch of the sturdy tower is a large, flat stone which may once have been used as a primitive altar. An Elizabethan building, Petty Hall, stands by the main road through the village, overlooking the spacious green, and in a garden nearby the owner defiantly displays an old Cumberland County sign, complete with crest – Orton having been in Westmorland!

A famous son of Orton was George Whitehead who became an early convert of George Fox and whose Quaker doctrines he preached fearlessly for 65 years. He died in 1723, aged 86, thus upholding the village's reputation for longevity – as at Broughton on the Duddon estuary.

CROSTON, *Lancs.* (on A581 7m W of Chorley), is now a dormitory village with some local industry, but there are several interesting, visible clues to its past. It is the only Croston in England – the name means 'village of the cross' – and the medieval base of a market cross remains at the end of a narrow, cobbled street that leads direct to the church door. The 18th-c cottages lining the street give a true picture of how many Lancashire villages would have appeared centuries ago. The packhorse bridge over the River Yarrow is of 1682. There remain six of the original ten inns in the village, although the juke-box at The Wheatsheaf has replaced the masques once enacted in the square beside it.

The church, once the centre of a far-flung parish, is of irregular design with massive oak doors and sturdy pews – even the tower is out of alignment. The churchyard is mown smooth and dotted with flat grave stones. The rectory has an interesting Jacobean-looking front, graced with down-spouts dated 1722 – as elegant a building as any incumbent might wish to live in. The old school on the banks of the now-tamed river was rebuilt and endowed in 1660; the oldest part of the village is over the bridge here.

To the W across the Moss and over the Leeds–Liverpool canal, completed in 1782, is **Rufford** village. Set in an oasis of trees is the Old Hall, and on the W outskirts the New Hall, a Georgian mansion surrounded by a lovely park and used as a hospital. Both Halls were seats of the Hesketh family, whose arms are emblazoned on Croston's church tower. Sir Thomas was reputed to have built the Old Hall in *c.* 1450 and his descendant, the 1st Lord Hesketh, gave it and the valuable contents to the National Trust in 1936.

The present building is of three parts, each of a distinct period – a half-timbered medieval great hall; a Carolean brick wing of 1662; and the old office wing of 1821. In the Old Hall is now housed the Philip Ashcroft village museum collection and this includes a dug-out canoe of *c.* 100 BC which was found on the reclaimed land of Martin Mere, 4m W, where the Wildfowl Trust has established a refuge and study centre. Between

the Old Hall, open from March to Christmas, and the parish church which, despite its forbidding appearance, is full of relics of vanished buildings, there stands an avenue of beech trees, carpeted with bluebells in May.

DALSTON, *Cumbria* (4m W of Carlisle), is on the Calder river and is now, like Wetheral to the E, a dormitory. The village square has one side taken up by the church of St Michael which, although simple without, has much to commend it within. Of special interest is the carved oak font cover by Robert Lorimer and the theme of this intricate work is based on the four traditional elements. The fabric of the church dates from the 12th c and in the churchyard are buried two Bishops of Carlisle, whose seat is at Rose Castle, 3m SW. The nucleus of the castle is the 13th-c pele tower, but the range of buildings of red sandstone was brought together *c.* 1830 by Rickman to create a rambling mansion. The grounds were landscaped by Paxton. The castle is not open to the public.

Dalston Hall, 2m S of Dalston, was the birthplace in 1847 of Musgrave Watson who, before a tragic early death, made his mark as a gifted sculptor, as witness his relief on Nelson's column in Trafalgar Square. The Hall itself is a Georgian house of classic proportions and $2\frac{1}{2}$ storeys high.

DENT, *Cumbria,* 5m SE of Sedbergh. After the Wars of the Roses there appeared in Dentdale the 'statesmen' or owner-farmers. Twenty-four of these statesmen have constituted a form of local government in Dent since 1429, and their family pews can be seen in the church. This body still exists and meets regularly.

The village – locally known as Dent Town – has narrow cobbled streets flanked by low cottages roofed with slabs of the local gritstone. In 1801 the population was 1733 – a self-contained community which practised many trades including making butter, breeding horses, quarrying black marble, mining coal and processing the local wool. The womenfolk of Dent were so proficient with their needles that they earned for themselves the doubtful title of 'the terrible knitters of Dent'. As an 18th-c rhyme claimed:

She knaws how to sing and knit
And she knaws how to carry t'kit
While she drives her kye to t'pasture

The wool was spun into a coarse thread of worsted called 'bump'.

The church of St Andrew was founded *c.* 1100. and has grown over the centuries. The tower is of 1772 and some of the old box pews remain.

Although Dent has lost many of the old industries, a new one in the form of glass-blowing and engraving is now established, and visitors are welcome to see this work carried out in the small factory.

Dent is on the extreme W of the Yorkshire Dales National Park which accounts in part for the excellent car parking and toilet arrangements

Geoffrey N. Wright

A cobbled street in Dent

for visitors. A large-scale map displayed by the car park and finger posts make it easy to find the many footpaths that can be followed in the valley; one of these strikes up the slope of the valley behind the village and skirts a waterfall formed out of the limestone slabs. Another path follows the banks of the River Dee whose waters have been harnessed once again to operate an old mill just upstream from Sedbergh.

DOWNHAM, *Lancs.,* 3m NE of Clitheroe. The massive whale-back ridge of Pendle Hill towers over this delightful little village. The memorial in the parish church to the last member of the Assheton family to have died is inscribed with the Latin legend that, loosely translated, claims, 'if any memorial should be needed just look around you'. This sums up the atmosphere of Downham, over which the Assheton family has exerted its benign influence for 400 years. The uniform, traditional design of the warm-coloured stone cottages remains, as do the old stocks, and the bridges over the stream that flows through the village green. The Asshetons (their present title is Lord Clitheroe) live in the Hall, whose long, low front of nine bays with a portico of Tuscan columns, built in 1835, conceals much older construction behind.

The church of St Leonard, whose tower has stood for 500 years, is, like all the village, very well kept and contains fine Assheton memorial reliefs. The brass chandelier is late-Georgian.

Across the N slopes of Pendle Hill and down into the head of the valley of the River Calder,

that joins the Ribble near Whalley, run the narrow roads to **Barrowford**. This is a long straggling village with many cottages dating from the early days of the Industrial Revolution. At the N end is a 17th-c farmhouse converted for use as a heritage study centre, with information and displays about local history and folk-lore. Naturally one room is devoted to the notorious witches of Pendle, and several other rooms tell the story of the cotton industry which has exerted such a great influence on this region.

On the other side of Pendle Hill, 3m S of Downham, is the peaceful village of **Pendleton** where stone-built houses stand either side of a stream. The Domesday survey recorded King Edward as having owned land here, and in the inn of The Swan with Two Necks, a 'regular' once auctioned his wife to the highest bidder. Bronze Age man had a settlement here, traces of which were recently found in a cottage garden.

DUFTON, *Cumbria* (3m N of Appleby), is at the foot of the 1578ft cone of Dufton Pike that rises boldly from the W flank of the Pennines. There is a broad village green, with an avenue of trees down the middle, and late 18th-c houses surrounding it, several of which provide 'bed and breakfast'. There is a fine Georgian pump, painted in the dark maroon so popular in these parts. Dufton Hall, now divided into three, dominates the S end of the village. The lovely church of St Cuthbert's is shared with **Knock**, 2m N, and stands by its old rectory of 1785 between the two villages. There is a fine Georgian symmetry about

Geoffrey N. Wright

Dufton village, with its Georgian pump, and Dufton Pike beyond

this simple church, which retains elegant brass numbers for each pew and the paraffin lamps at the gate into the churchyard. Set into the W end of the S aisle is a weathered stone which is finely carved with the symbols of bow, arrow and axe in Saxon times.

At **Appleby**, in about 1176, a massive stone keep was built high above the right bank of the River Eden. It came to be known as Caesar's Tower. It is now possible to visit all of its three floors and then stand on the roof, which has a turret with pretty lanterns at each corner. From atop the tower the layout of the castle buildings becomes clear and the views are well worth the climb. The castle belonged to the Viponts before it went to the Cliffords in the late 13th c. It remained Clifford property until the death of Lady Anne in 1676, when the Earl of Thanet, her son-in-law, inherited it. In 1383 the buildings were again strengthened, and traces of the 'hall-house' at the E end of the 'bailey' survive in the present 17th-c hall, set between massive square towers. Today the castle offers the visitor an opportunity to see how domestic architecture developed over six centuries. The ditches and ramparts of the Normans are now employed more peacefully to show to full advantage an impressive collection of rare breeds of domestic farm animals, together with an even more comprehensive collection of waterfowl, pheasants, poultry and owls. They make up a Rare Breeds Survival Trust Centre, the seventh of its kind.

GRASMERE, *Cumbria.* Mercifully this famous village is by-passed by the main N–S A591 route through the Lake District. 4m S, down the valley of the Rothay river and past Rydal is Ambleside, and to the N the col or 'raise' of Dunmail, named after a 10th-c Celtic chieftain; a huge heap of stones between the two carriageways marks the spot where he fought an unsuccessful battle.

The Norse settlers cleared the land around Grasmere, and the Easedale Valley to the W, for grazing pigs and sheep. (Gris – Old Norse for swine occurs in many local names.) The beautiful setting of the village, overlooked by Helm Crag, with its summit rocks resembling a lion couchant and a lamb, has secured a mention in every guidebook written about the Lakes since 1770, the year in which William Wordsworth was born at Cockermouth. In 1790 he came, with his sister Dorothy, to live at a simple lime-washed cottage at Town End where the last houses of Grasmere lay astride the old road leading up to White Moss Common and Rydal. The name of this cottage, once an inn called the Dove and Olive Branch, was shortened to 'Dove' and the Wordsworths spent an idyllic nine years there, entertaining literary friends such as Coleridge and Sir Walter Scott. Later Dove Cottage was let to Thomas de Quincey. In 1880 a Trust was established to preserve the building and in 1935 the museum across the road was opened, containing manuscripts, first editions and a model of a farm kitchen of 1800. The Trustees are in the process of creating a permanent study centre and exhibition in converted farm buildings nearby.

Wordsworth married in 1802 and in 1808 he moved his family to Allan Bank, a large house newly built in parkland W of the village. Although most of *The Excursion* was written there, he disliked the house, which is now National Trust property (not open to the public) having been bequeathed by Canon Rawnsley. Also owned by the Trust is Church Stile, a 16th-c house opposite the church, which was in the poet's day an inn strategically placed for church-goers, who hitched their horses to the rail outside. When the building was restored in 1969 a cockpit was found in the yard behind. By the lychgate into the churchyard is the old school where Grasmere gingerbread is made to Sarah Nelson's unique and secret recipe. The church, dedicated to St Oswald, stands on the site of a 12th-c chapel, and in the graveyard are buried William Wordsworth, his wife Mary, his sister Dorothy, and his beloved daughter, Dora Quillinan, and her husband. Hartley Coleridge's headstone is close by. The present building is noted for a two-storeyed continuous arcade, the lower dating from the 17th c. The pattern of black beams is a lesson of ingenuity in roof construction. Once the floor beneath was of beaten earth, covered each summer by rushes gathered by the children of the village. The rush-bearing ceremony continues to be observed on the Saturday nearest St Oswald's day (15 August) when floral emblems are paraded through the village. In the Hall is a large painting of the 1901 rush-bearing by Frank Bramley. It was given to the National Trust in 1913 and is occasionally put on view, especially during the annual exhibition of the Lake Artists Society held in the Hall during the late summer. In mid-August are held the Grasmere sports, when local sportsmen compete in Cumberland-style wrestling, fell-running and field events.

At Rydal Mount, in the hamlet of **Rydal**, at the S end of Rydal Water, Wordsworth lived for the rest of his life after leaving Grasmere in 1813. This house, beautifully sited in a terraced garden, is now owned by the poet's great-great granddaughter and is open to the public. Below it is a small piece of enclosed fell which Wordsworth bought and, in memory of his daughter Dora, planted with lent-lilies which now carpet the ground in April. The National Trust now owns Dora's Field. The Hall opposite Rydal Mount was until recently the seat of the Le Fleming family, who still own most of the hamlet and the park between here and Ambleside. Their original home was at Coniston Hall, an Elizabethan house with tall, cylindrical chimneys on the W shore of Coniston Water. Rydal Hall is now owned by the Diocese of Carlisle and is not open to the public.

HAWKSHEAD, *Cumbria.* The large car park E of the village is an indication of the popularity of this unique cluster of lime-washed houses, dominated by the church of St Michael and All Angels on its low hill. Hawkshead has flourished since Norse times – the very name derives from the Viking Haukr, who built the first stockaded settlement.

It is well placed at the junction of old packhorse routes which linked the Windermere ferries with the Coniston valley; as well as Ambleside to Newby Bridge. Markets flourished, with charcoal, bark and other products of the surrounding hard-woods and, of course, wool, finding ready buyers from Kendal and much further afield. The main square is dominated by the Market House or Shambles where the butchers had their stalls.

The village is a warren of small squares linked by flagged or cobbled alleys over which are several arches to make covered ways. As befits a market town there are several inns – in 1910 there were at least five with widows as licensees. Some spinning galleries remain, and there were many more when most households spun and prepared their own yarn. In season the small cottage gardens and window boxes full of flowers give Hawkshead rather a continental air.

The church, described by Wordsworth in 1788 as 'snow white . . . like a throned lady', is plain and sturdy, dating back to the 15th c. The long nave of 70ft is lined by massive columns which support round arches. A century later the roof was raised, clerestory windows were added and the N aisle was rebuilt. Remarkable are the mural paintings, some of which are attributed to James Addison in 1680; similar wall decorations are found in local farmhouses. Proof of the importance of the local wool industry is given by the 'Burial in Woollen' certificates kept in the church. One dated 1696 is on view. In the N aisle is the Sandys Chapel where a 16th-c table tomb reveres the memory of William and Margaret Sandys of Graythwaite, an estate a few miles S of Hawkshead where their descendants continue to live. Their son, Edwin, became Archbishop of York and founded the grammar school here in 1588. The present school building at the E gate to the churchyard is the original one, with a gymnasium – now converted into flats – opposite. The main ground-floor room is furnished with the desks and benches used by the scholars, of whom there were around 100 in 1785. William Wordsworth and his brother studied here between 1778 and 1787, and they lodged with the Tyson family at Green End Cottage in the hamlet of Colthouse, ½m E across the valley.

Nearby is a well-preserved Friends Meeting House of 1688 and, beside the road to Near Sawrey, their walled burial ground with simple grey headstones is a mass of wild flowers in season, beginning with the April lent-lilies.

On the E side of the smaller of the two squares in Hawkshead is the solicitor's office where Beatrix Potter's husband, William Heelis, once worked, and next door is the tiny shop where Tabatha Twitchit, in *The Tale of Samuel Whiskers,* once offered her wares. It is now an information point for the National Trust.

In the hamlet of **Near Sawrey,** 2m along the road to the Ferry, is Hill Top, the farmhouse bought by Beatrix Potter in 1903. Many of her children's books were based on the simple and contented life she led there until her death in 1943. Hill Top remains a working farmhouse, with a museum included, owned by the National Trust.

½m N of Hawkshead is the Old Hall, built by the monks of Furness Abbey who owned the land from here to Morecambe Bay until the Dissolution. There remains one corner building, now a private house, and the Courthouse which guards the approach to the cobbled courtyard through an archway. Inside, on the first floor, and approached by a flight of outside steps, is one long room where the manor courts were once held. It now houses an extension of the Museum of Lakeland Life and Industry at Abbot Hall in Kendal. The building is owned by the National Trust and is open to visitors in season.

HELMSHORE, *Lancs.,* 1m S of Haslingden. The Industrial Revolution caused such a profound change in the pattern of rural life and on the physical landscape in S Lancashire that it is instructive to visit a textile mill to see how these changes came about. In the small town of Helmshore one such mill is now preserved and it stands beside B6235, the Holcombe Road.

Higher Mill, for fulling woollen cloth, was built by the Turners in 1789 in this typical steep-sided valley through which runs the River Ogden. Power to the mill was supplied by a 14ft water wheel that developed 50hp, sufficient to drive the large hammers in the fulling stocks, as well as other machines necessary for the production of a cloth suitable for overcoats and blankets.

The wool would have been hand-spun and carded by the women and children in their cottages and farmhouses while the men were responsible for weaving the yarn into long lengths of cloth on the hand looms.

Nearly every cottage had at least one such loom, which usually measured 7–10ft across. Before the mills were built locally the cloth was collected by 'chapmen' and taken by packhorse across the moors to Rochdale.

The cloth, after fulling and washing, was stretched on frames, ringed with tenter-hooks, to be dried and this explains why the one solitary chimney-stack is sited up the hill away from the mill. This ensured that the soot from it would not fall on the clean, drying cloth – no matter should it fall on the roofs of the weavers' cottages!

In the Helmshore Higher Mill are now collected and displayed, in working condition, such historic machines as Arkwright's improved spinning frame and Samuel Crompton's 'mule', so called because it was a hybrid between Hargreave's jenny and Arkwright's frame! There are also examples of the looms and spinning wheels used in the weavers' cottages. The Mill only ceased working in 1967, and most of the fulling machinery is therefore intact. The County Council has now taken it over and opens it to the public in season.

HORNBY, *Lancs.* (8m NE of Lancaster), is a simple centre for a farming community, astride the

A683 and a natural halting place between Lancaster and Kirkby Lonsdale, hence the number of good inns! The castle is perhaps the most notable feature, a romantic pile on a bluff overlooking the River Wenning that runs into the Lune nearby. There is a pele tower of the 13th and 16th c, but the embattled building dates from 1849 and 1889. Sir Edward Stanley was responsible for the 16th-c tower and the present church of St Margaret was once the chapel for his castle. After the victory at Flodden Field in 1513 this gallant Knight, who became Lord Monteagle, built the octagonal church tower and then started on the chancel whose E end is a polygonal apse – a design seldom encountered. A treasure of this church is part of a unique Anglo-Saxon cross which was once embedded in the wall of an old barn built on the site of a priory nearby. A panel shows in relief the miracle of the 'Five loaves and two small fishes'.

Inside the church is an old box pew and a showcase containing needlework of *c.* 1725 taken from a private Maltese chapel. A processional wooden cross of the same date, made in Padua, hangs on the wall above.

On the river bank above the bridge leading to the main street are some attractive cottages forming a peaceful corner of the village on the edge of the open moor. A drinking well nearby is dated 1858.

1½m N of Hornby and over the graceful Loyn Bridge that spans the Lune is **Gressingham**, a village recorded in the Domesday survey and once placed under the Forest Laws of Henry I. Both foresters who held the land were charged with the care of the King's goshawks. The church of St John, rebuilt in 1734, is on a central mound chosen by the Saxons for their timber church – the head and piece of shaft of a cross dated AD 850 were unearthed in the graveyard and are now on view. The S doorway is 12th-c Trans, very Norman in appearance. Inside are box pews, well preserved hatchments and a pulpit of 1714. Gressingham Hall next door, with creeper-covered walls of grey sandstone, was built in 1688 and has an unusual continuous string-course over the mullioned windows.

INGLEWHITE, *Lancs.,* 6m N of Preston. Set amid prosperous farming country on the W edge of the Forest of Bowland, this straggling village surrounds two greens – one a 'goose' green with a market cross dated 1675 on a tall hexagonal plinth. This was once an important centre for local trade, renowned for sheep and cattle fairs. But the inns that once refreshed the dealers and drovers are private houses today and the horses now come from a large riding centre.

In the 18th c buttons from bone were carved in Button Row, while silk was woven in an old mill, now a farmhouse, a few yards away. The all important smithy was housed in the low stone building overlooking the green.

Beacon Fell to the NE is a Country Park and near its foot is the Georgian church of St James, enlarged and restored in Victorian times.

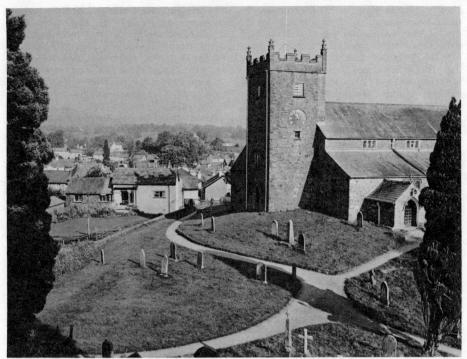

The church of St Michael and All Angels, dominating the village of Hawkshead

Through winding roads 3m S is **Goosnargh** with a pleasant cluster of inns, an interesting church and dominant hospital. Of chief interest is Old Chingle Hall, 1m SW, which has the reputation of being one of the most haunted houses in Britain. Born here was a Franciscan monk, John Wall, who was beheaded in 1679 for his faith. His severed head is supposed to be hidden in the Hall, which is well supplied with priests' holes.

KIRKOSWALD, *Cumbria,* 8m N of Penrith. No village green here but a compact line of red sandstone houses along the E slope of the valley of the River Eden, which is here crossed by a fine bridge leading to Lazonby on the left bank. The S approach to Kirkoswald is dominated both by the ruined tower of a 12th-c castle, surrounded by a deep moat and embankment, and, on another knoll nearer the river, by a solitary square 19th-c tower which belongs to the parish church, just down the hill. The church is dedicated to St Oswald who was killed in AD 642 on the Welsh border and thus became the first Christian hero king in British history.

In Norman times there was a small church whose only remains are two square piers and the base of the chancel arch. By 1240 the church was three-gabled, and in 1314 it was burnt by the Scots. In 1523 it became Collegiate and it was extensively restored in 1878. A spring rises under the nave and its crystal-clear water can be drunk from a well outside the W wall of the church. The

Priest's walk from opposite the College Gates to the churchyard, in which stand several ancient headstones, is paved with huge flags.

Immediately N of the church are the extensive buildings of the College, founded in 1523 and dissolved in 1547, after which it was sold by the Crown to the Featherstonhaugh family who have lived here ever since. The attractive red sandstone entrance and front elevation of the College are of 1696. A pele tower stood here in the 13th c, and inside there is Elizabethan panelling and an elaborate staircase. 2m NW is the nunnery, a building with a fine front built around a 13th-c core.

Across the bridge over the Eden to the SW, through Lazonby and up the left bank for 2m is the village of **Great Salkeld.** The church of St Cuthbert commands the one street with a fortified 14th-c tower that was built as a pele to frustrate the marauding Scots. The basement is tunnel-vaulted and the first floor has a fireplace.

MELMERBY, *Cumbria,* is strategically placed on A686 8m NE of Penrith, with an impressive backdrop of the Pennines, whose upper slopes retain patches of snow right into the summer. The village houses, many of the local red sandstone, are strung out around the broad common. In the NW corner is a Victorian church that retains windows and arches from a much earlier building. Nearby is the Hall, mainly 17th-c, with a range of outbuildings converted into a village bakery which uses wholemeal flour ground in the traditional way at Little Salkeld mill, 4m W. A whole range of delicious bread, cakes and local biscuits made to old Cumbrian recipes are baked here. 2m W is the small village of **Gamblesby**, quiet and secluded under the Hartside escarpment. Outside an old farmhouse a fine selection of old butter churns and agricultural implements is to be found.

2m SE is the scattered village of **Ousby**, surrounded by small fields with their boundaries of dry-stone walls. Cross Fell (2930ft) towers up behind. The simple church at Town Head, outside the village, is fortunate in owning a carved oak figure of a knight in armour whose crossed legs rest on his dog. Few such monuments remain in England and it is interesting to wonder at the circumstances that brought a 700-year-old effigy of a possible Crusader to this remote Cumbrian village.

MORLAND, *Cumbria,* 8m SE of Penrith. This delightful village is what most visitors would like to find. On the approach from the S and to the right of the road are the sheer faces of a limestone quarry, and the arched recesses of the kilns once used to burn the quarried stone. Low houses with painted walls then appear on either side of the beck, spanned by footbridges and crossed by a ford. There are two inns that have changed little over the years, and an arched bridge over a deep gill through which the water tumbles.

Through the tops of old yews rises the leaded spire of the church, which is approached by a narrow alley between high walls. An old building beside the street is converted to a showroom for musical instruments. The street forks at the top of the hill, the road to the S leading to the nearby hamlet of **Newby** where the Hall, now a farmhouse, is well worth the detour. The red sandstone panel above the front door bears the weathered coat of arms of the Nevison family and the date of 1685.

The church, dedicated to St Laurence, has a Saxon tower the like of which is found nowhere else W of the Pennines. It was probably built just after 1092 when King Rufus captured Carlisle from the Scots. Within the tower are massive oak ladders, hewn from one tree trunk. The church warden's accounts survive from the year of the Armada, 1588, and record a collection of brass for the founding of a new bell for the tower. Other items of interest in the church are box pews and a palimpsest brass with a recumbent figure engraved on the reverse side.

Not surprisingly Morland is a regular winner of the Best Kept Village competition organized annually within Cumbria.

4m N, just across A65 on the outskirts of **Temple Sowerby**, is Acorn Bank, or Temple Sowerby Manor as it is often called, at one time the Westmorland home of a Yorkshire dialect writer – Dorothy Una Ratcliffe. Once the halls of buildings that have stood on this site since Domesday echoed with epic tales told by Knights Templars and Knights Hospitallers after the various crusades and wars against the heathen. For these knights held the Manor until the Dissolution, when Henry VIII granted it to Thomas Dalston. On the large open fireplace in the entrance hall are mason's marks of *c.* 1171 identical with some at Aigues Mortes, in SE France, which was the starting point for the second Crusade.

The Manor is now owned by the National Trust and let to the Sue Ryder Foundation as a home for invalids. Visitors can only visit the house by appointment with the resident matron, but the grounds are open to the public six days a week in season, which begins in April with a superb display of daffodils along the Crowdundle beck behind the house. Beautiful wrought ironwork is everywhere. Two large and beautifully worked bronze Medici vases stand on either side of the front door, and in niches all over the front garden are delightful bronze putti that might once have graced a Tuscan villa. Beyond the SE wing is a Regency clock tower, and, in its shadow, a sheltered enclosure the Trust has transformed into a herb garden. Here over 140 varieties of herbs, all known to have been cultivated in England, are neatly planted and identified. To acquaint visitors with their multifarious uses the Trust has published a guide to all known English herbs.

PARBOLD, *Lancs.* The two best ways of appreciating the flat, fertile plain of W Lancs. are to survey it from the two beacons near Parbold – one on A5209 W of Junction 27 on M6, and the other 1m S. The Leeds–Liverpool canal snakes through the valley below, and, where the road crosses it in Parbold village, there are an old coaching inn, a wharf and a windmill. The two village churches have tall, slender steeples that show up impressively from Parbold Hill.

1m W is **Newburgh**, worth a stop in order to admire the old houses which surround the triangular green complete with market cross and shady trees. Very different from the new town of Skelmersdale – 'Skem' to the locals – whose geometric sweeps and terraces can be easily appraised from Beacon Hill behind. This is rich farming land which, on the reclaimed, low-lying levels, is very like the fens of East Anglia or even the Netherlands – after all, there is an Up-Holland and even a Down-Holland within a few miles of Parbold!

RAVENGLASS, *Cumbria.* The confluence of three rivers – the Irt, the Mite and the Esk – protected by a broken bar of sand dunes, has offered an ideal site for settlement since neolithic times on the W Cumbrian coast. The name is derived from the Celtic 'yr-afon-glas' – the grey-blue river – and was only changed to Glannaventa when the Romans established a supply base here. They had roads leading from here up and down the coast and also due E over the Hardknott and Wrynose passes to Ambleside (Galava to the Romans). A well-preserved bath house, ½m S of the village, is all that remains of an important Roman presence – the walls of red freestone a yard thick and in one a domed niche. Hardknott Fort, perched 800ft on an escarpment above the head of Eskdale, is another Roman ruin which evokes admiration for a race that colonized a wild area in such an effective way.

In 1208 King John granted Richard de Lucy, Lord of Egremont, the right to hold a Saturday market at Ravenglass and an annual fair on St James's Day. In 1675 this fair was a grand three-day affair with traders bringing goods from Scotland, Ireland and the Isle of Man.

The coming of the coast railway killed the market trade, and all that remains is a wide village street flanked by low-built cottages, some with attractive porches. Fresh fish is still available, however, from local boats. In 1875 a narrow-gauge railway was laid from Ravenglass up Eskdale to Boot to transport slate and minerals. This is now only used for passenger traffic but carries an increasing number of holidaymakers each year. The steam locomotives are made locally by the private railway company that successfully operates the line.

On the wooded headland W of Ravenglass is **Muncaster** Castle, a pele tower stronghold lived in by the Pennington family. In 1862 the castle was rebuilt by Anthony Salvin in a style that retained much of the original buildings. Although the castle boasts superb collections of silver and portraits, it is its setting in acres of wild garden that attracts the visitor, especially in May and June when the rhododendrons and azaleas are at their best.

Preserved in the castle is the famous Luck of Muncaster – a glass bowl, decorated in enamel and gilt, that a grateful monarch, Henry VI, gave to Sir John Pennington, who had given him shelter after the battle of Hexham. The prosperity of the Pennington family is reputed to depend upon the preservation of this bowl.

1m up the Mite is old Muncaster Mill where corn has been ground since 1470, although the present buildings date from the late 17th c. The railway company, whose line passes the mill, bought and restored it in 1975, and today the visitor can take a train to the mill and watch corn being ground on machinery proved by centuries of use. Note the loft with a 'floor' of perforated tiles where the corn was kiln-dried before grinding.

The sand dunes down this coastline provide nesting grounds for innumerable terns and gulls. Opposite Ravenglass itself the dunes are protected by the County Council and access is allowed to most of them; a map at the seaward end of the main street shows the access arrangements. S of the estuary are 167 acres of the Eskmeals dunes preserved by the Cumbria Naturalists Trust which allows the public access except during the nesting seasons.

RAVENSTONEDALE, *Cumbria* (5m SW of Kirkby Stephen), is best approached along the narrow lanes from the SE which wind past bare fells crowned with limestone outcrops. A peaty beck drops over shallow limestone ridges past the large churchyard, which is a suitable setting for a fine example of a Georgian church, rebuilt in 1744. The interior is very unusual in that tiered box pews face each other across the central aisle and the three-decker pulpit overlooks them all from the N side. In the E window is an interesting memorial to a female martyr who was the last woman to be burnt at the stake at Tyburn in 1685 – for performing an act of kindness! In the passageway at the foot of the W tower is preserved the clock face from the previous church with a brass plaque that gives the price – £10 – and the date – 1719. The oldest church relic is the shaft of a cross in the churchyard that was probably placed there 800 years ago.

The name Ravenstonedale is derived from the fact that as late as the 18th c a bounty of two pence was given for every raven's head that was produced.

SE on the road to Sedbergh is Tarn House, a 16th-c building with an unusual front elevation of mullioned windows and fronted by its own tarn. 1m W is the village of **Newbiggin** on the head waters of the Lune, an unpretentious cluster of traditional houses around a church with a Norman foundation.

RIBCHESTER, *Lancs.* (10m E of Preston in the Ribble valley), has been on the tourist map for many years, the visitors attracted by the remains of the Roman fort established here in AD 69–80. Camden visited 'Ribblechester' in 1582, and antiquarians have been digging and delving ever since. A fair selection of finds has been preserved in the museum, where an imaginative display includes a tombstone sculpture of a cavalry trooper of the 1st c, metal-work, glass, and the exact replica of a bronze parade helmet and mask which was unearthed in 1795. The original is in the British Museum.

The fort was identified as the Roman Bremetennacum by an inscribed votive stone dedicated to the 'God Apollo Maponus by the Sarmatian horsemen of Bremetennacum'. The same name occurs in the Ravenna Cosmography, which lists world place names known to the 7th-c compiler. Agricola, the Roman governor, had reached the Clyde by AD 83 and this fort was one of those established by him to control the route N. A much smaller garrison was based at Galava (Ambleside) about the same period. In the 3rd c a contingent of no less than 5000 Sarmatian horsemen from the Danube valley was stationed here, and many never returned to Europe but married local girls and became farmers and horse-breeders.

Little of the impressive fort now remains visible, especially as the river has eaten away much of it. Many of the artifacts seen in the museum were found on the bed of the river, and Tuscan pillars supporting the gallery in the church, and the porch of the White Bull Inn were very probably from Roman buildings. The foundations of the granaries, now preserved by the National Trust, can be seen behind the church, and in the museum are handfuls of burnt barley taken from them. The fort was abandoned *c.* AD 370, when the Romans moved to Lancaster on the estuary of the Lune.

The church of St Wilfrid is of simple EE design, with slender lancet windows and a Perp tower of the 14th c. There is fine woodwork on the Jacobean pulpit, the screens to two chapels, and the pews, the latter dated 1735 and 1761. The churchyard could well have been the site of the fort's Roman temple.

The church, the inn and the museum are focal points in the village, but there are also the steep banks of the Ribble on which to loiter and the narrow streets to explore. Craft shops have sprung up and there is usually the spectacle of an archaeological dig in progress.

Upstream is the fine three-arched bridge that carries the road to Whalley and Clitheroe, and 3m further up, just above where the Hodder and Ribble rivers merge, is the old, narrow bridge at Mitton over which Cromwell hurried his troops on the night before the battle of Preston.

RIVINGTON, *Lancs.,* 3m SE of Chorley. To provide for the many industries burgeoning in S and mid-Lancs. during the last century reservoirs had to be created. This need was directly responsible for some of the most attractive manmade scenery in the country, and there is no better place to appreciate this than in and around Rivington, a delightful village set in woodland E of the embankment that divides the upper and lower reservoirs of the same name. These were constructed in 1852–7 and immediately N of them is the Anglezarke reservoir of the same date. There is yet another, similar sheet of artificial water – Yarrow reservoir – slightly further E.

Man left traces of settlement in neolithic times on Anglezarke Moor, where a chambered tomb can be seen, and flint blades found nearby point to the early need to clear the dense forest that once covered this area. Overlooking the Moor from the S is the 1190ft high Rivington Pike, called by Henry VIII's antiquary, Leland, by the medieval name of 'Rivenpike'. A beacon was known to be established on the Pike in 1591 and the present stubby tower was built in 1733. All this land was once the hunting ground for the Lords of Manchester, but today it is a very popular 'lung' for the townsfolk, from Bolton especially, who climb to the top of the Pike to admire the superb view that, on a clear day, can extend as far as Black Combe, in the SW corner of the Lake District. An ascent to the Pike on Good Friday has been a long-held tradition.

Along the ridge to the N and towards the village is the Dovecote, a tower with two-light windows, which overlooks the moorland gardens created by Mawson for Lord Leverhulme in 1905. The Bungalow, a deceptive name for a luxurious dream-house also built by His Lordship nearby, is now demolished, but the terraces, once planted with shrubs of every hue, are once again to be cared for and the pathways cleared by this generation's

youth. In the early summer the rhododendrons glow with colour and in the autumn the rowan trees, which are supposed to have given the village it's name, are covered with bright berries.

The name Lever appears in parish records of Rivington as early as the reign of Edward III and it was fitting therefore that William Hesketh Lever became the Lord of the Manor in 1900. He was later to become Lord Leverhulme, the creator of Port Sunlight, the model industrial community outside Liverpool. In 1904 he bought Rivington Hall, a Georgian house with older parts dating back to the end of the 17th c, and laid out a park which is now the property of the local authority and designated a Country Park. Avenues of trees stretch in all directions, enclosing green swards and countless 'spots' for picnics and the setting-up of the tables and chairs that some families can never leave behind at home. Behind the Hall, once the family home of the Pilkingtons, is a well-preserved and restored tithe barn with medieval cruck beams. It is worth recording the dimensions of this barn – 105ft long and $57\frac{1}{2}$ft wide. Another barn, smaller and of Saxon origin, is beside the car park W of the Hall.

A Pilkington was responsible for the charming Anglican church that stands on a small knoll beside the road from the village green to the reservoirs. Built *c.* 1540, the church is small, with a bell-turret – a bell-house of the same period is in the churchyard and now used for tools – and was remodelled in 1666. The pulpit, with linen-fold panels, and a carved late Perp screen are to be noted, as are the inscribed 17th-c brasses. Perhaps most intriguing are the stone lintels and capital stones that are stacked beside the lychgate. Dates such as 1663 can be deciphered among the random patterns of symbols and initials, some of which can be traced back to houses connected with the Crusades. It is probable that these stones came from buildings that are now covered by the waters of the reservoirs.

Opposite the church is the village school, built in 1714 on the site of a free grammar school founded in 1566 by Bishop Pilkington who became known as the 'Good Old Bishop of Durham'. His portrait now hangs in the church.

Just up the road is the village green and on the uphill side is the Unitarian chapel, founded in the reign of Queen Anne as a Nonconformist meeting place. It is one of the oldest in the country and beautifully maintained, with a churchyard full of interesting headstones and a modern garden of remembrance round the back. Inside there are austere box pews and a centrally placed pulpit. Further along the green, past the post office, are the Mill House cottages, once known as Twig End, and near the site of the mill that was recorded as working as early as 1544.

A minor road winds north from Rivington, skirting Yarrow reservoir, and after 2m passes the old Manor House which overlooks yet another small sheet of impounded water. This house has a date stone of 1604. Past the N end of the Anglezarke reservoir and down a narrow lane is the small hamlet of **White Coppice** which can claim to have the most romantically sited cricket ground in the country, with Great Hill behind. The cottages here once were the homes of the weavers who worked in the mill demolished 100 years ago. Now many of the visitors to the lake country find their way here to admire the cottage gardens, bright with flowers, and picnic on the green – when it is not used for cricket.

ST BEES, *Cumbria.* The twin headlands of St Bees are the only real cliffs on the NW coast and their ledges are sanctuary for nesting sea birds. Between them is the narrow Fleswick Bay, famous not only for the rich assortment of stones found on the shingle banks, but also because, according to legend, the beautiful Irish Princess Bega was cast ashore in the 7th c after escaping from the Norse on the eve of her wedding to a chieftain. The Lord Egremont rashly promised her that she could have as much land as may be covered by snow on a midsummer's day – and true to Cumbrian weather the snow came and Bega established her nunnery on a 3m stretch of land around the headland. A Benedictine priory of St Bees arose on the site of St Bega's nunnery and was duly destroyed at the Dissolution except for part of the conventual church which was allowed to remain as the parish church. It is a cruciform structure of red St Bees sandstone with a choir of the 12th c and a clerestorial nave of about 50 years later. The Norman W door is exceptionally fine, as are the lancet windows in the chancel.

In the churchyard are ancient stones including a unique lintel of the 8th c, with the motif of St Michael and the Dragon. A distinguished native, Edmund Grindall, was educated at the priory school before its suppression, and became Archbishop of Canterbury in 1575. He obtained from Queen Elizabeth permission to found a free grammar school at St Bees in 1583, and today it remains essentially the public school for Cumberland although no longer free. The original Elizabethan schoolhouse makes up the N wing of the quadrangle.

At **Sandwith,** up the coast towards Whitehaven, is the large Marchon chemical factory that manufactures detergents, using as a raw material anhydrite (calcium sulphate) once extracted from 500ft under the headland of St Bees. There is now a large car park and promenade down by the beach of St Bees.

ST MICHAELS-ON-WYRE, *Lancs.* 10m E of Blackpool. When St Aidan, from Lindisfarne on the Northumbrian coast, came preaching the Gospel here in the 7th c, the land was heavily wooded and marshy. The River Wyre could be forded here so it was a strategic site for a chapel and in the Domesday Book is recorded 'Micheles cherche'; in the present church a board lists the names of incumbents since 1203.

From the busy A586 St Michaels today appears as a beautifully preserved haven of peace: a squat building with low-pitched roofs, walls and tower set at odd angles. Around it are many headstones full of history. Old yews give shelter, and just outside the E entrance of the churchyard is a low building that was once the day school, then a museum, and now a cottage.

Inside the tower is a clock whose large pendulum serenely records the time, and a bell, dated 1458, of probable French manufacture. Set in the modern windows of the N aisle are fragments of medieval glass, one of which depicts the clipping of sheep with shears that modern farmers could instantly recognize. Up the river, superbly sited on its bank, is the old vicarage built in the days when the vicar was also local squire.

3m W on A586 is the village of **Great Eccleston,** now by-passed but worth the detour. Two Bulls – the White and the Black – glare at each other across the large village square. Since before Domesday this predominantly farming community has tilled the flat, fertile fields. Rushes were a crop, and the small church of **Copp** (from the Old English *Copp* – a head) had its earth floor strewn with them, and a rushbearing ceremony is still held each summer. Norse names to streets, such as the Weind, also give clues to the age of this settlement. Lackonby House, near the SW corner of the main square, has original gateposts embedded in a brick wall and a plaque high up on the gable end is dated 1734. In a field behind is a brick dovecote.

The lowest ford on the Wyre is just N of the village and travellers took this route to Pilling on the coast. A bridge at Cartford was built in 1831 and remains one of the few private toll-bridges in the country.

SLAIDBURN, *Lancs.,* 8m N of Clitheroe on B6478. This delightful village used to be the administrative centre of the Forest of Bowland; the court room, next door to the inn rejoicing in the name Hark to Bounty, being used until 1913. The ancient route through the Trough of Bowland goes W from here to Lancaster via Dunsop Bridge, 4m down the Hodder valley, where a fine bridge is surrounded by unspoilt cottages.

Slaidburn is strategically sited on the valley bottom, surrounded by neat farmhouses and small fields enclosed by stone walls. There is an old grammar school of 1712 beside the church which, according to the list of vicars displayed inside, dates back to at least 1246. The interior is graced by a shining three-decker pulpit and a communion table that replaces the altar. On display are the dog whips wielded by the churchwardens to keep the farmers' collies in order while their masters were at church. The Vicar himself once had a dog called Bounty whose barking is immortalized in the name of the village inn mentioned above.

The triangular village green, complete with a War Memorial, a line of cottages leading down to the river, and another beautiful bridge, are all in fine order. A shop called the Jam Pot displays an interesting range of local crafts.

Geoffrey N. Wright

A 'statesman's' house at Townend, Troutbeck, home of the Browne family

The region of moorland and fell to the N and W has been known as the Forest of Bowland since Saxon times, and was given by William the Conqueror to Roger de Poictou. Through inheritance by John of Gaunt it again became Crown land and one of the principal officers appointed was the Bowbearer. In Charles II's reign Edward Parker of **Browsholme** held the office, but as the wild deer that once roamed the Forest were destroyed in 1805, it then became a titular honour. Today in Browsholme Hall, 8m S of Slaidburn, is preserved a silver 'doggange' or stirrup through which every dog belonging to the tenants within the Forest had to pass. This law effectively prevented the poaching of game by the use of large dogs. The Hall is a real history book in stone, and is still owned by the Parkers, who open it occasionally to the public.

TROUTBECK (Windermere), *Cumbria.* There are two Troutbecks in Cumbria – and neither of them was the home of John Peel! The 'Westmorland' Troutbeck is an old-fashioned village strung out for 1m along the W flank of a valley running into the fells NE of Windermere. The A592 up to Kirkstone Pass and beyond to Patterdale now runs in the valley-bottom, leaving the village a quiet and picturesque haven to be enjoyed at leisure. Most of the houses are 17th-c and some retain their spinning galleries and oak-mullioned windows. In the walls are set numerous drinking troughs once used for the horses before their long, hard climb up to Kirkstone. At the S end of the

village is Townend, an excellently preserved example of a yeoman farmer's, or statesman's house, which still contains the carved oak furniture, books, papers and domestic treen ware of the Browne family who were its owners and occupiers for 13 generations until 1944. The National Trust was given the property in 1948 and it is open to view, March to October. Opposite is the old range of farm buildings, which includes a spinning-gallery, with the spinning room at the N end, and a magnificent roof of carefully graded slate tiles.

At the other end of Troutbeck is an inn whose name, The Mortal Man, is culled from the famous irreverent verse:

Thou mortal man that lives by bread
How comes thy nose to be so red?
Thou silly ass that looks so pale,
It is by drinking Sally Birkett's ale!

Beyond this inn on the main road is another, The Queen's Head, where both bar and bedrooms boast four-poster beds. Just opposite it begins the lane that winds up to the head of the dale where Troutbeck Park farmhouse stands facing S beneath the Tongue – Old Norse *tunga*, 'a ridge between two valleys that join'. Once this 2000-acre property was emparked for deer which the Lords of Kendal hunted. In the time of Charles I it became a sheep-run for herdwick, the tough local breed of fell sheep, and in 1928 Mrs Heelis (Beatrix Potter) bought the farm in order to improve the traditional flock. The property – and the sheep – now belong to the National Trust.

Up on the fellside W of the Park are the remains of Hird House where a giant of a man called Hugh Hird lived. His prodigious strength enabled him to perform many feats, one of which was to slay the Scots invaders as they poured down Scots Rake, a steep section of the ancient Roman track that leads from High Street to Galava fort at Ambleside via the Troutbeck Valley. On the main road and isolated from the village is the church, twice rebuilt, with a simple 18th-c tower, a roof of fine oak beams and an oak altar table 300 years old. The churchyard is a mass of daffodils in April, and, inside, the E window is a thing of beauty, designed by Sir Edward Burne-Jones and executed by both him and his two contemporaries, William Morris and Ford Madox Brown, who were on a fishing holiday at the time.

TURTON, *Lancs.,* is a typical industrial community in the valley of the River Bradshaw whose fortunes were closely linked to the explosive growth of Bolton, 8m S, from 1790 onwards. The manufacturers who made their fortunes out of the cotton industry moved out to villages like this, taking over the houses once owned by landed gentry and establishing mills where the water ran pure from the moors above. Thus began the firm of Horrocks, a name now synonymous with high quality cotton products the world over, and the Turton Tower estate was taken over by Joseph Kay, a cotton spinner, in 1835. This building, constructed around a 15th-c pele tower and enlarged a century later, was given to the Council in 1930 and is now open to the public.

The N end of the village on the hill is called Chapeltown and is now designated as a Conservation Area because of the well-preserved links with the Industrial Revolution. Opening off the main street are the 'folds' or cobbled mews where both the workers and their master lived in the terraced cottages built from the local brown stone. In this street at No. 97 is the house that once belonged to Humphrey Chetham, who founded the grammar school in Manchester in 1653. Next door is a delightful little memorial garden where the stocks, which once were in constant use beside the Turton fairground, are safely preserved.

The church of St Anne, early Victorian, commands a fine view from its spacious churchyard beside the main street, which, when followed out of the village, soon brings the visitor to Edgeworth. The Roman Watling Street once crossed these moors and the present road from here to Blackburn follows the same direct line, whose final destination was Ribchester on the Ribble, once the key Roman fort of Bremetennacum.

Reservoirs to supply water for Bolton are found in every valley and the judicious planting of conifers around them is transforming the area into a miniature lakeland. The small village of **Belmont** lies across the moors W of Turton and above its own reservoir that is dotted with colourful sails

during the summer months. Its history is similar to that of the other communities affected by Bolton's growth; so here are found the same rows of weavers' cottages and a working mill engaged in bleaching and dyeing. The difference is that now the cottages are usually owned by those who can afford to commute to the big towns. Even the original independent sabbath school building of 1832 is now converted into a 'desirable residence', with a fenestration that makes mockery of the simple design of the building. Across the street from the erstwhile school and on the corner cottage are two elegant Georgian oval plaques that give the name of the street and the date – 1804. On the opposite side of the main street is the old Black Dog Inn which has an unusual mosaic of a dog set into the wall. Around the corner in the old stables a modern craftsman now makes chairs and pine furniture.

Here the church, whose slender spire can be seen from miles around, commands the head of the valley. The interior is plain, with box pews.

Samuel Crompton, the inventor of the spinning 'mule', met his wife in Turton whither she had moved from Warrington because of her father's financial losses. She found there ample and profitable employment spinning on Hargreave's jenny, a machine whose shortcomings gave Crompton the idea for his revolutionary invention.

WETHERAL, *Cumbria,* is a large village with a prosperous air about it, 4m E of Carlisle, and a dormitory for that city. The triangular village green is surrounded by well-built sandstone houses of the 18th c or later and from the E corner the road plunges down to the River Eden which is here 150ft wide. There is a lovely walk up the left bank of the river which has, through the centuries, carved a gorge with sheer, sandstone cliffs.

Holy Trinity Church stands in a commanding position above the river and its history is closely linked with that of the Priory, ½m upstream, whose monks officiated in the church before the Reformation. The Lady Marie Howard memorial within the church is a superb, lifesize study in white marble by Nollekens. There is another more ancient tomb worthy of note, that of Sir Richard Salkeld and his wife, *c.* 1500. In keeping with the village, this church is well furnished and cared for.

All that remains of the Benedictine priory, founded in *c.* 1100 by Ranulph de Meschines, is the 15th-c gatehouse; but the substantial farm buildings round about obviously arose from the ruins of the Priory. Immediately opposite across the river on the cliff is Corby Castle, a late Georgian mansion designed by Peter Nicholson with a 14th-c pele tower as its core. The Salkeld family built the tower to guard the river ford and were Lords of the Manor until Lord William Howard, a son of the Duke of Norfolk who was later executed for associating with Mary Queen of Scots, bought the estate in 1624. A branch of the Howard family, staunch Catholics, continues to live here. The grounds, open to the public, are on a grand scale, and include a cascade and a glorious broad walk along the river bank. At the S end is a classic temple with Tuscan columns and at the other are caves carved out of the red sandstone. Halfway along is a medieval salmon weir and trap which are used regularly at times and on dates determined centuries ago. Opposite are man-made caves, cut deep into the cliff and traditionally connected with St Constantine and the priory. The 21 acres of woods surrounding them are now owned by the National Trust and open for all to enjoy.

WHALLEY, *Lancs.,* 5m N of Accrington. With the appearance of a small town, this is really a large village and one with a past which the visitor can appreciate at leisure now that the by-pass has removed the worst traffic. The Nab, 607ft, to the S, is an excellent viewpoint. The railway viaduct spanning the Calder valley has 49 arches and was opened for use in 1850, a fine engineering feat.

Upstream, on the right bank, are the ruins of Whalley Abbey which flourished from 1300, when the Cistercian monks moved here from Stanlaw in Cheshire, until the Dissolution. At the height of its power the abbey's writ extended over a tenth of the present county, and in the monastery lived 110 persons and a continual stream of mendicants and visitors. Abbot Paslew and his monks unwisely joined the Pilgrimage of Grace and were convicted at Lancaster Assizes on charges of high treason. The Abbot was hanged outside his own gatehouse, but was spared the horror of drawing and quartering which two of his followers suffered. The demolition of the abbey did not begin until *c.* 1660, and many of the stones are now found in nearby buildings, including the Conference House which is used by the Diocese for retreats and many functions.

Some of the panelling found its way into the Toby Jug farmhouse in the village. The ruins of the church and cloisters are now beautifully maintained and open daily.

Immediately NW is the church of St Mary, established long before the abbey and now containing the stalls and misericords taken from it. They vie with the chancel screens, the rood screen and pews in their richness and ingenuity of carving. The fabric dates from Norman times through EE to late Perp. In the churchyard are three Celtic crosses that were set up when St Paulinus came to preach the Gospel here in AD 626–7, using the waters of the Calder for baptism.

There are several other interesting buildings in the village. The old grammar school that was founded by a charter of Edward IV in 1547 is at the N end of King Street – the straight stretch of pavement in front was once a rope-walk. At the other end is the cottage by the bridge over the river where Harrison Ainsworth wrote *The Lancashire Witches,* and opposite is a corn mill complete with mill wheel. Over the bridge is a terrace of weavers' cottages with a raised, iron balcony along the front.

WORSLEY, *Greater Manchester.* It is remarkable to find an identifiable village community with such important historical connections in this neighbourhood, where a motorway and various junctions now predominate. Just off Junction 13 on M62, signposted Swinton, is Worsley, with a village green created in 1907, a triangular oasis surrounded by half-timbered and stone houses on two sides. A forlorn memorial of classical proportions, sheltering a large stone chalice and covered with the inevitable graffiti, is on the green. Old cottages, well restored and with gleaming white walls, are up Mill Brow, behind the coaching inn on the roundabout. Overlooking the coal wharf on the canal is a half-timbered Court House, built in 1849; an impressive Tudor 'copy'.

Now overlooked by the speeding traffic on the motorway, but once in a commanding position, is the church of St Mark, built by Sir Gilbert Scott in 1846. The style is what Pevsner aptly describes as 'Middle Pointed' – a form of decorated geometric design which here means many gargoyles on the tower and gracing the down spouts. Inside is a monument to the 1st Earl of Ellesmere, who was responsible for this church. Opposite the church is Church Lodge which was once the entrance lodge to Worsley New Hall, now demolished. His Lordship had the Hall clock chime 13 so as to get his men back to work on time after the dinner break.

What draw people to Worsley are the rust-coloured waters in the basin of the Bridgewater Canal which the 3rd Duke of Bridgewater constructed to convey the coal from his coal mines at Worsley to Manchester. James Brindley was commissioned to undertake this major engineering feat that heralded the start of the transport revolution. Begun in 1759, the canal was finally completed in 1803. It involved constructing an aqueduct to take it over the River Irwell at Barton (now demolished). When the canal came into use the cost of coal in Manchester was immediately halved and undreamed-of prosperity came to SE Lancs. In the canal basin is still one of the exceedingly narrow boats in which the coal was brought from the levels through low tunnels 6m long and, at their terminus, 550ft underground.

Further E, at the S end of the Worsley road and on the bank of the canal, is the Bridgewater Mill where James Nasmyth established his works in 1836, an iron foundry that soon became nationally famous. Nearby in the suburb of Eccles is the early 16th-c church of St Mary, built from the local red sandstone and incorporating parts of a Norman chapel. A treasured possession is the remains of an Anglo-Saxon cross-shaft on which is carved the distinctive knot design.

FRANCIS TOWNE (1739–1816): Ambleside. Watercolour, 1786 (*Yale Center for British Art, Paul Mellon Collection*). Towne was the most individual of all the late eighteenth-century watercolourists, working in a highly personal way, on the basis of firm linear compositions with the pen. He made a tour of the Lake District in 1786.

FRANCIS NICHOLSON (1753–1844): The Elleemosynary at Fountains Abbey. Coloured lithograph by
C. Hullmandel, *c.* 1830 (*John Hadfield*). Nicholson was born at Pickering in Yorkshire.
He was a founder member of the Society of Painters in Watercolour in 1804, and he was
one of the first to realize the possibilities of the newly invented art of lithography.

Yorkshire

NORTH SOUTH AND WEST

Patrick and Biddy Nuttgens

Yorkshire is still the largest county in England in spite of losing fringe areas in the north-east to Cleveland, in the north-west to Lancashire, and the bulk of the East Riding to Humberside, in the local government reorganization of 1974. Villagers in these areas still speak of themselves as belonging to Yorkshire and consider the date on which the new boundaries came into force significant: All Fool's Day. Before this date Yorkshire was immemorially divided into three ridings, tridings or thirdings – North, West and East. Today we have North, West and South Yorkshire.

This is a much-lived-over county, and in every type of terrain there are settlements of picturesque or historic significance that are characteristic of their area. The pedigree of many of these villages goes back into archaeology: settlements have been built and rebuilt on the same site – by Iron Age tribes, Romans, Anglian settlers, Danes – and continuously since the Middle Ages. The two definitive influences have been agriculture (and, later, industry) and communications: which depend in their turn on the geographical and geological position of the settlement.

The county is heart-shaped, in two broad divisions. The uplands run roughly in an upside-down L. The top from east to west leaves only a narrow lowland strip along the border in the area north of Richmond. The north-to-south leg forms the Pennine chain between Yorkshire and Lancashire which in the south almost merges with the Derbyshire Peak District, south of Sheffield. The northern arm forms the limestone Dales area, a huge plateau slightly tilted towards the south-east, so that apart from the Esk, which runs into the sea at Whitby, all the other purely Yorkshire rivers – the Swale, the Ure, the Ouse, the Nidd, the Wharfe, the Derwent, the Aire, the Calder and the Don – find their way to join forces and eventually empty themselves out in the Humber. Across this plateau the main Dales – from north to south, Swaledale, Wensleydale and Wharfedale – run horizontally from west to east, crosshatched in places by smaller dales. In the angle of this L is the industrial area, based in the first instance on the woollen industry. The plateau comes to an end about half-way across the county, where the A1, the Great North Road, pursues its way up a wide lowland channel; but to the east of this a very different kind of upland starts again in the North Yorkshire Moors. This Jurassic plateau of mixed stone is heather-covered and stretches to the sea; the sheep population is sparser here than in the more westerly areas. Below the North Yorkshire Moors stretch the Vales of Pickering and Mowbray and the Plain of York: arable and cattle country down the east and middle of the county, and a stream of industrialism from the west which burrows under the fields. Coal measures are indeed the geological basis of this region.

The character of both planting and building depends very largely on the agricultural background. The earliest large-scale sheep farmers were the monks from abbeys such as Rievaulx, Fountains, Jervaulx and Kirkstall; they established granges up the smaller dales that formed the basis of later villages, and also originated another characteristic feature of upland Yorkshire: the dry-stone walling, used both to enclose animals and to mark boundaries. After the suppression of the monasteries in the sixteenth century many of these lands passed to the new great landowners who were to be instrumental in the changes on the face of the land throughout the eighteenth century.

The boundaries to fields are an excellent guide to the underlying geological structure. In the uplands, where the commissioners for the Land Enclosure Act made exact stipulations for the building of the dry-stone walls, which are all over the Dales today, dark walls indicate the rough sandstone called millstone grit, characteristic of the industrial Pennine area; white walls tell you you are in a limestone area. In lowland areas you must examine the hedges more minutely: on the magnesium limestone belt that runs up the centre of the county a mixture of plants form the hedges, such as hazel, maple, buckthorn, rose, and a variety of climbers like white and black bryony will crawl over the top; off the magnesium limestone, on the coal measures and alluvial soils, the hedges are almost entirely hawthorn.

The building materials are similarly easy to spot: grey sandstone and limestone in the Dales; darker millstone grit on the western Pennine range; a strand of gleaming magnesium limestone (of which York Minster is built) coming up the centre through the Lower Wharfe villages; more golden sandstone in the North Yorkshire Moors and the Howardian and Hambledon areas, and brick round York and to the south and west, roughly coinciding with the coal measures.

Communications have of course had a major effect on the siting of villages. Prehistoric tracks from west to east and south-west to north-east were often overlaid by the network of Roman roads. In addition Yorkshire is criss-crossed by a web of 'green roads', the ordinary paths of commerce. Some of these were strictly local, linking villages with churches in a region where often one church served a wide parish of little villages. Others ran across long distances. Roads looping over the hills from one dale to another might be followed from Northumberland or Scotland by drovers, taking flocks of sheep or herds of cattle to markets in the south, as well as by smugglers carrying booty. Along these roads too went the 'jaggers', the packmen who serviced the out-of-way areas with goods of all kinds.

Three developments gave a new shape and geometry to the pattern of communications. The turnpikes of the eighteenth century led to the building of coaching inns and coaching villages that often grew into something greater. The Great North Road was of crucial importance; villages sprang up along its length. The canals, following upon the navigations of the end of the seventeenth century, opened up new areas and carried much of the commercial cargo previously borne by the packmen. For Yorkshire they were particularly important in the developing industrial areas: the Aire and Calder Navigation, the Rochdale Canal, the Leeds–Liverpool Canal, and many others, linked the great industrial cities with smaller settlements. But it was the railways that transformed the North, a development affecting people as well as goods.

These changes, coinciding as they did with the use of steam for industrial power, had a crucial effect on the pattern of Yorkshire. The little villages of the cottage textile industry lost their importance: the work and the people moved down from the hill-top villages into valleys like the Calder valley, gaining access to water power and to the railways, roads and canals that could bring in coal and raw materials and distribute the finished products for sale. In the west the great industrial conurbations absorbed hundreds of little villages, many of which were swamped by building developments. A few strangely escaped and maintain a separate identity. The swamping of the little villages in the southern belt was due to coal-mining and the steel industry; few escaped sufficiently to warrant inclusion in our list. Yet the anachronistic little Hooton Pagnell (q.v.) still survives; and it is a fascinating area where

almost every settlement has ruins of value: Norman churches, moated farms, medieval walls.

The villages took shape in several waves of building. One such wave followed the Norman Conquest, growing round the great defensive castles: Skipton, Middleham (q.v.) and Richmond in the north; Conisbrough, Tickhill (q.v.) and Pontefract in the south. Following hard upon that was the building of the great abbeys and monasteries, which effectively were villages in themselves, communities of people, religious and secular, engaged in a variety of work; their ruins are sometimes, as at Rievaulx, incorporated into modern villages but more often, as at Fountains and Jervaulx, remain in haunting isolation as a reminder of former activity. Yorkshire is especially rich in them. The next great rebuilding took place, not as in the south of England in Elizabeth's reign, but after the Civil War. Though often rebuilt on older foundations, few rural Yorkshire houses date from before the late seventeenth century. That rebuilding led straight to the wide-spread changes of the eighteenth century, when agricultural expansion due to new techniques produced in the lowland central area and east the transformation or planning of estate villages and villages under the patronage of big country houses, as well as some rare and hardworking settlements by religious communities. A special and important development, which should not be ignored among Yorkshire villages, was the promotion of industrial villages by benevolent tycoons in the nineteenth century, and the first garden village early in the twentieth.

The villages described in the following pages have been selected to represent these periods as well as giving a geographical spread that reveals the wide variety of village types. It may be that we have been unduly attracted by the typical Anglian village plan – of houses round a green and a stream crossing. There are hundreds more to which these villages give an introduction, and which we have had to exclude regretfully, although well worth exploring.

GAZETTEER

ACKWORTH, *W. Yorks.* (2m S of Pontefract). Probably because of its Quaker school, Ackworth has retained an air of gracious living in this mining area. The village ambles along a ridge with an amazing number of large, beautiful houses of the 18th and 19th c, set in shady gardens – more what you would expect of the imposing suburbs of a city. There are some good examples of modern infilling, such as the row of houses on the green by the church. The 19th-c St Oswald's stands on a much older foundation: St Cuthbert's body is said to have lain here on its peregrinations to its final resting place in Durham Cathedral. On the green outside the church is a cross with a Tudor ball topping a medieval shaft, and elsewhere two very handsome Victorian signposts with carved dates. Opposite the church, Mary Lowther's Hospital, founded in 1741, appears to have been given over to the brambles; the pedimented doorway with the Gibbs surround is crumbling into dereliction. The range of buildings that form the Quaker school was built as a hospital for foundlings in 1758, and the smooth stonework and austere surroundings retain something of the cold uprightness of organized charity. It became a school 21 years later under the extraordinary Dr John Fothergill who, as well as helping to found hospitals in America, advocating cleaner air and vaccination against smallpox, was a botanist of repute who grew orchids. He was the supporter of numerous causes: he worked for peace in the American War of Independence, for the abolition of slavery and for prison reform. Not surprisingly, his school was educationally advanced: it was co-educational from the start. Its alumni include John Bright; visiting lecturers David Livingstone (who described how he had been shaken by a lion) and the naturalist Cherry Kearton; and in the depression of the 1930s craft classes were given in the school for out-of-work miners from the nearby pits.

ALDBOROUGH, *N. Yorks.* (1m E of Boroughbridge). When the 9th legion established their headquarters at an important junction of the supply routes to the armies in the N at the place we now call Aldborough they used the name Isurium Brigantium because this was the site of Iseur, capital town of the Brigantes, Britain's largest Celtic tribe. The Normans diverted attention to Boroughbridge, at the highest navigable point of the Ure close to its confluence with the Swale, and built a bridge where Carr's bridge was later to carry the Great North Road (the A1). Thus Aldborough was left, a sleepy little village with charming cottages and a market cross. Past the green where the maypole stands is the entrance to a café, the little museum and those Roman remains that have so far been excavated. Because the Roman village is directly under the modern one, viewing the remains involves a quaintly domesticated stroll. A delightful walk under trees full of birdsong leads past the remains of red sandstone walls, once 9ft thick and 20ft high, towards the quarry from which they came; then a sign indicates a path that runs through an orchard and skirts some allotments to reach two superb tesselated pavements, one of a panther under palm trees and the other showing an eight-pointed star, which are preserved inside little huts that smell of creosote. The 14th-c church of St Andrew stands on the site of the Temple of Mercury, and with rare Christian charity the battered statue of the god has been brought in from the cold and set at the W end. This church was once the centre of village life: voting was carried out here, using a tomb for a table; each Sunday 30 twopenny loaves were distributed to the poor; and the poisonous yews, essential for making longbows, grew on the sanctified ground of the churchyard where sheep might not graze. The lively parish records refer in one place to Oliver Cromwell as 'ye impious Arch Rebel', and record the baptism in 1537 of some poor unowned child as 'Elizabeth nobodie daughter of nobodie'. SE of the walls is the Roman burial area, and beyond, the site of the gladiatorial stadium. In the museum (founded 1864) can be seen many finds – not only coins and pieces of Samian ware, but the evocative trivia of everyday life: styli, dice and counters, gold earrings and spurs from cock-fights.

ARNCLIFFE, *N. Yorks.* Shortly after passing the impressive overhang of Kilnsey Crag on the B6160 from Grassington (q.v.) to Kettlewell, a road turns left up Littondale for Arncliffe. Littondale, a 9m valley cut out of the limestone by glacial action and watered by the effervescent little Skirfare, is a dale for all seasons, not only because of the changing colours of spring grass, bracken, turf and heather, but because of the marvellous tracery of limestone walling characteristic of the upper dales.

Arncliffe, 5½m up the Dale, is the loveliest and largest of the four villages set at intervals along the river. Sycamores lead up to a large green, too charming to need to be self-consciously neat, surrounded by the grey-walled or white-washed dwellings with grey slab roofs among which may be picked out small craftsman-built Georgian houses, some with 17th-c datestones from previous houses. Television addicts may recognize the Falcon Inn on the green as Amos Breerly's Woolpack in earlier episodes of *Emmerdale Farm* before the long-suffering villagers persuaded YTV to move its location elsewhere. Over the bridge and past the church, Bridge End appears – a grouping of millhouse, 17th-c cottages and a pocket-handkerchief lawn, edged with snowdrops and aconites in early spring, that seems to flow down unchecked into the beck. Here Charles Kingsley came to visit when he was cogitating *The Water Babies*, having walked over the hill from Malham Tarn House, now a field study centre, where he was staying. So it was from the chimneys of this great house that Tom, the chimney-sweep, came to emerge into the bedroom of the little white lady; and it is into the Skirfare at the edge of the lawn that Tom slips to become a water baby.

When Henry VI's church was rebuilt in 1793 the 1450 tower was retained, but the heavily restored interior is disappointing. A list on the wall of men of the Dale who fought at Flodden in 1513 reminds us of the intimate if hostile connections with Scotland. Henry Percy gave the tithes and living of this, the mother-church of Hubber-

Grazing on the green at Arncliffe

Kenneth Scowen

holme, to University College, Oxford, in 1443, and this has resulted in a series of erudite and interesting parsons. The Rev. Miles Wilson of Halton Gill, the next hamlet, is remembered for the endearing tract he wrote about a cobbler called Israel Jobson from Horton in Ribblesdale who built a ladder on Pen-y-ghent and climbed to the moon, but returned to earth when he found the food up there wasn't up to standard.

BAINBRIDGE, *N. Yorks.* In upper Wensleydale, Bainbridge's grey houses are set round the rim of an irregular saucer of green, wide enough to be criss-crossed by roads and rivers, and scattered with trees and seats and the old stocks. Entering from the Aysgarth end, a bridge crosses the River Bain, said to be the shortest river in England, which comes down from strange and secret Semerwater and is a magnificent sight in spate as it froths and spumes over a double-tiered weir right up against the walls of the houses. ¼m E, on Brough Hill (a drumlin left by glaciation on the valley floor), stood Verosidum, Roman Bainbridge, and one of a string of forts for policing and taxing. SW can be seen the Roman road, now a green road, to Ribblehead and Ingleton via Wether Fell. As an early Quaker village, Bainbridge has a Meeting House but no church. The Metcalfe family from Nappa Hall, a rare extant fortified farmhouse, are the traditional hornblowers of Bainbridge. At 9 p.m., from Hawes Back-End Fair (28 September) to Shrovetide, three eerie blasts are blown on the horn nightly, probably originally as a signal to the monks' herds to bring back the flocks into the safety of the village for the night.

Up Waldendale to the SE is **West Burton**, rough but compelling. A few miles to the N is **Askrigg**. The name means 'ash-tree ridge', but it is in fact a stark little village with something uncouth and alien about it – like the edge of the wild. The air is sharp from the moors behind, yet there is a distinctly urban feeling about its high, narrow three-storey houses, tightly packed up the steep main street with only the odd paved passageway cutting between. A cotton mill, opened in 1784, soon turned over to wool and supplied yarn for the cottage knitters. Clockmaking, which often ran in families, produced in the 18th c craftsmen like James Ogden, Mark Metcalfe and Christopher Caygill, who would decorate his clocks with angels and devils. The stately, late-Perp church with a fine wooden roof commands a two-way view: up the main street to the E, and to the W down Wensleydale.

BOSTON SPA, *W. Yorks* (4m SE of Wetherby), is the largest of a cluster of villages on the lower Wharfe built, like York Minster itself, of magnesium limestone from the Tadcaster quarries. The Royal Hotel, an old coaching inn, and the spreading new estates testify to a strategic position 1m off A1 and half-way between London and Edinburgh. Saline waters which relieved rheumatism were discovered in 1774, and the long High Street developed, twisting along parallel to the Wharfe and lined with handsome little Georgian houses, mostly set well back in bowery gardens. But Harrogate received Queen Victoria's accolade, and Boston Spa became a hydropathic backwater. Older residents still use the Victorian pronunciation 'Spaw' and recall the days when they rode by pony and trap to Newton Kyme station to catch the train for Scarborough and summer holidays.

A short, steep hill leads down from the middle of the High Street over an impressive bridge across the Wharfe to **Thorp Arch**, with its charming green and creeper-covered cottages. Upstream can be seen a shallow weir, beautiful and treacherous: angling is good here, swimming sometimes fatal. Thorp Arch has a hospital, an open prison and a remand centre. Behind lies a former royal ordnance factory with the dug-outs now converted into a trading estate and shopping centre; and here in 1962 was opened the National Lending Library for Science and Technology, now the British Library (Lending Division).

1m S of Boston is **Clifford**. On Clifford Moor Catholic gentlemen under Richard Conyers of Norton Conyers sought to muster troops for the Rising of the North in 1569, and the Royalists did the same during the Civil War, but it appears that 'Catholic' Clifford did not show much enthusiasm on either occasion. The building of their new church, St Edward's, at the bottom of the High Street in the 1840s was another matter: contributions were raised not only from local families like the Vavasours of Hazelwood Castle, but from the Duke of Parma, the King of Sardinia and the Queen of France. The tower, rising above the fields, is a landmark, and the E end, looking over the graveyard to fields where sheep graze, persuades bewildered visitors that they are entering a French village. It was in fact built by J. A. Hansom from the sketch designs of an architectural student, newly returned from a tour of Brittany and Normandy and dying of consumption. The tower is by Goldie and four stained-glass windows are by Pugin. Best of all are the round pillars individually carved at the whim of local craftsmen.

The Bramham by-pass has changed the A1 from the ruin of the village into an asset: the visitor turns off and under the A1, and sees **Bramham**, a huddle of creamy stone and red pantiled roofs, framed by the bridge. The special charm of Bramham Park, on the other side of the A1 from the village, lies in its combination of 1700 elegance with homely scale; the gardens, too, combine the 'manner of Versailles' with an English landscape of dancing trees and daffodils. The Bramham Moor Hunt has a considerable reputation.

Newton Kyme, a tiny village up a cul-de-sac off the Boston–Tadcaster road has a mossy 14th-c church where Milton often read the lesson; a tithe barn, now a private house; and a pillared Hall formerly approached by a lime avenue up which General Fairfax of the Civil War rides each Hallowe'en.

BRADFIELD, *S. Yorks.* A few miles from Sheffield off the B6077 and at the W tip of the Damflask Reservoir, Low Bradfield is a charming place to idle in the lush grass under the pine trees by the bridge. But it is only by climbing the steep street to where High Bradfield's grey cottages cluster around the embattled 15th-c church of St Nicholas, that the unique quality of these high Pennine villages is felt. The view from the church-yard is spectacular: a switchback of steep, in-dividual green hills heaving up from the valley floor, and the occasional glint of shining waters.

The number of large, stately gravestones, carved with intriguing verses, indicate that Brad-field parish covered a large area. The church key can be obtained from the gatehouse, built in 1745 as a watch house against body snatchers. Inside is a medieval font brought from Roche Abbey, S of Doncaster, an excellent 1930 stained-glass window of Yorkshire saints at the end of the S aisle, and an eagle lectern carved in oak by Robert Ellin of New York which won premier honours at the Philadelphia Exhibition of 1876. Beyond the farm behind the graveyard can be seen a medieval motte and bailey under clumps of trees, and there are indications of the prehistoric ditch and ram-parts of Bar Dyke. Reservoirs for Sheffield lie in the surrounding hills and local grandmothers still tell the story of the night the dam burst – how on 11 March 1864 waters from the Dale Dyke Dam flooded the valley, inundating the villages and drowning 244 people.

CAWOOD, *N. Yorks.* (4m NW of Selby), with its iron bridge, winding streets, rows of boats and passage of sugar-beet barges, seems very 20th c. Local people are concerned with the proximity of the new Selby coalfield and the flooding of the houses by the Ouse in recent winters. But the past looms up in the shape of a medieval tower seem-ingly embedded in a part of the street. This is what remains of 'The Castle', the seat of the Primates of the Northern Province. The site was probably given to the see of York by King Athelstan in about 930. Most of the house was probably built by Archbishop de Gray and crenellated by Arch-bishop Giffard in 1271. In its early days it was used as much by sovereigns as by the Church.

When Edward I, a week after his marriage to Marguerite of France, set off to subdue the Scots, he commanded his Queen to 'come to the North cuntre' to await his return. In the event the cam-paign lasted five years, most of which the Queen spent at Cawood. Their son Edward II, after the defeat of Bannockburn, crept back to Cawood to lick his wounds.

This was Cardinal Wolsey's castle, and it fell into neglect in his early years because he was never there; but after he fell from favour, he set about restoring it to its former grandeur. Wolsey was lying sick here when the Earl of Northumberland came to demand the keys of the palace and to arrest him on a charge of high treason; he must by then have established himself in the village for it is reported that there wasn't a dry eye as he was led away. Elizabeth made the palace the headquarters of the Royal Commission appointed to put down popery and rebellion; it was the Commissioners' job to quell the Rising of the North in 1569. During the Civil War the palace was passed back and forth between the two sides, and in 1646 the House of Commons resolved that the northern castles, including Cawood, Tickhill (q.v.), Bolton, Middleham (q.v.) and Crayke (q.v.), should be disgarrisoned and made untenable. If that ended Cawood's greatness, other functions prevailed. Stone from the Huddleston quarries was ferried down Bishop's Dyke (where today they catch fat eels) to Cawood for distribution for building edifices such as King's College, Cambridge.

COXWOLD, *N. Yorks.,* 8m SE of Thirsk. This Cotswoldy-looking village in the Vale of Mowbray snuggles between the Hambleton and the Howardian hills, on the green road called Hambledon Street. As you approach from Helms-ley, an enticing prospect opens out; the village clusters round a hill with the octagonal church tower topping it all. Once into the village you find a long street – almost an extended square – sloping upwards, with green banks, cobbles, rook-alive trees, plenty of colour: honey-coloured cottages and white walls striped vivid red and green by pyracantha. St Michael's Church, basically 15th-c although the chancel was rebuilt in the 17th, runs parallel to the street as you approach the top of the hill, and is so long that, driving past, you have a peculiar idea that you are passing a train on a parallel track.

Thomas, Earl of Fauconberg, married Oliver Cromwell's daughter Mary, an active lady who in 1662 endowed almshouses, the Fauconberg Hospital (one-storeyed with mullioned windows) further down the street on the N side; and is also thought to have brought her father's headless body back to Newburgh for burial. The 17th-c inn, the Fauconberg Arms, was once thatched.

But Coxwold is best remembered for its eccen-tric vicar, Laurence Sterne. The village had no vicarage, so Sterne settled into a humble 1½-storey brick house with a great chimney on the N side of the street and called it Shandy Hall – 'shandy' being a Yorkshire word for wild or eccentric. He lived there eight years, severely emaciated from tuberculosis, and wrote three novels including *A Sentimental Journey* and *Tristram Shandy.* In 1969 Kenneth Monkman, who runs the Sterne Trust at Shandy Hall, applied for Sterne's body when the graveyard in Bays-water, London, in which he was buried was being demolished, and brought it back to Coxwold. The inscription on his tombstone includes this verse:

*Sterne was the Man who with gigantic stride
Mow'd down luxuriant follies far and wide.*

CRAYKE, *N. Yorks.* (2½m E of Easingwold), is on top of a 'pimple' that rises sharply out of the Vale of York. It is also on the boundary of the

Geoffrey N. Wright

Shandy Hall, Coxwold, the home of Laurence Sterne

Forest of Galtres, the medieval forest that was once a royal hunting preserve when it stretched from York northwards to Easingwold. Crayke is an oddity in that until the 19th c it was not officially in Yorkshire: it was the property of the Palatine of Durham, having been given to St Cuthbert, Bishop of Durham, in the 7th c. The castellated castle was built either by Bishop Flambard of Durham or his successor, Bishop Hugh Pudsey, on the site of a Norman motte and bailey and probably of an earlier Saxon monastery, of neither of which are there any traces extant. The castle commands the village with its green and cobbled paths up to the red-brick cottages. It consists of two entirely separate 15th-c buildings, and is now privately owned. The church is of course St Cuthbert's. It is Perp with a good rood screen. A plaque on a cottage wall in the main street recalls that William Ralph Inge, the 'Gloomy Dean' of St Paul's, 'scholar, philosopher, writer', was born here in 1860.

Part of Crayke Hall is called Oliver's Mount, and the castle was besieged by the Roundheads in 1644. The outcome appears to have been uncertain, but when the battle was refought in 1970 by the Sealed Knot – a popular organization whose members dress in costumes of the Civil War and spend their weekends re-enacting battles – the Royalists won.

EAST WITTON, *N. Yorks.*, 4m SE of Leyburn. There is the church and the Victorian village school, closed only within the past few years, and then the road from Masham to Leyburn in Wensleydale curves right between the Holly Tree (once an inn) and the Blue Lion (still an inn), by-passing the village proper, which is a ring of unassuming detached cottages, each separated from the next only by the gate to its back yard, round a long sloping green. Its original foundation is ancient; but what you see today is the result of a total rebuilding in 1819 when it became the estate village of the Jervaulx Abbey estate. The houses are small, stone and similar to one another, but there is no planned uniformity: instead, a gentle sunny unanimity of truly organic architecture. On the green is a great boulder with a tap set into it – the original village water supply; and from the end of the green where grey tree boles stand against the light, a rutted road twists off to the secret valley of Coverdale. In April mats of purple aubretia are draped over every wall, and daffodils cluster along the road verges round the characteristic stone slab platforms, originally mounting blocks, where nowadays milk churns wait collection by the dairy cooperative.

Jervaulx is Norman French for 'Uredale' (Wensleydale takes its name from a village, not from its river), and the ruins of the Cistercian Abbey date from 1156. At the gate you can buy a list of one of its chief beauties – the wild flowers that swarm all over the grey ruins, for Jervaulx is privately owned and not subjected to herbicide sprays used on Government properties.

GOATHLAND, *N. Yorks.* There is little that is exceptional about the individual houses of Goathland, which are scattered round a wild common, rough with ditches and rushes – although St Mary's Church of the 1890s is of interest as being the work of York's great Art Nouveau architect, W. H. Brierly. The quality of the village depends on its central position in the North Yorkshire Moors, a strangely powerful landscape, pitted or heaving with prehistoric remains – tumuli, earthworks, crosses and standing stones – an eerie primitive landscape to which modern man's contribution, the three gigantic surrealistic 'ping-pong balls' of Fylingdales Early Warning System, seems peculiarly appropriate. But here and there this moorland plateau of browns and terra-cottas – red earth, dead bracken and dark heather – is slashed by lush green, wooded valleys down which water courses run eastwards to the sea. Retired people and visitors find combined here the benefits of sparkling moortop air with a variety of pleasant walks, by wooded crags and 'fosses' or waterfalls with charming names – Falling Foss, Nelly Ayre Foss, Thomason Foss, the Mallyan Spout and Water Ark – to neighbouring hamlets such as Beckhole, Grosmont and Egton Bridge.

There are sheep grazing everywhere. Horses figure, too, in the Goathland Hunt which dates back to 1750; Tom Ventris, the Hunt Whip, was better known than John Peel when he died in 1922 at the age of 101. The Roman Road, a 4-m stretch of Wade's Way from Malton to Whitby, is excitingly completed, with drainage culverts still visible. **Egton Bridge** is famous for gooseberries and priests. Every August, prizes are given for the best gooseberries at the Gooseberry Show. The 19th-c St Hedda's Church reminds us that this was a Catholic stronghold right back beyond penal times. In 1679 Egton's parish priest, Nicholas Postgate, aged 83, joined the company of the Forty English Martyrs when he was hanged on the Knavesmire at York for being caught baptizing a baby on a farm above charming **Littlebeck** in the 'green lost valley' of Eskdale, south of Whitby. His informer, an exciseman named Reeves, suffered remorse when he wasn't rewarded with the £20 he expected, and drowned himself in a pool called the Devil's Hole near Littlebeck.

Grosmont is the terminus of the N Yorkshire Moors Railway. Planned by George Stephenson himself in 1833, the railway was closed under the Beeching Plan, and reopened by a railway preservation society on 1 May 1973. In the early days of the railway an ingenious contraption was invented to pull the trains up to Goathland, involving a rope round a drum on the Bank Top which was attached to a series of empty wagons which were gradually filled with water to shift the balance.

GRASSINGTON, *N. Yorks.* This capital of upper Wharfedale has everything a tourist wants. Pleasingly individual grey limestone buildings group themselves in close architectural accord on either side of the steep main street that runs uphill through a cobbled square. Traction engines squash into the square each October for Grassington Feast, today's counterpart of the medieval three-day Michaelmas Feast. Streets called 'folds', marking the Anglian croft lands, run off on either side – Chamber End Fold, Jacob's Fold – and passageways have strange names like Jakey and The Woggins. There is a coaching inn, a smiddy, where the murdering blacksmith Tom Lee once worked, and plenty of antique and craft shops.

The Centre for the Yorkshire Dales National Park is at the top of the street. At Fort Gregory at the top of Grass Wood (now a botanist's paradise) or at Lea Green up Chapel Street, can be seen evidence of a fort and the Iron Age village of the Brigantes who lived here for 600 years and fought the Roman conquerors: hut circles, Celtic field systems, dewponds, sunken roads; 20th-c moles still throw up flint scrapers over 1600 years old. In the Middle Ages two important green ways crossed here: the monastic road from Fountains to the Lake District, and the road from Skipton to Wensleydale; and in 1281 a royal charter established a weekly market here. Later still, James I brought in miners from Derbyshire to extract lead ore up on Grassington and Hebden Moors, and the group of administrative buildings at Yarnbury, the cupola smelt mill chimney and some of the flues and shafts of the Duke of Devonshire's 18th-c workings can still be seen, although to explore them is dangerous. Still later, the village became a centre for the textile industry. In the arts field it can boast the prowess of its fiddlers, who played for the dancing at the fairs; and in Theatre Cottage, a barn converted to a theatre in the 19th c by an enterprising postmaster Tom Airey, Edmund Kean and Harriet Melon once performed. However, in the 1830s Mr Airey turned his talents to mail coaches and his family continued this business with a daily horse-bus service to Skipton until the end of the century.

GREAT AYTON, *N. Yorks.,* almost on the Cleveland border, is a jolly place, especially in high summer when visitors picnic on the green banks of the River Leven which runs virtually down the middle of the main street, and children paddle where the water slides almost imperceptibly downhill over wide, shallow steps. The village is full of bustle, with antique shops and cafés. The older church, All Saints, incorporates much of its Norman predecessor, and there are Saxon crosses and the family graves of the mother and siblings of Ayton's greatest son, Captain James Cook, to discover in the graveyard. There is now a museum in the upper storey of the red-brick school, built by Michael Postgate in 1704, in which Cook received his education from the age of eight. There are two greens. Round High Green stand the buildings of the Quaker School with classical façades and Doric columns to houses washed in soft pinks and greys, so that at first glance one presumes the buildings a group

Geoffrey N. Wright

The Brontë parsonage at Haworth

of gaily coloured hotels. It was started in 1842 for the children of Friends who had married out of the Society, and in the early days the curriculum centred round rural science. Roseberry Topping, a great lump of a hill resembling an upturned boat, provides a backdrop to the village; it is said that from here the boy Cook would gaze out over the moors to Whitby and the sea. A small obelisk marks the site where once stood the red-brick cottage with mullioned windows that Cook's father built for his family in 1755 from his savings from his job as farmhand to Squire Thomas Scottowe. The cottage itself was bought by the Government of Victoria, Australia, in 1934, dismantled and rebuilt in Melbourne. In 1827 Captain Cook's Monument by Robert Campion was erected at an elevation of 1064ft on Easby Moor and its inscription reads:

In Memory of Captain Cook
The celebrated navigator
A man in nautical knowledge inferior to none
In Zeal, Prudence and Energy superior to most
Regardless of Danger, he opened an Intercourse
with the Friendly Isles and other parts of the
Southern Hemisphere
Born at Marton in 1723
Massacred at Owkyee 1779

HAWORTH, *W. Yorks.,* Brontë devotees are often shocked to find that Haworth, far from being isolated on wuthering moors, is on the crest of a wave of industrialism that rolls uphill from the mill chimneys of the Worth Valley. The Black Bull, where Branwell drank, surprises by being just round the corner from the parsonage; and whether one approaches the village by the A629 from Keighley, or boards the train at Keighley and travels up part of the 5m track that is today operated by the Keighley and Worth Valley Railway Preservation Society, one observes the truth of Mrs Gaskell's comment: 'The town of Keighley never quite melts into countryside on the road to Haworth.' In the village itself, the atmosphere becomes devotional as one toils up the steep uneven street to the parsonage, between houses of blackish local millstone grit, almost every one now a shop selling mementoes that range from Californian shells and Indian bells to more genuine native products: Yorkshire wool, yellowed books, Brontë biscuits and liqueur.

In truth, the brilliant children of Patrick and Maria Brontë have lit up with romance a village so grim and stark by nature that it appalled Maria when her parson husband brought the family there in 1820. She died nine months later, and her last words were, 'O God, my poor children,

O God, my poor children'. Rapid expansion of the weaving industry in the 18th c had left Haworth a legacy of congested dwellings, polluted water and inadequate sanitation; pigs roamed the streets, there was a dunghill before each door, and typhus, cholera, dysentery and smallpox were rife. A Board of Health investigation in 1850 found that the average age at death was 28.5 years; so, at least in one respect, Branwell, Emily and Anne, dying in the three previous years at 31, 30 and 29, were pretty average. 'The little church rises above most of the houses in the village', describes Mrs Gaskell, 'and the graveyard rises above the church, and is terribly full of upright tombstones.'

That was the old church which an earlier incumbent, the Rev. William Grimshaw, had already put on the map in the mid-18th c by encouraging Charles Wesley and other early Methodists to preach there, and by his own eccentricities, which included emerging from the church during the singing of a long hymn and horse-whipping erring drunkards out of the nearby taverns and into his congregation. The present church, St Michael and All Angels, was built on the site in 1879 by a successor to Patrick Brontë. A brass plaque marks the crypt where all the Brontës, except Anne who died in Scarborough, are buried; and entries in the register may be seen, recording Emily's death in 1848 and Charlotte's marriage to the curate Arthur Bell Nicholls six years later. Across the lane is the 'new' schoolroom where Charlotte taught Sunday School.

The Rev. John Wade added in 1872 N and W wings (now used as museum space) to the plain Georgian parsonage. However, the Brontë Society, who acquired the house and opened it as a museum in 1928, has done wonders in collecting the family furniture and possessions, much of which had been dispersed in the 67 years since the last survivor, the old parson himself, had joined his family in the churchyard. Today, it is impossible not to be moved as one stands a foot from the dining-room sofa on which Emily died, or inspects the children's drawings of heads and figures on the whitewash of the nursery walls, or their father's pipe and book and spectacles laid down on the table in his sacrosanct study – as if he had just stepped into the kitchen to ask Tabby when she would be bringing his dinner. There is a wealth of relics: the miniature books ($2\frac{1}{2}$in × $1\frac{1}{2}$in) in which the children wrote up the adventures of Branwell's toy soldiers, Emily's comb, the pistol their father would fire into the air for effect, slippers small enough for a large doll which were Charlotte's – and, for serious scholars, the collection of manuscripts and drawings that started with the bequest of the Philadelphia publisher Henry Houston Bonnell in 1926. From the windows one looks out over the wild moors, as Charlotte, Branwell, Emily and Anne once did.

HEATH, *W. Yorks.* A scheme in 1894 to link Heath with Wakefield luckily aborted, and so this singular village of Georgian mansions remains, 2m E of Wakefield off A655 Normanton road. On a small hill above the industrial Calder Valley, it commands to the W an impressive panorama of the Wakefield skyline, and is reached by a road climbing over the heath that gave the village its name: the place where once Victorian lovers from Wakefield went to listen for the first cuckoo, now scruffy and grazed over by bedraggled horses from a Council gypsy encampment. The site is a wide rectangular common of about 230 acres whose SE corner has been pulled into a long triangle; the houses are scattered round the green facing inwards, the larger houses imposing and distinct with their outbuildings and grounds stretching behind, the cottages in groups. Most are listed buildings. The rough grass acres, uncluttered by shelters or monuments, are wide enough to accommodate an island of buildings clustering round the King's Head. The Grammar School, endowed by Lady Bolles in 1660, is off the side of the green; the church is 1m away at Kirkthorpe, and there is a primary school for 35 children. The Dower House dates back to the 1740s and has an interesting wrought-iron railing, edging a miniature ha-ha; Beech Lawns, home of a Quaker banking family, was once visited by W. G. Grace, who joined the village cricket team on the common. Most commanding are Heath House and Heath Hall. Heath House was totally reconstructed by the young James Paine on a narrow frontage with the grounds running back down to the River Calder. Heath Hall's pedigree goes back to the 17th c; Carr of York remodelled it extensively in the mid-18th c; and it was lovingly restored by Mr and Mrs Muir Oddie within the last twenty years. Heath Old Hall, attributed to the Smythsons, the Elizabethan architects, is tucked away behind trees on the NW corner of the site; in the 19th c it was a convent school run by Benedictine nuns, refugees from the French Revolution. However, undermined for coal, and since the 1950s nudged in the ribs with unpleasant intimacy by the Brotherton Power Station, the old house succumbed to decay and only a haunted ruin and Lady Anne Bolles' square water tower remain. Its pineapple-topped gateposts, restored as the village contribution to Architectural Heritage Year, today form a bizarre frame to a view of a cooling tower.

HEPTONSTALL, *W. Yorks.*, 3m NE of Todmorden. This hard, dark-stoned example of a Pennine textile village before the factory system took over, has reason to be history-conscious. The great plague swept its population in 1631. Twelve years later, while a Roundhead garrison, it was besieged by night by Royalist forces who suffered terrible losses in the encounter, some in battle, some by drowning in the River Calder, then in spate, and some crushed by boulders which the Roundheads rolled down the hill. But its greatest claim to history is that it is itself a three-tiered object lesson in the development of the Yorkshire woollen industry: on the

The village of Heptonstall   Geoffrey N. Wright

Halifax moortop graze the sheep; half-way down, clinging by their toe-nails to the steep face of the hills, are the villages of the home-weaving industry like Heptonstall and Luddenden (q.v.); and in the valley bottom are the power sinews of the later age of steam – the road, the railway, the river and the canal – and the towns they generated like Hebden Bridge and Luddenden Foot. The steep roads are paved with hard setts, and the village is tight and congested with church and graveyard at its heart. Here stands the shell of the 15th-c church, damaged in the great storm of 1847, beside the new church, built in 1854 in 15th-c style. There are reputed to be 10,000 bodies in this 'capacity' graveyard, where the stones are used twice and one set of inscriptions lies face down on the soil.

Chantry House at the bottom of the churchyard was once four weavers' cottages, and its reputation as haunted was greatly enhanced when reconstruction work in 1960 revealed it had once been a charnel house: the stairs were made of sawn-down coffin lids, the windowsills from tombstones, and cracks in floor and paving were packed with human bones. The octangular Methodist Chapel overlooking the valley is the oldest in the world, John Wesley himself having laid the foundation stone in 1764.

They speak 'broad' here: 'Top oth Town' reads a street sign; and they cherish old customs – in villages in this area the medieval story of St George and the Dragon, the 'Pace Eggers' Play', is still sometimes performed on Good Friday.

HOOTON PAGNELL, *S. Yorks.,* 6m NW of Doncaster. This strange area on either side of the A1 north of Doncaster has mines below the surface and flat arable land above, dotted here and there with ancient villages, in which the medieval – frequently Norman – church is often the best of what is left, as at **Burghwallis** with its herring-bone masonry and restored rood screen.

The exception is the Paganell family's farming village which is still in its rural medieval state, with warm, rounded golden stones, red pantiles, a tithe barn, the church on a daffodil-girt bank above the road, and the Hall with the arms of the Luttrell family (who intermarried with the Paganells) over the gateway and a dungeon inside where food was lowered to captives on a string. In the pictures that illustrate the Luttrell Psalter now in the British Museum, commissioned by the third Sir Geoffrey of that name about 1340, are preserved for us the kind of life that went on in Hooton Pagnell, including, as well as Sir Geoffrey on his charger, villeins ploughing with oxen, a woman milking a ewe, and a farmer shooting crows with a sling.

HOVINGHAM, *N. Yorks.* (8m W of Malton), a golden, relaxed village, below the Hambledon Hills, lies on the old trader's route, the Hambledon Street; and remains of a Roman villa in the grounds of the Hall and a Saxon tower and Norman arches in the church indicate an old lineage. The Hall is not separate from the village but is entered almost off the irregular green, opposite the low, Georgian Worsley Arms Hotel. One notices enormous chestnut leaves, a brief avenue of limes, and then, through the play of sun and shade, the tunnel-like entrance in the Hall gateway. This entry to a country house is unique. Sir Thomas Worsley, Surveyor General under George III, attended to his first great love when building the house in the mid-18th c: the visitor enters through a screen of Tuscan columns directly into a covered riding-school. The Worsley family still live here, opening the house for music festivals, for cricket on the superb pitch on the W lawn, and to seekers of history. The marriage of the late Sir William Worsley's daughter, Katherine, to the Duke of Kent in 1961 gave Yorkshire its first royal wedding in York Minster since Edward III married Phillippa of Hainault in 1328.

Kirby Hill: the former Grammar School is on the far right

Geoffrey N. Wright

HUTTON LE HOLE, *N. Yorks.*, 2½m N of the Helmsley–Pickering road. Inexplicably, planning permission has been given to a new house, totally unsympathetic in its colouring and detailing, above the beck right in the centre of a village that was often considered Yorkshire's greatest beauty spot. This village lies in a dip of the moor, but the sharp bite in the air and the fresh smell tell that one is near the moor top. The mellow houses, which date back to the Quaker foundation of the late 17th c, each in its patch of gay garden, are set on the shelves of the uneven terrain on either side of the watercourse; white railings and bridges mark the twisting path of the beck down through this lumpy, tussocky common. The Ryedale Folk Museum houses a fascinating collection of tools and implements from local crafts that go back to Domesday; and round it a folk park is being built up with reconstructed cruck cottages, a blacksmith's shop, a fire engine that was the latest thing at the Great Exhibition of 1851, a belt-driven corn-mill and an early tractor.

1m away across the moor is **Lastingham**, in a cleft in the ridge between Rosedale and lovely Farndale whose sheets of daffodils in 1920 earned it reprieve from flooding for a reservoir. The village is tucked away, a French-looking cluster of pantiled roofs and tufted trees. It is a strange and secret place for a centre of the early church. According to Bede who visited here, Bishop Cedd, one of four missionary brothers sent out by St Aidan of Lindisfarne, founded the tiny church in 654. The rare apsidal crypt, hardly touched since 1088, is quite clammy with awe and antiquity. Cedd also founded in this area, 1½m SW of Kirbymoorside, St Gregory's Minster, where

there is a Saxon sundial to be seen, and stories to be heard of how in 1821 William Buckland, Professor of Mineralogy from Oxford, found in a cave (now dug to nothing and overgrown) a hyena's den, containing the bones of an extraordinary collection of animal species, including lion, tiger, elephant, bison, rhinoceros, and reindeer as well as smaller animals.

HUTTON RUDBY, *N. Yorks.,* 6m S of Middlesbrough. This handsome Cleveland commuters' paradise, just E of M19, boasts an interestingly varied collection of warm gold sandstone houses round a spacious green, lots of flowering creepers and shrubs by the front doors, and a row of trees, ringed round with narcissi, planted by private subscription in 1878. An old saying records, 'Hutton Rudby Enterpen, More rogues than honest men'. But not presumably women. For here in 1642 came Mary Ward, founder of the Institute of the Blessed Virgin Mary, the Order that owns the Bar Convent, York (the oldest existing convent in the country), with '3 cochefulls' of her nuns to stay with Sir Thomas Gascoigne. Hotun and Rodebi figure in Domesday Book. The 14th-c church of All Saints is situated in Rudby, down the hill from Hutton's green, and on the other side of the bridge that crosses the Leven. The Perp tower of 100 years later is similar to that of Mount Grace Priory and may have been built by the same masons. Pevsner calls the box-shaped Elizabethan pulpit with inlaid marquetry panels 'a precious piece'. Opposite the N nave window in the churchyard may be seen the mound where the cholera victims of the 1832 plague were buried.

KILBURN, *N. Yorks.* (6m E of Thirsk), low-lying under the white horse carved out of the steep grassy side of Roulston Scar, is one of a garland of charming villages that encircle the Hambledons, and include Oldstead with its barrow and disused observatory, Coxwold (q.v.) and Wass with the ruins of Byland Abbey in be-tween, and **Ampleforth** where there is the well-known Benedictine public school of which Cardinal Hume was once abbot. It is rustic and hard-working, not smart like Coxwold; a straight beck runs beside the one street and slabs provide bridges to reach the cottages, a strange mixture of brick and stone in bright gardens; there are some very dilapidated houses in need of rescue, and a seat built round a tree for the village elders to sit on.

It is a village of animals and schoolboys. It was the local schoolmaster Thomas Hodgson who, returning inspired from a trip south to Uffington in 1857, went first to racing stables at Hambledon to sketch horses in training and then set his pupils to help carve out a white horse 314ft long and 228ft high, on whose eye twelve people can picnic. It is maintained by local enthusiasts including Ampleforth boys: not without difficulty, for the hill is not chalk, like the Berkshire Downs. An-other man, Robert Thompson, son of a joiner, also got local lads to help him when he started his wood-carving business, famed for the trademark of a little mouse carved on every piece. Thompson mice now run all over the country, even in West-minster Abbey and Peterborough Cathedral, and boys in the chapel or library at Ampleforth are reputed to while away the hours exploring the benches on which they sit to find where the mouse is hidden this time. Since Thompson himself died in 1953 his grandsons Robert and John Cartwright have carried on the business with 30 other craftsmen, all of whom must learn to carve little mice; and the founder's timber-framed cottage is now a workshop museum.

KIRBY HILL and RAVENSWORTH, *N. Yorks.,* 4m N of Richmond. The country here is gently hilly, and Ravensworth's broad, pleasant green lies open to the sun's embraces, sloping a little to the ruins of the Fitzhughs' Norman castle in the shallow bottom. The castle, part of the northern defence works, received a royal visit from King John in 1201; but since the 16th c its chief use has been by the locals as a quarry for building stone. The houses round the green date mostly from the 18th c to the present day and are an easy mixture of styles and materials: roofs, for instance, have pantiles, Yorkshire slabs, Welsh and Cumberland slates. From here the eye drifts down past the castle ruins and sharply up to the church and village on the hill.

This tiny gem, **Kirby Hill,** is by contrast close and secretive. The houses round its cobbled and grassy square, some attached, some standing apart, many with heavy window quoins, black on white like Scottish houses, all face inwards and shun the outer world. One feels life is complete in itself here, and is ready to believe, in spite of the fact that the houses are 17th- and 18th-c, that one is seeing the very village Leland described in the 16th c as 'a praty village on a little hilling ground'. Perhaps a straw-speckled ostler will peer suspi-ciously from the archway, or a servant lad sit by the trough under the great tree to whittle a stick while his master and his master's horses are re-freshed at the inn. Off the square on the edge of the hill looking down to Ravensworth is the church, with adjoining almshouses and the grammar school, now a parish centre, both founded by John Dakyn in the 16th c. The school wall that abuts onto the churchyard has a wonderful random collage of windows, including Gothic arches; and a sundial on the two-storey cottage which was the schoolmaster's house warns laconically *Mox, nox.* The curious custom for the biannual election of three trustees for the school was to enclose the nominees' names in little balls of wax which were then drawn from the top of a bowl of water on which they floated.

LINTON, *N. Yorks.* (1m S of Grassington), won an award for the 'loveliest village in the North' in 1949; however, the austerity of the stonework and the clear waters purling across the irregular green give it an astringency and dignity that make it more than a 'pretty village'. Based on a shallow lake left from a glacial moraine that spreads out to Cracoe, and in which flax was grown until it was drained in 1850, it has a typical Anglian village pattern, with houses in pictur-esque groupings round the green. Everywhere is evidence of care: in the 14th-c packhorse bridge, the clapper bridge, the third bridge and the step-ping-stones that cross the Eller beck, in the grass, the trees, the chain-link fencing, and in housing developments of the last century. St Michael's Church has an attractive short square bell tower, two Norman bays extant, and a window of about 1300 in the W aisle. But the most impressive build-ing is the amazingly long and grand Fountaine's Hospital, founded by Vanbrugh's timber mer-chant Richard Fountaine in 1721 for 'six poor men or women' – its size all the more surprising when one discovers it is all façade, being only one almshouse deep. Vanbrugh designed two identical almshouses with a chapel and four houses on the front, and the fifth and sixth houses forming little wings, intending the other one for his own parish in London, but it was never built. The old rectory is now a youth hostel.

Thorpe, off the road to Burnsall, suggests a set for *Lorna Doone,* with beautiful houses going back to the 17th c, some very ramshackle, a scrabble of farm buildings, much evidence of dung-heap and haystack. In fact Thorpe was in the 14th and 15th c both reivers' hideout and hiding-place for the Dalesmen from marauding Scots. This 'secret' village is tucked away under the 1660ft gritstone Thorpe Fell and between two 'reef knolls': grassy rounded limestone mounds full of shells and corals (as well, here, as lead seams) suggesting that these were once coral reefs.

LUDDENDEN, *W. Yorks.,* 2m W of Halifax.
'Foo-it! Foo-it!' the porters used to call as the
Pennine train, on one of the first passenger lines
to be opened in Britain, pulled along the valley,
beside the river and the canal, past the great
power-operated mills to Luddenden Foot. Halfway up the hill above 'Fooit' is the earlier village
of the cottage industry, crammed into the mouth
of a wedge-shaped cleft driven back into the hill
where the beck flows out. Although the streets are
hard cobbled and the dark gritstone houses are
often four storeys high – so high sometimes that
entry to the top two floors is made by a separate
path further up the street – and although the
serried ranks of thin narrow windows right across
the front of the houses give evidence in house after
house that here looms once clacked each day as
long as the light lasted, this village does not feel
urban. Rather 'like the bramble and the willow-
herb' it appears to grow out of the cleft in the rock.
It is full of birdsong and the sound of rushing
waters. The little square before the church proves
to be the heart of the village. Above is the school
with, on the ground floor side by side, two village
lock-ups for wrongdoers, labelled MIDGLEY and
WARLEY because at one time the boundary of
those two parishes ran through the middle of the
school. Here stands the Lord Nelson Inn, re-
christened from the Black Swan after Trafalgar,
where Branwell Brontë was a *habitué* in the brief
two years in which he managed to keep his job as
booking clerk at Luddenden Foot, paying his
membership of 4d a month to borrow from the
curious little library, mostly of theological books,
left to the inn by a local vicar. If life was hard for
the weavers, death was clearly seen as the entry to
paradise, for the churchyard is the most romantic
part of the village. Treading on paths and up
steps made from ancient gravestones, entry is
achieved by a bridge over the beck, and after that
paths wander freely under the trees in what, but
for the graves here and there, often hidden by
blossom and shrubs, appears to be a public park
stretching back up the slopes of the ravine. But
the two finest memorials to Thomas Murgatroyd,
the prosperous wool merchant with whose family
fortunes Luddenden's prosperity was tied up,
are not in the churchyard; they are his 1650

Lock-ups at Luddenden, 1825

Geoffrey N. Wright

mansion Kershaw House, where Tudor banquets
are held complete with mead, minstrels, wenches,
jesters and even a dancing bear; and the enormous family factory, seen standing all by itself
amid green fields away on the opposite slope of
the valley.

MIDDLEHAM, *N. Yorks.,* 2m S of Leyburn
on A6108. Middleham's population has increased little from the days when 600 inhabitants
made a town, which may explain its compact and
urbane character. The two cobbled squares, each
with its monument, are on a slope; and around
them, following the natural contours of the
ground, the houses of local stone have grown up
organically with characteristic vernacular individuality of colour, detailing and groupings.
S of the ruins of the Norman castle are traces of a
motte and bailey, and local tradition says that
he who runs nine times round this earthwork
without stopping will find the door to a fabulous
treasure, the hoard of Gilpatric the Dane. The
castle part, like Richmond and Skipton, of the
medieval northern defence system, and its keep
were built in the 1170s. The castle passed to the
Nevilles in the 13th c, and here Warwick the
Kingmaker kept such state that, according to
Lord Lytton, 'Middleham – not Windsor, nor
Sheen, nor Westminster, nor the Tower – seemed
the Court of England', and its appearance as a
scene-setting in Shakespeare's *Henry VI* speaks
of its part in the Wars of the Roses. But the hero of
this castle is Richard III – and not the villainous
Crookback of Shakespeare, either. He grew up
here. In 1474 at the age of 20, he married Anne,
who at 16 was already the widow of Edward, the
Lancastrian heir. They made their home at
Middleham and their only son Edward was born
here, probably in the Prince's Tower which still
stands, or in the nursery adjoining, built over the
bakehouse for warmth. The boy died the next
year and was buried at Sherrif Hutton, and a
chronicler records that the parents were in 'a
state bordering on madness by reason of their
sudden grief'.

This has always been horse country. 'Beware
Racehorses' say signs, and you may see them
being led out for exercise on the moor top. Richard
assisted Edward IV in setting up a chain of post-
houses for royal messengers which was later to
develop into the public posting system. Possibly
Horsehouse, up Coverdale, was one of them.
This was a racing centre before Newmarket.

The church is dedicated to St Alkelda, a Saxon
princess martyr, said to have been strangled about
AD 800 by two Danish women. Near the font
(which has an unusual canopy, 10ft high) is part
of a stone that may have marked her grave. Richard
III made the church collegiate, and Charles
Kingsley was one of the last canons.

MIDDLESMOOR, *N. Yorks.,* 7m NW of
Pateley Bridge, 965ft above sea-level, up a gradi-
ent of 1 in 3 and round a right-angled bend, is a
fitting consummation to a stunning trip up Nidder-

Geoffrey N. Wright

Middleham Castle in Wensleydale

dale from Pateley Bridge. On the way up, industrial archaeologists will be excited by a gigantic water-wheel at Foster's Beck; ornithologists by Canadian geese on steely Gouthwaite Reservoir, a bird sanctuary that resembles a Scottish loch. At its head is **Ramsgill**, famed for its son Eugene Aram who, as a schoolmaster in Knaresborough in the mid-18th c, fell into bad company and was eventually tried at York assizes and condemned for the murder of one Daniel Clark: the first man, it is said, to be convicted on circumstantial evidence bolstered by a confession in sleep-talk. Some say a carved head with fluffy hair and a bashed nose to be seen on the side of the schoolhouse is Eugene himself, others that it is Eugene's carving of his mother. But Ramsgill does not need this gloomy title to fame; it is a quite delicious hamlet where peacocks squawk and perch on the roof of what was once the Yorke family's shooting lodge, now the creeper-covered Yorke Arms Hotel; and great trees rustle on the sunlit green.

Unlike smiling Ramsgill, Middlesmoor looks like a French hill-top town, perched high and wrapped round itself against the bitter winds off the moors, offset by the 1866 church of St Chad, whose graveyard tumbles in sweet disorder down the hillside towards the climbing road. All is grey: bulging walls and sagging roofs; there are few gardens and no two houses appear to be on the same level; weeds grow on the steep, random-cobbled paths that twist between the houses. In contrast the churchyard and the sloping field below where lambs gambol seem all the greener. Tombstones here indicate the general direction in which the dead lie rather than mark specific graves. The view right down Nidderdale is superlative. Inside the church, a Norman font and an anvil-shaped cross inscribed 'Cross of St Ceadda' testify that this has long been a holy site. Here on St Barnabas' Day, 11 June, or the nearest Satur-

day, a bell festival is held to commemorate the gift of six bells to the church in 1868. From Lofthouse an old packhorse route crosses the moor to Masham.

MUKER, *N. Yorks.*, 7m N of Hawes. Above the point where the Swale comes from behind Kisdon Hill at the back of Muker, to flow down the valley that bears its name, the dale is narrow. Muker was once so inbred and so many people shared the same name that all sorts of colourful nicknames evolved: there was Tripy Tom and Tom Glowremour, Moor Close Jamie, Bill Up t'Steps, and Rough and Strong Metcalfe. Ecumenical sharing also has a long history here, for the church and the Methodist Chapel, built to celebrate Queen Victoria's Jubilee, occupy commanding positions both as regards the village and village life, and preachers and parties are often held in common. The church, heavily restored in the 19th c, is one of the few that date from Elizabeth's reign, and was built as a chapel of ease for Grinton. Before then, funeral parties from the upper dale had to follow the Swale down to the nearest consecrated ground at Grinton, often taking two days to the journey and resting the wickerwork coffin at traditional places, such as the corpse stone, still to be seen at Ivelet Bridge where the old road crosses the beck and today is reputed to be haunted, oddly, by a headless dog.

A plaque on the side of the 1678 schoolroom records that Richard and Cherry Kearton, the naturalist brothers, were educated there. Lead-mining was once the chief industry in this dale; today the valley has returned to keeping the black-faced Swaledale sheep and to welcoming tourists. Muker, which means 'meadow', is the calm centre for a variety of rugged walks.

It is well worth walking a few miles up the Swale to **Thwaite**, tightly grouped stone-flagged lead-miners' houses beside the river rushing over stones. There you can join the Pennine Way and follow it up to the tiny hamlet of **Keld**, so grey and stony on the hillside that it looks like another outcrop of rock. Here a character named Neddy Dick once discovered that different rocks gave out different notes when dropped, and made up his one-man rock band.

NEW EARSWICK, *N. Yorks.*, 3m N of York. Raymond Unwin and Barry Parker, the originators of the garden city, started with this garden village for Rowntree's Cocoa workers and other residents in 1902. Commissioned by Joseph Rowntree and managed by a trust, to which by a deed of 1904 all profits over 3½% were to be returned for the maintenance and extension of the village, it started with 28 houses and gradually extended to form the model village of 500 homes, widely spaced, freely grouped round a huge central green and a Folk Hall and School. Many of its features, today accepted parts of new town and estate building, were at that time innovatory: the cottage-style houses, often grouped round cul-de-sacs with turning circles; narrow roads with thick planting (the roads are appropriately called after trees) and space provided for children to play; the elimination of wasted pieces of back land by the careful planning of plots and gardens and by the use of flanking walls to create overall unity throughout the village. Inside, the 'through' living rooms, offering the architects greater choice in the orientation of the house, were a new feature; as were bathrooms on the first floor, the elimination of winders from the stairs, and outside stores built into the house.

An extensive programme of restoration in the 1970s brought the houses up to modern standards and included the regrouping of gardens to form some very attractive footways between the houses.

REETH, *N. Yorks.*, 9m W of Richmond. Reeth's white and black houses, spread out round a frank and ample green shelf on the side of Mount Calva, is a revelation. In spring it flutters with daffodils, planted by the local youth club; in summer, coaches park on the cobbles outside the 18th-c houses of High Row on the W side of the green, and their passengers busy themselves with buying local pottery, visiting the exhibition of Swaledale life in the folk museum in the old Methodist Sunday School, and eating Yorkshire ham and egg teas in the inns. In autumn there are sweeping views of the heather-purpled moors and sometimes the Swale will justify its name, which means 'swirling river', by 'coming out' and rushing down the valley in a wall of water. Such floods swept away bridges in 1547 and 1701; and in 1925 the valley viewed from Reeth looked like a lake. In 1895 the river froze, and skaters ventured as far up as Low Row.

Reeth and Grinton are Janus gateways to upper and lower Swaledale. The narrow upper dale is the common man's country of sheep and mines – tough and wiry. Reeth, a market town

from 1695, still holds the Reeth Show on 1 September and annual autumn sheep sales. It was also the centre for the lead-mining whose shafts honeycomb the hills behind. The mines ran up Arkengarthdale to the NW, and Tan Hill, now England's highest inn, used to be offices for the mining company. At the peak of the industry there were more miners than farmers in the dale, but the importing of Spanish lead caused a speedy decline between 1880 and 1900. Strangely, a knitting industry went along with mining: men as well as women went around knitting, often smoking pipes simultaneously.

Carr's bridge of 1773 at Fremington carries the road to **Grinton** which looks down-dale towards Richmond and the gentry's world of manors and abbeys. Originally a mission church to the wild dales run by the Augustinians of Bridlington, Grinton was for long the parish church for the dale up to Keld and beyond.

The Benedictine Abbey of Marrick on the Swale bank was founded in the 12th c by Roger de Aske, an ancestor of Robert Aske who led the Pilgrimage of Grace against the suppression of the monasteries in 1536 and was hung in chains over the castle at York. The rough tower can still be seen, built into a farm turned church youth centre.

RIPLEY, *N. Yorks.*, 4m N of Harrogate. This jolly village consists of a broad planned street of the 18th c, shaded with trees and smelling all summer of strawberries and icecream, and an older cobbled square with market cross and stocks. Beyond is the 15th-c gateway to the Tudor castle, built on the site of a feudal fortress and standing in lovely grounds watered by the Nidd. The orangery, the serpentine lake and the beech walk in bluebell time are particular attractions. A stone boar on the village fountain commemorates the granting of the Ripley estate to Thomas Ingilby 700 years ago, after he had saved the king from a charging boar in Knaresborough Forest; the family have been here ever since. They are a colourful clan. In the Civil War Sir William Ingilby took his sister, Trooper Jane, to fight with him on the Royalist side; and when in his absence Oliver Cromwell demanded shelter on the night after Marston Moor his wife showed no less spirit, keeping the Roundhead general sitting up all night with two pistols trained on him, to enforce his own and his men's good behaviour. Maybe it was this incident that piqued Cromwell into adding a line to a lengthy and florid eulogy on an Ingilby monument in the church: 'No pompe or pride: let God be honoured'. In the library hangs the portrait of a priest Ingilby who no doubt hid up in the priest's hole, which was only discovered in the wainscoting of the Knight's Chamber at the top of the tower in 1963; he was caught and hanged, drawn and quartered at York. In 1827–8 the eccentric Sir William Amcotts Ingilby recast the village in Alsatian style: he replaced the thatched cottages with Gothic or Tudor stone houses, styled the village hall the *Hôtel de Ville*, and his castle the schloss and his gatekeeper the Suisse: '*Parlez au Suisse*' says the notice on the archway. All Saints Church of the 14th c replaced the one sited on the round hill (since known as Kirk Sink) which subsided into the River Nidd about 1395. Bullet marks can be seen on the E wall where Cromwell had some Royalist prisoners shot after Marston Moor, and in the churchyard is the base of a weeping cross with niches for eight penitents to kneel in.

ROBIN HOOD'S BAY, *N. Yorks.*

Did the Abbot of Whitby offer Robin Hood a king's pardon if he would rid the coast of pirates? Or did Robert, Earl of Huntingdom, choose this spot for his summer residence by shooting an arrow? Either way, this settlement is older than Robin Hood. The brown scaurs (cliffs) are full of ammonites and other fossils. The Romans used the Ravenscar cliffs for a signalling station to Scarborough; the Danes left their sign of the raven in the name. Much later came smuggling, in which it is estimated that in 1800 every single resident in the Bay was involved, and a four-foot high chamber can be seen in the Raven Hall Hotel from where a lantern beam could be shone out to a waiting lugger. Today, the annual Lyke Wake Walk, 40m across the moors from Osmotherley, ends here, and the successful participants are awarded their coffin-shaped badges.

From a muddle of inferior streets on the hill top, the main street of the Bay proper, steep and cobbled, writhes its way down the ravine which the King's Beck has cut in the red-brown headland, to where the beach starts between, on one side, the Leeds University Marine Biology Station, and on the other the wall that shores up the Bay Hotel to prevent it succumbing to the embraces of the sea as its predecessor did in 1834. All the way down one is surrounded by a jumble of houses – some jutting over the ravine – shops, cafés, chapels, packed tight together and threaded through with a mesh of steps, twisting paths and alleys. One called The Bolts was built in 1709 as a smuggler's hideaway from the excisemen, or from the press gangs.

The soft oolitic limestone cliff recedes here at the rate of six inches every two years, and in 200 years as many houses have fallen into the sea. In the 19th c perhaps a hundred boats plied from here: inshore-fishing cobles, herring boats, coal boats, coastal traders and some who went as far as the Baltic or America. Today, holiday houses, artists and writers are the source of much of the income, but the dominance of the sea is still everywhere apparent: cottage rooms and the box pews of Old St Stephen's Church of 1821 are reminiscent of ships' cabins; they tell you how in one storm the bowsprit of a ship came through the window of the previous Bay Hotel; and in the churchyard a stone bemoans:

By storms at sea two sons I lost
Which sore distresses me
Because I could not have their bones
To anchor here with me.

RUNSWICK BAY, *N. Yorks.*, 9m NW of Whitby.

A straight hill catapults the motorist down into the small car-park above the perfect half-moon bay of white sand. This is the business end of the village: boats are upended for mending and tending, and the trim readiness of the lifeboat station reminds one of the harsh realities of life in a former fishing village. Its partner, the Robin Hood's Bay lifeboat, now closed, saved 91 lives between 1831 and 1931; jet, Yorkshire's oldest industry, was mined in the Hob Holes on the S side of Runswick Bay; and inhabitants here were once gripped with superstition as black as the jet: the women killed a cat with sacrificial ritual before the return of the fleet, and children lit bonfires on the hill-top to the spirit of the wind and danced around chanting 'Souther, wind, souther: blow father home to mother'. Today, holidaymakers leave any dark thoughts with the car at the car-park and take off into fantasy. The cliff appears to have been made into an enormous rockery in which whitewashed and gaily painted cottages have replaced the rocks. A network of little mossy paths, earth or cobbled, and flights of steps appear to be playing snakes and ladders between cascades of aubretia, gold and white alyssum, pansies and sweet peas according to the season. This unique village owes so little to modern ideas of planning that it is difficult to believe the houses are full size and that it isn't a gnome's town from some children's fairy tale. In fact, all but one house slipped into the sea in 1682, but since the warning signs of the landslide were spotted by some villagers coming back from a wake, everybody escaped to return and build a similar topsy-turvy village – roses above, pantiled roofs below, the inn and, later, the Methodist chapel where the organ commemorates lifeboat coxswain Robert Patton who lost his life in a rescue in 1934, wedged in any old how among the cottages to be chanced on as one twists delightedly around the corners of the maze.

SALTAIRE, *W. Yorks.*, N of Bradford.

In 1849 Sir Titus Salt, archetype of the successful Victorian manufacturer, Mayor of Bradford and Member of Parliament, decided to leave Bradford and set up a model community associated with his new mohair and alpaca factory in Shipley Glen beside the River Aire, the Leeds–Liverpool canal and the railway. He first built his mill, which was to employ between three and four thousand people – one of the most magnificent of Victorian industrial buildings, as long as St Paul's Cathedral, massive, solid and secure, finished in the Italian Renaissance style. The houses were started in 1853, the year in which the mill was opened on Sir Titus's 50th birthday, and within 20 years Saltaire was built. The architects Lockwood and Mawson laid out the village in straight streets of sandstone houses, varying in size and elaboration with the status of the occupiers. Italian Renaissance details were used selectively, but the groupings and shape of the houses and their back yards were more typical of

Yorkshire. There were 792 houses, almshouses, churches and chapels, a hospital and school, a steam laundry that Salt specified should have the clothes washed, mangled, dried and folded within one hour, public baths and a Turkish bath, and, most important, a 14-acre park complete with bandstand to cater for the West Riding passion for brass bands, and a statue of the patriarch himself staring calmly away from the town to which he devoted the remainder of his life. He had demonstrated in stone and grass that industry and ugliness are not inseparable. He is buried in the Salt mausoleum beside the church.

STAITHES, *N. Yorks.,* 8m E of Saltburn-by-the-Sea. In its fishing heyday in the 18th c, 400 Staithes men manned 70 cobles, and 14 fishing yawls of up to 60 tons sailed from the village. With steam trawlers, the traffic moved to Whitby in the 19th c, but there are still boats fishing from Staithes and it is the fifth lobster port in the kingdom. From the 16th c alum and jet were mined here, the jet industry getting a boost in Queen Victoria's reign as suitable court jewellery during mourning. Today people are employed in ironworks, chemicals or potash. The wild seas have three times washed away the Cod and Lobster Inn. The geological structure is rough and raw, for it looks as if giant hands have torn apart the cliff like a hunk of bread, and then crammed the village between the riven walls. Everything is rivetingly uncouth: the bright blue and yellow and white paintwork is weatherbeaten and peeling against the dark red of brick and pantiles; the main cobbled street is narrow and packed with tall houses clinging together against the wind; the red-brown stained cliff running inland up the estuary from the 666ft looming bulk of Boulby Head – the second highest point on the English coastline – is dotted all over with untidy white seabirds like so much litter. But the atmosphere is wonderful and exhilarating. There are lobster pots and broken mussels lying on doorsteps; cobbled alleyways and flights of steps give exciting views of the estuary, the boats, the jam-packed houses, the inevitable Methodist chapel, the sea. Who would not prefer, instead of the ubiquitous tourists' souvenirs, to buy a gull's egg, smooth with brown splodges, or a prickly sea urchin for which some local lad has just climbed or dived? On the harbour is the cottage where Captain Cook lodged when, at the age of 13, he was apprenticed to William Sanderson, grocer and haberdasher. The miracle moment to catch in Staithes is when overcast skies over the dark sodden cliffs give way to sunlight, the cliffs dry out and become gleaming white, and sea and village start to scintillate. Not surprisingly, artists, such as Dame Laura Knight, have drawn here; and writers, too, such as George du Maurier, who was so fascinated by the local headgear – frilly bonnets often pink or mauve or green for the women, and high-crowned hats for the men – that he used the men's hats in the first stage productions of *Trilby,* thereby launching the trilby hat.

Geoffrey N. Wright

Staithes

THORNTON DALE, *N. Yorks.,* 2m E of Pickering. Although it is the tourist heart along the stream that earns Thornton Dale its reputation as the loveliest village in Yorkshire, exploration of the fringes reveal interesting indications of past history. An area of scrappy modern development off the Pickering road has nevertheless alleys and passages often ending in surprising flowering backyards; a road, dusty with straw wisps, that climbs between worn stone cottages at the back of Lady Lumley's one-storey almshouses of 1657 towards the old mill area suggests older farming origins; and the terraced street leading to Scarborough wears an industrial aspect with no planting and high urban development.

Thornton Beck swirls through the village in a great S-shape. The cottages and Georgian villas are strung out usually along one side of the stream only, with gardens or the road on the other, necessitating pretty little bridges of stone or white-painted wood every thirty yards or so to give entry to the houses; intriguingly, the houses swap backwards and forwards from N to S bank as the shallow beck darts swiftly through past the blacksmith's and under the road. The church stands on a hill on the Scarborough road, close to the bridge and opposite Thornton Hall, now a hotel; the graveyard is perched atop a high wall, a good 6ft above the ground.

TICKHILL, *S. Yorks.,* 4m W of Bawtry. Licensed for tourneys by Richard I, Tickhill

Castle was one of a chain of Norman castles, with its neighbours Conisborough and Pontefract. Unlike Conisborough, the village has managed to preserve its identity in this gritty mining area, although the villagers say it has been badly mauled by uncontrolled development in the last two decades. Other than the timber-framed St Leonard's Hospital of 1470 in Northgate, the Maison Dieu almshouses believed to be founded by John of Gaunt, and a curious domed market cross standing on eight pillars in the market square, the most interesting features are to be found in the old area called the Lindricks. Here can be seen the high mound (above a 30ft ditch) on which the castle stood, together with the remains of the 12th-c curtain walling, pierced by a gatehouse that has a five-light Elizabethan window and a fireplace still in its upstairs room, but no roof. All are overgrown with trees and ivy. Before the castle ruins lies an unusually extensive millpond in a pleasant green and scented area; this is a popular place for people from the nearby industrial towns to sit and watch the ducklings scull across the glassy surface. The beautiful 14th-c Augustinian Friary on the Maltby road has for long been a private house, lived in first by Nicholas Booth, servant to the Earl of Shrewsbury, much later by Sheffield's Master Cutler, and now divided into two houses; look out for the monk's head on the gatepost. At the church of St Mary's, with its 124ft tower, a grand concert of birdsong and occasional outbreaks like 'The Minstrel Boy' and 'Home Sweet Home' on the bells keep the air sweet. The church has large aisle windows and is flooded with light. A Fitzwilliam knight with his lady adorn the top of a tomb in Italian Renaissance style; and there is the very moving alabaster tomb of Louisa Folijambe. She married in 1869 and died in childbirth two years later with the birth of this little second son; she lies with the baby in her arms under a rich braided cover under whose ample folds the inscription running round the side of the monument disappears in tantalizing fashion.

TONG, S. Yorks. Just over the Leeds boundary on the W side, Tong is basically one 18th-c street with Tong Hall of 1702 and the striking Georgian church of St James, both built by Sir George Tempest, grouped with the vicarage, gardens and cottages at one end. The village has been extended with considerable new building, sympathetically carried out in contemporary versions of local style of the period. The Hall is of brick, tall, with a three-bay centre front, approached up a short narrowing flight of steps with wrought-iron balustrades, and with a sundial by Henry Gyles in stained glass showing the sun and the four seasons over the front door. It is open as a museum at weekends. The vicarage, known as the Old Lantern House because of its lantern finials, which signified that it was exempt from taxes, once belonged to the Knights of St John of Jerusalem, who kept a hospital near Halifax.

Across the valley towards Pudsey can be seen the frontage of the **Fulneck** Moravian school strung out along a ridge of the hill, the chapel at the heart of the brick-fronted central block flanked on either side by the stone blocks that originally sheltered the communities of 'sisters' and 'brothers', and now house the girls' and boys' schools. This curiosity of a village, consisting of a single plain and worthy street, was built by the evangelistic sect from 1742 onwards as a self-sufficient settlement, complete down to its bake-houses and weaving sheds. Today one shop remains, and a dressmaker's quaintly labelled 'Seamstress'. A gate at one end leads into a graveyard like an orchard: under the trees the stones lie deep in grass and wild flowers. The motto 'Sure and Steadfast' with an anchor over a doorway recalls more rigid times, and old scholars remember the regular half-hour walk before and after Sunday chapel up and down the terrace 'but no further than the holly bush'. Colourful traditions are retained in the school, such as the nativity celebration of Christingles when the children sing carols and carry an orange to symbolize the world and a candle to symbolize Christ, light of the world. (*See illustration on page 63.*)

WEST TANFIELD, N. Yorks., 5m NW of Ripon. From under the three-arched bridge, dated 1734, which carries the Ripon road across the Ure, there is a magical view of West Tanfield, a row of cottages backing down to the river – a lovely patchwork composition of whitewash, yellow stone, mossy orange pantiles, further enhanced by gabled extensions in brick and wood and by tufty gardens. To the left rises the Perp tower of St Nicholas Church, and very close to it, 'just avoiding looking at one another' says Pevsner, the embattled gatehouse with turret stair and oriel window, which is all that remains of the manor house of the Marmions who came here in 1215. There are some lovely houses in this charming row approaching the church, where rooks caw in the trees and gardens are bright with flowers. Sir Walter Scott took only the name of his chivalrous hero, Lord Marmion of Flodden Field, from this family, but former knightly Marmions in state and alabaster stock the church, along with a handsome hearse over the burial place of Sir Robert de Marmion and his wife Laura, whose candle-prickets have inspired the modern gates on the porch, and carved wooden bench ends, one of a monk playing a harp. In 1871 a Miss Elizabeth Clarke of Tanfield Hall married Rookes Evelyn Bell Crompton, a pioneer of electricity. He set a waterwheel between the bank and an island in the Ure to drive a generator for his in-laws; his London home was the first in the land to be lit by electricity, and he later illuminated Buckingham Palace and Windsor, and started a supply system in Vienna.

A stream runs down the main street of **Well,** to the N, home of the Latimer family, one of whom, according to local legend, once bravely slew the dragon of Well; it is said that here were once the biggest Roman baths in Britain outside Bath itself, and legend survives in a ghostly manor house.

The North-East

CLEVELAND DURHAM TYNE AND WEAR NORTHUMBERLAND

Lyall Wilkes

Cleveland is a county of magnificent sea-cliff scenery – indeed the name Cleveland originally meant 'Cliffland'; and behind the sea cliffs there is much moorland with hard ironstone rock underneath, which with the salt of the ancient underground salt lakes enabled the iron and steel industry of Teesside to be founded. This ironstone sometimes gives the moorland streams a reddish colour. It is this hard rock with a limestone resistant to sea erosion which forms the high cliff scenery, notably between Boulby and Staithes, to a height of 660 feet – the highest cliffs throughout the whole length of the east coast of England. The interior landscape is terraced with a strong horizontal emphasis – flat-topped hills and crags and waterfalls formed of the limestone outcrops.

There must (one assumes) be good reason for the boundary lines of the new County of Cleveland. But they seem to have been drawn so as to exclude nearly all villages of architectural quality and coherence. Staithes is a few hundred yards outside the new boundary, as is Great Ayton. Hutton Rudby is also excluded, and one is tempted to describe the delightful little town of Yarm as a village – which spiritually it is, consisting as it does of one splendid brick street of mostly three-storeyed eighteenth- and early nineteenth-century houses. However, despite the village atmosphere, the presence of a market and a Town Hall rule it out.

The ancient capital of Cleveland, with its fourteenth-century priory, is Guisborough. But well outside the present county boundaries are villages with names like Carlton-in-Cleveland, Kirkby-in-Cleveland and others, reminding one that the historic region of Cleveland from the seventeenth century onwards was a much bigger region than the present county, and included even Stokesley.

But Cleveland is still a county of contrasts. Although most of the Cleveland Hills are outside the new county they form an impressive background, especially to the south. There is much moorland, and if the coastal resort of Saltburn, with its fine cliff scenery and large dignified Victorian hotels near the railway station, soon deteriorates to the north into a vast caravan site on clifftop and valley, that is apparently what the twentieth century demands. And since Cleveland is proud of its massive investment in steel, chemicals, oil and nuclear power, the landscape at Wilton and that to be seen from the A19 between Stockton and Middlesbrough is Satanic beyond anything which William Blake could have imagined. The strange thing is that only a quarter of a mile away from the Blakean landscape of Wilton lies the village of Kirkleatham – a fragile architectural gem. No greater contrast between the seventeenth and the twentieth century could be imagined.

If it is the steel and chemical industries and new industries based on twentieth-century technology that now threaten Kirkleatham and other areas of Cleveland, the Durham coalfield has provided in the past the same threat to many a Durham village. But Durham is a bigger county than the new Cleveland, the coal industry is declining, and fortunately for the landscape the coal reserves are concentrated between the centre and the coastal areas in the east, leaving a vast area of the Pennines and the moorlands of north-west Durham almost untouched by industrialism.

It is therefore quite wrong to regard Durham – as so many people do – as a mining county. That is part of the story, but only part. Durham can be divided into three landscapes; first, the coalfield extending from the centre to the east coast, then the north-west Durham Pennines and moorlands around Stanhope to beyond Allenheads and St John's Chapel, and third, the south-west of the county where the landscape around Staindrop and Gainford and Barnard Castle reflects the greater fertility of the land and the greater wealth of the community, giving rise to more ornate building and an eighteenth-century grace.

Some idea of the extent of the open spaces of County Durham can be seen when approaching Blanchland from Hexham, with the Pennines looming ahead, and even more vividly from the road leading from Allenheads to Cowshill, and then from St John's Chapel, taking the road down to Langdon Beck, Cronkley Fell, and Middleton-in-Teesdale, or by taking the Blanchland road to Rookhope. These great expanses of Pennine and moorland country are as wild as any parts of Exmoor, Yorkshire or Derbyshire. Indeed the dark grey dolerite rock of Cronkley Fell and elsewhere gives the Durham moorlands in storm and cloud a particularly dark and forbidding appearance which some may find romantic and others too severe for their taste.

Durham is second only to Northumberland as a centre of Christian religion and art. If the Lindisfarne Gospels and the earliest Christian missionaries were Northumbrian, Bede's History and the earliest Norman cathedral (begun in AD 1093) have their origin in what is now Durham County. But when St Cuthbert lived and died there was, of course, no County Durham because Northumberland meant literally what it said, and included all land north of the Humber to Edwinsburgh (Edinburgh). It was not until the twelfth century that Durham began to assume an identity of its own through the growing power and independence of the Bishops of Durham, who ruled like princes, with their own coinage and courts. Even now, parts of Northumberland such as Bedlingtonshire are still within the See of Durham, and even Norham until 1844 was part of what was called North Durham, although it was on the Scottish border. And still the most spectacular sight that Durham offers is that of the cathedral and castle on its rock high above the River Wear. Pevsner says that for something comparable one has to go to Avignon or Prague.

Although the people of Durham have more in common with the people of Northumberland in speech and temperament – especially the Northumbrian and Durham miners who share an almost common dialect with words derived from the Norse – building in County Durham is frequently closer in character to that of North Yorkshire (for example, Sedgefield, Hurworth, Gainford and Staindrop – q.v.) than to that of Northumberland, for Durham, like Yorkshire, is a mixed stone and brick county, with marble from Frosterley in addition, while Northumberland is almost entirely a county of stone, mostly sandstone of a beautiful soft grey colour. This is the stone which built Hadrian's Wall, the medieval castles and the fortified walls of Newcastle and Berwick as well as the villages. This is the stone which mostly built the dry-stone walls which in north Northumberland so largely take the place of hedges.

With a few exceptions, such as around Staindrop, Lambton and Lumley, Durham is a county of small farmers, whereas Northumberland, far from being dominated by the coalfield, as southerners believe, is still a county of great landowners. Northumbrians are fortunate in still being able to

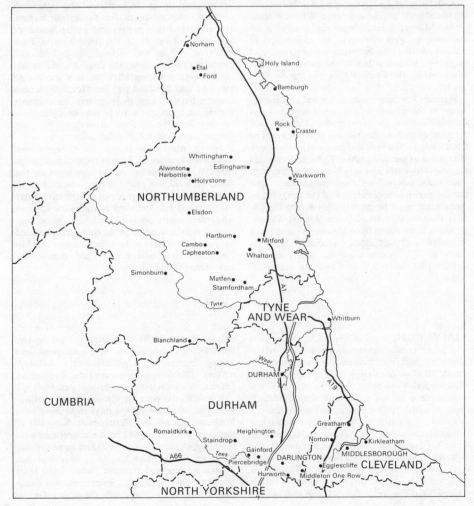

live on the landscape capital of the eighteenth and nineteenth centuries; and it shows in the great beeches, oaks and limes which make the lowland farms often look like parkland.

The famous sheep runs of the Cheviots provide a springy turf that make these rounded hills, green to their summits up to 2600 feet, the best walking country in England, where you can walk all day without meeting even a shepherd. The finer Cheviot grass pasture in contrast to the heather and rougher grass of the Pennines, gives to the rounded Cheviots a softness and more varied colour. The Cheviot hills, even in the worst weather, never appear hostile.

Northumberland, being the fifth largest county in England (70 miles long by 47 miles wide) has scope for an immense variety of scene between the Tweed at the north, the Tyne at the south, the Cheviot range at the west, and the North Sea at the east. The coalfield is mostly on or near the coastal plain, extending inland only for about twelve miles or so, and no further north than Amble, leaving the beaches unspoilt and overlooked by great castles such as Bamburgh and Dunstanburgh on their dolerite Whin Sill outcrops. Moving inland from the coastal plain and making for the centre you are soon in upland country, with large farms, wide horizons, and sweeping views. Further to the north and west you come to the Cheviot hills and the Scottish border.

Mention has been made of the military monuments to Northumbria's troubled history – its Roman Wall and the great medieval castles. But the great churches – St Aidan's at Bamburgh, St Cuthbert's at Norham and many others – speak of another aspect altogether. These churches are not only very early and very Northumbrian, with their squat towers, but their magnificence and size for parish churches speak of the pride felt in the fact that from the conversions made by Paulinus at Holystone in AD 627, and from St Aidan's arrival at Lindisfarne from Iona in 635, and from the mission of St Cuthbert from 664 until his death in 687, Northumberland had been the earliest and most active Christian centre in England, culminating in the first English Christian King, Oswald of Northumbria – later St Oswald. Embedded in many of the Norman churches are signs of the earlier Saxon church on the site, and these early churches and the monastic communities in Lindisfarne and Monkwearmouth were the centres not only of Christian life but were the source of the art of Northumbria's golden age in the eighth and ninth centuries – the Lindisfarne Gospels and other books, the sophistication and beauty of the carving on the Anglian and Saxon crosses, the Saxon churches, the work in silver and metal, and much else.

Signs of the difficult days ahead came with the beginning of the Danish raids on Lindisfarne in 793, which eventually in 875 compelled the monks to leave, carrying the coffin of St Cuthbert, the head of St Oswald, the bones of Aidan, their books and works of art, until they found a secure resting place in Durham over which the Cathedral was built. But it is the raids by the Scots and the general insecure state of the northern border which moulded the unique character of Northumbrian architecture up to the middle of the eighteenth century – the castles and fortified manor houses, the numerous pele towers and bastle houses of humbler folk built for the protection of their cattle as well as the villagers themselves. The predatory raids between the English and Scottish clans continued long after the two crowns of England and Scotland had been formally united under a Scottish king in 1603, and this accounts for the rarity of any seventeenth- or eighteenth-century building in Northumberland built for private delight rather than for defence.

Northumberland is famous for its beef farms, its sheep, its castles, its Roman remains and camps (notably at Corbridge and Housesteads on the Wall) its coal, its grey building stone, and its beaches; but its most precious commodity today lies in its solitude and silences and in the Cheviot wilderness where herds of wild goat can still be seen. It is to be hoped that the cold east winds and the size of the county will prevent tourism doing to Northumberland what it has already done to the Lake District and Cornwall.

GAZETTEER

BAMBURGH, *Northumberland.* Even for those who avoid coastal resorts and who have never quite recovered from their own or their children's seaside holidays Bamburgh must always be something special. First of all, it does not look like a seaside place. It has a pleasant sloping village street of mostly 19th-c houses and shops leading away from the castle to the triangular well-treed village green (called The Grove) ending near St Aidan's Church; secondly, whether due to the influence of Lord Armstrong or to some oversight, there are no amusement arcades, no bingo, no cheap cafés, no 'front', and no development at all (except for a few villas down the Wyndings) to detract from its village quality. Yet the nearby beaches are unexcelled, the hotels are good, and during the season the place is full of holidaymakers. The village has escaped the devastation gratuitously inflicted on Seahouses nearby.

It would have been scandalous if it were otherwise, for from early Saxon days there have been Kings and Saints and Castles here. King Ida of Bernicia in about AD 547 built a timber castle on the precipitous rock rising 150 feet from the sea. This earliest Christian kingdom, with St Aidan a close adviser and frequent visitor from Holy Island to King Oswald at Bamburgh, was under attack sometimes from Penda the pagan King of

Geoffrey N. Wright

Bamburgh Castle – 'perhaps the most tremendous spectacle of its kind in Britain'

Mercia and sometimes from the Welsh Cadwallader. Bede describes in his *History*, completed in AD 731, how Penda's men carried to Bamburgh a vast quantity of timber, brushwood and thatch and set fire to the timbered walls of the castle, and how Aidan from Farne Island, seeing the rising columns of smoke and flame, appealed to God and 'no sooner had he spoken than the winds shifted away from the city and drove back the flames on to those who had kindled them, so unnerving them that they abandoned their assault on a city so clearly under God's protection'.

The keep of the present stone castle, which is open to the public, is Norman. Few would dissent from Dr Thomas Sharp's opinion that it presents 'perhaps the most tremendous spectacle of its kind in Britain – dominating everything for miles around'. Yet a great deal of what one finds so breathtaking is a late 19th-c restoration by Lord Armstrong. (*See colour plate facing page 353.*)

Bamburgh, as the former seat of kings, so preserved its importance in spite of destruction by Dane and Norman, that in the Parliament of Edward I it sent two Members to Westminster. The only other Northumbrian towns represented were Corbridge and Newcastle. Even now, in the days of its lost grandeur, looking across the Grove to church and castle the sense of history remains. A house nearby carries a plaque saying 'Grace Darling died here', and is close to another one bearing the date 1692. At the church end of the village is a high late-17th-c wall built of Dutch brick, perhaps the garden wall of a house which has long disappeared, although it may be that it was the garden wall of the house of the Forster family opposite, which now has an attractive Georgian façade.

St Aidan's Church is so called because Aidan died in the Saxon church on the same site during a visit to King Oswald. There is no trace of this Saxon church, but the place of his death is marked inside the church. The nave of the church, with its two arcades of four arches springing from round pillars, dates from about 1170. As a parish church its magnificence in Northumberland is equalled only by Norham.

An effigy of Grace Darling is in the transept and to the W of the church is her monument, a few yards from her grave. Almost directly across the road is the Grace Darling Museum.

BLANCHLAND, *Northumberland.* There can be few (if any) English villages more beautiful than Blanchland; quite simply, it is too beautiful for its own good. Yet what the visitor now sees is not the grey stone medieval village it seems to be, but the restoration and repair carried out by Lord Crewe's Trustees from 1752 onwards, which kept to the collegiate layout of the medieval abbey and its buildings.

John Wesley preached in the village, and in his journal of 24 March 1747 wrote that 'the little town was little more than a heap of ruins'. This was partly the result of the raids by the Scots who had burnt the buildings, and partly the result of the dissolution of the Abbey in 1539 from which date the Abbey and the village had stood ruinous and roofless until 1752.

The abbey church was founded shortly after 1165, when the Praemonstratensian Order (a Norman order of monks of great strictness and self-denial) established themselves in Blanchland. The Order dressed in white robes and it is thought that this gave the village its name of Blanchland (Blanca Land or Whiteland).

The choir and the nave of the abbey were built in 1225 without transepts, aisles, or tower. Little is left of this 13th-c building except the N and S walls of the choir, the remains of the cloisters in the garden of the Lord Crewe Arms, and the ground floor walls of the inn itself, formerly the Abbey refectory and guest house. The tower was not completed until the 14th c; the font is Norman. Inside the abbey the tower arch is particularly fine. One of the early grave covers inside is shown to have been a woman's by the symbolic scissors carved on the stone; a huntsman's grave is carved with his hunting horn, his shield, arrow and sword; and the graves of two abbots, each with his pastoral staff, are inset nearby.

The present inn is, as already mentioned, on the site of the abbey refectory and guest house. The village consists of a series of L-shaped courtyards, mostly rebuilt in the 18th c. From the N you enter the village by the old gatehouse and from the S you enter by the beautiful bridge over the Derwent. The village is surrounded by fine moorland scenery and is well hidden in the valley, so that suddenly you come upon it without warning – an experience to be remembered.

CAMBO, *Northumberland,* 12m W of Morpeth. This delightful stone village was created as a model estate village by the Trevelyan family of Wallington Hall. Although it looks all of a period the replacement of the former medieval village (Camhoe) took from 1730, when Sir Walter Blackett demolished most of the old village and chapel, through to 1842 when the present church was built, right down to 1911 when Sir George Otto Trevelyan converted the old schoolhouse (to which Capability Brown had walked from nearby Kirkharle) into a village hall. Perhaps the greatest builder of Cambo was Sir Charles Edward Trevelyan, who added the tower to the church in 1883, cleared many old buildings away to make way for the present gardens and the village green, and built the Dolphin Fountain at the corner (dolphins are the supporters of the Trevelyan coat of arms). In 1941 Sir Charles Trevelyan gave Wallington and its large estates to the National Trust.

Although the village is by the side of the B6342 road, the sense of peace and quiet is total, perhaps because the village is enclosed in the shape of a rectangle, and, being sited on the ridge of a hill, the road lies below. The views over the countryside – especially from the little terrace of houses beginning with the post office (housed in the old pele tower) as far as the old vicarage – are particularly fine.

Near to this is the South Terrace (or Front Row) with the two larger houses having stone porches at each end. The one at the W end had been a coaching inn called The Two Queens, but when Sir Walter Trevelyan inherited the estate in 1846, he closed it down. Sir Walter was a temperance advocate who alarmed his relatives and visitors to Wallington, the great house 1m away from Cambo, by his often expressed intention to empty the contents of one of the best cellars in England into the Wansbeck. His wife Pauline made Wallington a Pre-Raphaelite centre in Northumberland, and it was there that Ruskin, Effie and John Millais stayed before setting off on their ill-starred Scottish journey in 1853. Wallington attracted many of the leading writers and artists of the day including Rossetti and Ruskin to this part of Northumberland. One of these, although living only 4m away, was the poet Algernon Charles Swinburne. He used often to ride over from Capheaton to Wallington and stay there. Until her early death Pauline gave Swinburne good advice about his behaviour and his mode of life, which, needless to say, he did not take.

Approaching **Capheaton** by crossing the A696 and taking a minor signposted road you pass under the best avenue of beeches in Northumberland before reaching the little estate village. The post office and general shop is at the corner of the village nearest the great gates of Capheaton designed, as was the Hall itself, by that eccentric genius in stone, Robert Trollope. The Hall is a highly decorated 17th-c masterpiece, but not to be seen by visitors except on special days, though Sir Edwin's great lake, designed by Capability Brown, is there to be seen by everyone. Past the terrace of estate houses there is a pleasant walk with the lake in view and to the right a Strawberry Hill Gothick tower.

CRASTER, *Northumberland,* 7m NE of Alnwick. Approaching Craster from Denwick, after leaving the A1, you will come to a castellated gateway across the road, an 18th-c folly built to set off nearby Craster Tower, the 14th-c pele tower house (seat of the Craster family), Georgianized and Gothickized in the 18th c. Pele towers are particularly common in this area (e.g. Dunstan and Rock) and were probably watch towers for the defence of Dunstanburgh Castle.

Craster is a rugged fishing village of character. The best view is from the harbour wall, the encircling line of cottages contrasting with the dramatic outline of Dunstanburgh on the pillared crags of the Whin Sill only 1m N. This largest of all Northumbria's castles was begun in 1313. Even when completed it would not have looked more spectacular than the jagged outline of its ruin.

One of the best short walks in Northumberland is the grassy walk by the cliff edge to Dunstanburgh; another, almost as fine, is the approach over the sand from Embleton. (Nobody should leave Craster without buying the locally smoked kipper – the best in England.)

Some 4m inland is **Rock**. It is easy to miss the village, which is down a narrow road to the left of the trees on the green. There is a landscaped lake on the left and a stone bridge over the stream which runs into it. On the other side of the road is a long row of picturesque mid-Victorian cottages with dormer windows (not unlike Matfen) with village green running in front. These are the estate cottages of the Bosanquet family, who bought the estate from the Salkelds in 1804. The green is bisected by the school built in 1855 as the square stone tablet on it indicates. Below this is a stone from the demolished building on the site, which bears the date 1623 and the Salkeld initials.

At the far end of the row is the post office. Opposite is an extremely small and beautiful church. The W doorway and the chancel arch are Norman and date from about 1170 and carry fine zigzag ornamentation: inside there is a memorial to Charles Bosanquet (1769–1850) who restored the church from a ruinous condition before Anthony Salvin's restoration of 1855. The Salkelds were a Royalist family and on the S wall of the chancel is a memorial to Colonel John Salkeld's 'constant, dangerous, and expensive loyalty'.

Exactly opposite the Norman doorway of the church is Rock Hall, incorporating a 15th-c pele tower, a Jacobean house, and a 19th-c addition by John Dobson. Approached through a rusticated 17th-c gateway the front bears the arms of the Salkelds and a sundial. It is now a Youth Hostel. The village is a delight and stirs the imagination.

EGGLESCLIFFE, *Cleveland.* This little known but rewarding village is not to be missed, although it is so difficult to find. Approaching it from Teesside on the A66, or from Darlington on the A67, you must turn sharply left off the road at the Blue Bell Inn, just before you reach the five-arched 15th-c bridge over the Tees into Yarm. You will see, high up above the river, half hidden by trees, the tower of St Mary's Church. This marks the site of the village. If there were cypresses instead of native English trees around the tower it would remind you of a hill village in Italy.

The best approach is by the path leading from the side of the Blue Bell up to the village, but before setting out on foot go to the rear of the inn, where tables are set in summer high above the river, and over a drink admire the view of the double line of arches – the five arches of the bridge and immediately above them the 43 arches of the viaduct, 2250ft long, completed in 1849. Up the path to the village St Mary's emerges on your left as you near the top; just past the church the path turns to the left and the village, with its delightful 18th-c and early 19th-c houses, gradually reveals itself. The second house you come to is the small 18th-c inn, the Pot and Glass. Immediately on your left, nearly hidden by trees, is the brick 18th-c rectory.

The large green is rectangular and banked, with many trees. A great variety of old village houses surrounds it on three sides, with all shapes and sizes of porches, windows and fanlights. Pear Tree House on the E side of the green was the former village shop, and next to it at the corner is The Fold, which, as its name implies, was the site of an animal pound or penfold. The village is fortunate in that there is no through road for vehicles.

Having admired the scene from one of the seats on the green you walk on to what is apparently the end of the village, but the path narrows and turns left and leads to the sad ruin of the still dignified 17th-c Old Hall, on the right.

On such an evocative hill site as this it is not surprising that there was a pre-Norman church before the present one; part of the Anglian cross shaft found in the buttress of the N wall and now in the porch is only one pointer to this. The S doorway is Norman, but the tower and most of what we now see from the outside is 15th-c. The chancel arch is 13th-c, but the most striking feature of the interior is the elaborate 17th-c woodwork in the Cosin Durham manner – the pews are divided by balusters, the screen has acanthus leaves and cherubs' heads, while the choir stalls have swags of fruit, poppy heads and balusters. Two effigies of cross-legged knights of the 13th c complete a handsome interior.

ELSDON, *Northumberland* (3½m E of Otterburn), is in the middle of moorland country that is desolate or magnificent according to taste, with Cheviot in the background. It consists of 18th- or early 19th-c houses facing a large triangular green, the 14th-c church of St Cuthbert, the fortified parsonage or Vicar's Pele, and the massive Mote Hills at the head of the village to the E of the Elsdon Burn. It was the capital of Redesdale – and indeed in earlier centuries was the largest settled community of this wild region. The Rev. Dodgson, later Bishop of Ossory, one of several rectors (1762–5) of intellectual distinction who have occupied the splendid Pele House, wrote 'Elsdon was once a market town, as some say, and a city according to others'. Professor G. M. Trevelyan wrote that Elsdon 'remains today as the spiritual capital of the Middle Marches – the capital of Redesdale when neither Scotland nor England existed'.

But the Mote Hills, although providing a fine site for the Norman timber motte-and-bailey castle built about AD 1080, take one back to Celtic and Saxon times as a seat of government. They are truly spectacular – the N hill is 63ft, the S hill 70ft above the burn, both fortified by earth ramparts respectively 60ft and 50ft wide, and 15ft and 12ft in height. Throughout the area are traces of large pre-Roman settlements, such as hill forts, ditches, earthworks, prehistoric cairns and large stones.

The Middle Marches, consisting primarily of Redesdale, Tynedale and Coquetdale, were synonymous with murder, plunder, and clan war. The system established in 1249 whereby wardens on both sides of the border were under oath to examine complaints and if justified to arrest the wrongdoer and bring him to trial at a time and place agreed by the Scottish and English wardens, did little to control the lawlessness.

William of Normandy gave Robert de Umfraville the duty of pacifying Redesdale and Tynedale, and the arms of the Umfravilles are still to be seen on the Vicar's Pele and inside the church. The present church was built in about AD 1400 just before the Vicar's Pele was built. What was on the site before this is uncertain but, as Tomlinson points out, there are signs of an earlier Norman church – two pilasters of about 1100 in the W gable, and two small round-headed windows in the W ends of the aisles. In 1810 against the N wall of the nave the bones of 100 men were discovered in double rows, 'with the skull of one row within the thigh bones of the other' and in 1877 1000 skulls were uncovered. These were men killed at the Battle of Otterburn and conveyed to Elsdon for mass burial in consecrated ground. Even more unexpected was the discovery in 1877 of a box containing the skeletons of three horses' heads inside the spire which tops the large square bell turret. Since the sacrifice of a horse was second only in solemnity to the sacrifice of a human being, Tomlinson suggests that a pagan form of sanctification of the building took place.

Elsdon Parsonage, sometimes called Elsdon Castle, is an impressive example of a large Northumbrian pele. The first floor is barrel-vaulted and there is a pitched roof instead of the more usual flat one. It ceased to be inhabited by the rector in 1962 and has been transformed since then into a most delectable country residence.

Walking round the green you pass a house with the figure of Bacchus in front which was once an inn. The church on the green is almost hidden from view by trees – a strange contrast with the Rev. Dodgson's complaint in the 1760s: 'There is not a single tree or hedgerow within twelve miles to break the force of the wind.' It is difficult to realize the former isolation of Elsdon since today it is only 1m from the A696 to Carter Bar, and good motor roads to Rothbury and Cambo and Otterburn now dissect its green instead of mud tracks over the moorland wastes. Whatever its isolation and however bloody its history it has been a place where for over 400 years shepherds and scholars have lived and shared hardship and danger.

ETAL, *Northumberland, 7m E of Cornhill-on-Tweed.* Some consider estate villages lifeless as compared with those that have developed naturally through many centuries. I do not think anyone could find Cambo (q.v.) lifeless, and Etal represents the self-conscious creation of an idyll that is perfect – 'too perfect', I can hear perfectionists mutter. At one end of the village Lord Joicey's 18th-c manor house closes the view, with Butterfield's St Mary's Church (1858) in the grounds just to the W of the house. In the chapel is a monument to an illegitimate son of King William IV, Lord Fitzclarence, whose widow, Lady Augusta Fitzclarence, lived at Etal. From the manor-house grounds very pleasant village houses line both sides of the street (five of them still thatched – a rarity in Northumberland), as well as an inn and a post office, down to the other end where Etal Castle closes the view. This original house of the Manners family was crenallated in 1341, only three years after nearby Ford Castle, evidence not only of the rivalry between the Manners and the Heron families but of the undoubted need for further strongholds against the Scots. The overwhelming defeat suffered by King James IV of Scotland at Flodden in 1513 makes one overlook the Scots' success at the beginning of the campaign, when Etal, Ford and Norham castles were taken.

Sufficient of the gatehouse tower with guard-room and vaulted chamber, and the four-storeyed keep or dwelling place with stairway and arched ribs, remains to show what a substantial second line of defence Etal was. The Manners' coat of arms is still above the gatehouse entrance. The castle is only a few yards from the River Till, very wide and beautiful at this point with a ford and a weir where the salmon leap spectacularly each year.

FORD, *Northumberland, 6m E of Cornhill-on-Tweed.* Those whose feelings are divided about estate villages can have a healthy argument about Ford, 1m from Etal. The steeply gabled Victorian

Kenneth Scowen
The pele tower of Elsdon parsonage

houses are certainly not Northumbrian in feeling at all. Thomas Sharp calls the village 'singularly unpleasant, being a bit of 19th-c suburban Surrey planted into these foreign parts'. Tomlinson, who was writing shortly after the houses were built, says, 'a sweeter little village than Ford could scarcely be imagined.'

The village is sited on a rising slope just out of sight of the castle and church. The green spaces and the gardens reconcile me to it as a period piece and an interesting reflection of late-Victorian taste. It is the creation of Louisa, Marchioness of Waterford. Lady Waterford was related to the Delavals who willed Ford to her, and when her husband in 1859 left her a young widow she retired there, with enough money to remodel the castle and build the village, and with enough energy and social ambition to entertain a wide circle of friends ranging from members of the Royal Family to John Ruskin and Augustus Hare.

The school is dated 1860 and over the next 22 years Lady Waterford covered the walls with large watercolours that can be viewed. They depict Biblical scenes but were something of a communal village effort for the people depicted are all portraits of the villagers and local friends, including the Vicar. Many visitors come to the school not expecting very much, or to scoff, but leave strangely moved. Ruskin was not impressed: 'I expected', he wrote, 'you would have done something better.'

Ford Castle has lost much of its original architectural interest through the 18th-c Strawberry Hill Gothick remodelling by the Delavals, which in its turn was mostly destroyed by Lady Waterford between 1861 and 1863. It is however an impressive looking fortress set on a commanding height, and because the original evocative design of four massive towers at each corner of a high curtain walled rectangle has been retained, few realize that with the exception of the N tower (King James's Tower), and the SW tower, which are both original, most of what is seen today is 19th-c. Spectacular views of Flodden Field and the surrounding countryside can be obtained from the castle, which is now used as an Adult Education Centre.

St Michael's Church is 18th-c. Near the church is a large Vicar's pele with walls 9ft thick, described in 1725, as a house 'strong and convenient', but now, alas, ruinous.

GAINFORD, *Durham,* 6m E of Barnard Castle. Few villages hide their beauty as successfully as Gainford. The busy A67 road to Darlington runs through it, and what one can see of Gainford from it is prosaic or downright ugly. Only a few know that by turning off the road down a narrow path by the Cross Keys they will come to a large village green surrounded on all four sides by 18th-c houses, with a late Norman church on the S side, very close to the steep bank of the River Tees.

There was a Saxon stone church on the site of the present 13th-c church, and during the 1864 restoration work a great quantity of Saxon stones were found in the church tower, and also Roman stones used in the building of the present church, brought from Piercebridge (q.v.). These included an altar dedicated to Jupiter and a stone marked LEG. VI V, now in Durham Cathedral.

After the dissolution of St Mary's Abbey by Henry VIII the King gave the tithes and the patronage of the living to Trinity College, Cambridge, and eight former vicars of Gainford have been Fellows of Trinity College. One of them, Dr Edlestone, was vicar from 1862 to 1895, and from the rear of the churchyard you can see the column his son brought from Stanwick to the garden of Edleston House. He was also in the habit of burying in the same garden, with much ceremony, any of his stud of 50 racehorses for whom he felt particular affection. He was Consul in the north for the Republic of San Marino, and bore the title of Baron Montalbo. After savouring from the churchyard the visible signs of clerical family eccentricity (worthy of a Trollope novel surely), there is a fine river walk to be enjoyed from the churchyard along the bank of the Tees.

The enclosed nature of the village was for defence – the Scots came down even further S than Gainford – for stock could be quickly brought within what amounted to a pen. And the enclosed character of the village has helped to defend it against much of the worst that the 20th c can do – with one or two exceptions.

If defence was the first purpose of the village, the second – with bad roads and no regular transport off the main coaching routes – was self-sufficiency. Today many in Gainford work in Darlington or Barnard Castle, but up to the Railway Age this was impossible. An 1856 Directory lists in Gainford five bootmakers, three blacksmiths, two tailors, and many other trades, although the population then was only about 700. An old lady told Mrs N. Deas (to whom I am much indebted for her permission to use information from her admirable *Brief History of Gainford*) that she remembers Mr and Mrs O'Neill who sat at the Market Cross and mended pots and pans.

The green slopes downward from High Green at the N to Low Green. To the W of the green is High Row, a curved terrace of 18th-c houses, some of them quite big, with impressive doorways, and others in the Row simple artisans' cottages – but nearly all with beautiful fanlights or some other attractive feature. Perhaps the cottages were for the servants of the family living in the adjacent larger houses? Whatever the reason for these variations in size the effect is both intimate and dignified as one walks past the doorways along the raised terrace which separates the houses from their gardens.

High Row ends at the Cross Keys Inn, and the terrace of High Green begins just over the road. These houses are the largest and architecturally the most important in Gainford, although some may prefer the intimacy of High Row to the grandeur of High Green.

We can no longer avert our gaze from the four modern houses built on Low Green in the late 1950s. All the other houses front the green, and their pleasant faces contribute to the green's beauty. However, these four recently built houses present their *ends* to the green, facing each other, so that there is a gap between each house. The green at this point therefore looks like an elegant woman with large gaps between her teeth. Next to these houses is the new vicarage, partly hidden by the high wall of Dr Edlestone's old vicarage, which is adjacent to the church. What can be seen of this new vicarage is a reticent new brick building of some character. It is the only new house visible from the green but it does not detract from the scene.

A good view of Edlestone Hall and its garden column can be seen from School Lane running W off Low Green. It is marked at its entrance 'No Through Road' and leads to the ford across the Tees. On the right can be seen the many decorated chimneys of Tudor Gainford Hall, built in 1600 by John Cradock, a former Vicar of Gainford.

GREATHAM, *Cleveland,* just off the A689, only about 5m from Hartlepool, is a village the centre-piece of which is (as in Kirkleatham, q.v.) an ancient hospital foundation. Greatham itself consists mostly of a long winding street of pleasant 19th-c houses with some earlier ones, and a small green opposite St John's Church. The Hospital was founded in 1272 by Robert Stichell, Prior of Finchale, who when the king seized the Manor of Greatham, fought and won his case against the seizure in the King's Council, and founded the charity and hospital on the land he had won.

Originally the Charity was for needy and

'decayed priests' but its clerical beneficiaries today constitute only half of those housed. The Master of the Hospital is the Vicar of Greatham. The Charity is a prosperous one, and its initiative in buying up houses as they became available has done much to prevent the village from being commuterised. It may not be a spectacular village but it is all of a piece. The Hospital's new buildings, including a small square of old people's bungalows, and new almshouses, are sensitively sited.

The present Hospital building (to be viewed from the pathway to the entrance to St John's Church) is by Jeffrey Wyatt (1803), and its most notable feature is a triple-arched loggia surmounted by a square clock tower and round bell tower. The Hospital chapel of 1788 is just behind the church. St John's was substantially restored in the 18th c, but two arches of the nave arcade have Norman zigzag decoration and the two altar pillars are Saxon, although not original to the site. The Master's stone house of 1725 (Greatham Hall) has recently been replaced by a brick house with a double bow by the Yorkshire architect, Francis Johnson, and is that rare thing, a truly elegant modern house.

HARBOTTLE, *Northumberland.* About 10m NW from Rothbury through Thropton is Harbottle. The sharp hill ridges of the Coquet Valley come down almost to enclose the village. To the right, just before the first village house, is a road leading to Harbottle Castle House, a 17th-c mansion remodelled in 1829 by John Dobson in his classical style. Just before its entrance and to the left, a path leads down to the River Coquet.

The village itself consists of a street of pleasing stone houses – so pleasing that they are increasingly bought as holiday or retirement homes to the detriment of village life. High above the village street behind the post office a small part of the ruin of Harbottle Castle in its mound can be seen. This immense and steep mound overlooking the Coquet is described by Pevsner as the finest medieval earthwork in Northumberland, but it is also thought to have been a Mote Hill of the ancient Britons. Henry II built the moated castle in 1160. It was the castle from which the Middle March was defended, and it had to withstand many attacks by the Scots since it is only 9m from the Scottish border, and dangerously exposed. Past the Manse a path leads to Harbottle Crag and the Drake stone (the Draag Stone of the Druids, says Tomlinson), a 30ft high stone associated, like the Castle Mound, with the rites of the ancient Britons. Harbottle Lough, a lonely tarn, is a short distance to the SW.

The hill scenery around Harbottle gets better the further along the Coquet Valley you go. **Alwinton,** the last village in England and only 7m from the Scottish Fence, is 1½m beyond Harbottle. It is noteworthy because of its surrounding landscape; it is the best centre for getting into the Cheviot wilderness through Clennel Street and by Usway Ford, and it has the atmosphere of a frontier village outpost. It is not surprising that its atmosphere is more noteworthy than its architecture when you read the names of surrounding hills – Bloody Bush Edge, Foulplay Head and Gallow Law. Sir Walter Scott was a visitor to Alwinton, drawn by the wild scenery, and wrote part of *Rob Roy* in the Rose and Thistle Inn.

Lady's Well and the statue of Paulinus at Holystone

Geoffrey N. Wright

½m S of Alwinton, and curiously isolated from the village, is the church of St Michael and All Angels. A good view of the surrounding hills is obtained from the top of its steeply sloped churchyard, and the steep site on which the church stands has necessitated ten steps up from the nave to the chancel and another three steps to the altar. The church is Norman in origin. Near the churchgate is a low building once used as the church stables, since most worshippers at this remote church could only get there by horse. Alwinton Shepherds' Show in October – the latest of all the Shows – with its Northumbrian pipes and its stress on the shepherding life, reflects the true spirit of Cheviot Northumberland. Beyond Alwinton the Coquet Valley narrows to a spectacular defile until the last farmhouses in England at Blindburn and Makendon are reached.

About halfway between Thropton and Harbottle there is a road off to the left to **Holystone**, 1m away – a compact and pretty village the houses standing at all angles to each other in pleasant informality. As one goes from the Salmon Inn towards St Mary's Church and the river, the remains of a Benedictine 12th-c priory can be seen to the right in what appears to be the end wall of a farm building; but if you stand in the road you can see in the gable-end a blocked-up pointed and arched window. The church is Norman in origin. Carved stones from the priory are inset into the church walls.

The combination of Roman roads with wells is not uncommon, but the well at Holystone, in a group of fir trees behind the Salmon Inn, is no common well. It lies close to the junction of two Roman roads, one from High Rochester, and it was here that in 627 Paulinus baptized 3000 Northumbrians in his earliest Christian mission. The crystal clear pool of water is surmounted by a Cross, and the statue of Paulinus at one end of the pool was brought here from Alnwick in 1780. The well for centuries has been called the Ladies' Well doubtless after the Nuns of the Priory. It is now owned by the National Trust and is open to visitors.

HARTBURN, *Northumberland*, 7m W of Morpeth. The first house you come to on the approach from Scots Gap is Dr Sharpe's Tower – the son of the Archdeacon Sharpe who was Lord Crewe's distinguished trustee and who left his mark on the restoration of Bamburgh, Blanchland and much besides. He was Vicar of Hartburn 1749–92. This castellated tower was built at the joint expense of Dr Sharpe and the parishioners to provide a house on the upper floor for the village schoolmaster and a schoolroom below with stables for the village hearse. It has an exterior staircase much as in the old Northumbrian bastle houses, and a large Gothic window. A later schoolhouse is next to it, built in 1844.

The siting of Hartburn is superb, but not apparent to anyone motoring through. On the N side (down from Dr Sharpe's Tower) there is a precipitous fall to the Hart burn, well over 100ft below, and a fall almost as steep to another stream on the S side. No wonder that (regrettably) several modern houses have been built here to enjoy the exciting view over river and dene. This view can be enjoyed by the visitor from the churchyard.

Proceeding past Dr Sharpe's Tower to the War Memorial in the middle of the road junction and turning left, the elegant Georgian vicarage embodying a pele tower *c*. AD 1250 comes into view. It was here that the Rev. John Hodgson, author of *The History of Northumberland*, lived as Vicar from 1833 until he died in 1845.

The church with its typically Northumbrian square low tower is late 12th-c. The nave piers are octagonal and date from *c*. AD 1250. At the top of one pillar near to the pulpit the early Christian symbol of a fish is carved. The font dates from 1250, as does the doorway with its dog tooth ornament. On the right-hand door post is carved a Maltese Cross and two daggers which indicate that the church must have been used by the Knights Templar as a meeting place.

HEIGHINGTON, *Durham*. Like Gainford, only 8m away, the fact that the older part of Heighington is contained within a rectangular green has protected it visually from the considerable amount of recent building which has taken place. That the green is very spacious and is on the slope of a hill 500ft above sea-level also adds to its charm, so that Sir Timothy Eden in his *History of Durham*, although expressing concern at its vulnerability, said it was 'as sweet a place of rural England as can be found in any county'. It is not now a village for the purist, but the spaciousness of the green preserves its unity, and the many fine buildings make walking round it a rewarding experience.

The church is St Michael and All Angels, a true Norman church although the S aisle is 13-c. The church arch, says Pevsner, has features which date it to the earliest ribs of Durham Cathedral (*c.* 1095). The old Georgian Vicarage was in the churchyard but was demolished in 1929 and the stones were used for the building of the new vicarage which is now opposite the church on the S of the East Green. Outside the churchyard by the N gate there is a terrace of three houses facing the church, the end one of which is particularly fine, *c.* 1760, with a scroll pedimented doorway and a side doorway with a good fanlight. Its neighbouring house is plainer but probably even older. The George and Dragon Inn is opposite.

There is a high curved wall and next to it in Church View is a long, low 18th-c house which formerly was a private Grammar School of some renown in its day. East Green runs at a right angle to the schoolhouse, and leads to the old Manor House, 1620, which also has a fine scroll pedimented doorway. Behind a recent stone wall at the E end of the green is yet another Georgian house, Eldon House. The new vicarage is next to it, but on the S side. The fine spectacle of the green depends on the mixture of houses, some large and important and some not, but all of equal importance to the green. On the West Green the Bay

Horse Inn is 17th-c, and just across the road which divides the green is one of the best houses in the village, with a columned porch. On this part of the green stands the stone pant erected by a vicar of the village in the first quarter of the 19th c; but unfortunately the duck pond has been filled in because the mothers of the village were frightened for the safety of their children – and, I dare say, for their husbands also after an evening in the Bay Horse or the George and Dragon. Heighington green is so large that in Fordyce's *History of Durham* we find it mentioned as one of the six places in Durham which held regular horse-race meetings in 1730 – the other places being Durham, Sedgefield, Stockton, Sunderland and Wolsingham.

Once there were gates to the village across the paths and across the gaps between the houses – the name Sneckgate is a reminder of this – to protect the grazing animals from raiders or thieves, and later, because Heighington was a bleaching village, to prevent outsiders stealing the linen off the green. The grazing of animals on the green continued until the increasing traffic through the village made it unsafe. When I last visited the village the only grazing animal on the green was a tethered goat. Near as it is to centres of population, this village retains its rural atmosphere to an astonishing degree.

HOLY ISLAND VILLAGE, *Northumberland.* I know no more romantic approach to any village than that to the village on Holy Island. Approaching, as one must, on the causeway, which is under water for several hours each day, and by which the island maintains a tenuous connection with the mainland, to the right Bamburgh Castle rises on its great rock, at one's back is the mass of Cheviot, snowcapped well into May, and ahead is Holy Island castle. Gradually the ridge on which the village is situated comes into view, the causeway and the swans and the waders are left behind, and one enters into the village.

This is the birthplace of Christianity in England. After the victory of King Oswald (later St Oswald) over the pagan Welsh prince Cadwallader at the Battle of Heavenfield, Oswald sent to Iona for Christian teachers to preach the Gospel in Northumbria. Not much progress was made until Aidan arrived with several Irish monks in AD 634. Coming from one island they settled on this other island, near to the royal city of Bamburgh, and throughout his mission Aidan remained a close and valued adviser to the king.

Aidan died in AD 651 and the place where he died is marked now by Bamburgh's magnificent St Aidan's Church. In 664 Cuthbert came to Holy Island as Prior, preached widely on the mainland, and then in 676 retired for nine years to a life of prayer and meditation on Farne Island. In 685 he reluctantly consented to the plea of King Ecgfrith to become Bishop of Lindisfarne. In 687 he died in his retreat on Farne Island.

Until the Danish raids began in 793, when they burnt the priory and robbed the church of silver and gold ornaments, life on the island was peaceful and artistically creative. The priory was soon rebuilt, and work and study continued until in 875, fearing more Viking raids, the monks left, carrying the bones of St Aidan, the head of St Oswald, the Lindisfarne Gospels and other works of art. They also carried St Cuthbert's coffin, and after several years of wandering, set it down at Durham, over which place the building of the cathedral in honour of St Cuthbert was begun.

Anglian art and civilization in Northumbria in the 7th, 8th and the first half of the 9th c reached a higher cultural level than anywhere else in Britain. The Lindisfarne Gospels and other illuminated books, the Anglian Crosses, and the works of Bede, are a reflection of this. Today the only signs of this early period on the Island, now that the Gospels are in the British Museum, are the finely carved and decorated stones in the Priory Museum. The priory itself, with its famous rainbow arch, was begun in 1093, and the building of St Mary's Church was begun in about 1145. The three E rounded arches in the church – separating the nave from the N aisle – belong to this Norman period, as distinct from the 13th-c pointed arches of the S arcade. The chancel is beautifully lit by eight narrow lancet-headed windows, and the carpet is a replica of a page from the Lindisfarne Gospels. There are photographs of this and other pages from the Lindisfarne Gospels in the Priory Museum.

At the N of the church just beyond the Priory Museum is the centre of the village, a pleasant green, and on it the market cross designed by John Dobson in 1828. It is a pity that the new houses allowed to be built have not been compelled to use replicas of the pleasing orange pantiled roofing used on so many of the 18th- and 19th-c houses. From the harbour, with its lobster pots, its nets, and its cobbles there is a fine view of the priory. The castle was restored by Sir Edwin Lutyens for Edward Hudson, the owner of *Country Life.* It was a fort and bulwark against the Scots, built in about 1550 from the stones of the ruined priory. It is now owned by the National Trust and can be visited.

It is to be hoped that the decline of the population over the last 200 years can be checked and the school remains open.

The older village houses are of peculiarly dark rough-cut Northumbrian stone, creating, with the almost white mortar, a pleasing marbling effect. In the gardens are vases of flowers and plant pots encrusted with sea shells. The village itself may not possess great architectural distinction, but its priory and church, its surrounding landscape, its harbour and its history, are riches enough.

HURWORTH, *Durham* (4m S of Darlington), is another of the lineal Durham villages (like Staindrop, q.v.) consisting almost entirely of one street some ¾m long. On one side of the road is a wide green behind which extremely attractive 18th- and early 19th-c houses face equally good

Geoffrey N. Wright

Sir William Turner's 'princely' Hospital at Kirkleatham

houses behind a narrow green on the other side of the road. The village is sited on a ridge immediately above the bank of the Tees, and the river and rich farmland beyond can be glimpsed between the trees and houses. It is remarkably unspoilt, and since it is little more than 10 minutes by car from Darlington it is not surprising that professional and business men who work there – especially solicitors – have chosen it as a place to live.

Many of the fanlights and doorways of the houses are very elegant. Opposite the post office are two older cottages with attractive stepped roofs and over one of the doorways are the dates 1453 and 1835 – the latter must be the date of restoration. A plaque on one of the houses (No. 24) states that William Emerson, 1701–82, lived in the house formerly on the site. This Emerson – son of the Hurworth village schoolmaster – was one of the most renowned mathematicians of his day, but his manners were so eccentric, his clothing so shabby, his behaviour so 'studiously vulgar', that he became almost as much renowned for this as for the fact that mathematicians came from all over England to visit him, and that he refused the honour of being made a Fellow of the Royal Society.

The village with its old houses ends abruptly to the E, with no modern accretions. New houses are to be seen at the W end of the village, but discreetly sited, so that they do not detract from the atmosphere of a more gracious age than our own. It is a village of many greens, sundials, river views,

trees and attractive doorcasings, and its centre has changed little since Jane Austen's day.

About 4m NE of Hurworth and very near to Middleton St George is **Middleton One Row** which consists of only one street and indeed of only one side of one street. This village is on a much higher and more spectacular ridge above the Tees than Hurworth. The ridge descends precipitously to the river giving the fortunate residents uninterrupted views over the river and the surrounding countryside. The row does not include houses of the same architectural quality as the best in Hurworth (except perhaps for an attractive hotel), but consists of a row of vernacular early 19th-c houses of much charm, diminished only slightly by the group of somewhat sombre late Victorian brick buildings whose centre is the Methodist church.

The Row and the views over the Tees are sufficiently attractive for one not to be surprised on a fine Sunday to see a line of cars bumper to bumper along the open river side of the village, even though all the car windows are closed, the radios switched on, and the occupants almost hidden by their Sunday newspapers.

KIRKLEATHAM, *Cleveland,* 2m S of Redcar. There could be no greater contrast to the Satanic landscape of Wilton, only ¼m away, than the 17th- and 18th-c architectural splendour of Kirkleatham. Sadly it has been allowed to decay, but in the last 15 years great efforts have been made by the Local Authority and by private individuals to improve matters. The modern concrete gibbets in the village have been replaced by Victorian lamp posts, the later accretions have been removed from the Old Hall (the Free School), and its renovation continues for re-opening to the public as a museum. Most important of all, the Sir William Turner Hospital was restored in the 1950s and modernization of the old people's apartments completed in 1978. The stonework of the magnificent chapel in the centre portion of this three-sided building has been damaged by the pollution of nearby Wilton, but this is soon to be remedied. This chapel is believed to be by James Gibbs, pupil and friend of Christopher Wren. Unfortunately Kirkleatham Hall, the former residence of the Turner family, a distinguished building by Carr of York, was demolished in 1955.

In 1623 the estate was bought by John Turner, and the Turner family's patronage of Gibbs and Carr was to produce four buildings within a short distance of each other which were un-equalled in Cleveland. One has to go as far afield as Castle Howard to find anything comparable. The Rev. John Graves in his *History of Cleveland* (1808) refers to Kirkleatham's 'princely grandeur'.

The key Turner is the second Turner, William, who was apprenticed in the wool trade in London and became a wealthy woollen draper. He became a friend of Pepys and Wren. In 1662 he was knighted, and he was Lord Mayor of London in 1668 and 1669. In 1676 he built and endowed his hospital at Kirkleatham for ten aged men and ten aged women – 'aged' according to the ideas of the time, for the qualifying age was 53. Ten boys and ten girls were also to be educated and provided for, the ages for entry ranged from eight to 11 years. The boys left at 15 to become apprentices.

The Gibbs Chapel can be seen by arrangement and is the centre piece of the hospital. It is as rich as anything Wren ever did in London and is redolent of his classicism. Inside are the standing figures of the founder, Sir William, in his mayoral robes, and John Turner, Sergeant-at-Law, who married a relative of Samuel Pepys.

Just over the road from the hospital is the Free School that Sir William instructed his son Cholmley Turner to build and which was built by him in 1709. It is a building of great dignity and strength and makes an unhappy contrast with the modern school building on the site of the former Turner family home opposite the church.

By the side of the gate into the nursery gardens is a small iron gate on the path to St Cuthbert's Church and some old village houses – four Victorian houses with arched doorways are set back from a terrace of three houses, the end one being a particularly good 18th-c house. Approaching the church there are three Georgian houses round one side of the churchyard, and the octagonal mausoleum with its pyramid comes into view. This was designed by Gibbs and built in 1740 at a time when there was a medieval church on the site. This was demolished and the present classical church built in 1763 – so it must be remembered

that this baroque mausoleum of 1740 was originally built onto the former medieval church. The mausoleum was built in memory of Marwood William Turner, son of Cholmley Turner who had died on the Grand Tour at the age of 23. His life-size statue in marble stands inside the mausoleum.

There is much of interest in the church, from a small child's stone coffin of the 9th c, to a large iron-bound chest of 1348, and St Cuthbert's window; but most noticeable of all is the plain grace of this Georgian church interior.

Leaving the church and crossing the road you enter between two isolated Vanbrugh-like rusticated pillars – the only sign of architectural elegance here – and arrive at the new school, about which the less said the better. But in an enclosure nearby is the great brick stable block, farm buildings, and coachyard, designed by Gibbs. These are architectural rarities and in sad need of repair.

In spite of past neglect and the near presence of Wilton it looks as if Kirkleatham, because of its rare quality, will survive.

MITFORD, *Northumberland,* 2m W of Morpeth. Across a steep wooded dene is the third and present home of the Mitford family, Mitford Hall, a neo-classical house built by the Newcastle architect John Dobson for the Mitford family in 1828. Further down the hill is the second home of the Mitfords, the 17th-c Manor House, of which unfortunately only the decorative central tower-entrance dated 1637 remains standing, and which is now embodied in a modern house; but the real drama is provided by the first house of the Mitfords, the Norman castle on its huge mound which comes into sight at the bottom of the hill. Nearby is the church of St Mary Magdalene, which goes back to the 12th c, with a priests' door on the S side of the chancel and dog-tooth Norman decorations in the chancel arch.

Mitford may be scattered, and as a village has little shape, but it has beauty and a sense of history. The thickly wooded valleys of the Font and Wansbeck rivers in which it is set are at this point particularly attractive. A bridge across the river takes you to a T-junction on the main road, and turning right you come to the post office and the Plough Inn. Across a beautiful 18th-c bridge over the Wansbeck you leave Mitford behind on the road to Morpeth and the 20th century.

NORHAM, *Northumberland* (9m SW of Berwick-upon-Tweed), consists of three streets: West Street with the Masons' Arms – a good 18th-c building with two bow windows; Castle Street leading to the castle; and Pedwell Way leading to St Cuthbert's Church and the River Tweed, very wide and impressive at this point with Scotland beginning on the far steep wooded bank. It is a linear stone village set on low ground between the river and the castle. It has a northern reticent look about it and is an example of how pleasant a sight plain stone building and green spaces can be. On one of these greens in Castle

JOHN SELL COTMAN (1782–1842): New Bridge, Durham. Watercolour, 1805 (*Private Collection*). This watercolour drawing from Cotman's finest period (which does not appear to have been reproduced in colour in any book about the artist) was said by Laurence Binyon to have been done not directly in the face of nature but in the studio. Whether idealized or not, it is a wonderful evocation of the Durham landscape in the early years of the nineteenth century. It is difficult to identify the exact location of the bridge.

THOMAS GIRTIN (1775-1802): Bamburgh Castle. Watercolour, *c.* 1797-99 (*Tate Gallery, London*). This powerful example of full-blooded Romanticism is especially interesting today as showing what the rocky ruins of Bamburgh Castle were like before the vast restoration undertaken by Lord Armstrong in the late nineteenth century.

Street stands the Market Cross with a medieval 13th-c base and a fish as its weather vane, reminding us of Norham's heavy dependence on salmon fishing. Each year, on 13 February, the Vicar still stands in a boat on the river at midnight to bless the opening of the salmon season.

If the village is plain and pleasant the castle is sheer melodrama. Of all the northern castles, none in ruin gives such an impression of power and strength. Leland tells us that when Marmion's lady presented her knight with a golden-crested helmet and told him 'that he should go to the daungerust place in England and there let the heaulme to be seene', the knight went to Norham. The castle area is immense, not only to accommodate the large garrison required, but to provide quarters for the Prince Bishop and his company, for until 1844 Norham with Holy Island and the Farnes was part of the County Palatinate of Durham, and was known as North Durham.

In about 1165 Bishop Pusey, the greatest builder in the long line of bishops, built the present Norman keep after King David of Scotland had destroyed Norham in 1138. At the same time he began to build St Cuthbert's Church, and used the same architect, Richard of Wolviston, for both. The castle was reduced to ruin by the cannon of James IV of Scotland just before Flodden, but after the defeat of the Scots at Flodden the military importance of Norham declined and Queen Elizabeth refused to repair it.

Returning from the castle down Castle Street and turning into Pedwell Way we come to St Cuthbert's. The first stone church was built in AD 830, probably to the E of the present church near the yew trees. Saxon stones from this early church have been cemented into a pillar in the church tower. In 1292 John Baliol successfully did homage in this church to King Edward I of England for the Scottish Crown and was eventually preferred to Robert Bruce in the arbitration which followed at Berwick.

The original Norman work is seen in the round arches on the S side of the aisle, and in three pillar bases on the N side of the nave. For 100 years after Flodden the church was roofless until restored by the people of Norham.

Walking from the church to the river nearby there is a good view of the castle on its precipitous hill, but the best view of the river and the village is from the castle hill itself.

NORTON, *Cleveland*. The character of the old village of Norton is sufficiently strong to preserve its Georgian identity, although a continuous built-up area straggles from it to Stockton to the S. The centre of the old village is at the green to its SW, and although it now has a traffic roundabout and a main road running through it, the green is so large and bold a feature it can take even this in its stride. The 18th- and early 19th-c houses are outnumbered by later houses not worthy of their setting, but the green is still attractive, embellished by some good 18th-c houses (No. 37 is one of the best in Norton) and by fine mature trees.

Just over the highway which divides the green, and on slightly raised ground, stands the church of St Mary the Virgin, from which the best view of the green is obtained; near to it is the smaller part of the green with a pleasant background of early 19th-c artisans' houses, and in the foreground a pond.

The church looks early, long and low with a squat tower, and is in origin an Anglo-Saxon church of the 11th c or even earlier. It has an almost complete Saxon crossing tower and small arched Saxon windows. There is later Norman dog-tooth decoration on the stones of the S porch and in the same porch is the effigy of a knight in chain-mail which Pevsner describes as 'the best effigy of its date in the county'. Adjacent to the church is one of the best of 18th-c vicarages, with a fine doorway. Sadly when I visited it (April 1979) it bore a 'For Sale' notice. It is hoped it has been bought by someone who will cherish it as it deserves.

The High Street is lined with a double row of trees and is extremely handsome. The best group of 18th-c houses is on the left side walking towards Stockton, from No. 96 to No. 106, but visitors will be able to choose their own favourite decorative fanlight or classical doorcasing from the many fine houses. Norton Priory, with two bow windows, on the other side of the road is particularly good. As one walks in the direction of Stockton, old Norton village is left behind, modern building takes over, but old Norton village is in no way diminished.

PIERCEBRIDGE, *Durham*, 6m W of Darlington. Approaching from the M1 on the B6275 you arrive first at an old inn, the George Hotel, and a few cottages, which are in Yorkshire; but the fine three-arched 18th-c bridge over the Tees is only a short distance ahead, hidden by a bend in the road – the rest of the village is on the other side of the Tees in Durham. The Tees is very beautiful at Piercebridge, and slightly to the W are the remains of the Roman bridge which carried the Roman road over it.

One is not conscious at all that this village is within the 11 acres or so of a 3rd-c Roman fort. It is a village built round a large rectangular green, that is enhanced by fine sycamores. Most of the houses are 18th- or early 19th-c, and although none of them is of great architectural distinction, whitewashed cream and white they form a most attractive composition. The houses vary from the single-storey bothie type to quite substantial ones, and near the bridge on the same side as St Mary's church are a pair of Victorian cottages with the steeply pointed high wooden porches more frequently met with in Wales. The oldest house is next to St Mary's, at right angles to a whitewashed farm building with red pantiled roof, both looking very picturesque. On the Durham side of the village is the Wheatsheaf.

The visual charm of Piercebridge must be obvious to everyone, but to the archaeologist and antiquarian its interest is still largely hidden. Most of the churches in the region – notably

Gainford's St Mary's – have in their walls some Roman stones taken from the camp here. Traces of a Roman villa have recently been uncovered and along the lane next to the church, leading away from the green, the visitor may stand and watch a site of many acres being excavated, and can see the foundations of the ancient buildings that have come to light.

ROMALDKIRK, *Durham,* 6m NW of Barnard Castle. Since the recent Local Government boundary changes Romaldkirk has been within the County of Durham. But the inhabitants of the village still feel they are part of the North Riding of Yorkshire, and what they feel is reinforced by the architecture of the village. Dr Pevsner's verdict is that Romaldkirk is perfection, and it would be difficult to find anyone to disagree.

It is a village of several greens; and scattered round the greens in an apparently haphazard way are stone houses. The balance of the picture made by the shapes and angles of the houses is superb. On a green in front of the Rose and Crown Inn is part of the old stocks. An adjacent larger green is dominated by the fine Georgian house of the veterinary surgeon. Opposite is the old rectory now being restored. (The rector here is also the Lord of the Manor.) The village is in a basin surrounded by distant moorland.

By the side of the Rose and Crown there is yet another green surrounded on two sides by cottages. A path by the side of the churchyard leads from this down to the 17th-c bridge to Egglestone and to Romaldkirk Mill, which ceased working about 100 years ago.

The village gets its name from the dedication to St Romald. Romald was the infant son of a Northumbrian king, when Northumbria comprised all the land N of the Humber, and the kingdom went as far N as Edinburgh. Romald's mother had fled from the N with her unborn son to escape the war between Northumbria and Mercia in about AD 800. So Romald was born in Buckingham, lived only three days, but made such an impression by his miraculous wisdom that when he died he became the patron Saint of Buckingham.

St Romald was of course a Saxon and the history of the village indicates a pre-Norman settlement with a Saxon church. The remains of this church are embodied in the present church and are to be found in the wall on either side of the chancel arch. The present nave and N aisle are 12th-c, and the tower is 15th-c.

In a village as attractive as this there must be a great demand for new housing which because of the open and unenclosed nature of the village would destroy it. Someone must have maintained a strict veto on new development and is consequently to be congratulated.

SIMONBURN, *Northumberland.* This beautiful village lies ½m E off the road from Hexham to Wark-on-Tyne. It cannot be approached from the W at all since there is no road to it over the wild moorland that stretches to the Scottish border. This region was part of the undefined and much fought-over border between England and Scotland, and after the Conquest for at least 150 years it formed part of the Kingdom of Scotland. King Alexander II and III of Scotland therefore appointed several of the rectors to Simonburn and the very name of its church, the church of St Mungo, speaks of its Scottish origin since St Mungo, the illegitimate son of a Pictish princess, became Bishop of Strathclyde and his fame is perpetuated by St Mungo's Cathedral in Glasgow, which he founded.

From the time when Simon of Senlis, Earl of Northumberland in 1136 (and himself a grandson of Waltheof, last of the Saxon Earls of Northumberland executed in 1076 by William the Conqueror), defended the North Tyne against his step-father David, King of Scotland, North Tynedale rivalled Redesdale as a region of blood-thirsty raid and counter-raid, so that in 1595 the rector designate refused the appointment 'deeming this body unable to live in so troublesome a place, and his nature not well brooking the perverse nature of so crooked a people.'

Today the village seems the very essence of idyllic peace. The rectangular green with magnificent chestnut trees is surrounded on three sides with whitewashed cottages built in the 18th and early 19th c. Over to the right behind the single-storey bothies are six late 19th-c houses with steeply pitched gables, the end one of which is the post office and general stores. The gardens of Simonburn are beautifully kept. The Red Lion Inn was closed a long time ago by Squire Allgood of nearby Nunwick Hall – an elegant Georgian house built in about 1760 by William Newton of Newcastle, who also in 1765 restored the church.

Entering the village, at the corner on the right is a handsome house, the Agent's or Steward's house, but the best house in the village is the three-storeyed rectory, with magnificent gateposts, built in about 1666 by Rector Allgood to replace the old fortified vicar's pele which stood in the rectory garden until 1832 when its stones were used to rebuild the garden wall. The rectory façade, Georgianized in 1725, fortunately does not quite disguise its origin in the age of Vanbrugh. Most of the church that one sees is 13th c but in the porch, discovered during the 1877 restoration work, are the remains of Anglian stone crosses of the 8th and 9th c. The stones bear tracings of vine, grape and bird carvings. There are good walks all around Simonburn – straight through the village for ½m to the remains of Simonburn Castle on its eminence near the joining of two burns between two steep ravines, or you can take the road to the left near the church and walk to the Teckitt Burn and its waterfall.

STAINDROP, *Durham,* 5m NE of Barnard Castle. In Staindrop you are in rich 18th-c watercolour country, and it is difficult to realize that the wild Pennine moorlands are little more than 10m away. It is a stone village with one of the longest greens – even in this county of long greens.

British Tourist Authority

The Hall at Raby Castle

Delectable fanlights, delicate as spiders' webs, above doorways of 18th-c and early 19th-c houses, face one another across the green throughout its length. There is scarcely a false note in this delightful village.

On the N side of the village is Staindrop parish church, originally dedicated to St Gregory. It is rare in England to find a church dedicated to St Gregory, and they are all of Saxon origin. A Saxon church was built on this site as early as the 8th c, and the Saxon part of the present church – the three arches on the N and S sides of the nave and the filled-in windows on the N side – date from that time. The line of the Saxon roof can still be seen above those windows. This church must therefore be only slightly later than the famous Saxon church at Escomb near Bishop Auckland only a few miles away.

It is now a church rich in atmosphere and furnishings. In the 12 c the present tower was added, and in the 13th c the chancel was extended to the E and decorated with the present fine sedilia. The porch is 14th-c, and in the 15th c a college for priests was established on the N side of the church beyond the churchyard. There are fine effigies in the church, notably a 13th-c effigy of a lady, and three of the 15th c representing a Neville, Earl of Westmorland, and his two wives.

The house of these Nevilles is nearby, NE of the village. This is Raby Castle, one of the largest and most impressive of the castles of the North, and open to visitors. The village, the church and the castle therefore should be seen as an historical and aesthetic unity, and each is superb.

STAMFORDHAM, *Northumberland,* 9m NE of Corbridge. The name means 'the homestead by the Stoney Ford', and if you take the path that goes downhill between the Bay Horse Inn and the church to the pretty hamlet of Hawkwell, you will come to the ford at the right-hand side of the little bridge over the River Pont. There are other things than its name that point to a Saxon past. A beautiful Anglian cross-shaft of the first half of the 8th c was discovered here and is now in the Cathedral Library at Durham; and although present opinion is that St Mary's Church goes back to the year 1200, its tower looks earlier.

Stamfordham, an important early settlement of the Angles, is planned round an enclosed green, the houses facing inwards. It was therefore well devised for keeping the cattle in and keeping out the Celts, wolves, boars, and later the Scots. There was a real danger of raids from the N as the Order of the Watch upon the Middle Marches, 27 October 1552, shows by enforcing a nightly watch at Stamfordham.

The Swinburnes of nearby Capheaton Hall (unsuspecting ancestors of Algernon Charles Swinburne, the poet) have been the most prominent family in and around Stamfordham for the past four centuries, as the memorials in the church make clear. A cattle market was established here in 1732 and lasted until the mid-1920s. The escapades that accompanied Market Day led to the building of the jail on the green in which many of the drovers spent the night to sober up. The market cross, which is not a cross at all but four arches supporting a stone steeply pitched roof with a square finial, a ball, and a weather vane, was presented to the village by Sir Edward Swinburne in 1735 and still bears the contemporary dedication although worn today.

In 1663 a Free Grammar School was established. As you approach the path to Hawkwell already mentioned, the old school building is the house on the left where the narrow path begins, and the two stones which held the old school bell can still be seen projecting from the gable end.

The entrance to the village from the E, past a large garage and some suburban houses, is the reverse of exciting: but after passing the early 18th-c red-brick house on the left the road curves to the left and the fine sweep of the village around its large green comes into view. The green slopes down from N to S. A fine Queen Anne red-brick bow-windowed house, Cross House, is the best house on the N side; and since we are in Jacobite country (the Old Pretender was first publicly proclaimed King in Hexham Market Place in 1715) the tradition is that the unfortunate James, Lord Derwentwater, later executed, met his friends on the bowling green at the rear of Cross House to plan the rebellion.

Stamfordham has preserved its village quality although close to Newcastle. There is a fine communal spirit; there are two good inns, two general stores and a fine rectory, part Tudor and part 18th-c that can be seen on the right as you walk down to Hawkwell. A planning decision to site the ugly toilets between the two entrances to St Mary's Church is inexplicable.

Just 4m W on the road out of Stamfordham
lies **Matfen.** The first sign of the village is the slim
spire of Holy Trinity Church, built in 1853,
soaring through the trees. Matfen is set in well-
treed parkland and is an estate village created by
the Blackett family in about 1850. The Blacketts
have owned this land since the beginning of the
18th c, and their influence has kept the village all
of a piece and free from damaging intrusion. A
Victorian village such as this is a rare delight. The
high pointed windows of the stone houses face
towards the green through which a stone-lined
channel carries water from the Catcleugh reservoir near the Scottish border to nearby Whittle-
dene Reservoir. Matfen Hall, built by Rickman
in 1828 for Sir Edward Blackett, has a Jacobean
exterior and a vast Gothic interior. It is now a
Cheshire Home having been leased to the Cheshire foundation by the Blackett family for a
nominal rent. There are two shops and two inns
in Matfen.

As this book goes to print there are disconcerting signs that new houses are to be built in Matfen
– disconcerting because in so few cases do modern
architects and builders succeed in designing and
building houses with any village (as distinct from
suburban) character.

Kenneth Scowen
The twelfth-century castle at Warkworth

WARKWORTH, *Northumberland,* 2m N of
Amble, is one of the wonders of Northumberland;
and the approach to it from the N, passing close
to the bridge built in 1379 with its tower (one of the
rare fortified bridges of England) over the wide
and wooded Coquet, and the view up the steep
street of 18th-c stone houses rising to the castle at
the top, is not excelled by many in England.

Warkworth Castle is one of the five great castles
of Northumberland – Norham (q.v.), Dunstanburgh, Bamburgh (q.v.), and Alnwick are the
others – and although built as a military engine of
war it is a work of great architectural and aesthetic
beauty, its character quite different from the
desolate grandeur of the others before 19th-c
remodelling 'civilized' Alnwick and Bamburgh.
This is due only partly to the great variation in
colour of the beautiful stone ranging from grey
and pink to yellow, to the polygonal bevelled-
edged turrets of the 15th-c keep, and to the fragments of Gothic tracery in the windows. Some of
the earlier parts of the castle below the level of the
keep date from the early 12th c. The steep banks
and the wide Coquet provided natural defences to
the E and W; to the S was the moat, and to the N
the fortified bridge. Throughout the 14th and 15th
c the castle was the main residence of the Percy
family, and three scenes in Shakespeare's *King
Henry the Fourth, Part One,* are set in Warkworth,
where the conspiracy of the Earl and his son Harry
Hotspur against the King was hatched.

In places the castle is surprisingly complete –
stone seats in the room where the pages sat to await
attendance in the nearby Hall, guardrooms at
the S gate with five arrow slits covering the approach across the most to the gate, the chapel in
the keep, the foundations of the 14th-c Col-

legiate Church, the Lion Tower with its ruffed and
almost mythological Percy Lion, and the kitchen
with two immense fireplaces. There are fine views
from the keep out to sea and over Amble Harbour
and Coquet Island.

A ferry takes the visitor up the river to the
unique Hermitage, where porch, cell, chapel,
kitchen and dormitory are hewn out of solid rock.

The 18th-c village street is still all of a piece,
with good doorways on the way from the castle
to the village cross, which bears the crescent sign
of the Percys. To the left is a short wide street
leading to St Lawrence's, an almost complete
Norman church heavily restored by John Dobson. The finest house in Warkworth is Bridge
End House, a five-bay house of *c.* 1730 with
moulded window and a pedimented doorway,
next to the old bridge from which the best views
of river, street and castle can be enjoyed.

WHALTON, *Northumberland,* 6m SW of
Morpeth. Nothing could look less warlike than
this delightful village, even if it is only 7m from
the ominously named Scots Gap. In fact it was
once a fortified village of bastle houses in the
ownership of the Scrope family, two sons of this
family being Wardens of the West March. On the
N side there is a raised terrace in front of the
houses situated behind a pleasant bank of green;
and the best view of Whalton's houses and the
tree-lined street is from this terrace. The houses
on the N side tend to be larger and earlier in date
than the houses on the S side. The Beresford
Arms on the N side is a well-known inn built of
the same stone as the rest of the village. The
church is mostly 13th-c, although the lower part
of the tower is 12th-c, and there is Norman dog-
tooth decoration in the N chapel.

Although only 15m from Newcastle the village shows no sign of being commuterized. There are plenty of council houses to the W of the village to ensure that it retains its link with work in the surrounding landscape and that the village remains a living and working community.

At the E end is the Manor House designed by Sir Edwin Lutyens in 1908, when he remodelled what had been originally four village houses into one, after Sir Robert Lorimer had remodelled two into one. (I am obliged to Mr Timothy Norton of the Manor House for this information.) It is a strikingly successful design with an entrance archway flanked by two large classical urns with Lutyens' signature of imaginative use of cobbled brick and stone on the pavements and entrances. The former vicarage, a fine 18th-c house with a circular lawn in front, is on the opposite side of the street.

WHITBURN, *Tyne and Wear.* Sometimes we find ourselves in 'carriage-lamp country' and personalized number plates stand outside unnerving versions of 'Georgian' doorways and three-car garages. An English village can die many kinds of death and this is one of them. With these sombre thoughts in mind, after an absence of many years I approached Whitburn, a village on the coast mid-way between Sunderland and South Shields and close to both.

To my relief there was not a single carriage-lamp in sight at the heart of the village, nor did I see an inappropriate doorway on the small 18th-c cottages or on the later Georgian houses. The Council has taken away the concrete gibbets which nowadays so often serve as lamp-posts, and has substituted in black painted ironwork a not unpleasing version of the Victorian lamp-post and gas lantern.

It is a very pretty village, with the village green on one side of the road and a raised grass-banked terrace on the N, from the top of which houses look across the green to the houses opposite. Both sides of the village are tree-lined. The green is almost divided into two by a recently renovated old house standing end on and at right angles. It is called Cross House – one supposes because it is near the old village cross of which I could find no trace. From the green the late Norman tower of St Mary's Church can be seen over the roofs of the houses to the S of the green. These houses seem to be the oldest houses in the village – some are 17th-c.

On the opposite side, on the raised terrace, are two particularly fine 18th-c houses flanking a remodelled later house whose main windows in a Georgian village of vertical windows have inexplicably been given a horizontal emphasis. At the E side of the raised terrace is the Victorian Whitburn House, which has been much Elizabethanized, and from the terrace you can see in the garden at the rear a fragment of St John's Church, Newcastle, removed from Newcastle in 1869. The date 1869 appears on the front of the house. Whitburn Hall is almost exactly opposite: its architecture ranges from the 17th c to the 1880s.

It has been left to decay and in places is now without a roof. Any modern development here would have a visually disastrous effect on the old village.

The old village ends to the W at the old buildings of the Glebe Farm and the mounting steps, at which point executive housing takes over, but at sufficiently tactful distance not to have too destructive an effect. Neither from the coastal nor from the inland approach is there any hint of the surprise in store for the visitor, for although only a short distance from industry and the crowds and the icecream stalls of Marsden it is 200 years away in atmosphere.

WHITTINGHAM, *Northumberland* (8m W of Alnwick,), lies in the most fertile vale of Northumberland, and the tall lime trees and sycamores on the green give it a prosperous look. Its air of peace and seclusion seems almost total, perhaps because in the early 19th c it ceased to be on the stage-coach route from Newcastle to Edinburgh and – thus by-passed – was able to retire from the everyday world.

The River Aln, narrow at this point, divides the village into two – the part surrounding St Bartholomew's, the rectory, the school, and a cluster of cottages, separated from the green with its cottages, the Castle Inn, the Court House, the shop, and the 14th-c pele tower.

The lower part of the tower and the W wall of St Bartholomew's date from King Ceolwulf's reign (*c.* 737) when the King resigned his crown and retired as a monk to Lindisfarne, and made a gift to Lindisfarne of five parishes including Edlingham, Eglingham and Whittingham. St Bartholomew's in 1839–40 was the scene of an almost unbelievable piece of architectural vandalism when John Green of Newcastle removed a considerable part of the top of the Saxon tower to Gothickize it; and even more unbelievably removed the round Norman pillars and arches on the N side of the aisle so that he could 'match' the pointed 13th-c arches of the octagonal pillars on the S side. But it is still a very beautiful church, and the initials C and E on the two front pews remind us that two great houses are close by – Callaly Castle and Eslington Hall.

Just off the green by the council houses (which illustrate by their simplicity how they can have a village quality which more pretentious 'executive' houses have not) is the pele tower. Its walls are 9ft thick, and in 1845 it was Gothickized at the top when, as the inscription on it states, it was 'repaired and otherwise embellished for the use and benefit of the deserving poor' by Lady Ravensworth of Eslington. It became an almshouse for women.

The fair is held on 24 September each year, and is the inspiration of the lovely ballad 'Whittingham Fair'.

Although only about 4m away from Whittingham, just off the B6341 road midway between Alnwick and Rothbury, **Edlingham** is in a different world. It is set in wild moorland scenery and your first sight is of Edlingham Castle. This

The old bridge over the Coquet at Warkworth

is a small castle and not a pele, and one of great beauty. It is good to see that the Department of the Environment is now repairing it. A short distance from the castle is Edlingham church, St John's. Eadwulf of Bamburgh, a relative of the King, had made his ham or home in the castle area and there has been a church on the site since *c.* 740; so castle and church have in some shape stood here for centuries before the Conquest. The only certain Saxon part of the church is that of the W wall of the nave, and the present church is essentially Norman with a 14th-c tower which is built like a pele for defence, with narrow arrow slits as windows and extremely thick walls. It is a vivid reminder of times when even churches had to be fortified. But the church with three 12th-c round pillars in the nave is as beautiful inside as it is grim outside. The tower has an unusual pyramidical shaped roof.

The village straggles uphill above the church and castle with fine views stretching over the moorland and hills.

Lincolnshire and Humberside

David L. Roberts

The underlying soil and rocks of Lincolnshire are distinctly marked in a north-to-south 'grain'. On the west lie the clays; then, centrally, the heath, often clearly marked by the steep scarp of the Lincoln Edge or 'Cliff' to the west; with the fen and marsh eastwards towards the sea. Between the stony but fertile soils of the heath and the fen is an irregular strip called the 'townland', alluvial soil that is well drained, and on which many early settlements were built – hence the name.

In Humberside the pattern of geology disintegrates. Erosion has carved a wide estuary for the Humber through the soft chalk and greeny sandstone of the Wold. North of the Humber lie the low, barely undulating clays and alluvial soils that overlie the rock. Geological variety governs not only the agriculture of the two counties but also the choice of building material in the villages. Churches, castles and the great houses ignored the imposed restriction by using materials carried for great distances. It is the farmhouses, cottages and work-a-day buildings of the communities that reflect geological factors. But canals, railways and the lorries of haulage contractors have progressively introduced alien material until the local style, based on the product of adjacent woodland, quarry or claypit, has been eliminated in all but a few villages.

Oak, cut from wind-blasted, stunted trees, was mixed with other hedgerow hardwoods – elm, ash and hazel or willow – in the framing of simple houses. The majority of framed buildings were of 'mud-and-stud' construction, where the wooden frame was covered in with lath, locally known as wands, which was the support for a covering of 'tempered earth': clay, pebbles, lime, dung, straw, hay and even acorns, trodden by man or animals to a sticky but hard-setting mass. Over the hardened mud a thin coat of plaster protected the wall exterior. 'Give it a good hat and good boots – it will last a century' was a frequent comment. The 'good hat' was thatch. A simple job with no fancy 'Norfolk work' on the ridge; the steeper the pitch of roof the poorer the covering might be. Old hay, sedge, straw or reed weathered grey and ruffled by birds is a rare sight in either county and most now lies below corrugated iron. 'Good boots' were the rubble footings or crude boulders of the wall foot. The wall posts were frequently set into the ground and consequently rotted quickly; the rotten feet and even the lower part of the wall itself are found 'underbuilt' with brick or other more durable materials in most surviving structures. 'Mud-and-stud' was a universal building material. The stone farmhouses of south Lincolnshire have their inner walls of mud-and-stud; the neat brick cottages of the clays are often found to be of mud-and-stud merely faced with brick. It was only during the eighteenth century that other materials really changed the streets and lanes in appearance. Brick, now common, was rare even in the late sixteenth century, although its revival dates back to the late fourteenth century in buildings in Lincoln or Thornton Abbey gatehouse. Stone, in the houses of working families, was exceptional too. In a tour of the counties many 'Red Houses' or 'Stone Houses' may still be identified by their name-boards.

Even in the most uninteresting villages it is rewarding to examine the method of bricklaying. The standard 'bonds' of the text book, Flemish and English, will be there no doubt, but 'garden-wall' bonds and altered characteristics show the hand of the villages' builders. A 'Flemish' bond of two headers and two stretchers alternating is quite common, particularly in west Lincolnshire. Up to 17 unbonded courses of stretchers have been recorded in an 'English garden-wall' bond wall of a brick farmhouse near Lincoln.

Stone building is in the 'Cotswold' tradition, which follows a distinct distribution from Somerset in the south to Yorkshire in the north. Lincolnshire has the greater concentration and the cold greyness of the weathered stone and more austere detailing give greater visual strength. The builder-architects of Stamford and Northamptonshire provided the stimulus for many village builders.

In the two counties the remains of open-field agriculture survive. Epworth (Humberside) still continues to be farmed in a weakened open structure; many of the other villages can show selion patterns through meadow grass, and here and there is a Sykes Lane or a North Field Farm to serve as a monument to a pre-Enclosure England. Village greens are not the predominant feature they once were, because of encroachment. Cattle, in most areas, are not so numerous, but the yards and sheltersheds or 'hovels' still stand by the village streets. 'Up corn, down horn', is the trend of modern farming; the 'corn' of course must be interpreted widely. The old pastures grow sugar-beet, carrots, celery and even daffodils and tulips.

The choice of villages representative of the two counties tries to avoid nostalgia. Attractive,

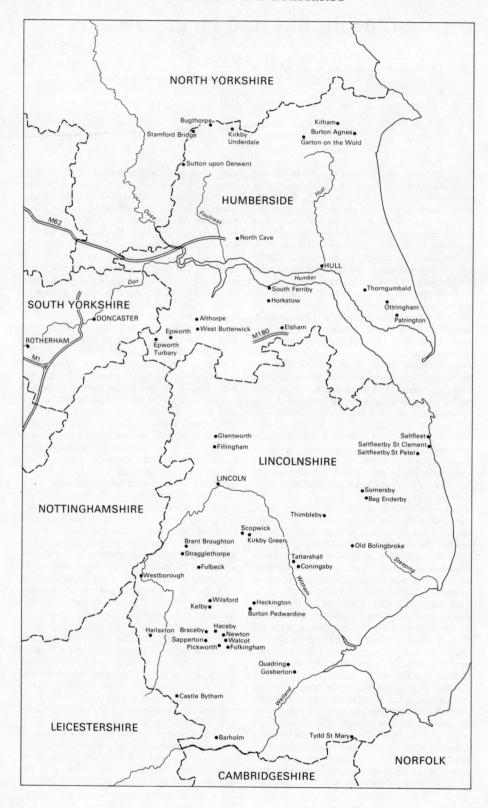

NORTH YORKSHIRE

Bugthorpe
Stamford Bridge
Kirkby Underdale
Kilham
Burton Agnes
Garton on the Wold

Sutton upon Derwent

HUMBERSIDE

Hull

Ouse
Foulness

M62

North Cave

HULL

Humber

Don

SOUTH YORKSHIRE

South Ferriby
Horkstow

Thorngumbald
Ottringham
Patrington

DONCASTER

ROTHERHAM

M1

Althorpe
Epworth
West Butterwick
Elsham
Epworth Turbary

M180

Glentworth
Fillingham

LINCOLNSHIRE

Saltfleet
Saltfleetby St Clement
Saltfleetby St Peter

LINCOLN

NOTTINGHAMSHIRE

Somersby
Bag Enderby

Thimbleby

Scopwick
Kirkby Green

Old Bolingbroke

Brant Broughton
Stragglethorpe
Fulbeck

Tattershall
Coningsby

Witham

Steeping

Westborough

Wilsford
Kelby
Heckington
Burton Pedwardine

Harlaxton
Braceby
Haceby
Sapperton
Newton
Pickworth
Walcot
Folkingham

Quadring
Gosberton

Castle Bytham

Welland

LEICESTERSHIRE

Barholm
Tydd St Mary

NORFOLK

CAMBRIDGESHIRE

unspoilt villages are rare and the desirable compromise between the unchanging picture-postcard village and the sprawling dormitory has yet to be reached. In many cases it is already far too late.

Lincolnshire and Humberside are out-of-the-way places, but even in their isolation their villages have suffered more indignities and injury in this age of planned environment than during almost all their long history. 'Standard' joinery has replaced the doors and elegant windows of the earlier carpenters. Even in the remote Wold the landscape is inexorably losing trees, shelter belts and hedges, as modern farming methods increase their hold. In only 30 years both village and landscape have lost much of that indefinable quality they once had. Occasionally glimpses of that former independence and informality show through the brash gloss of the commuters' improvements or the raw pseudo-Georgian enclaves that seem never destined to fit in with the old. Conservation Area policy has done little except to enhance property values in the 'designated areas'. Grossly large and alien windows scar gaunt old façades, and trim hedges have gone, to be replaced by perforated concrete block walls. Fortunately the hatred of trees is not universal; but, perversely, new planting, particularly of Japanese cherry and weeping willow in the suburban arcadias, is effete and detracts from the visual strength of ash, oak and walnut set in the old hawthorn hedges. To find a real village it is necessary to skirt the towns by up to 20 miles. But 30 miles from town and market probably spells desertion and destruction through neglect.

The great estates still hobble along on slender budgets, but even their conservative hand is loosening as houses and farms are sold to realize capital for costly machinery or asbestos buildings.

The villages of the two counties have the finest churches of almost any in England. Often the only reason for mention in guidebooks is the church buildings; but this book is about villages rather than architecture alone. Moreover it is about villages where Nonconformist worship had long been popular at the expense of the established church. Some parish churches have been declared redundant, and many chapels lie abandoned or serve as workshops. Dwindling congregations and the 'grouping' of parishes seem destined to destroy one of the main elements of the traditional village.

The buildings of the villages are also in peril. Improvement grants are too often accompanied by demands for standards quite unattainable within the shell of a small cottage. Grants for minor historic buildings are niggardly, and often it is only the commuter who can afford proper restoration. The two national institutions, the National Trust and the Department of the Environment, have only a meagre handful of monuments to show.

Any selection of villages representative of an area is difficult, and the rate of environmental change continues so rapidly that even that choice may lose its basis. Ever-widening ripples of suburban taste from the sprawl of the Grimsbys, Scunthorpes and Granthams erode the visual attractiveness or stern dignity of the village.

GAZETTEER

ALTHORPE, *Humberside* (4m W of Scunthorpe), is a village of largish farms combining the hamlets of Derrythorpe and Keadby. At Keadby Cut is the canal lock leading up from the Trent into the old canal network of England; it is still possible to reach Leeds or Liverpool from here by narrow-boat.

Althorpe's best house is an artisan mannerist brick L plan. Although poorly modernized it still has a pilastered doorcase with a floating pediment, friezeless over the coarse Tuscan detailing. The Wesleyan chapel (1864) is of red brick with yellow dressings and the Stevenson Memorial Hall (1903) is somewhat in the Italian style.

An asbestos garage trimmed with cedar boards asserts the right of everyman to ruin any pleasing prospect. It is sited 15ft from the fine church with its ashlar tower – a splendid exterior, weathered and silvery. Here and there among the coursed rubble and ashlaring is brick. Inside is an octagonal font on phaeon-stopped chamfers with fleuron squares in the frieze. The key to the locked church is at Fairview, a few yards S of the church porch, an interesting walk along the wide grass by the Trent edge all lined with reed and willow. The church is worth seeing if only for the sedilia –

buttressed and capped by castellated towers almost cut away by ogival arches and crocketed canopies. All was built (except for one fragment) by Sir John Neville, Kt, in 1483. Even the Victorian black and red floor has mellowed to the umbers and orange-rose pinks of an old Dutch picture. The S aisle was demolished and an 18th-c brick porch built in its place.

Opposite Manor Farm is the interestingly vernacular brickwork of a barn with bricknog venting.

BAG ENDERBY, *Lincs.* (6m E of Horncastle), is a U-shaped village lying N of the A158 down a minor road from Hagworthingham (an interesting village if only for its sadly decayed artisan mannerist Old Hall). The open centre of Bag Enderby is occupied by low, ivy-clad sheds of decaying wood and corrugated iron scattered among the trees and old drays and wagons. The former parsonage, now Ferndale Manor, is of early 18th-c origin with many later additions; its garden has dark evergreens and an odd collection of 'concretiana' – putti and squirrels, a toy house and weatherbeaten cats and dogs, all quite odd. The Hall, SE of the church, is built of pale ochre-washed brick. It has lateral stacks in the tradition of houses like Fenton Hall or Wykeham; chimneys like these seem the mark of a gentry house. Further to the E is evidence of modern farming in large asbestos sheds dwarfing the pantiled, whitewashed brick hovels that suited an earlier economy. A pretty two-bay single-storey house, whitewashed and under Norfolk thatch, lies down a dead-end lane W of the church. It has a late 18th-c stable and a barn with decorative brick venting. The building activity seems to have ended in the 1840s with a good pair of brick cottages.

The church is unaisled and built of greenstone. Albini of Enderby, who died in 1470, is responsible for both tower and church. Inside is an interesting font ornamented with passion symbols and a pieta. Franklin School, Spilsby, prepared a map, complete with crop distribution, in 1967, which is shown in the church with a good display of photographs. Delicately beautiful fragments of old glass survive. The screen is old but much restored. The heavy oak S door is perhaps 15th-c.

On leaving the village see the great tree-stump like a carving of a bear. Bag Enderby seems to have the highest density of cats in Lincs: my present count is ten, variegated.

BARHOLM, *Lincs.* (3m W of Market Deeping), is best approached from the W past a good stone house of the 1830s, three bays under a hipped stone-tiled roof, with a stone-walled garden. On the bend leading into the village is a good ashlar barn. The Old Hall, hidden behind its enormous stone barn, has a dovecote capped with a multitude of ball finials erected at about the time the house was cased in stone. There is only one pargeted gable (nothing elaborate, just the triangular

The Saxon–Norman doorway of
St Martin's, Barholm

Russell Read

impression of a trowel – up, down, up – giving an impression of diaperwork; a typically Northants. trait) to indicate the mass of oak framing that lies hidden behind the mullioned windowed front. The straggly village street has stone-tile, pantile and thatched (now under asbestos) roofs to the older houses; a few estate houses of the 1850s are dotted among them. E of the church is a large stone house in an orchard with, further E, a brick barn. The land is a sandy flat, with ponies, windbreaks and covert – hunting country.

There is an incredible array of Rococo tombstones, all beribboned, urned and finialled with angels amid the swags and gadrooned shellwork, in the churchyard of St Martin's. The Saxon-Norman S door has a tympanum with stone-cut diaper like the Old Hall pargeting. There is much Norman as well as Saxon work. The sedilia and piscina are EE lightly restored. The font is surely not the work of one generation: there is raised work, a jumble of Celtic motifs and a run of dogtooth on its octagonal flanks. There is a curious inscription on the armorial brass to Francis Fordham, Gent., 1641, and an 18th-c marble to Richard Walburgh. The tower, rebuilt in 1648 and raised in 1855, has a poignant inscription let into the re-used masonry (see the Saxon fragments). Before leaving, look to the E of the S porch for the blocked Saxon door with its scratchy carving and chopped ornament – it is well hidden and many visitors miss it.

BRACEBY, *Lincs.,* 7m E of Grantham. Limestone is the local building material, either as rubble, chopped and coursed or ashlar. Tiles, particularly pantiles, have replaced thatch as roof covering. Stone mullions and moulded ashlar show this to have been one of the centres of quarrying and masonry from early times. The houses are in part of 16th-c origin but the 17th c was the great period of stone building. Set back from the village street N of the churchyard is the long front of Manor Farm. The E part has a datestone LT 1653 but the W lengthening is undated (another datestone LT 1707 is built into a 19th-c barn at the rear; presumably this came from the house – as did the fragments of fireplace moulding and ashlar in a later drastic remodelling of the interior in the 1870s). Other, simpler houses form the rest of the village, and there is a roofless stone dovecote behind a whitewashed cottage with a box tree in its garden. An early 18th-c house of five bays under a hipped roof forms part of a group E of the church.

The tiny church of St Margaret is now just a nave and chancel since the demolition of both aisles. There is the start of an 'apprentice alphabet' on the W respond of the N arcade – he only got as far as 'G'. The nave capitals are just flared keel mouldings with some 'waterleaf'. The reset Dec tracery is of monolithic type – cut, like earlier plate-tracery, from a single block. The porch is much altered, and has reset fragments including a cross-head of spoked fleurons. The tub-font is scraped.

Russell Read

Manor Farm, Braceby, 1653 and 1707

One m to the E is the decaying village of **Haceby**. The gaunt church, dedicated, like that of Braceby, to St Margaret, is Norman, with an unbuttressed tower, EE lancets and larger Perp tracery ones. The porch has graffiti of 1677 and 1757. Locked and forlorn, it seems a symbol of the desertion of the villages of the Lincs. limestone heath. The S front of the great parsonage has collapsed, leaving only the rubble core to support its tile-less roof.

BRANT BROUGHTON, *Lincs.*, a predominantly Georgian village, lies in the Clays below the Edge, just off the A17 W of Leadenham. To the S is the tiny village of **Stragglethorpe** with an equally tiny church – ancient and unspoilt, pine Georgian interior – also the vastly enlarged and remodelled Elizabethan Hall and Vineyard (it does produce wine commercially). There are vernacular and estate houses.

It was politic in Georgian Lincs. to live in a 'rich' village, where there was little risk of a crippling contribution to the Poor. Itinerant labour from neighbouring villages supplemented the workforce on demand. The Poor Law Union system destroyed the financial advantages but left villages such as this more popular than ever in the eyes of the middle classes. Sir Robert Heron of nearby Stubton Hall built workhouses and made profit from them before the Union Workhouse was thought of. This explains to some extent the rich pattern of Georgian brick buildings in Brant Broughton.

Of the earlier village much is left. The Manor House (to the N) has a 17th-c history of addition and remodelling but the N wing is still timber-framed (*c.* 1500). The best house is the ashlar-fronted Priory of 1658; externally it is little altered but the plan has been completely reorganized, keeping some old detailing and the magnificent stair. Next to the Priory along Church Walk is the Old Hall, once a secondary seat of the Listers of

Coleby Hall, with a good five-bay brick front and ashlar detailing. Along the High Street and the narrow green with its curly iron seats under the trees, is a double row of houses that would take a day to describe. Grey Garth is a remodelled Carolean house with a wooden (Victorian) porch on balusters. Warburton House opposite the school (1871) preserves the name of Bishop William Warburton (rector here in 1728). It was obviously rebuilt in the 1800s. The rectory is built of orange brick with plum-coloured brick voussoirs to its three bays of sashes. Cobblers is early 18th-c and modernized – opposite is the picturesque old brick and stone forge with drop shutters, half-door and sliding casements. Here the church gates were hand-forged in the late 1920s: the tradition of fine ironwork is still carried on. Opposite and further on is a white five-bay house of the 1770s. The Hollies has plummy-orange brick walls and a pantiled roof – the sashes are four panes wide, a sign of early 19th-c work. Beyond again is a Flemish bond brick house with a towny Palladian front to the green. Corner House and the Quaker Meeting House (1701) are plain and brick. The most interesting house of the street lies to the E. It was originally a double-pile house of the 1630s (the stone-mullioned windows may still be seen from the narrow yard to the N) re-fronted in the Stamford style with a pedimented stone doorcase straight from Batty Langley's pattern books. The roofline has been destroyed by the addition of an attic floor in rendered brick. This is perhaps the key to the puzzling plan of the grid-like layout of the village – were there originally houses only to the E of the street? Almost opposite, down Guildford Lane, is a 16th-c stone dovecote in the spacious grounds of The Gables.

In the streets to the W is much of interest; almshouses with a sadly ruined well-house – Victorian. A tall, three-storeyed farmhouse in Flemish bond brick with vitrified headers has an old fanlight –

generous and typical of the larger farms further N on the Clays.

The church of St Helen has a spire visible for miles across the flat wooded vale of the River Brant. There is a perfect interior, despite demolition and rebuilding particularly in 1812 and 1876. The richly coloured interior has black-and-white diaper marble floors (1908), twinkling brass and the glow of faded gilt. Over the altar is a now famous painting – what a pity it was discovered to be valued in pound notes! It is not long since it could be appreciated just for itself. The glass in the windows was made by the Rev. Canon Frederick Sutton (Rector 1873–88) and fired and annealed in the kiln at Brant Broughton House.

The House is now an Educational Centre. In Heathcote Sutton's day it was the big house. Part 17th-c, part Georgian – a medley of stone and brick is held together by a brave attempt at symmetry. Two bays, canted of course, were added to the wings and a wooden Tuscan colonnade thrown across the front. Good stabling lies at the back (now converted) and, by the path to the church, a decaying wooden game larder, perhaps the last in the county.

BUGTHORPE, *Humberside,* 7m N of Pocklington. Approach the village from the A166 by the lane which runs across the wet meadows in the low fields below the selion-patterned enclosures surrounding the tofts and crofts. Beyond the village, to the N, is Bugthorpe beck, a small stream dividing Thoralby Hall from the main settlement. The spur of chalk wold on which the village stands has shallow earthworks and a pond down the quiet lane past the chapel. Perhaps the village site has changed dramatically over the centuries, although some houses and cottages have fragments of ragstone walling incorporated in later over-building which suggest a stone-built, but humble, group of houses of the late 16th c. The village farmsteads from which the tree-dotted landscape is worked are mostly built of variegated brick laid in English garden-wall bond, with three to five intervening courses of stretchers between the bonding header course. The only farms away from the nucleus seem to date from the period of enclosure when some of the old farmhouses in the village street were divided into labourers' cottages. To the W of the village is the vicarage, built of yellow brick with red brick bands under a slate roof, a canted brick bay in the centre of the S front: a typical clergy house of the late 1860s. To the E of the church is an attractive Victorian school, now a house, in a loosely Jacobean style built as an encroachment on the green.

In the spring the village is delightful, its grassy verges thick with snowdrops and daffodils. The crowning glory is the church of St Andrew. A weeping ash shades the S porch and late 18th-c tombstones stand in the grass. The urns and swags, incised letters and towny elegance are in complete contrast to the irregular mass of the greenstone and limestone of the church itself. Inside is a rich panoply of decoration built up over

centuries in a way that reconciles the Norman carving of the chancel arch, the fluttering Rococo cherubs of the Payler monument, the jolly baldachino, the Gothicized tower screen with the pomposity of the pseudo-City Church classical organ case 'presented in 1914' and the sparkle of the 18th-c six-branch chandelier. It is a church for those who delight in churches; obviously Goodhart-Rendel's work in 1936 for Lord Halifax kept all that was good. The chandeliers in the nave, gleaming brass again, have addorsed eagle finials – a problem of attribution for the enthusiast. Above all, the interior has a sense of colour elegantly set off against white.

CASTLE BYTHAM, *Lincs.* The county's best village? Although only 4m E of A1 (turn off 7m N of Stamford) it is remote in an area of interesting and tucked-away places. The plan of the village is T-shaped, confused by a system of lanes. An E–W street lies along and just below a limestone edge; here is the church, entered, as in so many replanned settlements, by the N porch. Below the churchyard and the romantically named Priory House is a tiny triangular green and the other street running N to Swayfield and Corby Glen. To the E are the massive, heaving earthworks of the castle slighted in 1221 by Henry III. Substantial fragments must have survived into the 18th c only to be robbed in the spate of building and rebuilding of the 1780s and '90s. It is well worth the steep climb if only to see the rich pattern of the village below. The roofs of the village are here the key to much of its history. Two at least are the survivors of the great open halls: Rectory Farmhouse at the N end and the Priory house next the church. Like many houses in the village their façades are unassuming, with perhaps the occasional distinction of a shallow rectangular bay of stone-mullioned lights. Below the inserted floors beneath the sooted rafters are the stone arcades of screen passages inserted from the 14th to the 16th c. At the rear of Pope's Farmhouse (remodelled in the 1870s) is a round dovecote – romantic rather than genuine. There are ducks on the pond and along the stream beneath the castle mound. The N side of the cruciform church with its cavernous porch is set in dark yews intermingled with pale green-lichened tombstones. From the churchyard there is another view across the village; to the W is the yellow pantile roof of the 17th-c Manor House (these tiles were perhaps fired at Little Bytham by the forerunners of the brick manufacturers there).

Inside the church of St James is full of an ochre silvery light. The nave roof has a low-pitched crown-post roof with roll-moulded tie-beams and stubby 'sprags' to the principals, typical of the 1520s. A large Dec tomb recess under an ogival canopy with a cap finial, enriched with ball-flower and crockets, is now used as an Easter sepulchre. The N arcade capitals have 'stiff-leaf' carving.

ELSHAM, *Humberside* (3m N of Brigg), is now famous for its gardens and Nature Trail (open except Good Friday and Christmas Day). The gardens belong to the Hall: seven bays, two and a half floors, grey cemented and grim, with more less formal building behind; the Orangery (1760) is an excellent foil. The Stables – by Carr or Perhaps Paine? – are good Georgian. Three pedimented brick pavilions are linked together and now serve as a crafts and antiques centre. The public unfortunately does not see the plasterwork in the old Rent Room: its fireplace with a 'sun in splendour' is now in the high garrets of the Hall. Its entrance stair has gone and only pigeons rest on its cornices and plaster mouldings, egg and dart with lugged panels. The yard behind is also 18th-c, designed for fatstock and storage of fodder, grain and roots.

The village has some vestiges of unspoilt houses in the intricate web of streets lined by pretty gardens, flowering shrubs and trees. All is well kept but bijou. Front Street has a large Georgian house in brick all painted yellow – may it weather to a better colour. It is still sashed and pantiled, and behind is the picturesque and unrestored yard under moss-grown roofs. Chapel Street has a pair of estate cottages, in brick with segmental arch lintels of yellow and vitrified brick and stone, built for Astley Corbett of the Hall, a colourful figure of the turf. There is an earthwork in the Park (Golf Course) amid coverts and plantings.

The church has much Norman and a little Saxon work amid the heavily restored and rebuilt Gothic (1874).

EPWORTH, *Humberside* (7m SW of Scunthorpe), is unusual. As the psychological centre of Methodist and Wesleyan pilgrimage it has buildings more suited to a town: the great campus of the Wesley Memorial Church, manse, school and house (1888–91), with an older chapel to the E refronted in 1868. The old chapel, sashed under segmental yellow-brick lintels, is a humble neighbour of the grandiose gothic revival of 1888. The rectory of the Wesley family stands in Albion Hill and is open daily (Sundays 2–4 p.m.); the Wesley brothers spent their childhood here. The irregular seven-bay front retains part of the old house burnt in 1709; the careful restoration has renewed the modillion cornice below the steep pantiled roof. Note the rafter feet exposed in the garrets – a locally common type of French derivation. The quoins to the façade are in cut brick.

The church of St Andrew stands apart from the village, N, on a hill (see how many capless and derelict mill towers there are on the horizon) up a flagged walk lined with trees. There is rough masonry to the aisles, a rendered clerestory, and an ashlar tower. The N porch was oddly rebuilt in 1721: it has a triple cusped arch with an old vault and masonry on brick footings. The Dec windows to the S side of the chancel are reticulated with flat tops – apparently original; the nave is an archaeological crossword puzzle.

At the foot of Church Walk there are Georgian houses, and beyond is Market Street (houses of 1843) and the partly cobbled Market Place

dominated by the generously proportioned four bays of the Red Lion. Here is the centre of the Conservation Area, round the stumpy 17th-c Market Cross on its circular stepped base. The Mechanic's Institute Library has a good italianate Victorian elevation: it must have looked better on paper than in dull brick, stone dressings and green-painted sashes.

Nearby, just in Queen Street, is a good five-bay Georgian house, whitewashed. In Hollingsworth Lane is the Magistrates' Court (the old police station, 1848) with tall sashes, stone dressings and a good interior.

There is modern development and 'bijou restoration': it is to be hoped that the neo-Georgian shopping group below the church and car park will mellow. Boothferry District Council has established a good picnic area to the N, near a reedy pond and willow trees.

S of the Burnham road crossing is a group of brick vernacular farmsteads; the White Bear Inn and a garden centre beyond. In the vestiges of open-field farming that survive in **Epworth Turbary**, a string of low-built shacks and single-bay houses. One two-unit house extended by a washhouse was the proud boast of its owner. 'I live in a three-storey house; but they built the — soidways.' Such is the humour of the Isle of Axholme.

FILLINGHAM, *Lincs.*, 9m N of Lincoln. The castle (alias Summer Castle) was built for Sir Cecil Wray (*see* Glentworth) from stone quarried in the park. Wray had for one of his 'gossips' or godparents Lady Vanbrugh, so this is perhaps a posthumous work of the Vanbrugh 'toy castle' idiom. The plan is simple; four rooms to a floor with 'an entry through all' and stair. Its derivation is from the sort of house built by minor gentry in the early 1600s (e.g. The Red Hall at Bourne) with the added display of Gothick towers and battlements. John Carr of York added a long wing (now almost all gone) and supplied the designs for the Great Barn and Stable as well as for the numerous castellated Lodges here and at Redbourne and Bishops Norton (Norton Place). It is a separate entity with gardens, saw-yard and smithy.

The village lies below the park at the foot of the Edge. It is a nucleated group of old freeholds 'bought in', with an old church revamped in Gothic. The tower has an open arcade in chisel-chipped, rustic ashlar with generous windows above – all Gothic and built as an eye-catcher for the vista from the castle to the serpentine lake; all of 1777. Much medieval and some Norman work has been incorporated in lightly handled remodelling of various dates. There is a Norman door arch, and the EE windows are perhaps reset. The aisles have disappeared. Inside is a carved chest of the 'Witham School' (the lid is new) and a series of restrained wall monuments of 1603, 1805, 1825 and 1852. The restoration was the work of the 'children, family and Tenantry of John Dalton' of the castle.

At the N end of the village is a tall whitewashed late Georgian house; opposite across the lawn and street is a good group of Georgian and Victorian farm buildings, hipped and pantiled. On the corner of Willingham Road three brick privies are exposed by demolition; nearby is a derelict 19th-c double-pile farmhouse. The Village Hall is 1840 Gothick. In Chapel Road the old smithy still has its tyring plate sunk in the grass outside; there is good Georgian vernacular building nearby. To the S is an enormously long low vernacular house with a massive brick-topped chimney. Early Jacobean no doubt, but elongated later; its odd silhouette suggests a cased timber frame.

The thatched Manor Farm House is ¼m NE of the church: 18th- and 19th-c buildings in stone.

There are good trees in the village, with specimen planting in the churchyard round the deliciously Gothic canopied monument to the Daltons – erected in 1854–5 – to the design by Keyworth of Hull. Fillingham is best approached from Lincoln through Cammeringham; along the road are magnificent views both E and W.

FOLKINGHAM, *Lincs.* (8m S of Sleaford), grew up at the foot of the early 14th-c castle of which only substantial earthworks remain. Its site was occupied by the House of Correction, a prison, of which only the picturesquely pompous gatehouse (1825) remains. The large green is surrounded by good, towny houses built, rebuilt or improved in the 1780s and '90s. Looking down the tapering green, S, is the old Court Room for Quarter Sessions and two ashlar limestone wings (remodelled in the 1720s). These seem to have been three buildings before they were joined to form the vast inn (*see illustration on page 22*). It is still possible to arrive in a coach and four: the stabling is adequate, having been built for forty, and there is all the spacious informality of the coaching era. The flanks of the green are lined with a variety of houses. The Manor House of the 1660s has a basement with three floors above, yet its plan was of only two rooms before the small E wing was added (note the storeyed pedimented porch); opposite is the warm cottagey brick of the Whipping Posts (a good foil for the cool greyness of the ashlar fronts of many others). There is a varied roofscape: pantile, slate and stone tile over mansard, hipped or gabled frames, thin brick chimneys or generous ashlar. Behind the grand five-bay, two-and-a-half storey houses W of the green is Chapel Lane; curious reset carvings are hidden in one yard – of drums, draped flags and trophies from some great building. What was the Good Intent of 1777 – surely not just a small malting? Spring Lane has good buildings of the late 17th c where Chapel Lane tails off into modern 'semis'.

The church of St Andrew is set back down a short street W of the Greyhound Inn. Its tall, four-stage Perp tower has a crown of 16 pinnacles visible for miles yet curiously unobtrusive in the village scene. Despite the restoration of 1857 the church is still richly mellow and architecturally ambitious. Fragments of Norman work survive in a church built in that curiously Lincolnshire style that hovers between Dec and Perp (e.g. the

ruined Wyeham chapel near Spalding). Further confusion is added by late EE work – or is it Dec? The furnishings include an 18th-c baluster font and an elegant Gothic screen that incorporates some fragments of old pew-ends.

It is difficult to believe that this village was once (*c.* 1780) of mud and stud, humble and dishevelled, centred on a pond and an untidy heap of scrap timber. It is fortunate that Thimbleby (q.v.) survives as a comparison.

FULBECK, *Lincs.,* 12m S of Lincoln. Follow the A607 through Navenby, Wellingore (see the unusual fragment of an L-plan ashlared house of the 1630s opposite the church, in Theaker's Yard: now a barn chock-full of modern machinery), past Welbourn (interesting house of the 1620s at the end of the lane by the church; a bee-hive rubble well house nearby – there are two more at Coleby) and on past Leadenham (good Hall, interesting village round a green with Jacobean and later houses – the George Inn has a good front) to the N end of Fulbeck – if the distraction of the other villages has not delayed the visit until darkness has fallen.

Here is the house of the old brickyard. Further S are two fine houses that, typically, turn their façades to the road rather than the fine views from the Cliff across the clays to the Trent. Fulbeck House is of the 1690s, five bays with a central Victorian doorcase replacing a window: the façade was originally doorless. It is convincingly 'Queen Anne', as remodelled; there are vast extensions of the 1830s behind. The Hall has fine wrought-iron gates to the tree-lined drive. After a fire in 1733, the Fanes added a new block to the remains of the earlier house. This block must be by a Stamford man (see No. 21 High Street, 1732): there are five bays of two-and-a-half floors, rusticated windows articulated by giant pilasters under a parapet, all in ashlar oolite. Nearby the Victorian 'Cottage' – a secondary Fane house – is large and brick-built. The Old Parsonage (an exchange for the 1860s one by the church) is Jacobean with a disastrous facelift of 1900.

S of this group, off A607 down a lane, is the old village clustered round a green and well-house (Victorian and timbered). Ermine House looks S down the green. Its silhouette and plan (two units divided by a stair, basement, two floors and garrets) looks early but it is an assembly of bits put together by an agent for several estates. The walling is rubble with brick dressings – of the 1830s – but the parapet is from another house, the stair (finely balustraded) and panelling convincingly put together but from various sources. Enlargements to the N are hidden by evergreens and trees. On the green is a good group of vernacular limestone buildings; these extend along the lanes towards the Low Fields. There is another group round Peacock Place.

The Fanes have been here since 1632 and there are several estate-type cottages in the village as well as farms out in the former open-field, e.g. Victoria Farm. The church was restored in 1888 at a cost of £1350; despite this there is much of interest. The Norman font is of arcaded stone (*see* Westborough) and fragments of another, square one are behind the pulpit. The dominant style is Perp with an eight-pinnacled tower looking over the Cliff towards its Notts. counterparts.

Somerton Castle (1281 and later) with some surviving building lies down the gated road from the Cliff: 7m N of Fulbeck, turn off A607 at Boothby Graffoe to the Low Road from Lincoln to Brant Broughton (q.v.) – there is a glimpse of the castle from here.

GLENTWORTH, *Lincs.,* 11m N of Lincoln, lies at the foot of the edge W of B1398 which follows the crest-line. The view from the road is good: the long 'flaring' brick front of the Hall (11 bays, by James Paine, *c.* 1753), the red-brick stables and the walled gardens – all in decay – in the foreground with a distant view across the flat clays towards the Trent. There is much planting of coppice, shelter-belt and covert and many hedgerow trees. St George's Hill is a sunken lane leading into the village. There is a neat stone house, sashed, amid brick building and old stockyards. N of the churchyard is a row of stone cottages, long and low but now raised in modern brick; opposite is Northlands House, with good Georgian sashes in ashlar-dressed chopped rubble walling. The roof is slate; the grounds well treed. Along Church Street some old houses mingle incongruously with modern development. The vicarage is a replacement of 1793; the Bassets were vicars or curates here from 1696 until 1850 (all presented by Lord Scarborough, rebuilder of the Hall, and his family). At the foot of Stony Lane, off Chapel Lane, is the church of St Michael. Seen over a Jacobean chancel and a nave of 1782, the tower is all Saxon but for the Perp window to the W with its excellent Victorian glass (1876): finely drawn and silvery with little strong colour yet richly decorative. St Raphael, St Michael and St Gabriel have fine wings and crowns. The tower bell-stage windows have mid-wall shafts (the S one with cabling) and a scratchy Saxon carving, a cross chevronny on the W window ashlar. Sir Christopher Wray, Queen Elizabeth's Chief Justice, who died in 1592, is commemorated by a monument, a towering *tour de force* in coloured marbles with kneeling mourners below and another in a niche above, and Corinthian columns in antis – the scale and fringe cornice as big as anything by Smythson. There is fine strapwork and foliage with a guilloched arch. Sir Christopher's prayer book, inkflask and pencase are carved just above his head in the tympanum. His son built the Hall, of which little is left: a courtyard house bigger than Blickling now reduced to a tiny wing behind the new Hall. He also built a new vicarage in 1612, in stone not mud and stud like its predecessor (now demolished). There is another fine Wray tomb of 1714 nearby.

HARLAXTON, *Lincs.,* 3m SW of Grantham. The Hall is dated 1837 and any louder trumpet-

Russell Read

The monument to Sir Christopher Wray in St Michael's church, Glentworth

blast of the Victorian Age's fanfare would be deafening. Anthony Salvin, his assistant James Deeson, and William Burn, with their patron, George de Ligne Gregory, worked on the design from 1822 (when the estate passed to Gregory). It was built to house an art collection that was to pass on to another family at the end of Gregory's life, leaving the vast echoing galleries, halls and corridors as empty as they are today. Russell Read's *Harlaxton* (Grantham, 1978) is a photographic memorial and record of this prodigious pile. The owners were old landed gentry, not new rich. The old Manor House was a long, low medieval and Jacobean house that provided some of the inspiration for the new. Fragments of its detailing are dotted about the new village.

Only four houses have substantial masonry of the 1630s: the best one is to the W of the churchyard. Only one house of the 1790s – a brick and pantile, rewindowed but with serpentine keystone lintels – stands intact by the W gate into the great park. The division of park, estate village and commercial village is very marked. The Drift is a double row of cottages – *ornées* and utilitarian – built down the sloping lane to the Nottingham-Grantham Canal. At the foot by the canal is an octagonal cottage – the best – dated GDG (George de Ligne Gregory) 1803. The initials ISG (Iohn Sherwin Gregory) also appear on this house; others are dated GDG 1808 – GDG 1810, GDG 1807 – 1810, GDG, 1820 (with later work). The Drift is separated from the estate village by A607 and the

Russell Read

Carved boss depicting a devil in the vaulted south aisle of St Andrew's, Kelby

Gregory Arms Hotel – its centre bow (now cemented over) has a brick counterpart in the village. The churchyard is a good place to start a tour; to the N is a three-bay brick (Flemish bond) house with three-light mullioned and leaded windows, the ground floor with transoms, the gables boarded and overhanging, and decorated brick stacks. There is no date, merely ISG over a newer porch of before 1869. There are scores of dated buildings (and dated alterations). Cottages, not necessarily of GDG's building, have 1788, 1789 (rebuilt *c.* 1860), 1791 and 1794 on their datestones. The rebuilding continues with GDG 1819, the village shop – brick arcaded front, sliding or leaded casements.

The village school incorporates some late Georgian work into its 'Disneyesque' fantasia of chevron half-timber (the construction is not just decorative), brick, ashlar dressings and terra cotta. In the court are an ashlared well house, pargeted timbered corner oriel, pantiles and a chimneyscape of astounding variety. The rectory is typical of the 1860s: brick and slate.

The church of St Mary and St Peter is, like the village, a work of addition and over-restoration throughout the Victorian era (£1200 was spent in 1890–1 alone). Solid Norman work ,and truly Gothic additions there are, even to one or two carved bits that have escaped recutting. There is a brass to William Strood (1498), several monuments to the de Ligne family (black marble altar-tomb 1686 to Sir Daniel) and their connections: Burrell (Dowsby and Ryhall), Cadwallader Glynne etc. Outside in the yard are good tombstones and Swithland slates of the 1790s.

Harlaxton was a freeholders' village bought in to make a setting for the Great House; the commons and open-field now lie below Park and Home Farm. The *raison d'être*, the monstrous Hall, is now an outpost of the University of Evansville, Indiana.

HECKINGTON, *Lincs.*, 5m E of Sleaford. Heckington Village Trust is only one sign of community spirit here. Its pressure has brought about the creation of the first Industrial Conservation Area in the county centred on the famous eight-sailed windmill. Several buildings are included: the station buildings, signal box, the former Railway Hotel and the 'Pea-House'. The latter was used by the local seed firm, Sharpes, for riddling peas; now it is to have a new lease of life as a Heritage Workshop and Exhibition Area. The project will house a basketmaker, a spinner and a weaver, among other craftsmen whose skills seem almost lost to the area. It is hoped that the whole complex will be open in 1980.

There has been no major change or demolition within the village for at least three years – a sharp contrast with almost every other place in Lincs. The parish church of St Andrew is one of the grandest in the county and perhaps the best-known example of Dec Gothic in the country. Victorian text books describe it in detail and their wood-engraved illustrations spread its influence far and wide during the Anglican Revival. Built shortly after 1300, it has an amazing display of infinitely varied window tracery and decorative carving. The Easter Sepulchre is perhaps the best of fine detail in the building; or is the sedilia with its carvings more assured? Outside there is much to see in the varied street pattern.

Two stone buildings, a derelict house in Hubbard's Yard off St Andrew's Street, and the Nag's Head Inn, Market Place (1684), are in the Lincolnshire–Cotswold tradition. The house in Hubbard's yard is of an uncommon plan: a tiny wood-mullioned window lights a small dairy at the end, a hall and parlour divided by a great chimney, and a lobby entrance with a fret baluster stair, form a two-and-a-half rather than three-unit house. The house has a parallel at Low Somerby dated 1632; the Heckington house was re-windowed in the early 1700s. The timber frame and mud-and-stud tradition is poorly represented by one house now divided into Nos. 35, 37 and 39 Eastgate (two bays are still under thatch). The Hall was drastically remodelled in the early part of the 20th c but old bits survive in the plinth masonry. In the trim garden, lined in clipped box, is a silted moat.

In Eastgate is Heckington Manor House, built originally of red brick; the 18th-c core was cased in fine white bricks face bedded to resemble ashlar. The detailing is also Victorian. A house in East Heckington has had similar treatment.

The green, now partially turned into a central car park, may at one time have been a market place (the base and shaft of a market cross were moved to the churchyard). To the N is a row of almshouses (1888) erected by Henry Godson; another row, now modernized (1975) was added in 1904 by Edward Godson in Vicarage Lane. Both are to the same design, single-storey brick laid in Flemish bond in a Tudoresque style with a covered porch all along the fronts. A plaque on a house near the W end of the church records the early attempts to relieve the poor without loss of dignity: a House of Industry rather than the workhouse.

The parish is large, over 5000 acres, and relied on a cattle-based economy until the 19th c. The vast common is now divided into farms.

KELBY, *Lincs.* (5m SW of Sleaford), is a tiny village, difficult to find but well worth a detour 1m S from **Wilsford** on A153. After passing through Wilsford, with its interesting church and 17th-c Home Farmhouse (note the willows near the site of the vanished priory that give the village its name – Willows Ford), the lane runs through the heavy ploughland of the Heath. Kelby occupies the centre of an E–W ridge of limestone amid the scrubby hedges and sparse trees. Here and at Heydour and Culverthorpe were the quarries of Ancaster Stone. Ancaster has only one small pit for field-walling stone, but the railway Bills of Lading were issued at Ancaster station.

The village is closely nucleated with large yards enclosed by dry-stone walls. At the E end is the pond and the green – a pretty sight with white ducks, all too rare in modern Lincs. Overlooking the pond is a fine 17th-c house of two-and-a-half units (*see* Heckington) and a small rubble cottage built in the early 18th c. A small group of outbuildings behind in the yard is alive with pigeons and poultry. W along the street is Heath, a steeply gabled house of the early 1700s, built of limestone rubble but with three brick chimneys. The windows were renewed as they decayed – *c*. 1800, 1860 and modern – and the porch with a wooden king post was added about 1900. To the W again is the Manor House, restored and almost rebuilt in the 1960s. Much old masonry survives; the gable kneelers and caps below the ball finials are designed for a roof pitch as steep as Heath's. Beyond the church as the lane turns S is a group of cottages and Glebe Farm and barn (1839) which have a few 17th-c fragments. In the hovel by the door of Glebe Farmhouse is an old 'ark' or hutch with a multitude of 'faggot-marks' used in counting grain sacks as they went into the granary (or the number of eggs laid). The rudimentary system was to record in 'I's to four (IIII) and then score a / across them to give units of five. The small churchyard has a laburnum, yews and 19th-c tombs: an ideal setting for the equally small church.

The barn-like chancel is attached to a beautifully minuscule aisled nave, tower and spire. The clerestory is 19th-c. Grotesquely carved medieval heads abound and the upper stage of the tower has rounded angle-shafts instead of quoins or buttresses. The church (St Andrew) is locked but the key is available from either Pond or Glebe Farmhouses. The sunlit S porch echoes to the noises of sheep and cattle in Glebe farmyard; its walls have old graffiti (1706 etc.) and on the bench is an oddly perforated stone which, when held correctly, spells out ?W ?R 177?8 – a puzzle indeed. In the nave is an almost complete set of poppy-head pews carved in the early 1500s. Blind tracery and heads in roundels '*à la Romayne*' are still sharply defined in the honey-grey oak. Almost every period and style is represented in the masonry; the fragment of herringbone masonry is perhaps

Lovers: another of the carved stone bosses in the roof of St Andrew's, Kelby

Saxon, the tower is part Norman, the N arcade EE, the S aisle Dec, a traceried window in the N aisle (Perp) is cut from a monolith. Plate tracery of this late type is not uncommon (*see* Westborough). The *tour de force* is the vaulted S aisle with its simple, carved bosses. An acrobat, a devil and a pair of lovers keep company with a jolly group of musicians. The vault responds are carved too: a petulant king, an escutcheoned cow and a contorted bishop.

An attempt has been made to cover the one blot – a bungalow – with saplings that one day may screen it as trees.

KILHAM, *Humberside,* lies 2m W of the village of **Burton Agnes,** famous for its great brick mansion of the first decade of the 17th c built to replace the surviving Norman upper-hall house. Kilham is 5m N of Great Driffield. Eleven roads, one of Roman origin, lead to the long, cranked village street lined with farmhouses. Behind the houses are long yards roughly based on the tofts and crofts of the medieval plan. These tofts are bounded by a typical back lane, and the ragged pattern of ditches and hedges seen from it gives an idea of how crofts were amalgamated to give a larger area for more recent cattle yards. At the W end of the nucleus, High Farm clearly shows the original layout fossilized under grass. High Farmhouse is built in three bays of irregular Flemish bond brick; its windows are sashed, four panes high and four panes wide – typical of very late country Georgian. Apart from the five-bay front of Hall Farm (1716) the village houses are all essentially of three bays. On the main street, opposite Driffield Road, is a sandstone-detailed white-brick house in English bond. Although it is built of alien materials and Victorian in detail, its basic plan and front still conform to the village idiom. Of the older farmhouses, Belgrave Lodge of *c*. 1845 has an added kitchen bay and an elaborate long wall to the yard with a curtsy-coped door and a round arch. The wall is in irregular English bond and the house is built with five courses of stretchers between the English bonding course of headers. The wooden doorcase to the house has reeded pilaster strips and an astragal fanlight under a triangular pediment; doorcases of similar type are scattered among the better houses.

Several modern intrusions show uneasily that the village is still alive, and the yard of a firm of agricultural contractors adds a splash of primary coloured machinery at the E end of the street. The village shop has paned bow windows to the street, of the 1830s rather than commuter 'Georgian'. Its side wall and trail of small storehouses tails off up the sunken lane to the toft ends; opposite is the flaring orange-brick Temperance Hall of 1886. Its front with dressings of Yorkstone and red brick is now scarred by a totally inappropriate modern porch. A Nonconformist chapel in raw red brick and white-stone Perp revival was built as late as 1920. Across the road from the church is the Star Inn, a former farmhouse still having its yard as well as a workshop of the type used by village craftsmen. At one time a stream must have run past the door; now the water is confined in a brick culvert beneath the street. Near the culvert outfall is the village pump. The pump is not an ordinary affair. Cast-iron Doric pillars support a metal-framed platform approached by iron steps; only a fragment of the decorative iron rail to the platform survives. The pump itself is a built-up blacksmith's job, with one spout for the village gossips' buckets and another, higher up and facing the road, for filling the water tanks of steam engines. There is a brick barn with intricately patterned vents in the nearby farmyard.

Standing a little apart is the splendid church with a most spectacular decorative Norman S door of six orders. All the arch voussoirs are in chevron. The whole originally formed a slightly projecting porticus with a great gable ornate with florets and circles in diaperwork; even the diaper ribs are cut with incised circles, arcading and paterae. Below, the arch is worked in alternating bands of chevron. The porch is now covered by a deeper 18th-c brick one which in its turn incorporates earlier fragments. Inside the porch is a small group of stone fragments: an intricately diapered and faceted nook shaft, an odd voussoir carved with a goat's head and part of a cross-shaft. The whitewashed interior has good, quiet monuments, and the Royal Arms of George III over the S door, (which is of fielded astragal panelling of a similar date). The five-bay chancel roof is unfortunate in design but, as a piece of wooden engineering, can have few peers.

This is a good working village, with the sound of lambs and livestock mingling with the rumble of tractors.

KIRKBY UNDERDALE, *Humberside,* 10m S of Malton. The modern fields of old grass-grown selions surround this Wold village. From the churchyard the surrounding landscape appears dotted with trees with long windbreaks crowning the low tops of the horizon. S of the village fields is A166, which cuts through a mass of tumuli and

earthworks on its way E after climbing Garrowby Hill. Below Garrowby Hill lies the late Victorian Hall built by the 2nd Viscount Halifax, a leader of the High Anglican movement. W of the nucleus of the village is Goman Castle Farm built amid the shallow silted earthworks of old fortification. The main settlement is now firmly established round the church and the wide street. Of particular note is the large U-plan brick house built early in the 18th c. At first sight it appears to be one of many pattern-book houses with its five-bay front and advanced centre bay. The heavy ornate brick cornice is oddly out of character – the last fling of what is now known as 'Artisan Mannerism'. The windows are wooden mullion and transom with the peculiarity of horizontally sliding sashes to the lower lights. S Humberside and Lincs. artisan mannerist houses have these windows, e.g. at Hagworthingham and Aslackby, which have never been recorded in other styles of building. It is unfortunate that the re-roofing may have swept away dormers and parapets in the extensive repairs of recent years.

The church of All Saints is partly built of Norman herringbone masonry into which is set a small Roman carving of Mercury (in the wall of the N aisle tower respond). Masonry older than the nave arcades must have been underpinned when the aisles were added; the arch masonry of the Norman windows is still visible over the inserted arcades. This underpinning is not unique and may be seen in Lincs. in the Saxon church at Hough on the Hill. The chancel arch has fine scallop capitals with roll mouldings. Although the chancel was rebuilt in the 1870s it is colourfully formal under its painted roof timbers; a contemporary hanging rood still remains. The incidentals are many: an armorial tomb-slab of 1532 to a Willberfoss of Garrowby, a reset Norman W door, and the tiny nail-head ornament to the mouldings of the S door. Outside in the breezy churchyard is a curious stone, perhaps a frith-stool, set sheltered by the yew trees.

10m E is the remarkable church of **Garton on the Wold**. This remains, apart from the upper stage of the tower, substantially an early 12th-c building externally. Inside almost all is High Victorian – a vision of Ravenna in Humberside. Sir Tatton Sykes, another adherent of the High Anglican movement, like his neighbour, Lord Halifax, had the interior painted in fresco, the floors laid with stone mosaic and the roof timbers painted. This must be the apogee of High Anglican restoration work.

NEWTON, *Lincs.,* 9m E of Grantham. This stone-built village grew around the rim of a small depression in the limestone heath 1m S of A52, at the top of Newton Bar, reputedly the highest point between Grantham and the Urals.

A shallow stream bisects an oval area that may once have been a central green. It is now occupied by buildings dating from the 1630s up to the 1870s when building virtually ceased; large open areas still survive. At the W end of the green is the pic-

Russell Read

*Corinthian door case in West Gate,
North Cave*

turesque group of the Red Lion, Woodruff Cottage (built in the 1600s and later remodelled), and a group of small cottages (c. 1830). Behind them lies Woodside Farm, a substantial house c. 1630 – three units and a through passage – hidden behind tall trees. The N elevation has three- and four-light ovolo-mullioned windows with a blocked ogival arch-lintel all in ashlar-dressed rubble. This was part of the great estate of the grandee Carre of Sleaford who made a fortune out of the Dissolution, sheep and depopulation. The grounds of the Victorian rectory run down to the lane that circles the village. The Hall (1839–41, 1870) lies behind, further N in a dense plantation; only a simple but elegant lodge on the roadside betrays its existence. Opposite the castellated entry to the rectory is the only brick house, the keeper's cottage, of the 1870s. The church of St Botolph (it is possible to see Boston alias Botolphstown from the Bar – particularly the Stump or great, lanterned W tower of Boston church) has a building history of jumbled Norman and EE articulated by a Dec remodelling; the interior is gloomy but good, all shod with pitch-pine (restoration of 1865–6). There are three hagioscopes.

On the lane from the church towards Folkingham (q.v.) is Moat House – Victorianized Georgian – standing by wet earthworks; there are cottages of the 1700s, large farmyards of the 1860s, and the former post office and shop – a building that was possibly the Manor House of the 1590s.

This is perhaps the best village on this part of the heath. **Walcot**, between here and Folkingham, has a fine church, St Nicholas, with an unusual spire amid interesting houses near the pond.

NORTH CAVE, *Humberside* (6m S of Market Weighton), is a village for the connoisseur of doorcases. The best are in West Gate – Nos. 72, 74 and 76 – a trio of unfluted Corinthian type on columns without bases, above, oddly ornate cornices – richly decorative but very rustic. No. 86 has console brackets; No. 14, Westgate House, has an oddly accented entasis to full columns supporting a flat entablature, the return with pilasters and so on. Just outside the village is the park of Hotham Hall, with a lodge entrance like a luxurious railway crossing keeper's – Italianate in yellow brick, stone dressings and yellow terracotta under a slate roof – opposite a signpost saying 'Ypres 347 miles' with terrible World War I statistics below. The picturesque lake and trees are separated from the village proper by a bridge.

N of the village is the Manor Farm and yard; there is a green-slated octagonal dovecote with a cupola in the double yard of buildings. A rubble wall to the roadside has brick tumbling. The vicarage is opposite in large grounds, with the church across the road. A booklet *Walking Round North Cave* (Heritage Trail), informative and invaluable, is available here or in the village shops. There is a good sense of community, and the villagers are proud of the place. One indication is the enthusiastic bell-ringing team – the church has six bells. The tower is Norman, with later interference. Much of the nave, aisles and chancel raises problems: is it in part 'churchwardens' Gothic' with renewed tracery? The church has transepts undefined by any crossing arcade. The solution is, perhaps, that here was a large platform type of rood screen stretching from chancel to the start of the nave arcading – such things are not unknown, and there is evidence for their existence in East Anglia. In the church furnishing there is much of interest: painted royal arms; monuments to the Clitherow, Metham and Burton families with two hatchments; a Carolean black-lettered Confession and Absolution is painted on the chancel S wall; two alabaster effigies lie bereft of their setting.

The school was built in 1833 and extended in 1870. A Primitive Methodist chapel (a replacement of 1871) is in Quaker Lane and a Temperance Hall (now British Legion) of 1851 stands in Blossom Lane. There is a former House of Industry (?1730s) now a farmhouse, in a yard off Westgate – redundant on the erection of Howdon Union Workhouse in 1839. A paper (and corn) mill by the stream is now a house, as is the upper mill of ?1730; to the W of Blossom Lane are Fishponds.

Parliamentary enclosure took place in 1765; from that date until the 1830s there was rebuilding of the village in brick, local oolite and ragstone bound by mud or lime. Rustic Georgian and Victorian building is the key to the village. Are the 'tudorbethan' brewers' timbering of the White Hart, plastic shop-signs and effete pastel paintwork the beginning of visual decay?

OLD BOLINGBROKE, *Lincs.* (6m SE of Horncastle), when approached from A155, is seen lying in a hollow of the Wold; a capless tower mill gleams white to the W, and nearer is the great Italianate whitewashed front of Haresby Hall. The landscape seems almost on the point of reversion to its pre-enclosure state. Trees and hedges have been grubbed out but some are still kept well trimmed and there is coppice and covert on the surrounding tops. Although the village is nucleated there are many outlying farms. The focal points of the village are John of Gaunt's church, low and without a clerestory, and the castle recently exposed dramatically from grass-grown mounds. The village houses mostly cluster round the open green centre by the castle. There is much variety. Church View, N of the church, is a typical three-bay house of the 1840s. The door is of six panels set in an odd triple pilastered doorcase (like those of Horncastle). A verge of 'Oxford glazing' in coloured glass surrounds its sashed windows. To the E is a fourth bay with a carriage arch with a Georgian sash above, flanked by blind recesses and curious sculptures. All this is surmounted by a curious coped pediment with a Diocletian window. A sadly mutilated pair of Tudoresque brick cottages is nearby; the diagonal stacks and hood moulds to curious sashes survive. The local brickwork is of Flemish bond accompanied by the usual village craftsmen's aberrations; some late building material is obviously brought in: for example, the lion-mask cast-iron guttering probably by Tupholm Foundry, Union Street, Horncastle (closed by 1860). A more polite house NE of the church is again of three bays but with 'venetians' to bays one and three separated by a reticent doorcase. Its hipped roof is well slated in the old way with graded tiers of slate diminishing towards the ridge. The slate, of course, is Welsh. Throughout the village are many other interesting houses: the Mill House over a small stream (the mill building disused and the machinery gone); Bolingbroke House, built in Flemish bond yellow brick, has a bizarre 19th-c set of elevations – canted battlemented turrets, curved windows set in curved facets of brick, ashlar dressings and a lugged and moulded doorcase – all quite symmetrical, but picturesque in its fine gardens with white pigeons and red-brick buildings in the back-court. Minor building retains a few fragments of mud-and-stud walling; more often the silhouette of a cottage betrays a casing of brick behind which the mutilated frame is preserved.

The school of 1841 is utilitarian but picturesque in tudor style. Gothic was the choice for the Methodist church of 1815 but a simple Greek revival doorcase has become entangled with the design; there is a schoolroom to match. The parish church, St Peter and St Paul, has been cut down in size; the present church is only the 14th-c S aisle with a N aisle of 1890. It seems more like a chancel with a tower. Inside there are signs of hacked-off canopies on the E window jambs. The arcade pillars have no capitals, and the moulding, except for one fascia that goes straight up into the arch, runs in a series of waves and rolls from floor

to apex. Some good Dec tracery is fitting company for a sedilia with cusped ogival canopies with crockets. The font has complex octagonal pyramid stops to octagonal pilasters on moulded bases – a rare group of early 17th-c date. All is covered in shallow graffiti. The founder, John of Gaunt, has two other monuments. One is the formal garden of recently planted Lancastrian Roses grown in Provins – the arms of Edmund, 1st Earl of Lancaster, and those of the Duchy of Lancaster hang nearby. The second is his castle, incorporating fragments of an earlier, Norman, one. Here Henry IV was born in 1367. Since the remaining part of the castle, the gatehouse, fell into disuse, even for rent-days, grass has covered the site. A dramatic restoration of the walls, which still stood to a height of some 14ft, has been carried out by the Department of the Environment (it is not yet officially open to the public). The plan has its counterparts in some Welsh castles; its site must have been low and marshy with additional earthworks to the S. It is possible to post cards in a box with the VR cypher built into the wall by the NW gate to the churchyard. It is a trim village with old gardens and conservatories; a delight to walk in. For the less active there is much to be seen from a slow-moving vehicle.

PATRINGTON, *Humberside*. After a succession of dormitory villages devoid of a sense of dignity, isolation and community, on A1033 from Kingston upon Hull to Spurn Head, Patrington comes as a surprise. The great cruciform church of St Patrick, with soaring spire set above the crocketed finials and intricate tracery, is just as interesting and beautiful inside. High in the roof of a transept is a rise and fall of steps across a gable; the small pillars and coiling figures are straight out of Honnecourt's drawings. Most of the carving is in the Heckington and Hawton school, with foliate delicacy. The E wall of the S transept has a canted bay for an oratory, carved and canopied in a unique piece of planning. The building history is involved: cruciform churches with central towers are not common. Some compromise in building has left a large pier base stranded just where a W tower ought to be. However, leave the archaeologist to ponder the problems, and enjoy the cake-decoration in stone of the gorgeously ornate font and the assured cutting of the sedilia and piscina. The Easter Sepulchre has a parallel in Lincolnshire at Heckington (q.v.) and there can be little doubt that the same craftsmen worked here and at Hawton (Notts.).

From the churchyard may be seen the flat, gaunt landscape stretching towards the grey and churning Humber. An equally gaunt long grey house of the 1820s blocks part of the view. In the village the brickwork is of interest: from the decaying Dutch paving outside the church door, spilling into the gravel, to the humbler locally made brick there is much to compare. The brickyard lay outside the village behind Winestead Garage; parts of the large works still exist, including a picturesquely decayed eight-bay pilastered

brick block. The kilns and chimney were on the site of the filling station. The flax mill at the corner has been demolished, and other buildings are ready to follow. A house built by the Ellis family in 1743 has been allowed to decay to ruin in Northside. The roof structure is exposed and the clasped purlin construction may easily be seen from the street. There are vast and colourful armorials on the whitewashed seven-bay front of the Hildyard Arms. No. 10, Northside is interesting. There are many Nonconformist chapels. Architecturally the wonder of them all is the Methodist Church; it seems that every architect from Inigo Jones to Carr of York has had some hand in the design. The date is 1811, perhaps the watershed of the battle of the styles – Gothic versus Classical. Even if only for the church, Greenshaw Lane is worth a visit.

The houses are mostly of brick of different colour, from ochre to flaring orange and brown-purple. Only a few are larger in size than three bays, or the occasional two, and almost all were built during the late 18th or early 19th c. Doorcases exhibit an extraordinary variety, from simple wooden affairs with reeded pilasters and plain fanlights to brick 'Saracenic' or Sienese Gothic of the Victorians.

SALTFLEET and the SALTFLEETBYS,

Lincs. 8m E of Louth is this fascinating group of settlements. Drive down the flattening edge of the Wold, across thousands of acres of flat plough-land, with nothing but the sea and the great tankers to bound the horizon. The bare land-scape is still dotted with old airfields left over from World War II. On the banks of the maze of drainage channels are those curiosities of the Fen, the 'half-houses'. These are of two bays, door and window, with a first floor and perhaps an outshot or addition for a kitchen. Many have the brick-work 'keyed' to receive an additional bay of building that never could be built in the depression following the Napoleonic Wars. They stand across the drain, approached by bridges with ornate cast-iron rails, built in spotty yellow or plum-red brick. Woodbine Cottage near **Saltfleetby St Peter** is a good example. All round are piles of clay land-drain pipe ready to replace the clogged drainage system of the Victorian farmers. Modern bungalows rub shoulders with corrugated iron sheds and the tiny old houses – quite incongruous. St Peter's tiny greenstone church with its bellcote is partly built of old masonry from the ruin of the old. Some larger houses, gaunt grand affairs of brick with tall sashes, look back towards the Wold. Saltfleetby House has a Prospect Tower, forlorn in a forlorn plantation. It is arcaded in brick with an octagonal lantern top. Old drove-roads to the now ploughed grazings intersect B1200, and there are numerous remains of old cattle yards.

The most picturesque house lies E of the old station site; three irregular bays of single-storey brick with tumbled brick dormers. The windows are Yorkshire casements: horizontally sliding sashes, under segmental brick arch-lintels. A dove-cote with its louvres blocked lies W of the house and a tiny cattleyard is sited to the E – all sur-rounded by ash trees and overgrown hedges. Its bridge across the drain is of re-used brick and stone. E again is Moat Hall: a grander affair in irregular Flemish bond, resashed and with some blocked windows, still the 17th-c vernacular plan translated into the Georgian idiom.

Saltfleetby All Saints church has a remarkably crooked tower and a delightfully irregular ex-terior. The nave N windows are Perp; a superb one to the W has triple ogival ornament to the transom with tall ogee lights above. The unusual arcaded wooden roof with collars and queen posts was repaired in 1611 and is probably of late 15th-c date despite the Renaissance overtones; there is no other local parallel. The interior has much of interest: a Jacobean pulpit with a dis-used and doubtfully Elizabethan one at the W end. A stone reredos, Norman capitals, EE transitional plate tracery and Perp additions and alterations all add up to an entertaining architec-tural puzzle. The few houses, late Georgian brick and pantile (one savagely rewindowed) are set in trees, in contrast to the bare yard of the now redundant church. Perhaps the now derelict three-unit house down the lane SW of the church is the last survivor of the older, larger settlement.

Saltfleetby St Clements lies behind the dunes that blocked the Haven centuries ago. Coastal trade was an important element in the economy of this group of villages. The few grass-grown selions between the road and the dunes still stand out clearly; as the road turns N they lie to the E with the level marsh and the isolated church all alone in a network of drains. The church appears to be a rebuilding of the 1880s but there is much EE work, including a five-bay arcade, that has sur-vived. The silvery oak lychgate, of a Voyseyesque, 1930s style, is attractive. There are low, mean houses along the banks of the drainage channels; single-storeyed and crooked with subsidence.

Saltfleet still has small boats moored in the silted Haven at the foot of the derelict brick tower mill. Although oppressed by bungalows and caravans, the place still has some of its old dignity. The 17th-c Manor House is built with its gable to the street and the remodelled five-bay 'show front' faces S. It was originally of two largish rooms separated by a balustraded stair in a hall; 18th- and 19th-c additions lie to the N. The stair balus-trading has been augmented by the addition of a section of early 17th-c communion rail – perhaps saved from the church which was washed away by the sea. Across the street is the tall brick New Inn; great trees line the court and the old green behind the inn. The four-bay front to the sea has cant bays to the first floor from which it is possible to see over the embankment to the greasy sea-flats. When the inn was built towards the end of the 18th c the view would have been one of busy shipping and beach fishing boats – not caravans. Some simple cottages and small houses survive on The Hill. St Botolph's, the new church, is in 'streaky bacon' brickwork, with an octagonal bellstage to a minuscule SW tower: a delightful lead-covered spirelet has fretted Gothic-revival woodwork. Pump Lane has some 18th- and 19th-c building; the post office and Home Farm are especially typical of the interesting local vernacular. There are several tumbled brick gables. Only one warehouse remains (W of the road) to give an impression of former trading bustle. The adjacent house, Sherwood, has a curiously twisted brick chimney at the rear. Attenuated S-shaped gable ties are common, but the wrought-iron initial or numeral type is absent.

The Methodist chapel and Sunday School still stand, as do other fragments of a long history. As late as the 1930s efforts were still being made to revive the Haven formed by the Withern Eau and Grayfleet, but to no purpose. The royal port – even worth an entry in Domesday – that supplied two ships and men for Edward III's invasion of Brittany in 1359 is but a memory along with the Market and Horse Fair (the area was famous for its foals and cart horses).

SAPPERTON, *Lincs*. (6m E of Grantham), is built on a low limestone hill. The old Hall has fragments of late medieval work that have survived the meddling alterations since the 1590s. It forms part of a picturesque grouping of church and hall, trees and stabling. A winding street forms the spine of this stone-built village. Cottages and farms of the 19th c have all but obscured the pattern of the early nucleated settlement. A stone-built double-pile farmhouse to the SE is typical of the local tudoresque popular in the 1840s. In the centre of the village is the former parsonage – a cut-down three-unit house – with 16th-c masonry below and 18th-c work above recorded by an obliquely worded Latin inscription, which may be translated 'It is not what we call ourselves but, much more, what we make of ourselves'.

The small spire of St Nicholas' Church is a visual stop to the street. The building is of interest and has much 13th- and 14th-c work; inside are good monuments.

Earthworks on the crown of the hill W of the old Hall are connected with an earlier village layout rather than the legendary house of the Saunders – reputed to have cost £15,000 in the early 1700s. Their house was built in part of Cranwell parish called Sapperton.

SCOPWICK, *Lincs*., 10m SE of Lincoln. The long village street lies alongside a small stream in a shallow dip of the Heath. The nucleated village lies across the A15, with the main settlement to the E and the farmland and fen even further E. This pattern is repeated in surrounding settlements such as Potter Hanworth and Nocton where the siting of the nucleus to the W of an attenuated parish stretching far to the E has encouraged minor settlements away from the village.

Of the building along the street by the stream that meanders through the narrow green there is much of interest. The solid front of the Royal Oak public house has massive lintels with a single, projecting keystone over sliding casements. Further along is the tall front of Lawn House. The rendering has been stripped from its squared-rubble walls during recent restoration: there is a good antique shop in the stabling and granary. Old cattleyards run right up to the boundary of the green, with largish barns and low cattle shelters. The farmhouses lie alongside interspersed with some infill, including a quite incongruous pair of suburban 'semis'.

No. 15 High Street is part of a group of irregular stone houses and yards; No. 60, built in the 1730s, has an outshot to the street, with cattleyard and barn to the E.

The church of Holy Cross is padlocked. Despite the scraping and recasing of the restoration, during which the aisles were rebuilt and the nave repaired (1882) the S porch rebuilt (1884) and a new chancel erected (1910), there is still something old to see. There is EE work in the tower (below the bell-stage of the 1630s) and the S door. The nave arcades also survive. Monuments to the Sewells and a flattened cross-legged effigy were also allowed to remain.

Past the unsightly caravan site, Braemar, is Kirby Green. Here, No. 9 Main Street has 17th-c masonry and gables overbuilt in the 19th: only a blocked window to the W gives the game away. Limestone and brick, under pantiles or occasionally slate, form the textural pattern. In the hamlet is a large farmhouse and barn, of limestone and brick, with old-fashioned pale-ochre paint: a typical Heath farmhouse and yard. The house is grand, four bays of double-pile, cant bayed and brick chimneyed, and hidden from the road by evergreens and a park-like garden – obviously the Hall. The church, Holy Cross, was 'archaeologically' rebuilt in 1848. Quite a success in its way, and a worthy precursor to others like St Lucia, Dembleby (1867–8). The building accounts survive and show the stone to have been hauled from near Wilsford and bricks from Dorrington yard. S of the Hall is the second sadly derelict mill and house, Georgian and picturesque.

There is here a sense of historical continuity combined with decay. Gaunt, ivy-grown trees and the shattered stumps of old ash in straggly hedges barely provide shelter to ploughland and small grass closes.

SOMERSBY, *Lincs*., 6m E of Horncastle. The moated Grange and the former rectory (birthplace of Alfred, Lord Tennyson) are fine houses S of the church. The Grange (Manor Farm) is of brick, early 18th-c, in the style of Vanbrugh's little 'castles', but by Robert Alfray rather than the master himself. Of the earlier village houses little may be seen except the sadly collapsing ruin NW of the churchyard. Two neat estate-pattern cottages lie beyond in a hen-pecked yard, and the village has its usual scatter of corrugated iron and wooden sheds in decay. The church of St Margaret is simple, with Victorian pine pews, pulpit and

Tennyson's birthplace, the former Rectory, Somersby. The Grange is the brick building beyond.

choir seats lightly carved or decorated with quatrefoils. An octagonal font is equally simple. A small case contains minor Tennyson relics and photographs. A copy of a bronze bust by Thomas Woolner was installed in 1911 in memory of the village Poet Laureate. Royal arms in high relief, coloured and gilt, a marble monument to Robert Burton 'citizen of London' (1753), and an armorial brass to George Littlebury of 1612 add to the interest of the interior. Outside is a complete cross, base, shaft and canopied crucifix: there are pyramidal stops to the ashlar facets.

Tennyson's birthplace, the former rectory, lies W of the Manor Farm. It is an irregular double-pile house extended E in cottagey style (this was the Gothick fantasia built by the poet's father and his coachman – all fantasy has gone now). Further W a sunken lane leads to Salmonby, crossing the brook of Tennyson's poem on its way. (There is some academic doubt as to the real identity of the 'Brook' but most believe this is the right one!) Beside the bridge is a quiet picnic spot sheltered by oak and ash. In spring or autumn all is solitude, but a fine summer day brings the tourists.

SOUTH FERRIBY, *Humberside* (4m W of Barton-on-Humber), is the only village to have any counterpart on the other bank. To many the very concept of the new Humberside is anathema. The wide greasy rush of water has divided rather than united the communities on either bank. A footpath leads from South Ferriby out to the dismal staithes where chalk and limestone cut from the eerie quarries were shipped in double-hulled keels and lighters. At low tide their eroded weed-hung ribs still protrude from the mud and

shingle, where they were sunk to prevent further erosion of Redcliff. Out in the estuary is a bell-buoy forever tolling a warning to steer off Read's Island. The grass-grown railways and abandoned machinery lie peacefully in the clay or sandy silt ploughland masked by coppice and windbreaks.

The roar of traffic on A1077 pervades the village and its gentle little dull-brick houses with tumbled gables. On the corner of Northend in Farrishes' Lane is a splendid cattleyard and shelter sheds full of good fat beasts; the adjoining farmhouse is a little later, perhaps of the 1840s, unspoilt – still sashed and with a pretty door with a Bohemian glass fanlight in a simple brick surround. There are many other similar houses and yards – one has a brick dovecote of 1788. Skinner's Lane has a few vernacular bits in bad brick with worse modernization. Low Street has the building of a long-defunct Total Abstainer's Hall (1882) that looks like a fire station. Throughout the village there is one peculiarity: the use of under- or over-fired brick in a sort of *opus reticulatum* without mortar. The piers of the old parsonage garden have normal brickwork with a cross laid in vitrified blackened brick as ornament, but the wall is all laid in diagonally set headers like the rest. The simple Methodist church is brick of two builds: the first Flemish bond (1839), the second English bond. In School Lane, opposite The Nelthorpe public house, is a solid barn of the early 1800s in cream-washed brick; the walling is capped by a dogset brick dentil-cornice, with no guttering to spoil the original effect.

The church is on a hill away from the village nucleus, across A1077. The Norman tympanum over the porch has a figure, perhaps St Nicholas, to whom is the dedication. There is Norman walling like Pope's description – some old dog-hole eked with the ends of wall – this time in brick, some 18th c, some Victorian. From the church-yard is an excellent view across the village away to North Humberside across the water. Just visible is the shattered parkscape of Sir John Nelthorpe's Hall, with the simple farmhouse-like elevations and additions that hide the front. Nearby is the former home farm, simply vernacular, dormered and grey with Victorian bits.

On the S fringe of the village is a good Georgian house and, further S, in pretty timbered grounds, a farmhouse with an enormously long façade of only four bays, generously proportioned. The first floor has only three bays, ashlar quoins and whitewash – all picturesque. The effect is totally shattered by an overhead 'feeder' from a quarry to nearby works passing over the road and too close to the yard, barns and gardens.

The B1204 continues S to **Horkstow** where Stubbs rented a farmhouse for his studies on *The Anatomy of the Horse*. It is now demolished. This is a village of good Georgian houses – the two best are in decay. Here is a place to question the effect of listing and grading – where are the con-servationists?

STAMFORD BRIDGE, *Humberside,* 7m E of York. Near the village is the site of the great victory of Harold over the forces of Tostig and Harald Hardrada in 1066: an event overshadowed by defeat days later at Hastings.

The best approach is from the N along A166, which passes through the village over an old bridge. By the bridge is a picnic area recently planted with trees in an attempt to screen modern but inoffensive cottagey development. From this point the great brick block of the mill dominates the scene. It stands astride the stream on stone piers and round arches which support the tall 'garden-wall' brickwork above. Its wheel is undershot, and much machinery is mixed with the bustle of a good restaurant. Information on the use of the building, including a brick-vaulted corn-drying chamber, is on display. Much of the machinery may be seen through protective grilles from outside. The houses surrounding the small sloping green are undistinguished but they do combine to give a strong settlement pattern. The Bay Horse public house at the top of the green has a painted sign hung on its drab brick wall; its frontage is typical of the rustic classical style of the surrounding buildings. The Nonconformist chapels are in a slightly more polite style: one has round-arched windows but even this now has a secular use. It was from villages such as this that the Nonconformists drew most support. After the decay of a chapel dedicated to St Edmund in the mid-16th c, there was no replacement until the present church, St John Baptist (1868), which now serves the united parish of Stamford Bridge with Ketton. Coupled lancet windows light a whitewashed interior with plain deal pews, a low

pulpit and simple font. The font cover is of scale ornament and fretwork, kneeling angels, gilt, at the corners. The roof slope is coffered with panels of diagonally set boarding. Outside the churchyard is a small but ornate Victorian house: it looks like a curate's house but was formerly part of the housing for workers in the now de-molished brewery. The railway station, like the brewery, has now gone, but the fine brick viaduct still stands. The central span is arched in iron with latticed spandrels. As befits a former East Riding village there is an exceptionally good fish-and-chip shop by the green. There are several brick houses with tumbled gables and original details; the usual discordant notes of inappropriate windows and twee taste are insufficient to spoil the place. Opposite, on the other bank of the river, is a crowded and obtrusive caravan site.

THIMBLEBY, *Lincs.,* 2m W of Horncastle. The unique survival of a group of three thatched mud-and-stud cottages makes this village the only place in the country where a good visual im-pression of the original rebuilt villages may still be seen. Even the houses of small market towns were once like these, until the Georgians and the Vic-torians pronounced them as little more than 'low, mean, mud-built hovels of the labouring class': and the only course for them then was demolition and speedy replacement in brick.

N of the E–W alignment of the village street lie the crofts and tofts of the medieval layout. At the W end of the street is a small single-storey farmhouse with a dormer window; behind is a simple traphouse and haystore making up one side of the cattleyard. The yard is divided from the former open-field by a very unprepossessing Fletton brick barn with a corrugated iron roof; inside, as with so many others, are the oak posts and roofing of the old vernacular tradition. To the E of the threshing-floor is an area of asphalt, which was used for coating the feet of geese that were to be driven to market.

Hall Garth Farm to the S of the street has an ornate and complex group of buildings. Although the stone-built mullioned-windowed house has gone there is a fragment of moat and traces of its once famous topiary garden.

The atmosphere is shattered by road traffic along B1190 as well as the unforgivable modern building intrusions. It is to be remembered that villages are not museums but working communi-ties; Thimbleby is also a dormitory for the nearby town of Horncastle. Trees do help to hide the mess, but the overhead cable-scape, telephone box and bus shelter are totally alien. The street is closed, visually, at its E end by an equally inappropriate and unmistakably Victorian church, St Margaret (1879), in a picturesque churchyard – clipped-top yews, stone tombs (one of 'fallen column' type probably by Broadgate of Horncastle) – on a sharp bend in the road.

It is the group of houses near the church that is so important to an understanding of Lincs. village topography in its evolution from the

Sixteenth-century mud-and-stud cottages with Norfolk thatched roofs, at Thimbleby

16th-c vestiges of feudalism to the more emancipated field farming of the mid-18th c. The three whitewashed houses N of the street are basically of 16th-c origin. The mud and stud on its boulder footing has patches of brick and fieldstone stopping further erosion. Two of the thatched roofs have Norfolk thatch with cut ridging but one is of the plain Lincolnshire sort. To the S is the brick farmhouse of the 1720s (see the insurance plate) with a larger toftstead than the older layout allowed: it has turned its back to the street and faces S into its yard of long, low building. It is a closely nucleated settlement and, even now, almost the only distant building visible is a capless, tapered brick mill tower away to the S.

TYDD ST MARY, *Lincs.* (5m N of Wisbech), is an island of building round an open oval centre planted with strawberries. To the NE the great house of the village has had its 17th-c shell crudely modernized under cement rendering. The Five Bells public house is in old ochre brick with a spotty orange string-course and tumbled gables, all overbuilt in modern brick and slated. A single-bay house, cream-washed under a tarred tin roof, was once a dovecote. Across the strawberries from the Five Bells is an interesting brick house (1785) much altered. Another tin roof, painted a virulent crimson, covers a row of cottages once a three-unit single-storey house; the S gable is tumbled with 'initial' tie irons to the purlins – S + H. NW of the strawberries is the brick-towered church with its white ashlar spire and lucarnes. Three 19th-c statues occupy the niches round the E tower door. There is brick Perp tracery over brick mullions in the three-light window of the N aisle, but set in ashlaring. The chancel has good reticulated tracery and Norman masonry, ashlar below and ragstone above. Crumbling stucco still clings to the brick in picturesque patches – a

Piperesque church with a foreground of straggly trees and Rococo tombstones. The main ensemble is completed by Georgian-style council houses (1925) in horrid kiss-marked brick. The A1101 runs across the E end of the village near a tall three-bay brick house with a Diocletian window to the W (masked by later additions).

The village straggles N with houses of variegated brick under slate roofs; grazing closes run right up to the road. Church Way peters out in modern development, separated from the old nucleus by a tiny architectural extravaganza in Italian taste cheerfully painted white and egg-yellow against dull brick. There are still reeds in the dikes and old pink carts mingled with cropsprayers. The road to Holbeach Clough and Saracen's Head is dotted with fine, Georgian houses amid tatty modern development; wooden 'shell' doorcases cling, rotting, to their fronts. Restoration has started but much is left for rescue.

From Crowland, itself set in the flat fen, to Tydd is an informative journey through the drainage system still largely the work of Cornelius Vermuyden and his drainers in the 17th c. The high-level drain carries flood water from further inland across the fen; water from natural drainage is pumped up into it (the windmill engines are, unfortunately, gone). On either side are houses crooked by fen shrinkage. There are few nucleated settlements, merely strung-out houses on the drain banks and droves. Across these miles of intensively cultivated fen there are scores of 19th-c two-bay houses in crumbling brick that stare out blankly, unoccupied and with tattered curtains blowing out through cracked sashes. The monotony is punctuated by the occasional brash 'Lego' bungalow or a house in 'farmers' executive' style.

WESTBOROUGH, *Lincs.* (8m NW of Grantham), was said by Arthur Mee to be the most remote village in the county. This is nonsense – particularly now A1 Long Bennington by-pass is only 1m E.

The village has been divided into two manors, East Hall and West Hall, since Saxon times. The East Hall belonged to Lord Lovell (of Minster Lovell, Oxfordshire). Now only silted and levelled earthworks survive but in times of flood the River Witham overflows to fill the triple Fishponds. The last Manor Court was held about 1760 before the building of the modernized brick cottage called the Manor House in the 1830s. The West Hall, now Dovecote House, still stands. Behind the Flemish bond brick front is an aisled hall with a cross-wing of chambers. This was part of a modernization scheme on the estates of the Constables (of Hough, Lincs., and Everingham, Humberside) immediately after 1491. The tenant-lords of the West Hall Manor were the Ellys family who emigrated from Everingham in the early 1400s: the last Ellis died unmarried in 1805 and is buried S of the church chancel under a superb Swithland slate headstone. Between the two Halls is the church of All Saints, which incorporates Saxon fragments in its gaunt Gothic emptiness. The body of the cruciform church is predominantly EE – see the lancets and the overall roofline (before the clerestory was added). The chancel-roof pitch was restored under pantiles quite recently, making the cut-off E window look Jacobean (the tracery and arch were removed when the roof was lowered). The S transept disappeared in the 1590s and the tower was virtually rebuilt and cased in ashlar (plain Gothic of 1752 – see masons' 'scrimshaw' on the quoins). Inside, above the Gothic screen, are the Royal Arms painted on canvas (1727); there are good but heavily restored pew ends in the chancel and a good Norman arcaded font (restored in neat cement!). A coped slab with an intricate fleuron cross and shaft on a stepped base – all in relief – has recently been rescued from the tree-shaded yard. It is now near the E end of the S aisle; other important fragments are in the S porch. S of the church is an intact churchyard cross.

Ignoring the brash modern building there is, N of the church, the five-bay brick front of the former rectory (1729 and later) built onto the stump of a house in lias walling and ashlar dressings with a *piano nobile* (cut down to transom level now) of the 1590s. The rectory grounds and adjacent paddock (Hemplands, now built over) are an encroachment on the green. The houses round the green were free-standing and surrounded by orchards and cattle or stackyards. Manor farmhouse, Village Farm, Potts' Farm (note the vernacular plan of the 1630s translated still in 1830s brick for the house), County Farm are all of brick, more or less mutilated, with good brick barns and buildings. Vestiges of timber-framing survive in Potts' Cottage and Bowler Arnolds' House. The houses W of the green are less spoilt (their gardens encroach beyond the stream boundary). Below the road is a brick culvert-drain of the 1830s (*see* Kilham). The only

fragment of old landscape left by the river is near the Grange (the rest destroyed by the Upper Witham Drainage Board – willows and all). Beyond Westborough Gate Farm (the limit of open-field to the W) are tiny closes marking the site of a totally deserted village, Thorpes by the River (Witham). N of Westborough Green at the cross-roads is the top step of the Green Cross (used as a vinegar dip against plague); 1m N across the Moor is an enclosure road leading to Dry Doddington.

WEST BUTTERWICK, *Humberside* (6m W of Scunthorpe), is a dour but surprisingly entertaining village within sight of Scunthorpe steelworks. It lies in open farmland sparsely dotted with farmhouses and groups of ageing trees; there are few hedges. The S approach to the village is undistinguished but the buildings are of interest – the more interesting the more derelict. Some are already demolished. Nearer the church is a (converted) brick dovecote rising above a yard full of strange animals – dragons, swans and 'Disneyesque' monsters – all in fibre-glass. Their brightly painted faces leer across the street at the shops of a monumental mason and a furniture restorer. The houses here are all later than the early 1800s. St Mary's Church is all of yellow brick (1841) in the London taste of the previous century. Perhaps Vanbrugh and Wren helped Wyatt and Soane let down the design from heaven – as did the cherub at Harlaxton Manor; the E end is a really original essay in Gothic revivalism. Better houses cluster round the church but none of more than three sashed bays, brick or cemented. South Street has the Ferry Boat Inn, all moulded brick tudoresque, opposite a typical three-bay, plum-brick farmhouse of 1898, with great trees, a large yard and barns. Just a few steps S of the inn is the River Trent flowing past the derelict smithy. The Three Horseshoes, North Street, is a brewery architect's job, out of keeping with the tumbled gable vernacular or the oddly detailed Victorian houses further N. These houses, with wooden Ionic-pilastered doorcases and odd door panelling, are about to be demolished. No. 26 North Street is a three-bay villa, the centre bay recessed and coupled Doric doorcase-pilasters, isolated behind a high wall – opposite a U-plan stable block stuccoed and reroofed when, doubtless, the pediment disappeared.

The vicarage is good Victorian stuff: asymmetrical, revival Gothic, with an iron ridge frill over the slate, streaky-bacon brickwork. There are, or were, two Methodist chapels and a Baptist chapel.

The narrow road winds N along the riverside and below the shallow concrete spans of the new bridge across the Trent. The brick sprawl of Scunthorpe is just across the river, and the completion of the bridge will have disastrous effects on the village and its neighbours. These are not pretty or remarkable, just typical of the area, adaptable to change and victims of visual erosion by neglect or over-enthusiasm.

Index of Places

Page numbers in roman type refer to the **bold** headings and subheadings in the gazetteers.
Page numbers in *italic* type indicate other text references, or illustrations.
The letter *f* before a page number indicates a colour plate facing that page.
A figure 2 in brackets immediately after a page number means that there are two
separate references to the subject on that page – either two references in the text
or one in the text and an illustration.